CONNECTIONS
A Multicultural Reader for Writers

CONNECTIONS
A Multicultural Reader for Writers

JUDITH A. STANFORD

Rivier College

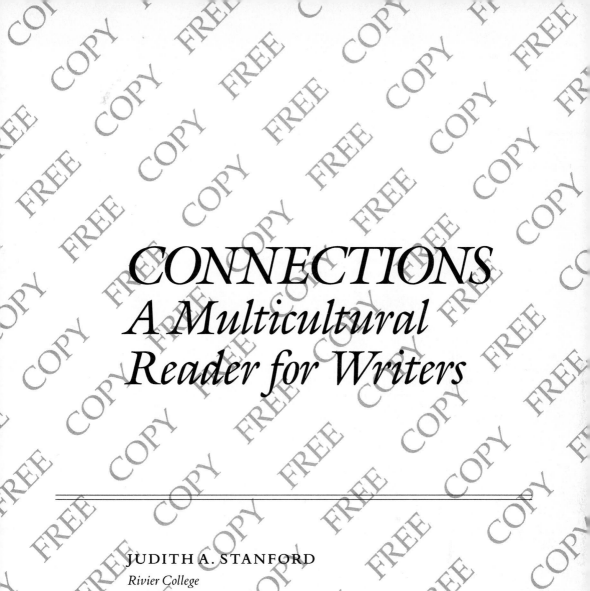

Mayfield Publishing Company

Mountain View, California
London • Toronto

For Arline Dupras

Copyright © 1993 by Mayfield Publishing Company

LIBRARY OF CONGRESS CATALOGING-IN-PUBLICATION DATA
Connections: a multicultural reader for writers / [compiled by]
   Judith A. Stanford.
      p.   cm.
   ISBN 1-55934-184-X
      1. Readers — Social sciences.   2. Pluralism (Social sciences) —
   Problems, exercises, etc.   3. English language — Rhetoric.
   4. College readers.   I. Stanford, Judith A.
   PE1127.S6C65   1992
   808′.0427 — dc20   92-32967
                                                             CIP

Manufactured in the United States of America
10 9 8 7 6 5 4 3 2 1

Mayfield Publishing Company
1240 Villa Street
Mountain View, California 94041

Sponsoring editor, Janet Beatty; managing editor, Linda Toy; production
editor, Carol Zafiropoulos; manuscript editor, Carol Beal; text and
cover design, David Bullen; cover art, *Garden Spiral*, 50″ × 50″,
Quilt. © Jane A. Sassaman. This text was set in 10/12 Bembo by
Thompson Type and printed on 50# Finch Opaque by Maple-Vail
Book Manufacturing Group.

ACKNOWLEDGMENTS AND COPYRIGHTS

Allen, Paula Gunn, "Where I Come From Is Like This." From *The Sacred
Hoop: Recovering the Feminine in American Indian Traditions* © 1986 by Paula
Gunn Allen. Reprinted by permission of Beacon Press, Boston.

Angelou, Maya, from *I Know Why the Caged Bird Sings* © 1969 by Maya
Angelou. Reprinted by permission of Random House, Inc.

Acknowledgments and copyrights continue at the back of the book on
pages 621–626, which constitute an extension of the copyright page.

PREFACE

"Only connect!" This injunction from E. M. Forster's *Howards End* is widely quoted. Yet Forster's character goes further: "Only connect the prose and the passion, and both will be exalted, and human love will be seen at its height. Live in fragments no longer."

A tall order, perhaps, yet this book faces the challenge by urging readers to make such connections. The structure, the apparatus, and the selections in *Connections* all lead students to seek relationships: among the processes of reading, writing, and thinking; among the ideas and emotions expressed by the writers; among the cultures that are represented by the eighty diverse selections; and, most of all, between the reading, writing, and thinking they are doing and the process of their own lives.

Connections does much more than simply provide a collection of readings that represent various cultures. The introductory section demonstrates critical-reading and -thinking skills and suggests that these skills become particularly important when readers encounter unfamiliar circumstances and ideas. In addition, this introductory section asks students to think carefully about the definition of culture and about the concept of reading, writing, and thinking across cultures.

Connections recognizes the importance of writing for a purpose, and so the book is organized by aims of writing and then by themes within those rhetorical aims. The readings are divided into three sections, each of which offers selections exemplifying one aim of writing: expressive, explanatory, and persuasive. Introductions to these three sections provide detailed discussions of the writing process as well as sample student essays demonstrating a possible process for each aim.

The writing apparatus has been carefully planned to involve students in a variety of roles and rhetorical situations. Each selection is introduced by a brief note on the author and the circumstances of the original publication, followed by a series of prereading prompts designed especially for journal writing, brief informal class writing, or discussion that will lead to thoughtful reading. Following each selection are a series of topics for writing and discussion as well as suggestions for research or for longer papers related to the reading. At the end of each thematic section, "Topics for Making Connections" asks students to stretch their responses beyond a single selection. Every writing suggestion encourages students to read closely, carefully, and with an open mind and seeks to engage students in meaningful writing that raises questions rather than simply answering them.

Preceding each thematic section are several photographs related to the theme as well as brief quotations taken from the selections that follow. The instructor's guide provides questions that give students the opportunity to respond to these photographs and quotations as a means of introduction to the theme. The instructor's guide also includes detailed discussion of each selection as well as innovative and flexible suggestions for using the text with various semester or quarter schedules.

Throughout the book, abundant student responses — sample discussions, journal entries, summaries, and papers in various stages of the writing process — demonstrate possible ways of reading, writing, and thinking, both individually and collaboratively.

Selections have been carefully chosen to provide diversity in terms of both the voices and the types of discourse represented. Readers will find an intriguing mix of letters, essays, newspaper columns, interviews, speeches, short stories, and poems. Again, the emphasis is on connection; selections represent an extraordinarily wide range of cultures. As one prepublication reviewer noted: "Rather than limiting the diversity and ethnic experiences to people of color or women, this text extends 'multicultural' to include accounts of immigrants, first-generation sons and daughters, the educated, the uneducated, and the poor — voices that all contribute to an American melody."

ACKNOWLEDGMENTS

Writing and Learning Center faculty as well as English Department faculty at Rivier College deserve sincere thanks for creating a working atmosphere that promotes sharing ideas, exploring new possibilities, and taking risks. My friend, colleague, and first coauthor, Rebecca Burnett, has offered suggestions, provided encouragement, and given support in ways that cannot be adequately acknowledged here. Kathleen Shine Cain and Bonnie Sunstein, as always, took time from their busy schedules to listen, to talk, and to offer valuable insights. My young friend Laura Gower thoughtfully offered the use of one of her books as I searched for selections. Lynn Quitman Troyka, Joyce Perkins, and Robert DiYanni have all taught me invaluable lessons about writing and have encouraged me to venture further into the world of textbook publishing. Joan O'Brien's ready wit, unflagging energy, and total commitment to the fine art of good teaching serve always as inspiration and reassurance.

Most especially, I wish to thank and praise my Writing and Learning Center colleague Lorraine Lordi, who has supported this project and accorded me loyal and unvarying friendship as this text has moved from proposal to final manuscript. Not only has she prepared the main sections of the detailed instructor's guide, but she has also recommended selections and, in addition, provided useful, apt, and creative suggestions for the apparatus that accompanies each of the selections.

I thank my husband, Don, for being a person who listens thoughtfully, who reads widely, and who truly enjoys a good conversation. His observations have helped to shape this book. My sons, David and Aaron—great readers and, definitely, critical thinkers—provide me with plenty of opportunity to discuss and argue about the issues addressed in *Connections*; someday soon I may even win one of those arguments. As always, my mother, Arline Dupras, to whom this book is dedicated, has given me help in every possible way. Editing, word processing, and proofreading are important, of course; but absolutely essential are the love of reading, the dedication to creative teaching, and the ever-hopeful view of life that she has passed on to me.

The reviewers of this text offered helpful and wise suggestions, which I greatly appreciate: Katherine Heenan, University of Connecticut; Nancy Shapiro, University of Maryland; Hildy Miller, University of Louisville; Molly Abel Travis, Tulane University; William E. Smith, Western Washington University.

At Mayfield Publishing Company, Carol Zafiropoulos skillfully guided the book through production, while Carol Beal offered excellent suggestions for fine-tuning as she copyedited the manuscript. I would like to thank Tom Broadbent, editorial director, for his help in shaping this book and his heroic work in collecting hundreds of articles and essays, many of which appear in the anthology sections. Most of all, I thank Senior Editor Jan Beatty, who has believed in this project from its beginning and who has shared not only her impressive expertise in publishing but also her love of reading. Her willingness to discuss ideas, to listen to possibilities, to anticipate pitfalls, and, above all, to convey a sense of absolute commitment to this book has made all the difference.

CONTENTS

READINGS ARRANGED BY RHETORICAL STRATEGY

Cause and Effect

1

Critical Reading and Thinking: An Approach to Crossing Cultures

How do you respond when you read and think about customs, actions, beliefs, or values that seem different from your own? Consider your reactions as you read the following essay, "Body Ritual among the Nacirema," by anthropologist Horace Miner. Miner examines a people he describes as obsessed with the idea "that the human body is ugly and that its natural tendency is to debility and disease."

HORACE MINER

Body Ritual among the Nacirema

The anthropologist has become so familiar with the diversity of ways in which different peoples behave in similar situations that he is not apt to be surprised by even the most exotic customs. In fact, if all of the logically possible combinations of behavior have not been found somewhere in the world, he is apt to suspect that they must be present in some yet undescribed tribe. This point has, in fact, been expressed with respect to clan organization by Murdock (1949:71). In this light, the magical beliefs and practices of the Nacirema present such unusual aspects that it seems desirable to describe them as an example of the extremes to which human behavior can go.

Professor Linton first brought the ritual of the Nacirema to the attention of anthropologists twenty years ago (1936:326), but the culture of this people is still very poorly understood. They are a North American group living in the territory between the Canadian Cree, the Yaqui and Tarahumare of Mexico, and the Carib and Arawak of the Antilles. Little is known of their origin, although tradition states that they came from the east. According to Nacirema mythology, their nation was originated by a culture hero, Notgnihsaw, who is otherwise known for two great feats of strength—the throwing of a piece of wampum across the river Pa-To-Mac and the chopping down of a cherry tree in which the Spirit of Truth resided.

Nacirema culture is characterized by a highly developed market economy which has evolved in a rich natural habitat. While much of the people's time is devoted to economic pursuits, a large part of the fruits of these labors and a considerable portion of the day are spent in ritual activity. The focus of this activity is the human body, the appearance and health of which loom as a dominant concern in the ethos of the people. While such a concern is certainly not unusual, its ceremonial aspects and associated philosophy are unique.

The fundamental belief underlying the whole system appears to be that the human body is ugly and that its natural tendency is to debility and disease. Incarcerated in such a body, man's only hope is to avert these characteristics through the use of the powerful influences of ritual and ceremony. Every household has one or more shrines devoted to this purpose. The more powerful individuals in the society have several shrines in their houses and, in fact, the opulence of a house is often referred to in terms of the number of such ritual centers it possesses. Most houses are of wattle and daub construction, but the shrine rooms of the more wealthy are walled with stone. Poorer families imitate the rich by applying pottery plaques to their shrine walls.

While each family has at least one such shrine, the rituals associated with it are not family ceremonies but are private and secret. The rites are normally only discussed with children, and then only during the period when they are being initiated into these mysteries. I was able, however, to establish sufficient rapport with the natives to examine these shrines and to have the rituals described to me. 5

The focal point of the shrine is a box or chest which is built into the wall. In this chest are kept the many charms and magical potions without which no native believes he could live. These preparations are secured from a variety of specialized practitioners. The most powerful of these are the medicine men, whose assistance must be rewarded with substantial gifts. However, the medicine men do not provide the curative potions for their clients, but decide what the ingredients should be and then write them down in an ancient and secret language. This writing is understood only by the medicine men and by the herbalists who, for another gift, provide the required charm.

The charm is not disposed of after it has served its purpose, but is placed in the charm-box of the household shrine. As these magical materials are specific for certain ills, and the real or imagined maladies of the people are many, the charm-box is usually full to overflowing. The magical packets are so numerous that people forget what their purposes were and fear to use them again. While the natives are very vague on this point, we can only assume that the idea in retaining all the old magical materials is that their presence in the charm-box, before which the body rituals are conducted, will in some way protect the worshipper.

Beneath the charm-box is a small font. Each day every member of the family, in succession, enters the shrine room, bows his head before the charm-box, mingles different sorts of holy water in the font, and proceeds with a brief rite of ablution. The holy waters are secured from the Water Temple of the community, where the priests conduct elaborate ceremonies to make the liquid ritually pure.

In the hierarchy of magical practitioners, and below the medicine men in prestige, are specialists whose designation is best translated "holy-mouth-men." The Nacirema have an almost pathological horror of and fascination with the mouth, the condition of which is believed to have a supernatural influence on all social relationships. Were it not for the rituals of the mouth, they believe that their teeth would fall out, their gums bleed, their jaws shrink, their friends desert them, and their lovers reject them. They also believe that a strong relationship exists between oral and moral characteristics. For example, there is a ritual ablution of the mouth for children which is supposed to improve their moral fiber.

The daily body ritual performed by everyone includes a mouth-rite. 10 Despite the fact that these people are so punctilious about care of the mouth, this rite involves a practice which strikes the uninitiated stranger as revolting. It was reported to me that the ritual consists of inserting a small bundle of hog hairs into the mouth, along with certain magical powders, and then moving the bundle in a highly formalized series of gestures.

In addition to the private mouth-rite, the people seek out a holy-mouth-man once or twice a year. These practitioners have an impressive set of paraphernalia, consisting of a variety of augers, awls, probes, and prods. The use of these objects in the exorcism of the evils of the mouth involves almost unbelievable ritual torture of the client. The holy-mouth-man opens the client's mouth and, using the above mentioned tools, enlarges any holes which decay may have created in the teeth. Magical materials are put into these holes. If there are no naturally occurring holes in the teeth, large sections of one or more teeth are gouged out so that the supernatural substance can be applied. In the client's view, the purpose of these ministrations is to arrest decay and to draw friends. The extremely sacred and traditional character of the rite is evident in the fact that the natives return to the holy-mouth-men year after year, despite the fact that their teeth continue to decay.

It is to be hoped that, when a thorough study of the Nacirema is made, there will be careful inquiry into the personality structure of these people. One has but to watch the gleam in the eye of a holy-mouth-man, as he jabs an awl into an exposed nerve, to suspect that a certain amount of sadism is involved. If this can be established, a very interesting pattern emerges, for most of the population shows definite masochistic tendencies. It was to these that Professor Linton referred in discussing a distinctive part of the daily body ritual which is performed only by men. This part of the rite involves scraping and lacerating the surface of the face with a sharp instrument. Special women's rites are performed only four times during each lunar month, but what they lack in frequency is made up in barbarity. As part of this ceremony, women bake their heads in small ovens for about an hour. The theoretically interesting point is that what seems to be a preponderantly masochistic people have developed sadistic specialists.

The medicine men have an imposing temple, or *latipso,* in every community of any size. The more elaborate ceremonies required to treat very sick patients can only be performed at this temple. These ceremonies involve not only the thaumaturge but a permanent group of vestal maidens who move sedately about the temple chambers in distinctive costume and headdress.

The *latipso* ceremonies are so harsh that it is phenomenal that a fair proportion of the really sick natives who enter the temple ever recover. Small children whose indoctrination is still incomplete have been known to resist attempts to take them to the temple because "that is where you go to die." Despite this fact, sick adults are not only willing but eager to undergo the protracted ritual purification, if they can afford to do so. No matter how ill the supplicant or how grave the emergency, the guardians of many temples will not admit a client if he cannot give a rich gift to the custodian. Even after one has gained admission and survived the ceremonies, the guardians will not permit the neophyte to leave until he makes still another gift.

The supplicant entering the temple is first stripped of all his or her 15 clothes. In every-day life the Nacirema avoids exposure of his body and its natural functions. Bathing and excretory acts are performed only in the secrecy of the household shrine, where they are ritualized as part of the body-rites. Psychological shock results from the fact that body secrecy is suddenly lost upon entry into the *latipso.* A man, whose own wife has never seen him in an excretory act, suddenly finds himself naked and assisted by a vestal maiden while he performs his natural functions into a sacred vessel. This sort of ceremonial treatment is necessitated by the fact that the excreta are used by a diviner to ascertain the course and nature of the client's sickness. Female clients, on the other hand, find their naked bodies are subjected to the scrutiny, manipulation, and prodding of the medicine men.

Few supplicants in the temple are well enough to do anything but lie on their hard beds. The daily ceremonies, like the rites of the holy-mouth-men, involve discomfort and torture. With ritual precision, the vestals awaken their miserable charges each dawn and roll them about on their beds of pain while performing ablutions, in the formal movements of which the maidens are highly trained. At other times they insert magic wands in the supplicant's mouth or force him to eat substances which are supposed to be healing. From time to time the medicine men come to their clients and jab magically treated needles into their flesh. The fact that these temple ceremonies may not cure, and may even kill the neophyte, in no way decreases the people's faith in the medicine men.

There remains one other kind of practitioner, known as a "listener." This witch-doctor has the power to exorcise the devils that lodge in the heads of people who have been bewitched. The Nacirema believe that parents bewitch their own children. Mothers are particularly suspected of putting a curse on children while teaching them the secret body rituals. The countermagic of the witch-doctor is unusual in its lack of ritual. The patient simply tells the "listener" all his troubles and fears, beginning with the earliest difficulties he can remember. The memory displayed by the Nacirema in these exorcism sessions is truly remarkable. It is not uncommon for the patient to bemoan the rejection he felt upon being weaned as a babe, and a few individuals even see their troubles going back to the traumatic effects of their own birth.

In conclusion, mention must be made of certain practices which have their base in native esthetics but which depend upon the pervasive aversion to the natural body and its functions. There are ritual fasts to make fat people thin and ceremonial feasts to make thin people fat. Still other rites are used to make women's breasts larger if they are small, and smaller if they are large. General dissatisfaction with breast shape is symbolized in the fact that the ideal form is virtually outside the range of human variation. A few women afflicted with almost inhuman hypermammary development are so idolized that they make a handsome living by simply going from village to village and permitting the natives to stare at them for a fee.

Reference has already been made to the fact that excretory functions are ritualized, routinized, and relegated to secrecy. Natural reproductive functions are similarly distorted. Intercourse is taboo as a topic and scheduled as an act. Efforts are made to avoid pregnancy by the use of magical materials or by limiting intercourse to certain phases of the moon. Conception is actually very infrequent. When pregnant, women dress so as to hide their condition. Parturition takes place in secret, without friends or relatives to assist, and the majority of women do not nurse their infants.

Our review of the ritual life of the Nacirema has certainly shown them 20 to be magic-ridden people. It is hard to understand how they have managed to exist so long under the burdens which they have imposed upon themselves. But even such exotic customs as these take on real meaning when they are viewed with the insight provided by Malinowski when he wrote (1948:70):

> Looking from far and above, from our high places of safety in the developed civilization, it is easy to see all the crudity and irrelevance of magic. But without its power and guidance early man could not have mastered his practical difficulties as he has done, nor could man have advanced to the higher stages of civilization.

References Cited

LINTON, RALPH. 1936. *The Study of Man.* New York, D. Appleton-Century Co.
MALINOWSKI, BRONISLAW. 1948. *Magic, Science, and Religion.* Glencoe, The Free Press.
MURDOCK, GEORGE P. 1949. *Social Structure.* New York, The Macmillan Co.

Most readers encountering Miner's essay for the first time agree with his observation that these practices strike "the uninitiated stranger as revolting." These initial responses change, however, as the reader continues reading the essay and notes such details as the twice yearly visit to the "holy-mouth-man" who engages in "unbelievable ritual torture" by enlarging "any holes which decay may have created in the teeth" and inserting "magical materials" into these holes. It soon becomes clear that Miner has been figuratively pulling the reader's leg (or tooth, perhaps) by describing aspects of modern American ("Nacirema" spelled backward) culture in unfamiliar ways. With his exaggerations and distorted viewpoints, he gently pokes fun at what he sees as the American obsession with health and cleanliness. Perhaps more important, he insists that we pay attention to our tendency to look at customs, actions, beliefs, and values that seem different from our own and quickly judge them as strange, odd, or even "revolting."

WHAT IS CULTURE?

The title of Miner's essay, "Body Ritual among the Nacirema," leads us to expect that we will be reading about a culture different from our own. To understand the responses often triggered by this expectation, we need first to recognize what is meant by the word *culture*.

Culture may be defined as the ideas, customs, values, skills, and arts of a specific group of people. Most of us belong not to one cultural group but to several. For instance, our age places us in a culture such as childhood, youth, or middle age. We may be called "baby boomers" or "children of the eighties," and these phrases may trigger certain images or values in other people's minds. In addition, we are all either male or female, and the way various societies treat gender differences has traditionally created cultural distinctions between men and women. Another group we belong to relates to the country of our birth or to the country where our ancestors were born. We may be Norwegian, Japanese, Native American, Irish-American, or African-American, or we may come from a combination of ethnic roots. The selections in this book all look at some aspect of the various cultures that make up the United States.

WHY READ AND THINK TO CROSS CULTURES?

Learning to read and to think critically in the context of different cultures are essential skills not only for reading this book but also for fully appreciating many other college courses. In addition, these skills are necessary for working effectively in an increasingly diverse environment and for living with tolerance and understanding for the many groups of people who comprise the citizens of the United States — and of the world.

In many other courses — for example, history, sociology, psychology, business, science, literature, art, music, and religion — you will study aspects of other cultures. Similarly, in your future professional life you will almost certainly work with people from different cultural groups who are making significant contributions to your chosen field. Developing the patterns of thinking encouraged in this book will help you to communicate — to read, to speak, and to write — as a fully aware citizen of the multicultural world in which we live.

Exercise 1

Make a list of as many cultural groups as possible to which you see yourself as belonging. These cultural groups may relate to your age, your ethnic background, your religious preference, your political beliefs, and your current work status.

After making the list, choose one of the cultural groups to which you belong and write a paragraph describing the ideas, customs, values, skills, and/or arts of that group that you see as positive.

Exercise 2

Write a paragraph or two responding to one of the following topics.
A. Describe an example of something you read or heard in another class that revealed a cultural perspective different from your own. Explain what new ideas or possibilities were suggested by this perspective.
B. Describe an incident from a television program or a film you have seen that showed you a cultural perspective different from your own. Explain what new ideas or possibilities were suggested by this perspective.
C. Describe an event from your work that showed you a cultural perspective different from your own. Explain what new ideas or possibilities were suggested by this perspective.

STRATEGIES FOR READING AND THINKING ACROSS CULTURES

Reading cross-cultural selections thoughtfully and productively calls for both skill and courage. It requires the skill necessary for understanding and evaluating any complex idea or issue. More importantly, it asks for the courage to approach each writer's work with a mind that remains open to multiple possibilities and points of view. It demands the willingness to see and acknowledge differences yet also to look for similarities and connections. Most of all, reading across cultures asks the reader to avoid hasty judgments, to discard clichéd responses, and to tolerate ambiguity.

Reading to Respond

When you first read any work, fiction or nonfiction, one of the best strategies is to skim through, noting your responses as you move quickly from point to point. Being aware of initial responses is particularly important when you read across cultures because when you encounter unfamiliar ideas, images, and values, it's easy to feel overwhelmed with new vocabulary, with unexpected examples, or with evaluations that are different from your own.

During a first reading, try not to censor your responses, whether they be negative, positive, or neutral. On the other hand, no matter how much you may agree or disagree with what you are reading, try expressing some of your reactions in the form of questions or open-ended statements that could lead to, rather than close off, discussion. By working with these structures, you'll keep an honest record of your thoughts and feelings; yet you'll also help yourself to remain alert to many different possibilities and directions.

MARGINAL NOTES As an example of initial responses, consider the notes one student, Alyssa Clark, wrote in the margins of her book as she read this excerpt from "What's American about America?" an essay by black American novelist, poet, and editor Ishmael Reed. The original version of this selection appeared in Reed's 1983 nonfiction book, *Writin' Is Fightin'*.

ISHMAEL REED

From "What's American about America"

Were all these people U.S. citizens? Tourists? New immigrants?

① An item from the *New York Times,* June 23, 1983: "At the annual Lower East Side Jewish Festival yesterday, a Chinese woman ate a pizza slice in front of Ty Thuan Duc's Vietnamese grocery store. Beside her a Spanish-speaking family patronized a cart with two signs: 'Italian Ices' and 'Kosher by Rabbi Alper.' And after the pastrami ran out, everybody ate knishes."

② On the day before Memorial Day, 1983, a poet called me to describe a city he had just visited. He said that one section included mosques, built by the Islamic people who dwelled there. Attending his reading, he said, were large numbers of Hispanic people, 40,000 of whom lived in the same city. He was not talking about a fabled city located in some mysterious region of the world. The city he'd visited was Detroit.

Where do Islamic people usually live (Not in Detroit?)

③ A few months before, as I was visiting Texas, I heard the taped voice used to guide passengers to their connections at the Dallas Airport announcing items in both Spanish and English. This trend is likely to continue; after all, for some southwestern states like Texas, where the largest minority is now Mexican-American, Spanish was the first written language and the Spanish style lives on in the western way of life.

Do other airports do this? Other languages?

Should Spanish be second language in U.S.? Why? / Why not?

④ Shortly after my Texas trip, I sat in a campus auditorium at the University of Wisconsin at Milwaukee as a Yale professor — whose original work on the influence of African cultures upon those of the Americas has led to his ostracism from some intellectual circles — walked up and down the aisle like an old-time Southern evangelist, dancing and drumming the top of the lectern, illustrating his points before some Afro-American intellectuals and art-

Why is he ostracized for this?

ists who cheered and applauded his performance. The professor was "white." *[margin note: Why the quotes?]* After his lecture, he conversed with a group of Milwaukeeans — all of whom spoke Yoruban, though only the professor had ever traveled to Africa.

⑤ One of the artists there told me that his paintings, which included 5 African and Afro-American mythological symbols and imagery, were hang- *[margin note: Great idea!]* ing in the local McDonald's restaurant. The next day I went to McDonald's and snapped pictures of smiling youngsters eating hamburgers below paintings that could grace the walls of any of the country's leading museums. The *[margin note: What makes him think this?]* manager of the local McDonald's said, "I don't know what you boys are doing, but I like it," as he commissioned the local painters to exhibit in his restaurant.

⑥ Such blurring of cultural styles occurs in everyday life in the United States to a greater extent than anyone can imagine. The result is what the above-mentioned Yale professor, Robert Thompson, referred to as a cultural *[margin note: meaning?]* bouillabaisse. Yet members of the nation's present educational and cultural elect still cling to the notion that the United States belongs to some vaguely *[margin note: who does he mean?]* defined entity they refer to as "Western civilization," by which they mean, presumably, a civilization created by people of Europe, as if Europe can even *[margin note: meaning?]* be viewed in monolithic terms. Is Beethoven's Ninth Symphony, which includes Turkish marches, a part of Western civilization? Or the late-nineteenth- *[margin note: Yes! because it's mostly Western!]* and twentieth-century French paintings, whose creators were influenced by Japanese art? And what of the cubists, through whom the influence of African art changed modern painting? Or the surrealists, who were so impressed *[margin note: Questions are really examples]* with the art of the Pacific Northwest Indians that, in their map of North America, Alaska dwarfs the lower forty-eight states in size?

[left margin notes: Yes — Examples here on campus — students wear clothing from different cultures. Questions are really examples]

As Alyssa read this article, she jotted in the margin any question or observation that came to mind. While most people don't stop to analyze their responses, it may be helpful to look closely not only at the *content* of Alyssa's notes but also at the *types* of comments and questions she wrote. You'll notice that many of her marginal observations fall loosely into the following categories:

1. Questions that ask about people (paragraph 1)
2. Questions that ask about places (paragraph 2)
3. Questions that ask about actions (paragraphs 3, 4)
4. Questions that ask about policies, laws, or customs (paragraph 4)
5. Questions that address the writer's style (such as choice of example, vocabulary, sentence structure, or even unusual punctuation) (paragraphs 4, 6)
6. Questions or comments that challenge or call for closer examination of the writer's observations, judgments or evaluations, or inferences (paragraphs 5, 6)
7. Comments that affirm or expand on the writer's observations, judgments, evaluations, or inferences (paragraphs 5, 6)

While there are many more ways of responding to reading, this list suggests the wide variety of ways readers react when they encounter a text. As you form your first responses, never be afraid of these early reactions — don't worry that tentative, initial probings will be wrong, silly, or simplistic. Of course, it's true that you may later change your mind and decide to revise or even reject entirely one or more of your original reactions. But these changes — which you'll base on rereading, on writing in response to reading, and, perhaps, on discussions with your fellow classmates and your instructor — represent progress and development. Rather than indicating that your first responses were unworthy or embarrassing, such changes demonstrate your willingness to apply critical thinking and to remain open to new possibilities.

JOURNAL ENTRIES Another useful way of responding to reading is to keep a reading journal. Reading journals take many different forms. They may be kept strictly as individual, exploratory writing, or they may be a course requirement. If you write a journal as a class assignment, the instructor may ask you to write a certain number of entries each week and may specify approximately how long these entries should be. The instructor may also suggest topics or approaches to help you determine the focus of the entries.

Whether or not you are keeping a journal as a requirement, writing entries in response to your initial readings can be a helpful way of engaging your mind with the ideas and feelings the writer expresses. Here are several examples of journal entries that students wrote following their first quick reading of Ishmael Reed's "What's American about America?"

1. I like the way the writer, I. Reed, looks at the positive side. His example of the quote from the *New York Times* in the first paragraph, for example. Here you are shown people from five different nationalities all getting along. But, on the other hand, this seems too ideal to me. From what I've seen and from what you see on television all the time on the news, I would think a situation like this festival would be a place for fights or at least name-calling. *Frank Pagiano*

2. He (Reed) just describes all these other people who live in these places, but he doesn't talk about the regular Americans. What I don't understand is why he keeps saying "Islamic" or "Hispanic" or "Vietnamese." Aren't these people American? And why does he put quotes when he says "white"? Does he think only white people are real Americans? I can't really figure out his point which he says in his title: "What's American about America?" *Lee Ann Jamross*

3. When I read about hearing the announcements in Spanish and English, my reaction was, Why should the announcements be in both languages, because this is the U.S. and English is our language. Why should we have to have another language? I know in some places the

ballots and other papers like that have to be printed in Spanish and my question is, Why? *Stan O'Brien*

4. The airport description made me think of traveling in other countries. My family is military and we've lived in Germany, Italy, and Japan. At the civilian airports in major cities, the announcements are in many different languages. And English is always one which I am glad for, because when I am traveling I don't know the language of the country if it's not English. What I noticed was that in most other countries people know more than one language, and I think this is a good idea because it gives you more possibilities of ways to communicate. I think it would be a good idea in this country if we were more aware of other languages and maybe started to learn them in the early grades instead of one or two years in high school. *Danya Mielewski*

5. "Bouillabaisse." I circled this word as one I didn't know, and I had to look it up because it seemed to me to be important in regard to what the paragraph was saying. Well, it means "a chowder made with several kinds of fish and shellfish, vegetables, and seasoning." At first I thought, well, this is like the "melting pot" which you hear as a way to describe this country. But then I thought, no, because in a melting pot everything just goes together and becomes one big mass and you can't tell the different parts. But in this "bouillabaisse," which Reed says Robert Thompson calls America, you would still see all the parts (like the different kind of fish and the different vegetables). So they would still be themselves, but they would be working together to make something different, too (which would be the chowder). So I'm thinking if America is like this. Do all the different groups stay separate in some ways but work together in others? *William Ferguson*

As you can see from these journal entries, readers respond very differently to what they read. The following list briefly evaluates and comments on each of the entries.

1. Frank Pagiano identifies one particular detail that he admires in the essay and then explains his reasons. His comment goes on, however, to show some reservations he feels about the accuracy of this detail.
2. In her entry, Lee Ann Jamross asks many questions about the terms Reed uses to describe groups of people. Her final questions raise points concerning definition: She wonders exactly how Reed defines "Americans."
3. Stan O'Brien's initial response is to challenge an assumption Reed makes. O'Brien doesn't flatly reject Reed's point about the Spanish language announcements, but the tone of his questions show that he is not entirely convinced.

4. Taking a viewpoint quite different from Stan O'Brien's, Danya Mielewski addresses the same issue: the use of more than one language within the United States. Mielewski uses personal examples as a way of exploring the ideas that were inspired by Reed's essay.

5. William Ferguson focuses on one unfamiliar word in Reed's essay. Because this word seemed central to the meaning of the paragraph in which it occurred, and because he couldn't figure out the meaning of the word from the context in which it was used, Ferguson used a dictionary to help him get started. After finding the dictionary definition, he spent time pondering the implications of the comparison Robert Thompson (cited by Reed) makes between the American culture and the chowder called bouillabaisse. By looking at language closely and by refusing to be discouraged or put off by a word he didn't know, Ferguson discovered an idea he considered worth pursuing.

These five entries suggest ways of writing journal entries as initial responses to reading. Notice that many of the entries focus on questions and that most of them keep possibilities open rather than seeking one simple, easy answer. These entries also reflect the way early responses draw heavily on the reader's own experiences and knowledge. In addition, note that two of the sample entries (3 and 4) disagree with each other, yet each asks thoughtful questions and raises important issues. The point here is that there is no one "correct" way to respond to any piece of reading. In addition, when these students returned to Reed's essay to read it for a second or third time, many of them changed or modified their initial responses. Points that may have seemed puzzling during the first reading became clear during the second; issues that seemed straightforward revealed previously unnoted complexities; opinions that seemed convincing now appeared unsupported by sufficient evidence. The richness in reading — and particularly in reading across cultures — lies in the diversity and the possibilities it offers.

Exercise 3

Read the following essay written by Gloria Bonilla, who fled her native El Salvador in 1981 and came to the United States. This essay was originally published in 1988 in *You Can't Drown the Fire: Latin American Women Writing in Exile.*

As you read, make notes in the margins to record your responses. Then write a journal entry expanding on at least one of those responses.

GLORIA BONILLA

Leaving El Salvador
January 4, 1988

I saw my friend Alicia this afternoon while I was at the post office waiting in line. We began chatting of things, projects, etc. The book, her deadline. El Salvador. Incredible! It has been almost seven years since I left. I have not been back since.

— Write something, write about your feelings —

It is so difficult to write, to think, to reflect on it. My experience. It is still painful to remember.

I fled El Salvador, leaving behind my family and friends, my undergraduate studies, a job, and all short- and long-term personal goals, in April of 1981 to escape government persecution. In an effort to remain in the United States more than three months at one time, and map out bits and pieces of an unknown future, I was required to change my tourist visa to a student visa. Because the United States recognized then, and continues to recognize today, the government of El Salvador, I have been unable to enter the United States as a refugee, nor can I realistically expect to receive political asylum.

My story does not differ very much from the stories that most Salva- 5 dorans tell. I consider myself more fortunate because I did not have to cross the Mexican border and enter the United States illegally. I was also able to maintain a legal status which allows me to continue my education in the United States.

I think, like my parents, I have learned through life quite a bit. My father used to say that we never stop learning in life. He did not go to college. I remember him very much because most of what he knew he had learned on his own. My first recollections of the history of El Salvador were through my father and mother. That history was not in print.

My trip to the United States was sudden, precipitous. I, like many other Salvadorans, finally realized that El Salvador was no longer a safe place to live.

I arrived in Washington, D.C., in April of 1981. When I arrived, my good friend, John, was waiting for me at the airport, carrying a heavy coat, assuming I would have no winter clothing. I met John in El Salvador back in the seventies when he was a Peace Corps volunteer. After he came back to the United States, he kept in touch with me, until the political conditions in El Salvador reached serious and dangerous proportions. Then he invited me to come to the United States, an invitation which I did not decline, but which I postponed until I could no longer remain in El Salvador. One day, I called John from Guatemala to let him know I was on my way.

I knew no one in Washington except John, who sheltered me until I was able to support myself. John introduced me to his friends, some of whom are my friends still. As insiders, they helped me to become familiar with the United States. I am grateful for all their help.

A lot has happened since that moment on that spring day in 1981, when   10
I arrived in the United States.

I underwent a metamorphosis. I went from a period of mutiny, in which
I encapsulated myself like a larva in a cocoon, to a period of awakening and
rebirth. The process was painful and difficult. But I survived. Because I left
El Salvador so quickly, I hardly had the chance to reflect on what was happening. When I came to the United States, I carried with me my past, which tied
me to people and a land that I had to give up.

There is no medicine to take care of heartache and homesickness — not
even here in the United States where there are drugs for almost everything,
mostly for pain. I believe we unconsciously or consciously develop methods
to cope with those ailments. So, I made up a prescription of my own to help
me stay sane and survive in my new niche. I filled my hours, my days, without
respite, so I had no time to think, cry or break.

I forced myself to learn English. I took intensive English courses from
9:00 A.M. to 2:00 P.M. I worked in the afternoons. Later, I got a full-time job
and I enrolled at the university, finished college and went straight for a master's degree in sociology. I did it all in five and a half years.

I did not do it alone, but with the support of friends. I had moments of
despair in which I felt lost, with little or no hope. My driving force was that I
had no relatives in Washington to look after me. Therefore, I could not afford
to lose my most precious commodity, my mind. Some call it pride; for others
it is survival instinct. I experienced both.

The United States Immigration and Naturalization Service regulates,   15
controls, and restricts the free access of foreigners to society and subsequently
to its benefits. For example, I had a legal status that allowed me to study and
remain in the United States as long as I attended school full time. On the other
hand, that same status forbade me to work and compete freely for jobs that I
thought I was qualified for.

I maintained that legal status as long as I went to school full time. I paid
my bills as long as I worked full time. I had no choice. My constant concerns
were basic: food, shelter, education, legal status.

A legal status which allows an immigrant to work is an imperative. In
my case, the choice was to apply for political asylum or for permanent residence. The best bet was permanent residence.

Political asylum, in the case of Salvadorans, becomes a dead end since
U.S. immigration law requires the applicant to provide evidence of a well-
founded fear of persecution. A subjective condition, when you think about
it. For example, the army did not need any evidence to determine that I was a
"suspicious individual," and to break into my home and my parents' home in
1981. Ironically, it is the same subjective reasoning used by a U.S. immigration
judge that determines the non-eligibility of a Salvadoran for political asylum.
Salvadorans in exile in the United States have been required to all but present
a signed affidavit from their persecutors in order to prove their well-founded
fear of persecution.

I believe I had good enough reasons to be granted political asylum back in 1981 if I had applied. But a U.S. judge might have disagreed with me, since I did not have concrete evidence of my fear of persecution. Worse, I came from a country whose government is friendly to the United States.

I eliminated the political asylum option from the very beginning. Sal- 20 vadorans had, back in the early 1980s, little or no chance of having a political asylum application approved; later, it became pointless, since the Reagan administration had invested so much money "democratizing" El Salvador.

I am only an example of what Salvadorans could do if given the chance. In my case, maintaining a student visa gave me access to education, something most Salvadorans have not been able to attain. That is why Salvadorans in the United States hold occupations that require little or no formal education.

I think Salvadorans have tried their best to prove their worth. Our future in the United States does not look promising. Lawmakers had an opportunity to offer better conditions to Salvadorans. The Immigration Reform and Control Act proves it. The United States had a chance to review the law and to review the Central American question, but did not. I believe Salvadorans in the United States have been sentenced without trial. When you think about it, it is not very different from the way our people are treated in El Salvador.

Reading to Understand

After you explore your initial responses to something you have read, the next step is to return to the selection and reread carefully to be certain you have an accurate understanding of what the writer is saying and how he or she is saying it. It is easy, during the first reading, to skip over essential points, to miss important evidence, or to be overwhelmed by the emotions the piece arouses.

Writing down and talking about initial responses and then returning to the text before you make firm evaluations are essential parts of critical thinking. While these steps are part of any careful, thoughtful reading, they are particularly important for reading across cultures. When we read something written from a cultural viewpoint that is different from our own perspective, we may jump to unwarranted conclusions or fail to see the point the author is making.

One way to delay the rush to judgment as you read and reread is to look for the author's main idea as well as for the points that support that idea. Until you fully understand what the writer is saying, it's impossible to move from an initial response to a logical and carefully thought-out evaluation of those ideas.

SUMMARIZING TO IDENTIFY THE MAIN IDEA AND SUPPORTING IDEAS A useful strategy for gaining a clear sense of what the author is saying is to try writing a summary of the selection. When you summarize, you move from your own initial responses to an objective view of the writer's ideas. In a summary, you briefly restate in your own words the author's main idea or ideas and, often, the most important supporting points.

Useful summaries usually share the following qualities:

1. They clearly identify the author's main point or points.
2. They identify the most important supporting points.
3. They make clear the relationship between the main point and the supporting points.
4. They condense these points without omitting essential ideas.
5. They are stated primarily in your own words. If you use any of the author's words, they should be enclosed in quotation marks and properly documented.
6. They focus on the author's ideas and feelings and do not include your own observations or evaluations.

Here are sample paragraphs written by three different students who had read "Leaving El Salvador" and had been asked to write a summary of what they had read. As you read these paragraphs, consider which one best demonstrates the qualities just listed for summaries and note your reasons for making this judgment.

A. Gloria Bonilla left El Salvador to escape government persecution, and she had to change her tourist visa to a student visa. She learned the history of El Salvador from her parents. She came to Washington, D.C., in April 1981, and she stayed with her friend John, whom she had called from Guatemala. She was homesick, but she forced herself to study and to get a job. She had the support of friends. She had trouble with the U.S. immigration service, and the army broke into her home in 1981. But she could not get political asylum. She explains why many Salvadorans have not done very well: because they don't have the education. She also thinks immigration laws are unfair and that Salvadorans have been sentenced without trial.

B. The central idea of this essay is that the author came from El Salvador to the United States to try to find a better life. But all she does is complain about the different laws and problems. She got a college education here and even a master's degree, so I don't see what she is complaining about. It seems like she wants the United States to change the immigration laws, but she doesn't say why. Also, what does she mean by "it is not very different from the way our people are treated in El Salvador"?

C. In her essay "Leaving El Salvador," Gloria Bonilla describes the reasons she left El Salvador to come to the United States. She explains the problems and conditions in her native country, but the real central point of the essay is to describe the problems she encountered after she came here, to explain what caused the problems, and to tell how she tried to solve them. Although being homesick was a difficulty at first, the main obstacles Bonilla describes did not come from inside herself but from the regulations and rules established by the U.S. immigration service. She gives many examples of the complex issues Salvadorans must face if they want to come to this country. For example, she argues that she was able to succeed only because she managed to get a student visa and was able to get a college education, "something most Salvadorans have not been able to attain" (p. 15). She ends her essay with a statement that compares the way the U.S. immigration service treats Salvadoran immigrants to the way the government in El Salvador treated the same people when they were citizens of that country.

Example A does not fit the definition of a summary. First, this sample does not clearly identify the central point, and it does not differentiate between main ideas and supporting ideas. Instead, it simply plows through the essay chronologically, picking up details here and there. Some of the details are important points — for example, "Gloria Bonilla left El Salvador to escape government persecution." Yet in the same sentence, and given equal emphasis, is a much less important point: "she had to change her tourist visa to a student visa." In addition, several details in the sample, such as the second sentence, "She learned the history of El Salvador from her parents," are only marginally related to the main points the author makes.

Another problem with Example A shows up in this sentence, "She had trouble with the U.S. immigration service and the army broke into her home in 1981." As written, the sentence implies that the U.S. army broke into her home. Careful reading shows, however, that Bonilla cites this detail as an example of her persecution by the government in El Salvador.

Finally, several sentences take words directly from the essay without enclosing them in quotation marks or providing correct documentation. For instance, note the final sentence, which takes the phrase "have been sentenced without trial" from the next-to-last sentence in the essay. In addition to using the words without quotations, the writer fails to provide a proper context. Bonilla uses the image of sentencing without trial as a metaphor to describe the way she believes Salvadorans have been treated by the U.S. immigration service. In the sample, however, the phrase seems to mean that they have actually been sentenced by a judge without a trial.

This example demonstrates two problems that can arise from failing to read carefully: (1) not establishing a clear overview of the author's ideas, and (2) not understanding how the author uses details, reasons, and examples to support that idea.

Example B is not really a summary at all. Instead, it is a response. While responding freely to a text is essential, a different process is required for summarizing. Without summarizing (or using a similar clarifying strategy), the reader never moves beyond initial responses to carefully considered judgments.

The writer of Example B starts off with a sentence that might well start a summary, since it does suggest Bonilla's main idea. The rest of Example B, however, expresses opinions and asks questions. While it's important to react and respond to what you read throughout the reading process, it's also essential to be able to set aside those responses at some point and to look objectively at what the author is saying. You cannot move on to evaluate the author's ideas — or to evaluate your own responses to those ideas — until you understand the main and supporting points clearly.

Example C is a useful summary of "Leaving El Salvador." In the opening sentence, the writer provides a context by mentioning both the author's name and the title of the essay and by suggesting one of the author's purposes. In the second sentence, the writer moves from the initial purpose to the central idea of the essay; this sentence shows that the writer understands the objective of the first section of the essay. The first section discusses the author's leaving El Salvador and arriving in the United States, but it serves primarily as a long introduction to the author's main point: describing "the problems she encountered after she came here, [explaining] what caused the problems, and [telling] how she tried to solve them." This student has read through the entire essay and has seen how the parts of the essay fit together. Rather than writing a summary that simply moves chronologically through the essay, the student provides an overview of what happens throughout (see sentence 2) and then offers examples that develop this overview.

This student correctly uses quotation marks and documentation to identify words taken directly from Bonilla's essay and refrains from making evaluations. The act of writing the summary, then, accomplishes at least two goals: It allows the student writer to understand clearly what Bonilla is saying, and it provides time to think and thus to avoid the rush to unconsidered judgments.

Exercise 4

Reread the excerpt from Ishmael Reed's "What's American about America?" Then read the following summaries of that excerpt. Applying the criteria given on page 16, and following the process used in the evaluations on pages 17–18, state which summary you believe demonstrates the clearest understanding of Reed's observations, and explain the reasons for your choice.

A. In Ishmael Reed's article "What's American about America?" he seems to wonder about all the different kinds of people in this country. He lists a lot of examples of the different kinds of people, like Italian, Islamic, and Spanish. He is saying that announcements on speakers at airports should be in Spanish, too. Also, he wants professors to talk about other cultures, even if they're white. But maybe if a professor was white, he wouldn't be as much of an expert on another culture, so I would say that this point is a problem.

B. Ishmael Reed in his article "What's American about America?" tells about an item he read in the *New York Times* that describes a festival attended by people of many different nationalities. He also tells about a poet who talked to Hispanic people in Detroit who were Islamic. While in Texas, Reed heard an airport announcement in both Spanish and English; and when he returned, he listened to a Yale professor whose original work on African cultures led to his ostracism from some intellectual circles. This professor was a white man.

Reed also went to a McDonald's and took pictures of kids eating hamburgers. Then he talks about a cultural bouillabaisse and about Beethoven's Ninth Symphony, the cubists, and the surrealists.

C. In this excerpt from his essay "What's American about America?" Ishmael Reed gives a series of examples that illustrate the question he asks in the title. This question suggests that it is difficult, if not impossible, to give any one single definition of "American." Instead, as the examples show, America is made up of many different kinds of people from many different backgrounds. Some of the groups he mentions are religious, for example, Jewish and Islamic. Other groups relate to the country where these people or their ancestors came from, for example, Chinese, African, and Hispanic. All the examples lead to the final paragraph, where Reed quotes Yale professor Robert Thompson, who calls the United States "a cultural bouillabaisse" (p. 9). This comparison reinforces the main idea by showing that American culture is like a soup made of many different ingredients, where each ingredient stays separate yet also combines in an interesting way with the other ingredients.

Exercise 5

Choose a selection from Sections 2–4 of this book, read it carefully, and then write a summary. As you write, keep in mind the examples you have just read as well as the qualities of a strong summary listed on page 16.

READING TO UNDERSTAND INFERENCES   When you make inferences, you use hints or suggestions to understand more completely what a writer or speaker is saying. For example, if you show your uncle the hiking boots you have decided to buy, he might note that the high tops of the boots will be uncomfortable on summer hikes. While your uncle has not stated that you should reconsider your decision, you can infer that meaning from his comment. In other words, you have to go beyond an understanding of his literal statement and recognize the implications of what he has said.

In a similar manner, to understand fully what you are reading, you need to go beyond identifying the author's main points and supporting points. You need to think more deeply so that you can recognize ideas, feelings, and values that are not directly stated but are, instead, implied.

When you make inferences, you use hints or suggestions in what you read to understand more completely what the writer is saying. For instance, in the excerpt from "What's American about America?" Ishmael Reed mentions listening to a Yale professor speak on "the influence of African cultures upon those of the Americas." Nowhere in that paragraph does Reed directly state his attitude toward the professor or toward those he describes as disapproving of the professor. Yet the words and images he chooses allow the reader to infer that Reed admires the speaker and scorns those who fail to see the worth of his work. For example, he shows us the professor "dancing and drumming the top of the lectern." These activities would be interpreted by many readers as lively, energetic (and, therefore, positive) actions — as opposed to the negative "ostracism" the professor encounters from some "intellectual circles." We can infer that these "intellectual circles" who shun the professor are probably white. Certainly, they are not black, since in the next sentence we are told that he is "cheered and applauded" by "Afro-American intellectuals and artists." From these details, the reader can infer Reed's disapproval of the white intellectuals' response, his affirmation of the Afro-American intellectuals' responses, and his admiration for the professor.

When you read to make inferences, you "read between the lines" to see what the writer suggests as well as what he or she actually states. As you develop your ability to make inferences, keep in mind the following suggestions:

1. Notice the writer's choice of words and be sensitive to the *connotation* (the emotional associations of the words) as well as the *denotation* (the dictionary definition of the words).
2. Notice the examples the writer chooses to describe an individual or a place or to explain a point. Consider the responses these examples evoke from readers.
3. Notice any value judgments the writer makes and consider whether these stated judgments help you to understand the writer's attitude toward other topics he or she discusses.
4. Notice any biases the writer states and consider how these views might relate to what he or she discusses.

Exercise 6

Reread Gloria Bonilla's essay "Leaving El Salvador," noting carefully her choice of words as she describes her experiences in her native country and her choice of words as she describes her experiences in the United States. Note also the examples she chooses to illustrate these experiences.

Then list the inferences you can make about (1) Bonilla's attitude toward El Salvador and (2) Bonilla's attitude toward the United States. Does she seem to admire one country more than the other? Or does she see them as equally negative? Explain your reasons.

Next, write a brief paragraph discussing the inferences you can make about Bonilla's feelings concerning her fellow Salvadoran immigrants. Remember to go beyond what is actually stated and consider what is implied. For instance, what does she imply about the way she believes many U.S. citizens view Salvadoran immigrants.

Reading to Evaluate

While the process of reading is highly complex and varies widely from individual to individual, most effective critical reading moves through the two stages just described — responding and understanding — to a third stage: evaluating.

To evaluate what you read (and your responses to what you read), you need to think carefully both about what the author states and implies and about the way you initially react to those statements and inferences. When you are reading selections from a wide variety of cultural backgrounds, you have to work diligently to establish intelligent, fair criteria (standards) by which to evaluate what you have read. Then you use these criteria to make sensible, balanced judgments that you can explain in speaking or writing.

ESTABLISHING CRITERIA When you make judgments about anything, you begin by establishing your criteria. For example, suppose you want to buy a new pair of shoes. Before you even begin looking, you start making a list of criteria in your head. These criteria are, of course, affected by many circumstances, and, obviously, they do not remain exactly the same for every pair of shoes you buy. For instance, if you are buying shoes to wear on a job that requires you to stand on your feet for eight hours a day, your criteria might include comfortable fit, sturdy material, cushioned innersoles, and low cost. On the other hand, if you are buying shoes to wear as part of a wedding party, your criteria might change to include a formal style, a specific color, comfortable fit, and low cost. Notice that while some of the criteria changed to suit the specific circumstances, other criteria (comfortable fit and low cost) remained the same.

As you develop criteria to evaluate what you read, you'll find that the process is similar. Some criteria will remain important to you no matter what you are reading. Other criteria may need to be established to fit the particular selection. For instance, if you are reading an essay written by someone from a culture very different from your own, you may find that to make a fair judgment, you have to revise or even discard some of your old standards. You may need to look at this writing in an entirely new way.

As you develop criteria for evaluating what you read, keep the following suggestions in mind:

1. *Consider the author.* What do you know about the author? (In this book, the headnotes that precede each piece give some information about the author.) Do the author's credentials give you confidence in

his or her knowledge of the topic? Do you have any reason to expect bias in the selection?

2. *Consider the audience.* For whom was the author originally writing? (In this book, the headnote often provides this information by telling you where the selection was first published.) To what extent do you believe the author would have been successful in communicating with this audience? For instance, how well does he or she seem to consider both *who* the readers are (their age, sex, ethnic background, political philosophy, religious beliefs, occupation, economic status) and *what they might already know* (level of education, experience with the topic, preconceptions about the topic).

 To what extent do you believe this author is successful in communicating with you and your fellow students as an audience? (Consider the same aspects related to audience analysis that are listed in the previous paragraph.)

3. *Consider the author's purpose.* While it's usually not possible to ascribe one specific reason for an author's writing any given selection, keep in mind three broad aims for writing:

 A. *Writing to express emotions, ideas, incidents, observations.* When authors write expressively, they are usually describing something, often by telling a true story about a situation they have experienced or observed. Their purpose is to create a picture made of words that will show the reader a new way of looking at some aspect of life.

 B. *Writing to explain.* When authors write to explain, they convey information and, often, prove a point about the subjects they explore. To accomplish their purpose, they may analyze, evaluate, synthesize, describe a process, make a comparison, define an unfamiliar concept, or explain the causes and effects of an action or decision — or they may use a combination of two or more of these strategies.

 C. *Writing to persuade.* When authors write to persuade, they offer evidence or make emotional appeals designed to convince the reader to acknowledge and accept as true the idea they are promoting. Often, in addition to urging readers to accept a certain idea, the author also hopes to move them to make certain actions.

 Identifying the author's aim allows you to establish criteria to determine how well he or she has accomplished that aim.

4. *Consider the author's use of details, reasons, and examples.* After you have identified the author's intended audience and purpose, you need to look carefully at the way he or she works to communicate to the audience and, thus, accomplish the aim. Depending on the audience and aim you have identified, you may want to consider either or both of the following:

 A. *Use of evidence.* Does the author provide evidence that convincingly supports the points he or she is making? For instance, if statistics are used, are they clearly explained and do they come from sources you believe to be reliable? If the author quotes experts, are these individuals' qualifications mentioned so that you can determine their reliability?

B. *Use of emotional appeals.* Does the author use examples, anecdotes (brief stories), or specific words that appeal particularly strongly to the readers' emotions? If so, do these emotional appeals help the writer to communicate effectively, or are these appeals a hindrance? Many readers find that emotional appeals enhance a writer's efforts when the appeals seem honest. When emotional appeals seem manipulative, many readers resent them. There are no easy tests to separate an "honest" use of emotion from a "manipulative" use. You'll need to establish your own reading sensibilities to make such judgments.

5. *Consider the values represented.* In addition to evaluating how effectively the author communicates with the audience, you may also evaluate the values suggested by what he or she has written. You might, for example, read a selection that you believe communicates strongly, yet you might disagree with what the author has to say.

When you make judgments about an author's values, you also think about and explore your own values, which serve as your criteria for evaluating the writer. As you read selections written by writers who may share some, but not all, of your own values, you'll often need to rethink both the views the author holds and the views you hold. This rethinking is the most challenging — and, often, disturbing — part of reading critically. It is challenging because it requires you to examine what you believe to be true about the way humans should interact with each other, with their institutions, and with their environment. It can be disturbing because as you read the thoughts and feelings of writers with views different from your own, you may find yourself questioning some of your own beliefs and ideals. The process may be less distressing if you consider that changing an opinion or belief — or, conversely, affirming in a new way an old belief or opinion — is an essential part of becoming an educated man or woman. If you were to pass through college entirely untouched by what you read or heard, you would be wasting a great deal of time and money.

USING CRITERIA TO EVALUATE: JOURNAL ENTRIES Once you have thought about the criteria you are using to evaluate a selection, you need to apply them. Writing journal entries is one way to do this.

An explanation of journal writing and several models of journal entries appear on pages 10–12. While these samples show students' responses rather than evaluations, the process is basically the same. You simply sit down and put on paper the evaluations that come to your mind as you are considering your criteria. In a journal entry, you are not worrying about formal aspects of writing such as organization, style, and mechanics; instead, you are using writing as a way of thinking. Here are two sample journal entries evaluating aspects of Gloria Bonilla's "Leaving El Salvador."

> As I read Gloria Bonilla's essay, I noticed that she uses a lot of examples to convince you that the U.S. legal system should have treated her better. As part of her point, she says that she believes she "had good enough reasons to be granted political asylum back in 1981." The thing is that when I looked at her examples closely, most of them had to do with what happened to her after she got here. Only one that I could find really talked about what happened to her in El Salvador and that was that the army broke into her house. She doesn't give enough information for me to be convinced that she should have been given political asylum, and it seems to me that this omission weakens the case she is making. How can she say it is as bad here as in El Salvador when she doesn't really show much of what happens there? *Cathy Lively*

> What I noticed was that Bonilla uses a lot of metaphors to describe what happened to her and for me they really made her picture come to life. For instance, she compares herself to a "larva in a cocoon" and you can picture that she stayed in there and then emerged gradually and became the beautiful butterfly who is her current self. She is now well-educated and a successful author who has had her essay published in a book. Also she talks about "heartache and homesickness" as though they were diseases and then she says she wrote her own "prescription." This is a metaphor that explains how and why she filled her days with work. For me, these metaphors make her story come to life, and I think she uses them effectively to tell about the changes she has lived through. These images remind me of my own feelings when I first came to this country and make me sympathetic with her experience. *Amy Ishigami*

These journal entries look at Bonilla's essay in markedly different ways, yet both make evaluations. Cathy Lively bases her evaluation on the evidence Bonilla offers to support her contention that she could have qualified for political asylum. Amy Ishigami, on the other hand, considers Bonilla's use of language as the main criterion for making a judgment. Lively's entry is somewhat critical of Bonilla's essay, while Ishigami's entry indicates approval. Just as there is no one correct response to a reading selection, so also there is no one correct evaluation. Evaluations differ according to the criteria used and the way those criteria are applied.

USING CRITERIA TO EVALUATE: DISCUSSIONS Discussing what you have read with others provides another way to explore your responses and to develop evaluations. An instructor may ask you to participate in class discussions or small-group discussions, or you may form your own group with other students to talk about what you have read. The great advantage to discussion is that it provides multiple viewpoints and keeps your responses and evaluations fluid. That is, you often find yourself developing new ideas or revising old ideas in reaction to what you hear. As an example of the way discussions can help readers to discover and explore ideas, consider the following transcript. It records the comments and questions of several students who had read and written journal entries responding to Ishmael Reed's "What's American about America?"

Frank: He's just not realistic — he doesn't — I don't think — he doesn't see the bad side to all this together stuff. To me, this fiesta or festival — whatever — couldn't happen today.

Lee Ann: But that's just one example. He doesn't — well, I don't think he's saying that this happens all the time because here in — in this paragraph here (paragraph 5) — he shows about the "ostracism," as he says, of the white professor. So he does see that conflict and that's realistic, I think.

Stan: He's realistic about the so-called intellectual circle — and you can see they're white — or they're not black, anyway because of paragraph 4, about the "Afro-American intellectuals." But he's not realistic about expecting announcements to be in two languages.

Danya: Everybody keeps saying "realistic" but what exactly do you mean? Does it have to be something that really happens all the time? Does it have to be something like — what I'm wondering is — like an actual current fact everywhere to be worth reading about it? Is that what it has to be for it to be realistic? I mean, it could be like the "I Have a Dream" which they play all the time on Martin Luther King's birthday. Which is something that is what you hope for but it may not be happening everywhere — or maybe it's going to happen in the future.

William: But if it's like a dream — so it isn't realistic — then what about all the examples he gives? They're supposed to be real, as far as I can see. I mean, he doesn't — there's no place where he says, "I wish this would happen."

Lee Ann: Well, maybe not a dream like future fantasy or something but like looking at the best possible case — in his opinion that is. So like maybe "idealistic" is the word instead of "realistic" or "dream."

In this short sample discussion, the participants express their own ideas, and, in addition, they listen carefully to what others have to say. Not only do they state opinions, but they also ask questions and indicate an openness to change. For example, they start out working with the idea of "realism" as a possible way to describe (and perhaps evaluate) the essay. As the discussion moves along, they explore the possibility of seeing Reed's ideas as a "dream" and then move to considering "idealistic" as perhaps a better description. The discussion is by no means finished; it's easy to see that there are many different directions it could take. Also, note that a discussion like this need not have as its goal finding one consensual "answer." Groups working together do not always have to agree. In fact, rather than insisting on compromise and closure, the most fruitful discussions usually value the way multiple voices open fresh possibilities and raise new questions.

When you discuss what you read with others, keep the following suggestions in mind:

1. Before the discussion, read thoughtfully and carefully, making notes that record your questions and observations.
2. When you come to the discussion, bring notes, summaries, journal entries — anything you've written that may help you participate in the discussion.
3. Respect your own ideas and come prepared to support them with specific references to what you have read.
4. Respect the ideas of others and listen with full attention, rather than planning what you are going to say next while others are speaking.
5. Remember that disagreeing with what someone else says or offering a different viewpoint is a legitimate — and useful — part of discussion.
6. Ask for clarification whenever you are not sure what a person means (for example, if someone uses a term like *courage, duty* or *patriotic,* you might want to ask for a definition).
7. Encourage quiet participants to enter into the conversation — perhaps by asking them their opinion on a specific point.

Exercise 7

Read a selection in Sections 2, 3, or 4. As you read, make notes in the margins, and then write a journal entry describing an initial response to the selection.

Next, reread the selection carefully, identifying the main idea and the primary supporting ideas. Then write a summary of no more than two paragraphs showing that you understand the main and supporting ideas.

Finally, consider ways to evaluate what you have read. If possible, discuss the selection with other students. Then write a journal entry that evaluates some aspect of the selection.

As you do this exercise, keep in mind the following summary of the critical-reading process, remembering that these approaches do not always proceed in this exact order. For example, many readers make inferences as they first read and respond. And most readers develop new responses throughout the reading process, not just when they first encounter a text.

Summary: Critical-Reading Process

1. Initial responding
2. Second responding (responding to responses)
3. Clarifying meaning (summarizing, making inferences)
4. Evaluating (establishing criteria, forming judgments)

2

Expressive Writing

The selections in Section 2 focus on three themes, "Arrivals," "Parents and Children," and "Ways of Learning." Each thematic section offers essays, interviews, letters, short stories, poems, and excerpts from books that demonstrate writers expressing their thoughts and feelings about a wide variety of subjects. As these authors write, they tell stories and describe people, places, and events to communicate both their external and their internal experiences to readers.

In the section "Arrivals," the selections relate the experiences of people coming to new places for the first time. Most of the selections focus on immigrants who arrive willingly in the United States, but "Slave Ship" and "Arrival at Manzanar" tell the stories of people who were forcibly taken from their homes and made to face unfamiliar and sometimes hostile circumstances. Selections in "Parents and Children" provide a close look at the similarities as well as differences between sons and daughters and their mothers and fathers. Most of the selections consider the cultural contrasts between immigrant parents and the children they are raising in the United States. On the other hand, both "My Father's Life" and "I Remember Papa" show sons looking at the ramifications of the economic and social backgrounds they shared with their fathers while growing up in the United States. Selections in "Ways of Learning" look not only at diverse school experiences but also at people who discovered ways to learn outside traditional institutions. For instance, Maya Angelou describes lessons she learned in a kitchen. Judith Ortiz Cofer reveals the wisdom gained through discussions in her grandmother's living room, and Frederick Douglass and Mike Rose explain how they were inspired to develop their own plans for self-education.

READING EXPRESSIVE WRITING

As you read expressive writing, you'll notice ways the author's view of the world is similar to or different from your own. Your strongest initial responses may come from identifying with or reacting against those similarities and differences. As you return to reread each selection, consider carefully what you believe to be the writer's central idea. Sometimes, the central idea will be clearly stated in a sentence or two occurring in the first or second paragraph. But often when you read expressive writing, you'll need to infer the author's main point from thinking about the anecdotes, examples, and descriptions he or she provides.

WRITING EXPRESSIVELY

For any selection in this section, your first tasks will include reading and rereading; writing exploratory notes, journal entries, and summaries; and discussing the selection. Then you may be asked to write a formal paper in response to what you have read. This response can take many different directions. One way of responding to what you have read is to write an expressive essay. In expressive writing, like the selections presented in this section, you provide a brief story (or perhaps several anecdotes) as well as carefully planned descriptive examples to convey to your readers your thoughts and feelings about a particular person, place, or events. Your aim is to recreate in words the subject you have chosen so that the reader can understand your perception of that subject.

SAMPLE EXPRESSIVE ESSAY

As an example of expressive writing, consider Rosalie Bryant's process as she responded to the following assignment:

> After reading Mary Antin's "The Promised Land," write an essay that expresses your responses to arriving in a new place. Like Antin, consider not only the place you came to but also the place you came from.

(Before you read Rosalie's response to this writing topic, read "The Promised Land" [p. 58].)

Exploring Ideas: Making Lists

After reading Antin's essay several times, making notes in the margins, and writing journal entries both about the essay and about the assignment, Rosalie decided to sort through her own responses as well as Antin's responses by making lists. As the following list (on the left) suggests, Rosalie noticed her strongest responses related Antin's reactions to differences between her native country and her new home and to Antin's memories of her former life.

Once she saw this pattern, Rosalie returned to Antin's essay to gather additional details related to the contrast between the old and the new.

As she wrote the list on the left, Rosalie began to see that Antin's first impressions of her new home had some similarities to Rosalie's own memories of her first venture onto the campus where she now attended classes. In addition, Antin's thoughts of her old life prompted Rosalie to recall memories of her own previous schooling. She then made notes in response to Antin's observations, noting where she saw similarities and where she saw differences.

Antin's Responses to Arrival in United States	*My Responses — First Time on Campus*
Met by father; acts like guide	Accompanied by cousin; constant advice
Amazed by big buildings and brick sidewalks — had not seen anything like it before	Surprised at size of campus and at number of classroom buildings — almost like a city; drove around three times
Interprets people at open windows as friendly	Everyone seemed busy with their own stuff — interpreted as unfriendly
Impressed with new home; mainly only had necessities; some things strange: "mysterious iron structure" turns out to be stove; mainly impressed because these things were "American"	Looked in empty classrooms — could these ever be "home"? Saw computers in many places — anxiety about using them; but impressed with the bare-walled classrooms; seem filled with serious intention
First meal; father gave them new food (bananas, had to give up on them); tin cans of food not cooked	First meal in cafeteria "mystery meat"; unidentifiable mixed vegetables
Education free; schooling important because of this	Education not free; important because of this
People who are angels "of deliverance"	Admissions people who helped me
Getting rid of "despised immigrant clothing"	Getting rid of "despised housewife clothing"
Antin's Memories	*My Memories*
Used to be rich; new place less fancy	Used to think college only for "other" people (smarter, richer)

Antin's Memories	*My Memories*
Everything in Russia cost money: school; lights to go through street	High school was "free"; you got your books "free," your paper "free" — but you didn't feel free
Officials told you what to do	Teachers and principal told you what to do

Writing the Draft

After making these lists, Rosalie saw that her experiences on her first visit to campus could, indeed, qualify as worthy material for an essay expressing her thoughts and feelings as she arrived at a new and strange place. She read "The Promised Land" one more time, noticing particularly Antin's use of details to create the sense of her experience; and then she began drafting. The draft printed here shows what she came up with after writing and revising three other drafts.

As you read this draft, notice that Rosalie uses some of the points in her list, but not all of them. Part of the process of drafting is to decide which ideas to use and which to eliminate. You do not have to fit every thought from your prewriting into your draft.

Notice also that Rosalie's paper is clearly organized. She arranges the events of her first trip to campus chronologically. And when she refers to memories in the past, she provides *transitions* (connecting words and phrases) to show how those memories relate to her main narrative (the story of her going to sign up for the class). Working toward a clear organization is also an important part of drafting.

MY PROMISED LAND

Rosalie Bryant

I sat in my kitchen, accompanied by a sink full of dirty dishes, a dog whining to be fed, and two laundry baskets heaped with my son's and daughter's clothes. As I drank my second cup of coffee, I thought about the long morning ahead while the two of them were at school. To avoid looking at the sink, the dog, or the laundry, I grabbed the nearest piece of reading material. Was it just by chance that what I grabbed was the flyer from Mt. Suffolk Community College?

Every year, I received these flyers, and every year I read them from cover to cover, looking at all the classes offered and thinking about what they might be like. Some sounded interesting, like "The Child in Literature" and "Parents and the Schools." Others sounded so intimidating; I couldn't understand the titles or the explanations. My eyes sped right past "Introduction to Finite Math" and "Principles of Anatomy and Physiology." This year, the same titles — and some new ones — caught my attention. "You have the time to take a class now," I thought.

And I could hear my husband, Paul, encouraging me, "Rosalie, go to school, if you want to!" But other voices quickly came in to squash that idea.

I heard my Uncle Joe, during Christmas vacation of my freshman year in high school. After he looked at my brother's report card and then at mine he said, "Well, Rosalie, good thing you're good-looking 'cause it looks like Dave got the brains in the family." Uncle Joe wasn't the only one who thought I lacked brains. My guidance counselor told me to forget about a college course and recommended that I sign up for classes that would help me get a job. "You'll need to work until you get married," he said, as if getting married was like going to the bank. (I wish he could see me now, working two nights and Sundays to help make the mortgage payments.) These old voices, and others, echoed in my head and told me I was foolish to think of college.

But I had another voice I could think of—one that had continued to be a support in my life for as long as I could remember. I grabbed the phone and called that "old voice," my cousin Susan, and before I lost my courage, I blurted out to her my thoughts about the college class. Of course, as always, she took right over! "Stay right there," she ordered, "I'm coming to get you." Within fifteen minutes she drove in the yard, and before I knew what was happening, Sue had talked me into getting in the car. "We'll just drive over to the college," she said. "We don't have to go in."

Sue is four years older than I am, and she's always been a major support in my life. She never went to college herself, but she reads all the time and she's always giving me books. We talk about what we read, and once I remember she told me I was "college material." I don't know why, but somehow deep inside there was something in me that believed her. Now, here she was literally driving me to college.

As we turned off the highway, following the signs to the college, I felt a large lump growing in my throat and, to accompany the lump, I felt butterflies hatching in my stomach in record numbers. "Let's just drive around," I told Sue, in a trembling voice. She started to pull into a parking space, but she looked at me, and I said again, more loudly, "Sue, keep driving!" We drove slowly around the road that surrounds the college. On the third pass by the parking lot, Sue said, "Well, I can do this until I run out of gas." I guess I must have nodded or something, because we turned into the parking lot and drove by what seemed like hundreds of parked cars as my cousin looked for a place to put her VW Rabbit. Finally, she found a place, and as we got out, I looked over past the parking lot to what looked to me like a whole city of multistory brick buildings. Even if I wanted to sign up for a class, how would I know which building?

As I read Mary Antin's description of her first day in Boston, I thought of this first day at Mt. Suffolk Community College. Like Mary,

I couldn't stop looking around. Everything seemed so new and different. Mary had her father acting as a guide, and I had Sue who didn't know anything more about the place than I did but who was firmly giving me orders. "Watch where you're going! Don't keep looking around like that! Look serious, like a college student!" Not knowing how to "look like a college student" and not wanting to show any more of my ignorance, I just followed Sue, moving fast to try to keep up with her steady pace. From time to time, I tried to hang back because I was terrified and having a hard time getting my breath, but Sue kept me going.

As we walked, I noticed that most of the other people we saw moved along quickly like my cousin. They all seemed to be looking beyond me or above me; no one smiled or said hello. I thought of the safety of the kitchen I had left. Even the dirty dishes, the unfolded laundry, and the whining dog seemed pleasing and comforting as I thought of them. Why had I ever let myself be talked into this? Or, to be more honest, why had I talked myself into this?

As we got closer to the nearest brick building, Sue stopped one of the hurrying students and asked where you'd sign up for a class. The student kept walking but pointed to a building with large granite steps and a sign that proclaimed "Administration." Now even Sue slowed down. The granite steps seemed to stretch up forever. I knew I couldn't climb them, even though several dozen other people were clearly making their way very easily. Finally, Sue took a deep breath and said, "Come on." I truly don't know how I got from the bottom to the top of the steps. But once we made it inside the door, things suddenly got much easier.

A large, hand-lettered sign proclaimed "Registration — Continuing Education," and an arrow pointed at a door that was slightly opened and seemed to invite me in. As I moved through the door, I saw lines of people. Most of them were my age or older, which was a relief, since I had visions of being the only "older woman" on campus. As I looked around, a little dazed with the hum and buzz of so many voices, a very short white-haired woman appeared next to me. Mary Antin uses the phrase "an angel of deliverance" to describe the neighbor who taught her mother to use the stove; in the next few minutes, I came to see the white-haired woman as my fairy godmother.

She introduced herself as Doris Reece, and she explained that she was the Administrative Assistant for the Dean of Continuing Education. I didn't know what to say, but Sue stepped in and said, "My cousin wants to take a class here." Doris looked at me questioningly; and as the lump in my throat began to melt and the butterflies in my stomach started to calm down, I silently nodded. She then sat down with me for a few minutes and suggested that I take English 101 as my first course. I felt better because I love to read, and I knew English would mean reading.

After that, I got into line, filled in the forms, and made out the required check. Then Sue and I left. My feelings were entirely changed from when we first arrived on campus. I was a college student at last!

Revising

Rosalie had already done a great deal of revising by the time she got to this third draft. (For more information on revising and for a revision checklist, see pp. 217–219.)

As a final step in revising, she asked a friend of hers, Janice Rule, who was also taking the English class, to read what she had written. She also asked Janice to suggest any improvements that would help her to communicate her experience more effectively. After reading Rosalie's draft, Janice returned it with this note.

Rosalie,

I really like what you've said. You used a lot of details like the dog and the laundry that made me be able to see where you were. Also, you told about things like the "old voices" and you gave examples so that I could also tell how you were feeling. Another thing I liked was that you used conversation, which you quoted so that I also could hear what it was like when you and your cousin Sue were talking.

The one thing I think you should change is your last paragraph. It just seems to come to an end that is too blah and doesn't show me enough about the change you said you had in your feelings. I guess you weren't nervous any more, but I'd like you to explain more what you mean.

Janice

Rosalie thought about what Janice said and, after several tries, came up with this new, revised final paragraph.

Somehow, I got into the right line, filled in the forms, and made out the required check. As Sue and I left, the granite steps didn't seem so steep. I was amazed to notice there were only five of them. And the students didn't seem so grim or so rushed. Several smiled and nodded to me. I suppose it was because I was smiling so much myself. After so many Septembers of reading the catalogue and throwing it away, I was finally a college student!

Revising means, literally, "re-seeing." Rosalie's revision shows that she did more than just add a detail or two. Instead, she spent time thinking about how she could show Janice (and any other readers) exactly how she felt as she left the administration building. As she reread her paper, she focused on her description of the steps. She realized that the steps had seemed much bigger and higher to her when she went into the building than when she came out. Recognizing this one detail helped her to draft a new conclusion. With other minor changes and proofreading, the third draft (the one printed on pp. 30–33) with the revised conclusion (preceding this paragraph) became her final paper.

Suggestions for Writing Expressively

1. Allow plenty of time for *prewriting,* note taking, summarizing, journal writing, listing, and so on.

2. As you think about your subject and plan to start your draft, consider your *audience.* Think about what your readers already know, what you will need to tell them, and how you can choose words that will communicate to them the feelings and ideas you want to express.

3. As you plan your draft, consider how you will *organize* the details and examples you want to use. For an expressive essay, some sort of chronological arrangement usually works well. If you move back and forth between the past and the present (or into the future), be sure to provide clear transitions to show how these time frames work together to communicate your experience in a unified way that makes sense to your readers.

4. When you write the *opening* of an expressive essay, move right into the topic without stopping to announce the subject. (Rosalie's first paragraph would have lost much of its power if she had begun by saying, "I'm going to describe how nervous I was when I first came to school to sign up for a class.")

5. As you write — and especially as you revise — keep in mind the importance of the *details* you select. Be specific; yet remember that you do not have to include everything that was part of the experience you are describing. (Note again Rosalie's list and compare it with her final draft. She omits many of the details that originally came to her mind.)

6. As you write — and especially as you revise — keep in mind the importance of *diction* (choice of words). For example, try to select words that not only convey the meaning but also communicate shades of emotion. (Rosalie says that her "eyes sped right past" the descriptions of courses she found intimidating. This choice of words suggests that her eyes moved of their own accord and that she is not entirely in control of how she feels about these courses. This phrase says so much more than "When I saw a course name I didn't understand, I just didn't read any more about it.")

7. As you write — and especially as you revise — keep in mind the possibility of using *directly quoted conversation.* Reporting a person's exact words is often more effective than simply giving a summary of what he or she said.

8. As you write — and especially as you revise — consider your *conclusion* carefully. You want a strong image, detail, or example to leave your readers fully recognizing and acknowledging the experience you are expressing.

You do not want a paragraph that goes on at length summing up your experience and making it sound like a moral lesson. On the other hand, you do not want to end too abruptly, leaving your reader with a sense of letdown or disappointment.

Arrivals

Previews: ARRIVALS

About twenty persons were seized in our village at the time I was; and amongst these were three children so young that they were not able to walk or to eat any hard substance. The mothers of these children had brought them all the way with them and had them in their arms when we were taken on board this ship.

From: *Slave Ship,* CHARLES BALL

That was the time, you see, when America was known to foreigners as the land where you'd get rich. There's gold on the sidewalk — all you have to do is pick it up. So people left that little village and went to America.

From: *From Steerage to Sweat Shop,* PAULINE NEWMAN

I came to the island [Ellis Island], too, so I could tell the ghosts that I was one of them, and that I honored them — their stoicism, and their innocence, the fear that turned them inward, and their pride. I wanted to tell them that I liked them better than the Americans who made them pass through the Great Hall and stole their names and chalked their weaknesses in public on their clothing.

From: *More Than Just a Shrine: Paying Homage to the Ghosts of Ellis Island,* MARY GORDON

I was here for two months before I started working, and then my uncle got me a job, first in the celery fields picking celery, washing it, packing it, and later picking prunes. Then, all of a sudden, one day the Immigration showed up, and I ran and I hid in a river that was next to the orchard. The man saw me and he questioned me, and he saw I didn't have any papers.

From: *Crossing the Border,* MIGUEL TORRES

RICHARD FRETHORNE
Letter from Virginia, 1623

> *This letter is one of three that remain to bear testimony to the homesickness, illness, poverty, and loneliness that this young, indentured servant experienced during his first months in what he and his parents would have called the New World. While living with and working for a family who lived near the Jamestown colony in Virginia, Frethorne sent this letter to his parents, which provides a personal look at the struggles and difficulties faced by the earliest immigrants.*

Prereading/Journal-Writing Suggestions

1. Write about the first time you went away from home. Were you homesick? What did you miss most about not being home? How did you get through this time?
2. Write about a place or an event that didn't quite live up to your expectations. Try to describe what you expected versus what you received. How did you handle the situation? Did you change in any way? Did you learn anything?

Loving and kind father and mother:

My most humble duty remembered to you, hoping in God of your good health, as I myself am at the making hereof. This is to let you understand that I your child am in a most heavy case by reason of the nature of the country, [which] is such that it causeth much sickness, as the scurvy and the bloody flux and diverse other diseases, which maketh the body very poor and weak. And when we are sick there is nothing to comfort us; for since I came out of the ship I never ate anything but peas, and loblollie (that is, water gruel). As for deer or venison I never saw any since I came into this land. There is indeed some fowl, but we are not allowed to go and get it, but must work hard both early and late for a mess of water gruel and a mouthful of bread and beef. A mouthful of bread for a penny loaf must serve for four men which is most pitiful. . . . People cry out day and night — Oh! that they were in England without their limbs — and would not care to lose any limb to be in England again, yea, though they beg from door to door. For we live in fear of the enemy every hour, yet we have had a combat with them on the Sunday before Shrovetide, and we took two alive and made slaves of them. But it was by policy, for we are in great danger; for our plantation is very weak by reason of the death and sickness of our company. For we came but twenty for the merchants, and they are half dead just; and we look every hour when two more should go. Yet there came some four other men yet to live with us, of which there is but one alive; and our Lieutenant is dead, and his father and his brother. And there was some five or six of the last year's twenty, of which there is but three left, so that we are fain to get other men to plant with us; and yet we are but 32 to fight against 3000 if they should come. And the nighest help that we have is ten miles of us, and when the rogues overcame this place last they slew 80 persons. . . .

And I have nothing to comfort me, nor there is nothing to be gotten here but sickness and death, except that one had money to lay out in some things for profit. But I have nothing at all — no, not a shirt to my back but two rags (2), nor no clothes but one poor suit, nor but one pair of shoes, but one pair of stockings, but one cap, but two bands. My cloak is stolen by one of my own fellows, and to his dying hour [he] would not tell me what he did with it; but some of my fellows saw him have butter and beef out of a ship, which my cloak, I doubt [not], paid for. So that I have not a penny, nor a penny worth, to help me to either spice or sugar or strong waters, without the which one cannot live here. For as strong beer in England doth fatten and strengthen them, so water here doth wash and weaken these here [and] only keeps life and soul together. But I am not half a quarter so strong as I was in England, and all is for want of victuals; for I do protest unto you that I have eaten more in [one] day at home than I have allowed me here for a week. You have given more than my day's allowance to a beggar at the door; and if Mr. Jackson had not relieved me, I should be in a poor case. But he like a father and she like a loving mother doth still help me. . . .

Goodman Jackson pitied me and made me a cabin to lie in always when I come up . . . which comforted me more than peas or water gruel. Oh, they be very godly folks, and love me very well, and will do anything for me. And he much marvelled that you would send me a servant to the Company; he saith I had been better knocked on the head. And indeed so I find it now, to my great grief and misery; and saith that if you love me you will redeem me suddenly, for which I do entreat and beg. And if you cannot get the merchants to redeem me for some little money, then for God's sake get a gathering or entreat some good folks to lay out some little sum of money in meal and cheese and butter and beef. Any eating meat will yield great profit. Oil and vinegar is very good; but, father, there is great loss in leaking. But for God's sake send beef and cheese and butter, or the more of one sort and none of another. But if you send cheese, it must be very old cheese; and at the cheese-monger's you may buy very good cheese for twopence farthing or halfpenny, that will be liked very well. But if you send cheese, you must have a care how you pack it in barrels; and you must put cooper's chips between every cheese, or else the heat of the hold will rot them. And look whatsoever you send me — be it never so much — look, what[ever] I make of it, I will deal truly with you. I will send it over and beg the profit to redeem me; and if I die before it come, I have entreated Goodman Jackson to send you the worth of it, who hath promised he will. . . . Good father, do not forget me, but have mercy and pity my miserable case. I know if you did but see me, you would weep to see me; for I have but one suit. . . . Wherefore, for God's sake, pity me. I pray you to remember my love to all my friends and kindred. I hope all my brothers and sisters are in good health, and as for my part I have set down my resolution that certainly will be; that is, that the answer of this letter will be life or death to me. Therefore, good father, send as soon as you can; and if you send me any thing let this be the mark.

ROT   Richard Frethorne,
                                                              Martin's Hundred

---

Suggestions for Writing and Discussion
1. After reading this piece through one time, what is your initial reaction to the writer's experience or to Frethorne himself?
2. Do you think you would have survived under the circumstances Frethorne describes? Why or why not?
3. In your opinion, what type of person is Frethorne? Is he a whiner? A hero? An opportunist? A fool? Something else? Please look closely at the words he chooses to describe his circumstances and cite specific examples to support your answer.
4. Why might so many people like Frethorne — the earliest immigrants to the United States — have been unprepared to survive on their own?
5. Frethorne writes that "we live in fear of the enemy every hour." Who is the enemy? Besides encountering people he describes as "the enemy," what other experiences were foreign to Frethorne?
6. What might Frethorne have expected this land to be like before he came to America, and why might he have wanted to come to this new land?

Suggestions for Extended Thinking and Research
1. Write a personal narrative about a struggle you have encountered and surmounted in your own life. Try to focus on your survival "process" — who helped you, why you kept trying, what you needed to do, how long your struggle took.
2. Search for another account of the early Jamestown experience, and compare this account with Richard Frethorne's experiences.

CHARLES BALL

Slave Ship

> *This narrative, published originally in 1854, is one of many gathered by Julius Lester and reprinted in his book* To Be a Slave *(1968). Like so many before him, Charles Ball was forcibly taken from his native village in Africa, brought aboard a slave ship, and sold to a plantation owner in Charleston, South Carolina. Ball was one of thousands of blacks who escaped from the South and told their stories to northern abolition groups just before and during the Civil War. These narratives were recorded and published as powerful tools to garner support for the emancipation of slaves.*

Prereading/Journal-Writing Suggestions

1. Think back to a time you left familiar surroundings and people to visit a new or strange place (your first day at school or at summer camp; your first plane ride alone; your first sleep-over with a friend or relative). Write about the actual trip you took — from your departure to your arrival. As you describe the details of the trip, include both the external physical details and your inner thoughts and feelings.

2. Before you read this piece, jot down a list or write a few sentences explaining what you know about the issue of slavery in the United States. Do you know any names, dates, events, or places connected with this issue? After reading what you have written, evaluate what you know about slavery. Would you consider yourself an expert or a novice as far as this period in history is concerned? Explain your reasons.

At the time we came into this ship, she was full of black people, who were all confined in a dark and low place, in irons. The women were in irons as well as the men.

About twenty persons were seized in our village at the time I was; and amongst these were three children so young that they were not able to walk or to eat any hard substance. The mothers of these children had brought them all the way with them and had them in their arms when we were taken on board this ship.

When they put us in irons to be sent to our place of confinement in the ship, the men who fastened the irons on these mothers took the children out of their hands and threw them over the side of the ship into the water. When this was done, two of the women leaped overboard after the children — the third was already confined by a chain to another woman and could not get into the water, but in struggling to disengage herself, she broke her arm and died a few days after of a fever. One of the two women who were in the river was carried down by the weight of her irons before she could be rescued; but the other was taken up by some men in a boat and brought on board. This woman threw herself overboard one night when we were at sea.

The weather was very hot whilst we lay in the river and many of us died every day; but the number brought on board greatly exceeded those who died, and at the end of two weeks, the place in which we were confined was so full that no one could lie down; and we were obliged to sit all the time, for the room was not high enough for us to stand. When our prison could hold no more, the ship sailed down the river; and on the night of the second day after she sailed, I heard the roaring of the ocean as it dashed against her sides.

After we had been at sea some days, the irons were removed from the 5 women and they were permitted to go upon deck; but whenever the wind blew high, they were driven down amongst us.

We had nothing to eat but yams, which were thrown amongst us at random — and of these we had scarcely enough to support life. More than one third of us died on the passage and when we arrived at Charleston, I was not able to stand. It was more than a week after I left the ship before I could straighten my limbs. I was bought by a trader with several others, brought up the country and sold to my present master. I have been here five years.

Suggestions for Writing and Discussion

1. This oral slave narrative is told in the first person. What tone does the speaker use to describe his agonizing ordeal? Identify specific words, phrases, and images that support your observation.
2. How old do you think the narrator is at the time he is speaking? How old do you picture him at the time of his capture? What details can you infer about the speaker from what he says in his narrative?
3. This narrative was probably originally used by white northerners just before and during the Civil War to gain sympathy for the antislavery cause. How effective do you think this narrative would be in reaching its intended audience and accomplishing its purpose? Pay attention to the connotations and denotations of the narrator's words as you explain your response.
4. Besides the main narrator, there are many other individuals mentioned in this short piece. Adopt another person's point of view and write this piece from that individual's perspective (one of the women, another slave, a young child, a white slave trader).
5. This narrative presents a general overview of the conditions and events surrounding one slave's journey. However, few details are provided. Choose one small scene in this piece and write a descriptive essay in which you use your imagination to supply intricate details. Concentrate on strong, sensory language that includes powerful verbs. Consider also using dialogue.

Suggestions for Extended Thinking and Research

1. Find another primary source written by a black American right after the Civil War. Compare or contrast this document with Ball's experience.
2. Read several other historical documents written at this same time in the United States (government documents, newspaper articles, personal letters, for example). Then write a paper describing what you have learned about some aspect of society during that time period.

PAULINE NEWMAN

From Steerage to Sweatshop

> *Born in 1893, Pauline Newman emigrated from Russia with her mother and two sisters. She joined her brother and another sister who had been sent ahead to earn enough money to bring over the rest of the family. Like many immigrants, Newman had been told that America was a land where there was "gold on the sidewalk." She soon learned from her experiences at the Triangle Shirtwaist Factory, where she started work at the age of eight, that survival — rather than getting rich — would be her main goal. In spite of the difficulties she faced, Newman remained determined to lead her life with dignity. Following the disastrous fire at the Triangle Factory, which claimed the lives of many of her friends, Newman became an organizer and tireless worker for the International Ladies Garment Workers' Union.*

Prereading/Journal-Writing Suggestions

1. In your journal, freewrite about what you consider to be your hometown. Let the writing lead you in any direction it chooses. After writing for about ten minutes, come to some conclusion: Is this a place you want to stay forever? Why or why not?
2. For what social cause would you be willing to volunteer your time? Would you be willing to actually fight for this cause? Explain why or why not.

   The village I came from was very small. One department store, one synagogue, and one church. There was a little square where the peasants would bring their produce, you know, for sale. And there was one teahouse where you could have a glass of tea for a penny and sit all day long and play checkers if you wanted.

   In the winter we would skate down the hilltop toward the lake, and in the summer we'd walk to the woods and get mushrooms, raspberries. The peasants lived on one side of the lake, and the Jewish people on the other, in little square, thatched-roofed houses. In order to go to school you had to own land and we didn't own land, of course. Very few Jews did. But we were allowed to go to Sunday School and I never missed going to Sunday School. They would sing Russian folk songs and recite poetry. I liked it very much. It was a narrow life, but you didn't miss anything because you didn't know what you were missing.

   That was the time, you see, when America was known to foreigners as the land where you'd get rich. There's gold on the sidewalk — all you have to do is pick it up. So people left that little village and went to America. My brother first and then he sent for one sister, and after that, a few years after that, my father died and they sent for my mother and my other two sisters and me. I was seven or eight at the time. I'm not sure exactly how old, because the village I came from had no registration of birth, and we lost the family Bible on the ship and that was where the records were.

Of course we came steerage. That's the bottom of the ship and three layers of bunks. One, two, three, one above the other. If you were lucky, you got the first bunk. Of course you can understand that it wasn't all that pleasant when the people on the second bunk or the third bunk were ill. You had to suffer and endure not only your own misery, but the misery from the people above you.

My mother baked rolls and things like that for us to take along, because 5 all you got on the boat was water, boiled water. If you had tea, you could make tea, but otherwise you just had the hot water. Sometimes they gave you a watery soup, more like a mud puddle than soup. It was stormy, cold, uncomfortable. I wasn't sick, but the other members of my family were.

When we landed at Ellis Island our luggage was lost. We inquired for it and they said, "Come another time. Come another time. You'll find it. We haven't got time now." So we left and we never saw our luggage again. We had bedding, linen, beautiful copper utensils, that sort of thing.

From Ellis Island we went by wagon to my brother's apartment on Hester Street. Hester Street and Essex on the Lower East Side. We were all bewildered to see so many people. Remember we were from a little village. And here you had people coming and going and shouting. Peddlers, people on the streets. Everything was new, you know.

At first we stayed in a tiny apartment with my brother and then, finally, we got one of our own. Two rooms. The bedroom had no windows. The toilets were in the yard. Just a coal stove for heat. The rent was ten dollars a month.

A cousin of mine worked for the Triangle Shirtwaist Company and she got me on there in October of 1901. It was probably the largest shirtwaist factory in the city of New York then. They had more than two hundred operators, cutters, examiners, finishers. Altogether more than four hundred people on two floors. The fire took place on one floor, the floor where we worked. You've probably heard about that. But that was years later.

We started work at seven-thirty in the morning, and during the busy 10 season we worked until nine in the evening. They didn't pay you any overtime and they didn't give you anything for supper money. Sometimes they'd give you a little apple pie if you had to work very late. That was all. Very generous.

What I had to do was not really very difficult. It was just monotonous. When the shirtwaists were finished at the machine there were some threads that were left, and all the youngsters — we had a corner on the floor that resembled a kindergarten — we were given little scissors to cut the threads off. It wasn't heavy work, but it was monotonous, because you did the same thing from seven-thirty in the morning till nine at night.

What about the Child Labor Laws?

Well, of course, there were laws on the books, but no one bothered to enforce them. The employers were always tipped off if there was going to be an inspection. "Quick," they'd say, "into the boxes!" And we children would climb into the big boxes the finished shirts were stored in. Then some shirts were piled on top of us, and when the inspector came—no children. The factory always got an okay from the inspector, and I suppose someone at City Hall got a little something, too.

The employers didn't recognize anyone working for them as a human being. You were not allowed to sing. Operators would have liked to have sung, because they, too, had the same thing to do and weren't allowed to sing. We weren't allowed to talk to each other. Oh, no, they would sneak up behind if you were found talking to your next colleague. You were admonished: "If you keep on you'll be fired." If you went to the toilet and you were there longer than the floor lady thought you should be, you would be laid off for half a day and sent home. And, of course, that meant no pay. You were not allowed to have your lunch on the fire escape in the summertime. The door was locked to keep us in. That's why so many people were trapped when the fire broke out.

My pay was $1.50 a week no matter how many hours I worked. My sisters made $6.00 a week; and the cutters, they were the skilled workers, they might get as much as $12.00. The employers had a sign in the elevator that said: "If you don't come in on Sunday, don't come in on Monday." You were expected to work every day if they needed you and the pay was the same whether you worked extra or not. You had to be there at seven-thirty, so you got up at five-thirty, took the horse car, then the electric trolley to Greene Street, to be there on time.

At first I tried to get somebody who could teach me English in the 15 evening, but that didn't work out because I don't think he was a very good teacher, and, anyhow, the overtime interfered with private lessons. But I mingled with people. I joined the Socialist Literary Society. Young as I was and not very able to express myself, I decided that it wouldn't hurt if I listened. There was a Dr. Newman, no relation of mine, who was teaching in City College. He would come down to the Literary Society twice a week and teach us literature, English literature. He was very helpful. He gave me a list of books to read, and, as I said, if there is a will you can learn. We read Dickens, George Eliot, the poets. I remember when we first heard Thomas Hood's "Song of the Shirt." I figured that it was written for us. You know, because it told the long hours of "stitch, stitch, stitch." I remember one of the girls said, "He didn't know us, did he?" And I said, "No, he didn't." But it had an impact on us. Later on, of course, we got to know Shelley. Shelley's known for his lyrics, but very few people know his poem dealing with slavery, called "The Masque of Anarchy." It appealed to us, too, because it was a time when we were ready to rise and that helped us a great deal. [*Recites:* "Rise like Lions after slumber."]

I regretted that I couldn't go even to evening school, let alone going to day school; but it didn't prevent me from trying to learn and it doesn't have to prevent anybody who wants to. I was then and still am an avid reader. Even if I didn't go to school I think I can hold my own with anyone, as far as literature is concerned.

Conditions were dreadful in those days. We didn't have anything. If the season was over, we were told, "You're laid off. Shift for yourself." How did you live? After all, you didn't earn enough to save any money. Well, the butcher trusted you. He knew you'd pay him when you started work again. Your landlord, he couldn't do anything but wait, you know. Sometimes relatives helped out. There was no welfare, no pension, no unemployment insurance. There was nothing. We were much worse off than the poor are today because we had nothing to lean on; nothing to hope for except to hope that the shop would open again and that we'd have work.

But despite that, we had good times. In the summer we'd go to Central Park and stay out and watch the moon arise; go to the Palisades and spend the day. We went to meetings, too, of course. We had friends and we enjoyed what we were doing. We had picnics. And, remember, in that time you could go and hear Caruso for twenty-five cents. We heard all the giants of the artistic world — Kreisler, Pavlova. We only had to pay twenty-five cents. Of course, we went upstairs, but we heard the greatest soloists, all for a quarter, and we enjoyed it immensely. We loved it. We'd go Saturday night and stand in line no matter what the weather. In the winter we'd bring blankets along. Just imagine, the greatest artists in the world, from here and abroad, available to you for twenty-five cents. The first English play I went to was *Peer Gynt*. The actor's name was Mansfield. I remember it very well. So, in spite of every-thing, we had fun and we enjoyed what we learned and what we saw and what we heard.

I stopped working at the Triangle Factory during the strike in 1909 and I didn't go back. The union sent me out to raise money for the strikers. I apparently was able to articulate my feelings and opinions about the criminal conditions, and they didn't have anyone else who could do better, so they assigned me. And I was successful getting money. After my first speech before the Central Trade and Labor Council I got front-page publicity, including my picture. I was only about fifteen then. Everybody saw it. Wealthy women were curious and they asked me if I would speak to them in their homes. I said I would if they would contribute to the strike, and they agreed. So I spent my time from November to the end of March upstate in New York, speaking to the ladies of the Four Hundred [the elite of New York's society] and sending money back.

Those ladies were very kind and generous. I had never seen or dreamed 20 of such wealth. One Sunday, after I had spoken, one of the women asked me to come to dinner. And we were sitting in the living room in front of a fireplace; remember it was winter. A beautiful library and comfort that I'd never seen before and I'm sure the likes of me had never seen anything like it either. And the butler announced that dinner was ready and we went into the dining room and for the first time I saw the silver and the crystal and the china and the beautiful tablecloth and vases — beautiful vases, you know. At that moment I didn't know what the hell I was doing there. The butler had probably never seen anything like me before. After the day was over, a beautiful limousine took me back to the YWCA where I stayed.

In Buffalo, in Rochester, it was the same thing. The wealthy ladies all asked me to speak, and they would invite me into their homes and contribute money to the strike. I told them what the conditions were that made us get up: the living conditions, the wages, the shop conditions. They'd probably never heard anything like this. I didn't exaggerate. I didn't have to. I remember one time in Syracuse a young woman sitting in front of me wept.

We didn't gain very much at the end of the strike. I think the hours were reduced to fifty-six a week or something like that. We got a 10 percent increase in wages. I think that the best thing that the strike did was to lay a foundation on which to build a union. There was so much feeling against unions then. The judge, when one of our girls came before him, said to her: "You're not striking against your employer, you know, young lady. You're striking against God," and sentenced her to two weeks on Blackwell's Island, which is now Welfare Island. And a lot of them got a taste of the club.

I can look back and find that there were some members of the union who might very well be compared to the unknown soldier. I'll never forget one member in the Philadelphia union. She was an immigrant, a beautiful young woman from Russia, and she was very devoted to the local union. And one Friday we were going to distribute leaflets to a shop that was not organized. They had refused to sign any agreement and we tried to work it that way to get the girls to join. But that particular day — God, I'll never forget the weather. Hail, snow, rain, cold. It was no weather for any human being to be out in, but she came into my office. I'd decided not to go home because of the weather and I'd stayed in the office. She came in and I said, "You're not going out tonight. I wouldn't send a dog out in weather like this." And I went to the window and I said, "Look." And while my back was turned, she grabbed a batch of leaflets and left the office. And she went out. And the next thing I heard was that she had pneumonia and she went to the hospital and in four days she was gone. I can't ever forget her. Of course, perhaps it was a bit unrealistic on her part, but on the other hand, I can't do anything but think of her with admiration. She had the faith and the will to help build the organization and, as I often tell other people, she was really one of the unknown soldiers.

After the 1909 strike I worked with the union, organizing in Philadelphia and Cleveland and other places, so I wasn't at the Triangle Shirtwaist

Factory when the fire broke out, but a lot of my friends were. I was in Philadelphia for the union and, of course, someone from here called me immediately and I came back. It's very difficult to describe the feeling because I knew the place and I knew so many of the girls. The thing that bothered me was the employers got a lawyer. How anyone could have *defended* them — because I'm quite sure that the fire was planned for insurance purposes. And no one is going to convince me otherwise. And when they testified that the door to the fire escape was open, it was a lie! It was never open. Locked all the time. One hundred and forty-six people were sacrificed, and the judge fined Blank and Harris seventy-five dollars!

Conditions were dreadful in those days. But there was something that 25 is lacking today and I think it was the devotion and the belief. We *believed* in what we were doing. We fought and we bled and we died. Today they don't have to.

You sit down at the table, you negotiate with the employers, you ask for 20 percent, they say 15, but the girls are working. People are working. They're not disturbed, and when the negotiations are over they get the increases. They don't really have to fight. Of course, they'll belong to the union and they'll go on strike if you tell them to, but it's the inner faith that people had in those days that I don't see today. It was a terrible time, but it was interesting. I'm glad I lived then.

Even when things were terrible, I always had that faith. . . . Only now, I'm a little discouraged sometimes when I see the workers spending their free hours watching television — trash. We fought so hard for those hours and they waste them. We used to read Tolstoy, Dickens, Shelley, by candlelight, and they watch the "Hollywood Squares." Well, they're free to do what they want. That's what we fought for.

Suggestions for Writing and Discussion

1. After reading this piece, what three characteristics would you choose to describe the author, Pauline Newman?
2. Compare the immigrants' preconceived notions of America with the realities of living there.
3. Explain how, even though she never received formal schooling, Pauline Newman became such an educated and articulate woman.
4. Newman states that "we were much worse off than the poor are today." What evidence does she offer to support this claim? What evidence can you find in this piece that supports the notion that in some ways the poor in the early 1900s were better off than the poor today?
5. Respond to the ending of this piece. In your own words, what is the point that Newman is making? Do you find this ending effective? Why or why not?

6. Agree or disagree with Newman's claim that people today lack the devotion and inner faith of the early factory union workers. Offer specific examples to support your claim.

Suggestions for Extended Thinking and Research

1. Consult the *New York Times Index* to find news articles about the Triangle Shirtwaist Factory. Write a report from the standpoint of an eyewitness to this tragic event. Assume the role of a factory worker, a boss, a bystander, a fire fighter, or any other role of your choice. Try to blend concrete facts with your imagination for this assignment.
2. Consult two other resources in order to learn more about the problems and successes that took place while unions were first being formed in this country.

MARY GORDON

*More Than Just a Shrine: Paying Homage
to the Ghosts of Ellis Island*

> *Born in 1949, Mary Gordon attended Barnard College and the Writing
> Program at Syracuse University. Best known for her acclaimed novels* Final
> Payments *(1978),* The Company of Women *(1981), and* Men and Angels
> *(1985), Gordon is also a regular contributor and reviewer for the* New York
> Times, *where she first published "More Than Just a Shrine." In this essay, she
> tells the story of her own journey to Ellis Island, a pilgrimage she made to help
> her better understand the experiences of her ancestors who passed through this
> huge — and, to many, intimidating — processing center when they arrived as Irish
> immigrants in New York.*

Prereading/Journal-Writing Suggestions

1. What do you know about your own ancestry? Write a few paragraphs
   retelling some of the stories you've heard about your grandparents or
   great-grandparents. Do any of these stories deal with injustice, with personal triumphs, with family tragedies? Pick one story from your family's
   past to write about more extensively.
2. If you were entertaining a student from another country, what one landmark within driving distance of where you live or go to school would you
   want to share with this visitor? Explain the significance you see in this
   landmark.
3. If the United States had to suggest one item or monument to the United
   Nations as a representative symbol, what would you propose? Write a
   paragraph or two in support of your proposal.

I once sat in a hotel in Bloomsbury trying to have breakfast alone. A
Russian with a habit of compulsively licking his lips asked if he could join
me. I was afraid to say no; I thought it might be bad for détente. He explained
to me that he was a linguist, and that he always liked to talk to Americans to
see if he could make any connection between their speech and their ethnic
background. When I told him about my mixed ancestry — my mother is Irish
and Italian, my father a Lithuanian Jew — he began jumping up and down in
his seat, rubbing his hands together, and licking his lips even more frantically.

"Ah," he said, "so you are really somebody who comes from what is
called the boiling pot of America." Yes, I told him, yes I was, but I quickly
rose to leave. I thought it would be too hard to explain to him the relation of
the boiling potters to the main course, and I wanted to get to the British
Museum. I told him that the only thing I could think of that united people

whose backgrounds, histories, and points of view were utterly diverse was that their people had landed at a place called Ellis Island.

I didn't tell him that Ellis Island was the only American landmark I'd ever visited. How could I describe to him the estrangement I'd always felt from the kind of traveler who visits shrines to America's past greatness, those rebuilt forts with muskets behind glass and sabers mounted on the walls and gift shops selling maple sugar candy in the shape of Indian headdresses, those reconstructed villages with tables set for fifty and the Paul Revere silver gleaming? All that Americana — Plymouth Rock, Gettysburg, Mount Vernon, Valley Forge — it all inhabits for me a zone of blurred abstraction with far less hold on my imagination than the Bastille or Hampton Court. I suppose I've always known that my uninterest in it contains a large component of the willed: I am American, and those places purport to be my history. But they are not mine.

Ellis Island is, though; it's the one place I can be sure my people are connected to. And so I made a journey there to find my history, like any Rotarian traveling in his Winnebago to Antietam to find his. I had become part of that humbling democracy of people looking in some site for a past that has grown unreal. The monument I traveled to was not, however, a tribute to some old glory. The minute I set foot upon the island I could feel all that it stood for: insecurity, obedience, anxiety, dehumanization, the terrified and careful deference of the displaced. I hadn't traveled to the Battery and boarded a ferry across from the Statue of Liberty to raise flags or breathe a richer, more triumphant air. I wanted to do homage to the ghosts.

I felt them everywhere, from the moment I disembarked and saw the   5 building with its high-minded brick, its hopeful little lawn, its ornamental cornices. The place was derelict when I arrived; it had not functioned for more than thirty years — almost as long as the time it had operated at full capacity as a major immigration center. I was surprised to learn what a small part of history Ellis Island had occupied. The main building was constructed in 1892, then rebuilt between 1898 and 1900 after a fire. Most of the immigrants who arrived during the latter half of the nineteenth century, mainly northern and western Europeans, landed not at Ellis Island but on the western tip of the Battery at Castle Garden, which had opened as a receiving center for immigrants in 1855.

By the 1880s the facilities at Castle Garden had grown scandalously inadequate. Officials looked for an island on which to build a new immigration center because they thought that on an island immigrants could be more easily protected from swindlers and quickly transported to railroad terminals in New Jersey. Bedloe's Island was considered, but New Yorkers were aghast at the idea of a "Babel" ruining their beautiful new treasure, "Liberty Enlightening the World." The statue's sculptor, Frédéric Auguste Bartholdi, reacted to the prospect of immigrants landing near his masterpiece in horror; he called it a "monstrous plan." So much for Emma Lazarus.

Ellis Island was finally chosen because the citizens of New Jersey petitioned the federal government to remove from the island an old naval powder magazine that they thought dangerously close to the Jersey shore. The explosives were removed; no one wanted the island for anything. It was the perfect place to build an immigration center.

I thought about the island's history as I walked into the building and made my way to the room that was the center in my imagination of the Ellis Island experience: the Great Hall. It had been made real for me in the stark, accusing photographs of Louis Hine and others who took those pictures to make a point. It was in the Great Hall that everyone had waited — waiting, always, the great vocation of the dispossessed. The room was empty, except for me and a handful of other visitors and the park ranger who showed us around. I felt myself grow insignificant in that room, with its huge semicircular windows, its air, even in dereliction, of solid and official probity.

I walked in the deathlike expansiveness of the room's disuse and tried to think of what it might have been like, filled and swarming. More than sixteen million immigrants came through that room: approximately 250,000 were rejected. Not really a large proportion, but the implications for the rejected were dreadful. For some, there was nothing to go back to, or there was certain death; for others, who left as adventurers, to return would be to adopt in local memory the fool's role, and the failure's. No wonder that the island's history includes reports of three thousand suicides.

Sometimes immigrants could pass through Ellis Island in mere hours, 10 though for some the process took days. The particulars of the experience in the Great Hall were often influenced by the political events and attitudes on the mainland. In the 1890s and the first years of the new century, when cheap labor was needed, the newly built receiving center took in its immigrants with comparatively little question. But as the century progressed, the economy worsened, eugenics became both scientifically respectable and popular, and World War I made American xenophobia seem rooted in fact.

Immigration acts were passed; newcomers had to prove, besides moral correctness and financial solvency, their ability to read. Quota laws came into effect, limiting the number of immigrants from southern and eastern Europe to less than 14 percent of the total quota. Intelligence tests were biased against all non-English-speaking persons and medical examinations became increasingly strict, until the machinery of immigration nearly collapsed under its own weight. The Second Quota Law of 1924 provided that all immigrants be inspected and issued visas at American consular offices in Europe, rendering the center almost obsolete.

On the day of my visit, my mind fastened upon the medical inspections, which had always seemed to me most emblematic of the ignominy and terror the immigrants endured. The medical inspectors, sometimes dressed in uniforms like soldiers, were particularly obsessed with a disease of the eyes called trachoma, which they checked for by flipping back the immigrants' top eyelids with a hook used for buttoning gloves — a method that sometimes resulted in the transmission of the disease to healthy people. Mothers feared that if their children cried too much, their red eyes would be mistaken for a symptom of the disease and the whole family would be sent home. Those immigrants suspected of some physical disability had initials chalked on their coats. I remembered the photographs I'd seen of people standing, dumbstruck and innocent as cattle, with their manifest numbers hung around their necks and initials marked in chalk upon their coats: "E" for eye trouble, "K" for hernia, "L" for lameness, "X" for mental defects, "H" for heart disease.

I thought of my grandparents as I stood in the room; my seventeen-year-old grandmother, coming alone from Ireland in 1896, vouched for by a stranger who had found her a place as a domestic servant to some Irish who had done well. I tried to imagine the assault it all must have been for her; I've been to her hometown, a collection of farms with a main street — smaller than the athletic field of my local public school. She must have watched the New York skyline as the first- and second-class passengers were whisked off the gangplank with the most cursory of inspections while she was made to board a ferry to the new immigration center.

What could she have made of it — this buff-painted wooden structure with its towers and its blue slate roof, a place *Harper's Weekly* described as "a latter-day watering place hotel"? It would have been the first time she'd have heard people speaking something other than English. She would have mingled with people carrying baskets on their heads and eating foods unlike any she had ever seen — dark-eyed people, like the Sicilian she would marry ten years later, who came over with his family, responsible even then for his mother and sister. I don't know what they thought, my grandparents, for they were not expansive people, nor romantic; they didn't like to think of what they called "the hard times," and their trip across the ocean was the single adventurous act of lives devoted after landing to security, respectability, and fitting in.

What is the potency of Ellis Island for someone like me — an American, 15 obviously, but one who has always felt that the country really belonged to the early settlers, that, as J. F. Powers wrote in "Morte D'Urban," it had been "handed down to them by the Pilgrims, George Washington and others, and that they were taking a risk in letting you live in it." I have never been the victim of overt discrimination; nothing I have wanted has been denied me because of the accidents of blood. But I suppose it is part of being an American to be engaged in a somewhat tiresome but always self-absorbing process of national definition. And in this process, I have found in traveling to Ellis Island an important piece of evidence that could remind me I was right to feel my differentness. Something had happened to my people on that island, a result of the eternal wrongheadedness of American protectionism and the predictabilities of simple greed. I came to the island, too, so I could tell the ghosts that I was one of them, and that I honored them — their stoicism, and their innocence, the fear that turned them inward, and their pride. I wanted to tell them that I liked them better than the Americans who made them pass through the Great Hall and stole their names and chalked their weaknesses in public on their clothing. And to tell the ghosts what I have always thought: that American history was a very classy party that was not much fun until they arrived, brought the good food, turned up the music, and taught everyone to dance.

Suggestions for Writing and Discussion

1. Why do you think Gordon begins this piece by discussing her experience in another country? What can you infer about her character from the details she provides about her meeting with the Russian linguist?
2. Gordon says she has never visited any other American landmarks except Ellis Island, and yet she goes on to describe the commercialism of other historical places, such as Gettysburg and Plymouth Rock. In your opinion, is it fair of her to assess landmarks she's never visited? Explain your reasons. Do your own experiences with such landmarks lead you to agree or disagree with Gordon's observations?
3. Gordon's grandmother came from Ireland when she was seventeen years old. This was "the single adventurous act" of her life. Looking back on your life, what has been your most adventurous act? Describe the act and explain why you consider it adventurous. Do you regret the act or are you proud of it? What insights and lessons (if any) came from the act?
4. Throughout this essay, Gordon seems to discount a connection between her own past and that of early American settlers. What does she gain or lose by using this approach? Are you sympathetic with her sentiments? Explain.
5. Gordon's last sentence clearly expresses her main point. In what ways does her final metaphor of a party connect to her main theme? What other metaphors for describing our connection with America's past can you suggest? Choose one metaphor and write a paragraph explaining it.

Suggestions for Extended Thinking and Research

1. Gordon explains that immigrants had to prove "moral correctness and financial solvency" in order to remain in America. Imagine that in order to remain in this country today, you, too, have to prove "moral correctness and financial solvency." Write a persuasive essay in which you prove that, based on the above criteria, you do, indeed, deserve to remain here.
2. Interview older relatives — aunts, uncles, grandparents, great-aunts, great-uncles — to learn about their experiences or their ancestors' experiences when they were younger. Using your interviews, write an essay in which you focus on the "single adventurous act" in their lives so far.
3. Find some photographs of the Ellis Island experience taken by photographers such as Louis Hine. Choose the one that you respond to most strongly, and write an essay describing the details of this photograph. As

you write your description, choose words, phrases, and images that will convey the emotions you feel as you look at and think about the picture.

4. Read other narratives and descriptions of the Ellis Island experience. Then write a creative narrative in which you imagine yourself to be an immigrant arriving at Ellis Island from any country you choose and during any time period you choose. Remember to be true to the historical details you discovered in your research.

MARY ANTIN

The Promised Land

> *Born to an affluent Russian Jewish family in 1881, Mary Antin saw her family lose their wealth and security to the growing oppression of czarist Russia. This excerpt from Antin's autobiography,* The Promised Land *(1912), shows her optimistic view of the immigrant experience. Neither the journey in steerage nor the difficult living circumstances in her family's crowded Boston apartment dampen her hope for a new and better life.*

Prereading/Journal-Writing Suggestions

1. Think back to your earliest memories when life was still full of mystery and magnificence. Describe from this childhood vantage point one specific memory. Include as many details as you can to bring this experience to life for your readers. (*Suggestions:* Consider significant "firsts," such as a first birthday party, a first move, a first best friend, a first disappointment, a first discovery.)
2. Describe and explain the significance of a place that to others may appear commonplace but to you is special.
3. Describe the greatest change in your life so far. How has that change affected you? Consider both what you may have lost and what you may have gained.

Anybody who knows Boston knows that the West and North Ends are the wrong ends of that city. They form the tenement district, or, in the newer phrase, the slums of Boston. Anybody who is acquainted with the slums of any American metropolis knows that that is the quarter where poor immigrants foregather, to live, for the most part, as unkempt, half-washed, toiling, unaspiring foreigners; pitiful in the eyes of social missionaries, the despair of boards of health, the hope of ward politicians, the touchstone of American democracy. The well-versed metropolitan knows the slums as a sort of house of detention for poor aliens, where they live on probation till they can show a certificate of good citizenship.

He may know all this and yet not guess how Wall Street, in the West End, appears in the eyes of a little immigrant from Polotzk. What would the sophisticated sight-seer say about Union Place, off Wall Street, where my new home waited for me? He would say that it is no place at all, but a short box of an alley. Two rows of three-story tenements are its sides, a stingy strip of sky is its lid, a littered pavement is the floor, and a narrow mouth its exit.

But I saw a very different picture on my introduction to Union Place. I saw two imposing rows of brick buildings, loftier than any dwelling I had ever lived in. Brick was even on the ground for me to tread on, instead of common earth or boards. Many friendly windows stood open, filled with uncovered heads of women and children. I thought the people were interested in us, which was very neighborly. I looked up to the topmost row of windows, and my eyes were filled with the May blue of an American sky!

In our days of affluence in Russia we had been accustomed to upholstered parlors, embroidered linen, silver spoons and candlesticks, goblets of gold, kitchen shelves shining with copper and brass. We had featherbeds heaped halfway to the ceiling; we had clothes presses dusky with velvet and silk and fine woollen. The three small rooms into which my father now ushered us, up one flight of stairs, contained only the necessary beds, with lean mattresses; a few wooden chairs; a table or two; a mysterious iron structure, which later turned out to be a stove; a couple of unornamental kerosene lamps; and a scanty array of cooking-utensils and crockery. And yet we were all impressed with our new home and its furniture. It was not only because we had just passed through our seven lean years, cooking in earthen vessels, eating black bread on holidays and wearing cotton; it was chiefly because these wooden chairs and tin pans were American chairs and pans that they shone glorious in our eyes. And if there was anything lacking for comfort or decoration we expected it to be presently supplied — at least, we children did. Perhaps my mother alone, of us newcomers, appreciated the shabbiness of the little apartment, and realized that for her there was as yet no laying down of the burden of poverty.

Our initiation into American ways began with the first step on the new soil. My father found occasion to instruct or correct us even on the way from the pier to Wall Street, which journey we made crowded together in a rickety cab. He told us not to lean out of the windows, not to point, and explained the word "greenhorn." We did not want to be "greenhorns," and gave the strictest attention to my father's instructions. I do not know when my parents found opportunity to review together the history of Polotzk in the three years past, for we children had no patience with the subject; my mother's narrative was constantly interrupted by irrelevant questions, interjections, and explanations.

The first meal was an object lesson of much variety. My father produced several kinds of food, ready to eat, without any cooking, from little tin cans that had printing all over them. He attempted to introduce us to a queer, slippery kind of fruit, which he called "banana," but had to give it up for the time being. After the meal, he had better luck with a curious piece of furniture on runners, which he called "rocking-chair." There were five of us newcomers, and we found five different ways of getting into the American machine of perpetual motion, and as many ways of getting out of it. One born and bred to the use of a rocking-chair cannot imagine how ludicrous people can make themselves when attempting to use it for the first time. We laughed immoderately over our various experiments with the novelty, which was a wholesome way of letting off steam after the unusual excitement of the day.

In our flat we did not think of such a thing as storing the coal in the bathtub. There was no bathtub. So in the evening of the first day my father conducted us to the public baths. As we moved along in a little procession, I was delighted with the illumination of the streets. So many lamps, and they burned until morning, my father said, and so people did not need to carry lanterns. In America, then, everything was free, as we had heard in Russia. Light was free; the streets were as bright as a synagogue on a holy day. Music was free; we had been serenaded, to our gaping delight, by a brass band of many pieces, soon after our installation on Union Place.

Education was free. That subject my father had written about repeatedly, as comprising his chief hope for us children, the essence of American opportunity, the treasure that no thief could touch, not even misfortune or poverty. It was the one thing that he was able to promise us when he sent for us; surer, safer than bread or shelter. On our second day I was thrilled with the realization of what this freedom of education meant. A little girl from across the alley came and offered to conduct us to school. My father was out, but we five between us had a few words of English by this time. We knew the word school. We understood. This child, who had never seen us till yesterday, who could not pronounce our names, who was not much better dressed than we, was able to offer us the freedom of the schools of Boston! No application made, no questions asked, no examinations, rulings, exclusions; no machinations, no fees. The doors stood open for every one of us. The smallest child could show us the way.

This incident impressed me more than anything I had heard in advance of the freedom of education in America. It was a concrete proof—almost the thing itself. One had to experience it to understand it.

It was a great disappointment to be told by my father that we were not 10 to enter upon our school career at once. It was too near the end of the term, he said, and we were going to move to Crescent Beach in a week or so. We had to wait until the opening of the schools in September. What a loss of precious time—from May till September?

Not that the time was really lost. Even the interval on Union Place was crowded with lessons and experiences. We had to visit the stores and be dressed from head to foot in American clothing; we had to learn the mysteries of the iron stove, the washboard, and the speaking-tube; we had to learn to trade with the fruit peddler through the window, and not to be afraid of the policeman; and, above all, we had to learn English.

The kind people who assisted us in these important matters form a group by themselves in the gallery of my friends. If I had never seen them from those early days till now, I should still have remembered them with gratitude. When I enumerate the long list of my American teachers, I must begin with those who came to us on Wall Street and taught us our first steps. To my mother, in her perplexity over the cookstove, the woman who showed her how to make the fire was an angel of deliverance. A fairy godmother to us children was she who led us to a wonderful country called "uptown," where, in a dazzlingly beautiful palace called a "department store," we exchanged our hateful homemade European costumes, which pointed us out as "greenhorns" to the children on the street, for real American machine-made garments, and issued forth glorified in each other's eyes.

With our despised immigrant clothing we shed also our impossible Hebrew names. A committee of our friends, several years ahead of us in American experience, put their heads together and concocted American names for us all. Those of our real names that had no pleasing American equivalents they ruthlessly discarded, content if they retained the initials. My mother, possessing a name that was not easily translatable, was punished with the undignified nickname of Annie. Fetchke, Joseph, and Deborah issued as Frieda, Joseph, and Dora, respectively. As for poor me, I was simply cheated. The name they gave me was hardly new. My Hebrew name being Maryashe in full, Mashke for short, Russianized into Marya (*Mar-ya*), my friends said that it would hold good in English as *Mary:* which was very disappointing, as I longed to possess a strange-sounding American name like the others.

I am forgetting the consolation I had, in this matter of names, from the use of my surname, which I have had no occasion to mention until now. I found on my arrival that my father was "Mr. Antin" on the slightest provocation, and not, as in Polotzk, on state occasions alone. And so I was "Mary Antin," and I felt very important to answer to such a dignified title. It was just like America that even plain people should wear their surnames on week days.

As a family we were so diligent under instruction, so adaptable, and so   15 clever in hiding our deficiencies, that when we made the journey to Crescent Beach, in the wake of our small wagon-load of household goods, my father had very little occasion to admonish us on the way, and I am sure he was not ashamed of us. So much we had achieved toward our Americanization during the two weeks since our landing.

Suggestions for Writing and Discussion

1. In "The Promised Land," the writer's life changed from affluence to sparseness. Despite her losses, the writer seems to feel fortunate and overwhelmed with her new life. Speculate on why the writer feels so grateful for the meager life to which she has come.

2. If, as a child, you had had to wait a summer in order to go to school, would you have regarded the delay as "a loss of precious time"? What is the author's attitude toward education? Why do she and her family consider education a valued gift, a privilege? To what extent do you share her views? How does your own view of education contrast with hers?

3. Antin writes that in the United States even "light was free." List, as quickly as you can, all the things in your daily life that are "free." As far as you know, are these things "free" in other countries? Can you think of things that are free in other countries that are not free here?

4. Antin writes that her new Americanized name gives her a "dignified title." Why does this matter to her? Why is it so important that she and her family discard their original names? Have you ever changed your name in any way? Why did you make the change, and how did you feel about it? If you have never changed your name, would you consider doing so? Explain.
5. Compare the values of the Antin family with the modern American families as portrayed on television or in films. What similarities do you see? What differences?

Suggestions for Extended Thinking and Research

1. How do you think elementary and secondary education in this country would change if such schooling suddenly became a privilege extended only to certain people rather than a right extended to all? Interview professors on your campus, local elementary and secondary teachers, and students at various levels to gather data leading to your response to this question.
2. Compare the way you saw something as a child with the way you see it today. What do the similarities and differences you see tell you about the ways you have stayed the same and the ways you have changed?
3. Write an essay describing the steps necessary to begin something new. Base this essay on your own experience with a new project. Where did you start? What obstacles did you face? Where did you find support? What did you have to learn? What did you have to change?
4. Antin and her family fled czarist Russia to avoid oppression because of their Jewish heritage. Locate other primary sources written by Russian immigrants during this time period. From reading these sources, write an essay describing the kinds of oppression people suffered and their responses to these outrages.

JEANNE WAKATSUKI HOUSTON
AND JAMES D. HOUSTON

Arrival at Manzanar

> *Born in California in 1935, Jeanne Wakatsuki was among thousands of Americans of Japanese descent who were rounded up and sent to internment camps during World War II (following the Japanese attack on Pearl Harbor in December 1941). She remained at the camp in Manzanar from the age of seven to the age of eleven. Later, while studying journalism at San Jose State University, she met her future husband, novelist James D. Houston. Together they wrote* Farewell to Manzanar *to document her life there and to describe the impact of the internment on the Wakatsuki family as well as other families who spent the duration of the war at the camp.*
>
> *Like the other selections in this section, Jeanne Wakatsuki's story describes leaving a familiar place and arriving at a strange place. However, she and her family are unwilling "immigrants" to their new home.*

Prereading/Journal-Writing Suggestions

1. Think back to what happened in your life between the ages of seven and eleven. Start off by listing as many events and as many experiences as you can remember. Include the people you met, the things you learned, the books you read, the places you saw, the events that mattered, both personally and nationally. Then draw some conclusions that explain how and why those four years were important to you. How did you grow? How did you change? What made you happy, angry, puzzled, sad, surprised?

2. All families experience challenges at one time or another. Write about one such time in your own family. How did you react? How did other members of the family react? How did the family change as a result of facing this challenge?

In December of 1941 Papa's disappearance didn't bother me nearly so much as the world I soon found myself in.

He had been a jack-of-all-trades. When I was born he was farming near Inglewood. Later, when he started fishing, we moved to Ocean Park, near Santa Monica, and until they picked him up, that's where we lived, in a big frame house with a brick fireplace, a block back from the beach. We were the only Japanese family in the neighborhood. Papa liked it that way. He didn't want to be labeled or grouped by anyone. But with him gone and no way of knowing what to expect, my mother moved all of us down to Terminal Island. Woody already lived there, and one of my older sisters had married a Terminal Island boy. Mama's first concern now was to keep the family together; and once the war began, she felt safer there than isolated racially in Ocean Park.

But for me, at age seven, the island was a country as foreign as India or Arabia would have been. It was the first time I had lived among other Japanese, or gone to school with them, and I was terrified all the time.

This was partly Papa's fault. One of his threats to keep us younger kids in line was "I'm going to sell you to the Chinaman." When I had entered kindergarten two years earlier, I was the only Oriental in the class. They sat me next to a Caucasian girl who happened to have very slanted eyes. I looked at her and began to scream, certain Papa had sold me out at last. My fear of her ran so deep I could not speak of it, even to Mama, couldn't explain why I was screaming. For two weeks I had nightmares about this girl, until the teachers finally moved me to the other side of the room. And it was still with me, this fear of Oriental faces, when we moved to Terminal Island.

In those days it was a company town; a ghetto owned and controlled by the canneries. The men went after fish, and whenever the boats came back — day or night — the women would be called to process the catch while it was fresh. One in the afternoon or four in the morning, it made no difference. My mother had to go to work right after we moved there. I can still hear the whistle — two toots for French's, three for Van Camp's — and she and Chizu would be out of bed in the middle of the night, heading for the cannery.

The house we lived in was nothing more than a shack, a barracks with   5
single plank walls and rough wooden floors, like the cheapest kind of migrant workers' housing. The people around us were hardworking, boisterous, a little proud of their nickname, *yo-go-re,* which meant literally *uncouth one,* or roughneck, or dead-end kid. They not only spoke Japanese exclusively, they spoke a dialect peculiar to Kyushu, where their families had come from in Japan, a rough, fisherman's language, full of oaths and insults. Instead of saying *ba-ka-ta-re,* a common insult meaning *stupid,* Terminal Islanders would say *ba-ka-ya-ro,* a coarser and exclusively masculine use of the word, which implies gross stupidity. They would swagger and pick on outsiders and persecute anyone who didn't speak as they did. That was what made my own time there so hateful. I had never spoken anything but English, and the other kids in the second grade despised me for it. They were tough and mean, like ghetto kids anywhere. Each day after school I dreaded their ambush. My brother Kiyo, three years older, would wait for me at the door, where we would decide whether to run straight home together, or split up, or try a new and unexpected route.

None of these kids ever actually attacked. It was the threat that frightened us, their fearful looks, and the noises they would make, like miniature Samurai, in a language we couldn't understand.

At the time it seemed we had been living under this reign of fear for years. In fact, we lived there about two months. Late in February the navy decided to clear Terminal Island completely. Even though most of us were American-born, it was dangerous having that many Orientals so close to the Long Beach Naval Station, on the opposite end of the island. We had known something like this was coming. But, like Papa's arrest, not much could be done ahead of time. There were four of us kids still young enough to be living with Mama, plus Granny, her mother, sixty-five then, speaking no English, and nearly blind. Mama didn't know where else she could get work, and we had nowhere else to move *to*. On February 25 the choice was made for us. We were given forty-eight hours to clear out.

The secondhand dealers had been prowling around for weeks, like wolves, offering humiliating prices for goods and furniture they knew many of us would have to sell sooner or later. Mama had left all but her most valuable possessions in Ocean Park, simply because she had nowhere to put them. She had brought along her pottery, her silver, heirlooms like the kimonos Granny had brought from Japan, tea sets, lacquered tables, and one fine old set of china, blue and white porcelain, almost translucent. On the day we were leaving, Woody's car was so crammed with boxes and luggage and kids we had just run out of room. Mama had to sell this china.

One of the dealers offered her fifteen dollars for it. She said it was a full setting for twelve and worth at least two hundred. He said fifteen was his top price. Mama started to quiver. Her eyes blazed up at him. She had been packing all night and trying to calm down Granny, who didn't understand why we were moving again and what all the rush was about. Mama's nerves were shot, and now navy jeeps were patrolling the streets. She didn't say another word. She just glared at this man, all the rage and frustration channeled at him through her eyes.

He watched her for a moment and said he was sure he couldn't pay more 10 than seventeen fifty for that china. She reached into the red velvet case, took out a dinner plate and hurled it at the floor right in front of his feet.

The man leaped back shouting, "Hey! Hey, don't do that! Those are valuable dishes!"

Mama took out another dinner plate and hurled it at the floor, then another and another, never moving, never opening her mouth, just quivering and glaring at the retreating dealer, with tears streaming down her cheeks. He finally turned and scuttled out the door, heading for the next house. When he was gone she stood there smashing cups and bowls and platters until the whole set lay in scattered blue and white fragments across the wooden floor.

The name Manzanar meant nothing to us when we left Boyle Heights. We didn't know where it was or what it was. We went because the government ordered us to. And, in the case of my older brothers and sisters, we went with a certain amount of relief. They had all heard stories of Japanese homes being attacked, of beatings in the streets of California towns. They were as frightened of the Caucasians as Caucasians were of us. Moving, under what appeared to be government protection, to an area less directly threatened by the war seemed not such a bad idea at all. For some it actually sounded like a fine adventure.

Our pickup point was a Buddhist church in Los Angeles. It was very early, and misty, when we got there with our luggage. Mama had bought heavy coats for all of us. She grew up in eastern Washington and knew that anywhere inland in early April would be cold. I was proud of my new coat, and I remember sitting on a duffel bag trying to be friendly with the Greyhound driver. I smiled at him. He didn't smile back. He was befriending no one. Someone tied a numbered tag to my collar and to the duffel bag (each family was given a number, and that became our official designation until the camps were closed), someone else passed out box lunches for the trip, and we climbed aboard.

I had never been outside Los Angeles County, never traveled more than 15
ten miles from the coast, had never even ridden on a bus. I was full of excitement, the way any kid would be, and wanted to look out the window. But for the first few hours the shades were drawn. Around me other people played cards, read magazines, dozed, waiting. I settled back, waiting too, and finally fell asleep. The bus felt very secure to me. Almost half its passengers were immediate relatives. Mama and my older brothers had succeeded in keeping most of us together, on the same bus, headed for the same camp. I didn't realize until much later what a job that was. The strategy had been, first, to have everyone living in the same district when the evacuation began, and then to get all of us included under the same family number, even though names had been changed by marriage. Many families weren't as lucky as ours and suffered months of anguish while trying to arrange transfers from one camp to another.

We rode all day. By the time we reached our destination, the shades were up. It was late afternoon. The first thing I saw was a yellow swirl across a blurred, reddish setting sun. The bus was being pelted by what sounded like splattering rain. It wasn't rain. This was my first look at something I would soon know very well, a billowing flurry of dust and sand churned up by the wind through Owens Valley.

We drove past a barbed-wire fence, through a gate, and into an open space where trunks and sacks and packages had been dumped from the baggage trucks that drove out ahead of us. I could see a few tents set up, the first rows of black barracks, and beyond them, blurred by sand, rows of barracks that seemed to spread for miles across this plain. People were sitting on cartons or milling around, with their backs to the wind, waiting to see which friends or relatives might be on this bus. As we approached, they turned or stood up, and some moved toward us expectantly. But inside the bus no one stirred. No one waved or spoke. They just stared out the windows, ominously silent. I didn't understand this. Hadn't we finally arrived, our whole family intact? I opened a window, leaned out, and yelled happily. "Hey! This whole bus is full of Wakatsukis!"

Outside, the greeters smiled. Inside there was an explosion of laughter, hysterical, tension-breaking laughter that left my brothers choking and whacking each other across the shoulders.

We had pulled up just in time for dinner. The mess halls weren't completed yet. An outdoor chow line snaked around a half-finished building that broke a good part of the wind. They issued us army mess kits, the round metal kind that fold over, and plopped in scoops of canned Vienna sausage, canned string beans, steamed rice that had been cooked too long, and on top of the rice a serving of canned apricots. The Caucasian servers were thinking the fruit poured over rice would make a good dessert. Among the Japanese, of course, rice is never eaten with sweet foods, only with salty or savory foods. Few of us could eat such a mixture. But at this point no one dared protest. It would have been impolite. I was horrified when I saw the apricot syrup seeping through my little mound of rice. I opened my mouth to complain. My mother jabbed me in the back to keep quiet. We moved on through the line and joined the others squatting in the lee of half-raised walls, dabbing courteously at what was, for almost everyone there, an inedible concoction.

After dinner we were taken to Block 16, a cluster of fifteen barracks that 20 had just been finished a day or so earlier — although finished was hardly the word for it. The shacks were built of one thickness of pine planking covered with tarpaper. They sat on concrete footings, with about two feet of open space between the floorboards and the ground. Gaps showed between the planks, and as the weeks passed and the green wood dried out, the gaps widened. Knotholes gaped in the uncovered floor.

Each barracks was divided into six units, sixteen by twenty feet, about the size of a living room, with one bare bulb hanging from the ceiling and an oil stove for heat. We were assigned two of these for the twelve people in our family group; and our official family "number" was enlarged by three digits — 16 plus the number of this barracks. We were issued steel army cots, two brown army blankets each, and some mattress covers, which my brothers stuffed with straw.

The first task was to divide up what space we had for sleeping. Bill and Woody contributed a blanket each and partitioned off the first room: one side for Bill and Tomi, one side for Woody and Chizu and their baby girl. Woody also got the stove, for heating formulas.

The people who had it hardest during the first few months were young couples like these, many of whom had married just before the evacuation began, in order not to be separated and sent to different camps. Our two rooms were crowded, but at least it was all in the family. My oldest sister and her husband were shoved into one of those sixteen-by-twenty-foot compartments with six people they had never seen before — two other couples, one recently married like themselves, the other with two teenage boys. Partitioning off a room like that wasn't easy. It was bitter cold when we arrived, and the wind did not abate. All they had to use for room dividers were those army blankets, two of which were barely enough to keep one person warm. They argued over whose blanket should be sacrificed and later argued about noise at night — the parents wanted their boys asleep by 9:00 p.m. — and they continued arguing over matters like that for six months, until my sister and her husband left to harvest sugar beets in Idaho. It was grueling work up there, and wages were pitiful, but when the call came through camp for workers to alleviate the wartime labor shortage, it sounded better than their life at Manzanar. They knew they'd have, if nothing else, a room, perhaps a cabin of their own.

That first night in Block 16, the rest of us squeezed into the second room — Granny, Lillian, age fourteen, Ray, thirteen, May, eleven, Kiyo, ten, Mama, and me. I didn't mind this at all at the time. Being youngest meant I got to sleep with Mama. And before we went to bed I had a great time jumping up and down on the mattress. The boys had stuffed so much straw into hers, we had to flatten it some so we wouldn't slide off. I slept with her every night after that until Papa came back.

___

Suggestions for Writing and Discussion

1. Wakatsuki Houston's father was a "jack-of-all-trades" and, in addition, a man who liked his family to live among all types of people. What do these characteristics say about him? Do you agree with his view of the kind of community he wanted for his family? Explain.
2. Consider Houston's portrayal of different members of her family. If they lived in your neighborhood today, do you think you and your family would become close friends with them? Good neighbors? Distant neighbors? Have no relationship with them? Would you prefer to be friends with some of the Wakatsuki family members and not with others? Explain.
3. Because of the authors' various lively anecdotes, the child's perspective shines through in this piece. What do you think Wakatsuki Houston was like as a child? What kind of outlook did she have? What kind of personality? How would you characterize her approach to life?
4. Imagine you were in the same room when the dealer was bargaining with Mama over the dishes. How would you have reacted to this scene? If you have a strong response, write a letter to someone who was not there. In the letter, briefly describe the event and then describe your reaction, explaining whether (and why) you defend or condemn Mama's decision to break the dishes.
5. Imagine you are one of the author's older siblings. Then choose one specific scene and rewrite it from your point of view.
6. If six members of your family had to live together in a space the size of a small living room, what problems or conflicts could you foresee? If you had to share this same space with five strangers for six months, what other types of difficulties or conflicts would arise? How do you think you would approach or try to solve any problems you can foresee?

___

Suggestions for Extended Thinking and Research

1. Locate several articles and editorials from the *New York Times* during the month of December 1941. Is there any mention of America's reaction to the Japanese? Can you find anything about Terminal Island? Check this

same source for editorials in February 1942. Keep researching from this date on until you find several editorials on America's concern with the Japanese. Write an essay showing how these articles compare and contrast with the information Wakatsuki Houston offers.

2. Find other primary sources describing the experiences of Japanese-Americans who were interned during World War II. Compare these narratives with Wakatsuki Houston's. You may also want to read the book from which the excerpt included here was taken, *Farewell to Manzanar*.

MIGUEL TORRES

Crossing the Border

> At the time Miguel Torres told his story to an interpreter, he was twenty years old and was employed in a mushroom plant in California. He told the interviewer that he had entered the United States illegally four times during the past year. His story is representative of those of the many illegal aliens from various countries who take great risks to find the employment in the United States that they believe will bring them better lives.

Prereading/Journal-Writing Suggestions

1. Under what circumstances would you leave your home and your country for a foreign land?
2. In your journal, describe your ideal country, your idea of utopia. What about your utopia is possible in this country? What seems improbable?

I was born in a small town in the state of Michoacán in Mexico. When I was fifteen, I went to Mexico City with my grandmother and my mother. I worked in a parking lot, a big car lot. People would come in and they'd say, "Well, park my car." And I'd give them a ticket and I'd park the car and I'd be there, you know, watching the cars. I got paid in tips.

But I wanted to come to the United States to work and to earn more money. My uncle was here, and I thought if I could come to him, I could live with him and work and he would help me.

It's not possible to get papers to come over now. So when I decided to come, I went to Tijuana in Mexico. There's a person there that will get in contact with you. They call him the Coyote. He walks around town, and if he sees someone wandering around alone, he says, "Hello, do you have relatives in the United States?" And if you say yes, he says, "Do you want to visit them?" And if you say yes, he says he can arrange it through a friend. It costs $250 or $300.

The Coyote rounded up me and five other guys, and then he got in contact with a guide to take us across the border. We had to go through the hills and the desert, and we had to swim through a river. I was a little scared. Then we come to a highway and a man was there with a van, pretending to fix his motor. Our guide said hello, and the man jumped into the car and we ran and jumped in, too. He began to drive down the highway fast and we knew we were safe in the United States. He took us to San Isidro that night, and the next day he took us all the way here to Watsonville. I had to pay him $250 and then, after I'd been here a month, he came back and I had to give him $50 more. He said I owed him that.

I was here for two months before I started working, and then my uncle 5
got me a job, first in the celery fields picking celery, washing it, packing it,
and later picking prunes. Then, all of a sudden, one day the Immigration
showed up, and I ran and I hid in a river that was next to the orchard. The
man saw me and he questioned me, and he saw I didn't have any papers. So
they put me in a van and took me to Salinas, and there was some more illegals
there and they put us in buses and took us all the way to Mexicali near the
border. We were under guard; the driver and another one that sleeps while one
drives. The seats are like hard boards. We'd get up from one side and rub, you
know, that side a little bit and then sit on the other side for a while and then
rub that side because it's so hard. It was a long trip.

When we arrived in Mexicali, they let us go. We caught a bus to Tijuana,
and then at Tijuana, that night, we found the Coyote again and we paid him
and we came back the next day. I had to pay $250 again, but this time he knew
me and he let me pay $30 then and $30 each week. Because he knew me, you
know. He trusted me.

We came through the mountains that time. We had to walk through a
train tunnel. It all lasted maybe about three hours, through the tunnel. It was
short; for me it was short. We're used to walking, you know. Over in Mexico
we have to walk like ten miles to go to work or to go home or to go to school,
so we're used to walking. To me it was a short distance to walk for three
hours. And after we got out of the tunnel, we got into a car; and from there,
from the tunnel, we came all the way into Los Angeles. That was the second
time. We didn't see any border patrol either time.

The second time I was here for three months. My uncle managed to get
me a job in the mushroom plant. I was working there when the Immigration
came. There's this place where they blow air between the walls to make it
cool and I hid there. And I was watching. The Immigration was looking
around the plant everywhere. There was another illegal there, and he just kept
on picking the mushrooms. He'd only been back a couple of days himself.
The Immigration walked over there, and that kid turned around and looked
at the Immigration and said, "What's the matter? What happened?" And the
Immigration looked at him and said, "Oh, nothing," and the kid kept right
on picking mushrooms. Yet he was an illegal! He knew how to act, play it
cool. If you just sit tight they don't know you're illegal.

Well, the Immigration looked between the walls then and he caught me
again. That was the second time. They put handcuffs on me with another guy
and we were handcuffed together all the way from California to Mexicali.

Altogether I've been caught three times this year and made the trip over 10
here four times. It's cost me one thousand dollars but it's still better than what
I was making in Mexico City.

It's the money. When you come back here you get more money here than
you do over there. Right now, the most, the most that I'd be getting in Mexico
would be from 25 to 30 pesos a day, which is maybe $2.00, $2.50. And here,
with overtime, sometimes I make a $150 a week. Things are expensive here,

but it's expensive over there, too. And I like the way people live here. All the — what do you call it — all the facilities that you have here, all the things you can get and everything.

The boss at the mushroom factory doesn't ask for papers. He doesn't say anything about it. The last time, he hired me back as soon as I got back here, without any questions.

I learned to hide my money when the Immigration catch me. You know, if you have a lot on you, they take you fifteen or twenty miles from the border in Mexico. But if you have just two dollars or so, they let you go right in Tijuana. Then it's easier to come back. You can just walk right down the street and find the Coyote or someone like him. A man I know was hitchhiking along the road near San Diego and someone picked him up and it was the Immigration man who had just brought him back to Mexico! The Immigration laughed and said, "You got back faster than I did." Of course, he took him back to Mexico again then. But that man is back in Watsonville now, working in the brussels sprouts. It takes a longer time for the Immigration to catch us than it does for us to come back. [*Laughs.*]

I'd like to be able to stay here, to live here and work; but the only way now is to find someone that'll say, "Well, I'll marry you, I'll fix your papers for you." There's a lot of them who do that. I'd be willing to if I could find someone that would do it for me. You pay them, you know. You don't sleep together or even live in the same house, but they marry you. A long time ago you could fix up papers for your nephew or brother, a friend, a cousin. It was real easy then. But now it has to be close relations: mother, father, wife, son, or daughter. My uncle can't do it for me. The only way I could do it would be if I could marry an American citizen.

I'd like to learn English because it would be easier for me. There is a   15 night school here, but I don't like to go because after work I like to go out and mess around and goof off. [*Laughs.*] Maybe I'll go later. If I could just learn a tiny bit of English, you know, I could turn around and tell the Immigration, "What's the matter with you? What do you want?" and I wouldn't be recognized as an illegal.

Suggestions for Writing and Discussion
1. Reread the first paragraph of this piece. From the details and language used in these six sentences alone, what can you infer about Miguel's life before he turned fifteen?
2. What would you say are Miguel's personal strengths? What are his weaknesses? Is he someone you would probably have as a friend? Why or why not?
3. Analyze Miguel's reactions for each of the three times he is caught. Do his reactions change over the course of this year? Please explain.
4. Which life do you feel is better for Miguel — life in America with his uncle, or life in Mexico City with his mother and grandmother? Explain.

5. Make a prediction for Miguel's life ten years from the time of this interview. Where might he be living? What might he be doing? Would you see
his life as better than his life at the age of fifteen?
6. Is Miguel's presence in America a hindrance or a contribution to this
country? Please support your answer with inferences and facts from the
text itself. You may also offer any personal experience as support as well.

Suggestions for Extended Thinking and Research
1. Rewrite this piece from the immigration officer's point of view.
2. Research current immigration laws and the means by which an emigrant
can enter and live in America.
3. Research the controversies raised in several states that have experienced a
recent influx of illegal immigrants, particularly in California and Texas.

VO THI TAM

A Boat Person's Story

After the Communist takeover of South Vietnam, following the fall of Saigon in 1975, thousands of Vietnamese fled. Many of these people attempted to escape on overloaded boats, where they faced long journeys with little food or water. In addition, they were vulnerable to attacks from pirates; and if they survived, they often found themselves unwelcome in the countries they attempted to enter. In an interview, Vo Thi Tam describes her 1979 escape from Vietnam.

Prereading/Journal-Writing Suggestions

1. Writing can be public — that is, it can be shared with others. But writing can also be private. Private writing offers an opportunity to consider and reconsider various issues and problems. Try writing a private journal entry in which you think back to what might be the hardest experience you have encountered.
2. Think about the one modern appliance you depend upon most. Now write about what would happen if you couldn't use that appliance for two weeks.

My husband was a former officer in the South Vietnamese air force. After the fall of that government in 1975, he and all the other officers were sent to a concentration camp for reeducation. When they let him out of the camp, they forced all of us to go to one of the "new economic zones," that are really just jungle. There was no organization, there was no housing, no utilities, no doctor, nothing. They gave us tools and a little food, and that was it. We just had to dig up the land and cultivate it. And the land was very bad.

It was impossible for us to live there, so we got together with some other families and bought a big fishing boat, about thirty-five feet long.

Altogether, there were thirty-seven of us that were to leave — seven men, eight women, and the rest children. I was five months pregnant.

After we bought the boat we had to hide it, and this is how: We just anchored it in a harbor in the Mekong Delta. It's very crowded there and very many people make their living aboard the boats by going fishing, you know. So we had to make ourselves like them. We took turns living and sleeping on the boat. We would maneuver the boat around the harbor, as if we were fishing or selling stuff, you know, so the Communist authorities could not suspect anything.

Besides the big boat, we had to buy a smaller boat in order to carry   5 supplies to it. We had to buy gasoline and other stuff on the black market — everywhere there is a black market — and carry these supplies, little by little, on the little boat to the big boat. To do this we sold jewelry and radios and other things that we had left from the old days.

On the day we left we took the big boat out very early in the morning — all the women and children were in that boat and some of the men. My husband and the one other man remained in the small boat, and they were to rendezvous with us outside the harbor. Because if the harbor officials see too many people aboard, they might think there was something suspicious. I think they were suspicious anyway. As we went out, they stopped us and made us pay them ten taels of gold — that's a Vietnamese unit, a little heavier than an ounce. That was nearly all we had.

Anyway, the big boat passed through the harbor and went ahead to the rendezvous point where we were to meet my husband and the other man in the small boat. But there was no one there. We waited for two hours, but we did not see any sign of them. After a while we could see a Vietnamese navy boat approaching, and there was a discussion on board our boat and the end of it was the people on our boat decided to leave without my husband and the other man. [*Long pause.*]

When we reached the high seas, we discovered, unfortunately, that the water container was leaking and only a little bit of the water was left. So we had to ration the water from then on. We had brought some rice and other food that we could cook, but it was so wavy that we could not cook anything at all. So all we had was raw rice and a few lemons and very little water. After seven days we ran out of water, so all we had to drink was the sea water, plus lemon juice.

Everyone was very sick and, at one point, my mother and my little boy, four years old, were in agony, about to die. And the other people on the boat said that if they were agonizing like that, it would be better to throw them overboard so as to save them pain.

During this time we had seen several boats on the sea and had waved to 10 them to help us, but they never stopped. But that morning, while we were discussing throwing my mother and son overboard, we could see another ship coming and we were very happy, thinking maybe it was people coming to save us. When the two boats were close together, the people came on board from there — it happened to be a Thai boat — and they said all of us had to go on the bigger boat. They made us all go there and then they began to search us — cutting off our blouses, our bras, looking everywhere. One woman, she had some rings she hid in her bra, and they undressed her and took out everything. My mother had a statue of our Lady, a very precious one, you know, that she had had all her life — she begged them just to leave the statue to her. But they didn't want to. They slapped her and grabbed the statue away.

Finally they pried up the planks of our boat, trying to see if there was any gold or jewelry hidden there. And when they had taken everything, they put us back on our boat and pushed us away.

They had taken all our maps and compasses, so we didn't even know which way to go. And because they had pried up the planks of our boat to look for jewelry, the water started getting in. We were very weak by then. But we had no pump, so we had to use empty cans to bail the water out, over and over again.

That same day we were boarded again by two other boats, and these, too, were pirates. They came aboard with hammers and knives and everything. But we could only beg them for mercy and try to explain by sign language that we'd been robbed before and we had nothing left. So those boats let us go and pointed the way to Malaysia for us.

That night at about 9:00 p.m. we arrived on the shore, and we were so happy finally to land somewhere that we knelt down on the beach and prayed, you know, to thank God.

While we were kneeling there, some people came out of the woods and began to throw rocks at us. They took a doctor who was with us and they beat him up and broke his glasses, so that from that time on he couldn't see anything at all. And they tied him up, his hands behind him like this [*demonstrates*], and they beat up the rest of the men, too. They searched us for anything precious that they could find, but there was nothing left except our few clothes and our documents. They took these and scattered them all over the beach.

Then five of the Malaysian men grabbed the doctor's wife, a young woman with three little children, and they took her back into the woods and raped her—all five of them. Later, they sent her back, completely naked, to the beach.

After this, the Malaysians forced us back into the boat and tried to push us out to sea. But the tide was out and the boat was so heavy with all of us on board that it just sank in the sand. So they left us for the night. . . .

In the morning, the Malaysian military police came to look over the area, and they dispersed the crowd and protected us from them. They let us pick up our clothes and our papers from the beach and took us in a big truck to some kind of a warehouse in a small town not far away. They gave us water, some bread, and some fish, and then they carried us out to Bidong Island. . . .

Perhaps in the beginning it was all right there, maybe for ten thousand people or so, but when we arrived there were already fifteen to seventeen thousand crowded onto thirty acres. There was no housing, no facilities, nothing. It was already full near the beach, so we had to go up the mountain and chop down trees to make room for ourselves and make some sort of a temporary shelter. There was an old well, but the water was very shallow. It was so scarce that all the refugees had to wait in a long line, day and night, to get our turn of the water. We would have a little can, like a small Coke can at the end of a long string, and fill that up. To fill about a gallon, it would take an hour, so we each had to just wait, taking our turn to get our Coke can of water. Sometimes one, two, or three in the morning we would get our water. I was pregnant, and my boys were only four and six, and my old mother with me was not well, but we all had to wait in line to get our water. That was just for cooking and drinking of course. We had to do our washing in the sea.

The Malaysian authorities did what they could, but they left most of the administration of the camp to the refugees themselves, and most of us were sick. There were, of course, no sanitary installations, and many people had diarrhea. It was very hard to stop sickness under those conditions. My little boys were sick and my mother could hardly walk. And since there was no man in our family, we had no one to chop the wood for our cooking, and it was very hard for us just to survive. When the monsoons came, the floor of our shelter was all mud. We had one blanket and a board to lie on, and that was all. The water would come down the mountain through our shelter, so we all got wet.

After four months in the camp it was time for my baby to be born. Fortunately, we had many doctors among us, because many of them had tried to escape from Vietnam, so we had medical care but no equipment. There was no bed there, no hospital, no nothing, just a wooden plank to lie down on and let the baby be born, that was all. Each mother had to supply a portion of boiling water for the doctor to use and bring it with her to the medical hut when it was time. It was a very difficult delivery. The baby came legs first. But, fortunately, there were no complications. After the delivery I had to get up and go back to my shelter to make room for the next woman.

When we left Vietnam we were hoping to come to the United States, because my sister and her husband were here already. They came in 1975 when the United States evacuated so many people. We had to wait in the camp a month and a half to be interviewed, and then very much longer for the papers to be processed. Altogether we were in the camp seven months.

All this time I didn't know what had happened to my husband, although I hoped that he had been able to escape some other way and was, perhaps, in another camp, and that when I came to the United States I would find him.

We flew out here by way of Tokyo and arrived the first week in July. It was like waking up after a bad nightmare. Like coming out of hell into paradise. . . .

[*Shortly after she arrived in this country, Vo Thi Tam learned that her husband had been captured on the day of their escape and was back in a "reeducation" camp in Vietnam.*]

Suggestions for Writing and Discussion

1. Which one, single hardship in this account would you personally find the most difficult to bear? How do you think Vo Thi Tam survived this?
2. Analyze the possible reasons why people like Vo Thi Tam could endure such agony, such tragedy.
3. What might Tam's life have been like "in the old days," before the 1970s? Explain your answer.
4. What explanations can you offer for the matter-of-fact, detached tone in this piece? Take one scene from this piece and rewrite it in an emotional way. Which tone do you think most readers would find most appealing? Why?
5. Tam writes that she and her family spent seven months in Malaysia before they could leave. Use the details provided and your imagination to write a piece on how she probably spent a typical day in Malaysia.

Suggestions for Extended Thinking and Research

1. Consult 1975 issues of the *New York Times* for news articles on the boat people. Write an article in which you synthesize the new information you find with Tam's account.
2. Take a chance at writing a poem. You can write one from the third-person point of view, using vivid details and facts from this account. You could also write it from Tam's point of view or from her mother's or children's viewpoints.

BILL MOYERS, Interviewer

Dreaming Big Dreams: An Interview with Bharati Mukherjee

Bharati Mukherjee grew up in India and later emigrated first to Canada and then to the United States, where she has written and published several books, including The Middleman, *a collection of short stories focusing on the experiences of Asian immigrants who settled in America.* The Middleman *won the National Book Critics Circle Award in 1988. Mukherjee's most recent novel,* Jasmine, *follows the travels of a young Punjabi woman who, like the author, moves from India to America and then migrates throughout the United States. Mukherjee now teaches at the University of California at Berkeley, where she is a writer in residence.*

Bill Moyers is a highly respected television journalist who is well known for his insightful reporting at both PBS and CBS news. He has written several books and articles, many based on the perceptive interviews he has conducted in his work as a reporter. His books include The Power of Myth, *which was inspired by his conversations with educator and mythologist Joseph Campbell.*

Prereading/Journal-Writing Suggestions

1. If you were being interviewed, how would you respond to this question: "Where is your home?" Would it be the place you now live? Why or why not? What is it that makes the place you name "home" for you?

2. Have you ever been in a situation where you suddenly became acutely aware of differences between yourself and others because of the class you see yourself as belonging to? If so, describe that situation and your reactions. If not, comment on whether or not you see class as a significant issue in the culture of the United States. Use examples from your own experiences to support and explain your observations.

Moyers: You once said that your life has been a long process of searching for a home. Have you found it yet?

Mukherjee: Oh yes, absolutely. I feel very American. I've lived in many different countries, and I make many trips outside the United States for lectures or readings, but I'm always eager to come back here.

Moyers: To what? What is it that makes you feel as if finally, after all of these wanderings, you belong somewhere?

Mukherjee: I knew the moment I landed as a student in 1961, at the Writer's Workshop at the University of Iowa, that this is where I belonged. It was an instant kind of love, a feeling of being at one.

You see for me, America is an idea. It is a stage for transformation. I 5 felt when I came to Iowa City from Calcutta that suddenly I could be a new person. I didn't have to be the daughter of a very upper-class patriarch, a daughter who was guarded every moment of her life by bodyguards and so on.

Moyers: So home is not a place. Home is an ideal, a state of mind, an attitude.

Mukherjee: Home is a state of mind. And that's a big change from what I was brought up to believe. In Bengali, the word for home is *desh,* which means "region." As a child, when I was asked, "Where is your home?" I would have to cite the name of the village, Faridpur, now in Bangladesh, where my father was born, even though I hadn't ever been there. So making the change from thinking of home as a place, to thinking of it as an idea, was a radical metamorphosis for me.

Moyers: What does America mean to you as an idea?

Mukherjee: What America offers me is romanticism and hope. I came out of a continent of cynicism and irony and despair. A traditional society where you are what you are, according to the family that you were born into, the caste, the class, the gender. Suddenly, I found myself in a country where — theoretically, anyway — merit counts, where I could choose to discard that part of my history that I want, and invent a whole new history for myself.

Moyers: That's what Americans have been doing for two hundred years, 10 isn't it? Inventing, often romantically, an identity, a sense of themselves.

Mukherjee: Well, America as romanticism is what appeals to me. It's that capacity to dream and then try to pull it off, if you can. I think that the traditional societies in which people like me were born really do not allow the individual to dream. To dream big.

Moyers: That's what America is to Jasmine, the character in your new novel. She has big dreams. She leaves Florida, comes to New York, leaves New York, goes to Iowa, then leaves for California, dreaming big dreams, "greedy with dreams," I think the phrase is, and "reckless with hope."

Mukherjee: What's also exciting for me about America is that my soul is always at risk here. The immigrant's soul is always at risk. There are no comforting stereotypes to fit into. I have to make up the rules as I go along. No one has really experienced what the nonwhite, non-European immigrants are going through in the States. We can't count on the wisdom and experience of the past of the old country; and we can't quite fit into the traditional Euro-centric experiences of Americans.

Many of my characters in fact are like Joseph Conrad's in their ambiguous morality, and their need for risky adventures. They have some call from the unconscious that forces them to undertake these journeys outside their circumscribed little, petty villages, and it gets them off and in trouble. It certainly gets Jasmine in trouble. But there's a morality and a purification involved in that. If Conrad had the "Heart of Darkness," I'm exploring the heart of light, if you like, through Jasmine.

Moyers: And the light is — 15

Mukherjee: Where the Conradian character might say, "The horror, the horror," I am saying, "The wonder, the wonder." And light is tricky, too.

Light can daze, light can blind. But it's coming in from the outside into the lighted interior, and one has to open one's eyes wide.

Moyers: You have said a new American epic was washing up on our shores in the eighties.

Mukherjee: I meant new epic themes. We are going through lives that are larger than real in many ways, we new immigrants. And we're coming with such a hunger to find new meanings. We're coming with so much energy and curiosity in order to make new lives for ourselves, that to me, those are big stories to tell, very dense lives to chronicle. In a way, I am disappointed with the kind of fiction in magazines like *The New Yorker* or *The Atlantic,* which constantly records neat, miniaturized, suburban lives, and small crises, as opposed to the raw, raucous, messy lives that we nonwhites are leading during the same decade. It's as though some of the fiction editors don't want to acknowledge the rawness and messiness out there in America.

I think of it sometimes as fiction of fear. Of panic reaction to the changes that are going on in the country. Minimalist writing, with its codes, with its shorthand, with its very white suburban emphasis, is, I feel, an ostrich-with-head-in-the-sand kind of fiction.

Moyers: So many of these editors have their roots in Central Europe, 20 Poland, Italy, Germany — that part of the world that is itself white. Their parents and grandparents came here, and went through that raucous transformation that you and other Asians are now experiencing. How's this old-guard immigrant group reacting to the newcomer?

Mukherjee: In many ways, the Asian immigrant identifies with some significant aspects of the European immigration. We too believe in family-centeredness, and in education, and working very hard to improve oneself. But we're very different too because of race and religion.

Also, a lot of the South Asians, Pakistanis, and Indians have come in jets, rather than steerage. We've come with sophisticated degrees. We've come with the confidence to succeed in one generation, rather than wait for our children and our grandchildren to slowly cash in on America's promise. So in significant ways we have to deal with racism. If I have a message to deliver to America, it is a message of inclusiveness. That instead of thinking of the new Americans as new, or "we" versus "they," we should be thinking of all of us as a new kind of American.

Moyers: Well, I hear that. But I don't see any evidence that the newcomers are integrating into the mainstream. I mean Pakistanis live here, and Indians live there, and Russians live there, and Thais live here, and Vietnamese live there, and El Salvadorans live there. They live to themselves. I don't see this integration taking place.

Mukherjee: I think psychologically, emotionally, it is occurring with the children who came when they were two years old, let's say, or who were born over here. They want to be American. But I sometimes think that liberal whites, out of their need to appease guilt of some sort, want the non-European to preserve her or his original culture. Multiculturalism, in a sense, is well intentioned; but it ends up marginalizing the person. And what I'm witnessing through my travels, and in the enormous amount of mail I get from immigrants, is that the parents quite often, out of either arrogance about their native culture or fear of American culture, will try to retreat back into an unreal, frozen image of the old world. Whereas the children want to be very American.

Moyers: They want to become something new.   25

Mukherjee: A new being. Which is not to say that they want to be Anglo-Saxons, but yes, part of the new world. So I'm talking about psychological changes. Something has to be done at every level about marginalizing people into ghettos.

Moyers: Have you experienced any racism here?

Mukherjee: Not in the United States, not personally, but I did in Canada. My husband, Clark Blaise, is also a writer, and his parents were Canadian. So when Clark and I were looking for our first jobs, after our degrees from the University of Iowa, we looked only in Montreal, and we went there in 1966. In the beginning, Montreal was a perfect city for a bi-racial, bi-cultural, multilingual couple like us. But by the early seventies, racism reared its ferocious head. And by 1980, I felt that not only was racism institutional there, but had gotten physically virulent.

Moyers: Did you experience it physically?

Mukherjee: Yes, absolutely. I was spat on, and thrown to the back of the   30
bus, and ejected from the lobby of a fancy hotel, and called a whore. These were not just my personal experiences, but they were every South Asian Canadian's experience during the seventies. I blame some of that on the mosaic theory of absorbing immigrants.

Moyers: You mean the theory that culture is a variety of pieces placed side by side. They don't blend, or fuse into each other. It's just a mosaic.

Mukherjee: A mosaic, exactly, where the government and the national mythology encourage the newcomer to hang onto old-world cultures, old-world psyches. The intention was good. But if, in a multicultural system, unequal value is put on the various cultures, then I'm afraid that marginalization tends to work against the nonwhite immigrant. I wrote an essay called "An Invisible Woman" that was my good-bye to Canada. I said that the American system, in which everyone is encouraged to think of himself or herself as an American first, and then something else, works to the advantage of people like me, newcomers.

Moyers: How did Canadians respond?

Mukherjee: This was the very first time that a writer of credibility was calling Canadians on racism, so initially there was shock and outrage among the mainstream Canadians. In the seventies the Canadians tended to believe that all racism occurred south of the border, in the United States, and that they were humane in their treatment of foreigners. But I got enormous amounts of mail on that essay, which showed that others too, German war-brides and so on, had also felt otherized, marginalized. On the last trip that I made to Toronto, which was just October of last year, I saw that letters to the editor and newspaper editorials are now agreeing with the ideas I had tried to bring into the consciousness of people in 1981.

Moyers: Have you thought about why you would experience racism 35 more in Canada than here?

Mukherjee: Yes. I think that we nonwhite new immigrants have profited in the United States from the long history of black-white racial conflict. The civil rights laws are already in place in the United States. I want for all of us to remember what it was like when there was no such equality, so that we don't relapse into racism again. In Canada, there hadn't been open conflict until the 1970s because, I think, the minorities hadn't challenged the mainstream. So there was a kind of smugness. And there was no constitution guaranteeing us rights. Canada depended in those days on good will, rather than law.

Moyers: Your characters certainly experience some racism. Jasmine recognizes in America an infinite possibility for evil. Small wonder, since no sooner has she arrived than she's involved in a rape and in a murder. Even so, she manages never to feel like a victim.

Mukherjee: All American writers, even those who are offering messages of hope and possibility, must be very clear-eyed about the potential for evil. I hope that the stories in *The Middleman and Other Stories* or *Jasmine* present a full picture, a complicated picture of America. But I like to think that I, as well as my characters, constantly fight evil. We don't retreat from battle. And we don't like to be flattened altogether.

Moyers: She fights back. Sometimes with an eye for an eye and a tooth for a tooth. I don't sense that *you've* done that, except through your stories.

Mukherjee: Have I murdered someone, have I blackmailed, did I come as 40 an illegal alien? No, I didn't. But we, the new pioneers, who are still thinking of America as frontier country, do have a kind of ambiguous morality. We are improvising morality as we go along. And so Jasmine, who does murder, who does blackmail, is nonetheless true to herself, and keeps her integrity in the course of her adventures.

I want to think that my work has a moral center, that there is a very deep sense of right and wrong located inside the novel. But it does not necessarily have to be conventional Judaeo-Christian morality. Not all my characters are virtuous. Pioneering does not necessarily equate with virtue. I think that the original American pioneers had to have been in many ways hustlers, and capable of a great deal of violence, in order to wrest the country from the original inhabitants and to make a new life and a new country for themselves. So I like to think my characters have that vigor of possessing the land.

Moyers: What has it taken for a Third World woman to survive in this culture?

Mukherjee: A lot of discipline, a lot of strength, a lot of optimism.

Moyers: Weren't you brought up in India, like most Indian women, to please?

Mukherjee: Yes. To be very adaptable. Not to look a man straight in the 45 eye. To sit right. And to be elegant and decorative. But I guess I was into subversion.

Moyers: How did that happen? Who planted the seeds of subversion?

Mukherjee: I went outside India for the first time when I was eight years old. I went with my family to a school in England and Switzerland for three years. Suddenly, being removed from a very predictable world in which every second of my life was programmed, into a world in which I had some independence and just seeing the world out there was very exciting. I knew right then and there that I wanted more than what my family, my father, my privileged life could afford in Calcutta. I wanted psychological freedom.

Moyers: Why did you leave to come to this country in the first place in 1961? What were you looking for?

Mukherjee: I thought, when I came as a student to Iowa, that I was coming simply to get a Master of Fine Arts degree in creative writing at the Writer's Workshop in the heartland. But now, thinking back on it, I realize that I was looking for more out of life; that I never really intended to go back to that very circumscribed, safe life that my parents had promised. While I was a student living in a dorm in Iowa City, Iowa, my parents did find for me the perfect Bengali groom for an arranged marriage. I didn't know the first name of this man. He had seen my photograph, and he'd said, "Terrific, I'll take her." I was expected, certainly, to do what girls of my class normally did — be happy in an arranged marriage; be content, anyway, in an arranged marriage. But deep down, I must have rejected that safe, circumscribed life. So fate sometimes is full of happy accidents, and I fell in love with a fellow student, Clark Blaise. After a two-week whirlwind courtship, we got married during lunchtime. And therefore, I made my life in this country.

Moyers: What did you mean when you said some people, like your 50 character Jasmine, like yourself, although born oceans away, are born American at heart?

Mukherjee: It's that capacity for dreaming. The desire for change, for seizing the good life; meaning not a bigger house and bigger car, but freedom from fate, from a predetermined life. The desire to discard the traditional world, and sink or swim in a new world, without rules.

Moyers: Jasmine wants to reposition the stars. Is that what you wanted to do?

Mukherjee: I didn't know it when I actually left India, but yes. I want to reposition the stars. I want to conquer. I want to love and possess this country. I don't want to be simply an expatriate who always has her bags packed and is looking for greener pastures elsewhere.

Moyers: What's the difference between an expatriate and an immigrant?

Mukherjee: An expatriate is someone who is nourished by the old world, 55 whose psychic life is still totally attached to the discarded world thousands of miles away. An immigrant is someone who in psychological, social, psychic ways, has made herself or himself over in the new world. Who's accepting the new world as her own.

Moyers: How do you become an American? How do you let go of the past and invent the future when you're up against a culture of which you have only the dimmest, if not crudest, understanding?

Mukherjee: I think you invent an America for yourself. America is a total and wondrous invention. Letting go of the old culture, allowing the roots to wither is natural; change is natural. But the unnatural thing is to hang on, to retain the old world. What is the point of hanging on to a culture that's thousands of miles away, and that probably not you, not your children, not your grandchildren, will ever see? Why not adjust and accommodate to the world around you?

Moyers: It's hard. When I travel to foreign cultures, I've been hostage to nostalgia, to homesickness.

Mukherjee: I think nostalgia is a reaction of fear. It's a very understandable reaction, but it's one of panic or fear. Or it also can be in the case of, say, non-European immigrants, cultural arrogance. They feel that everything American is somehow inferior culturally to what they've left behind. I think if you've made the decision to come to America, to be American, you must be prepared to really, emotionally, become American and put down roots. Make that emotional commitment.

Moyers: Roots are more than geographical implants. 60

Mukherjee: Absolutely. In doing that, we very painfully, sometimes violently, murder our old selves. That's an unfortunate, perhaps, but inevitable process. I want to think that it's a freeing process. In spite of the pain, in spite of the violence, in spite of the bruising of the old self, to have that freedom to make mistakes, to choose a whole new history for oneself, is exciting.

Moyers: Even though you have not yourself experienced racism in the United States, I'm sure that you know that many Asians have. I can give you chapter and verse from South Texas to Chicago.

Mukherjee: There's going to be an increase in interminority violence in the nineties, I'm afraid. There's been a kind of disinvestment in America in the eighties that may continue in the nineties. People have not invested in the country. Instead they've been asking, "What part of the pie is for me?" They're privatizing, instead of saying, what kind of an America do we want? What kind of an America can we build?

As a result, I think that we are seeing large numbers of disenchanted minority groups who watch new immigrants from Asia come in, work hard, and in their perception, do rather well. They hold down jobs, move into good homes, buy big cars. There's a real resentment against the Asians. They're misperceived as the model minority.

I was standing by a newspaper kiosk which is staffed by an Indian- 65 American, and a homeless Afro-American came up and said, "Why is it that all the foreigners are taking over our jobs, and doing so well, while we are nowhere?" There's that kind of climate of scapegoating. We must do whatever is necessary, as a nation, as a whole country, to try and prevent that scapegoating. The Asians must make a commitment to America. If they've chosen to be Americans, then I think that they must really invest in their neighborhoods, invest in projects that help the homeless, or help solve problems for other minorities.

Moyers: What have you learned since you've been here about the American language? Your novels and short stories are so precise in their slang, in their understanding of American pop culture. You seem to have a gift for listening.

Mukherjee: I can't help it. I find myself mimicking every person that I listen to for more than fifteen minutes. It's also a hunger to know America. My love for the country translates itself into a kind of hunger to absorb it whole. I'm married to a fellow writer who's very American, who has dragged me to endless baseball games, and I have to thank him for giving me access to American trivia. I usually say that I'm a four-hundred-year-old lady, because I've lived through colonial and post-colonial history in India, and then have ingested wholesale two-hundred-odd years of American history.

Moyers: One of the most fascinating chapters in our story is coming now in the nineties, as the face of America is being changed by people who bring new ideas and are changed by the ideas that are here. Our story is changing even as we sit here.

Mukherjee: Yes. I think that we are creating American culture, daily. It is not something static. But through our art, and through the dangerous, improvised lives that we have to lead, we are creating a new American culture.

Moyers: Dangerous lives? 70

Mukherjee: Well, there are no comforts, no old mythologies to cling to. We have to invent new American mythologies.

Moyers: So tell me, your basic Protestant white male with Anglo-Saxon roots, what to expect from this new epic that is washing up on our shores.

Mukherjee: Vigor and energy and passion, and the hunger to belong to whatever mythology or dream this country can still offer. Maybe for the white, Anglo-Saxon males, the country is become depressing or no longer a dream. But the rest of us are coming with an eagerness to refashion ourselves. Letting go of the old notions of what America was shouldn't be seen as a loss. I hope that as we all mongrelize we will build a better and more hopeful nation.

Moyers: You write of Americans that we're overalert but underinformed, suspicious but ignorant, coddled like babies by our politicians, and rattled by the media drum beat. Have you figured out this country, what makes it tick?

Mukherjee: No. I hope I haven't figured it out. Part of the excitement is 75 constantly retooling and refashioning, trying to discover. My subject is not nostalgia for a known world, or chronicling of a real world — it's a continual discovery. I don't think of myself as a realistic writer, even though I hope that all the details ring true, whether it's about Iowa farmers going crazy, or Iowa bankers with their midlife crises shacking up with eighteen-year-old undocumented Punjabi girls like Jasmine.

But really, I'm writing a fable for the times. I'm trying to create a mythology that we can live by as we negotiate our daily lives. A mythology, a fable that can help us retain our integrity.

Moyers: Do you think America has a soul?

Mukherjee: Oh yes. That's why I'm here. I would have left if I didn't believe that America has a soul. Whenever I come back from trips outside, I heave a sigh of relief when I come into this country. I know it's unfashionable to believe so wholeheartedly, but I do.

Moyers: What is it you believe in?

Mukherjee: The visionariness of the Founding Fathers. The American 80 Constitution, whether it is practiced every day or not, absolutely entrances me. The protection of human rights, at least in theory. I'm seeing the world through very fresh eyes, whereas I felt jaded, even though I was a very young person when I lived in India. I felt I was a jaded child, looking through large jaded, bulging eyes at the world. Irony was my natural form of expression. Here, I'm not afraid to be impassioned. I'm not afraid to make mistakes. And I certainly have made many.

Moyers: We think of the immigrants in literature and in movies as sometimes pathetic figures. Whimpering, frightened creatures. You're painting a different portrait of the immigrant in America today.

Mukherjee: Yes. I'm not a pathetic creature, and my heroines are not pathetic creatures, because they don't think of themselves as victims. On the contrary, they think of themselves as conquerors. We have come not to passively accommodate ourselves to someone else's dream of what we should be. We've come to America, in a way, to take over. To help build a new culture. So we're pioneers, with the same guts and energy and feistiness that the original American Pilgrims had.

Suggestions for Writing and Discussion

1. Early in the interview, Moyers notes that Jasmine, one of Mukherjee's fictional characters, moves around the United States pursuing her dreams. As you read the interview, what dreams does Mukherjee, herself, seem to be pursuing? How would you compare her dreams with your own? Describe an incident from your own life that shows how your hopes and goals are similar to or different from Mukherjee's.

2. From your own observations and experiences, respond to Mukherjee's contention that immigrants who strive to preserve their own culture — and those citizens who encourage them to preserve their own culture — are actually doing the immigrants harm and "marginalizing" them.

3. Explain the contrasts Mukherjee sees between American and Canadian society. How does she use the analogy of the "mosaic theory" to support her contentions? Develop another analogy to describe the process Mukherjee seems to be recommending as most likely to serve both new immigrants and their new culture best.

4. Mukherjee characterizes American pioneers as "in many ways hustlers, and capable of a great deal of violence, in order to wrest the country from the original inhabitants and to make a new life and a new country for themselves." Further, she contends that "pioneering does not necessarily equate with virtue." What is your response to these observations? Is your first inclination to see her statements as an attack on American pioneers? If so, would you be inclined to defend them or to agree with her? If you do not see her views as necessarily negative, explain why.

5. In what ways do you see Mukherjee as rebelling against the culture in which she grew up? In what ways do you see her as affirming her cultural roots? Explain your response to the values implied both by her acts of rebellion and by her acts of affirmation.

Suggestions for Extended Thinking and Research

1. Mukherjee says that she sees the fiction in magazines like the *New Yorker* and the *Atlantic* as disappointing, because it "constantly records neat, miniaturized, suburban lives, and small crises, as opposed to the raw, raucous, messy lives that we nonwhites are leading." Read several stories from recent issues of these magazines, and then write your own response explaining whether you agree or disagree with Mukherjee's observation.

2. Do research on racial discrimination in Canada. In addition to seeking materials from the library, try to interview people who have lived in Canada for at least a year during the past decade. Then compare your findings with Mukherjee's observations.

ABRAHAM CAHAN

I Discover America

> *Abraham Cahan (1860–1951), himself an immigrant to the United States, creates a fictional version of the experience in his 1917 novel* The Rise of David Levinsky. *In this excerpt, the hero contrasts his dreams of the new world with the reality he encounters when he arrives.*

Prereading/Journal-Writing Suggestions

1. Use your journal to write about your biggest dreams for yourself. Don't hold back — really dare to dream for fifteen minutes. However, after your dream is complete, come back down to earth and analyze whether or not any of these dreams are possible for you to achieve.
2. Do you consider yourself a dreamer or a realist? A person caught in the past or geared toward the future? An optimist or a pessimist? A believer or a skeptic? A doer or a thinker? Choose any two of these pairs and explain a little bit about the type of person you are and the type of person you are not.

Two weeks later I was one of the multitude of steerage passengers on a Bremen steamship on my way to New York. Who can depict the feeling of desolation, homesickness, uncertainty, and anxiety with which an emigrant makes his first voyage across the ocean? I proved to be a good sailor, but the sea frightened me. The thumping of the engines was drumming a ghastly accompaniment to the awesome whisper of the waves. I felt in the embrace of a vast, uncanny force. And echoing through it all were the heart-lashing words:

"Are you crazy? You forget your place, young man!"

When Columbus was crossing the Atlantic, on his first great voyage, his men doubted whether they would ever reach land. So does many an American-bound emigrant to this day. Such, at least, was the feeling that was lurking in my heart while the Bremen steamer was carrying me to New York. Day after day passes and all you see about you is an unbroken waste of water, an unrelieved, a hopeless monotony of water. You know that a change will come, but this knowledge is confined to your brain. Your senses are skeptical.

In my devotions, which I performed three times a day, without counting a benediction before every meal and every drink of water, grace after every meal and a prayer before going to sleep, I would mentally plead for the safety of the ship and for a speedy sight of land. My scanty luggage included a pair of phylacteries and a plump little prayer-book, with the Book of Psalms at the end. The prayers I knew by heart, but I now often said psalms, in addition, particularly when the sea looked angry and the pitching or rolling was unusually violent. I would read all kinds of psalms, but my favorite among them was the 104th, generally referred to by our people as "Bless the Lord, O my soul," its opening words in the original Hebrew. It is a poem on the power and wisdom of God as manifested in the wonders of nature, some of its verses dealing with the sea. It is said by the faithful every Saturday afternoon during the fall and winter: so I could have recited it from memory; but I preferred to read it in my prayer-book. For it seemed as though the familiar words had changed their identity and meaning, especially those concerned with the sea. Their divine inspiration was now something visible and audible. It was not I who was reading them. It was as though the waves and the clouds, the whole far-flung scene of restlessness and mystery, were whispering to me:

"Thou who coverest thyself with light as with a garment, who stretches 5
out the heavens like a curtain: who layeth the beams of his chambers in the waters: who maketh the clouds his chariot: who walketh upon the wings of the wind. . . . So is this great and wide sea wherein are things creeping innumerable, both small and great beasts. There go the ships: there is that leviathan whom thou hast made to play therein. . . ."

The relentless presence of Matilda in my mind worried me immeasurably, for to think of a woman who is a stranger to you is a sin, and so there was the danger of the vessel coming to grief on my account. And, as though to spite me, the closing verse of Psalm 104 reads, "Let the sinners be consumed out of the earth and let the wicked be no more." I strained every nerve to keep Matilda out of my thoughts, but without avail.

When the discoverers of America saw land at last they fell on their knees and a hymn of thanksgiving burst from their souls. The scene, which is one of the most thrilling in history, repeats itself in the heart of every immigrant as he comes in sight of the American shores. I am at a loss to convey the peculiar state of mind that the experience created in me.

When the ship reached Sandy Hook I was literally overcome with the beauty of the landscape.

The immigrant's arrival in his new home is like a second birth to him. Imagine a new-born babe in possession of a fully developed intellect. Would it ever forget its entry into the world? Neither does the immigrant ever forget his entry into a country which is, to him, a new world in the profoundest sense of the term and in which he expects to pass the rest of his life. I conjure up the gorgeousness of the spectacle as it appeared to me on that clear June morning: the magnificent verdure of Staten Island, the tender blue of sea and sky, the dignified bustle of passing craft — above all, those floating, squatting, multitudinously windowed palaces which I subsequently learned to call ferries. It was all so utterly unlike anything I had ever seen or dreamed of before. It unfolded itself like a divine revelation. I was in a trance or in something closely resembling one.

"This, then, is America!" I exclaimed, mutely. The notion of something 10
enchanted which the name had always evoked in me now seemed fully borne out.

In my ecstasy I could not help thinking of Psalm 104, and, opening my little prayer-book, I glanced over those of its verses that speak of hills and rocks, of grass and trees and birds.

My transport of admiration, however, only added to my sense of helplessness and awe. Here, on shipboard, I was sure of my shelter and food, at least. How was I going to procure my sustenance on those magic shores? I wished the remaining hour could be prolonged indefinitely.

Psalm 104 spoke reassuringly to me. It reminded me of the way God took care of man and beast: "Thou openest thine hand and they are filled with good." But then the very next verse warned me that "Thou hidest thy face, they are troubled: thou takest away their breath, they die." So I was praying God not to hide His face from me, but to open His hand to me; to remember that my mother had been murdered by Gentiles and that I was going to a strange land. When I reached the words, "I will sing unto the Lord as long as I live: I will sing praise to my God while I have my being," I uttered them in a fervent whisper.

My unhappy love never ceased to harrow me. The stern image of Matilda blended with the hostile glamour of America.

One of my fellow-passengers was a young Yiddish-speaking tailor 15 named Gitelson. He was about twenty-four years old, yet his forelock was gray, just his forelock, the rest of his hair being a fine, glossy brown. His own cap had been blown into the sea and the one he had obtained from the steerage steward was too small for him, so that gray tuft of his was always out like a plume. We had not been acquainted more than a few hours, in fact, for he had been seasick throughout the voyage and this was the first day he had been up and about. But then I had seen him on the day of our sailing and subsequently, many times, as he wretchedly lay in his berth. He was literally in tatters. He clung to me like a lover, but we spoke very little. Our hearts were too full for words.

As I thus stood at the railing, prayer-book in hand, he took a look at the page. The most ignorant "man of the earth" among our people can read holy tongue (Hebrew), though he may not understand the meaning of the words. This was the case with Gitelson.

"Saying, 'Bless the Lord, O my soul'?" he asked, reverently. "Why this chapter of all others?"

"Because — Why, just listen." With which I took to translating the Hebrew text into Yiddish for him.

He listened with devout mien. I was not sure that he understood it even in his native tongue, but, whether he did or not, his beaming, wistful look and the deep sigh he emitted indicated that he was in a state similar to mine.

When I say that my first view of New York Bay struck me as something 20 not of this earth it is not a mere figure of speech. I vividly recall the feeling, for example, with which I greeted the first cat I saw on American soil. It was on the Hoboken pier, while the steerage passengers were being marched to the ferry. A large, black, well-fed feline stood in a corner, eyeing the crowd of new-comers. The sight of it gave me a thrill of joy. "Look! there is a cat!" I said to Gitelson. And in my heart I added, "Just like those at home!" For the moment the little animal made America real to me. At the same time it seemed unreal itself. I was tempted to feel its fur to ascertain whether it was actually the kind of creature I took it for.

We were ferried over to Castle Garden. One of the things that caught my eye as I entered the vast rotunda was an iron staircase rising diagonally against one of the inner walls. A uniformed man, with some papers in his hands, ascended it with brisk, resounding step till he disappeared through a door not many inches from the ceiling. It may seem odd, but I can never think of my arrival in this country without hearing the ringing footfalls of this official and beholding the yellow eyes of the black cat which stared at us at the Hoboken pier.

The harsh manner of the immigration officers was a grievous surprise to me. As contrasted with the officials of my despotic country, those of a republic had been portrayed in my mind as paragons of refinement and cordiality. My anticipations were rudely belied. "They are not a bit better than Cossacks," I remarked to Gitelson. But they neither looked nor spoke like Cossacks, so their gruff voices were part of the uncanny scheme of things that surrounded me. These unfriendly voices flavored all America with a spirit of icy inhospitality that sent a chill through my very soul.

The stringent immigration laws that were passed some years later had not yet come into existence. We had no difficulty in being admitted to the United States, and when I was I was loath to leave the Garden.

Many of the other immigrants were met by relatives, friends. There were cries of joy, tears, embraces, kisses. All of which intensified my sense of loneliness and dread of the New World. The agencies which two Jewish charity organizations now maintain at the Immigrant Station had not yet been established. Gitelson, who like myself had no friends in New York, never left my side. He was even more timid than I. It seemed as though he were holding on to me for dear life. This had the effect of putting me on my mettle.

"Cheer up, old man!" I said, with bravado. "America is not the place to 25 be a ninny in. Come, pull yourself together."

In truth, I addressed these exhortations as much to myself as to him: and so far, at least, as I was concerned, my words had the desired effect.

I led the way out of the big Immigrant Station. As we reached the park outside we were pounced down upon by two evil-looking men, representatives of boarding-houses for immigrants. They pulled us so roughly and their general appearance and manner were so uninviting that we struggled and protested until they let us go — not without some parting curses. Then I led the way across Battery Park and under the Elevated railway to State Street. A train hurtling and panting along overhead produced a bewildering, a daunting effect on me. The active life of the great strange city made me feel like one abandoned in the midst of a jungle. Where were we to go? What were we to do? But the presence of Gitelson continued to act as a spur on me. I mustered courage to approach a policeman, something I should never have been bold enough to do at home. As a matter of fact, I scarcely had an idea what his function was. To me he looked like some uniformed nobleman — an impression that in itself was enough to intimidate me. With his coat of blue cloth, starched linen collar, and white gloves, he reminded me of anything but the policemen of my town. I addressed him in Yiddish, making it as near an approach to German as I knew how, but my efforts were lost on him. He shook his head. With a witheringly dignified grimace he then pointed his club in the direction of Broadway and strutted off majestically.

"He's not better than a Cossack, either," was my verdict.

At this moment a voice hailed us in Yiddish. Facing about, we beheld a middle-aged man with huge, round, perpendicular nostrils and a huge, round, deep dimple in his chin that looked like a third nostril. Prosperity was written all over his smooth-shaven face and broad-shouldered, stocky figure. He was literally aglow with diamonds and self-satisfaction. But he was unmistakably one of our people. It was like coming across a human being in the jungle. Moreover, his very diamonds somehow told a tale of former want, of a time when he had landed, an impecunious immigrant like myself; and this made him a living source of encouragement to me.

"God Himself has sent you to us," I began, acting as the spokesman: 30 but he gave no heed to me. His eyes were eagerly fixed on Gitelson and his tatters.

"You're a tailor, aren't you?" he questioned him.

My steerage companion nodded. "I'm a ladies' tailor, but I have worked on men's clothing, too," he said.

"A ladies' tailor?" the well-dressed stranger echoed, with ill-concealed delight. "Very well; come along. I have work for you."

That he should have been able to read Gitelson's trade in his face and figure scarcely surprised me. In my native place it seemed to be a matter of course that one could tell a tailor by his general appearance and walk. Besides, had I not divined the occupation of my fellow-passenger the moment I saw him on deck?

As I learned subsequently, the man who accosted us on State Street was 35 a cloak contractor, and his presence in the neighborhood of Castle Garden was anything but a matter of chance. He came there quite often, in fact, his purpose being to angle for cheap labor among the newly arrived immigrants.

We paused near Bowling Green. The contractor and my fellow-passenger were absorbed in a conversation full of sartorial technicalities which were Greek to me, but which brought a gleam of joy into Gitelson's eye. My former companion seemed to have become oblivious of my existence.

As we resumed our walk up Broadway the bejeweled man turned to me.

"And what was your occupation? You have no trade, have you?"

"I read Talmud," I said confusedly.

"I see, but that's no business in America," he declared. "Any rela- 40 tives here?"

"No."

"Well, don't worry. You will be all right. If a fellow isn't lazy nor a fool he has no reason to be sorry he came to America. It'll be all right."

"All right" he said in English, and I conjectured what it meant from the context. In the course of the minute or two which he bestowed upon me he uttered it so many times that the phrase engraved itself upon my memory. It was the first bit of English I ever acquired.

The well-dressed, trim-looking crowds of lower Broadway impressed me as a multitude of counts, barons, princes. I was puzzled by their preoccupied faces and hurried step. It seemed to comport ill with their baronial dress and general high-born appearance.

In a vague way all this helped to confirm my conception of America as 45 a unique country, unlike the rest of the world.

When we reached the General Post-Office, at the end of the Third Avenue surface line, our guide bade us stop. "Walk straight ahead," he said to me, waving his hand toward Park Row. "Just keep walking until you see a lot of Jewish people. It isn't far from here." With which he slipped a silver quarter into my hand and made Gitelson bid me good-by.

The two then boarded a big red horse-car.

I was left with a sickening sense of having been tricked, cast off, and abandoned. I stood watching the receding public vehicle, as though its scarlet hue were my last gleam of hope in the world. When it finally disappeared from view my heart sank within me. I may safely say that the half-hour that followed is one of the worst I experienced in all the thirty-odd years of my life in this country.

The big, round nostrils of the contractor and the gray forelock of my young steerage-fellow haunted my brain as hideous symbols of treachery.

With twenty-nine cents in my pocket (four cents was all that was left of 50 the sum which I had received from Matilda and her mother) I set forth in the direction of East Broadway.

Suggestions for Writing and Discussion

1. What does the speaker achieve by focusing on the vastness and mystery of the sea in the opening paragraphs of this piece?
2. Analyze the main character's topics of reflection in paragraphs 3–7. What do these topics reveal about this character?
3. If you were a passenger on this boat, would you befriend the main character? Why or why not?
4. What are the possible reasons you can offer for this character's decision to come to America?
5. Reread the speaker's description of Gitelson in paragraph 15. Which statements are based on fact? Which ones are based on imagination or opinion? What conclusions can you draw about the main character's ability to judge people?
6. How does the main character's "poetic" outlook on life help him on this journey? How does it hinder him?
7. At the end of this piece, the speaker believes he has been "tricked, cast off,

abandoned" by Gitelson and the tailor. Is the speaker merely overreacting at this time, or can you find any support to these allegations?

8. What has the speaker really "discovered" in this piece?

Suggestions for Extended Thinking and Research

1. Stretch your creative writing talents: Describe the next three events that happen to this character!

2. Find a firsthand account of an immigrant's journey to America and arrival at Ellis Island. Consider, also, Mary Gordon's observations on the Ellis Island experience (pp. 52–56). From these accounts, how much of this story would you classify as "fiction"?

Carved on the Walls: Poetry by Early Chinese Immigrants

> *From 1910 to 1940, Angel Island in San Francisco Bay served as the entry point to the United States for approximately 175,000 Chinese immigrants. Less well known than Ellis Island, Angel Island served the same purpose: as a processing and detention headquarters for those seeking entrance to the United States. The poems reprinted here were discovered by park ranger Alexander Weiss in 1970; they were carved on the walls of the detention barracks where Chinese men and women waited to learn whether they would be admitted or deported. In 1980, Him Mark Lai, Genny Lim, and Judy Yung recorded these poems in* Island: Poetry and History of Chinese Immigrants on Angel Island, 1910–1940.

Prereading/Journal-Writing Suggestions

1. Nearly all of us have felt like outsiders at one time or another. Write a descriptive narrative about a time and a place where you didn't "fit in." (*Suggestions:* Describe a place where you never felt comfortable; describe a time when you were overlooked or unappreciated; describe an event where everyone except you seemed to know one another; describe a school experience — either in or out of the classroom — when you were left out of a group; describe a lonely feeling in a familiar place.)
2. Graffiti are anonymous ways of publishing ideas in slogans or short statements. If there were a wall on campus or in your town where you could write graffiti, what statements would you make? Explain your reasons.

From "The Voyage"

5

Four days before the Qiqiao Festival,
I boarded the steamship for America.
Time flew like a shooting arrow.
Already, a cool autumn has passed.
Counting on my fingers, several months have elapsed.   5
Still I am at the beginning of the road.
I have yet to be interrogated.
My heart is nervous with anticipation.

8

Instead of remaining a citizen of China, I willingly became an ox.
I intended to come to America to earn a living.

The Western styled buildings are lofty; but I have not the luck to live in them.
How was anyone to know that my dwelling place would be a prison?

From "The Detainment"

20

Imprisonment at Youli, when will it end?
Fur and linen garments have been exchanged; it is already another autumn.
My belly brims with discontent, too numerous to inscribe on bamboo slips.
Snow falls, flowers wilt, expressing sorrow through the ages.

30

After leaping into prison, I cannot come out.
From endless sorrows, tears and blood streak.
The *jingwet* bird carries gravel to fill its old grudge.
The migrating wild goose complains to the moon, mourning his
    harried life.
When Ziqing was in distant lands, who pitied and inquired after him?   5
When Ruan Ji reached the end of the road, he shed futile tears.
The scented grass and hidden orchids complain of withering and falling.
When can I be allowed to rise above as I please?

By Li Jingbo of Taishan District

31

There are tens of thousands of poems composed on these walls.
They are all cries of complaint and sadness.
The day I am rid of this prison and attain success,
I must remember that this chapter once existed.
In my daily needs, I must be frugal.   5
Needless extravagance leads youth to ruin.
All my compatriots should be mindful.
Once you have some small gains, return home early.

By One From Xiangshan

From "The Weak Shall Conquer"

35

Leaving behind my writing brush and removing my sword, I came to
    America.
Who was to know two streams of tears would flow upon arriving here?

If there comes a day when I will have attained my ambition and become
   successful,
I will certainly behead the barbarians and spare not a single blade of grass.

38

Being idle in the wooden building, I opened a window.
The morning breeze and bright moon lingered together.
I reminisce the native village far away, cut off by clouds and mountains?
On the little island the wailing of cold, wild geese can be faintly heard.
The hero who has lost his way can talk meaninglessly of the sword.   5
The poet at the end of the road can only ascend a tower.
One should know that when the country is weak, the people's spirit dies.
Why else do we come to this place to be imprisoned?

42

The dragon out of water is humiliated by ants;
The fierce tiger who is caged is baited by a child.
As long as I am imprisoned, how can I dare strive for supremacy?
An advantageous position for revenge will surely come one day.

Suggestions for Writing and Discussion

1. If you had to leave your homeland, what — other than people there —
   would you miss the most? Explain your response.
2. From the images and the tone in poem 5, how would you describe the
   writer? (Consider age, sex, occupation, personality.)
3. What is your response to poem 8? Do you agree that where one lives is
   primarily a matter of luck?
4. In poem 31, the author writes that "there are tens of thousands of poems
   composed on these walls." What would you imagine to be the motivation
   of these Chinese immigrants who wrote on the walls? Why didn't most of
   them sign their names?
5. What is the tone in poem 35? From the details suggested by this poem and
   the others, do you agree that the treatment of these immigrants was
   "barbaric"?
6. Imagine poem 35 or poem 38 put to music. What do you hear? Describe
   the instruments as well as the tone, melody, discord, or whatever. Would
   you choose similar or distinctly different music for these two poems?
   Explain.
7. Reread these poems, looking for any images that might suggest a central
   theme or idea that ties them together.

Suggestions for Extended Thinking and Research

1. Write your own short poem in response to the eight selections from Angel Island. Use a structure similar to one of these poems.
2. Research and read the history of Angel Island. Explain what you discovered through your research and how those findings compare with the impressions of Angel Island conveyed by the poems.
3. In poem 31, the author writes, "I must remember that this chapter once existed." Write an essay in which you examine a difficult past chapter in your life. How did you face it? How have you changed as a result? If you could go back in time, would you erase this chapter? Why or why not?

TOPICS FOR MAKING CONNECTIONS: ARRIVALS

1. Many people around the world still view the United States as the land of promise and opportunity. Despite the losses and cruel treatment that many immigrants suffered, why did so many choose to remain in this country and to encourage their relatives to follow? Refer to several selections in this section as you write your response.
2. Some argue that the concept of America as a "melting pot" is not entirely accurate. In a melting pot, everything blends into a new whole. In a short essay, defend this metaphor as accurate, or explain in detail a different metaphor that you believe better represents this country.
3. As Mary Antin's "The Promised Land" shows us, many immigrants came to this country with the intention of becoming part of American society. However, as other selections attest, many immigrants preferred to hold on to their native culture and values. Write an essay analyzing the benefits of each approach. Explain which approach you would most likely adopt if you were to move to another country.
4. Each author in this section has a strong sense of what *freedom* really is, although no one comes out and defines this term. Referring to at least three of these readings, develop your own definition of freedom. (You may agree or disagree with the concepts implied by the writers you choose.)
5. Most of the immigrants whose experiences are described in these pieces arrive at new places of their own free will. This is not the case in "Slave Ship" and the Houston's essay "Arrival at Manzanar." What similarities do you see between the experiences of the slave and those of the Wakatsuki family? How do these experiences reflect values held by Americans at the time of the forced "arrivals"? Do you believe those values have changed? Somewhat? A great deal? Only a little? Not at all? Explain.
6. Bill Moyers notes that many people "think of the immigrants in literature and in movies as sometimes pathetic figures. Whimpering, frightened creatures" (p. 87). Describe your impression of immigrants from the readings in this section. Do these individuals fit the image Moyers suggests? Or do they in some ways defy this stereotype? Explain your responses.

Parents and Children

Previews: PARENTS AND CHILDREN

Then I looked again at this thief, this "Loaf-of-bread gunman" as the papers had tagged him. He had taken five loaves of bread, along with twelve dollars. Suddenly I could not stay there condemning this man, my father. It seemed such a waste, this magnificently strong man sitting there, his tremendous chest barely moving, hands resting quietly, talking to me, his whole being showering torrents of words about me.

From: *I Remember Papa*, HARRY DOLAN

My mother is not soft; the girl with the small nose and dimpled underlip is soft. My mother is not humorous, not like the girl at the end who lifts her mocking chin to pose like Girl Graduate. My mother does not have smiling eyes; the old woman teacher (Dean Woo?) in front crinkles happily, and the one faculty member in the western suit smiles westernly. Most of the graduates are girls whose faces have not yet formed; my mother's face will not change anymore, except to age. She is intelligent, alert, pretty. I can't tell if she's happy.

From: *Photographs of My Parents*, MAXINE HONG KINGSTON

Today at the beach my chubby-legged, brown-skinned daughter ran laughing into the water as fast as she could. My wife and I laughed watching her, until we heard behind us a low guttural curse and then an unpleasant voice raised in an imitation war whoop.

From: *For My Indian Daughter*, LEWIS P. JOHNSON

After the service at the funeral home, after we had moved outside, a woman I didn't know came over to me and said, "He's happier where he is now." I stared at this woman until she moved away. I still remember the little knob of a hat she was wearing. Then one of my dad's cousins — I didn't know the man's name — reached out and took my hand. "We all miss him," he said, and I knew he wasn't saying it just to be polite.

I began to weep for the first time since receiving the news. I hadn't been able to before. I hadn't had the time, for one thing. Now, suddenly, I couldn't stop. I held my wife and wept while she said and did what she could do to comfort me there in the middle of that summer afternoon.

From: *My Father's Life*, RAYMOND CARVER

TRAN THI NGA

Letter to My Mother

> *Tran Thi Nga, who was born in China in 1927, was a social worker in Vietnam. In addition, she has worked as a journalist in both Asia and the United States. This letter suggests the connections she feels to her mother as well as the differences she sees between their lives and the places they live.*

Prereading/Journal-Writing Suggestions

1. Write a tribute to an older relative in your family. In this tribute, describe what you admire most about this person. What have you learned from observing and hearing about this person's life experiences and everyday values?
2. At this point in your life, what is the greatest sacrifice you have made? What is the greatest sacrifice someone else has made for you? Write a descriptive narrative responding to either of these questions.
3. If you could make one wish for either one, or both, of your parents, what would be your wish? Explain the significance of your response.

Dear Mother,

I do not know if you are receiving my letters, but I will keep writing to you as you are always in my mind.

We have been here three years now. I have moved from Greenwich and have a wooden shingled house in Cos Cob. We have a garden in the back where we plant vegetables, flowers in the front the way we used to when we were together. I have a pink dogwood tree that blooms in spring. It looks like the Hoa dai tree, but has no leaves, only flowers.

We worked for months to clear away the poison ivy, a plant that turns your skin red and makes you itch.

We are near a beach, a school and a shopping center. Green lawns go down to the streets and there are many cars and garages. I am even learning to drive.

When we got our new house, people from the church came and took us 5 to "Friendly's" for ice cream. Americans celebrate with ice cream. They have so many kinds — red like watermelon, green for pistachio, orange sherbet like Buddha's robes, mint chocolate chip. You buy it fast and take it away to eat.

Our house is small, but a place to be together and discuss our daily life. At every meal we stare at the dishes you used to fix for us and think about you. We are sorry for you and for ourselves.

If we work hard here, we have everything, but we fear you are hungry and cold and lonesome. Last week we made up a package of clothes. We all tried to figure out how thin you must be now. I do not know if you will ever receive that package wrapped with all our thoughts.

I remember the last days when you encouraged us to leave the country and refused to go yourself. You said you were too old, did not want to leave your home and would be a burden to us. We realize now that you sacrificed yourself for our well-being.

You have a new grandson born in the United States. Thanh looked beautiful at her wedding in a red velvet dress and white veil, a yellow turban in her dark hair. She carried the chrysanthemums you love.

You always loved the fall in Hanoi. You liked the cold. We don't. We have just had the worst winter in a century, snow piled everywhere. I must wear a heavy coat, boots, fur gloves, and a hat. I look like a ball running to the train station. I feel that if I fell down, I could never get up.

Your grandson is three, in nursery school. He speaks English so well that we are sad. We made a rule. We must speak Vietnamese at home so that the children will not forget their mother tongue.

We have made an altar to Father. We try to keep up our traditions so that we can look forward to the day we can return to our country, although we do not know when that will be.

Here we are materially well off, but spiritually deprived. We miss our country. Most of all we miss you. Should Buddha exist, we should keep praying to be reunited.

Dear Mother, keep up your mind. Pray to Buddha silently. We will have a future and I hope it will be soon.

We want to swim in our own pond.   15
Clear or stinky, still it is ours.

Your daughter,
Nga

Suggestions for Writing and Discussion

1. Describe the tone of Tran Thi Nga's letter to her mother. From the words and images she chooses to use, explain how you think she feels about the United States and about her homeland.

2. In much of this letter, Nga writes about common, everyday scenes and events. She describes flowers, her neighborhood, ice cream, the clothing she wears, and even the weather. Why do you think she spends so much time explaining these simple things? What do you surmise she wants to convey to her mother?

3. Look again at the parts of her life Nga chooses to share with her mother. Can you speculate on parts of her life she does not mention? What are possible explanations for these omissions?

4. From reading this letter, do you think Nga believes that she will see her mother someday? Do you believe she will return to her homeland? Support

your response with specific evidence or well-founded inferences from the text itself.

5. In her last two lines, Nga writes: "We want to swim in our own pond/ Clear or stinky, still it is ours." Stop and think about this metaphor. What exactly is she comparing to a pond — her old way of life, her homeland, her neighborhood, her yard, or something else? What does the metaphor of the pond imply about her life now?

Suggestions for Extended Thinking and Research

1. Assume the part of Nga's mother. Write to your daughter responding to the letter from her that you have just read.
2. What was China like in 1927? Research this time and place in history to get a feel of what life was like the year Nga's mother gave birth to her daughter.
3. Read (or reread) Pearl S. Buck's *The Good Earth*. Examine the values and hierarchy within the Chinese family as suggested by the relationships among Wang Lung, O-'lan, their families and their children. Write an essay discussing the roles and values of each member of Wang Lung and O-'lan's family.

HARRY DOLAN

I Remember Papa

> *In this essay, which first appeared in* From the Ashes: Voices of Watts, *edited by Budd Schulberg, Harry Dolan shows the pitfalls his parents faced as they struggled with poverty, illness, and negative racial stereotypes. By explaining his father's life, Dolan urges readers to examine and, perhaps, reconsider their own views of families like his and, particularly, of the choices made by the men who are the fathers of those families.*

Prereading/Journal-Writing Suggestions

1. Describe the earliest memories you have of your father (or grandfather, uncle, older brother, stepfather). Try to focus on specific, vivid images: eyes, hands, gestures, facial expressions, bits of conversation.
2. If you were in charge of writing a manual that defined a "good" father, what would you include? List the top ten qualifications, in order of their importance to you, that you believe all fathers should possess. Then reflect on the reasons for your choices and for the order in which you arranged your choices.
3. Describe a time when someone in your family embarrassed you; explain what happened and why you responded as you did.

The other night after attending a gratifying function which had been initiated to help the black man, specifically to help build a nursery for children of working mothers, and after seeing and hearing white people make speeches professing their understanding and desire to go to any length to help, I found myself suddenly cornered and forced to defend the fabled laziness of the black man.

What was especially surprising was the fact that I assumed this white acquaintance—since he had paid thirty dollars to attend this dinner held for the purpose of helping the black man—did, at least in part, have some sympathy with what his, the white people, had tried to accomplish.

As I stood there watching his eyes I became suspect of my own sincerity, for I stood attentively nodding my head and smiling. I lit a cigarette, raised an eyebrow, performed all of the white man's laws of etiquette, and all the while I knew if it had been others of my black brothers, they would have cursed him for his smugness and invited him outside to test his theory of black man's courage and laziness. Of course I did none of these things. I grinned as he indicated in no uncertain terms that as soon as the black man got off his lazy butt and took advantage of all the blessings that had been offered him for the last two hundred years, then he, the white man, would indeed be willing to help.

I could have answered him — and was tempted to, for he was obviously sincere. Instead, I found an excuse to slip away and let a white man fight my battle, a friend, even a close friend. I went to a far corner and blindly played a game of pool by myself as the voices of this man and my friend dissected me. I stacked the pool balls, leaned over the table, and remembered a black man I had known.

It was said of him later in his life that he had let his family down. He'd 5 been lazy, no-account, a troublemaker. Maybe so, maybe so, but I can't help remembering nights of his pacing the squeaking floor muttering to himself, coming back across the floor, sitting down, his legs trembling as he listened to the woman plead for him not to do anything bad.

"I'll go to hell first before I'll let you and the children starve." God, how many times had I heard him say that! How many other men standing bunched in helpless stagnation have I heard vow to take a gun and get some food for their children! Yes, they were planning to commit a crime; yes, they were potential criminals. Then. They are usually black too — another crime, it seems.

I remember that man, but more I remember his woman, my mother. Curiously though, I never remember her dancing, running, playing; always lying down, the smell of disinfectant strong, the deep continuous coughing, the brown paper bag filled with the toilet paper red with bubbly spit and blood, lying half concealed under the bed.

I never remember her eating food such as bread, meat, potatoes; only apples and only Delicious apples. In those days five cents apiece. She was a small woman, barely five foot.

"Junior," she would say softly. She never spoke above a whisper. "Go to the store and get me an apple." The thin trembling hand would reverse itself and slide up and under the covers and under the pillow and then return as though of its own volition, the weight almost too much, and as I'd start out the door, she would always smile and say, "Hurry, Junior."

I'd nod, and always, always there seemed to be a need to hurry. Those 10 trips were always made with a feeling of breathless fear. I didn't know why then, only that for some reason I must always come back as soon as possible.

I was returning with an especially large apple, walking along, tempted to bite just a tiny piece, when I turned the corner and saw the black police ambulance standing in front of my door. Suddenly I had to go to the bathroom so bad I couldn't move. I stood watching as two uniformed men came out with the stretcher, and then the sound of my mother's shrill voice hit me.

"Mama, Mama," she was screaming. I could see her twisting and swinging at the lady next door as she was held back. I stood there feeling the hot piss run down my trembling legs, feeling cold chills spatter through my body, causing frozen limbs to spasmodically begin to move. I forced myself toward the police wagon as the men opened the doors and slid the stretcher along the bare metal. I saw my mother's head bounce on the floor.

"Wait," I moaned, "don't hurt her." Then I was running, screaming, "Please don't hurt her."

I looked down at her pain-filled face, and she smiled, even then she smiled. I showed her the apple. The effort to nod seemed a terrible effort but she did, her eyes so very bright, so very shiny.

"You eat it, Junior, you and sis." 15

"What's wrong, Mama?" I asked softly. "You really, really sick now?"

She nodded.

"Your father will be home soon. Tell him I'm at the General Hospital. Tell him to — to hurry."

"I'll tell him, Mama," I promised. "I'll tell him to hurry, Mama." She nodded sadly and puckered her lips as she always did since we weren't allowed to kiss her.

That was the last time I saw my mother except at the grave. My father 20 came to the funeral with two white men who stood on each side of him all the time. There were people crying all around us. My grandmother kept squeezing me and moaning. I saw my father try to cover his face but one of the men said something and he stood up stiffly after that. I didn't cry, because my mother seemed to look happier, more rested than I had ever seen her. For some reason, I was glad she was dead. I think maybe, except for us, she was too.

I was nine, my sister five. It was not until ten years later that I saw my father again.

We sat on opposite sides of a screen and talked into telephones. I had come there to tell him that in spite of my beginning, I had made it. I was nineteen, and a radioman in the U.S. Coast Guard, ready to fight and die for my country. There had been something mysterious about his smile.

"I'm proud of you, boy," he said. "You're a real man. You know I volunteered for the front lines too, but they turned me down."

We don't want you, I thought, we're not criminals, we're honest, strong. Then I looked again at this thief, this "Loaf-of-bread gunman" as the papers had tagged him. He had taken five loaves of bread, along with twelve dollars. Suddenly I could not stay there condemning this man, my father. It seemed such a waste, this magnificently strong man sitting there, his tremendous chest barely moving, hands resting quietly, talking to me, his whole being showering torrents of words about me.

"Be careful, boy, there are so many ways to fail, the pitfall sometimes 25 seems to be the easiest way out. Beware of my future, for you must continue, you must live. You must, for in you are all the dreams of my nights, all the ambitions of my days."

A bell rang and we stood up and a man pointed me toward a heavy door. I looked back, and saw him standing easy, hands at his side, so very calm, yet my mind filled to overflowing with the many things he had not said. It was to be ten years before he walked again as a free man, that is, as a physically free man.

I remember an earlier time, an earlier chapter of my growing up. I remember the first time my mother said we were taking lunch to my father's job. We had been down to the welfare line and I had stood with her, our feet burning against the hot pavement, and slowly moved forward in the sun. Years later I stood in chow lines over half of the world, but no desert, no burning deck was as hot as that day.

At last we reached the man sitting at the desk and my mother handed him the book of stamps. She smiled, a weak almost timid smile, as he checked her name and thumbed her to the food line.

As we headed home, my wagon was loaded with cans of corned beef, powdered milk, powdered eggs, and white margarine that she would later color yellow to look like butter.

At home we made sandwiches and off we went to my father's job, to take him his lunch. I pulled my sister along in my wagon, a Red Flyer.   30

It was to be a picnic, a celebration really, my father's new job.

I remember the wagon did not have a tongue or handle but only a rope with which I pulled it wobbling along. We were excited, my sister and I, as we left our district of dirt streets and unpaved sidewalks and began to make our way along roads called boulevards and malls we had never had occasion to travel. The streets themselves were fascinating, so different. They were twice as wide, and there were exotic trees along the sidewalks and lo and behold trees down the center of the street as far as I could see and then we turned the corner and before us stretched an overwhelming sight. An overhead highway was being built. Columns rose to staggering heights, bulldozers thrust what seemed to me mountains of dirt before them, and hundreds, no thousands of men seemed to be crawling like ants hurrying from one point to another. Cranes lifted nets of steel and laid them in rows on the crushed rock.

I stared in awe at important-looking white men in metal hats, carrying rolls of papers which they intermittently studied, then pointing into space at what to me seemed only emptiness.

And then I saw my father. He sat among fifty other black men, all surrounded by great boulders marked with red paint. They all held steel chisels with which they cut along the marked lines. They would strike a certain point and the boulder would split into smaller pieces and as we approached there was a silence around them except for the pinging of the hammer against the chisel. In all the noise it was a lonely sound, futile, lost, oppressive. My father seemed to be concentrating, his tremendous arm whipping the air. He was stripped to the waist, black muscles popping sweat, goggled eyes for the metal and stone only. We stood there, the three of us, my mother, my sister, and I, and watched my father work for us, and as he conquered the huge boulder my chest filled with pride. Each stroke shouted for all the world to hear: This is my family and I love them! No one can tell me this was the act of a lazy man.

Suddenly a white man walked up and blew a whistle and the black men all looked up and stopped working. My father glanced over at me, grinned and winked. He was glistening with sweat, the smell strong and powerful.   35

He dropped his big hand on my shoulder and guided me to a large boulder.

"Hey, boy, you see me beat that thing to bits? This one's next," he said, indicating the one that shaded us from the sun. "I'll pound it to gravel by nightfall." It was a challenge he expected, he welcomed. That was my lazy, shiftless father.

And then one day they brought him home, his thumb, index, and middle finger gone from his left hand. They sat him in the kitchen chair and mumbled something about carelessness. He sat there for two hours before he answered our pleadings.

"Chain broke, I—I was guiding boulder. I couldn't, I just couldn't get my hand out from under in time—I, goddam it, Jean, they took my fingers off. I layed right there, my hand under the rock, and they nipped them like butchering a hog. Look at my goddam hand."

My mother held him in her arms and talked to him. She spoke softly, so softly my sister and I, standing in the corner, couldn't hear the words, only the soothing softness of her voice.

"Joe, Joe, we can." And then he began to cry like—like I sometimes did 40 when I was hurt deep inside and couldn't do anything about it.

After that there was a change in him. My father had been a fighter. He had feared no man white or black. I remember the time we were sitting on a streetcar and a woman had forgotten her fare—or maybe she never had any in the first place. Anyway, the driver slammed the doors on her and held her squeezed between them.

My father jumped up, snatched the driver out of the seat, and let the woman out. He and the driver had words that led to battle and Pop knocked the driver down just as a patrolman arrived. The patrolman didn't listen to any of the people that tried to explain what had happened. He just began to swing his night stick at my father's head. It was a mistake. My father hit him once and even today I can see all the people laughing at the funny look on the policeman's face as he staggered back all the way across the street and up against a building, slowly sagging down.

The police wagon arrived with four other policemen and one told him they were going to beat his brains in when they got him down town.

My pop had laughed then and backed against the building.

"I guess ain't no sense me going peaceable then." 45

They knocked out all his upper front teeth that day, but as he said later, "Them four white boys will think of me every time they shave."

They finally overpowered him and dragged him, still struggling, to the wagon. One of them kept muttering, "He's one fighting son of a black bitch, he's a fighting son of a bitch."

All the time I hadn't said a word or cried or yelled as they stomped and kicked him. I had shut my eyes and held my lips tightly pressed together and I had done just as he'd always told me.

"You stay out of it, boy, stay real quiet, and when that wagon leaves, you run behind and keep it in sight. If they lose you, you ask someone where the closest police station is — that's where I'll be. You go home and tell your mother."

That's the way he had been before losing his left hand. Afterwards, well, 50 it took a lot from him. He told me one day, laughing and shaking the nub as he called it, "If I'd only had the thumb, just the lousy thumb, I'd have it made."

Gradually he lost the ability to see humor in the nub. I think the whole thing came to a head the night I killed the kitten.

We hadn't had meat or potatoes for over two weeks. Even the grease drippings were gone and my mother was too sick to raise her head from the pillow. So I had gotten the skillet and put it in the open grate. We had two cups of flour so I mixed water with it and poured it into the greasy skillet. I can still recall the coldness of the room on my back and the warmth from the grate on my face as my sister and I knelt and hungrily watched the flour brown.

You know, today my wife marvels at how, no matter what she puts before me, I eat with relish. My children say that I eat very fast. I pray to God they never have to experience the causes of my obsession. But back to the story — the flour finally hardened and I broke a piece for my sister and a piece for my mother and left mine in the skillet on the table.

I took my mother's piece over to the bed and put it in her hand. She didn't move so I raised her hand to her mouth and she began to suck on it. Then I heard my sister scream, "Topsy is eating your food, Junior, Topsy's eating your food!" I turned around to see the cat tearing at my tiny piece of hard dough. I went wild. I leaped across the room and grabbed the kitten by the tail and began slamming her against the wall.

"That's my food," I kept yelling, "my food!" At last I heard my sister 55 screaming, "She's bleeding, you're killing Topsy. Here, here, eat my bread. Please don't kill her."

I stopped, horrified, staring at the limp nothing I now held. It was two weeks later that they got me to speak and that same night my father left the house for the last time. I don't say that what he did was right. No, it most assuredly was wrong. But what I do ask is, what else could he have done? I need an answer quickly now, today, right away, for I tell you this, my children will not starve, not here, not in this time of millions to foreign countries and fountains to throw tons of water upward to the sky, and nothing to the hungry, thirsty multitudes a stone's throw away.

Suggestions for Writing and Discussion

1. How does Dolan feel about white people? Give specific evidence from the essay to support your response.
2. Dolan entitles this piece, "I Remember Papa." However, he writes that "I remember that man, but more I remember his woman, my mother." Why

then, doesn't he include the word "Mama" in his title? In your opinion, is this title a contradiction or an apt phrase that reflects his central idea?

3. Describe Dolan's mother. What type of a person was she? How does Dolan's father compare or contrast to her? Why do you think he would remember her more than he remembers his father?

4. Imagine you are a rider on the bus when Dolan's father frees the woman from the bus door and then fights with four policemen. What is your response? Is he heroic? Foolish? Wise? Noble? Headstrong? Or something else? Explain your answer.

5. Dolan provides close-up, detailed views of several events in which his father plays a role. Examine these events and make inferences about how Dolan, as an adult writing this piece, feels about his father. How does this adult view compare with his views as a young boy and as a young man?

Suggestions for Extended Thinking and Research

1. By examining Dolan's childhood and adult views of his father, and by examining your own childhood and adult views of parents or other authority figures, think about how we try to discover what is true in our lives. How do our past memories embellish, cloud, tint, or taint our present perceptions? To what extent should we pay heed to our memories, and to what extent should we disregard them?

2. Argue for or against the following proposition: It is acceptable to commit a crime when your family's survival is on the line.

3. Dolan's father leaves his sick wife and two small children for the last time after his son frantically flings a kitten against the wall. Dolan says, "I don't say what he did was right. No, it most assuredly was wrong. But what I do ask is, what else could he have done?" Write an essay responding to Dolan's question. Did his father have any other options? What were the roadblocks in his way? Did he have anything or anyone who could have helped him out?

GRACE MING-YEE WAI
Chinese Puzzle

> Grace Ming-Yee Wai, a first-generation Chinese-American, grew up in Memphis, Tennessee. When she was ten years old, her father was shot to death during a robbery that netted the killer $26 in change. In the following essay, Wai offers a collage of episodes from her childhood as a way of describing her father and of suggesting how both his life and his death affected the values she developed.

Prereading/Journal-Writing Suggestions
1. Describe what you would consider to be the ideal family. In what ways is your own family similar or different from this ideal?
2. Take twenty minutes today to write about your father in your journal. After you do this freewriting, come to some conclusions about what you know and don't know about your father.

I am a first generation Chinese-American woman educated in both private and public American schools. I grew up in the mid-South city of Memphis, Tennessee, where there were very few other Asian families. We lived in the South, I realized after my teens, primarily for economic reasons. Although there were more Asians in cities such as New York, Los Angeles, or San Francisco, it would have been very expensive to live in those cities, and our grocery store would have had much more competition. My parents immigrated to the United States from Hong Kong before I was born, for a better life for themselves and their children. Neither had a college education, but both emphasized hard work and the importance of education. Like all parents, they hoped their children would be fortunate enough to receive a quality education that would provide future opportunity and financial security.

My sister, brother, and I have been lucky to receive an education and all of us have reached or are near our goals, but not without pain and sacrifices. When I was 10 years old, my father was shot and killed while being robbed for $26 in change. He was the favorite son of seven living children. He took in one of my cousins from Hong Kong so she could study nursing. My youngest uncle was the only one of their generation to become a professional, primarily because he was lucky enough to have the opportunity to go to dental school at the University of Tennessee in Memphis.

Dad owned a small grocery store in a poor neighborhood. My parents worked more than 12 hours a day, seven days a week. We lived above the store in five rooms and one bathroom. At different times, my grandmother, three uncles, an aunt and her two sons also lived with us. My brother, sister and I had a maid who came six days a week to take care of us. I became very attached to her and cried on her day off. I still send Willie Christmas cards every year.

My father had a fierce temper. Whenever something upset him a little, he yelled a lot, so my brother, sister, and I shuddered at the thought of angering him. His bark was worse than his bite, however. He was also very fair. He loved us all very much. He and Mom worked hard for us, for the family. Family meant everything.

Since Mom and Dad worked so much, there was not much time for us kids. We occasionally went to Shoney's for a hamburger. It was a big treat to pat the statue of Big Boy on the stomach upon entering and exiting the restaurant. Dad took me to the dog track once because I wanted to go with him. I think I just wanted very much to have him for myself since he was always helping other people and working in the store with Mom.

I was the first to go to school because I was the oldest child. When I was four years old, I went to prekindergarten at a small, private, Episcopal school. On my first day, Dad drove me to the door, but he would not take me to my class. I knew where my class was located because we visited earlier to meet my teachers. My heart was pounding with a force I did not know my little body had when I jumped out of the car, and I know fear was evident on my face, but Dad didn't budge. I asked, "Daddy, aren't you coming with me?" He replied, "No, Grace, you know where your class is and who your teachers are. You can go by yourself." He was teaching me to be self-sufficient at four. Still, it must have been difficult for him to watch his firstborn walk alone into a world of which he would not have a part. It was my first day of independence.

I clearly remember my sixth birthday because Dad was in the hospital with pneumonia. He was working so hard he paid very little attention to his health. As a result, he spent almost the entire summer before I entered first grade in the hospital. Mom visited him nightly. On my birthday I was allowed to see him. I have memories of sitting happily in the lobby of the hospital talking to the nurses, telling them with a big smile that I was going to see my dad because it was my birthday. I couldn't wait to see him because children under 12 were not allowed to visit patients, so I had not seen him in a long time. When I entered his hospital room, I saw tubes inserted into his nose and needles stuck in his arm. He was very, very thin. I was frightened and wanted to cry, but I was determined to have a good visit. So I stayed for a while, and he wished me a happy birthday. When it was time to go, I kissed him good-bye and waited until I left his room to cry.

In first grade, I lived with my grandparents because a public elementary school was just across the street. My father bought the house for my grandparents with plans for us three children to attend Levi Elementary School since it was close and convenient. My brother and sister stayed with my parents because Nancy was only four, and Robert was in kindergarten at my old school which was near the store. I felt very isolated and alone in that great big house away from my immediate family.

I learned from my father while in first grade one valuable lesson that still affects me now: never be afraid to ask questions. I was very self-conscious and timid in school. My grades were falling. My father asked me: "How are you going to learn if you don't ask questions?" Even then, when I was six years of age, he tried to make me realize the importance of taking initiative in school. He made me realize improving in school was up to me because he could not be with me all the time.

In those days, my grandmother took care of me. She had moved to 10 America when I was three years old to be with my youngest uncle when he came to go to college. My grandfather joined us three years later. Every morning my grandmother got me dressed and made my breakfast. While I sat at the dining room table, she combed and brushed my hair to prepare me for school. She spoke no English, so we conversed in Cantonese. Every day after school, I called the store to talk to my mother. I really missed being with my parents, brother, and sister and looked forward to their weekly visits. Of course, only one parent visited at a time because someone had to be at the store. I was very jealous that Robert and Nancy were able to stay with my parents.

After school, my grandfather liked to see what I learned that day. It was always a treat to show him the new words I was taught to write in school. Every night I rewrote all the new words for him. He always smiled with approval. Sometimes he helped me with my mathematics. My grandfather played with numbers a lot and actually had an abacus on his desk, which he used daily.

My grandmother did not read or write English. I was learning material she would never understand. She was my caretaker. She cooked and cleaned the house. She fed and bathed me. Neither of my grandparents worked. At that time, they were in their mid-sixties. They had no desire to learn the culture of the new land. Their livelihood depended upon my father, and they were happy merely to be near their children's families.

In the summer, my sister and brother joined me at our grandparents' house. We played a lot more since we had a yard. At the store, we stayed upstairs mostly. When summer was over, I was alone with my grandparents again. That year, in second grade, I was often chased around by Albert, a little black boy in my class. He would try to kiss me. Other children were fascinated by my straight black hair, and would constantly try to touch it. I was jeered at by other children for being Chinese, for having squinty eyes and a flat nose. I was almost ashamed of being Chinese, and being so young I did not understand it at all. I had grown up around other blacks who had frequented our store. Many were my friends, but in school I was having trouble — with black and white children. There were no other Chinese children in my school.

I refrained from telling my parents about Albert because earlier in the school year, I had been hit on the head during recess by a classmate with a baseball bat and had to have stitches. My father told me I should not have been playing so recklessly in school. But one day, in my attempt to hide from Albert, I fell and scraped both knees badly. The principal found me and told me that I should tell my teacher if he did it again. After the next episode, I told my teacher, but made the mistake of embarrassing myself by telling in front of the class. What hurt even more was the fact that my teacher did not do anything about it. Finally, I decided I must tell my parents. I think I feared they would think I had done something wrong, that it was my fault — that perhaps I provoked the boy. I also feared my father's temper.

First I told my mother, and she encouraged me to tell my dad about it. 15 He would make the final decision. I sighed and then proceeded to creep upstairs where he was taking a nap and sat outside their bedroom. When my father awoke, fearfully, I told him about what was happening to me in school. Dad was so understanding. To my relief, he was calm and collected, not angry. He asked me what I wanted to do. He asked if I would like to go to the private school my brother and sister attended. Would I! I was so happy. Yes! I wanted to go back to school with Robert and Nancy! That meant, also, that I would be moving back to the store to live with my parents.

I realize now that Dad was very angry. Not at me, but angry with the teachers and the principal of my elementary school for ignoring my distress. He took me out of Levi in the middle of the year. I feel for the people Dad dealt with to get me out of school. I imagine he probably went there red-faced and smoking with anger to fill out the necessary paperwork. It is funny, though, how Dad let me feel I made the decision to leave Levi.

My father was a loving and devoted son to my grandparents. He made sure they were happy and comfortable. He wanted them with us so he was assured of their well-being. My grandfather had fallen ill when I was around seven years old. The doctors thought he had cancer. Twenty years ago, that meant certain death. The night the diagnosis was given, I was alone with my parents after the store was closed. Dad was crying. I was frightened because I had never before seen him cry. Taking off his glasses and looking at me with red, teary eyes and unmistakable pain, he asked me, "Do you love your Ye-Ye?" It was difficult to speak to him when he seemed so vulnerable, but with all the courage I could muster and tears welling up in my eyes, I answered, "Yes." Mom was behind Dad comforting him. At seven years of age, I was learning what it is to love your parents, and I was learning even Dads cry. Thankfully, my grandfather's cancer went into remission after treatment.

When Dad caught wind of the fact that I was doing poorly on my multiplication tables in third grade, he drilled me nightly in the back of the store where he stood behind the meat counter. I remember sweating and feeling extremely apprehensive and fearful of his wrath if I answered incorrectly. I quickly learned my multiplication tables inside out.

On the day he died, Dad came to my grandparents' house where my brother, sister, and I were staying for Thanksgiving weekend. He planned to go car-shopping with his older brother. I went along with them. We had lunch at Shoney's afterward, at my suggestion, of course. I did not care about car-shopping. I just wanted to spend time with Dad, even if we were with my uncle. I chattered away while we had lunch. When we returned to my grandparents' house, he took a nap in my bedroom before going back to work at the store. I was to wake him in an hour. Upon leaving, he picked me up for a big hug and kiss good-bye. I had my arms around his neck and my head on his shoulder. He told me to be good before putting me down. I did not know it would be the last time I would see him alive.

Later, in the afternoon, I heard my grandfather making dozens of phone 20 calls, saying with grief and shock: "Ah, Davey say joh loh, Davey say joh loh!" meaning, "Davey's dead, Davey's dead!" I couldn't believe his words and rushed to tell my sister and brother, who responded with disbelief and dismay. They thought I was lying to them, playing a cruel trick on them. Later, when we had heard the grown-ups talking and were in fact sure Dad was killed, the three of us went up to our favorite spot in the attic where we cried and cried and hugged one another. We were in the way of the adults. They did not know how to talk to us, nor would they answer our questions. We only had each other for comfort.

My aunts and uncles from various parts of the country left their families to rush to Memphis the day Dad was shot. We had a full house of people who came by to bring food, to pay respects. It was very late in the evening before all but family were left in our house. It seemed peaceful once again. My best friend brought a plant the next day. We were both at a loss for words — we did not need them. It was enough just to see her.

The next day, there was an article in the newspaper about what happened. My aunt said it did not do my father justice. The robber was never caught by the police. In fact, the police later found the bag of change lying in an alley nearby. My mom's reaction was calm as she told me, "Even if they find him, it won't bring your daddy back, Grace."

The day of my father's funeral was rainy and cold. There was a long procession of cars on the way to the cemetery. My father was well respected by others in the community and had many friends. My grandmother did not attend the funeral. As long as I knew her, she never once set foot in a hospital, nor did she go to funerals. My grandfather also elected not to attend, but as the hearse passed by their house, he ran out, down the long walkway to the gate with a black raincoat held above his head. He wished to open the coffin to see his son one more time, but it was nailed shut. It was only possible for him to touch the casket.

All my teachers and the principal of our school attended Dad's funeral. Willie was there too. We were all crying when they came to see us. Later, my best friend told me the teachers didn't think we would be returning to school for a while. They were surprised to find us in class the following day. My friends did not know how to react to me, and in homeroom, my teacher asked, in front of everyone, if I was okay. I was not okay. I was in pain, but what could I do? I lost my father. He was never coming back. I tried to be strong, and looking down at my desk, I said, "Yes, I'm okay."

We were so young: Robert eight, and Nancy seven. Now we are grown 25 adults. I wonder what it would have been like if Dad were living during our developing years. I suspect I would be a very different person. I am very much a feminist and a professional now. I don't think he would have allowed me to move 1,000 miles from home to live on my own after college. I probably would not have been allowed to participate in many things such as dating, parties, and school activities if he were alive during my adolescence, for he was extremely strict.

We visited his gravesite every year on his birthday, on the anniversary of his death, and on holidays such as New Year's and Christmas. Following my grandmother's Asian traditions, we brought incense to burn at the gravesite, and food: a bowl of rice, fruit, a main dish for his spirit to eat. We also burned special paper, which my grandmother stated represented money for Dad to spend in the afterlife. We did these things for her since she would not go to the cemetery. Following American tradition, we also brought flowers. When the incense was lit, the money burning, and the food set out with chopsticks along with tea and sometimes scotch (he had to have something to drink as well as utensils!), we took turns paying our respects by bowing to the headstone three times and silently told his spirit whatever we wanted to tell him, whatever was on our minds. When done, we bowed again three times to bid farewell until the next time.

I write this now because it is more than 14 years since my father's death. I think about how fast those 14 years have gone by and all the changes and growing that have taken place. I wonder if he is proud of me now. I wonder what I would be like today if he were alive. Even though I only had him in the first 10 years of my life, I know there is much of him in me. I have his temperament, his strictness, and his self-righteous nature. I have his sense of fairness, generosity, and loyalty. He taught me much in those first 10 years. There are also scars from his death because my family did not talk about our loss. We took the blow and went on with life.

In the last four years, I have also lost both grandparents. They are buried with my father. One day, my mother and uncles will join them. Whenever I return to Memphis to visit family and friends, I also go to the cemetery to visit my father and grandparents. I don't follow all the traditions my grandmother so treasured, but I do carry incense and flowers with me. I still bow and have my talk with each. Those are always peaceful and contemplative moments. Sometimes I drive by the old store, the old house, and the private elementary school to relive some of my past.

Death does not get easier. The people I love will not be with me forever. That hurts. Death, however, is a part of life we all face at some point. Nevertheless, it is a comfort to me to believe that after death, those I love go somewhere nice and comfortable. My grandmother always wished to return as a bird — to fly over the earth — soaring and free. I hope she made it.

Suggestions for Writing and Discussion

1. Describe the relationship between Wai and her father. Were they close? Distant? Comfortable with one another? Something else?

2. Compare and contrast the values held within Wai's Chinese family with the values held within a typical American family today. How do you account for any differences?

3. Why might Wai have had trouble with some of the children in school but not with the same children in her neighborhood?

4. In paragraph 17, Wai writes that she "was learning what it is to love your parents." What does she mean by this statement?

5. What do the events surrounding the father's funeral signify about the relationship between Wai's family and the surrounding community?

6. In paragraph 27, Wai muses, "I wonder if he is proud of me now." What do you think? From his expectations for his young daughter, would he be proud of this grown one? Explain.

Suggestions for Extended Thinking and Research

1. Interview a Chinese-American person in order to discover his or her view on how one goes about "blending" cultures.

2. Research the Chinese beliefs regarding the meaning of death. Report to the class on your findings.

MAXINE HONG KINGSTON
Photographs of My Parents

> *Best known for her collections of essays,* The Woman Warrior *(1976) and* China Men *(1980), Maxine Hong Kingston is also the author of a significant article related to multicultural studies: "Cultural Misreading by American Reviewers," in* Asian and Western Writer in Dialogue: New Cultural Identities *(1982). Born in Stockton, California, in 1940, she grew up listening to the stories of the friends and relatives who gathered in the laundry her parents operated. Following her graduation from Berkeley, Kingston began to think deeply about how those stories had influenced her life, and she started writing down her reminiscences. "Photographs of My Parents" suggests the respect and admiration Kingston holds for her parents as well as the conflicts she has encountered between their values and the values of their adopted country.*

Prereading/Journal-Writing Suggestions

1. Find a picture (or recall one from memory) of your parents when they were younger (young adults), perhaps a wedding or graduation picture. Carefully describe the details in these photos. Can you come to any conclusions about your parents' lives at the time this photograph was taken? Can you see any clues about what they might have been thinking or feeling?

2. Look at (or recall) a photograph of yourself when you were younger. First, simply describe the picture. Then, try to remember what you were thinking or feeling at the time the picture was taken. What were the surrounding events of this day and time? Who else might have been in the background? What do you remember that is not shown in the picture?

3. What do you think your mother (or other female relative) is most proud of in her life? What is her most valued possession? Write short answers to these questions. Then after writing, ask the person for her response. If her answers differ from yours, write a paragraph or two describing what you discover.

Once in a long while, four times so far for me, my mother brings out the metal tube that holds her medical diploma. On the tube are gold circles crossed with seven red lines each—"joy" ideographs in abstract. There are also little flowers that look like gears for a gold machine. According to the scraps of labels with Chinese and American addresses, stamps, and postmarks, the family airmailed the can from Hong Kong in 1950. It got crushed in the middle, and whoever tried to peel the labels off stopped because the red and gold paint came off too, leaving silver scratches that rust. Somebody tried to pry the end off before discovering that the tube pulls apart. When I open it, the smell of China flies out, a thousand-year-old bat flying heavy-headed out of the Chinese caverns where bats are as white as dust, a smell that comes from long ago, far back in the brain. Crates from Canton, Hong Kong, Singapore, and Taiwan have that smell too, only stronger because they are more recently come from the Chinese.

Inside the can are three scrolls, one inside another. The largest says that in the twenty-third year of the National Republic, the To Keung School of Midwifery, where she has had two years of instruction and Hospital Practice, awards its Diploma to my mother, who has shown through oral and written examination her Proficiency in Midwifery, Pediatrics, Gynecology, "Medecine," "Surgary," Therapeutics, Ophthalmology, Bacteriology, Dermatology, Nursing and Bandage. This document has eight stamps on it: one, the school's English and Chinese names embossed together in a circle; one, as the Chinese enumerate, a stork and a big baby in lavender ink; one, the school's Chinese seal; one, an orangish paper stamp pasted in the border design; one, the red seal of Dr. Wu Pak-liang, M.D., Lyon, Berlin, president and "Ex-assistant étranger à la clinique chirugicale et d'accouchement de l'université de Lyon"; one, the red seal of Dean Woo Yin-kam, M.D.; one, my mother's seal, her chop mark larger than the president's and the dean's; and one, the number 1279 on the back. Dean Woo's signature is followed by "(Hackett)." I read in a history book that Hackett Medical College for Women at Canton was founded in the nineteenth century by European women doctors.

The school seal has been pressed over a photograph of my mother at the age of thirty-seven. The diploma gives her age as twenty-seven. She looks younger than I do, her eyebrows are thicker, her lips fuller. Her naturally curly hair is parted on the left, one wavy wisp tendrilling off to the right. She wears a scholar's white gown, and she is not thinking about her appearance. She stares straight ahead as if she could see me and past me to her grandchildren and grandchildren's grandchildren. She has spacy eyes, as all people recently from Asia have. Her eyes do not focus on the camera. My mother is not smiling; Chinese do not smile for photographs. Their faces command relatives in foreign lands — "Send money" — and posterity forever — "Put food in front of this picture." My mother does not understand Chinese-American snapshots. "What are you laughing at?" she asks.

The second scroll is a long narrow photograph of the graduating class with the school officials seated in front. I picked out my mother immediately. Her face is exactly her own, though forty years younger. She is so familiar, I can only tell whether or not she is pretty or happy or smart by comparing her to the other women. For this formal group picture she straightened her hair with oil to make a chinlength bob like the others'. On the other women, strangers, I can recognize a curled lip, a sidelong glance, pinched shoulders. My mother is not soft; the girl with the small nose and dimpled underlip is soft. My mother is not humorous, not like the girl at the end who lifts her mocking chin to pose like Girl Graduate. My mother does not having smiling eyes; the old woman teacher (Dean Woo?) in front crinkles happily, and the one faculty member in the western suit smiles westernly. Most of the graduates are girls whose faces have not yet formed; my mother's face will not change anymore, except to age. She is intelligent, alert, pretty. I can't tell if she's happy.

The graduates seem to have been looking elsewhere when they pinned   5 the rose, zinnia, or chrysanthemum on their precise black dresses. One thin girl wears hers in the middle of her chest. A few have a flower over a left or right nipple. My mother put hers, a chrysanthemum, below her left breast. Chinese dresses at that time were dartless, cut as if women did not have breasts; these young doctors, unaccustomed to decorations, may have seen their chests as black expanses with no reference points for flowers. Perhaps they couldn't shorten that far gaze that lasts only a few years after a Chinese emigrates. In this picture too my mother's eyes are big with what they held — reaches of oceans beyond China, land beyond oceans. Most emigrants learn the barbarians' directness — how to gather themselves and stare rudely into talking faces as if trying to catch lies. In America my mother has eyes as strong as boulders, never once skittering off a face, but she has not learned to place decorations and phonograph needles, nor has she stopped seeing land on the other side of the oceans. Now her eyes include the relatives in China, as they once included my father smiling and smiling in his many western outfits, a different one for each photograph that he sent from America.

He and his friends took pictures of one another in bathing suits at Coney Island beach, the salt wind from the Atlantic blowing their hair. He's the one in the middle with his arms about the necks of his buddies. They pose in the cockpit of a biplane, on a motorcycle, and on a lawn beside the "Keep Off the Grass" sign. They are always laughing. My father, white shirt sleeves rolled up, smiles in front of a wall of clean laundry. In the spring he wears a new straw hat, cocked at a Fred Astaire angle. He steps out, dancing down the stairs, one foot forward, one back, a hand in his pocket. He wrote to her about the American custom of stomping on straw hats come fall. "If you want to save your hat for next year," he said, "you have to put it away early, or else when you're riding the subway or walking along Fifth Avenue, any stranger can snatch it off your head and put his foot through it. That's the way they celebrate the change of seasons here." In the winter he wears a gray felt hat with his gray overcoat. He is sitting on a rock in Central Park. In one snapshot he is not smiling; someone took it when he was studying, blurred in the glare of the desk lamp.

There are no snapshots of my mother. In two small portraits, however, there is a black thumbprint on her forehead, as if someone had inked in bangs, as if someone had marked her.

"Mother, did bangs come into fashion after you had the picture taken?" One time she said yes. Another time when I asked, "Why do you have fingerprints on your forehead?" she said, "Your First Uncle did that." I disliked the unsureness in her voice.

The last scroll has columns of Chinese words. The only English is "Department of Health, Canton," imprinted on my mother's face, the same photograph as on the diploma. I keep looking to see whether she was afraid. Year after year my father did not come home or send for her. Their two children had been dead for ten years. If he did not return soon, there would be no more children. ("They were three and two years old, a boy and a girl. They could talk already.") My father did send money regularly, though, and she had nobody to spend it on but herself. She bought good clothes and shoes. Then she decided to use the money for becoming a doctor. She did not leave for Canton immediately after the children died. In China there was time to complete feelings. As my father had done, my mother left the village by ship. There was a sea bird painted on the ship to protect it against shipwreck and winds. She was in luck. The following ship was boarded by river pirates, who kidnapped every passenger, even old ladies. "Sixty dollars for an old lady" was what the bandits used to say. "I sailed alone," she says, "to the capital of the entire province." She took a brown leather suitcase and a seabag stuffed with two quilts.

Suggestions for Writing and Discussion

1. What audience might Kingston have had in mind when she was writing the book from which this selection is taken? Do you think some readers would have a more positive response than others? Explain.
2. Smells, psychologists tell us, are often great sensory triggers to our past. When Kingston opens the tube that contains her mother's scrolls, "the smell of China flies out." Describe and explain the significance of the scents in your own life that take you back to other times and other places.
3. Certainly Kingston's mother's most valuable possession was her medical diploma. Explain why the circumstances related to the diploma give it special significance for her.
4. Compare the description of Kingston's mother with the description of her father. How would you characterize each of them? Do you feel more empathetic with one than with the other? What inferences can you make about their relationship with each other? From Kingston's descriptions, how do you think she feels about each of her parents?
5. What do the descriptions of Kingston's mother and father suggest about the differences in values between their native culture and that of their adopted country?

Suggestions for Extended Thinking and Research

1. Make a list of questions that you would like to ask someone of your parents' generation about his or her life as a young adult. Choose questions that truly interest you. Then find a person willing to be interviewed; carefully

record the responses to your questions. After thinking about these responses, write an essay analyzing the most significant differences and similarities you see between your life as a young adult and the young adult life of the person you interviewed.

2. Imagine you are Kingston's mother. On opening the tube for the first time, what are your reactions to the scrolls?

3. Research approaches to health care in China. Note especially alternative ways of treating patients. Write an essay comparing these approaches with medical treatment you have encountered or observed here in the United States.

LEWIS P. JOHNSON

For My Indian Daughter

> *Born in 1935, Lewis Johnson grew up in Harbor Springs, Michigan, where his great-grandfather lived out his final days as the last recognized chief of the Potawatomi Ottawas. A surveyor by profession, Johnson has done extensive research on Indian approaches to interpretive dreams. He has written many essays, like "For My Indian Daughter," that suggest the complexities raised by the modern juxtaposition of Native American culture and values with traditional Western European culture and values.*

Prereading/Journal-Writing Suggestions

1. Choose one story from your family's past — one in which you take a great deal of pride. After describing the incident, explain what you think it reveals about your family's values.
2. Write about a time someone ridiculed or belittled you. How did you react? How do you evaluate the episode now that you can look back at it?
3. In three minutes, list all the words, phrases, and images that come to your mind when you hear the word *Indian*. Then read over your list and reflect on what you have written. What is first on your list? What words did you end with? Can you see any groups of words or phrases that go together?

My little girl is singing herself to sleep upstairs, her voice mingling with the sounds of the birds outside in the old maple trees. She is two and I am nearly 50, and I am very taken with her. She came along late in my life, unexpected and unbidden, a startling gift.

Today at the beach my chubby-legged, brown-skinned daughter ran laughing into the water as fast as she could. My wife and I laughed watching her, until we heard behind us a low guttural curse and then an unpleasant voice raised in an imitation war whoop.

I turned to see a fat man in a bathing suit, white and soft as a grub, as he covered his mouth and prepared to make the Indian war cry again. He was middle-aged, younger than I, and had three little children lined up next to him, grinning foolishly. My wife suggested we leave the beach, and I agreed.

I knew the man was not unusual in his feelings against Indians. His beach behavior might have been socially unacceptable to more civilized whites, but his basic view of Indians is expressed daily in our small town, frequently on the editorial pages of the county newspaper, as white people speak out against Indian fishing rights and land rights, saying in essence, "Those Indians are taking our fish, our land." It doesn't matter to them that we were here first, that the U.S. Supreme Court has ruled in our favor. It matters to them that we have something they want, and they hate us for it.

Backlash is the common explanation of the attacks on Indians, the bumper stickers that say, "Spear an Indian, Save a Fish," but I know better. The hatred of Indians goes back to the beginning when white people came to this country. For me it goes back to my childhood in Harbor Springs, Michigan.

Theft

Harbor Springs is now a summer resort for the very affluent, but a   5 hundred years ago it was the Indian village of my Ottawa ancestors. My grandmother, Anna Showanessy, and other Indians like her, had their land there taken by treaty, by fraud, by violence, by theft. They remembered how whites had burned down the village at Burt Lake in 1900 and pushed the Indians out. These were the stories in my family.

When I was a boy my mother told me to walk down the alleys in Harbor Springs and not to wear my orange football sweater out of the house. This way I would not stand out, not be noticed, and not be a target.

I wore my orange sweater anyway and deliberately avoided the alleys. I was the biggest person I knew and wasn't really afraid. But I met my comeuppance when I enlisted in the U.S. Army. One night all the men in my barracks gathered together and, gang-fashion, pulled me into the shower and scrubbed me down with rough brushes used for floors, saying, "We won't have any dirty Indians in our outfit." It is a point of irony that I was cleaner than any of them. Later in Korea I learned how to kill, how to bully, how to hate Koreans. I came out of the war tougher than ever and, strangely, white.

I went to college, got married, lived in La Porte, Indiana, worked as a surveyor and raised three boys. I headed Boy Scout groups, never thinking it odd when the Scouts did imitation Indian dances, imitation Indian lore.

One day when I was 35 or thereabouts I heard about an Indian powwow. My father used to attend them and so with great curiosity and a strange joy at discovering a part of my heritage, I decided the thing to do to get ready for this big event was to have my friend make me a spear in his forge. The steel was fine and blue and iridescent. The feathers on the shaft were bright and proud.

In a dusty state fairground in southern Indiana, I found white people   10 dressed as Indians. I learned they were "hobbyists," that is, it was their hobby and leisure pastime to masquerade as Indians on weekends. I felt ridiculous with my spear, and I left.

It was years before I could tell anyone of the embarrassment of this weekend and see any humor in it. But in a way it was that weekend, for all its silliness, that was my awakening. I realized I didn't know who I was. I didn't have an Indian name. I didn't speak the Indian language. I didn't know the Indian customs. Dimly I remembered the Ottawa word for dog, but it was a baby word, *kahgee*, not the full word, *muhkahgee,* which I was later to learn. Even more hazily I remembered a naming ceremony (my own). I remembered legs dancing around me, dust. Where had that been? Who had I been?

"Suwaukquat," my mother told me when I asked, "where the tree begins to grow."

That was 1968, and I was not the only Indian in the country who was feeling the need to remember who he or she was. There were others. They had powwows, real ones, and eventually I found them. Together we researched our past, a search that for me culminated in the Longest Walk, a march on Washington in 1978. Maybe because I now know what it means to be Indian, it surprises me that others don't. Of course there aren't very many of us left. The chances of an average person knowing an average Indian in an average lifetime are pretty slim.

Circle

Still, I was amused one day when my small, four-year-old neighbor looked at me as I was hoeing in my garden and said, "You aren't a real Indian, are you?" Scotty is little, talkative, likable. Finally I said, "I'm a real Indian." He looked at me for a moment and then said, squinting into the sun, "Then where's your horse and feathers?" The child was simply a smaller, whiter version of my own ignorant self years before. We'd both seen too much TV, that's all. He was not to be blamed. And so, in a way, the moronic man on the beach today is blameless. We come full circle to realize other people are like ourselves, as discomfiting as that may be sometimes.

As I sit in my old chair on my porch, in a light that is fading so the leaves are barely distinguishable against the sky, I can picture my girl asleep upstairs. I would like to prepare her for what's to come, take her each step of the way saying, there's a place to avoid, here's what I know about this, but much of what's before her she must go through alone. She must pass through pain and joy and solitude and community to discover her own inner self that is unlike any other and come through that passage to the place where she sees all people are one, and in so seeing may live her life in a brighter future.

Suggestions for Writing and Discussion

1. Why do you think Johnson wrote this piece? Who might his intended audience be? Primarily his daughter? Other Indians? Non-Indians? All Americans? Himself?
2. What inferences does Johnson make about the middle-aged man on the beach? On what evidence does he base these inferences? What do you think of Johnson's reaction? Was it appropriate, cowardly, overreacting, something else? Explain.
3. Do you agree with Johnson's claim that the feelings suggested by the man's actions are not "unusual"? Explain.
4. Why is the middle section of this piece called "Theft" and the final section entitled "Circle"?

5. Describe and evaluate Johnson's feelings and reactions when he attends the powwow.

Suggestions for Extended Thinking and Research

1. In the last paragraph of the section called "Theft," Johnson says, "That was 1968, and I was not the only Indian in the country who was feeling the need to remember who he or she was." Research the mood and events in America in 1968 by using the *New York Times Index* or by skimming several 1968 issues of popular magazines such as *Newsweek, Time,* and *Life*. What conclusions can you draw about the attitudes and concerns during this year in U.S. history?

2. Find accounts of the Longest Walk on Washington in 1978 (mentioned by Johnson in the final paragraph of the "Theft" section). You might use the *New York Times Index* or the *Reader's Guide to Periodical Literature* to aid your research. After locating several sources, write a detailed account of one moment during the walk. Before you begin to write, adopt the point of view of someone who was on the scene, perhaps a participant, a conservative U.S. senator, a reporter, or a police officer who is on duty.

3. Find information on the Native Americans who live (or lived) in or near your part of the country. Write an essay describing beliefs, rituals, family life, and actions of these people.

RAYMOND CARVER

My Father's Life

> *Born in Clatskanie, a logging town in Oregon, Raymond Carver (1938–1988) graduated from California State University at Humbolt. Following a year at the Writer's Workshop at the University of Iowa, he taught writing at the University of California, the University of Texas, and at Syracuse University. When he was not teaching, he worked at a series of jobs, including truck driver, custodian, and deliveryman, to support himself while he wrote poetry and fiction. In this memoir of his father, Carver evaluates the effects of the hardships his father faced as a laborer during the Great Depression of the 1930s. He also examines the impact of his father's psychological depression on his family.*

Prereading/Journal-Writing Suggestions

1. It's a fact: Most people don't even come close to developing their full potential and talents. Freewrite about what your talents are and whether or not you're making the most of these talents today.
2. What is your definition of success? Keeping this definition in mind, what do you believe a person needs to do to succeed? Think about people you know who have, according to your definition, achieved some degree of success in order to answer this question. Also think about those who have failed to achieve what you see as success.

My dad's name was Clevie Raymond Carver. His family called him Raymond and friends called him C.R. I was named Raymond Clevie Carver Jr. I hated the "Junior" part. When I was little my dad called me Frog, which was okay. But later, like everybody else in the family, he began calling me Junior. He went on calling me this until I was thirteen or fourteen and announced that I wouldn't answer to that name any longer. So he began calling me Doc. From then until his death, on June 17, 1967, he called me Doc, or else Son.

When he died, my mother telephoned my wife with the news. I was away from my family at the time, between lives, trying to enroll in the School of Library Science at the University of Iowa. When my wife answered the phone, my mother blurted out, "Raymond's dead!" For a moment, my wife thought my mother was telling her that I was dead. Then my mother made it clear *which* Raymond she was talking about and my wife said, "Thank God. I thought you meant *my* Raymond."

My dad walked, hitched rides, and rode in empty boxcars when he went from Arkansas to Washington State in 1934, looking for work. I don't know whether he was pursuing a dream when he went out to Washington. I doubt it. I don't think he dreamed much. I believe he was simply looking for steady work at decent pay. Steady work was meaningful work. He picked apples for a time and then landed a construction laborer's job on the Grand Coulee Dam. After he'd put aside a little money, he bought a car and drove back to Arkansas to help his folks, my grandparents, pack up for the move west. He said later that they were about to starve down there, and this wasn't meant as a figure of speech. It was during that short while in Arkansas, in a town called Leola, that my mother met my dad on the sidewalk as he came out of a tavern.

"He was drunk," she said. "I don't know why I let him talk to me. His eyes were glittery. I wish I'd had a crystal ball." They'd met once, a year or so before, at a dance. He'd had girlfriends before her, my mother told me. "Your dad always had a girlfriend, even after we married. He was my first and last. I never had another man. But I didn't miss anything."

They were married by a justice of the peace on the day they left for 5 Washington, this big, tall country girl and a farmhand-turned-construction worker. My mother spent her wedding night with my dad and his folks, all of them camped beside the road in Arkansas.

In Omak, Washington, my dad and mother lived in a little place not much bigger than a cabin. My grandparents lived next door. My dad was still working on the dam, and later, with the huge turbines producing electricity and the water backed up for a hundred miles into Canada, he stood in the crowd and heard Franklin D. Roosevelt when he spoke at the construction site. "He never mentioned those guys who died building that dam," my dad said. Some of his friends had died there, men from Arkansas, Oklahoma, and Missouri.

He then took a job in a sawmill in Clatskanie, Oregon, a little town alongside the Columbia River. I was born there, and my mother has a picture of my dad standing in front of the gate to the mill, proudly holding me up to face the camera. My bonnet is on crooked and about to come untied. His hat is pushed back on his forehead, and he's wearing a big grin. Was he going in to work or just finishing his shift? It doesn't matter. In either case, he had a job and a family. These were his salad days.

In 1941 we moved to Yakima, Washington, where my dad went to work as a saw filer, a skilled trade he'd learned in Clatskanie. When war broke out, he was given a deferment because his work was considered necessary to the war effort. Finished lumber was in demand by the armed services, and he kept his saws so sharp they could shave the hair off your arm.

After my dad had moved us to Yakima, he moved his folks into the same neighborhood. By the mid-1940s the rest of my dad's family — his brother, his sister, and her husband, as well as uncles, cousins, nephews, and most of their extended family and friends — had come out from Arkansas. All because my dad came out first. The men went to work at Boise Cascade, where my dad worked, and the women packed apples in the canneries. And in just a little while, it seemed — according to my mother — everybody was better off than my dad. "Your dad couldn't keep money," my mother said. "Money burned a hole in his pocket. He was always doing for others."

The first house I clearly remember living in, at 1515 South Fifteenth 10
Street, in Yakima, had an outdoor toilet. On Halloween night, or just any
night, for the hell of it, neighbor kids, kids in their early teens, would carry
our toilet away and leave it next to the road. My dad would have to get
somebody to help him bring it home. Or these kids would take the toilet and
stand it in somebody else's backyard. Once they actually set it on fire. But
ours wasn't the only house that had an outdoor toilet. When I was old enough
to know what I was doing, I threw rocks at the other toilets when I'd see
someone go inside. This was called bombing the toilets. After a while,
though, everyone went to indoor plumbing until, suddenly, our toilet was the
last outdoor one in the neighborhood. I remember the shame I felt when my
third-grade teacher, Mr. Wise, drove me home from school one day. I asked
him to stop at the house just before ours, claiming I lived there.

I can recall what happened one night when my dad came home late to
find that my mother had locked all the doors on him from the inside. He was
drunk, and we could feel the house shudder as he rattled the door. When he'd
managed to force open a window, she hit him between the eyes with a colander and knocked him out. We could see him down there on the grass. For
years afterward, I used to pick up this colander — it was as heavy as a rolling
pin — and imagine what it would feel like to be hit in the head with something
like that.

It was during this period that I remember my dad taking me into the
bedroom, sitting me down on the bed, and telling me that I might have to go
live with my Aunt LaVon for a while. I couldn't understand what I'd done
that meant I'd have to go away from home to live. But this, too — whatever
prompted it — must have blown over, more or less, anyway, because we stayed
together, and I didn't have to go live with her or anyone else.

I remember my mother pouring his whiskey down the sink. Sometimes
she'd pour it all out and sometimes, if she was afraid of getting caught, she'd
only pour half of it out and then add water to the rest. I tasted some of his
whiskey once myself. It was terrible stuff, and I don't see how anybody could
drink it.

After a long time without one, we finally got a car, in 1949 or 1950, a
1938 Ford. But it threw a rod the first week we had it, and my dad had to have
the motor rebuilt.

"We drove the oldest car in town," my mother said. "We could have had 15
a Cadillac for all he spent on car repairs." One time she found someone else's
tube of lipstick on the floorboard, along with a lacy handkerchief. "See this?"
she said to me. "Some floozy left this in the car."

Once I saw her take a pan of warm water into the bedroom where my
dad was sleeping. She took his hand from under the covers and held it in the
water. I stood in the doorway and watched. I wanted to know what was going
on. This would make him talk in his sleep, she told me. There were things she
needed to know, things she was sure he was keeping from her.

Every year or so, when I was little, we would take the North Coast
Limited across the Cascade Range from Yakima to Seattle and stay in the

Vance Hotel and eat, I remember, at a place called the Dinner Bell Cafe. Once we went to Ivar's Acres of Clams and drank glasses of warm clam broth.

In 1956, the year I was to graduate from high school, my dad quit his job at the mill in Yakima and took a job in Chester, a little sawmill town in northern California. The reasons given at the time for his taking the job had to do with a higher hourly wage and the vague promise that he might, in a few years' time, succeed to the job of head filer in this new mill. But I think, in the main, that my dad had grown restless and simply wanted to try his luck elsewhere. Things had gotten a little too predictable for him in Yakima. Also, the year before, there had been the deaths, within six months of each other, of both his parents.

But just a few days after graduation, when my mother and I were packed to move to Chester, my dad penciled a letter to say he'd been sick for a while. He didn't want us to worry, he said, but he'd cut himself on a saw. Maybe he'd got a tiny sliver of steel in his blood. Anyway, something had happened and he'd had to miss work, he said. In the same mail was an unsigned postcard from somebody down there telling my mother that my dad was about to die and that he was drinking "raw whiskey."

When we arrived in Chester, my dad was living in a trailer that belonged 20 to the company. I didn't recognize him immediately. I guess for a moment I didn't want to recognize him. He was skinny and pale and looked bewildered. His pants wouldn't stay up. He didn't look like my dad. My mother began to cry. My dad put his arm around her and patted her shoulder vaguely, like he didn't know what this was all about, either. The three of us took up life together in the trailer, and we looked after him as best we could. But my dad was sick, and he couldn't get any better. I worked with him in the mill that summer and part of the fall. We'd get up in the mornings and eat eggs and toast while we listened to the radio, and then go out the door with our lunch pails. We'd pass through the gate together at eight in the morning, and I wouldn't see him again until quitting time. In November I went back to Yakima to be closer to my girlfriend, the girl I'd made up my mind I was going to marry.

He worked at the mill in Chester until the following February, when he collapsed on the job and was taken to the hospital. My mother asked if I would come down there and help. I caught a bus from Yakima to Chester, intending to drive them back to Yakima. But now, in addition to being physically sick, my dad was in the midst of a nervous breakdown, though none of us knew to call it that at the time. During the entire trip back to Yakima, he didn't speak, not even when asked a direct question. ("How do you feel, Raymond?" "You okay, Dad?") He'd communicate if he communicated at all, by moving his head or by turning his palms up as if to say he didn't know or care. The only time he said anything on the trip, and for nearly a month afterward, was when I was speeding down a gravel road in Oregon and the car muffler came loose. "You were going too fast," he said.

Back in Yakima a doctor saw to it that my dad went to a psychiatrist. My mother and dad had to go on relief, as it was called, and the county paid for the psychiatrist. The psychiatrist asked my dad, "Who is the President?" He'd had a question put to him that he could answer. "Ike," my dad said. Nevertheless, they put him on the fifth floor of Valley Memorial Hospital and began giving him electroshock treatments. I was married by then and about to start my own family. My dad was still locked up when my wife went into this same hospital, just one floor down, to have our first baby. After she had delivered, I went upstairs to give my dad the news. They let me in through a steel door and showed me where I could find him. He was sitting on a couch with a blanket over his lap. *Hey,* I thought. *What in hell is happening to my dad?* I sat down next to him and told him he was a grandfather. He waited a minute and then he said, "I feel like a grandfather." That's all he said. He didn't smile or move. He was in a big room with a lot of other people. Then I hugged him, and he began to cry.

Somehow he got out of there. But now came the years when he couldn't work and just sat around the house trying to figure what next and what he'd done wrong in his life that he'd wound up like this. My mother went from job to crummy job. Much later she referred to that time he was in the hospital, and those years just afterward, as "when Raymond was sick." The word *sick* was never the same for me again.

In 1964, through the help of a friend, he was lucky enough to be hired on at a mill in Klamath, California. He moved down there by himself to see if he could hack it. He lived not far from the mill, in a one-room cabin not much different from the place he and my mother had started out living in when they went west. He scrawled letters to my mother, and if I called she'd read them aloud to me over the phone. In the letters, he said it was touch and go. Every day that he went to work, he felt like it was the most important day of his life. But every day, he told her, made the next day that much easier. He said for her to tell me he said hello. If he couldn't sleep at night, he said, he thought about me and the good times we used to have. Finally, after a couple of months, he regained some of his confidence. He could do the work and didn't think he had to worry that he'd let anybody down ever again. When he was sure, he sent for my mother.

He'd been off from work for six years and had lost everything in that time—home, car, furniture, and appliances, including the big freezer that had been my mother's pride and joy. He'd lost his good name too—Raymond Carver was someone who couldn't pay his bills—and his self-respect was gone. He'd even lost his virility. My mother told my wife, "All during that time Raymond was sick we slept together in the same bed, but we didn't have relations. He wanted to a few times, but nothing happened. I didn't miss it, but I think he wanted to, you know."

During those years I was trying to raise my own family and earn a living. But, one thing and another, we found ourselves having to move a lot. I couldn't keep track of what was going down in my dad's life. But I did have a chance one Christmas to tell him I wanted to be a writer. I might as well have told him I wanted to become a plastic surgeon. "What are you going to write about?" he wanted to know. Then, as if to help me out, he said, "Write about stuff you know about. Write about some of those fishing trips we took." I said I would, but I knew I wouldn't. "Send me what you write," he said. I said I'd do that, but then I didn't. I wasn't writing anything about fishing, and I didn't think he'd particularly care about, or even necessarily understand, what I was writing in those days. Besides, he wasn't a reader. Not the sort, anyway, I imagined I was writing for.

Then he died. I was a long way off, in Iowa City, with things still to say to him. I didn't have the chance to tell him goodbye, or that I thought he was doing great at his new job. That I was proud of him for making a comeback.

My mother said he came in from work that night and ate a big supper. Then he sat at the table by himself and finished what was left of a bottle of whiskey, a bottle she found hidden in the bottom of the garbage under some coffee grounds a day or so later. Then he got up and went to bed, where my mother joined him a little later. But in the night she had to get up and make a bed for herself on the couch. "He was snoring so loud I couldn't sleep," she said. The next morning when she looked in on him, he was on his back with his mouth open, his cheeks caved in. *Graylooking,* she said. She knew he was dead — she didn't need a doctor to tell her that. But she called one anyway, and then she called my wife.

Among the pictures my mother kept of my dad and herself during those early days in Washington was a photograph of him standing in front of a car, holding a beer and a stringer of fish. In the photograph he is wearing his hat back on his forehead and has this awkward grin on his face. I asked her for it and she gave it to me, along with some others. I put it up on my wall, and each time we moved, I took the picture along and put it up on another wall. I looked at it carefully from time to time, trying to figure out some things about my dad, and maybe myself in the process. But I couldn't. My dad just kept moving further and further away from me and back into time. Finally, in the course of another move, I lost the photograph. It was then that I tried to recall it, and at the same time make an attempt to say something about my dad, and how I thought that in some important ways we might be alike. I wrote the poem when I was living in an apartment house in an urban area south of San Francisco, at a time when I found myself, like my dad, having trouble with alcohol. The poem was a way of trying to connect up with him.

Photograph of My Father in His Twenty-Second Year

October. Here in this dank, unfamiliar kitchen
I study my father's embarrassed young man's face.
Sheepish grin, he holds in one hand a string
of spiny yellow perch, in the other
a bottle of Carlsberg beer.

In jeans and flannel shirt, he leans
against the front fender of a 1934 Ford.
He would like to pose brave and hearty for his posterity,

wear his old hat cocked over his ear.
All his life my father wanted to be bold.

But the eyes give him away, and the hands
that limply offer the string of dead perch
and the bottle of beer. Father, I love you,
yet how can I say thank you, I who can't hold my liquor either
and don't even know the places to fish.

The poem is true in its particulars, except that my dad died in June and ₃₀ not October, as the first word of the poem says. I wanted a word with more than one syllable to it to make it linger a little. But more than that, I wanted a month appropriate to what I felt at the time I wrote the poem—a month of short days and failing light, smoke in the air, things perishing. June was summer nights and days, graduations, my wedding anniversary, the birthday of one of my children. June wasn't a month your father died in.

After the service at the funeral home, after we had moved outside, a woman I didn't know came over to me and said, "He's happier where he is now." I stared at this woman until she moved away. I still remember the little knob of a hat she was wearing. Then one of my dad's cousins—I didn't know the man's name—reached out and took my hand. "We all miss him," he said, and I knew he wasn't saying it just to be polite.

I began to weep for the first time since receiving the news. I hadn't been able to before. I hadn't had the time, for one thing. Now, suddenly, I couldn't stop. I held my wife and wept while she said and did what she could do to comfort me there in the middle of that summer afternoon.

I listened to people saying consoling things to my mother, and I was glad that my dad's family had turned up, had come to where he was. I thought I'd remember everything that was said and done that day and maybe find a way to tell it sometime. But I didn't. I forgot it all, or nearly. What I do remember is that I heard our name used a lot that afternoon, my dad's name and mine. But I knew they were talking about my dad. *Raymond,* these people kept saying in their beautiful voices out of my childhood. *Raymond.*

Suggestions for Writing and Discussion

1. From the opening paragraph alone, what do you know about Carver, his father, and their relationship?
2. Why do you think Carver's mother continued to stay on with her husband despite all his apparent failings as a husband? If you could have given her advice at any time during her life, would you have urged her to stay or to leave? Explain.
3. What do you think about the father's advice to his son regarding writing (paragraph 26)? Why doesn't Carver initially take his father's advice? Why does he finally decide to follow this advice?

4. What forces, both external and internal, contribute to the downfall of Carver's father?

5. Describe Carver's relationship with his father and also with his mother. With whom was he closest? Explain.

6. In the poem, Carver shows a picture of his father with a string of fish in one hand and a beer in the other. Why does he choose these two particular images?

7. In his poem, Carver writes that he loved his dad but he couldn't thank him. From the details in the poem, explain what he loved about his father, and explain why he cannot thank him.

Suggestions for Extended Thinking and Research

1. Write a personal narrative describing your relationship with your father or your mother. Refrain from telling the reader too much about your feelings or the depth of this relationship. Instead, focus on specific events and specific details in order to show the reader (and perhaps yourself) what the relationship was all about.

2. Model Carver's poem by writing a poem of your own, for either your father or your mother.

3. Research the causes and effects of alcoholism.

4. Was Carver's father a good father or a poor one? Write a paper in which you argue for either one of these positions. To write this paper, you'll need to develop a definition of either a good father or a poor father (or, perhaps, of both).

BHARATI MUKHERJEE
Fathering

> *Currently a professor of English at the University of California, Berkeley, Bharati Mukherjee was born in India in 1940 and has lived in the United States and Canada for more than thirty years. Mukherjee's novels (particularly* Wife *[1975] and* Jasmine *[1989]) and short stories often look at the cultural differences she has observed between her native India and the United States. "Fathering" first appeared in her collection of short stories,* The Middleman and Other Stories, *which won the 1988 National Book Critics Circle award. (An interview between Bill Moyers and Mukherjee appears on pp. 79–87.)*

Prereading/Journal-Writing Suggestions

1. In recent years, the Vietnam experience has been portrayed in films and on television. From any of these you may have seen, as well as from anything you may have heard or read about this war, what is your reaction to the war and to the Americans who fought there?
2. In what ways do you hope your generation will contribute to the next generation?
3. "Am I my brother's keeper?" What do you think this question means? How would you respond to it? Do you think your response is typical of most Americans your age?

Eng stands just inside our bedroom door, her fidgety fist on the doorknob which Sharon, in a sulk, polished to a gleam yesterday afternoon.

"I'm starved," she says.

I know a sick little girl when I see one. I brought the twins up without much help ten years ago. Eng's got a high fever. Brownish stains stiffen the nap of her terry robe. Sour smells fill the bedroom.

"For God's sake leave us alone," Sharon mutters under the quilt. She turns away from me. We bought the quilt at a garage sale in Rock Springs the Sunday two years ago when she moved in. "Talk to her."

Sharon works on this near-marriage of ours. I'll hand it to her, she really does. I knead her shoulders, and I say, "Easy, easy," though I really hate it when she treats Eng like a deaf-mute. "My girl speaks English, remember?"

Eng can outcuss any freckle-faced kid on the block. Someone in the killing fields must have taught her. Maybe her mama, the honeyest-skinned bar girl with the tiniest feet in Saigon. I was an errand boy with the Combined Military Intelligence. I did the whole war on Dexedrine. Vietnam didn't happen, and I'd put it behind me in marriage and fatherhood and teaching high school. Ten years later came the screwups with the marriage, the job,

5

women, the works. Until Eng popped up in my life, I really believed it didn't happen.

"Come here, sweetheart," I beg my daughter. I sidle closer to Sharon, so there'll be room under the quilt for Eng.

"I'm starved," she complains from the doorway. She doesn't budge. The robe and hair are smelling something fierce. She doesn't show any desire to cuddle. She must be sick. She must have thrown up all night. Sharon throws the quilt back. "Then go raid the refrigerator like a normal kid," she snaps.

Once upon a time Sharon used to be a cheerful, accommodating woman. It isn't as if Eng was dumped on us out of the blue. She knew I was tracking my kid. Coming to terms with the past was Sharon's idea. I don't know what happened to *that* Sharon. "For all you know, Jason," she'd said, "the baby died of malaria or something." She said, "Go on, find out and deal with it." She said she could handle being a stepmother — better a fresh chance with some orphan off the streets of Saigon than with my twins from Rochester. My twins are being raised in some organic-farming lesbo commune. Their mother breeds Nubian goats for a living. "Come get in bed with us, baby. Let Dad feel your forehead. You burning up with fever?"

"She isn't hungry, I think she's sick," I tell Sharon, but she's already 10 tugging her sleeping mask back on. "I think she's just letting us know she hurts."

I hold my arms out wide for Eng to run into. If I could, I'd suck the virus right out of her. In the jungle, VC mamas used to do that. Some nights we'd steal right up to a hootch — just a few of us intense sons of bitches on some special mission — and the women would be at their mumbo jumbo. They'd be sticking coins and amulets into napalm burns.

"I'm hungry, Dad." It comes out as a moan. Okay, she doesn't run into my arms, but at least she's come as far in as the foot of our bed. "Dad, let's go down to the kitchen. Just you and me."

I am about to let that pass though I can feel Sharon's body go into weird little jerks and twitches when my baby adds with emphatic viciousness, "Not her, Dad. We don't want her with us in the kitchen."

"She loves you," I protest. Love — not spite — makes Eng so territorial; that's what I want to explain to Sharon. She's a sick, frightened, foreign kid, for Chrissake. "Don't you, Sharon? Sharon's concerned about you."

But Sharon turns over on her stomach. "You know what's wrong with 15 you, Jase? You can't admit you're being manipulated. You can't cut through the 'frightened-foreign-kid' shit."

Eng moves closer. She comes up to the side of my bed, but doesn't touch the hand I'm holding out. She's a fighter.

"I feel fire-hot, Dad. My bones feel pain."

"Sharon?" I want to deserve this woman. "Sharon, I'm so sorry." It isn't anybody's fault. You need uppers to get through peace times, too.

"Dad. Let's go. Chop-chop."

"You're too sick to keep food down, baby. Curl up in here. Just for 20 a bit?"

"I'd throw up, Dad."

"I'll carry you back to your room. I'll read you a story, okay?"

Eng watches me real close as I pull the quilt off. "You got any scars you haven't shown me yet? My mom had a big scar on one leg. Shrapnel. Boom boom. I got scars. See? I got lots of bruises."

I scoop up my poor girl and rush her, terry robe flapping, to her room which Sharon fixed up with white girlish furniture in less complicated days. Waiting for Eng was good. Sharon herself said it was good for our relationship. "Could you bring us some juice and aspirin?" I shout from the hallway.

"Aspirin isn't going to cure Eng," I hear Sharon yell. "I'm going to call 25 Doctor Kearns."

Downstairs I hear Sharon on the phone. She isn't talking flu viruses. She's talking social workers and shrinks. My girl isn't crazy; she's picked up a bug in school as might anyone else.

"The child's arms are covered with bruises," Sharon is saying. "Nothing major. They look like . . . well, they're sort of tiny circles and welts." There's nothing for a while. Then she says, "Christ! no, Jason can't do enough for her! That's not what I'm saying! What's happening to this country? You think we're perverts? What I'm saying is the girl's doing it to herself."

"Who are you talking to?" I ask from the top of the stairs. "What happened to the aspirin?"

I lean as far forward over the railing as I dare so I can see what Sharon's up to. She's getting into her coat and boots. She's having trouble with buttons and snaps. In the bluish light of the foyer's broken chandelier, she looks old, harrowed, depressed. What have I done to her?

"What's going on?" I plead. "You deserting me?" 30

"Don't be so fucking melodramatic. I'm going to the mall to buy some aspirin."

"How come we don't have any in the house?"

"Why are you always picking on me?"

"Who was that on the phone?"

"So now you want me to account for every call and every trip?" She ties 35 an angry knot into her scarf. But she tells me. "I was talking to Meg Kearns. She says Doctor Kearns has gone hunting for the day."

"Great!"

"She says he has his beeper on him."

I hear the back door stick and Sharon swear. She's having trouble with the latch. "Jiggle it gently," I shout, taking the stairs two at a time. But before I can come down, her Nissan backs out of the parking apron.

Back upstairs I catch Eng in the middle of a dream or delirium. "They got Grandma!" she screams. She goes very rigid in bed. It's a four-poster with canopy and ruffles and stuff that Sharon put on her MasterCard. The twins slept on bunk beds. With the twins it was different, totally different. Dr. Spock can't be point man for Eng, for us.

"She bring me food," Eng's screaming. "She bring me food from the forest. They shoot Grandma! Bastards!"

"Eng?" I don't dare touch her. I don't know how.

"You shoot my grandmother?" She whacks the air with her bony arms. Now I see the bruises, the small welts all along the insides of her arms. Some have to be weeks old, they're that yellow. The twins' scrapes and cuts never turned that ochre. I can't help wondering if maybe Asian skin bruises differently from ours, even though I want to say skin is skin; especially hers is skin like mine.

"I want to be with Grandma. Grandma loves me. I want to be ghost. I don't want to get better."

I read to her. I read to her because good parents are supposed to read to their kids laid up sick in bed. I want to do it right. I want to be a good father. I read from a sci-fi novel that Sharon must have picked up. She works in a camera store in the mall, right next to a B. Dalton. I read three pages out loud, then I read four chapters to myself because Eng's stopped up her ears. Aliens have taken over small towns all over the country. Idaho, Nebraska: No state is safe from aliens.

Some time after two, the phone rings. Since Sharon doesn't answer it on the second ring, I know she isn't back. She carries a cordless phone everywhere around the house. In the movies, when cops have bad news to deliver, they lean on your doorbell; they don't call. Sharon will come back when she's ready. We'll make up. Things will get back to normal.

"Jason?"

I know Dr. Kearns's voice. He saw the twins through the usual immunizations.

"I have Sharon here. She'll need a ride home. Can you drive over?"

"God! What's happened?"

"Nothing to panic about. Nothing physical. She came for a consultation."

"Give me a half hour. I have to wrap Eng real warm so I can drag her out in this miserable weather."

"Take your time. This way I can take a look at Eng, too."

"What's wrong with Sharon?"

"She's a little exercised about a situation. I gave her a sedative. See you in a half hour."

I ease delirious Eng out of the overdecorated four-poster, prop her against my body while I wrap a blanket around her. She's a tiny thing, but she feels stiff and heavy, a sleepwalking mummy. Her eyes are dry-bright, strange.

It's a sunny winter day, and the evergreens in the front yard are glossy with frost. I press Eng against my chest as I negotiate the front steps. Where the gutter leaks, the steps feel spongy. The shrubs and bushes my ex-wife planted clog the front path. I've put twenty years into this house. The steps, the path, the house all have a right to fall apart.

I'm thirty-eight. I've let a lot of people down already.

The inside of the van is deadly cold. Mid-January ice mottles the wind-shield. I lay the bundled-up child on the long seat behind me and wait for the engine to warm up. It feels good with the radio going and the heat coming on. I don't want the ice on the windshield to melt. Eng and I are safest in the van.

In the rearview mirror, Eng's wrinkled lips begin to move. "Dad, can I have a quarter?"

"May I, kiddo," I joke.   60

There's all sorts of junk in the pockets of my parka. Buckshot, dimes and quarters for the vending machine, a Blistex.

"What do you need it for, sweetheart?"

Eng's quick. Like the street kids in Saigon who dove for cigarettes and sticks of gum. She's loosened the blanket folds around her. I watch her tuck the quarter inside her wool mitt. She grins. "Thanks, soldier."

At Dr. Kearns's, Sharon is lying unnaturally slack-bodied on the lone vinyl sofa. Her coat's neatly balled up under her neck, like a bolster. Right now she looks amiable, docile. I don't think she exactly recognizes me, although later she'll say she did. All that stuff about Kearns going hunting must have been a lie. Even the stuff about having to buy aspirins in the mall. She was planning all along to get here.

"What's wrong?"   65

"It's none of my business, Jason, but you and Sharon might try an honest-to-goodness heart-to-heart." Then he makes a sign to me to lay Eng on the examining table. "We don't look so bad," he says to my daughter. Then he excuses himself and goes into a glass-walled cubicle.

Sharon heaves herself into a sitting position of sorts on the sofa. "Everything was fine until she got here. Send her back, Jase. If you love me, send her back." She's slouched so far forward, her pointed, sweatered breasts nearly touch her corduroy pants. She looks helpless, pathetic. I've brought her to this state. Guilt, not love, is what I feel.

I want to comfort Sharon, but my daughter with the wild, grieving pygmy face won't let go of my hand. "She's bad, Dad. Send *her* back."

Dr. Kearns comes out of the cubicle balancing a sample bottle of pills or caplets on a flattened palm. He has a boxer's tough, squarish hands. "Miraculous stuff, this," he laughs. "But first we'll stick our tongue out and say *ahh*. Come on, open wide."

Eng opens her mouth real wide, then brings her teeth together, hard, 70 on Dr. Kearns's hand. She leaps erect on the examining table, tearing the disposable paper sheet with her toes. Her tiny, funny toes are doing a frantic dance. "Don't let him touch me, Grandma!"

"He's going to make you all better, baby." I can't pull my alien child down, I can't comfort her. The twins had diseases with easy names, diseases we knew what to do with. The thing is, I never felt for them what I feel for her.

"Don't let him touch me, Grandma!" Eng's screaming now. She's hopping on the table and screaming. "Kill him, Grandma! Get me out of here, Grandma!"

"Baby, it's all right."

But she looks through me and the country doctor as though we aren't here, as though we aren't pulling at her to make her lie down.

"Lie back like a good girl," Dr. Kearns commands.

But Eng is listening to other voices. She pulls her mitts off with her   75
teeth, chucks the blanket, the robe, the pajamas to the floor; then, naked, hysterical, she presses the quarter I gave her deep into the soft flesh of her arm. She presses and presses that coin, turning it in nasty half-circles until blood starts to pool under the skin.

"Jason, grab her at the knees. Get her back down on the table."

From the sofa, Sharon moans. "See, I told you the child was crazy. She hates me. She's possessive about Jason."

The doctor comes at us with his syringe. He's sedated Sharon; now he wants to knock out my kid with his cures.

"Get the hell out, you bastard!" Eng yells. "*Vamos!* Bang bang!" She's   80
pointing her arm like a semiautomatic, taking out Sharon, then the doctor. My Rambo. "Old way is good way. Money cure is good cure. When they shoot my grandma, you think pills do her any good? You Yankees, please go home." She looks straight at me. "Scram, Yankee bastard!"

Dr. Kearns has Eng by the wrist now. He has flung the quarter I gave her on the floor. Something incurable is happening to my women.

Then, as in fairy tales, I know what has to be done. "Coming, pardner!" I whisper. "I got no end of coins." I jiggle the change in my pocket. I jerk her away from our enemies. My Saigon kid and me: we're a team. In five minutes we'll be safely away in the cold chariot of our van.

Suggestions for Writing and Discussion

1. Read this selection all the way through without stopping. After doing so, write for five minutes without stopping, jotting down your immediate reactions. Put the response you have written away for a few minutes. Then reread it and evaluate your reactions. Do you think you are responding primarily to the images and events in the essay? To some event in your own life? To a general principle? Or some combination? Explain.

2. What is your impression of the three main characters? With whom can you identify most strongly? Sharon? Eng? Jason? Explain your reasons.

3. What do you think of Jason's way of fathering? What do you think of his treatment of Eng? What do you think of Sharon's treatment of Eng? Besides the obvious reasons, why do Sharon and Jason treat Eng in such different fashions? If you were to give Sharon and Jason advice, how would you suggest they respond to Eng?

4. Do you think Jason will succeed in forming a relationship with Eng? Explain your response, using specific details from the story.
5. Write a journal entry from Jason's point of view. In the entry, explain what causes him to insist so strongly on taking care of Eng.

Suggestions for Extended Thinking and Research

1. View several of the films about the Vietnam War (*Apocalypse Now; Good Morning, Vietnam; Platoon; Born on the Fourth of July,* for example). Compare the views of the war, and of the people who fought in this war, as they are presented in these films.
2. Find several sources that focus on the father's role in raising his children. From your reading, summarize your conclusions concerning what experts believe children need from their fathers. Then compare these conclusions with your own observations and experiences. To what extent do you agree with the authorities you have consulted? To what extent do you disagree? Explain.
3. Research the effects of the Vietnam War on the children who were born in Vietnam to American servicemen and Vietnamese mothers. What has become of these children? What kind of life do they now lead? Write a paper explaining your findings and suggesting possible solutions for any problems you have uncovered.

CATHY SONG

The Youngest Daughter

> *Cathy Song, born in 1955, grew up in Honolulu, Hawaii, with her Chinese mother and Korean father. She attended Wellesley College and received a master's degree in Creative Writing from Boston University in 1981. Her first book of poems,* Picture Bride, *won the Yale Series of Younger Poets Award in 1983. The poems in this book exemplify Song's interest in the intersections and connections of the generations that comprise families. The poem presented here, "The Youngest Daughter," shows a balance between Song's sense of her Asian heritage and her commitment to the growth of her Asian-American self.*

Prereading/Journal-Writing Suggestions

1. What is your place in the birth order of your family (being the oldest, youngest, or only child, for example)? How do you think this order has affected the role you play in the family and the way you look at and think about yourself?
2. What do you think your life will be like when you grow old? How do you envision yourself at, say, sixty-five, seventy, or older? Where do you think you will live? Who will be the important people in your life? What will you be doing?

The sky has been dark
for many years.
My skin has become as damp
and pale as rice paper
and feels the way   5
mother's used to before the drying sun
parched it out there in the fields.

   Lately, when I touch my eyelids,
my hands react as if
I had just touched something   10
hot enough to burn.
My skin, aspirin colored,
tingles with migraine. Mother
has been massaging the left side of my face
especially in the evenings   15
when the pain flares up.

This morning
her breathing was graveled,

her voice gruff with affection
when I wheeled her into the bath.   20
She was in a good humor,
making jokes about her great breasts,
floating in the milky water
like two walruses,
flaccid and whiskered around the nipples.   25
I scrubbed them with a sour taste
in my mouth, thinking:
six children and an old man
have sucked from these brown nipples.

I was almost tender   30
when I came to the blue bruises
that freckle her body,
places where she has been injecting insulin
for thirty years. I soaped her slowly,
she sighed deeply, her eyes closed.   35
It seems it has always
been like this: the two of us
in this sunless room,
the splashing of the bathwater.

In the afternoons   40
when she has rested,
she prepares our ritual of tea and rice,
garnished with a shred of gingered fish,
a slice of pickled turnip,
a token for my white body.   45
We eat in the familiar silence.
She knows I am not to be trusted,
even now planning my escape.
As I toast to her health
with the tea she has poured,   50
a thousand cranes curtain the window,
fly up in a sudden breeze.

Suggestions for Writing and Discussion

1. Many of the images in this poem could be grouped together as being hard and painful. List several of these images and then discuss what connection they have to Song's underlying message or theme.
2. Speculate on what Song means by her opening lines, "The sky has been dark/for many years."
3. Describe your first reaction to the speaker's description of her mother in the bath.

4. What does the mother do for the daughter? What is the daughter's reaction to her mother's care?

5. In line 46, the speaker says, "We eat in the familiar silence." Sometimes silence can be more powerful than words. In this poem, what is the silence "saying"? During the next few days, notice "silences" in your own life. How do you interpret these silences?

Suggestions for Extended Thinking and Research

1. Research what authorities say about the importance and effects of birth order on our personalities and development. After thinking about what you have read, write an essay that briefly explains your findings and then provides an evaluation of those findings, based on your own observations and experiences.

2. People in different cultures have different ways of treating their elderly. Research a specific culture either within or outside the United States, and write about their customs and expectations for treating the elderly. Compare what you have learned with what you have observed about the treatment of the elderly within the culture group to which you belong.

3. Should children be responsible (morally and legally) for caring for their aging parents? Explain the reasons for your beliefs.

TOPICS FOR MAKING CONNECTIONS: PARENTS AND CHILDREN

1. Referring to at least three of the selections in this section, write an essay comparing different approaches to parenting. As part of the comparison, evaluate these approaches and explain which you most admire.

2. What do children contribute to their parents' lives? Refer to at least three selections in this section as you respond to this question.

3. Are parents to blame for how children turn out? Write an essay that takes a stand on this issue. For support, use reference sources you have consulted, your own experience, and several selections from this section.

4. Analyze the inequalities and pressures that men and women experience at certain ages. Choose one specific age period (childhood, adolescence, young adulthood, middle age, old age). As you write on this topic, use reference sources (including interviews of people currently in the age group you chose) and, in addition, refer to examples in selections in this section.

5. Choose an author or a person described in one of the selections in this section. Write a letter from that individual's point of view to the author or a person described in one of the other selections. To complete this task,

you'll need to consider what the writer might want to say to the recipient of the letter. What advice, consolation, or observations might he or she offer? (For example, what might Maxine Hong Kingston say to the speaker in Cathy Song's poem? What advice might Harry Dolan give to Jason in "Fathering" or to Raymond Carver as he looks back at his father's life?)

Ways of Learning

Previews: WAYS OF LEARNING

I lived in Master Hugh's family about seven years. During this time, I succeeded in learning to read and write. In accomplishing this, I was compelled to resort to various stratagems. I had no regular teacher. My mistress, who had kindly commenced to instruct me, had, in compliance with the advice and direction of her husband, not only ceased to instruct, but had set her face against my being instructed by anyone else.

From: *Learning to Read and Write,* FREDERICK DOUGLASS

All teachers were to be respected like gods, and God Himself was the greatest of all school superintendents. Long after I had ceased to believe that our teachers could see with the back of their heads, it was still understood, by me, that they knew everything.

From: *Brownsville Schooldays,* ALFRED KAZIN

It was on these rockers that my mother, her sisters, and my grandmother sat on these afternoons of my childhood to tell their stories, teaching each other, and my cousin and me, what it was like to be a woman, more specifically, a Puerto Rican woman. They talked about life on the island, and life in *Los Nueva Yores,* their way of referring to the United States from New York City to California: the other place, not home, all the same.

From: *Casa: A Partial Remembrance of a Puerto Rican Childhood,* JUDITH ORTIZ COFER

In our isolated Greek village, my mother had bribed a cousin to teach her to read, for girls were not supposed to attend school beyond a certain age. She had always dreamed of her children receiving an education. She couldn't be there when I graduated from Boston University, but the person who came with my father and shared our joy was my former teacher, Marjorie Hurd. We celebrated not only my bachelor's degree but also the scholarships that paid my way to Columbia's Graduate School of Journalism. There, I met the woman who would eventually become my wife. At our wedding and at the baptisms of our three children, Marjorie Hurd was always there, dancing alongside the Greeks.

From: *The Teacher Who Changed My Life,* NICHOLAS GAGE

FREDERICK DOUGLASS

Learning to Read and Write

Born a slave in Talbot County, Maryland, in 1818, Frederick Douglass grew up on a plantation and was later sent to Baltimore to live with and work for the Auld family. During this period of his life, Douglass became aware of the essential relationship between literacy and independence. Although the Auld family thwarted him whenever they could, he discovered innovative ways of learning to read and write. He describes this phase of his education in the following excerpt from his autobiography, Narrative of the Life of Frederick Douglass, an American Slave, Written by Himself *(1845).*

Prereading/Journal-Writing Suggestions

1. Do you believe an educated person has advantages over an uneducated person? Explain the advantages (or lack of advantages) you see.
2. Do you think it is important to be a good listener? Explain your reasons. Are you a good listener? If so, how do you think you developed this skill?
3. What is the best advice anyone ever gave you? Did you heed this advice or not? What happened as a result of paying attention to or ignoring this advice?

I lived in Master Hugh's family about seven years. During this time, I succeeded in learning to read and write. In accomplishing this, I was compelled to resort to various stratagems. I had no regular teacher. My mistress, who had kindly commenced to instruct me, had, in compliance with the advice and direction of her husband, not only ceased to instruct, but had set her face against my being instructed by anyone else. It is due, however, to my mistress to say of her, that she did not adopt this course of treatment immediately. She at first lacked the depravity indispensable to shutting me up in mental darkness. It was at least necessary for her to have some training in the exercise of irresponsible power, to make her equal to the task of treating me as though I were a brute.

My mistress was, as I have said, a kind and tender-hearted woman; and in the simplicity of her soul she commenced, when I first went to live with her, to treat me as she supposed one human being ought to treat another. In entering upon the duties of a slaveholder, she did not seem to perceive that I sustained to her the relation of a mere chattel, and that for her to treat me as a human being was not only wrong, but dangerously so. Slavery proved as injurious to her as it did to me. When I went there, she was a pious, warm, and tender-hearted woman. There was no sorrow or suffering for which she had not a tear. She had bread for the hungry, clothes for the naked, and comfort for every mourner that came within her reach. Slavery soon proved its ability to divest her of these heavenly qualities. Under its influence, the tender heart became stone, and the lamblike disposition gave way to one of tiger-like fierceness. The first step in her downward course was in her ceasing to instruct me. She now commenced to practice her husband's precepts. She finally became even more violent in her opposition than her husband himself. She was not satisfied with simply doing as well as he had commanded; she seemed anxious to do better. Nothing seemed to make her more angry than to see me with a newspaper. She seemed to think that here lay the danger. I have had her rush at me with a face made all up of fury, and snatch from me a newspaper, in a manner that fully revealed her apprehension. She was an apt woman; and a little experience soon demonstrated, to her satisfaction, that education and slavery were incompatible with each other.

From this time I was most narrowly watched. If I was in a separate room any considerable length of time, I was sure to be suspected of having a book, and was at once called to give an account of myself. All this, however, was too late. The first step had been taken. Mistress, in teaching me the alphabet, had given me the *inch,* and no precaution could prevent me from taking the *ell.*

The plan which I adopted, and the one by which I was most successful, was that of making friends of all the little white boys whom I met in the street. As many of these as I could, I converted into teachers. With their kindly aid, obtained at different times and in different places, I finally succeeded in learning to read. When I was sent on errands, I always took my book with me, and by doing one part of my errand quickly, I found time to get a lesson before my return. I used also to carry bread with me, enough of which was always in the house, and to which I was always welcome; for I was much better off in this regard than many of the poor white children in our neighborhood. This bread I used to bestow upon the hungry little urchins, who, in return, would give me that more valuable bread of knowledge. I am strongly tempted to give the names of two or three of those little boys, as a testimonial of the gratitude and affection I bear them; but prudence forbids — not that it would injure me, but it might embarrass them; for it is almost an unpardonable offence to teach slaves to read in this Christian country. It is enough to say of the dear little fellows, that they lived on Philpot Street, very near Durgin and Bailey's ship-yard. I used to talk this matter of slavery over with them. I would sometimes say to them, I wished I could be as free as they would be when they got to be men. "You will be free as soon as you are twenty-one, *but I am a slave for life!* Have not I as good a right to be free as you have?" These words used to trouble them; they would express for me the liveliest sympathy, and console me with the hope that something would occur by which I might be free.

I was now about twelve-years-old, and the thought of being *a slave for* 5 *life* began to bear heavily upon my heart. Just about this time, I got hold of a book entitled "The Columbian Orator." Every opportunity I got, I used to read this book. Among much of other interesting matter, I found in it a dialogue between a master and his slave. The slave was represented as having run away from his master three times. The dialogue represented the conversation which took place between them, when the slave was retaken the third time. In this dialogue, the whole argument in behalf of slavery was brought forward by the master, all of which was disposed of by the slave. The slave was made to say some very smart as well as impressive things in reply to his master — things which had the desired though unexpected effect; for the conversation resulted in the voluntary emancipation of the slave on the part of the master.

In the same book, I met with one of Sheridan's mighty speeches on and in behalf of Catholic emancipation. These were choice documents to me. I read them over and over again with unabated interest. They gave tongue to interesting thoughts of my own soul, which had frequently flashed through my mind, and died away for want of utterance. The moral which I gained from the dialogue was the power of truth over the conscience of even a slaveholder. What I got from Sheridan was a bold denunciation of slavery, and a powerful vindication of human rights. The reading of these documents enabled me to utter my thoughts, and to meet the arguments brought forward to sustain slavery; but while they relieved me of one difficulty, they brought on another even more painful than the one of which I was relieved. The more I read, the more I was led to abhor and detest my enslavers. I could regard them in no other light than a band of successful robbers, who had left their homes, and gone to Africa, and stolen us from our homes, and in a strange land reduced us to slavery. I loathed them as being the meanest as well as the most wicked of men. As I read and contemplated the subject, behold! that very discontentment which Master Hugh had predicted would follow my learning to read had already come, to torment and sting my soul to unutterable anguish. As I writhed under it, I would at times feel that learning to read had been a curse rather than a blessing. It had given me a view of my wretched condition, without the remedy. It opened my eyes to the horrible pit, but to no ladder upon which to get out. In moments of agony, I envied my fellow-slaves for their stupidity. I have often wished myself a beast. I preferred the condition of the meanest reptile to my own. Anything, no matter what, to get rid of thinking! It was this everlasting thinking of my condition that tormented me. There was no getting rid of it. It was pressed upon me by every object within sight or hearing, animate or inanimate. The silver trump of freedom had roused my soul to eternal wakefulness. Freedom now appeared, to disappear no more forever. It was heard in every sound, and seen in every thing. It was ever present to torment me with a sense of my wretched condition. I saw nothing without seeing it, I heard nothing without hearing it, and felt nothing without feeling it. It looked from every star, it smiled in every calm, breathed in every wind, and moved in every storm.

I often found myself regretting my own existence, and wishing myself dead; and but for the hope of being free, I have no doubt but that I should have killed myself, or done something for which I should have been killed. While in this state of mind, I was eager to hear anyone speak of slavery. I was a ready listener. Every little while, I could hear something about the abolition-ists. It was some time before I found what the word meant. It was always used in such connections as to make it an interesting word to me. If a slave ran away and succeeded in getting clear, or if a slave killed his master, set fire to a barn, or did anything very wrong in the mind of a slaveholder, it was spoken of as the fruit of *abolition*. Hearing the word in this connection very often, I set about learning what it meant. The dictionary afforded me little or no help. I found it was "the act of abolishing"; but then I did not know what was to be abolished. Here I was perplexed. I did not dare to ask anyone about its mean-ing, for I was satisfied that it was something they wanted me to know very little about. After a patient waiting, I got one of our city papers, containing an account of the number of petitions from the North, praying for the aboli-tion of slavery in the District of Columbia, and of the slave trade between the States. From this time I understood the words *abolition* and *abolitionist,* and always drew near when that word was spoken, expecting to hear something of importance to myself and fellow-slaves. The light broke in upon me by degrees. I went one day down on the wharf of Mr. Waters; and seeing two Irishmen unloading a scow of stone, I went, unasked, and helped them. When we had finished, one of them came to me and asked me if I were a slave. I told him I was. He asked, "Are ye a slave for life?" I told him that I was. The good Irishman seemed to be deeply affected by the statement. He said to the other that it was a pity so fine a little fellow as myself should be a slave for life. He said it was a shame to hold me. They both advised me to run away to the North; that I should find friends there, and that I should be free. I pretended not to be interested in what they said, and treated them as if I did not under-stand them; for I feared they might be treacherous. White men have been known to encourage slaves to escape, and then, to get the reward, catch them and return them to their masters. I was afraid that these seemingly good men might use me so; but I nevertheless remembered their advice, and from that time I resolved to run away. I looked forward to a time at which it would be safe for me to escape. I was too young to think of doing so immediately; besides, I wished to learn how to write, as I might have occasion to write my own pass. I consoled myself with the hope that I should one day find a good chance. Meanwhile, I would learn to write.

The idea as to how I might learn to write was suggested to me by being in Durgin and Bailey's shipyard, and frequently seeing the ship carpenters, after hewing, and getting a piece of timber ready for use, write on the timber the name of that part of the ship for which it was intended. When a piece of timber was intended for the larboard side, it would be marked thus — "L." When a piece was for the starboard side, it would be marked thus — "S." A piece for the larboard side forward, would be marked thus — "L.F." When a piece was for starboard side forward, it would be marked thus — "S.F." For larboard aft, it would be marked thus — "L.A." For starboard aft, it would be marked thus — "S.A." I soon learned the names of these letters, and for what they were intended when placed upon a piece of timber in the shipyard. I immediately commenced copying them, and in a short time was able to make the four letters named. After that, when I met with any boy who I knew could write, I would tell him I could write as well as he. The next word would be, "I don't believe you. Let me see you try it." I would then make the letters which I had been so fortunate as to learn, and ask him to beat that. In this way I got a good many lessons in writing, which it is quite possible I should never have gotten in any other way. During this time, my copy-book was the board fence, brick wall, and pavement; my pen and ink was a lump of chalk. With these, I learned mainly how to write. I then commenced and continued copying the Italics in *Webster's Spelling Book,* until I could make them all without looking on the book. By this time, my little Master Thomas had gone to school, and learned how to write, and had written over a number of copy-books. These had been brought home, and shown to some of our near neighbors, and then laid aside. My mistress used to go to class meeting at the Wilk Street meeting-house every Monday afternoon, and leave me to take care of the house. When left thus, I used to spend the time in writing in the spaces left in master Thomas's copy-book, copying what he had written. I continued to do this until I could write a hand very similar to that of Master Thomas. Thus, after a long, tedious effort for years, I finally succeeded in learning how to write.

Suggestions for Writing and Discussion

1. List as many reasons as you can for the "mistress's" anger when she saw Douglass with a newspaper. What was she worried about?
2. What emotions and ambitions led Douglass, a black slave, to make friends with the poor white boys in his town?
3. What did Douglass learn about his own life through the readings he encountered?
4. At times, Douglass writes, reading was a curse for him, for he was faced with truths that were painful and depressing. Have you ever felt like this about things you have read? Is it preferable to live in ignorance than to have old ideas and ways of thinking challenged? What, if anything, is gained by learning disturbing truths? What, if anything, is lost?
5. What does Douglass mean by the phrase "the light broke in upon me by degrees"? Could you use this phrase to describe the process of your own education? If so, explain why. If not, think of a more apt phrase and explain why you chose that description.
6. How did Douglass learn to write? Who or what was his teacher? How does his way of learning to write compare with yours? Compare the advantages and disadvantages of each process.
7. This essay outlines the many steps Douglass took to learn to read and write. Using his combination of description and anecdote, explain the steps you took to learn something new.

Suggestions for Extended Thinking and Research

1. Find one of Douglass's famous speeches. Analyze this document and reach some conclusions about the audience Douglass hoped to reach. To help in this analysis, find several sources that describe what this country was like at the time Douglass was writing.
2. Find several sources that document Douglass's life. Write a biographical sketch focusing either on the early influences in his life or on the influence Douglass had on America's history. Select two or three specific incidents as the basis of your paper.

ALFRED KAZIN
Brownsville Schooldays

> *Although Alfred Kazin became a renowned journalist, biographer, and literary critic, he never forgot the feelings of fear and anxiety instilled during his early schooling in Brownsville, New York. Born in 1915 in New York City, Kazin grew up in a family of Jewish immigrants. In his acclaimed books* On Native Ground *(1942) and* Starting Out in the Thirties *(1965), Kazin called on his ethnic background as a way to explore and analyze the literary and cultural life of American cities and of the writers these cities produced. In this essay, Kazin looks at his early years in school and describes the lessons he learned — both academic and nonacademic.*

Prereading/Journal-Writing Suggestions

1. Looking back at your early school years, describe your image of yourself as a student. On what do you base this image? Your grades? Your actions? Your teachers' opinions? Your parents' opinions? Your friends' opinions? Describe an early event, explaining how you developed this image of yourself.
2. Describe what your first school looked like. Imagine your five- or six-year-old self in a specific place (a classroom, the playground, the cafeteria). What are your initial impressions? How do you react to what you see and hear? What emotions do you experience? What do you most fear? What do you most enjoy?
3. Describe a time when a teacher exercised a great sense of power over you. Was this a positive or negative experience? How did you react? How do you look at this incident from your current adult perspective?

All my early life lies open to my eye within five city blocks. When I passed the school, I went sick with all my old fear of it. With its standard New York public-school brown brick courtyard shut in on three sides of the square and the pretentious battlements overlooking that cockpit in which I can still smell the fiery sheen of the rubber ball, it looks like a factory over which has been imposed the façade of a castle. It gave me the shivers to stand up in that courtyard again; I felt as if I had been mustered back into the service of those Friday morning "tests" that were the terror of my childhood.

It was never learning I associated with that school: only the necessity to succeed, to get ahead of the others in the daily struggle to "make a good impression" on our teachers, who grimly, wearily, and often with ill-concealed distaste watched against our relapsing into the natural savagery they expected of Brownsville boys. The white, cool, thinly ruled record book sat over us from their desks all day long, and had remorselessly entered into it each day — in blue ink if we had passed, in red ink if we had not — our attendance, our conduct, our "effort," our merits and demerits; and to the last possible decimal point in calculation, our standing in an unending series of "tests" — surprise tests, daily tests, weekly tests, formal midterm tests, final tests. They never stopped trying to dig out of us whatever small morsel of fact we had managed to get down the night before. We had to prove that we were really alert, ready for anything, always in the race. That white thinly ruled record book figured in my mind as the judgment seat; the very thinness and remote blue lightness of its lines instantly showed its cold authority over me; so much space had been left on each page, columns and columns in which to note down everything about us, implacably and forever. As it lay there on a teacher's desk, I stared at it all day long with such fear and anxious propriety that I had no trouble believing that God, too, did nothing but keep such record books, and that on the final day He would face me with an account in Hebrew letters whose phonetic dots and dashes looked strangely like decimal points counting up my every sinful thought on earth.

All teachers were to be respected like gods, and God Himself was the greatest of all school superintendents. Long after I had ceased to believe that our teachers could see with the back of their heads, it was still understood, by me, that they knew everything. They were the delegates of all visible and invisible power on earth — of the mothers who waited on the stoops every day after three for us to bring home tales of our daily triumphs; of the glacially remote Anglo-Saxon principal, whose very name was King; of the incalculably important Superintendent of Schools who would someday rubberstamp his name to the bottom of our diplomas in grim acknowledgment that we had, at last, given satisfaction to him, to the Board of Superintendents, and to our benefactor the City of New York — and so up and up, to the government of the United States and to the great Lord Jehovah Himself. My belief in teachers' unlimited wisdom and power rested not so much on what I saw in them — how impatient most of them looked, how wary — but on our abysmal humility, at least in those of us who were "good" boys, who proved by our ready compliance and "manners" that we wanted to get on. The road to a professional future would be shown us only as we pleased *them. Make a good impression the first day of the term, and they'll help you out. Make a bad impression, and you might as well cut your throat.* This was the first article of school folklore, whispered around the classroom the opening day of each term. You made the "good impression" by sitting firmly at your wooden desk, hands clasped; by silence for the greatest part of the live-long day; by standing up obsequiously when it was so expected of you; by sitting down noiselessly when you had answered a question; by "speaking nicely," which meant reproducing their painfully exact enunciation; by "showing manners," or an ecstatic submissiveness in all things; by outrageous flattery; by bringing little gifts at Christmas, on their birthdays, and at the end of the term — the well-known significance of these gifts being that they came not from us, but from our parents, whose eagerness in this matter showed a high level of social consideration, and thus raised our standing in turn.

It was not just our quickness and memory that were always being tested. Above all, in that word I could never hear without automatically seeing it raised before me in gold-plated letters, it was our *character*. I always felt anxious when I heard the word pronounced. Satisfactory as my "character" was, on the whole, except when I stayed too long in the playground reading; outrageously satisfactory, as I can see now, the very sound of the word as our teachers coldly gave it out from the end of their teeth, with a solemn weight on each dark syllable, immediately struck my heart cold with fear — they could not believe I really had it. Character was never something you had; it had to be trained in you, like a technique. I was never very clear about it. On our side *character* meant demonstrative obedience; but teachers already had it — how else could they have become teachers? They had it; the aloof Anglo-Saxon principal whom we remotely saw only on ceremonial occasions in the assembly was positively encased in it; it glittered off his bald head in spokes of triumphant light; the President of the United States had the greatest conceivable amount of it. Character belonged to great adults. Yet we were constantly being driven onto it; it was the great threshold we had to cross. *Alfred Kazin, having shown proficiency in his course of studies and having displayed satisfactory marks of character* . . . Thus someday the hallowed diploma, passport to my further advancement in high school. But there — I could already feel it in my bones — they would put me through even more doubting tests of character; and after that, if I should be good enough and bright enough, there would be still more. *Character* was a bitter thing, racked with my endless striving to please. The school — from every last stone in the courtyard to the battlements frowning down at me from the walls — was only the stage for a trial. I felt that the very atmosphere of learning that surrounded us was fake — that every lesson, every book, every approving smile was only a pretext for the constant probing and watching of me, that there was not a secret in me that would not be decimally measured into that white record book. All week long I lived for the blessed sound of the dismissal gong at three o'clock on Friday afternoon.

I was awed by this system, I believed in it, I respected its force. The alternative was "going bad." The school was notoriously the toughest in our tough neighborhood, and the dangers of "going bad" were constantly impressed upon me at home and in school in dark whispers of the "reform school" and in examples of boys who had been picked up for petty thievery, rape, or flinging a heavy inkwell straight into a teacher's face. Behind any failure in school yawned the great abyss of a criminal career. Every refractory attitude doomed you with the sound "Sing Sing." Anything less than absolute perfection in school always suggested to my mind that I might fall out of the daily race, be kept back in the working class forever, or — dared I think of it? — fall into the criminal class itself.

I worked on a hairline between triumph and catastrophe. Why the odds should always have felt so narrow I understood only when I realized how little my parents thought of their own lives. It was not for myself alone that I was expected to shine, but for them — to redeem the constant anxiety of their existence. I was the first American child, their offering to the strange new God; I was to be the monument of their liberation from the shame of being — what they were. And that there was shame in this was a fact that everyone seemed to believe as a matter of course. It was in the gleeful discounting of themselves — what do we know? — with which our parents greeted every fresh victory in our savage competition for "high averages," for prizes, for a few condescending words of official praise from the principal at assembly. It was in the sickening invocation of "Americanism" — the word itself accusing us of everything we apparently were not. Our families and teachers seemed tacitly agreed that we were somehow to be a little ashamed of what we were. Yet it was always hard to say why this should be so. It was certainly not — in Brownsville! — because we were Jews, or simply because we spoke another language at home, or were absent on our holy days. It was rather that a "refined," "correct," "nice" English was required of us at school that we did not naturally speak, and that our teachers could never be quite sure we would keep. This English was peculiarly the ladder of advancement. Every future young lawyer was known by it. Even the Communists and Socialists on Pitkin Avenue spoke it. It was bright and clean and polished. We were expected to show it off like a new pair of shoes. When the teacher sharply called a question out, then your name, you were expected to leap up, face the class, and eject those new words fluently off the tongue.

There was my secret ordeal: I could never say anything except in the most roundabout way; I was a stammerer. Although I knew all those new words from my private reading — I read walking in the street, to and from the Children's Library on Stone Avenue; on the fire escape and the roof; at every meal when they would let me; read even when I dressed in the morning, propping my book up against the drawers of the bureau as I pulled on my long black stockings — I could never seem to get the easiest words out with the right dispatch, and would often miserably signal from my desk that I did not know the answer rather than get up to stumble and fall and crash on every word. If, angry at always being put down as lazy or stupid, I did get up to speak, the black wooden floor would roll away under my feet, the teacher would frown at me in amazement, and in unbearable loneliness I would hear behind me the groans and laughter: *tuh-tuh-tuh-tuh.*

The word was my agony. The word that for others was so effortless and so neutral, so unburdened, so simple, so exact, I had first to meditate in advance, to see if I could make it, like a plumber fitting together odd lengths and shapes of pipe. I was always preparing words I could speak, storing them away, choosing between them. And often, when the word did come from my mouth as a great and terrible birth, quailing and bleeding as if forced through a thornbush, I would not be able to look the others in the face, and would walk out in the silence, the infinitely echoing silence behind my back, to say it all cleanly back to myself as I walked in the streets. Only when I was alone in the open air pacing the roof with pebbles in my mouth, as I had read Demosthenes had done to cure himself of stammering; or in the street, where all words seemed to flow from the length of my stride and the color of the houses as I remembered the perfect tranquility of a phrase in Beethoven's *Romance In F* I could sing back to myself as I walked—only then was it possible for me to speak without the infinite premeditations and strangled silences I toiled through whenever I got up at school to respond with the expected, the exact answer.

It troubled me that I could speak in the fullness of my own voice only when I was alone on the streets, walking about. There was something unnatural about it; unbearably isolated. I was not like the others! I was not like the others! At midday, every freshly shocking Monday noon, they sent me away to a speech clinic in a school in East New York, where I sat in a circle of lispers and cleft palates and foreign accents holding a mirror before my lips and rolling difficult sounds over and over. To be sent there in the full light of the opening week, when everyone else was at school or going about his business, made me feel as if I had been expelled from the great normal body of humanity. I would gobble down my lunch on my way to the speech clinic and rush back to the school in time to make up for the classes I had lost. One day, one unforgettable dread day, I stopped to catch my breath on a corner of Sutter Avenue, near the wholesale fruit markets, where an old drugstore rose up over a great flight of steps. In the window were dusty urns of colored water floating off iron chains; cardboard placards advertising hairnets, Ex-Lax; a great illustrated medical chart headed THE HUMAN FACTORY, which showed the exact course a mouthful of food follows as it falls from chamber to chamber of the body. I hadn't meant to stop there at all, only to catch my breath; but I so hated the speech clinic that I thought I would delay my arrival for a few minutes by eating my lunch on the steps. When I took the sandwich out of my bag, two bitterly hard pieces of hard salami slipped out of my hand and fell through a grate onto a hill of dust below the steps. I remember how sickeningly vivid an odd thread of hair looked on the salami, as if my lunch were turning stiff with death. The factory whistles called their short, sharp blasts stark through the middle of noon, beating at me where I sat outside the city's magnetic circle. I had never known, I knew instantly I would never in my heart again submit to, such wild passive despair as I felt at that moment, sitting on the steps before THE HUMAN FACTORY, where little robots gathered and shoveled the food from chamber to chamber of the body. They had put me out into the streets, I thought to myself; with their mirrors and their everlasting pulling at me to imitate their effortless bright speech and their stupefaction that a boy could stammer and stumble on every other English word he carried in his head, they had put me out into the streets, had left me high and dry on the steps of that drugstore staring at the remains of my lunch turning black and grimy in the dust.

In the great cool assembly hall, dominated by the gold sign above the 10 stage, KNOWLEDGE IS POWER, the windowsills were lined with Dutch bulbs, each wedged into a mound of pebbles massed in a stone dish. Above them hung a giant photograph of Theodore Roosevelt. Whenever I walked in to see the empty assembly hall for myself, the shiny waxed floor of the stage dangled in the middle of the air like a crescent. On one side was a great silk American flag, the staff crowned by a gilt eagle. Across the dry rattling of varnish-smelling empty seats bowing to the American flag, I saw in the play of the sun on those pebbles wildly sudden images of peace. *There* was the other land, crowned by the severe and questioning face of Theodore Roosevelt, his eyes above the curiously endearing straw-dry mustache, behind the pince-nez glittering with light, staring and staring me through as if he were uncertain whether he fully approved of me.

The light pouring through window after window in that great empty varnished assembly hall seemed to me the most wonderful thing I had ever seen. It was that thorough varnished cleanness that was of the new land, that light dancing off the glasses of Theodore Roosevelt, those green and white roots of the still raw onion-brown bulbs delicately flaring up from the hill of pebbles into which they were wedged. The pebbles moved me in themselves, there were so many of them. They rose up around the bulbs in delicately strong masses of colored stone, and as the sun fell between them, each pebble shone in its own light. Looking across the great rows of empty seats to those pebbles lining the windowsills, I could still smell summer from some long veranda surrounded by trees. On that veranda sat the family and friends of Theodore Roosevelt. I knew the name: Oyster Bay. Because of that picture, I had read *The Boy's Life of Theodore Roosevelt;* knew he had walked New York streets night after night as Police Commissioner, unafraid of the Tenderloin gangsters; had looked into *Theodore Roosevelt's Letters to His Children,* pretending that those hilarious drawings on almost every page were for me. *There* was America, I thought, the real America, *his* America, where from behind the glass on the wall of our assembly hall he watched over us to make sure we did right, thought right, lived right.

"Up, boys! Up San Juan Hill!" I still hear our roguish old civics teacher, a little white-haired Irishman who was supposed to have been with Teddy in Cuba, driving us through our Friday morning tests with these shouts and cries. He called them "Army Navy" tests, to make us feel big, and dividing the class between Army and Navy, got us to compete with each other for a coveted blue star. Civics was city government, state government, federal government; each government had functions; you had to get them out fast in order to win for the Army or the Navy. Sometimes this required filling in three or four words, line by line, down one side of the grimly official yellow foolscap that was brought out for tests. (In the tense silence just before the test began, he looked at us sharply, the watch in his hand ticking as violently as the sound of my heart, and on command, fifty boys simultaneously folded their yellow test paper and evened the fold with their thumbnails in a single dry sigh down the middle of the paper.) At other times it meant true-or-false tests; then he stood behind us to make sure we did not signal the right answers to each other in the usual way—for true, nodding your head; for false, holding your nose. You could hear his voice barking from the rear. *"Come on now, you Army boys! On your toes like West Point cadets! All ready now? Get set! Go! Three powers of the legislative branch? The judiciary? The executive? The subject of the fifteenth amendment? The capital of Wyoming? Come on, Navy! Shoot those landlubbers down! Give 'em a blast from your big guns right through the middle! The third article of the Bill of Rights? The thirteenth amendment? The sixteenth? True or false, Philadelphia is the capital of Pennsylvania. Up and at 'em, Navy! Mow them down! COME ON!!!"* Our "average" was calculated each week, and the boys who scored 90 percent or over were rewarded by seeing *their own names* lettered on the great blue chart over the blackboard. Each time I entered that room for a test, I looked for my name on the blue chart as if the sight of it would decide my happiness for all time.

Down we go, down the school corridors of the past smelling of chalk, lysol out of the open toilets, and girl sweat. The staircases were a gray stone I saw nowhere else in the school, and they were shut in on both sides by some thick unreflecting glass on which were pasted travel posters inviting us to spend the summer in the Black Forest. Those staircases created a spell in me that I had found my way to some distant, cool, neutral passageway deep in the body of the school. There, enclosed within the thick, green boughs of a classic summer in Germany, I could still smell the tense probing chalk smells from every classroom, the tickling high surgical odor of lysol from the open toilets, could still hear that continuous babble, babble of water dripping into the bowls. Sex was instantly connected in my mind with the cruel openness of those toilets, and in the never-ending sound of the bowls being flushed I could detect, as I did in the maddeningly elusive fragrance of cologne brought into the classroom by Mrs. B., the imminence of something severe, frightening, obscene. Sex, as they said in the "Coney Island" dives outside the school, was like going to the toilet; there was a great contempt in this that made me think of the wet rings left by our sneakers as we ran down the gray stone steps after school.

Outside the women teachers' washroom on the third floor, the tough guys would wait for the possible appearance of Mrs. B., whose large goiterous eyes seemed to bulge wearily with mischief, who always looked tired and cynical, and who wore thin chiffon dresses that affected us much more than she seemed to realize. Mrs. B. often went about the corridors in the company of a trim little teacher of mathematics who was a head shorter than she and had a mustache. Her chiffon dresses billowed around him like a sail; she seemed to have him in tow. It was understood by us as a matter of course that she wore those dresses to inflame us; that she *was* tired and cynical, from much practice in obscene lovemaking; that she was a "bad one" like the young Polish blondes from East New York I occasionally saw in the "Coney Island" dives sitting on someone's lap and smoking a cigarette. How wonderful and unbelievable it was to find this in a teacher; to realize that the two of them, after we had left the school, probably met to rub up against each other in the faculty toilet. Sex was a grim test where sooner or later you would have to prove yourself doing things to women. In the smell of chalk and sweat and the unending smirky babble of the water as it came to me on the staircase through my summer's dream of old Germany, I could feel myself being called to still another duty — to conquer Mrs. B., to rise to the challenge she had whispered to us in her slyness. I had seen pictures of it on the block — they were always passing them around between handball games — the man's face furious, ecstatic with lewdness as he proudly looked down at himself; the woman sniggering as she teased him with droplets from the contraceptive someone had just shown me in the gutter — its crushed, filmy slyness the very sign of the forbidden.

They had never said anything about this at home, and I thought I knew 15 why. Sex was the opposite of books, of pictures, of music, of the open air, even of kindness. They would not let you have both. Something always lingered to the sound of those toilets to test you. In and out of the classroom they were always testing you. *Come on, Army! Come on, Navy!* As I stood up in that school courtyard and smelled again the familiar sweat, heard again the unending babble from the open toilets, I suddenly remembered how sure I had always been that even my failures in there would be entered in a white, thinly ruled, official record book.

Suggestions for Writing and Discussion

1. Kazin says that going back to his first school gave him "shivers," he was so terrorized. Imagine a visit back to a school you have attended and describe what you see, whom you meet, and how you respond.
2. What was it that Brownsville teachers expected of their students? What are your responses to these expectations? Do you find them reasonable? Unreasonable? Useful for later life? Explain.
3. Do you think it is true that the "good" student is one who simply doesn't cause trouble? What's your definition of a good student?
4. Kazin writes that "the very atmosphere of learning that surrounded us was fake." What exactly does he mean by fake? Have you ever detected similar qualities in your own school surroundings? Choose specific examples to support your response.
5. When he was alone, Kazin had no trouble thinking about problems or questions and finding possible answers. When he was forced to come up with "the expected exact answer," however, he began stuttering. What is your response to his dilemma. Do most questions posed in school have "right" answers? In all subjects? In some subjects? Explain.
6. What do you think about the teaching approach Kazin ascribes to the "little white-haired Irishman"? Is this an approach that fosters learning? What might students gain, if anything, from this approach? What might they lose?

7. Kazin has pursued a distinguished career as a writer. Would you say his Brownsville school days were a hindrance or a help in achieving success?

Suggestions for Extended Thinking and Research

1. Many educators believe that competition in schools fosters learning; others believe just as strongly that cooperation is far more effective. Do research to investigate these two ways of learning. Then from what you have read, as well as from your own learning experiences, explain which side of the controversy you support.
2. Imagine that you are Kazin's mother or father. Write a letter to the school's principal in which you express your displeasure or pleasure with the education your son is receiving.
3. Kazin talks about Roosevelt's America. Do research about the United States under Theodore Roosevelt's leadership to discover what Kazin means by this phrase.
4. How much power should a teacher have over students? Write a response based on your own educational experiences.
5. What is knowledge? Write an essay defining this term.

JUDITH ORTIZ COFER

Casa: *A Partial Remembrance of a Puerto Rican Childhood*

> *Born in Puerto Rico in 1952, Judith Ortiz Cofer spent her early years moving from place to place in Puerto Rico and on the mainland United States in accordance with the orders received by her career Navy father. Because of these moves, she attended school in many different cultural environments, eventually earning a master's degree in English from the University of Florida and pursuing further graduate work at Oxford University in England. In "Casa," Cofer focuses not on formal schooling but, rather, on the lessons she learned during afternoons spent at her grandmother's house, visiting and talking with her mother, her aunts, and her grandmother.*

Prereading/Journal-Writing Suggestions

1. What tales has your family handed down from generation to generation? Pick your favorite scandal or heroic episode and tell it as you have heard it from your relatives.
2. Describe the room in your house where you feel most comfortable to sit and talk.

At three or four o'clock in the afternoon, the hour of *café con leche,* the women of my family gathered in Mamá's living room to speak of important things and retell familiar stories meant to be overheard by us young girls, their daughters. In Mamá's house (everyone called my grandmother Mamá) was a large parlor built by my grandfather to his wife's exact specifications so that it was always cool, facing away from the sun. The doorway was on the side of the house so no one could walk directly into her living room. First they had to take a little stroll through and around her beautiful garden where prize-winning orchids grew in the trunk of an ancient tree she had hollowed out for that purpose. This room was furnished with several mahogany rocking chairs, acquired at the births of her children, and one intricately carved rocker that had passed down to Mamá at the death of her own mother.

It was on these rockers that my mother, her sisters, and my grandmother sat on these afternoons of my childhood to tell their stories, teaching each other, and my cousin and me, what it was like to be a woman, more specifically, a Puerto Rican woman. They talked about life on the island, and life in *Los Nueva Yores,* their way of referring to the United States from New York City to California: the other place, not home, all the same. They told real-life stories though, as I later learned, always embellishing them with a little or a lot of dramatic detail. And they told *cuentos,* the morality and cautionary tales told by the women in our family for generations: stories that became a part of

my subconscious as I grew up in two worlds, the tropical island and the cold
city, and that would later surface in my dreams and in my poetry.

One of these tales was about the woman who was left at the altar. Mamá
liked to tell that one with histrionic intensity. I remember the rise and fall of
her voice, the sighs, and her constantly gesturing hands, like two birds
swooping through her words. This particular story usually would come up
in a conversation as a result of someone mentioning a forthcoming engage-
ment or wedding. The first time I remember hearing it, I was sitting on the
floor at Mamá's feet, pretending to read a comic book. I may have been eleven
or twelve years old, at that difficult age when a girl was no longer a child who
could be ordered to leave the room if the women wanted freedom to take their
talk into forbidden zones, nor really old enough to be considered a part of
their conclave. I could only sit quietly, pretending to be in another world,
while absorbing it all in a sort of unspoken agreement of my status as silent
auditor. On this day, Mamá had taken my long, tangled mane of hair into her
ever-busy hands. Without looking down at me and with no interruption of
her flow of words, she began braiding my hair, working at it with the quickness and determination that characterized all her actions. My mother was
watching us impassively from her rocker across the room. On her lips played
a little ironic smile. I would never sit still for *her* ministrations, but even then,
I instinctively knew that she did not possess Mamá's matriarchal power to
command and keep everyone's attention. This was never more evident than in
the spell she cast when telling a story.

"It is not like it used to be when I was a girl," Mamá announced. "Then,
a man could leave a girl standing at the church altar with a bouquet of fresh
flowers in her hands and disappear off the face of the earth. No way to track
him down if he was from another town. He could be a married man, with
maybe even two or three families all over the island. There was no way to
know. And there were men who did this. Hombres with the devil in their
flesh who would come to a pueblo, like this one, take a job at one of the
haciendas, never meaning to stay, only to have a good time and to seduce the
women."

The whole time she was speaking, Mamá would be weaving my hair   5
into a flat plait that required pulling apart the two sections of hair with little
jerks that made my eyes water; but knowing how grandmother detested
whining and *boba* (sissy) tears, as she called them, I just sat up as straight and
stiff as I did at La Escuela San Jose, where the nuns enforced good posture
with a flexible plastic ruler they bounced off of slumped shoulders and heads.
As Mamá's story progressed, I noticed how my young Aunt Laura lowered
her eyes, refusing to meet Mamá's meaningful gaze. Laura was seventeen, in
her last year of high school, and already engaged to a boy from another town
who had staked his claim with a tiny diamond ring, then left for Los Nueva
Yores to make his fortune. They were planning to get married in a year. Mamá
had expressed serious doubts that the wedding would ever take place. In
Mamá's eyes, a man set free without a legal contract was a man lost. She

believed that marriage was not something men desired, but simply the price they had to pay for the privilege of children and, of course, for what no decent (synonymous with "smart") woman would give away for free.

"María La Loca was only seventeen when *it* happened to her." I listened closely at the mention of this name. María was a town character, a fat middle-aged woman who lived with her old mother on the outskirts of town. She was to be seen around the pueblo delivering the meat pies the two women made for a living. The most peculiar thing about María, in my eyes, was that she walked and moved like a little girl though she had the thick body and wrinkled face of an old woman. She would swing her hips in an exaggerated, clownish way, and sometimes even hop and skip up to someone's house. She spoke to no one. Even if you asked her a question, she would just look at you and smile, showing her yellow teeth. But I had heard that if you got close enough, you could hear her humming a tune without words. The kids yelled out nasty things at her, calling her *La Loca,* and the men who hung out at the bodega playing dominoes sometimes whistled mockingly as she passed by with her funny, outlandish walk. But María seemed impervious to it all, carrying her basket of *pasteles* like a grotesque Little Red Riding Hood through the forest.

María La Loca interested me, as did all the eccentrics and crazies of our pueblo. Their weirdness was a measuring stick I used in my serious quest for a definition of normal. As a Navy brat shuttling between New Jersey and the pueblo, I was constantly made to feel like an oddball by my peers, who made fun of my two-way accent: a Spanish accent when I spoke English, and when I spoke Spanish I was told that I sounded like a *Gringa.* Being the outsider had already turned my brother and me into cultural chameleons. We developed early on the ability to blend into a crowd, to sit and read quietly in a fifth story apartment building for days and days when it was too bitterly cold to play outside, or, set free, to run wild in Mamá's realm, where she took charge of our lives, releasing Mother for a while from the intense fear for our safety that our father's absences instilled in her. In order to keep us from harm when Father was away, Mother kept us under strict surveillance. She even walked us to and from Public School No. 11, which we attended during the months we lived in Paterson, New Jersey, our home base in the states. Mamá freed all three of us like pigeons from a cage. I saw her as my liberator and my model. Her stories were parables from which to glean the *Truth*.

"María La Loca was once a beautiful girl. Everyone thought she would marry the Méndez boy." As everyone knew, Rogelio Méndez was the richest man in town. "But," Mamá continued, knitting my hair with the same intensity she was putting into her story, "this *macho* made a fool out of her and ruined her life." She paused for the effect of her use of the word "macho," which at that time had not yet become a popular epithet for an unliberated man. This word had for us the crude and comical connotation of "male of the species," stud; a *macho* was what you put in a pen to increase your stock.

I peeked over my comic book at my mother. She too was under Mamá's spell, smiling conspiratorially at this little swipe at men. She was safe from

Mamá's contempt in this area. Married at an early age, an unspotted lamb, she had been accepted by a good family of strict Spaniards whose name was old and respected, though their fortune had been lost long before my birth. In a rocker Papá had painted sky blue sat Mamá's oldest child, Aunt Nena. Mother of three children, stepmother of two more, she was a quiet woman who liked books but had married an ignorant and abusive widower whose main interest in life was accumulating wealth. He too was in the mainland working on his dream of returning home rich and triumphant to buy the *finca* of his dreams. She was waiting for him to send for her. She would leave her children with Mamá for several years while the two of them slaved away in factories. He would one day be a rich man, and she a sadder woman. Even now her life-light was dimming. She spoke little, an aberration in Mamá's house, and she read avidly, as if storing up spiritual food for the long winters that awaited her in Los Nueva Yores without her family. But even Aunt Nena came alive to Mamá's words, rocking gently, her hands over a thick book in her lap.

Her daughter, my cousin Sara, played jacks by herself on the tile porch 10 outside the room where we sat. She was a year older than I. We shared a bed and all our family's secrets. Collaborators in search of answers, Sara and I discussed everything we heard the women say, trying to fit it all together like a puzzle that, once assembled, would reveal life's mysteries to us. Though she and I still enjoyed taking part in boys' games — chase, volleyball, and even *vaqueros,* the island version of cowboys and Indians involving cap-gun battles and violent shoot-outs under the mango tree in Mamá's backyard — we loved best the quiet hours in the afternoon when the men were still at work, and the boys had gone to play serious baseball at the park. Then Mamá's house belonged only to us women. The aroma of coffee perking in the kitchen, the mesmerizing creaks and groans of the rockers, and the women telling their lives in *cuentos* are forever woven into the fabric of my imagination, braided like my hair that day I felt my grandmother's hands teaching me about strength, her voice convincing me of the power of storytelling.

That day Mamá told how the beautiful María had fallen prey to a man whose name was never the same in subsequent versions of the story; it was Juan one time, José, Rafael, Diego, another. We understood that neither the name nor any of the *facts* were important, only that a woman had allowed love to defeat her. Mamá put each of us in María's place by describing her wedding dress in loving detail: how she looked like a princess in her lace as she waited at the altar. Then, as Mamá approached the tragic denouement of her story, I was distracted by the sound of my Aunt Laura's violent rocking. She seemed on the verge of tears. She knew the fable was intended for her. That week she was going to have her wedding gown fitted, though no firm date had been set for the marriage. Mamá ignored Laura's obvious discomfort, digging out a ribbon from the sewing basket she kept by her rocker while describing María's long illness, "a fever that would not break for days." She spoke of a mother's despair: "that woman climbed the church steps on her knees every morning, wore only black as a *promesa* to the Holy Virgin in exchange for her daughter's health." By the time María returned from her honeymoon with death, she was ravished, no longer young or sane. "As you can see, she is almost as old as her mother already," Mamá lamented while tying the ribbon to the ends of my hair, pulling it back with such force that I just knew I would never be able to close my eyes completely again.

"That María's getting crazier every day." Mamá's voice would take a lighter tone now, expressing satisfaction, either for the perfection of my braid, or for a story well told—it was hard to tell. "You know that tune María is always humming?" Carried away by her enthusiasm, I tried to nod, but Mamá still had me pinned between her knees.

"Well, that's the wedding march." Surprising us all, Mamá sang out, "Da, da, dara . . . da, da, dara." Then lifting me off the floor by my skinny shoulders, she would lead me around the room in an impromptu waltz— another session ending with the laughter of women, all of us caught up in the infectious joke of our lives.

Suggestions for Writing and Discussion

1. From the stories these women tell, what was life like for them? Do you think their experiences paralleled women's experiences in general at that time, regardless of their geographical and cultural background? Explain.
2. The tales the older women tell all have a moral. What is the moral of the story about María La Loca? Do you see this moral as pertinent to young women today? Explain.
3. Explain the allusion to Little Red Riding Hood. How does this reference support the main idea of this essay?
4. What do these women think about men? Do you think they are being fair? Are men, in general, like the men in the stories they tell?
5. Cofer recalls the family secrets she shared with her cousin, Sara. If you had a confidante while you were growing up (family member, best friend), describe this person. Explain what you gained from the time you spent together and from the conversations you shared.
6. What is your reaction to the ending of this piece, where Mamá reveals that María, the crazy woman, has been humming the wedding march for years on end? Why do you think the women laugh at this revelation?

Suggestions for Extended Thinking and Research

1. The women in Cofer's family had a special talent for creating parables (brief stories that convey a moral or message). Try your own hand at writing a parable designed to carry a lesson you believe to be important for an audience of your choice (young people; parents; children; young men; young women).
2. What memories do you have of the women or men in your family? Write your own "Partial Remembrance," using Cofer's format as a model.

MAYA ANGELOU
Finishing School

> *Originally named Marguerita Johnson, Maya Angelou was born in St. Louis in 1928. She and her brother grew up in Stamps, Arkansas, under the watchful, loving eye of their grandmother, who they called "Momma." In this selection, a chapter from Angelou's highly praised autobiography,* I Know Why the Caged Bird Sings *(1969), she tells the story of a painful lesson she learns in a white woman's kitchen that she ironically terms her "finishing school."*

Prereading/Journal-Writing Suggestions

1. How do you feel about your name? In other words, if someone calls you something slightly different from your name ("Cathy" instead of "Kate," for instance), does it bother you? How important is your name to you?
2. Write about a significant educational experience you have had *outside* the classroom.

Recently a white woman from Texas, who would quickly describe herself as a liberal, asked me about my hometown. When I told her that in Stamps my grandmother had owned the only Negro general merchandise store since the turn of the century, she exclaimed, "Why, you were a debutante." Ridiculous and even ludicrous. But Negro girls in small Southern towns, whether poverty-stricken or just munching along on a few of life's necessities, were given as extensive and irrelevant preparations for adulthood as rich white girls shown in magazines. Admittedly the training was not the same. While white girls learned to waltz and sit gracefully with a tea cup balanced on their knees, we were lagging behind, learning the mid-Victorian values with very little money to indulge them. . . .

We were required to embroider and I had trunkfuls of colorful dish-towels, pillowcases, runners and handkerchiefs to my credit. I mastered the art of crocheting and tatting, and there was a life-time's supply of dainty doilies that would never be used in sacheted dresser drawers. It went without saying that all girls could iron and wash, but the finer touches around the home, like setting a table with real silver, baking roasts and cooking vegetables without meat, had to be learned elsewhere. Usually at the source of those habits. During my tenth year, a white woman's kitchen became my finishing school.

Mrs. Viola Cullinan was a plump woman who lived in a three-bedroom house somewhere behind the post office. She was singularly unattractive until she smiled, and then the lines around her eyes and mouth which made her look perpetually dirty disappeared, and her face looked like the mask of an impish elf. She usually rested her smile until late afternoon when her women friends dropped in and Miss Glory, the cook, served them cold drinks on the closed-in porch.

The exactness of her house was inhuman. This glass went here and only here. That cup had its place and it was an act of impudent rebellion to place it anywhere else. At twelve o'clock the table was set. At 12:15 Mrs. Cullinan sat down to dinner (whether her husband had arrived or not). At 12:16 Miss Glory brought out the food.

It took me a week to learn the difference between a salad plate, a bread 5 plate and a dessert plate.

Mrs. Cullinan kept up the tradition of her wealthy parents. She was from Virginia. Miss Glory, who was a descendant of slaves that had worked for the Cullinans, told me her history. She had married beneath her (according to Miss Glory). Her husband's family hadn't had their money very long and what they had "didn't 'mount to much."

As ugly as she was, I thought privately, she was lucky to get a husband above or beneath her station. But Miss Glory wouldn't let me say a thing against her mistress. She was very patient with me, however, over the house-work. She explained the dishware, silverware and servants' bells. The large round bowl in which soup was served wasn't a soup bowl, it was a tureen. There were goblets, sherbet glasses, ice-cream glasses, wine glasses, green glass coffee cups with matching saucers, and water glasses. I had a glass to drink from, and it sat with Miss Glory's on a separate shelf from the others. Soup spoons, gravy boat, butter knives, salad forks and carving platter were additions to my vocabulary and in fact almost represented a new language. I was fascinated with the novelty, with the fluttering Mrs. Cullinan and her Alice-in-Wonderland house.

Her husband remains, in my memory, undefined. I lumped him with all the other white men that I had ever seen and tried not to see.

On our way home one evening, Miss Glory told me that Mrs. Cullinan couldn't have children. She said that she was too delicate-boned. It was hard to imagine bones at all under those layers of fat. Miss Glory went on to say that the doctor had taken out all her lady organs. I reasoned that a pig's organs included the lungs, heart and liver, so if Mrs. Cullinan was walking around without those essentials, it explained why she drank alcohol out of unmarked bottles. She was keeping herself embalmed.

When I spoke to Bailey about it, he agreed that I was right, but he also 10 informed me that Mr. Cullinan had two daughters by a colored lady and that I knew them very well. He added that the girls were the spitting image of their father. I was unable to remember what he looked like, although I had just left him a few hours before, but I thought of the Coleman girls. They were very light-skinned and certainly didn't look very much like their mother (no one ever mentioned Mr. Coleman).

My pity for Mrs. Cullinan preceded me the next morning like the Cheshire cat's smile. Those girls, who could have been her daughters, were beautiful. They didn't have to straighten their hair. Even when they were caught in the rain, their braids still hung down straight like tamed snakes. Their mouths were pouty little cupid's bows. Mrs. Cullinan didn't know what she missed. Or maybe she did. Poor Mrs. Cullinan.

For weeks after, I arrived early, left late and tried very hard to make up for her barrenness. If she had her own children, she wouldn't have had to ask me to run a thousand errands from her back door to the back door of her friends. Poor old Mrs. Cullinan.

Then one evening Miss Glory told me to serve the ladies on the porch. After I set the tray down and turned toward the kitchen, one of the women asked, "What's your name, girl?" It was the speckled-faced one. Mrs. Cullinan said, "She doesn't talk much. Her name's Margaret."

"Is she dumb?"

"No. As I understand it, she can talk when she wants to but she's usually 15 quiet as a little mouse. Aren't you, Margaret?"

I smiled at her. Poor thing. No organs and couldn't even pronounce my name correctly.

"She's a sweet little thing, though."

"Well, that may be, but the name's too long. I'd never bother myself. I'd call her Mary if I was you."

I fumed into the kitchen. That horrible woman would never have the chance to call me Mary because if I was starving I'd never work for her. . . .

That evening I decided to write a poem on being white, fat, old and 20 without children. It was going to be a tragic ballad. I would have to watch her carefully to capture the essence of her loneliness and pain.

The very next day, she called me by the wrong name. Miss Glory and I were washing up the lunch dishes when Mrs. Cullinan came to the doorway. "Mary?"

Miss Glory asked, "Who?"

Mrs. Cullinan, sagging a little, knew and I knew. "I want Mary to go down to Mrs. Randall's and take her some soup. She's not been feeling well for a few days."

Miss Glory's face was a wonder to see. "You mean Margaret, ma'am. Her name's Margaret."

"That's too long. She's Mary from now on. Heat that soup from last 25 night and put it in the china tureen and, Mary, I want you to carry it carefully."

Every person I knew had a hellish horror of being "called out of his name." It was a dangerous practice to call a Negro anything that could be loosely construed as insulting because of the centuries of their having been called niggers, jigs, dinges, blackbirds, crows, boots and spooks.

Miss Glory had a fleeting second of feeling sorry for me. Then as she handed me the hot tureen she said, "Don't mind, don't pay that no mind. Sticks and stones may break your bones, but words . . . You know, I been working for her for twenty years."

She held the back door open for me. "Twenty years. I wasn't much older than you. My name used to be Hallelujah. That's what Ma named me, but my mistress give me 'Glory,' and it stuck. I likes it better too."

I was in the little path that ran behind the houses when Miss Glory shouted, "It's shorter too."

For a few seconds it was a tossup over whether I would laugh (imagine being named Hallelujah) or cry (imagine letting some white woman rename you for her convenience). My anger saved me from either outburst. I had to quit the job, but the problem was going to be how to do it. Momma wouldn't allow me to quit for just any reason.

"She's a peach. That woman is a real peach." Mrs. Randall's maid was talking as she took the soup from me, and I wondered what her name used to be and what she answered to now.

For a week I looked into Mrs. Cullinan's face as she called me Mary. She ignored my coming late and leaving early. Miss Glory was a little annoyed because I had begun to leave egg yolk on the dishes and wasn't putting much heart in polishing the silver. I hoped that she would complain to our boss, but she didn't.

Then Bailey solved my dilemma. He had me describe the contents of the cupboard and the particular plates she liked best. Her favorite piece was a casserole shaped like a fish and the green glass coffee cups. I kept his instructions in mind, so on the next day when Miss Glory was hanging out clothes and I had again been told to serve the old biddies on the porch, I dropped the empty serving tray. When I heard Mrs. Cullinan scream, "Mary!" I picked up the casserole and two of the green glass cups in readiness. As she rounded the kitchen door I let them fall on the tiled floor.

I could never absolutely describe to Bailey what happened next, because each time I got to the part where she fell on the floor and screwed up her ugly face to cry, we burst out laughing. She actually wobbled around on the floor and picked up shards of the cups and cried, "Oh, Momma. Oh, dear Gawd. It's Momma's china from Virginia. Oh, Momma, I'm sorry."

Miss Glory came running in from the yard and the women from the porch crowded around. Miss Glory was almost as broken up as her mistress. "You mean to say she broke our Virginia dishes? What we gone do?"

Mrs. Cullinan cried louder, "That clumsy nigger. Clumsy little black nigger."

Old speckled-faced leaned down and asked, "Who did it, Viola? Was it Mary? Who did it?"

Everything was happening so fast I can't remember whether her action preceded her words, but I know that Mrs. Cullinan said, "Her name's Margaret, goddamn it, her name's Margaret." And she threw a wedge of broken plate at me. It could have been the hysteria which put her aim off, but the flying crockery caught Miss Glory right over her ear and she started screaming.

I left the front door wide open so all the neighbors could hear.

Mrs. Cullinan was right about one thing. My name wasn't Mary.

Suggestions for Writing and Discussion

1. Why do you think Margaret had to learn the "finer touches" around a home? Did all girls at that time learn these same things?

2. Based on the physical description alone, what type of person do you imagine Mrs. Cullinan to be? Can you describe someone you know (changing names to protect the guilty) who comes close to matching her?

3. Why do Miss Glory's cup and Margaret's cup sit on a separate shelf?

4. Angelou writes that she felt sorry for Mrs. Cullinan's "barrenness," so she tried to make up for it by working extra hard. What does this tell you about Angelou's personality and character? When and why does her attitude change toward Mrs. Cullinan?

5. What do you think of Miss Glory? In what ways is she like Margaret? In what ways do they differ? Why do you think Miss Glory has stayed with Mrs. Cullinan for so many years? What do their different decisions suggest about their values? With whom do you more closely identify? Why?

6. Angelou makes several references to Alice in Wonderland in this piece. In what ways do these allusions connect to the central idea she conveys?

7. Mrs. Cullinan says that the name Margaret is too long, so she shortens it to Mary. She also does this to Glory's name. What do you see as the deeper implications of these changes? What goes on in Mrs. Cullinan's conscious or subconscious mind as she alters her employees' names?

8. What do you think of Bailey's solution to Margaret's dilemma? Could she have solved her problem any other way? Explain.

Suggestions for Extended Thinking and Research

1. Margaret says that in order to really capture someone, you have to watch very carefully. Practice the art of observation yourself. Watch someone very carefully, making notes about what the person does and says. Then draw some conclusions based on your notes.

2. Read historical accounts of women who have worked as domestic servants. Explain how the accounts you read differ from or support the description of this work that Angelou gives.

MIKE ROSE

"I Just Wanna Be Average"

> *Born to immigrant Italian parents in 1944, Mike Rose is an outstanding scholar and teacher, known especially for his autobiographical book on the school experiences of America's underclass,* Lives on the Boundary *(1989). "I Just Wanna Be Average," a chapter from that book, shows the terrifying ways students can slip through the cracks in the educational system. Rose also shows, however, that there is hope for the individual lucky enough to encounter a caring teacher and to find the motivation to actively pursue learning both in and out of school.*

Prereading/Journal-Writing Suggestions

1. Do you see yourself (or perhaps a close friend or sibling) as having had a "label" during your school years? For instance, did your teachers or classmates see you (or your friend or sibling) as the class clown, the brain, or the quiet one? In what ways was this label fitting? What might a teacher have missed because of this label?

2. Describe your attitude toward school during your high school years. What interested you? What did school mean to you? What were your best moments? Your worst?

3. If you could go back and change anything about your past educational experiences, what would you change? How? Why?

It took two buses to get to Our Lady of Mercy. The first started deep in South Los Angeles and caught me at midpoint. The second drifted through neighborhoods with trees, parks, big lawns, and lots of flowers. The rides were long but were livened up by a group of South L.A. veterans whose parents also thought that Hope had set up shop in the west end of the country. There was Christy Biggars, who, at sixteen, was dealing and was, according to rumor, a pimp as well. There were Bill Cobb and Johnny Gonzales, grease-pencil artists extraordinaire, who left Nembutal-enhanced swirls of "Cobb" and "Johnny" on the corrugated walls of the bus. And then there was Tyrrell Wilson. Tyrrell was the coolest kid I knew. He ran the dozens like a metric halfback, laid down a rap that outrhymed and outpointed Cobb, whose rap was good but not great—the curse of a moderately soulful kid trapped in white skin. But it was Cobb who would sneak a radio onto the bus, and thus underwrote his patter with Little Richard, Fats Domino, Chuck Berry, the Coasters, and Ernie K. Doe's mother-in-law, an awful woman who was "sent from down below." And so it was that Christy and Cobb and Johnny G. and Tyrrell and I and assorted others picked up along the way passed our days in the back of the bus, a funny mix brought together by geography and parental desire.

Entrance to school brings with it forms and releases and assessments. Mercy relied on a series of tests, mostly the Stanford-Binet, for placement, and somehow the results of my tests got confused with those of another student named Rose. The other Rose apparently didn't do very well, for I was placed in the vocational track, a euphemism for the bottom level. Neither I nor my parents realized what this meant. We had no sense that Business Math, Typing, and English-Level D were dead ends. The current spate of reports on the schools criticizes parents for not involving themselves in the education of their children. But how would someone like Tommy Rose, with his two years of Italian schooling, know what to ask? And what sort of pressure could an exhausted waitress apply? The error went undetected, and I remained in the vocational track for two years. What a place.

My homeroom was supervised by Brother Dill, a troubled and unstable man who also taught freshman English. When his class drifted away from him, which was often, his voice would rise in paranoid accusations, and occasionally he would lose control and shake or smack us. I hadn't been there two months when one of his brisk, face-turning slaps had my glasses sliding down the aisle. Physical education was also pretty harsh. Our teacher was a stubby ex-lineman who had played old-time pro ball in the Midwest. He routinely had us grabbing our ankles to receive his stinging paddle across our butts. He did that, he said, to make men of us. "Rose," he bellowed on our first encounter; me standing geeky in line in my baggy shorts. "'Rose'? What the hell kind of name is that?"

"Italian, sir," I squeaked.

"Italian! Ho. Rose, do you know the sound a bag of shit makes when it 5 hits the wall?"

"No, sir."

"Wop!"

Sophomore English was taught by Mr. Mitropetros. He was a large, bejeweled man who managed the parking lot at the Shrine Auditorium. He would crow and preen and list for us the stars he'd brushed against. We'd ask questions and glance knowingly and snicker, and all that fueled the poor guy to brag some more. Parking cars was his night job. He had little training in English, so his lesson plan for his day work had us reading the district's required text, *Julius Caesar*, aloud for the semester. We'd finish the play way before the twenty weeks was up, so he'd have us switch parts again and again and start again: Dave Snyder, the fastest guy at Mercy, muscling through Caesar to the breathless squeals of Calpurnia, as interpreted by Steve Fusco, a surfer who owned the school's most envied paneled wagon. Week ten and Dave and Steve would take on new roles, as would we all, and render a water-logged Cassius and a Brutus that are beyond my powers of description.

Spanish I—taken in the second year—fell into the hands of a new re-cruit. Mr. Montez was a tiny man, slight, five foot six at the most, soft-spoken and delicate. Spanish was a particularly rowdy class, and Mr. Montez was as prepared for it as a doily maker at a hammer throw. He would tap his pencil to a room in which Steve Fusco was propelling spitballs from his heavy lips, in which Mike Dweetz was taunting Billy Hawk, a half-Indian, half-Spanish, reed-thin, quietly explosive boy. The vocational track at Our Lady of Mercy mixed kids traveling in from South L.A. with South Bay surfers and a few Slavs and Chicanos from the harbors of San Pedro. This was a dangerous miscellany: surfers and hodads and South-Central blacks all ablaze to the metronomic tapping of Hector Montez's pencil.

One day Billy lost it. Out of the corner of my eye I saw him strike out 10 with his right arm and catch Dweetz across the neck. Quick as a spasm, Dweetz was out of his seat, scattering desks, cracking Billy on the side of the head, right behind the eye. Snyder and Fusco and others broke it up, but the room felt hot and close and naked. Mr. Montez's tenuous authority was finally ripped to shreds, and I think everyone felt a little strange about that. The charade was over, and when it came down to it, I don't think any of the kids really wanted it to end this way. They had pushed and pushed and bullied their way into a freedom that both scared and embarrassed them.

Students will float to the mark you set. I and the others in the vocational classes were bobbing in pretty shallow water. Vocational education has aimed at increasing the economic opportunities of students who do not do well in our schools. Some serious programs succeed in doing that, and through exceptional teachers — like Mr. Gross in *Horace's Compromise* — students learn to develop hypotheses and troubleshoot, reason through a problem, and communicate effectively — the true job skills. The vocational track, however, is most often a place for those who are just not making it, a dumping ground for the disaffected. There were a few teachers who worked hard at education; young Brother Slattery, for example, combined a stern voice with weekly quizzes to try to pass along to us a skeletal outline of world history. But mostly the teachers had no idea of how to engage the imaginations of us kids who were scuttling along at the bottom of the pond.

And the teachers would have needed some inventiveness, for none of us was groomed for the classroom. It wasn't just that I didn't know things — didn't know how to simplify algebraic fractions, couldn't identify different kinds of clauses, bungled Spanish translations — but that I had developed various faulty and inadequate ways of doing algebra and making sense of Spanish. Worse yet, the years of defensive tuning out in elementary school had given me a way to escape quickly while seeming at least half alert. During my time in Voc. Ed., I developed further into a mediocre student and a somnambulant problem solver, and that affected the subjects I did have the wherewithal to handle: I detested Shakespeare; I got bored with history. My attention flitted here and there. I fooled around in class and read my books indifferently — the intellectual equivalent of playing with your food. I did what I had to do to get by, and I did it with half a mind.

But I did learn things about people and eventually came into my own socially. I liked the guys in Voc. Ed. Growing up where I did, I understood and admired physical prowess, and there was an abundance of muscle here. There was Dave Snyder, a sprinter and halfback of true quality. Dave's ability and his quick wit gave him a natural appeal, and he was welcome in any clique, though he always kept a little independent. He enjoyed acting the fool and could care less about studies, but he possessed a certain maturity and never caused the faculty much trouble. It was a testament to his independence that he included me among his friends — I eventually went out for track, but I was no jock. Owing to the Latin alphabet and a dearth of *R*s and *S*s, Snyder sat behind Rose, and we started exchanging one-liners and became friends.

There was Ted Richard, a much-touted Little League pitcher. He was chunky and had a baby face and came to Our Lady of Mercy as a seasoned street fighter. Ted was quick to laugh and he had a loud, jolly laugh, but when he got angry he'd smile a little smile, the kind that simply raises the corner of the mouth a quarter of an inch. For those who knew, it was an eerie signal. Those who didn't found themselves in big trouble, for Ted was very quick. He loved to carry on what we would come to call philosophical discussions: What is courage? Does God exist? He also loved words, enjoyed picking up big ones like *salubrious* and *equivocal* and using them in our conversations — laughing at himself as the word hit a chuckhole rolling off his tongue. Ted didn't do all that well in school — baseball and parties and testing the courage he'd speculated about took up his time. His textbooks were *Argosy* and *Field and Stream*, whatever newspapers he'd find on the bus stop — from the *Daily Worker* to pornography — conversations with uncles or hobos or businessmen he'd meet in a coffee shop, *The Old Man and the Sea*. With hindsight, I can see that Ted was developing into one of those rough-hewn intellectuals whose sources are a mix of the learned and the apocryphal, whose discussions are both assured and sad.

And then there was Ken Harvey. Ken was good-looking in a puffy way 15 and had a full and oily ducktail and was a car enthusiast . . . a hodad. One day in religion class, he said the sentence that turned out to be one of the most memorable of the hundreds of thousands I heard in those Voc. Ed. years. We were talking about the parable of the talents, about achievement, working hard, doing the best you can do, blah-blah-blah, when the teacher called on the restive Ken Harvey for an opinion. Ken thought about it, but just for a second, and said (with studied, minimal affect), "I just wanna be average." That woke me up. Average? Who wants to be average? Then the athletes chimed in with the clichés that make you want to laryngectomize them, and the exchange became a platitudinous melee. At the time, I thought Ken's assertion was stupid, and I wrote him off. But his sentence has stayed with me all these years, and I think I am finally coming to understand it.

Ken Harvey was gasping for air. School can be a tremendously disorienting place. No matter how bad the school, you're going to encounter notions that don't fit with the assumptions and beliefs that you grew up with — maybe you'll hear these dissonant notions from teachers, maybe from the other students, and maybe you'll read them. You'll also be thrown in with all kinds of kids from all kinds of backgrounds, and that can be unsettling — this is especially true in places of rich ethnic and linguistic mix, like the L.A.

basin. You'll see a handful of students far excel you in courses that sound exotic and that are only in the curriculum of the elite: French, physics, trigonometry. And all this is happening while you're trying to shape an identity, your body is changing, and your emotions are running wild. If you're a working-class kid in the vocational track, the options you'll have to deal with this will be constrained in certain ways: you're defined by your school as "slow"; you're placed in a curriculum that isn't designed to liberate you but to occupy you, or, if you're lucky, train you, though the training is for work the society does not esteem; other students are picking up the cues from your school and your curriculum and interacting with you in particular ways. If you're a kid like Ted Richard, you turn your back on all this and let your mind roam where it may. But youngsters like Ted are rare. What Ken and so many others do is protect themselves from such suffocating madness by taking on with a vengeance the identity implied in the vocational track. Reject the confusion and frustration by openly defining yourself as the Common Joe. Champion the average. Rely on your own good sense. Fuck this bullshit. Bullshit, of course, is everything you — and the others — fear is beyond you: books, essays, tests, academic scrambling, complexity, scientific reasoning, philosophical inquiry.

The tragedy is that you have to twist the knife in your own gray matter to make this defense work. You'll have to shut down, have to reject intellectual stimuli or diffuse them with sarcasm, have to cultivate stupidity, have to convert boredom from a malady into a way of confronting the world. Keep your vocabulary simple, act stoned when you're not or act more stoned than you are, flaunt ignorance, materialize your dreams. It is a powerful and effective defense — it neutralizes the insult and the frustration of being a vocational kid and, when perfected, it drives teachers up the wall, a delightful secondary effect. But like all strong magic, it exacts a price.

My own deliverance from the Voc. Ed. world began with sophomore biology. Every student, college prep to vocational, had to take biology, and unlike the other courses, the same person taught all sections. When teaching the vocational group, Brother Clint probably slowed down a bit or omitted a little of the fundamental biochemistry, but he used the same book and more or less the same syllabus across the board. If one class got tough, he could get tougher. He was young and powerful and very handsome, and looks and physical strength were high currency. No one gave him any trouble.

I was pretty bad at the dissecting table, but the lectures and the textbook were interesting: plastic overlays that, with each turned page, peeled away skin, then veins and muscle, then organs, down to the very bones that Brother Clint, pointer in hand, would tap out on our hanging skeleton. Dave Snyder was in big trouble, for the study of life — versus the living of it — was sticking in his craw. We worked out a code for our multiple-choice exams. He'd poke me in the back: once for the answer under *A*, twice for *B*, and so on; and when he'd hit the right one, I'd look up to the ceiling as though I were lost in thought. Poke: cytoplasm. Poke, poke: methane. Poke, poke, poke:

William Harvey. Poke, poke, poke, poke: islets of Langerhans. This didn't work out perfectly, but Dave passed the course, and I mastered the dreamy look of a guy on a record jacket. And something else happened. Brother Clint puzzled over this Voc. Ed. kid who was racking up 98s and 99s on his tests. He checked the school's records and discovered the error. He recommended that I begin my junior year in the College Prep program. According to all I've read since, such a shift, as one report put it, is virtually impossible. Kids at that level rarely cross tracks. The telling thing is how chancy both my placement into and exit from Voc. Ed. was; neither I nor my parents had anything to do with it. I lived in one world during spring semester, and when I came back to school in the fall, I was living in another.

Switching to College Prep was a mixed blessing. I was an erratic student. I was undisciplined. And I hadn't caught onto the rules of the game: why work hard in a class that didn't grab my fancy? I was also hopelessly behind in math. Chemistry was hard; toying with my chemistry set years before hadn't prepared me for the chemist's equations. Fortunately, the priest who taught both chemistry and second-year algebra was also the school's athletic director. Membership on the track team covered me; I knew I wouldn't get lower than a *C*. U.S. history was taught pretty well, and I did okay. But civics was taken over by a football coach who had trouble reading the textbook aloud—and reading aloud was the centerpiece of his pedagogy. College Prep at Mercy was certainly an improvement over the vocational program—at least it carried some status—but the social science curriculum was weak, and the mathematics and physical sciences were simply beyond me. I had a miserable quantitative background and ended up copying some assignments and finessing the rest as best I could. Let me try to explain how it feels to see again and again material you should once have learned but didn't.

You are given a problem. It requires you to simplify algebraic fractions or to multiply expressions containing square roots. You know this is pretty basic material because you've seen it for years. Once a teacher took some time with you, and you learned how to carry out these operations. Simple versions, anyway. But that was a year or two or more in the past, and these are more complex versions, and now you're not sure. And this, you keep telling yourself, is ninth- or even eighth-grade stuff.

Next it's a word problem. This is also old hat. The basic elements are as familiar as story characters: trains speeding so many miles per hour or shadows of buildings angling so many degrees. Maybe you know enough, have sat through enough explanations, to be able to begin setting up the problem: "If one train is going this fast . . ." or "This shadow is really one line of a triangle . . ." Then: "Let's see . . ." "How did Jones do this?" "Hmmmm." "No." "No, that won't work." Your attention wavers. You wonder about other things: a football game, a dance, that cute new checker at the market. You try to focus on the problem again. You scribble on paper for a while, but the tension wins out and your attention flits elsewhere. You crumple the paper and begin daydreaming to ease the frustration.

The particulars will vary, but in essence this is what a number of students go through, especially those in so-called remedial classes. They open their textbooks and see once again the familiar and impenetrable formulas and diagrams and terms that have stumped them for years. There is no excitement here. *No* excitement. Regardless of what the teacher says, this is not a new challenge. There is, rather, embarrassment and frustration and, not surprisingly, some anger in being reminded once again of long-standing inadequacies. No wonder so many students finally attribute their difficulties to something inborn, organic: "That part of my brain just doesn't work." Given the troubling histories many of these students have, it's miraculous that any of them can lift the shroud of hopelessness sufficiently to make deliverance from these classes possible.

Through this entire period, my father's health was deteriorating with cruel momentum. His arteriosclerosis progressed to the point where a simple nick on his shin wouldn't heal. Eventually it ulcerated and widened. Lou Minton would come by daily to change the dressing. We tried renting an oscillating bed — which we placed in the front room — to force blood through the constricted arteries in my father's legs. The bed hummed through the night, moving in place to ward off the inevitable. The ulcer continued to spread, and the doctors finally had to amputate. My grandfather had lost his leg in a stockyard accident. Now my father too was crippled. His convalescence was slow but steady, and the doctors placed him in the Santa Monica Rehabilitation Center, a sun-bleached building that opened out onto the warm spray of the Pacific. The place gave him some strength and some color and some training in walking with an artificial leg. He did pretty well for a year or so until he slipped and broke his hip. He was confined to a wheelchair after that, and the confinement contributed to the diminishing of his body and spirit.

I am holding a picture of him. He is sitting in his wheelchair and smiling 25 at the camera. The smile appears forced, unsteady, seems to quaver, though it is frozen in silver nitrate. He is in his mid-sixties and looks eighty. Late in my junior year, he had a stroke and never came out of the resulting coma. After that, I would see him only in dreams, and to this day that is how I join him. Sometimes the dreams are sad and grisly and primal: my father lying in a bed soaked with his suppuration, holding me, rocking me. But sometimes the dreams bring him back to me healthy: him talking to me on an empty street, or buying some pictures to decorate our old house, or transformed somehow into someone strong and adept with tools and the physical.

Jack MacFarland couldn't have come into my life at a better time. My father was dead, and I had logged up too many years of scholastic indifference. Mr. MacFarland had a master's degree from Columbia and decided, at twenty-six, to find a little school and teach his heart out. He never took any credentialing courses, couldn't bear to, he said, so he had to find employment in a private system. He ended up at Our Lady of Mercy teaching five sections of senior English. He was a beatnik who was born too late. His teeth were stained, he tucked his sorry tie in between the third and fourth buttons of his shirt, and his pants were chronically wrinkled. At first, we couldn't believe this guy, thought he slept in his car. But within no time, he had us so startled with work that we didn't much worry about where he slept or if he slept at all. We wrote three or four essays a month. We read a book every two to three weeks, starting with the *Iliad* and ending up with Hemingway. He gave us a quiz on the reading every other day. He brought a prep school curriculum to Mercy High.

MacFarland's lectures were crafted, and as he delivered them he would pace the room jiggling a piece of chalk in his cupped hand, using it to scribble on the board the names of all the writers and philosophers and plays and novels he was weaving into his discussion. He asked questions often, raised everything from Zeno's paradox to the repeated last line of Frost's "Stopping by Woods on a Snowy Evening." He slowly and carefully built up our knowledge of Western intellectual history — with facts, with connections, with speculations. We learned about Greek philosophy, about Dante, the Elizabethan world view, the Age of Reason, existentialism. He analyzed poems with us, had us reading sections from John Ciardi's *How Does a Poem Mean?*, making a potentially difficult book accessible with his own explanations. We gave oral reports on poems Ciardi didn't cover. We imitated the styles of Conrad, Hemingway, and *Time* magazine. We wrote and talked, wrote and talked. The man immersed us in language.

Even MacFarland's barbs were literary. If Jim Fitzsimmons, hung over and irritable, tried to smart-ass him, he'd rejoin with a flourish that would spark the indomitable Skip Madison — who'd lost his front teeth in a hapless tackle — to flick his tongue through the gap and opine, "good chop," drawing out the single "o" in stinging indictment. Jack MacFarland, this tobacco-stained intellectual, brandished linguistic weapons of a kind I hadn't encountered before. Here was this *egghead,* for God's sake, keeping some pretty difficult people in line. And from what I heard, Mike Dweetz and Steve Fusco and all the notorious Voc. Ed. crowd settled down as well when MacFarland took the podium. Though a lot of guys groused in the schoolyard, it just seemed that giving trouble to this particular teacher was a silly thing to do. Tomfoolery, not to mention assault, had no place in the world he was trying to create for us, and instinctively everyone knew that. If nothing else, we all recognized MacFarland's considerable intelligence and respected the hours he put into his work. It came to this: the troublemaker would look foolish rather than daring. Even Jim Fitzsimmons was reading *On the Road* and turning his incipient alcoholism to literary ends.

There were some lives that were already beyond Jack MacFarland's ministrations, but mine was not. I started reading again as I hadn't since elementary school. I would go into our gloomy little bedroom or sit at the dinner table while, on the television, Danny McShane was paralyzing Mr. Moto with the atomic drop, and work slowly back through *Heart of Darkness,* trying to catch the words in Conrad's sentences. I certainly was not MacFarland's best student; most of the other guys in College Prep, even my fellow slackers, had better backgrounds than I did. But I worked very hard, for MacFarland had hooked me. He tapped my old interest in reading and creating stories. He gave me a way to feel special by using my mind. And he provided a role model that wasn't shaped on physical prowess alone, and something inside me that I wasn't quite aware of responded to that. Jack MacFarland established a literacy club, to borrow a phrase of Frank Smith's, and invited me — invited all of us — to join.

There's been a good deal of research and speculation suggesting that the 30 acknowledgement of school performance with extrinsic rewards — smiling faces, stars, numbers, grades — diminishes the intrinsic satisfaction children experience by engaging in reading or writing or problem solving. While it's certainly true that we've created an educational system that encourages our best and brightest to become cynical grade collectors and, in general, have developed an obsession with evaluation and assessment, I must tell you that venal though it may have been, I loved getting good grades from MacFarland. I now know how subjective grades can be, but then they came tucked in the back of essays like bits of scientific data, some sort of spectroscopic readout that said, objectively and publicly, that I had made something of value. I suppose I'd been mediocre for too long and enjoyed a public redefinition. And I suppose the workings of my mind, such as they were, had been private for too long. My linguistic play moved into the world; . . . these papers with their circled, red B-pluses and A-minuses linked my mind to something outside it. I carried them around like a club emblem.

One day in the December of my senior year, Mr. MacFarland asked me where I was going to go to college. I hadn't thought much about it. Many of the students I teach today spent their last year in high school with a physics text in one hand and the Stanford catalog in the other, but I wasn't even aware of what "entrance requirements" were. My folks would say that they wanted me to go to college and be a doctor, but I don't know how seriously I ever took that; it seemed a sweet thing to say, a bit of supportive family chatter, like telling a gangly daughter she's graceful. The reality of higher education wasn't in my scheme of things: no one in the family had gone to college; only two of my uncles had completed high school. I figured I'd get a night job and go to the local junior college because I knew that Snyder and Company were going there to play ball. But I hadn't even prepared for that. When I finally said, "I don't know," MacFarland looked down at me — I was seated in his office — and said, "Listen, you can write."

My grades stank. I had A's in biology and a handful of B's in a few English and social science classes. All the rest were C's — or worse. Mac-Farland said I would do well in his class and laid down the law about doing well in the others. Still, the record for my first three years wouldn't have been acceptable to any four-year school. To nobody's surprise, I was turned down flat by USC and UCLA. But Jack MacFarland was on the case. He had received his bachelor's degree from Loyola University, so he made calls to old professors and talked to somebody in admissions and wrote me a strong letter.

Loyola finally accepted me as a probationary student. I would be on trial for the first year, and if I did okay, I would be granted regular status. MacFarland also intervened to get me a loan, for I could never have afforded a private college without it. Four more years of religion classes and four more years of boys at one school, girls at another. But at least I was going to college. Amazing.

In my last semester of high school, I elected a special English course fashioned by Mr. MacFarland, and it was through this elective that there arose at Mercy a fledgling literati. Art Mitz, the editor of the school newspaper and a very smart guy, was the kingpin. He was joined by me and by Mark Dever, a quiet boy who wrote beautifully and who would die before he was forty. MacFarland occasionally invited us to his apartment, and those visits became the high point of our apprenticeship: we'd clamp on our training wheels and drive to his salon.

He lived in a cramped and cluttered place near the airport, tucked away in the kind of building that architectural critic Reyner Banham calls a *dingbat*. Books were all over: stacked, piled, tossed, and crated, underlined and dog eared, well worn and new. Cigarette ashes crusted with coffee in saucers or spilled over the sides of motel ashtrays. The little bedroom had, along two of its walls, bricks and boards loaded with notes, magazines, and oversized books. The kitchen joined the living room, and there was a stack of German newspapers under the sink. I had never seen anything like it: a great flophouse of language furnished by City Lights and Café le Metro. I read every title. I flipped through paperbacks and scanned jackets and memorized names: Gogol, *Finnegans Wake,* Djuna Barnes, Jackson Pollock, *A Coney Island of the Mind,* F. O. Matthiessen's *American Renaissance,* all sorts of Freud, *Troubled Sleep,* Man Ray, *The Education of Henry Adams,* Richard Wright, *Film as Art,* William Butler Yeats, Marguerite Duras, *Redburn, A Season in Hell, Kapital.* On the cover of Alain-Fournier's *The Wanderer* was an Edward Gorey drawing of a young man on a road winding into dark trees. By the hotplate sat a strange Kafka novel called *Amerika,* in which an adolescent hero crosses the Atlantic to find the Nature Theater of Oklahoma. Art and Mark would be talking about a movie or the school newspaper, and I would be consuming my English teacher's library. It was heady stuff. I felt like a Pop Warner athlete on steroids.

Art, Mark, and I would buy stogies and triangulate from MacFarland's 35 apartment to the Cinema, which now shows X-rated films but was then L.A.'s premier art theater, and then to the musty Cherokee Bookstore in Hollywood to hobnob with beatnik homosexuals — smoking, drinking bourbon and coffee, and trying out awkward phrases we'd gleaned from our mentor's bookshelves. I was happy and precocious and a little scared as well, for Hollywood Boulevard was thick with a kind of decadence that was foreign to the South Side. After the Cherokee, we would head back to the security of MacFarland's apartment, slaphappy with hipness.

Let me be the first to admit that there was a good deal of adolescent passion in this embrace of the avant-garde: self-absorption, sexually charged pedantry, an elevation of the odd and abandoned. Still it was a time during which I absorbed an awful lot of information: long lists of titles, images from expressionist paintings, new wave shibboleths, snippets of philosophy, and names that read like Steve Fusco's misspellings — Goethe, Nietzsche, Kierkegaard. Now this is hardly the stuff of deep understanding. But it was an introduction, a phrase book, a Baedeker to a vocabulary of ideas, and it felt good at the time to know all these words. With hindsight I realize how layered and important that knowledge was.

It enabled me to do things in the world. I could browse bohemian bookstores in far-off, mysterious Hollywood; I could go to the Cinema and see events through the lenses of European directors; and, most of all, I could share an evening, talk that talk, with Jack MacFarland, the man I most admired at the time. Knowledge was becoming a bonding agent. Within a year or two, the persona of the disaffected hipster would prove too cynical, too alienated to last. But for a time it was new and exciting: it provided a critical perspective on society, and it allowed me to act as though I were living beyond the limiting boundaries of South Vermont.

Suggestions for Writing and Discussion

1. In what way does Rose's title, "I Just Wanna Be Average," reflect the central idea of this excerpt from his book? What is ironic about the title?
2. Rose's experience was based on what is known in education as tracking or homogeneous grouping. Did the schools you attended use this system of grouping? How did grouping (or nongrouping) work out for you? From your own experiences, what do you see as the advantages and disadvantages of tracking?
3. Rose gives five examples of different teachers in his high school. What are the general characteristics each teacher displays? Do you think these characteristics are representative of teachers today? Explain.
4. After Brother Clint discovered that Rose was misplaced in his classes, Rose says he hadn't quite "caught onto the rules of the game: why work hard in a class that didn't grab my fancy?" What are the "rules of the game" in education today? What advice would you give to a student who finds a particular (required) class boring?
5. Rose's most influential teacher, Jack MacFarland, "immersed" his class in language. What subjects (if any) have you been immersed in during your educational experience? What subjects were taught to you on a surface, cursory level? What effect did each approach have on you?

Suggestions for Extended Thinking and Research

1. What effect do grades really have on students? Consult the *Education Index* at your library to find several sources on this subject. Write an essay describing the findings of several authorities who have differing opinions on

this subject. Which opinions do you favor, based on your own experiences? Explain.

2. After reading several sources on the pros and cons of tracking, research the schools in your area to determine what approach they take toward tracking. Interview educators, principals, parents, and (with permission) students. Then write a report explaining your findings.

NICHOLAS GAGE

The Teacher Who Changed My Life

Born in Greece in 1940, Nicholas Gage has written movingly of the torture and murder in 1948 of his mother Eleni Gatzoyiannis. In his best-selling book Eleni, *he describes the events leading to her death at the hands of Communist guerrillas when she sent her children to live in the United States. In his book* A Place for Us, *from which this essay is taken, Gage describes the difficult adjustment he and his sisters faced after arriving in their new country and pays tribute to the teacher he sees as the inspiration and motivating force behind his later success as a writer.*

Prereading/Journal-Writing Suggestions

1. Write about someone you see as your mentor, your inspiration.
2. Describe your past experiences with writing, especially in a school environment. How did you learn to write? How do you feel about writing? How would you assess your writing ability at this point in your life?
3. What three characteristics are most important for a good teacher to possess? Explain your answer by describing your own specific experiences with good teachers.

The person who set the course of my life in the new land I entered as a young war refugee — who, in fact, nearly dragged me onto the path that would bring all the blessings I've received in America — was a salty-tongued, no-nonsense schoolteacher named Marjorie Hurd. When I entered her classroom in 1953, I had been to six schools in five years, starting in the Greek village where I was born in 1939.

When I stepped off a ship in New York Harbor on a gray March day in 1949, I was an undersized 9-year-old in short pants who had lost his mother and was coming to live with the father he didn't know. My mother, Eleni Gatzoyiannis, had been imprisoned, tortured and shot by Communist guerrillas for sending me and three of my four sisters to freedom. She died so that her children could go to their father in the United States.

The portly, bald, well-dressed man who met me and my sisters seemed a foreign, authoritarian figure. I secretly resented him for not getting the whole family out of Greece early enough to save my mother. Ultimately, I would grow to love him and appreciate how he dealt with becoming a single parent at the age of 56, but at first our relationship was prickly, full of hostility.

As Father drove us to our new home — a tenement in Worcester, Mass. — and pointed out the huge brick building that would be our first school in America, I clutched my Greek notebooks from the refugee camp, hoping that my few years of schooling would impress my teachers in this cold, crowded country. They didn't. When my father led me and my 11-year-old sister to Greendale Elementary School, the grim-faced Yankee principal put the two of us in a class for the mentally retarded. There was no facility in those days for non-English-speaking children.

By the time I met Marjorie Hurd four years later, I had learned English, been placed in a normal, graded class and had even been chosen for the college preparatory track in the Worcester public school system. I was 13 years old when our father moved us yet again, and I entered Chandler Junior High shortly after the beginning of seventh grade. I found myself surrounded by richer, smarter and better-dressed classmates who looked askance at my strange clothes and heavy accent. Shortly after I arrived, we were told to select a hobby to pursue during "club hour" on Fridays. The idea of hobbies and clubs made no sense to my immigrant ears, but I decided to follow the prettiest girl in my class — the blue-eyed daughter of the local Lutheran minister. She led me through the door marked "Newspaper Club" and into the presence of Miss Hurd, the newspaper adviser and English teacher who would become my mentor and my muse.

A formidable, solidly built woman with salt-and-pepper hair, a steely eye and a flat Boston accent, Miss Hurd had no patience with layabouts. "What are all you goof-offs doing here?" she bellowed at the would-be journalists. "This is the Newspaper Club! We're going to put out a *newspaper*. So if there's anybody in this room who doesn't like work, I suggest you go across to the Glee Club now, because you're going to work your tails off here!"

I was soon under Miss Hurd's spell. She did indeed teach us to put out a newspaper, skills I honed during my next 25 years as a journalist. Soon I asked the principal to transfer me to her English class as well. There, she drilled us on grammar until I finally began to understand the logic and structure of the English language. She assigned stories for us to read and discuss; not tales of heroes, like the Greek myths I knew, but stories of underdogs — poor people, even immigrants, who seemed ordinary until a crisis drove them to do something extraordinary. She also introduced us to the literary wealth of Greece — giving me a new perspective on my war-ravaged, impoverished homeland. I began to be proud of my origins.

One day, after discussing how writers should write about what they know, she assigned us to compose an essay from our own experience. Fixing me with a stern look, she added, "Nick, I want you to write about what happened to your family in Greece." I had been trying to put those painful memories behind me and left the assignment until the last moment. Then, on a warm spring afternoon, I sat in my room with a yellow pad and pencil and stared out the window at the buds on the trees. I wrote that the coming of spring always reminded me of the last time I said goodbye to my mother on a green and gold day in 1948.

I kept writing, one line after another, telling how the Communist guerrillas occupied our village, took our home and food, how my mother started planning our escape when she learned that the children were to be sent to re-education camps behind the Iron Curtain and how, at the last moment, she couldn't escape with us because the guerrillas sent her with a group of women to thresh wheat in a distant village. She promised she would try to get away on her own, she told me to be brave and hung a silver cross around my neck, and then she kissed me. I watched the line of women being led down into the ravine and up the other side, until they disappeared around the bend — my mother a tiny brown figure at the end who stopped for an instant to raise her hand in one last farewell.

I wrote about our nighttime escape down the mountain, across the 10 minefields and into the lines of the Nationalist soldiers, who sent us to a refugee camp. It was there that we learned of our mother's execution. I felt very lucky to have come to America, I concluded, but every year, the coming of spring made me feel sad because it reminded me of the last time I saw my mother.

I handed in the essay, hoping never to see it again, but Miss Hurd had it published in the school paper. This mortified me at first, until I saw that my classmates reacted with sympathy and tact to my family's story. Without telling me, Miss Hurd also submitted the essay to a contest sponsored by the Freedoms Foundation at Valley Forge, Pa., and it won a medal. The Worcester paper wrote about the award and quoted my essay at length. My father, by then a "five-and-dime-store chef," as the paper described him, was ecstatic with pride, and the Worcester Greek community celebrated the honor to one of its own.

For the first time I began to understand the power of the written word. A secret ambition took root in me. One day, I vowed, I would go back to Greece, find out the details of my mother's death and write about her life, so her grandchildren would know of her courage. Perhaps I would even track down the men who killed her and write of their crimes. Fulfilling that ambition would take me 30 years.

Meanwhile, I followed the literary path that Miss Hurd had so forcefully set me on. After junior high, I became the editor of my school paper at Classical High School and got a part-time job at the Worcester *Telegram and Gazette*. Although my father could only give me $50 and encouragement toward a college education, I managed to finance four years at Boston University with scholarships and part-time jobs in journalism. During my last year of college, an article I wrote about a friend who had died in the Philippines — the first person to lose his life working for the Peace Corps — led to my winning the Hearst Award for College Journalism. And the plaque was given to me in the White House by President John F. Kennedy.

For a refugee who had never seen a motorized vehicle or indoor plumbing until he was 9, this was an unimaginable honor. When the Worcester paper ran a picture of me standing next to President Kennedy, my father rushed out to buy a new suit in order to be properly dressed to receive the congratulations of the Worcester Greeks. He clipped out the photograph, had it laminated in plastic and carried it in his breast pocket for the rest of his life to show everyone he met. I found the much-worn photo in his pocket on the day he died 20 years later.

In our isolated Greek village, my mother had bribed a cousin to teach   15
her to read, for girls were not supposed to attend school beyond a certain age. She had always dreamed of her children receiving an education. She couldn't be there when I graduated from Boston University, but the person who came with my father and shared our joy was my former teacher, Marjorie Hurd. We celebrated not only my bachelor's degree but also the scholarships that paid my way to Columbia's Graduate School of Journalism. There, I met the woman who would eventually become my wife. At our wedding and at the baptisms of our three children, Marjorie Hurd was always there, dancing alongside the Greeks.

By then, she was Mrs. Rabidou, for she had married a widower when she was in her early 40s. That didn't distract her from her vocation of introducing young minds to English literature, however. She taught for a total of 41 years and continually would make a "project" of some balky student in whom she spied a spark of potential. Often these were students from the most troubled homes, yet she would alternately bully and charm each one with her own special brand of tough love until the spark caught fire. She retired in 1981 at the age of 62 but still avidly follows the lives and careers of former students while overseeing her adult stepchildren and driving her husband on camping trips to New Hampshire.

Miss Hurd was one of the first to call me on Dec. 10, 1987, when President Reagan, in his television address after the summit meeting with Gorbachev, told the nation that Eleni Gatzoyiannis' dying cry, "My children!" had helped inspire him to seek an arms agreement "for all the children of the world."

"I can't imagine a better monument for your mother," Miss Hurd said with an uncharacteristic catch in her voice.

Although a bad hip makes it impossible for her to join in the Greek dancing, Marjorie Hurd Rabidou is still an honored and enthusiastic guest at all family celebrations, including my 50th birthday picnic last summer, where the shish kebab was cooked on spits, clarinets and *bouzoukis* wailed, and costumed dancers led the guests in a serpentine line around our Colonial farmhouse, only 20 minutes from my first home in Worcester.

My sisters and I felt an aching void because my father was not there to   20
lead the line, balancing a glass of wine on his head while he danced, the way he did at every celebration during his 92 years. But Miss Hurd was there,

surveying the scene with quiet satisfaction. Although my parents are gone, her presence was a consolation, because I owe her so much.

This is truly the land of opportunity, and I would have enjoyed its bounty even if I hadn't walked into Miss Hurd's classroom in 1953. But she was the one who directed my grief and pain into writing, and if it weren't for her I wouldn't have become an investigative reporter and foreign correspondent, recorded the story of my mother's life and death in *Eleni* and now my father's story in *A Place for Us,* which is also a testament to the country that took us in. She was the catalyst that sent me into journalism and indirectly caused all the good things that came after. But Miss Hurd would probably deny this emphatically.

A few years ago, I answered the telephone and heard my former teacher's voice telling me, in that won't-take-no-for-an-answer tone of hers, that she had decided I was to write and deliver the eulogy at her funeral. I agreed (she didn't leave me any choice), but that's one assignment I never want to do. I hope, Miss Hurd, that you'll accept this remembrance instead.

Suggestions for Writing and Discussion

1. Right from the start, Gage attributes his success in America to his seventh-grade English teacher. After reading this piece, what other factors do you see that may have contributed to Gage's success in writing?

2. Miss Hurd opens up a new world for Gage, and at the same time she makes him proud of his origins. Think back to your own school days. Did you ever have a teacher who made you feel proud? Describe this teacher as well as you can, and describe the incidents that encouraged your pride.

3. What do you think about Miss Hurd's advice — to compose an essay based on one's own experience? Do you think this type of assignment might be particularly effective for seventh graders, or do you think it would be very difficult for most of them? Explain.

4. Gage writes poignantly about how the spring makes him remember the last time he saw his mother. Do you, too, associate a particular season with a powerful memory (either sad or joyful)? If so, write about the season. Describe specifically what you see, hear, and smell that triggers thoughts of the past.

5. Miss Hurd succeeded in finding the potential in her students. Have you ever had a teacher who sparked your potential? If so, describe this person and explain what talent or ability this person helped you to develop. Explain the process as well as the effects of discovering this ability.

6. Gage describes Miss Hurd as a catalyst in his life. What does he mean by this metaphor? List other metaphors to describe the good teachers in your own life. Then explain why you chose these metaphors.

Suggestions for Extended Thinking and Research

1. When Gage's piece was published, he realized how powerful language can be. Consider trying to publish something yourself. Start off writing about something that deeply concerns you — perhaps an issue in your school or community. Rewrite this piece as a letter to the editor and send it out to your local or school newspaper.

2. Gage recounts how he and his sister were initially put into a room with mentally retarded students because the school had no English-as-a-second-language program. Research how non-English-speaking children are ac-climated into the schools today. (You might want to read the selections in this text on bilingual education by Angelo Gonzalez and Richard Rodri-guez.) What programs are offered? How successful do you believe these programs are?

3. Write a letter thanking a "teacher" (either in or out of the school system) who has done something special for you. Explain the difference that he or she has made in your life. Consider tracking down this person's address so that you can send the letter and thus make it more than an assignment for a class.

GRACE PALEY

The Loudest Voice

> *Born into a family of socialist Russian Jews in 1922, Grace Paley spent hours listening to the tales of her parents, uncles, and aunts. These stories, told alternately in Russian, English, and Yiddish, inspired Paley, as she explained in an interview with* Shenandoah *magazine (1981). When she first began writing, she found herself too focused on "me — me — me." To get beyond this point, she started listening carefully to "other people's voices" and integrating them into her work by "writing with an accent." In "The Loudest Voice," she offers a fictional picture of a young Jewish girl who learns to listen to the voices around her and to value them all, yet to recognize that her own voice is especially important.*

Prereading/Journal-Writing Suggestions

1. What is one ability that makes you feel proud of yourself — something you can do better than most others?
2. If you could play a starring role in any play or film you've seen, which would you choose? Explain.

There is a certain place where dumbwaiters boom, doors slam, dishes crash; every window is a mother's mouth bidding the street shut up, go skate somewhere else, come home. My voice is the loudest.

There, my own mother is still as full of breathing as me and the grocer stands up to speak to her. "Mrs. Abramowitz," he says, "people should not be afraid of their children."

"Ah, Mr. Bialik," my mother replies, "if you say to her or her father 'Ssh,' they say, 'In the grave it will be quiet.'"

"From Coney Island to the cemetery," says my papa. "It's the same subway; it's the same fare."

I am right next to the pickle barrel. My pinky is making tiny whirlpools 5 in the brine. I stop a moment to announce: "Campbell's Tomato Soup. Campbell's Vegetable Beef Soup. Campbell's S-c-otch Broth . . ."

"Be quiet," the grocer says, "the labels are coming off."

"Please, Shirley, be a little quiet," my mother begs me.

In that place the whole street groans: Be quiet! Be quiet! but steals from the happy chorus of my inside self not a tittle or a jot.

There, too, but just around the corner, is a red brick building that has been old for many years. Every morning the children stand before it in double lines which must be straight. They are not insulted. They are waiting anyway.

I am usually among them. I am, in fact, the first, since I begin with "A." 10

One cold morning the monitor tapped me on the shoulder. "Go to Room

409, Shirley Abramowitz," he said. I did as I was told. I went in a hurry up a down staircase to Room 409, which contained sixth-graders. I had to wait at the desk without wiggling until Mr. Hilton, their teacher, had time to speak.

After five minutes he said, "Shirley?"

"What?" I whispered.

He said, "My! My! Shirley Abramowitz! They told me you had a particularly loud, clear voice and read with lots of expression. Could that be true?"

"Oh, yes," I whispered.

"In that case, don't be silly; I might very well be your teacher someday. 15 Speak up, speak up."

"Yes," I shouted.

"More like it," he said. "Now, Shirley, can you put a ribbon in your hair or a bobby pin? It's too messy."

"Yes!" I bawled.

"Now, now, calm down." He turned to the class. "Children, not a 20 sound. Open at page 39. Read till 52. When you finish, start again." He looked me over once more. "Now, Shirley, you know, I suppose, that Christmas is coming. We are preparing a beautiful play. Most of the parts have been given out. But I still need a child with a strong voice, lots of stamina. Do you know what stamina is? You do? Smart kid. You know, I heard you read 'The Lord is my shepherd' in Assembly yesterday. I was very impressed. Wonderful delivery. Mrs. Jordan, your teacher, speaks highly of you. Now listen to me, Shirley Abramowitz, if you want to take the part and be in the play, repeat after me, 'I swear to work harder than I ever did before.'"

I looked to heaven and said at once, "Oh, I swear." I kissed my pinky and looked at God.

"That is an actor's life, my dear," he explained. "Like a soldier's, never tardy or disobedient to his general, the director. Everything," he said, "absolutely everything will depend on you."

That afternoon, all over the building, children scraped and scrubbed the turkeys and the sheaves of corn off the schoolroom windows. Goodbye Thanksgiving. The next morning a monitor brought red paper and green paper from the office. We made new shapes and hung them on the walls and glued them to the doors.

The teachers became happier and happier. Their heads were ringing like the bells of childhood. My best friend Evie was prone to evil, but she did not get a single demerit for whispering. We learned "Holy Night" without an error. "How wonderful!" said Miss Glacé, the student teacher. "To think that some of you don't even speak the language!" We learned "Deck the Halls" and "Hark! The Herald Angels." . . . They weren't ashamed and we weren't embarrassed.

Oh, but when my mother heard about it all, she said to my father: "Misha, you don't know what's going on there. Cramer is the head of the Tickets Committee."

"Who?" asked my father. "Cramer? Oh yes, an active woman."

"Active? Active has to have a reason. Listen," she said sadly, "I'm surprised to see my neighbors making tra-la-la for Christmas."

My father couldn't think of what to say to that. Then he decided: "You're in America! Clara, you wanted to come here. In Palestine the Arabs would be eating you alive. Europe you had pogroms. Argentina is full of Indians. Here you got Christmas. . . . Some joke, ha?"

"Very funny, Misha. What is becoming of you? If we came to a new country a long time ago to run away from tyrants, and instead we fall into a creeping pogrom, that our children learn a lot of lies, so what's the joke? Ach, Misha, your idealism is going away."

"So is your sense of humor."   30

"That I never had, but idealism you had a lot of."

"I'm the same Misha Abramovitch, I didn't change an iota. Ask anyone."

"Only ask me," says my mama, may she rest in peace. "I got the answer."

Meanwhile the neighbors had to think of what to say too.

Marty's father said: "You know, he has a very important part, my boy." 35

"Mine also," said Mr. Sauerfeld.

"Not my boy!" said Mrs. Klieg. "I said to him no. The answer is no. When I say no! I mean no!"

The rabbi's wife said, "It's disgusting!" But no one listened to her. Under the narrow sky of God's great wisdom she wore a strawberry-blond wig.

Every day was noisy and full of experience. I was Right-hand Man. Mr. Hilton said: "How could I get along without you, Shirley?"

He said: "Your mother and father ought to get down on their knees 40 every night and thank God for giving them a child like you."

He also said: "You're absolutely a pleasure to work with, my dear, dear child."

Sometimes he said: "For God's sakes, what did I do with the script? Shirley! Shirley! Find it."

Then I answered quietly: "Here it is, Mr. Hilton."

Once in a while, when he was very tired, he would cry out: "Shirley, I'm just tired of screaming at those kids. Will you tell Ira Pushkov not to come in till Lester points to that star the second time?"

Then I roared: "Ira Pushkov, what's the matter with you? Dope! Mr. 45 Hilton told you five times already, don't come in till Lester points to that star the second time."

"Ach, Clara," my father asked, "what does she do there till six o'clock she can't even put the plates on the table?"

"Christmas," said my mother coldly.

"Ho! Ho!" my father said. "Christmas. What's the harm? After all, history teaches everyone. We learn from reading this is a holiday from pagan times also, candles, lights, even Chanukah. So we learn it's not altogether

Christian. So if they think it's a private holiday, they're only ignorant, not patriotic. What belongs to history, belongs to all men. You want to go back to the Middle Ages? Is it better to shave your head with a secondhand razor? Does it hurt Shirley to learn to speak up? It does not. So maybe someday she won't live between the kitchen and the shop. She's not a fool."

I thank you, Papa, for your kindness. It is true about me to this day. I am foolish but I am not a fool.

That night my father kissed me and said with great interest in my career, 50 "Shirley, tomorrow's your big day. Congrats."

"Save it," my mother said. Then she shut all the windows in order to prevent tonsillitis.

In the morning it snowed. On the street corner a tree had been decorated for us by a kind city administration. In order to miss its chilly shadow our neighbors walked three blocks east to buy a loaf of bread. The butcher pulled down black window shades to keep the colored lights from shining on his chickens. Oh, not me. On the way to school, with both my hands I tossed it a kiss of tolerance. Poor thing, it was a stranger in Egypt.

I walked straight into the auditorium past the staring children. "Go ahead, Shirley!" said the monitors. Four boys, big for their age, had already started work as propmen and stagehands.

Mr. Hilton was very nervous. He was not even happy. Whatever he started to say ended in a sideward look of sadness. He sat slumped in the middle of the first row and asked me to help Miss Glacé. I did this, although she thought my voice too resonant and said, "Show-off!"

Parents began to arrive long before we were ready. They wanted to 55 make a good impression. From among the yards of drapes I peeked out at the audience. I saw my embarrassed mother.

Ira, Lester, and Meyer were pasted to their beards by Miss Glacé. She almost forgot to thread the star on its wire, but I reminded her. I coughed a few times to clear my throat. Miss Glacé looked around and saw that everyone was in costume and on line waiting to play his part. She whispered, "All right . . ." Then:

Jackie Sauerfeld, the prettiest boy in first grade, parted the curtains with his skinny elbow and in a high voice sang out:

"Parents dear
We are here
To make a Christmas play in time.
It we give
In narrative
And illustrate with pantomime."

He disappeared.

My voice burst immediately from the wings to the great shock of Ira, Lester, and Meyer, who were waiting for it but were surprised all the same.

"I remember, I remember, the house where I was born . . ." 60

Miss Glacé yanked the curtain open and there it was, the house — an old hayloft, where Celia Kornbluh lay in the straw with Cindy Lou, her favorite doll. Ira, Lester, and Meyer moved slowly from the wings toward her, sometimes pointing to a moving star and sometimes ahead to Cindy Lou.

It was a long story and it was a sad story. I carefully pronounced all the words about my lonesome childhood, while little Eddie Braunstein wandered upstage and down with his shepherd's stick, looking for sheep. I brought up lonesomeness again, and not being understood at all except by some women everybody hated. Eddie was too small for that and Marty Groff took his place, wearing his father's prayer shawl. I announced twelve friends, and half the boys in the fourth grade gathered round Marty, who stood on an orange crate while my voice harangued. Sorrowful and loud, I declaimed about love and God and Man, but because of the terrible deceit of Abie Stock we came suddenly to a famous moment. Marty, whose remembering tongue I was, waited at the foot of the cross. He stared desperately at the audience. I groaned, "My God, my God, why hast thou forsaken me?" The soldiers who were shieks grabbed poor Marty to pin him up to die, but he wrenched free, turned again to the audience, and spread his arms aloft to show despair and the end. I murmured at the top of my voice, "The rest is silence, but as everyone in this room, in this city — in this world — now knows, I shall have life eternal."

That night Mrs. Kornbluh visited our kitchen for a glass of tea.

"How's the virgin?" asked my father with a look of concern.

"For a man with a daughter, you got a fresh mouth, Abramovitch." 65

"Here," said my father kindly, "have some lemon, it'll sweeten your disposition."

They debated a little in Yiddish, then fell in a puddle of Russian and Polish. What I understood next was my father, who said, "Still and all, it was certainly a beautiful affair, you have to admit, introducing us to the beliefs of a different culture."

"Well, yes," said Mrs. Kornbluh. "The only thing . . . you know Charlie Turner — that cute boy in Celia's class — a couple others? They got very small parts or no part at all. In very bad taste, it seemed to me. After all, it's their religion."

"Ach," explained my mother, "what could Mr. Hilton do? They got very small voices; after all, why should they holler? The English language they know from the beginning by heart. They're blond like angels. You think it's so important they should get in the play? Christmas . . . the whole piece of goods . . . they own it."

I listened and listened until I couldn't listen any more. Too sleepy, I 70 climbed out of bed and kneeled. I made a little church of my hands and said, "Hear, O Israel . . ." Then I called out in Yiddish, "Please, good night, good night. Ssh." My father said, "Ssh yourself," and slammed the kitchen door.

I was happy. I fell asleep at once. I had prayed for everybody: my talking family, cousins far away, passersby, and all the lonesome Christians. I expected to be heard. My voice was certainly the loudest.

Suggestions for Writing and Discussion

1. What kind of a person is Shirley Abramowitz? If you were in sixth grade with her, do you think you two would be friends? Explain.
2. Shirley has a reputation for a "loud, clear voice." When you were in sixth grade, were you known for any outstanding characteristic?
3. Mr. Hilton tells Shirley that an actor's life is much like a soldier's: She cannot be late, and she must always listen to the general (the director). Create an analogy that explains what your life as a student is like. Develop and explain the comparison you make.
4. Although both are practicing Jews, Shirley's parents find themselves divided on the issue of letting her participate in the Christmas program. Describe each parent's reactions. Do you sympathize equally with each position, or do you find yourself favoring one or the other? Explain.
5. Only Mrs. Klieg won't allow her son to be in the Christmas play. In your opinion, when most parents are under pressure related to a controversial issue, do they give in so as to please their children? So as to please the school? Explain your answer.
6. What does the Christmas tree on the corner symbolize to the Jewish residents who live nearby?
7. Shirley's mother comes to the performance even though she is embarrassed and against her daughter's performing. Why then, does she come? What does her action say about her?
8. What point does Mrs. Kornbluh make when she expresses her concern with the children who got such small parts in the play? How does her view of the selection of the cast differ from Mr. Hilton's? What are his primary concerns as he casts the play?
9. Why, in the end, does Shirley see the Christians as "lonesome"? What is your response to this observation?

Suggestions for Extended Thinking and Research

1. This story is told from Shirley's point of view. Rewrite any episode in the story through the eyes of another character.
2. If you (or one of your children) were asked to take part in a religious celebration that was contrary to your own religious beliefs, would you do it? Would you allow your child to do it? Why or why not?
3. Research the holy days and special observances of several different religions. Write an essay discussing significant similarities and differences you discovered.

ANNA LEE WALTERS
A Teacher Taught Me

> *Anna Lee Walters was born in Oklahoma in 1946. A Pawnee/Otoe, she currently lives with the Navaho Nation and serves as an educational consultant and curriculum specialist at Navajo Community College. She has written many poems and short stories, which have been anthologized in such collections as* Voices of the Rainbow *(1975) and* The Remembered Earth *(1978). In "A Teacher Taught Me," Walters questions the lessons Native American children learned from their white teachers and classmates.*

Prereading/Journal-Writing Suggestions

1. What did your school books and teachers teach you about Native Americans? What impression did you get from these school sources?
2. Did someone ever defend you because you were different? Did you ever defend someone else who was singled out as different? Write about one of these experiences.

I

a teacher taught me
more than she knew
patting me on the head
putting words in my hand
— "pretty little *Indian* girl!"   5
saving them —
going to give them
back to her one day . . .
show them around too
cousins and friends   10
laugh and say — "aye"

II

binding by sincerity
hating that kindness
eight years' worth
third graders heard her   15
putting words in my hand
— "we should bow our heads
in shame for what we did
to the American Indian"
saving them —   20
going to give them

III

in jr. hi
a boy no color
transparent skin
except sprinkled freckles
followed me around   30
putting words in my hand
— "squaw, squaw, squaw"
(not that it mattered,
hell, man, I didn't know
what squaw meant . . .)   35
saving them —
going to give them
back to him one day . . .
show them around too
cousins and friends   40
laugh and say — "aye"

back to her one day . . .
show them around too
cousins and friends
laugh and say — "aye"   25

IV

slapping open handed
transparent boy
across freckled face
knocking glasses down   45
he finally sees
recollect a red
handprint over minutes
faded from others
he wears it still   50
putting words in my hand
— "sorry, so sorry"
saving them —
going to give them
back to him one day   55
show them around too
cousins and friends
laugh and say — "aye"

Suggestions for Writing and Discussion

1. What did the teacher teach the student in this poem?
2. What's the difference between putting "words in a head" and putting "words in a hand"?
3. Why does the student say that she saves the words? What does she mean by this?

Suggestions for Extended Thinking and Research

1. Read several accounts of how Native American children were taught before white people came to this country. What were the lessons they learned? How does their education differ from the education obtained through schools? What do you see as the benefits and drawbacks of such education?

2. Read several sources describing the history of the education of Native American children by the United States government. Then write an essay explaining the strengths and weaknesses you see in the ways they have been taught.

TOPICS FOR MAKING CONNECTIONS: WAYS OF LEARNING

1. Use at least four sources from this section and, in addition, consider your own educational experiences as you plan and write an essay on this question: What are the most important factors to consider when planning a child's education?
2. Write an essay proposing a utopian grade school. Base your description on your personal educational philosophies and experiences; in addition, refer to the selections in this section.
3. Referring to at least four selections, define what it means to be an educated person.
4. Write an essay exploring two alternatives to public schooling: private schools and home schooling. Refer to selections in this section, and do additional research as you plan and write this paper.
5. Compare and contrast the learning experiences of at least three people whose stories appear in this section. Come to some conclusions about why and how these individuals learn or fail to learn.
6. Write an essay agreeing or disagreeing with the following statement: The trouble with education in the United States today is that it is a guaranteed right, whether or not a student wants to learn. To be effective, education must be a privilege, not a right.
7. Who is ultimately responsible for a child's education? The parents? The schools? Individual teachers? The community? The child? Referring to at least four of the selections in this section, write an essay exploring the responsibilities of all these parties. As a conclusion, discuss who you see as most responsible.
8. Compare the approaches of four different teachers (not necessarily from school settings) described in this section. Use these teachers as examples to develop your definition of the ideal teacher.

3

Writing to Explain

Selections in Section 2 tell stories and offer descriptions that re-create for the reader people, events, and emotions important to the writers' lives. A primary aim of these selections is to show readers pictures of places, times, and experiences they could otherwise never know or appreciate. In Section 3, many of the selections also incorporate description and stories; but rather than seeking mainly to express personal thoughts and feelings, these pieces share a different common aim: They explain ideas, processes, or concepts. For example, in the first thematic section, "Roots and Memories," Toni Morrison's "Site of Memory" analyzes the role of childhood experiences in the development of her creative writing. Charlene Spretnak in "Ecofeminism: Our Roots and Flowering" develops a complex analogy to explore questions related to the relationship between modern society and nature. Adrienne Rich compares the two sides of her heritage — Protestant and Jewish — to trace her search for identity. Mark Mathabane and Jay Ford explain the processes they followed as they sought the significance of their African roots. In "Rootlessness," David Morris evaluates the problems caused by lack of what he calls "neighborliness" in modern American society and suggests possible ways to solve these problems.

Selections that represent the second theme, "American Dreams and Creations," explain creative impulses that are unique to the United States. In "Elvis, Thailand, and I," Nitaya Kanchanawan analyzes the impact of Elvis Presley and his music on her native Thai society. William Zinsser explores and evaluates the responses of students at a Chinese conservatory as they listen to two American performers introduce a classic American art form — jazz improvisation. In "Black Music in Our Hands," Bernice Reagon traces the changes in her own perception of black music and explains how her definition of this music has become increasingly broad and complex. "Halo of the Sun" by Noël Bennett defines the author's process as she learns the significance of both skill and tradition in the art of Navaho weaving. Michael Dorris's "Indians in Aspic" offers an analysis of the way Native Americans are portrayed by recent Hollywood films. Jim Sagel explains the obstacles faced and overcome by Sandra Cisneros, an American with Hispanic roots, in her quest to become a writer. In "Quilts and Women's Culture," Elaine Hedges begins by observing, "Women's needlework has been a universal form of activity, uniting women of different classes, races, and nations," and she goes on to delineate both the positive and negative implications of this shared activity.

The final theme in this section, "Men and Women," offers selections that address gender-related issues in various cultural contexts. Paula Gunn Allen explains the roles of men and women in the Native American communities where she grew up and where she now lives. In "Between a Rock and a Soft Place," Peter Filene traces the changing image of manhood in America during the past hundred years, and Alexis de Toqueville's essay offers an explanation of how Americans view equality between the sexes. Brent Staples describes the public perception of black men and analyzes the effects of that perception. Taking another tack, Alice Walker outlines the historic relationship between white men and black women as a way of exploring the question of abortion.

READING AND UNDERSTANDING
WRITING THAT EXPLAINS

Writing that explains takes many different forms, but all forms share the broad purpose of seeking to convey new information to readers. Writers explain by using a variety of approaches; so as you begin to read an essay, article, or book that explains, you may find it helpful to identify the writer's approach. Although these approaches cannot be neatly labeled and are rarely used in isolation, it's helpful to understand some of the ways writers choose to convey new ideas or to offer new ways of looking at familiar ideas.

1. *Informing*. When writers seek to inform, they usually are concerned mainly with providing facts: giving readers access to details, statistics, anecdotes, and so on, with which they were previously unacquainted. An essay that is strictly informative almost always takes an objective stance. That is, the writer does not offer an opinion about the information provided. Rather, the author provides the data, usually ends with a brief summary, and leaves the reader to draw conclusions or to discover the implications of the new information. Articles in scientific journals are often written primarily to inform. On a more mundane level, a set of directions telling someone how to get to a previously unvisited location is also an example of informative writing.

   More common than the strictly informative essay, however, is writing that offers information but, in addition, uses that information for another purpose — for example, *defining, analyzing, synthesizing, or evaluating.*

2. *Defining.* A writer who contemplates a complex concept may explain ideas about that concept by developing a detailed, extended definition. Obviously, such an essay goes far beyond the brief notations given in dictionaries. Rather than providing the short — and often simplistic — definitions found in reference books, selections that explain through defining explore complexities and ambiguities, offering examples and details that help the reader see the richness of the subject being discussed.

   In Section 3, selections that provide extended definitions include Charlene Spretnak's look at ecofeminism (pp. 228–238), Bernice Reagon's thoughtful consideration of her own changing and developing views of black music (pp. 306–310), and Alexis de Toqueville's exploration of the American definition of equality of the sexes (pp. 376–380).

3. *Analyzing.* Analysis means looking at the parts to see how they work together to create the whole. To write an analysis, a writer looks closely at the aspects and qualities that comprise a place, a person, an idea, an emotion, or, perhaps, a work of literature or an object of art. Then, focusing on those aspects or qualities that seem most significant, the writer explains what he or she has discovered. Note particularly that the purpose of analysis is not simply to see the components of a whole but, rather, to see the significance of those components in relationship with each other.

   A practical example of analysis is the process most of us go through when we are trying to fix something that isn't working as it should. Consider, for example, a photocopier that refuses to make clean, clear copies. To solve the problem, we would probably consult the "Owner's Guide." After identifying the components of the copier, we would recognize that the paper tray, the power plug, and the front cover could not be sources of the problem; but we'd certainly want to check the glass, the chargers, and the toner box. We'd consider how these parts should be working together to produce a readable copy. And if our analysis is successful, we'd learn what needs to be done to get the machine functioning smoothly once again.

   A writer who makes an analysis may look at a complicated principle, at a common assumption, at a geographic phenomenon, at a distinguished and unusual person's life. By looking at the parts that make up any of these (or many other) subjects, the writer discovers new and significant ideas and possibilities, which she or he then explains to the reader. Examples of selections in Section 3 that analyze include "The Site of Memory" by Toni Morrison (pp. 223–227),

"Elvis, Thailand, and I" by Nitaya Kanchanawan (pp. 287–292), "Indians in Aspic" by Michael Dorris (pp. 321–324), and "Where I Come From Is Like This" by Paula Gunn Allen (pp. 351–358).

4. *Synthesizing.* The ability to synthesize information, ideas, and observations is essential for anyone truly interested in learning and growing. This process is particularly important for thinking, reading, and writing across cultures; because when you synthesize, you look for connections, disjunctions, differences, and similarities. More important, you look for the significance of the comparisons and contrasts you have observed. Writers who explain through synthesis work to see relationships among apparently different people, places, ideas, concepts, or emotions.

   We all use the process of synthesis when we meet a new person who will be significant in our lives (co-worker, roommate, supervisor, in-law). Of course, we observe differences between ourselves and these people as we strive to discover how we'll address those differences. However, we also look for similarities and for ways to make connections with those who are important to us.

   Several selections in Section 3 provide examples of writers who explain their ideas through making syntheses. Adrienne Rich strives to see the relationships between her Jewish heritage and her Protestant heritage in "Split at the Root" (pp. 239–249). William Zinsser in "Shanghai Blues" (pp. 293–305) weaves together the creative impulses behind traditional Chinese music and those behind American jazz improvisation. In "The Right to Life" (pp. 386–390), Alice Walker observes mainly disjunctions and contrasts yet explains her ideas by synthesizing the past experiences of black women with the present challenges and obstacles faced by those same women.

5. *Evaluating.* When writers evaluate, they provide readers with information about a particular person, place, idea, action, or theory. Then they go on to define or imply criteria for judging this subject and to apply those criteria. Making an evaluation requires the writer to form an opinion about the subject and to provide evidence to convince the reader that this opinion deserves attention. An evaluation may be as straightforward as formulating a judgment of a book or film. For example, when we recommend a particular movie to a friend and then offer reasons why we think this movie is worthwhile, we are making and expressing an evaluation.

   A more complex, yet equally common, way of evaluating is for a writer to define a problem and then explain what he or she sees as the significant causes or effects of that problem. An evaluation of a problem may also include suggestions for solving the problem. Selections in Section 3 that provide evaluations include "Rootlessness" by David Morris (pp. 265–269), "Quilts and Women's Culture" by Elaine Hedges (pp. 331–336), and "Just Walk on By" by Brent Staples (pp. 381–385).

WRITING TO EXPLAIN

As you read the selections in this section, you'll almost certainly notice that many of your own writing tasks require explanation of one kind or another. For example, professors may ask you to write a review or critique of an article, essay, book, or chapter in a book. Such an assignment calls for evaluation. Also, many essay exams require you to compare or contrast various aspects of the course's subject. The exam may not directly state that you are to give the significance you see in these similarities and differences. But you are usually expected to synthesize the information you have gathered, providing a useful conclusion rather than merely a list of things that are alike and things that are not alike. As another example, a history instructor may assign a paper on the causes and effects of the French Revolution or the Great Depression, a writing task that can be accomplished through analysis. Or a philosophy course may focus on a semester-long exploration of a concept such as truth or love that leads to a paper defining the complexities of one of these terms.

To write papers that explain requires developing a process that allows you to explore ideas, gather data effectively, and formulate a clear *thesis* (central idea) that will serve as your focus. Whatever approach you take to explaining — informing, defining, analyzing, synthesizing, or evaluating — you need to keep in mind that your primary purpose is to convey new information or a new way of thinking to your reader. To convince readers that this new information or new way of thinking is worthy of their attention and consideration, you need to provide details, reasons, and examples that will show — not just tell — them what you want them to think about. Remember, also, that when you write to explain, you rarely use one approach exclusively. For instance, a paper that analyzes may also include an extended definition of an important term. An essay that synthesizes two apparently different ideas may also evaluate the significance the writer sees in newly discovered similarities between these two ideas.

Exercise

Write a short commentary (perhaps a journal entry) reflecting on an exam or paper you have written for another class and explaining how you used any of the approaches just discussed. In addition, suggest any revisions you would make to the exam or paper after thinking about the various strategies for writing to explain.

SAMPLE ESSAY: WRITING TO EXPLAIN

As an example of an essay that explains, we will consider Harue Hashimoto's process as she responded to the following assignment.

After reading Adrienne Rich's "Split at the Root," write an essay that explains a contradiction you see in your own life or in the life of someone you know well. As you write, keep in mind that your writing should lead the reader to see the significance you give to this contradiction.

Before you read Harue's response to this assignment, you may want to read "Split at the Root" (pp. 239–249).

Exploring Ideas: Freewriting and Outlining

After reading Rich's essay several times, making notes in the margins, and participating in a discussion of the essay, Harue — along with her fellow students — spent the final ten minutes of class doing a *freewriting* in response to one of the topics the instructor suggested. Freewriting is a process that encourages writers to explore the far corners of their minds by writing without stopping (usually for a given period of time). This process can help writers get past a "blocked" feeling and can lead to finding new ideas and approaches at any stage in the writing process. For instance, as you begin a writing project, you might use freewriting to discover or narrow a topic; later, you may again freewrite to find details and examples that will successfully develop a weak or thin section of a draft.

Sometimes, freewriting begins with whatever thought first pops into the writer's mind; sometimes, it begins with a question, observation, or assignment. When the writer has a specific topic or assignment in mind, this strategy is called *focused freewriting*. Here's part of the focused freewriting Harue worked on as she began thinking about her topic.

> So — write about contradiction and do not stop — do not stop — contradict contradict mother says "do not contradict" — father just silent — mother and father I do not understand why mother and father get along — big gap — father simple old Japanese character — shy, vague, conservative — thinks about World War II — "demons" — people who spoke English — mother modern/open-minded — liberal ideas/wanted to study in U.S. Mother wanted English for us — problem with Japanese school system — severe strict — my mother's teaching — feel like a race horse — just being trained to run a race and win for owner — mother-as-owner/but father, too? He wanted the other side — traditional culture/ calligraphy/flower arrangement/tea ceremony — confusion — confusion — where am I going here? — keep writing — keep writing — confusion — confusion with English — loved English — radio — American songs — language like rhythmical music — problem with grades/not as good as my older sister — turned away from mother's dream to live through the daughters — father delights to teach Japanese culture/to encourage Japanese womanhood — still no answer — what about these two parts????

As Harue looked at the freewriting, she saw a contradiction between her father's and mother's goals for their own lives. She saw additional and related contradictions between their hopes for their children's lives. Since she was asked to explain the significance she saw in this contradiction, Harue decided to write an informal outline to delineate her mother's values and her father's values.

An informal outline, which a writer uses to think out ideas, does not require roman numerals, capital letters, and so on, as does a formal outline, which would be submitted to an instructor, an editor, or a supervisor at work. Instead, most people who use outlining during the early, discovery stages of writing simply number their ideas as a way of organizing them. Here's the informal outline Harue wrote.

Father

1. Shy — values quiet contemplation
2. Conservative — does not like change
3. Speaks only Japanese — very patriotic
4. Thinks daughters (and all girls) should learn Japanese arts — takes traditional approach
5. Goal for daughters: to follow traditional roles of Japanese women — wives, mothers

Mother

1. Outgoing — values communication, talking to others
2. Wanted to study in the U.S. — ambitious
3. Challenges old way of doing things — became a teacher (not a mother who stays at home)
4. Speaks English as well as Japanese (teaches English)
5. Thinks daughters (and all girls) should have a chance to be completely educated (same subjects as boys)
6. Goals for daughters: to be competitive, to learn English perfectly (sister better than I am), to study in the U.S.

Conclusions

1. First tried to please mother
2. Then felt like failure in languages
3. Next tried to please father
4. Now trying to find my own way

Planning and Writing a Draft

After making these outlines, Harue was still not sure what her thesis (main idea) would be. But she knew that her aim (her purpose for writing) would be to explain the contradictions and conflicts she saw between her

mother's values and her father's values. She decided to write a *discovery draft*—
a draft that would explore the ideas she wanted to explain even though those
ideas were not yet clearly focused or fully organized.

As she wrote, she knew she needed to keep in mind her *audience*—those
who would read her essay. Of course, her instructor was part of the audience.
In addition, she would be working in class with other students as peer editors,
so she knew she had to consider them, too. As she thought about audience,
Harue used the following suggestions provided by her instructor.

Suggestions for Thinking about Audience

1. *Keep in mind how much your audience knows about your subject.* What
   information, explanations, and definitions do you need to provide?
   On the one hand, you do not want to insult readers by telling them
   things that they already know. On the other hand, you do not want
   them to be puzzled because your subject matter or approach is entirely unfamiliar.

2. *Keep in mind your readers' values.* You determine readers' values in
   many different ways. Sometimes, you will have talked with your
   readers, and they will have told you that, for instance, they consider
   getting an education absolutely essential or, conversely, that they
   believe practical experience to be more important than the theories
   learned in formal schooling. Sometimes, you can guess at readers'
   values if you know, say, their political affiliations or their religious
   beliefs (or rebellion against certain religious beliefs). While it's dangerous to make generalizations without recognizing exceptions, you
   can guess that a group whose motto is "Save the Whales" will hold
   considerably different values than a group who sums up their philosophy with the phrase "Save Jobs, Not Owls." If you were writing a
   paper on environmental issues, knowing that most of your readers
   belonged to one or the other of these groups would most certainly
   affect the way you approach your topic.

   If the values you are explaining are significantly different from
   those of your readers, consider how you will approach your discussion. You do not want your audience to become alienated immediately or to dismiss your ideas as irrelevant because they are looking
   at only a difference. You want them to see the significance of that
   difference—or the possible connections with their own values.

3. *Keep in mind that your audience will probably not be made up entirely of a
   single, easily definable group.* Occasionally, you may write for readers
   who have very nearly the same level of knowledge about your subject
   and who hold similar values relating to your subject. More often,
   however, you'll be writing for people who are alike in some ways,
   but are dramatically different in others. For instance, within an introductory writing class, there will often be students whose ages,

ethnic background, work experience, and previous education vary widely. When you are writing to such a mixed audience, you have to decide how to meet the needs of as many readers as possible without making your paper a mishmash that fails to communicate clearly because it is trying to be all things to all people.

Harue knew that most people in her class were somewhat familiar with Japanese culture, but she also decided that she needed to explain certain aspects of the Japanese education system. In addition, she knew that some students might be uncomfortable with a discussion of her father's views toward his daughters' education and with her own agreement with some of those views. At first, she thought about giving a detailed explanation of her father's background, including many details about his childhood and his relationship with his parents. In the end, she decided not to take that approach — both because she was afraid it would lead her too far away from her original subject and because she did not want her paper to sound like an apology.

Here is Harue's first draft.

MY FRUSTRATION

I do not understand why my mother and father get along with each other, because certainly there is a big gap between them. My father is a simple old Japanese character, shy, vague and conservative. Because of a long period of isolation from the rest of the world, Japanese have joined together to protect the original race. That is why Japanese think that group harmony is very much more important than individual opinions, and they are concerned about what people think about them. My father, especially, experienced World War II, and at that time he thought the people who spoke English were demons.

On the other hand, my mother is more open-minded. She has been interested in English since she was a university student. Once she worked at a foreign embassy as an interpreter. In addition, when she was a student, she had a chance to study abroad, but her parents, who are also old-type Japanese, opposed it. My mother gave up this chance, but she became an English teacher and she still teaches junior high school students. She can speak her opinion openly and has very liberal ideas.

My mother began to teach me English when I was in the fourth grade. I was filled with the delight of knowing a language totally different from Japanese. English allowed me to have a bright, new world. I was very happy to share the same thing with my mother. I was excited to learn some English letters and words which were like mathematical signs to me. My mother always listened to the English radio station. I still remember that the sound of English speaking was a kind of rhythmical music to me. When I entered junior high school, I really began to study English. I did very good unexpectedly. So I was so awfully delighted with it. My friends who were around me took it for granted because I was the daughter of an English teacher. In addition, even my mother expected me not to disgrace her occupation. The only thing I had to take care of was to keep good grades in English. It invaded the relationship between my mother and me. English was then becoming a burden for me, because I thought that English alone was the glue to connect us.

The Japanese educational system is very severe, strict, and competitive, because the academic background decides the way people are valued in society. That is why Japanese parents hope their children will enter a prestigious university. My mother was no exception. Without thinking of their children's feelings, adults compare their children as either better or inferior to others. I studied so as not to disappoint my mother's expectation and to be superior to others in this vehement competition. I was like a racing horse. I lost myself because I was driven by my purpose, but I still did not have any security. My mother began to seem not like a mother to me but like a Japanese woman with an American mask on her face. I now began to hate English.

My older sister has been so smart that she can speak English without difficulty. I thought that my mother loved her more because she was the daughter my mother expected. Before I was aware, my English grades went down. I was very lonely, and in my loneliness, I turned to my father's way of thinking. It is his belief that daughters be educated to the old ways. Thinking about his view, I tried to adopt Japanese traditional cultures such as calligraphy, flower arrangement, and doing tea ceremonies instead of learning English. Through practicing those things, I recognized the Japanese spirit. This isolated island, my homeland, had created such a sensitive race and elegant and refined culture. My father was very delighted to teach me about it.

I can see now that the big gap between my mother and father is that of new ideas versus the old ones. I cannot argue which is better except that there is a large frustration in trying to reconcile them. Right now, as a Japanese woman, I see conflicts because I value my home culture, including the isolation from others, yet I also see how much modern Japan has learned from other cultures all over the world. For instance, although my father still remembers World War II and thinks of the United States as an enemy, my mother points out that behind today's Japanese prosperity, there has been American relief. Also, here I am in America where my mother often dreamed to go for study. Although I came with some reluctance, I think again that this country is great. It provides me with relief from the frustration I felt in Japan of having to choose between my mother's view and my father's view. From the time I was a young girl, I wanted only to please one parent or to please the other. Now, in this country, I see young people who do what they want to do. Now I understand real liberty means not following someone else's ways. Here I can become educated but also value my traditions. I don't have to be my mother or my father. This is my life and I am me.

Revising

After Harue finished writing her discovery draft, she put it away for several days. When she read it again, she immediately noticed several points of concern. To help in the revision process, she jotted down the following questions and observations to use as she worked with peer editors in class workshop sessions, as she visited the campus writing center for tutoring, and as she consulted with her professor during office hours.

Revision Notes

1. What is my central idea? Should I focus on contradictions between the Japanese education system and the American education system and way of life? On the contradiction between my mother's and father's values? On the contradiction between what my mother wants for me and what I want for myself?
2. Do all the paragraphs relate to my general subject of contradiction? (Example: Does ¶ 5 get off the topic by talking about my sister?)
3. I talk more about my mother and her ideas than about my father and his ideas, but the aim of my paper is to compare them and their influence in my life. Should I talk about both the same amount?
4. Does my conclusion say enough? Does it follow from the stories and examples I have given in the paper?
5. I have the same ideas in different places. Do I repeat too much?
6. Is it all right that I use "I" in this paper? In my English classes before I was told not to, but the essay we read in the textbook ("Split at the Root") did use "I."
7. Do I use "is" and "was" too much? I did this on my last paper. How can I change these words?
8. Do I use apostrophes and commas right? I have problems with this.
9. Do I change the tense of the verbs when this is not necessary?

Harue's revision notes fall into three categories. Her first five questions address *global issues*. These questions look at the content and meaning of her essay. When writers revise, they notice many aspects of their writing. Most experienced writers try to focus on the larger, global issues before they move to issues of *style* (which questions 6 and 7 address) or issues of *grammar* and *mechanics* (which questions 8 and 9 address). As you revise your own work, you may want to consider the following list, which suggests global issues, issues of style, and issues of grammar and mechanics.

REVISION CHECKLIST

Global Issues

1. Have you focused on a subject that is specific enough to allow full treatment in a paper of the length you've been asked to write?
2. Do you have a clear understanding of the purpose of your paper?

Do you communicate the purpose of your paper to your readers? (Perhaps through a *thesis statement* — a sentence or two that not only gives your subject but also tells what you intend to say about that subject.)

3. Have you organized the ideas, information, and descriptions you are presenting so that they make sense to your audience?
4. Does each paragraph deal with one main idea, and does each paragraph logically follow the paragraph before it?
5. Does every paragraph offer sufficient information (details, examples, reasons) to support the idea it expresses?
6. Do all paragraphs relate clearly to the purpose of your paper?
7. Have you analyzed and evaluated your audience, considering their abilities, beliefs, values, opinions, knowledge, and interest? And have you written with your audience analysis in mind?
8. Have you provided an opening paragraph that catches the interest of your audience and makes them want to read further?
9. Have you written a concluding paragraph that provides an original analysis, evaluation, solution, option, insight? (A strong conclusion usually does more than simply summarize what you've already said.)
10. Does every paragraph in the paper lead logically to the conclusion?

Issues of Style

1. Have you used a variety of sentence structures to avoid sounding dull and monotonous?
2. Have you chosen words carefully, considering both *denotation* (the dictionary meaning) and *connotation* (the emotional overtones readers attach to words)?
3. Have you avoided *repetition* (unless, of course, the repetition is used for emphasis)?
4. Have you avoided overuse of *passive voice* (sentences where the subject is acted upon rather than acting)?
   > *Example: Passive Voice* The map was read by the visitor.
   > *Active Voice* The visitor read the map.
5. Have you avoided using long, pretentious words when shorter, more concise words will convey your meaning just as accurately?
6. Have you avoided using unnecessary words (for example, saying "due to the fact that" when you could just as easily say "because")?

Issues of Grammar and Mechanics

1. Does each sentence express a complete thought?
2. Have you avoided fusing two complete thoughts together with no mark of punctuation or with only a comma?
3. Do descriptive words or phrases *(modifiers)* relate clearly to the word or words they are intended to describe?

4. Do all subjects and verbs agree?
5. Does every pronoun have a clear *antecedent* (a noun to which it refers)?
6. Do all pronouns agree with their antecedents?
7. Is the *tense* (time reference) of verbs consistent throughout the paper (except when you intend to indicate change in time)?
8. Are commas, semicolons, and other punctuation marks used correctly?
9. Are possessives formed correctly, using apostrophes with nouns (the girl's book; two girls' books) but not with personal pronouns (the book is hers; its cover is torn).
10. Are all words spelled correctly?

THE REVISION PLAN After Harue talked with other students, with her tutor, and with her instructor, she realized that she did need a clearer focus. Her paper definitely had a purpose—to explain the contrasts she saw between her mother's values and her father's values—but her introduction didn't show why Harue saw these conflicting values as important. She realized that although her mother and father were essential to the idea she was explaining, it was her own conflict that was really the subject of the essay. She tried writing a list of several possible thesis statements and finally settled on this one:

> From the time of my earliest memory, I've always tried to understand why I am a person who is determined to go forward yet who always feels drawn back toward the past. Recently, as I was thinking about this question, I realized that the conflict I feel within myself is reflected in my mother and father and the values they hold.

As Harue considered how she would use this idea to focus her paper, she at first thought she would eliminate references to her sister and to the Japanese education system, because they didn't seem to be clearly related to her own conflict. After trying this strategy, she realized that she would lose parts of her paper she really liked and that she knew were important to the significance she saw in her parents' differences. So she decided not to drop the story of her sister and the evaluation of the Japanese education system but, rather, to provide transitions that would connect these points more clearly with her central idea.

Harue agreed with her readers that there was no problem with her discussing her mother more than her father. As her revised conclusion notes, her mother's values are the ones that motivated her most strongly as well as the ones she needed most to rebel against.

In addition to making the global revisions outlined here, Harue also worked on correcting punctuation and on using more active verbs rather than relying so heavily on forms of the verb *to be*.

After writing several drafts, Harue turned in the following finalized paper.

MY FRUSTRATION

From the time of my earliest memory, I've always tried to understand why I am a person who is determined to go forward yet who always feels drawn back toward the past. Recently, as I was thinking about this question, I realized that the conflict I feel within myself reflects the values my mother and father hold. I do not understand why my mother and father get along with each other, because certainly a big gap exists between them, which can be represented by the way each one thinks about the English language.

My father is a simple, old Japanese character, shy, vague, and conservative. Like many other Japanese people, he thinks that group harmony is very much more important than individual opinions, and he worries about what other people think about him. He thinks that preserving the old ways is best, and he doesn't try to see things in a new way. For example, he and many of his friends experienced World War II, and at that time they thought the people who spoke English were demons; my father still does not speak English and does not like to hear any of his family speak English.

On the other hand, my mother thinks with a more open mind. She has been interested in English since she was a university student. Once she worked at a foreign embassy as an interpreter. In addition, during her student days, she had a chance to study in the United States, but her parents, who are also old-type Japanese, opposed it. To please her parents, my mother gave up this chance, but she became an English teacher, and now she teaches junior high school students. She speaks her opinion openly and has very liberal ideas.

From my early years, I knew my father's beliefs, but my mother was the one who took care of me most of the time. In one way, at least, I was like my father from the beginning: I really cared what other people thought of me. I wanted my mother to think well of me; I wanted to please her. She began to teach me English when I was in the fourth grade, and I was filled with the delight of knowing a language totally different from Japanese. English allowed me to have a bright, new world and to develop an interest I was very happy to share with my mother. I was excited to learn some English letters and words, which were like mathematical signs to me.

During those years, I remember my father often leaving the house while my mother listened to the English radio station. I still can picture myself listening with her. To me the sound of English speaking was a kind of rhythmical music. When I entered junior high school, I really began to study English. Although my mother never said anything directly, I could tell from some hints that she expected me not to disgrace her profession. I started my English class with some dread, but I, to my delight, did very well with it. As I continued to study, however, I found I lost the pleasure of hearing enjoyable music in the English language. The only thing I had to take care of was to keep good grades. This pressure for high marks invaded the relationship between my mother and me. English was then becoming a burden for me, because I thought that English alone was the glue to connect us.

My mother realized that the Japanese educational system is very severe, strict, and competitive, and she knew that the academic background decides the way people are valued in society. That is why, like other modern Japanese parents, she hoped her children would enter a prestigious university. Without thinking of their children's feelings, my mother and her friends and colleagues compared their children as either better than or inferior to others. I studied so as not to disappoint my mother's expectation and to be superior to others in this vehement competition. I was like a racing horse. I lost myself, and my own pleasure in English, because I was driven by my purpose, but I still did not have any security. My mother began to seem not like a mother to me but like a Japanese woman with an American mask on her face. I now began to hate English.

To make things worse, my mother began talking to me more and more about my older sister, who was so smart that she learned to speak English without difficulty. As I heard my mother make more and more of these comparisons, I thought that she loved my sister more because she was the daughter my mother expected. Before I was aware, my English grades went down and my mother was very unhappy with me. She did not scold me, but no longer did we share the harmonies of the American radio programs.

One day when she turned on the radio, I was feeling very lonely. In my loneliness, I followed my father out the door as he left to take a walk. For the first time, I listened to him talk about his thoughts about the English language. He explained that for a long time Japan was isolated from other countries and that we had to depend on ourselves. Even now, we had to preserve our culture. I saw myself as that isolated island, and I turned to my father's way of thinking. It is his belief that daughters be educated to the old ways so that when they are wives and mothers they may carry on our customs. Thinking about his view, I tried to adopt Japanese traditional cultures such as calligraphy, flower arrangement, and tea ceremonies instead of studying English. Through practicing those things, I recognized the Japanese spirit. I saw that this isolated island, my homeland, had created such a sensitive race and elegant and refined culture. My father was very delighted to teach me about it.

Now I had my father's approval, but I was still not happy. I saw that I was giving up one important part of myself—studying English—just because I was angry at the pressure my mother put on me. When I told my father I was going to study English again, I could see that he was sad. But I let him know that I was not going to forget all the Japanese culture I had learned. He said he did not see how that was possible, but still when my mother urged me to accept the chance to study in the United States, he did not try to keep me behind.

I can see now that the big gap between my mother and father is that of new ideas versus the old ones. My frustration came from trying always to think which way was best. Right now, as a Japanese woman, I see conflicts because I value my home culture, including the isolation from others; yet I also see how much modern Japan has learned from other cultures all over the world. For instance, although my father still remembers World War II and thinks of the United States as an enemy, my mother points out that behind today's Japanese prosperity, there has been American relief. Also, here I am in America where my mother often dreamed to go for study. Although I came with some reluctance, I think that this country is great. Here I find relief from the frustration I felt in Japan of having to choose between my mother's view and my father's view. From the time I was a young girl, I wanted only to please one parent or to please the other. Now, in the United States, I see young people who do what they want to do. Now I understand real liberty means not following someone else's ways. Here I can become educated and study the English language but also value my traditions. I don't have to be my mother or my father. This is my life and I am me.

Suggestions for Writing to Explain

1. As you are prewriting, keep in mind the many approaches that help a writer to explain: informing, defining, analyzing, synthesizing, and evaluating.

2. As you think about your subject and plan your draft, consider your audience. Consider such things as their knowledge, interests, concerns, and values.

3. As you write the opening of an essay that informs, remember that your audience needs to understand your purpose. Readers need to know the subject of your essay as well as what you are going to say about that subject. A standard way to convey this information is in a thesis statement (a sentence or two that sums up your main idea).

4. As you develop your ideas, remember that your purpose is to inform readers of a new idea or a new way of looking at the world. To accomplish this purpose, you'll need to provide specific details, reasons, and examples. You want to show your readers what you are talking about rather than overwhelming, and perhaps confusing, them with unsupported generalizations.

5. As you write your conclusion, remember that it should follow logically from the information you have given your reader in the rest of the essay. Remember, too, that the conclusion should do more than summarize. It should provide an original analysis, evaluation, solution, option, or insight.

Roots and Memories

Previews: ROOTS AND MEMORIES

So the nature of my research begins with something as ineffable and as flexible as a dimly recalled figure, the corner of a room, a voice. I began to write my second book, which was called *Sula,* because of my preoccupation with a picture of a woman and the way in which I heard her name pronounced.

From: *The Site of Memory,* TONI MORRISON

In Kenya I felt more free than I have ever felt before. The only thing holding me captive was the earth which would grow the food, the sky which would quench the earth of its thirst, and the sun which would warm and help all things to grow. But these masters were sure to give back all that you have put in.

From: *20/20 Hindsight,* JAY FORD

We were taught that any mention of skin color in the presence of colored people was treacherous, forbidden ground. In a parallel way, the word "Jew" was not used by polite gentiles. I sometimes heard my best friend's father, a Presbyterian minister, allude to "the Hebrew people" or "people of the Jewish faith." The world of acceptable folk was white, gentile (christian, really), and had "ideals" (which colored people, white "common" people, were not supposed to have).

From: *Split at the Root: An Essay on Jewish Identity,* ADRIENNE RICH

Americans are a rootless people. Each year one in six of us changes residences; one in four changes jobs. We see nothing troubling in these statistics. For most of us, they merely reflect the restless energy that made America great.

From: *Rootlessness,* DAVID MORRIS

TONI MORRISON
The Site of Memory

> *Born Chloe Anthony Wofford in Lorain, Ohio, in 1931, Toni Morrison graduated from Howard and Cornell Universities. In 1964, after several years as a faculty member at Howard, she became an editor with Random House publishing company. In addition, she wrote steadily, publishing many stories and essays and, in 1970, her first novel,* The Bluest Eye. *Morrison's other novels include* Sula *(1973),* Song of Solomon *(1977),* Tar Baby *(1981), and* Beloved *(1987). "The Site of Memory" is an excerpt from a talk Morrison gave at the New York Public Library in 1986.*

Prereading/Journal-Writing Suggestions

1. List four or five of your earliest memories. Don't try to reconstruct entire events. Just jot down images that come to mind. Let one image lead to another as you include any people, places, objects, colors, sounds, scents, or tastes that you remember. Choose one of these memories and explain why you believe it has lingered in your mind for so many years.
2. Write about your earliest memory of writing. Include as many details as possible: What did you write about? Why did you write? Did you find writing easy, hard, discouraging, challenging, intriguing? Were you happy with what you wrote? Did you have any readers? If so, what were their responses?
3. When you begin a piece of writing — when you are in the thinking stage — do you see images or hear words or both? Explain by using specific examples.

I can't tell you how I felt when my father died. But I was able to write *Song of Solomon* and imagine, not him, and not his specific interior life, but the world that he inhabited and the private or interior life of the people in it. And I can't tell you how I felt reading to my grandmother while she was turning over and over in her bed (because she was dying, and she was not comfortable), but I could try to reconstruct the world that she lived in. And I have suspected, more often than not, that I *know* more than she did, that I *know* more than my grandfather and my great-grandmother did, but I also know that I'm no wiser than they were. And whenever I have tried earnestly to diminish their vision and prove to myself that I know more, and when I have tried to speculate on their interior life and match it up with my own, I have been overwhelmed every time by the richness of theirs compared to my own. Like Frederick Douglass talking about his grandmother, and James Baldwin talking about his father, and Simone de Beauvoir talking about her mother, these people are my access to me; they are my entrance into my own interior life. Which is why the images that float around them — the remains, so to speak, at the archeological site — surface first, and they surface so vividly and so compellingly that I acknowledge them as my route to a reconstruction of a world, to an exploration of an interior life that was not written and to the revelation of a kind of truth.

So the nature of my research begins with something as ineffable and as flexible as a dimly recalled figure, the corner of a room, a voice. I began to write my second book, which was called *Sula,* because of my preoccupation with a picture of a woman and the way in which I heard her name pronounced. Her name was Hannah, and I think she was a friend of my mother's. I don't remember seeing her very much, but what I do remember is the color around her — a kind of violet, a suffusion of something violet — and her eyes, which appeared to be half closed. But what I remember most is how the women said her name: how they said "Hannah Peace" and smiled to themselves, and there was some secret about her that they knew, which they didn't talk about, at least not in my hearing, but it seemed *loaded* in the way in which they said her name. And I suspected that she was a little bit of an outlaw but that they approved in some way.

And then, thinking about their relationship to her and the way in which they talked about her, the way in which they articulated her name, made me think about friendship between women. What is it that they forgive each other for? And what is it that is unforgivable in the world of women? I don't want to know any more about Miss Hannah Peace, and I'm not going to ask my mother who she really was and what did she do and what were you laughing about and why were you smiling? Because my experience when I do this with my mother is so crushing: she will give you *the* most pedestrian information you ever heard, and I would like to keep all of my remains and my images intact in their mystery when I begin. Later I will get to the facts. That way I can explore two worlds — the actual and the possible.

What I want to do this evening is to track an image from picture to meaning to text — a journey which appears in the novel that I'm writing now, which is called *Beloved.*

I'm trying to write a particular kind of scene, and I see corn on the cob. 5 To "see" corn on the cob doesn't mean that it suddenly hovers; it only means that it keeps coming back. And in trying to figure out "What is all this corn doing?" I discover what it *is* doing.

I see the house where I grew up in Lorain, Ohio. My parents had a garden some distance away from our house, and they didn't welcome me and my sister there, when we were young, because we were not able to distinguish between the things that they wanted to grow and the things that they didn't, so we were not able to hoe, or weed, until much later.

I see them walking, together, away from me. I'm looking at their backs and what they're carrying in their arms: their tools, and maybe a peck basket.

Sometimes when they walk away from me they hold hands, and they go to this other place in the garden. They have to cross some railroad tracks to get there.

I also am aware that my mother and father sleep at odd hours because my father works many jobs and works at night. And these naps are times of pleasure for me and my sister because nobody's giving us chores, or telling us what to do, or nagging us in any way. In addition to which, there is some feeling of pleasure in them that I'm only vaguely aware of. They're very rested when they take these naps.

And later on in the summer we have an opportunity to eat corn, which is the one plant that I can distinguish from the others, and which is the harvest that I like the best; the others are the food that no child likes — the collards, the okra, the strong, violent vegetables that I would give a great deal for now. But I do like the corn because it's sweet, and because we all sit down to eat it, and it's finger food, and it's hot, and it's even good cold, and there are neighbors in, and there are uncles in, and it's easy, and it's nice.

The picture of the corn and the nimbus of emotion surrounding it 10 became a powerful one in the manuscript I'm now completing.

Authors arrive at text and subtext in thousands of ways, learning each time they begin anew how to recognize a valuable idea and how to render the texture that accompanies, reveals, or displays it to its best advantage. The process by which this is accomplished is endlessly fascinating to me. I have always thought that as an editor for twenty years I understood writers better than their most careful critics, because in examining the manuscript in each of its subsequent stages I knew the author's process, how his or her mind worked, what was effortless, what took time, where the "solution" to a problem came from. The end result — the book — was all that the critic had to go on.

Still, for me, that was the least important aspect of the work. Because, no matter how "fictional" the account of these writers, or how much it was a product of invention, the act of imagination is bound up with memory. You know, they straightened out the Mississippi River in places, to make room for houses and livable acreage. Occasionally the river floods these places. "Floods" is the word they use, but in fact it is not flooding; it is remembering. Remembering where it used to be. All water has a perfect memory and is forever trying to get back to where it was. Writers are like that: remembering where we were, what valley we ran through, what the banks were like, the light that was there, and the route back to our original place. It is emotional memory — what the nerves and the skin remember as well as how it appeared. And a rush of imagination is our "flooding."

Along with personal recollection, the matrix of the work I do is the wish to extend, fill in, and complement slave autobiographical narratives. But only the matrix. What comes of all that is dictated by other concerns, not least among them the novels' own integrity. Still, like water, I remember where I was before I was "straightened out."

Suggestions for Writing and Discussion

1. Throughout this piece, Morrison raises questions and then moves on, content to let the question float on the page. One of her first questions is this: "What is . . . unforgivable in the world of women?" What do you think she means by "the world of women"? After defining this phrase, write your own response to Morrison's question or to a parallel question, "What is unforgivable in the world of men?"

2. Morrison would prefer to let some things remain mysteries so that she can use her imagination as well as actual facts. Do you subscribe to this philosophy? Explain.

3. How would you evaluate the period of childhood Morrison describes? What was her life like? Her family relationships? What do you see as positive? As negative?

4. List the emotions and images Morrison associates with corn. Then choose your favorite food and freewrite about the times and places and people you relate to that food. Write for ten minutes without stopping; then read what you have written. Finally, write an essay explaining what you have discovered.

5. What advice about writing does Morrison offer? Evaluate this advice, using your own approach to writing as a basis for the evaluation. Do you find yourself agreeing or disagreeing with her observations? What significance do you see in the differences and similarities between your process and hers?

6. Morrison says that, for her, the end result of writing—the book or the finished product—is the "least important aspect of the work." What, then, is most important to her? Explain why you think she values this part of writing. In addition, explain what part of writing is most important to you (discovering ideas, doing research, drafting, revising, seeing the finished product).

7. List at least five tools Morrison believes a person needs to use to be a good writer; then evaluate her choices. As a writer, why would you choose or reject these tools? What tools might you add?

Suggestions for Extended Thinking and Research

1. Research your favorite author to discover how he or she wrote a work that you particularly admire. How did this writer discover the ideas? What were the most difficult stages of writing this work? What evaluations did the author make about the work? How did his or her evaluations compare with those of scholars or reviewers who have written about this work?

2. Take one or two favorite passages from something written by an author you admire. First, copy the paragraphs two times by hand (no typing or word processing). Then write a paragraph of your own, on your own

topic, using the copied paragraphs as models. Try to capture the exact rhythm of the passages you have copied. Pay attention to such issues as word choice, sentence length, word order, use of repetition, and use of figures of speech or irony. After you have completed this exercise, write an analysis of this author's style of writing by comparing it with your own natural style of writing.

3. Morrison says her writing is "a flood." From reading this piece, do you find the metaphor appropriate? Suggest several possible metaphors for your own writing process, and explain why you chose these comparisons. Then think carefully about a specific writing task you've faced, and use one of these metaphors to trace the process you followed as you completed that assignment.

CHARLENE SPRETNAK

Ecofeminism: Our Roots and Flowering

As a founder of the Feminist Writers Guild and cofounder of the Green Committees of Correspondence, Charlene Spretnak is a widely acclaimed speaker and writer on both feminist and ecological issues. She is the author of Lost Goddesses of Early Greece *(1987) and* The Spiritual Dimension of Green Politics *(1986). This essay comes from her 1990 book* Reweaving the World: The Emergence of Ecofeminism.

Prereading/Journal-Writing Suggestions

1. What would you define as the three greatest problems facing the world today. Are you taking any direct action to help remedy any of these problems? If so, explain why. If you are not doing anything, explain why not.
2. Write about a time when you were particularly moved or affected by a specific aspect of nature. Describe the aspect (a storm, an aging tree, a wild animal) and explain its effect on you.
3. If an almighty being had to have a gender, would this being be male or female? Take a distinct position and explain your answer.

Our roots, our beginning, the increasing allure of "eco" for feminists offer some answers to a question of great immediacy: *What are the experiences through which humans raised in industrialized, modern society connect on a deep level with nature?* Our flowering, our insights, our growing impact on political philosophy and practice offer answers to another key question of our time: *What is the purpose of cultivating ecological wisdom at this postmodern moment in human history?*

Our Roots

Our situation as a species is the following: the life-support systems of this almost impossibly beautiful planet are being violated and degraded, causing often irreparable damage, yet only a small proportion of humans have focused on this crisis. In our own country, our farms are losing 4 billion tons of topsoil a year; the groundwater and soil are being poisoned by pesticide runoff and toxic dumping; the groundwater table itself, accumulated over thousands of years, is being recklessly depleted to serve the profits of agribusiness and developers; the nuclear power industry has generated much more than enough plutonium to poison every creature and ecosystem on Earth and has no idea how to store it safely; we're losing 200,000 to 300,000 acres of wetland habitat every year; and the songbirds, which used to herald the coming of spring, are now perishing in large numbers every winter when they migrate to the devastated land in Central and South America that formerly was majestic tropical rain forest.

Is this many-faceted ecocrisis a focus of awareness in our society? Hardly. In the 1987 State of the Union address, our president did not mention the present and pending environmental disasters at all. When the opposition party was given response time on national television and radio, no one mentioned this absence in the president's account of our problems. When members of the media, female and male, commented on the address, the glaring absence of ecological concern, let alone ecological wisdom, again went unmentioned. In the State of the Union addresses for the previous two years, the story was the same, except for the president's brief tip of the hat in 1986 to the Superfund (ridiculously underfunded for the cleanup of toxic dump sites) and his promising the previous year not to grant drilling and mining leases inside the national park system!

That politicians, the media, and the public barely noticed the crucial omission in the president's annual assessment of our national situation is merely one indication of pervasive alienation from the realities of nature. A powerful industrial giant like us lives on *top* of nature, it is understood, free to do with it what we will. The arrogance and ignorance behind that deadly folly are being challenged to varying extents by environmentalist organizations and to a much deeper extent by a loose aggregate of movements whose members are sometimes called the "new" ecologists: ecofeminism, deep ecology, Green politics, bioregionalism, creation-centered spirituality, animal rights, and others. Their numbers are not a large portion of our 242 million, but they are carrying on extremely significant work, feeling their way out of alienation toward a way of being that is infused with ecological wisdom. *Something* connected those people with nature; some event or accumulation of experiences woke them up to the centrality of ecology.

In the case of ecofeminism, there are many paths into our rich and fertile garden, each with its own occasions for awakening. What cannot be said, though, is that women are drawn to ecology and ecofeminism simply because we are female. The very first issue of *Audubon Magazine* in 1887 contained an article by Celia Thaxter titled "Woman's Heartlessness," on the resistance she and other activists met in trying to get women to stop wearing on their hats the feathers and stuffed bodies of birds: "Not among the ignorant and uncultured so much as the educated and enlightened do we find the indifference and hardness that perplexes us . . . I think I may say in two-thirds of the cases to which we appeal. One lady said to me, 'I think there is a great deal of sentiment wasted on the birds. There are so many of them, they will never be missed, any more than mosquitoes.'" Clearly those ladies were team players, defenders of patriarchal, anthropocentric values, which is exactly what we were raised to be, too—until we figured out that the game was dreadfully wrong.

Ecofeminism grew out of radical, or cultural, feminism (rather than from liberal feminism or socialist feminism), which holds that identifying the dynamics—largely fear and resentment—behind the dominance of male over female is the key to comprehending every expression of patriarchal culture with its hierarchical, militaristic, mechanistic, industrialist forms. The first tendrils of ecofeminism appeared not in the exuberant season of Earth Day 1970 — for feminists were quite preoccupied with the birthing of our own movement then — but in mid-decade. Our sources of inspiration at the time were not Thoreau, John Muir, or even Rachel Carson (though we have certainly come to appreciate those beacons since then) but, rather, our own experiential explorations.

One path into ecofeminism was the study of political theory and history. Radical/cultural feminists who had been exposed to Marxist analysis in the 1960s as well as those who had gone on to study critical theory and social ecology in the early 1970s built upon the framework of dominance theory. They rejected the Marxist assertion that domination is based solely on money and class: if there is a universally dominated class, surely it is women. Experiencing and naming the inadequacies of classical dominance theory, which ignores nature as well as women, such radical feminists moved in the direction of ecofeminism. Another source of radical/cultural feminist dominance theory was the work of cultural historians who explored the roots of patriarchy.

A second path into ecofeminism is exposure to nature-based religion, usually that of the Goddess. In the mid-1970s many radical/cultural feminists experienced the exhilarating discovery, through historic and archaeological sources, of a religion that honored the female and seemed to have as its "good book" nature itself. We were drawn to it like a magnet, but only, I feel, because both of those features were central. We would not have been interested in "Yahweh with a skirt," a distant, detached, domineering godhead who happened to be female. What was cosmologically wholesome and healing was the discovery of the Divine as immanent in and around us. What was intriguing was the sacred link between the Goddess in her many guises and totemic animals and plants, sacred groves, and womblike caves, in the moon-rhythm blood of menses, the ecstatic dance — the experience of *knowing* Gaia, her voluptuous contours and fertile plains, her flowing waters that give life, her animal teachers. For who among us would ever again see a snake coiled around the arms of an ancient Goddess statue, teaching lessons of cyclic renewal and regeneration with its shedding of skins, as merely a member of the ophidian order in the reptilian class of the vertebrate phylum? That period of discovery — which would certainly not have been news to primal peoples, but was utterly earthshaking for us Judeo-Christian women of a thoroughly modern culture — inspired art, music, poetry, and the resurrection of long-forgotten sacred myth and ritual, usually held out of doors, of course, often on the Earth's holy days of cosmic alignment, the solstices and equinoxes. They are rituals of our own creation that express our deepest feelings of a spirituality infused with ecological wisdom and wholeness. At the beginning of that period, ecology was not on our minds; since moving out of that period into activism, ecology has never left our minds. Today we work for ecopeace, ecojustice, ecoeconomics, ecopolitics, ecoeducation, ecophilosophy, ecotheology, and for the evolution of ecofeminism.

A third path into ecofeminism comes from environmentalism. For many women with careers in public policy, science and technology, public-interest environmental organizations, and environmental studies programs in universities, their initial connection with feminism was the liberal-feminist attention to how and why their progress on the career ladder was blocked. From there they eventually encountered a book, an article, or a lecture with ecofeminist analysis — and suddenly their career work was framed with a radically different meaning. Similarly, women and men who become involved with Green politics for environmental reasons discover ecofeminism and deep ecology there. College students, male and female, who feel that feminism was merely an issue for their mothers' generation and who enroll in an environmental studies course are often exposed to ecofeminist analysis and recognize a depth not present in their textbooks.

There are many variations of these three well-trodden paths into our garden, and perhaps other paths altogether. I have delineated them in order to acknowledge our diversity, which brings strength, but also in the hope that the social and political theory evolving within ecofeminism will address not only the interlinked dynamics in patriarchal culture of the terror of nature and the terror of the elemental power of the female but also the ways *out* of the mesmerizing conditioning that keeps women and men so cut off from our grounding in the natural world, so alienated from our larger sense of self in the unfolding story of the universe. If we look into this matter further, I think we'll find that many people connected with nature on a deep level through a ritual moment of awakening, or perhaps several of them. These moments may have occurred in the context of spiritual practice. They may have occurred in childhood. They are the precious moments we need to acknowledge and to cultivate, to refuse to let the dominant culture pave them over any longer with a value system made of denial, distancing, fear, and ignorance.

The moment of awakening, however, is only the beginning. After that comes a great deal of work if we really want to transform patriarchal culture into new possibilities informed by justice, wisdom, and compassion. We have to be willing to do intellectual work — to explore the books and articles, the speeches and debates that contribute to the evolving social and political theory of ecofeminism. We have to be willing to seek a holistic understanding of ecofeminism, to make an effort to learn about the priorities and experiential wisdom of ecofeminists who came from paths different from our own. We have to be willing to pursue self-education in ecology since our schooling for the most part failed us in that, to read an ecology textbook, for instance. We have to be willing to educate ourselves about the major ecological issues of our day and to understand the economic and political forces at work.

Extremely important is a willingness to deepen our experience of communion with nature. This can be done in the mountains, at the ocean, in a city park, or a backyard garden. My own life is a rather embarrassing example of how long one can be absorbed in ecofeminist intellectual thought, political activism, and ritual honoring of nature *after* the moment of awakening and still know almost nothing of the richness and profound depth of communion that nature can offer. Several years ago I was invited to a conference on bioregionalism and Green politics in Santa Fe and met the environmental editor of the journal that was then called *CoEvolution Quarterly*. We went for a walk, conversing all the while, and when we returned a colleague asked if the editor, who was wearing a large pair of binoculars on a strap around his neck, had seen any birds. "I didn't see any, but I heard four," he replied. "What?!" I thought to myself, "Four birds? On that walk? Just now? I didn't hear anything. Four birds?!" It was at that moment that I realized that, despite my intellectual and political understanding of ecofeminism, I was a tourist in the natural world. In the intervening years, I have gone on many birding hikes, which I love, as well as canoe and backpacking trips into the wilderness. Nature has given me gifts, teachings, and revelations, but none more intense than those times in the wilderness I approached in silence, simply observing and being aware of the sensations I was experiencing, until eventually I was enfolded by the deep, deep silence and the oneness that is almost palpable. At that moment the distinction between inner and outer mind dissolves, and we meet our larger self, the One Mind, the cosmic unfolding. I feel that various intensities of that mystery are revealed to us during the postorgasmic state and during certain kinds of meditation and also ritual, but the grandeur and majesty of oneness I have found only in nature. A starting point for ecofeminists who are as backward in their direct knowledge of nature as I certainly was might be to learn about ten birds and ten plants native to their bioregion. The rest will come quite naturally.

All these kinds of work are the nutrient-rich compost that has yielded the vibrant flowering of ecofeminism today. Composting good soil takes time, and the work of ecofeminism goes back more than a dozen years. In fact, it goes back to a number of feminist writers (including Simone de Beauvoir in 1947) who mentioned in passing the attitudes of men (under patriarchy) to nature and to women and the connection between the two. The first conference to address this idea was "Women and the Environment," organized by Sandra Marburg and Lisa Watson at the University of California, Berkeley, in 1974. In 1980, spurred by the Three Mile Island catastrophe, Ynestra King, Celeste Wesson, Grace Paley, Anna Gyorgy, Christina Rawley, Nancy Jack Todd, and Deborah Gaventa organized a conference in Amherst, Massachusetts, on "Women and Life on Earth: Ecofeminism in the 1980s." Prior to learning of that gathering, Susan Adler and other spiritually aware women at Sonoma State University in California began planning a 1981 conference entitled "Women and the Environment: The First West Coast Ecofeminist Conference." In London, an ecofeminist conference called "Women and Life on Earth" was also held that year. The number of ecofeminist books and articles as well as running debates in anthologies and journals is far too great to cite here, but certainly *Woman and Nature* by Susan Griffin (New York: Harper & Row, 1978) and *The Death of Nature* by Carolyn Merchant (San Francisco: Harper & Row, 1980) were particularly important contributions. Both of those books were begun many years earlier, but they were immediately recognized as the ecofeminist classics that they are because so many radical/cultural feminists had moved in that direction during the second half of the 1970s.

Our Flowering

So those are our roots. Today ecofeminists address the crucial issues of our time, from reproductive technology to Third World development, from toxic poisoning to the vision of a new politics and economics — and much more. We support and join our sisters fighting for equal pay, for battered women's shelters, for better child care, and for all the efforts to stop the daily exploitation and suffering of women. But we see those efforts as bandages on a very unhealthy system. Radical/cultural feminism is sometimes called "big-picture" feminism because we examine the deepest assumptions, values, and fears that inform the structures and expectations of patriarchal culture. The reason we insist on integrating radical analysis with ecological perspective is best understood in the larger framework of the fate of our species and all life on Earth: *What is the purpose of cultivating ecological wisdom at this postmodern moment in human history?*

Our society is facing a crisis in agriculture, a crisis in education and 15 literacy, a crisis in national security and the arms race, a crisis in the international debt situation, and a crisis in the state of the global environment. For the first time in the modern era, there is widespread agreement that something is very wrong. The assumptions of modernity, the faith in technological "progress" and rapacious industrialism, along with the militarism necessary to support it, have left us very lost indeed. The quintessential malady of the modern era is free-floating anxiety, and it is clear to ecofeminists that the whole culture is free floating — from the lack of grounding in the natural world, from the lack of a sense of belonging in the unfolding story of the universe, from the lack of a healthy relationship between the males and females of the species. We are entangled in the hubris of the patriarchal goal of dominating nature and the female. On August 29, 1986, the *New York Times* published a lead editorial titled "Nature as Demon," reminding everyone that the proper orientation of civilization is to advance itself *in opposition* to nature. The editorial advised that disasters such as "Hiroshima, DDT, Bhopal, and now Chernobyl" simply require "improving the polity," that is, fine-tuning the system. Such smugness, of course, is the common response of guardians of the status quo: retrenchment and Band-Aids.

But ecofeminists say that the system is leading us to ecocide and species suicide because it is based on ignorance, fear, delusion, and greed. We say that people, male or female, enmeshed in the *values* of that system are incapable of making rational decisions. They pushed nuclear power plants when they did not have the slightest idea what to do with the plutonium wastes — because, after all, someone always comes along later to clean up like Mom. They pushed the nuclear arms race because those big phallic missiles are so "technologically sweet." They are pushing reproductive technology with the gleeful prediction that children of the future, a result of much genetic selection, will often have a donor mother, an incubator mother, and social mother who raises them — making motherhood as disembodied and discontinuous as fatherhood, at last! They are pushing high-tech petroleum-based agriculture, which makes the soil increasingly brittle and lifeless and adds millions of tons of toxic pesticides to our food as well as our soil and water, because *they* know how to get what they want from the Earth — a far cry from the peasant rituals that persisted in parts of Europe even up to World War I where women would encircle the fields by torchlight and symbolically transfer their fertility to the land they touched. Women and men in those cultures participated in the cycles of nature with respect and gratitude.

Such attitudes have no place in a modern, technocratic society fueled by the patriarchal obsessions of dominance and control. They have been replaced by the managerial ethos, which holds efficiency of production and short-term gains above all else — above ethics or moral standards, above the health of community life, and above the integrity of all biological processes, especially those constituting the elemental power of the female. The experts guiding our society seek deliverance from their fears of nature, with which they have no real communion or deep connection, through their seeming victories over the great forces: their management of the vast watersheds and forests of the planet and its perilously thin layer of topsoil; their management of the economics and daily conditions of people of color throughout the Third World (the so-called developing nations) and the Fourth World (the indigenous peoples); their management of "improved animal tools" for agribusiness; their management of women's economic status; and finally — so very technologically sweet — their management of women's birthing power, beginning first with control over labor and delivery, then control over breastfeeding (which the AMA almost succeeded in phasing out between the 1930s and the mid-1970s), and now control over conception and gestation, with the prediction that they will one day colonize the universe by sending frozen human embryos or cells for clones into space to colonize planets.

The technological experts of the modern era, with their colleagues in business, government, and the military, are waging an antibiological revolution in human contact. The moral systems of Western ethics and religion are nearly powerless in this struggle because those systems themselves are largely devoid of ecological wisdom. The crying need right now — if we have any hope of charting a postmodern, posthumanist, and postpatriarchal transition to the Age of Ecology — is for a new philosophical underpinning of civilization. We need an ecophilosophy that speaks the truth with great immediacy in language that everyone can understand.

That work has already been started by ecofeminists and by the deep ecology movement, many of whose pioneering members are philosophy professors drawing on ecology, ethics, philosophy, and religion. There has been little serious contact between these two movements, a situation that I hope both parties will work to change, for ecofeminism has a great deal to add to the evolution of ecophilosophy. The following are a few examples. Deep ecologists write that Western philosophy, religion, and culture in general are estranged from nature, being anthropocentric. Ecofeminists say, "Yes, but surely you've noticed something else about them, haven't you? They're intensely *androcentric*. And surely you've noticed that Western conquest and degradation of nature are based on fear and resentment; we can demonstrate that that dynamic is linked closely to patriarchal fear and resentment of the elemental power of the female." Deep ecologists write that our estrangement from nature began with classic Greek humanism and the rise of Judeo-Christian culture. But ecofeminists say, "Actually, it began around 4500 B.C. with the Indo-European invasions of nomadic tribes from the Eurasian steppes, who replaced the nature-based and female-honoring religion of the Goddess in Europe, the Near East, Persia, and India with their thunderbolt God, removing that which is held sacred and revered from the life processes of the Earth to the distant realm of an omnipotent, male Sky-God. It is in the Indo-European Revolution, not in the Scientific Revolution of the sixteenth and seventeenth centuries, that one finds the earliest sources of desacralized nature, the foundation of a mechanistic worldview." Deep ecologists write that the only incidence of ecological wisdom in Christianity was Saint Francis of Assisi. But ecofeminists say, "There were many other creation-centered great mystics of the medieval era, including Hildegard of Bingen, Mechtild of Mageburg, Julian of Norwich, and Meister Eckhart, who said he learned much from the Beguines, a female lay order." Deep ecologists write that the well-being and flourishing of human and nonhuman life on Earth has value in itself and that humans have no right to reduce the richness and diversity of life forms except to satisfy vital human needs. Ecofeminists agree but wonder how much one's concept of "vital needs" is shaped by the values of patriarchal culture.

There are also some philosophical ecologists who favor abstract schemes 20 such as "ecological process analysis" to explain the natural world. But ecofeminists find such approaches alone to be sterile and inadequate, a veiled attempt, yet again, to distance oneself from wonder and awe, from the emotional involvement and caring that the natural world calls forth.

To care empathetically about the person, the species, and the great family of all beings, about the bioregion, the biosphere, and the universe is the framework within which ecofeminists wish to address the issues of our time. The problem of world population, for example, is one that attracts no dearth of single-minded solutions. The New Left claims that any population-control program proposed for the Third World is genocide of people of color. The Reagan administration cut off U.S. money for abortion operations in Third World countries and talked of cutting off support for contraception on the grounds that growth always brings prosperity — meaning, I suspect, that Third World fetuses are viewed as future markets. Ecologists point out that the Earth's ecosystems are strained almost beyond their carrying capacity and that a major collapse is imminent if human population continues to soar. Radical feminists say that any population control is patriarchal domination of women's wombs.

The reality that many Third World countries are facing is one with half of their populations under age 18, roaming shanty towns in overcrowded cities looking for food and work while ecosystems die around them. An ecofeminist response to this suffering would involve the following elements: (1) the health of the biosphere demands that the rate of population growth level off *everywhere* and then decline (with the exception of tribal peoples in danger of extinction); (2) Third World women have made it clear that they are not interested in contraception unless health and economic conditions are improved (studies have shown that when the death rate of children goes down, the birth rate goes down); (3) women at the regional level must be involved with the planning of population-control programs, health care, education, and nonexploitative small-scale economic opportunities; (4) the political struggles between indigenous cultural nations and the capitalist or socialist states that have been created around them (a freedom fight that accounts for 78 percent of the current wars globally, according to one study) must be resolved so that the women of the ethnic nations are no longer pressured to have many babies in order to outnumber their oppressors; (5) governments and institutions must address the patriarchal attitudes that condition men to demand a large number of offspring in order to prove their virility — as well as the patriarchal attitudes that bring such misery, and sometimes death, to young mothers who give birth to a female under China's "successful" one-child-only policy.

It is our refusal to banish feelings of interrelatedness and caring from the theory and practice of ecofeminism that will save our efforts from calcifying into well-intentioned reformism, lacking the vitality and wholeness that our lives contain. We need to find our way out of the technocratic alienation and nihilism surrounding us by cultivating and honoring our direct connections with nature.

In my own life I have found that many of those connections have been long since buried. In thinking about ecofeminism recently, I remembered an event that took place sixteen years ago, which I had nearly lost from memory. When my daughter was about three days old and we were still in the hospital, I wrapped her up one evening and slipped outside to a little garden in the warmth of late June. I introduced her to the pine trees and the plants and the flowers, and they to her, and finally to the pearly moon wrapped in a soft haze and to the stars. I, knowing nothing then of nature-based religious ritual or ecofeminist theory, had felt an impulse for my wondrous little child to meet the rest of cosmic society. Perhaps it was the ultimate coming-out party! The interesting thing is that that experience, although lovely and rich, was so disconnected from life in a modern, technocratic society that I soon forgot all about it. Last year when I heard about a ritual of the Omaha Indians in which the infant is presented to the cosmos, I waxed enthusiastic and made copies of the prayer for friends who were planning a baptism — but forgot completely that I, too, had once been there, so effective is our cultural denial of nature.

I cannot imagine a challenge greater than that addressed by ecofemin- 25 ism. We know that we are of one fabric with all life on this glorious blue-green planet, that the elements in our bodies and in the world around us were forged by the fireball at the moment the universe was born, and that we have no right to destroy the integrity of the Earth's delicately balanced ecosystems, whose histories are far longer than our own. Around us we see the immensely destructive thrashing of patriarchal leaders *who cannot even name the pain and ignorance that drive their greed.* In their frenzy, they push 10,000 species into extinction each year, a figure that is ever increasing. Can ecofeminism and the related grassroots movements heal those people, heal ourselves, and heal the planet?

Our society is lost and very confused. Perhaps the most effective strategy for us — and certainly the most difficult — is to lead by example: to contribute to the new philosophical base and to work in its new ecopolitics and ecoeconomics; to organize around the concrete issues of suffering and exploitation; to speak out clearly but without malice against those who further policies of injustice and ecological ignorance; to nurture the relationships with our colleagues, never feeling that we must ridicule and crush those with whom we disagree — but most of all, to unlock our memories; to follow the "body parables" of our sexuality; to cultivate our spiritual impulses; to act, as best we can, with pure mind/pure heart; to celebrate with gratitude the wonders of life on Earth; and to seek intimate communion with the natural world. All of these are the flowering of ecofeminism.

Suggestions for Writing and Discussion

1. In this essay, Charlene Spretnak synthesizes various themes concerning nature and modern life. What ideas does her synthesis suggest concerning the world and nature? Our country and nature? Females and nature? The individual and nature?

2. Who, do you suppose, is Spretnak's intended audience? In what specific publications would you expect to find an article like this? Explain through reference to specific details in the article why you think it would appeal to the audience you have identified and defined.

3. How would you define *ecofeminism,* as Spretnak uses this term? Does her definition imply that men are not concerned, not moved by, ecological concerns? Explain your response.

4. Analyze the historical paths that have led to the ecofeminist movement. Which of these precursors as explained by Spretnak do you find most plausible? Do any of the causes listed seem illogical or disconnected to the present movement? Has Spretnak overlooked any other cause?

5. Analyze the significance of the garden metaphor throughout this essay, especially in terms of Spretnak's main point. As this metaphor branches out, trace the effectiveness of the extended parts of the garden.

6. Spretnak writes that today our whole culture is "free floating." Given the details in the article, how would you define this term? For example, in one

passage she notes "the lack of a sense of belonging . . . the lack of a healthy relationship between the males and females of the species." Do you agree with this assessment of our modern world?

7. Write a thoughtful, detailed definition of Spretnak's term *ecophilosophy*.
8. Paragraph 23 consists only of two sentences. Paraphrase these sentences in your own words to make that message and its interpretation less formal and more direct.
9. In the end, Spretnak advises us — her readers — to "unlock our memories," to "cultivate our spiritual impulses," to "celebrate with gratitude the wonders of life," and to "seek intimate communion with the natural world." Suggest one specific action that might fit each of these recommendations, and explain the effects you think might result from such an action (undertaken individually or by a small or large group of people).

Suggestions for Extended Thinking and Research

1. You are asked to write a review of Spretnak's essay for the "Today's Living" section of your daily newspaper. Include in this review a summary of the main points, an analysis of these points, and an evaluation of the overall effectiveness of this essay, based on issues such as audience, topic, logic, language, tone, and style.
2. Research a culture (past or present) that celebrates nature-based religions. Compare these beliefs, values, and rituals with the patriarchal religions that are more common in Western culture today.
3. Read Simone de Beauvoir's book *The Second Sex*. Identify several ideas in de Beauvoir's book that you see as affirming or challenging the points Spretnak makes in her article. Write an essay evaluating the similarities and differences you find in the two writers' philosophies.
4. Write an essay in which you support or challenge several points Spretnak makes in this essay. Be sure to use good reasons and adequate development for each of your points.

ADRIENNE RICH

Split at the Root: An Essay on Jewish Identity

> *Noted poet and essayist Adrienne Rich (b. 1929) grew up with a strong sense of divided identity. In her long poem "Sources," written in 1960, she explores her relationships with her father and her husband, both of whom represent Jewish heritage. Speaking of herself, she asks, "From where does your strength come, you Southern Jew/split at the root, raised in a castle of air?" This essay, written many years later, in 1982, investigates her question further and explains the ambiguities and complexities Rich sees in the traditions from which she comes.*

Prereading/Journal-Writing Suggestions

1. From a scale of 1–5 (1 being low, 5 being high), rate how important honesty is to you. Is honesty one of the qualities you look for in a friendship? In work-related relationships? In the politicians you support? Do you think most people are naturally honest? Explain.

2. What's the one thing about yourself that concerns you the most? What's the one thing about your family that concerns (and, perhaps, irritates) you the most? Is there any connection between these two?

3. Give a different answer for each of the following questions.

   Who are you?
   Who are you?
   Who are you?
   Who are you?
   Who are you?

   Now, on the basis of these answers, analyze in a sentence or two who you really are.

For about fifteen minutes I have been sitting chin in hand in front of the typewriter, staring out at the snow. Trying to be honest with myself, trying to figure out why writing this seems to be so dangerous an act, filled with fear and shame, and why it seems so necessary. It comes to me that in order to write this I have to be willing to do two things: I have to claim my father, for I have my Jewishness from him and not from my gentile mother; and I have to break his silence, his taboos; in order to claim him I have in a sense to expose him.

And there is, of course, the third thing: I have to face the sources and the flickering presence of my own ambivalence as a Jew; the daily, mundane anti-Semitisms of my entire life.

These are stories I have never tried to tell before. Why now? Why, I asked myself sometime last year, does this question of Jewish identity float so impalpably, so ungraspably around me, a cloud I can't quite see the outlines of, which feels to me to be without definition?

And yet I've been on the track of this longer than I think.

In a long poem written in 1960, when I was thirty-one years old, I described myself as "Split at the root, neither Gentile nor Jew, / Yankee nor Rebel." I was still trying to have it both ways: to be neither/nor, trying to live (with my Jewish husband and three children more Jewish in ancestry than I) in the predominantly gentile Yankee academic world of Cambridge, Massachusetts.

But this begins, for me, in Baltimore, where I was born in my father's workplace, a hospital in the Black ghetto, whose lobby contained an immense white marble statue of Christ.

My father was then a young teacher and researcher in the department of pathology at the Johns Hopkins Medical School, one of the very few Jews to attend or teach at that institution. He was from Birmingham, Alabama; his father, Samuel, was Ashkenazic, an immigrant from Austria-Hungary, and his mother, Hattie Rice, a Sephardic Jew from Vicksburg, Mississippi. My grandfather had had a shoe store in Birmingham, which did well enough to allow him to retire comfortably and to leave my grandmother income on his death. The only souvenirs of my grandfather, Samuel Rich, were his ivory flute, which lay on our living-room mantel and was not to be played with; his thin gold pocket watch, which my father wore; and his Hebrew prayer book, which I discovered among my father's books in the course of reading my way through his library. In this prayer book there was a newspaper clipping about my grandparents' wedding, which took place in a synagogue.

My father, Arnold, was sent in adolescence to a military school in the North Carolina mountains, a place for training white southern Christian gentlemen. I suspect that there were few, if any, other Jewish boys at Colonel Bingham's, or at "Mr. Jefferson's university" in Charlottesville, where he studied as an undergraduate. With whatever conscious forethought, Samuel and Hattie sent their son into the dominant southern WASP culture to become an "exception," to enter the professional class. Never, in describing these experiences, did he speak of having suffered — from loneliness, cultural alienation, or outsiderhood. Never did I hear him use the word *anti-Semitism*.

It was only in college, when I read a poem by Karl Shapiro beginning "To hate the Negro and avoid the Jew / is the curriculum," that it flashed on me that there was an untold side to my father's story of his student years. He looked recognizably Jewish, was short and slender in build with dark wiry hair and deep-set eyes, high forehead and curved nose.

My mother is a gentile. In Jewish law I cannot count myself a Jew. If it is true that "we think back through our mothers if we are women" (Virginia Woolf) — and I myself have affirmed this — then even according to lesbian theory, I cannot (or need not?) count myself a Jew.

The white southern Protestant woman, the gentile, has always been there for me to peel back into. That's a whole piece of history in itself, for my gentile grandmother and my mother were also frustrated artists and intellectuals, a lost writer and a lost composer between them. Readers and annotators of books, note takers, my mother a good pianist still, in her eighties. But there was also the obsession with ancestry, with "background," the southern talk of family, not as people you would necessarily know and depend on, but as heritage, the guarantee of "good breeding." There was the inveterate romantic heterosexual fantasy, the mother telling the daughter how to attract men (my mother often used the word "fascinate"); the assumption that relations between the sexes could only be romantic, that it was in the woman's interest to cultivate "mystery," conceal her actual feelings. Survival tactics of a kind, I think today, knowing what I know about the white woman's sexual role in the southern racist scenario. Heterosexuality as protection, but also drawing white women deeper into collusion with white men.

It would be easy to push away and deny the gentile in me—that white southern woman, that social christian. At different times in my life I have wanted to push away one or the other burden of inheritance, to say merely *I am a woman; I am a lesbian.* If I call myself a Jewish lesbian, do I thereby try to shed some of my southern gentile white woman's culpability? If I call myself only through my mother, is it because I pass more easily through a world where being a lesbian often seems like outsiderhood enough?

According to Nazi logic, my two Jewish grandparents would have made me a *Mischling, first-degree*—nonexempt from the Final Solution.

The social world in which I grew up was christian virtually without needing to say so—christian imagery, music, language, symbols, assumptions everywhere. It was also a genteel, white, middle-class world in which "common" was a term of deep opprobrium. "Common" white people might speak of "niggers"; *we* were taught never to use that word—*we* said "Negroes" (even as we accepted segregation, the eating taboo, the assumption that Black people were simply of a separate species). Our language was more polite, distinguishing us from the "rednecks" or the lynch-mob mentality. But so charged with negative meaning was even the word "Negro" that as children we were taught never to use it in front of Black people. We were taught that any mention of skin color in the presence of colored people was treacherous, forbidden ground. In a parallel way, the word "Jew" was not used by polite gentiles. I sometimes heard my best friend's father, a Presbyterian minister, allude to "the Hebrew people" or "people of the Jewish faith." The world of acceptable folk was white, gentile (christian, really), and had "ideals" (which colored people, white "common" people, were not supposed to have). "Ideals" and "manners" included not hurting someone's feelings by calling her or him a Negro or a Jew—naming the hated identity. This is the mental framework of the 1930s and 1940s in which I was raised.

(Writing this, I feel dimly like the betrayer; of my father, who did not 15 speak the word; of my mother, who must have trained me in the messages; of my caste and class; of my whiteness itself.)

Two memories: I am in a play reading at school of *The Merchant of Venice.* Whatever Jewish law says, I am quite sure I was *seen* as Jewish (with a reassuringly gentile mother) in that double vision that bigotry allows. I am the only Jewish girl in the class, and I am playing Portia. As always, I read my part aloud for my father the night before, and he tells me to convey, with my voice, more scorn and contempt with the word "Jew": "Therefore, Jew . . ." I have to say the word out, and say it loudly. I was encouraged to pretend to be a non-Jewish child acting a non-Jewish character who has to speak the word "Jew" emphatically. Such a child would not have had trouble with the part. But *I* must have had trouble with the part, if only because the word itself was really taboo. I can see that there was a kind of terrible, bitter bravado about my father's way of handling this. And who would not dissociate from Shylock in order to identify with Portia? As a Jewish child who was also a female, I loved Portia — and, like every other Shakespearean heroine, she proved a treacherous role model.

A year or so later I am in another play, *The School for Scandal,* in which a notorious spendthrift is described as having "many excellent friends . . . among the Jews." In neither case was anything explained, either to me or to the class at large, about this scorn for Jews and the disgust surrounding Jews and money. Money, when Jews wanted it, had it, or lent it to others, seemed to take on a peculiar nastiness; Jews and money had some peculiar and unspeakable relation.

At this same school — in which we had Episcopalian hymns and prayers, and read aloud through the Bible morning after morning — I gained the impression that Jews were in the Bible and mentioned in English literature, that they had been persecuted centuries ago by the wicked Inquisition, but that they seemed not to exist in everyday life. These were the 1940s, and we were told a great deal about the Battle of Britain, the noble French Resistance fighters, the brave, starving Dutch — but I did not learn of the resistance of the Warsaw ghetto until I left home.

I was sent to the Episcopal church, baptized and confirmed, and attended it for about five years, though without belief. That religion seemed to have little to do with belief or commitment; it was liturgy that mattered, not spiritual passion. Neither of my parents ever entered that church, and my father would not enter *any* church for any reason — wedding or funeral. Nor did I enter a synagogue until I left Baltimore. When I came home from church, for a while, my father insisted on reading aloud to me from Thomas Paine's *The Age of Reason* — a diatribe against institutional religion. Thus, he explained, I would have a balanced view of these things, a choice. He — they — did not give me the choice to be a Jew. My mother explained to me when I was filling out forms for college that if any question was asked about "religion," I should put down "Episcopalian" rather than "none" — to seem to have no religion was, she implied, dangerous.

But it was white social christianity, rather than any particular christian 20 sect, that the world was founded on. The very word *Christian* was used as a synonym for virtuous, just, peace-loving, generous, etc., etc.[1] The norm was christian: "religion: none" was indeed not acceptable. Anti-Semitism was so intrinsic as not to have a name. I don't recall exactly being taught that the Jews killed Jesus — "Christ killer" seems too strong a term for the bland Episcopal vocabulary — but certainly we got the impression that the Jews had been caught out in a terrible mistake, failing to recognize the true Messiah, and were thereby less advanced in moral and spiritual sensibility. The Jews had actually allowed *moneylenders in the Temple* (again, the unexplained obsession with Jews and money). They were of the past, archaic, primitive, as older (and darker) cultures are supposed to be primitive; christianity was lightness, fairness, peace on earth, and combined the feminine appeal of "The meek shall inherit the earth" with the masculine stride of "Onward, Christian Soldiers."

Sometime in 1946, while still in high school, I read in the newspaper that a theater in Baltimore was showing films of the Allied liberation of the Nazi concentration camps. Alone, I went downtown after school one afternoon and watched the stark, blurry, but unmistakable newsreels. When I try to go back and touch the pulse of that girl of sixteen, growing up in many ways so precocious and so ignorant, I am overwhelmed by a memory of despair, a sense of inevitability more enveloping than any I had ever known. Anne Frank's diary and many other personal narratives of the Holocaust were still unknown or unwritten. But it came to me that every one of those piles of corpses, mountains of shoes and clothing had contained, simply, individuals, who had believed, as I now believed of myself, that they were intended to live out a life of some kind of meaning, that the world possessed some kind of sense and order; yet *this* had happened to them. And I, who believed my life was intended to be so interesting and meaningful, was connected to those dead by something — not just mortality but a taboo name, a hated identity. Or was I — did I really have to be? Writing this now, I feel belated rage that I was so impoverished by the family and social worlds I lived in, that I had to try to figure out by myself what this did indeed mean for me. That I had never been taught about resistance, only about passing. That I had no language for anti-Semitism itself.

When I went home and told my parents where I had been, they were not pleased. I felt accused of being morbidly curious, not healthy, sniffing around death for the thrill of it. And since, at sixteen, I was often not sure of the sources of my feelings or of my motives for doing what I did, I probably accused myself as well. One thing was clear: there was nobody in my world with whom I could discuss those films. Probably at the same time, I was reading accounts of the camps in magazines and newspapers; what I remember were the films and having questions that I could not even phrase, such as *Are those men and women "them" or "us"?*

[1] In a similar way the phrase "That's white of you" implied that you were behaving with the superior decency and morality expected of white but not of Black people.

To be able to ask even the child's astonished question *Why do they hate us so?* means knowing how to say "we." The guilt of not knowing, the guilt of perhaps having betrayed my parents or even those victims, those survivors, through mere curiosity — these also froze in me for years the impulse to find out more about the Holocaust.

1947: I left Baltimore to go to college in Cambridge, Massachusetts, left (I thought) the backward, enervating South for the intellectual, vital North. New England also had for me some vibration of higher moral rectitude, of moral passion even, with its seventeenth-century Puritan self-scrutiny, its nineteenth-century literary "flowering," its abolitionist righteousness, Colonel Shaw and his Black Civil War regiment depicted in granite on Boston Common. At the same time, I found myself, at Radcliffe, among Jewish women. I used to sit for hours over coffee with what I thought of as the "real" Jewish students, who told me about middle-class Jewish culture in America. I described my background — for the first time to strangers — and they took me on, some with amusement at my illiteracy, some arguing that I could never marry into a strict Jewish family, some convinced I didn't "look Jewish," others that I did. I learned the names of holidays and foods, which surnames are Jewish and which are "changed names"; about girls who had had their noses "fixed," their hair straightened. For these young Jewish women, students in the late 1940s, it was acceptable, perhaps even necessary, to strive to look as gentile as possible; but they stuck proudly to being Jewish, expected to marry a Jew, have children, keep the holidays, carry on the culture.

I felt I was testing a forbidden current, that there was danger in these 25 revelations. I bought a reproduction of a Chagall portrait of a rabbi in striped prayer shawl and hung it on the wall of my room. I was admittedly young and trying to educate myself, but I was also doing something that *is* dangerous: I was flirting with identity.

One day that year I was in a small shop where I had bought a dress with a too-long skirt. The shop employed a seamstress who did alterations, and she came in to pin up the skirt on me. I am sure that she was a recent immigrant, a survivor. I remember a short, dark woman wearing heavy glasses, with an accent so foreign I could not understand her words. Something about her presence was very powerful and disturbing to me. After marking and pinning up the skirt, she sat back on her knees, looked up at me, and asked in a hurried whisper: "You Jewish?" Eighteen years of training in assimilation sprang into the reflex by which I shook my head, rejecting her, and muttered, "No."

What was I actually saying "no" to? She was poor, older, struggling with a foreign tongue, anxious; she had escaped the death that had been intended for her, but I had no imagination of her possible courage and foresight, her resistance — I did not see in her a heroine who had perhaps saved many lives, including her own. I saw the frightened immigrant, the seamstress hemming the skirts of college girls, the wandering Jew. But I was an American college girl having her skirt hemmed. And I was frightened myself, I think, because she had recognized me ("It takes one to know one," my friend Edie at Radcliffe had said) even if I refused to recognize myself or her, even if her recognition was sharpened by loneliness or the need to feel safe with me.

But why should she have felt safe with me? I myself was living with a false sense of safety.

There are betrayals in my life that I have known at the very moment were betrayals: this was one of them. There are other betrayals committed so repeatedly, so mundanely, that they leave no memory trace behind, only a growing residue of misery, of dull, accreted self-hatred. Often these take the form not of words but of silence. Silence before the joke at which everyone is laughing; the anti-woman joke, the racist joke, the anti-Semitic joke. Silence and then amnesia. Blocking it out when the oppressor's language starts coming from the lips of one we admire, whose courage and eloquence have touched us: *She didn't really mean that; he didn't really say that.* But the accretions build up out of sight, like scale inside a kettle.

1948: I come home from my freshman year at college, flaming with new insights, new information. I am the daughter who has gone out into the world, to the pinnacle of intellectual prestige, Harvard, fulfilling my father's hopes for me, but also exposed to dangerous influences. I have already been reproved for attending a rally for Henry Wallace and the Progressive party. I challenge my father: "Why haven't you told me that I am Jewish? Why do you never talk about being a Jew?" He answers measurably, "You know that I have never denied that I am a Jew. But it's not important to me. I am a scientist, a deist. I have no use for organized religion. I choose to live in a world of many kinds of people. There are Jews I admire and others whom I despise. I am a person, not simply a Jew." The words are as I remember them, not perhaps exactly as spoken. But that was the message. And it contained enough truth—as all denial drugs itself on partial truth—so that it remained for the time being unanswerable, leaving me high and dry, split at the root, gasping for clarity, for air.

At that time Arnold Rich was living in suspension, waiting to be appointed to the professorship of pathology at Johns Hopkins. The appointment was delayed for years, no Jew ever having held a professional chair in that medical school. And he wanted it badly. It must have been a very bitter time for him, since he had believed so greatly in the redeeming power of excellence, of being the most brilliant, inspired man for the job. With enough excellence, you could presumably make it stop mattering that you were Jewish; you could become the *only* Jew in the gentile world, a Jew so "civilized," so far from "common," so attractively combining southern gentility with European cultural values that no one would ever confuse you with the raw, "pushy" Jews of New York, the "loud, hysterical" refugees from eastern Europe, the "overdressed" Jews of the urban South.

We—my sister, mother, and I—were constantly urged to speak quietly in public, to dress without ostentation, to repress all vividness or spontaneity, to assimilate with a world which might see us as too flamboyant. I suppose that my mother, pure gentile though she was, could be seen as acting "common" or "Jewish" if she laughed too loudly or spoke aggressively. My father's mother, who lived with us half the year, was a model of circumspect behavior, dressed in dark blue or lavender, retiring in company, ladylike to an extreme, wearing no jewelry except a good gold chain, a narrow brooch, or a string of pearls. A few times, within the family, I saw her anger flare, felt the passion she was repressing. But when Arnold took us out to a restaurant or on a trip, the Rich women were always tuned down to some WASP level my father believed, surely, would protect us all — maybe also make us unrecognizable to the "real Jews" who wanted to seize us, drag us back to the *shtetl,* the ghetto, in its many manifestations.

For, yes, that *was* a message — that some Jews would be after you, once they "knew," to rejoin them, to re-enter a world that was messy, noisy, unpredictable, maybe poor — "even though," as my mother once wrote me, criticizing my largely Jewish choice of friends in college, "some of them will be the most brilliant, fascinating people you'll ever meet." I wonder if that isn't one message of assimilation — of America — that the unlucky or the unachieving want to pull you backward, that to identify with them is to court downward mobility, lose the precious chance of passing, of token existence. There was always within this sense of Jewish identity a strong class discrimination. Jews might be "fascinating" as individuals but came with huge unruly families who "poured chicken soup over everyone's head" (in the phrase of a white southern male poet). Anti-Semitism could thus be justified by the bad behavior of certain Jews; and if you did not effectively deny family and community, there would always be a remote cousin claiming kinship with you who was the "wrong kind"of Jew.

I have always believed his attitude toward other Jews depended on who they were. . . . It was my impression that Jews of this background looked down on Eastern European Jews, including Polish Jews and Russian Jews, who generally were not as well educated. This from a letter written to me recently by a gentile who had worked in my father's department, whom I had asked about anti-Semitism there and in particular regarding my father. This informant also wrote me that it was hard to perceive anti-Semitism in Baltimore because the racism made so much more intense an impression: *I would almost have to think that blacks went to a different heaven than the whites, because the bodies were kept in a separate morgue, and some white persons did not even want blood transfusions from black donors.* My father's mind was predictably racist and misogynist; yet as a medical student he noted in his journal that southern male chivalry stopped at the point of any white man in a streetcar giving his seat to an old, weary Black woman standing in the aisle. Was this a Jewish insight — an outsider's insight, even though the outsider was striving to be on the inside?

Because what isn't named is often more permeating than what is, I believe that my father's Jewishness profoundly shaped my own identity and our family existence. They were shaped both by external anti-Semitism and my father's self-hatred, and by his Jewish pride. What Arnold did, I think, was call his Jewish pride something else: achievement, aspiration, genius, idealism. Whatever was unacceptable got left back under the rubric of Jewishness or the "wrong kind" of Jews — uneducated, aggressive, loud. The message I got was that we were really superior: nobody else's father had collected so many books, had traveled so far, knew so many languages. Baltimore was a musical city, but for the most part, in the families of my school friends, culture was for women. My father was an amateur musician, read poetry, adored encyclopedic knowledge. He prowled and pounced over my school papers, insisting I use "grownup" sources; he criticized my poems for faulty technique and gave me books on rhyme and meter and form. His investment in my intellect and talent was egotistical, tyrannical, opinionated, and terribly wearing. He taught me, nevertheless, to believe in hard work, to mistrust easy inspiration, to write and rewrite; to feel that I *was* a person of the book, even though a woman; to take ideas seriously. He made me feel, at a very young age, the power of language and that I could share in it.

The Riches were proud, but we also had to be very careful. Our behavior had to be more impeccable than other people's. Strangers were not to be trusted, nor even friends; family issues must never go beyond the family; the world was full of potential slanderers, betrayers, *people who could not understand*. Even within the family, I realize that I never in my whole life knew what my father was really feeling. Yet he spoke — monologued — with driving intensity. You could grow up in such a house mesmerized by the local electricity, the crucial meanings assumed by the merest things. This used to seem to me a sign that we were all living on some high emotional plane. It was a difficult force field for a favored daughter to disengage from.

Easy to call that intensity Jewish; and I have no doubt that passion is one of the qualities required for survival over generations of persecution. But what happens when passion is rent from its original base, when the white gentile world is softly saying "Be more like us and you can be almost one of us"? What happens when survival seems to mean closing off one emotional artery after another? His forebears in Europe had been forbidden to travel or expelled from one country after another, had special taxes levied on them if they left the city walls, had been forced to wear special clothes and badges, restricted to the poorest neighborhoods. He had wanted to be a "free spirit," to travel widely, among "all kinds of people." Yet in his prime of life he lived in an increasingly withdrawn world, in his house up on a hill in a neighborhood where Jews were not supposed to be able to buy property, depending almost exclusively on interactions with his wife and daughters to provide emotional connectedness. In his home, he created a private defense system so elaborate that even as he was dying, my mother felt unable to talk freely with his colleagues or others who might have helped her. Of course, she acquiesced in this.

The loneliness of the "only," the token, often doesn't feel like loneliness but like a kind of dead echo chamber. Certain things that ought to don't resonate. Somewhere Beverly Smith writes of women of color "inspiring the behavior" in each other. When there's nobody to "inspire the behavior," act out of the culture, there is an atrophy, a dwindling, which is partly invisible.

Sometimes I feel I have seen too long from too many disconnected angles: white, Jewish, anti-Semite, racist, anti-racist, once-married, lesbian, middle-class, feminist, exmatriate southerner, *split at the root* — that I will never bring them whole. I would have liked, in this essay, to bring together the meanings of anti-Semitism and racism as I have experienced them and as I believe they intersect in the world beyond my life. But I'm not able to do this yet. I feel the tension as I think, make notes: *If you really look at the one reality, the other will waver and disperse.* Trying in one week to read Angela Davis and Lucy Davidowicz;[2] trying to hold throughout to a feminist, a lesbian, perspective — what does this mean? Nothing has trained me for this. And sometimes I feel inadequate to make any statement as a Jew; I feel the history of denial within me like an injury, a scar. For assimilation has affected *my* perceptions; those early lapses in meaning, those blanks, are with me still. My ignorance can be dangerous to me and to others.

Yet we can't wait for the undamaged to make our connections for us; 40 we can't wait to speak until we are perfectly clear and righteous. There is no purity and, in our lifetimes, no end to this process.

This essay, then, has no conclusions: it is another beginning for me. Not just a way of saying, in 1982 Right Wing America, *I, too, will wear the yellow star.* It's a moving into accountability, enlarging the range of accountability. I know that in the rest of my life, the next half century or so, every aspect of my identity will have to be engaged. The middle-class white girl taught to trade obedience for privilege. The Jewish lesbian raised to be a heterosexual gentile. The woman who first heard oppression named and analyzed in the Black Civil Rights struggle. The woman with three sons, the feminist who hates male violence. The woman limping with a cane, the woman who has stopped bleeding are also accountable. The poet who knows that beautiful language can lie, that the oppressor's language sometimes sounds beautiful. The woman trying, as part of her resistance, to clean up her act.

Suggestions for Writing and Discussion
1. Writers choose their details very selectively. In paragraph 6, what details does Rich give us about the place of her birth? Speculate on details she may have omitted and on why she chose to include just these three. How are these particular details important to the rest of this essay?
2. What souvenirs does Rich associate with her grandfather? Analyze the significance of these three items in relation to Rich's identity.
3. From the details provided in the essay, explain why Rich's father, Arnold, does not talk about his Jewish experience. Why didn't he insist that his

---

[2]Angela Y. Davis, *Woman, Race and Class* (New York: Random House, 1981); Lucy S. Davidowicz, *The War against the Jews 1933–1945* (New York: Bantam, 1979).

children learn the teachings of his ancestors? Explain whether or not, and why, you agree with his decisions and actions (or lack of actions).

4. What does Rich mean when she says "it was white social christianity . . . that the world was founded on"? Given the details and examples in this essay, what do you believe to be her definition of "white social christianity"? What is her definition of "the world"? Do you agree with her observations? Explain.

5. Why did Rich consider it "dangerous" for her to be "flirting with identity"? Explain the possible effects of flirting with one's identity.

6. What does Rich mean by the "wrong kind of Jew"? Is she overgeneralizing here? Does her statement serve to perpetuate stereotypes or to face them down? Explain.

7. According to Rich, what happens when people lose their culture? Evaluate the role of culture in your own family. For example, how important is an ethnic background or a religion, or both, to you?

8. In some ways, Rich is arguing that in order to keep a culture alive, a person must openly live, openly profess the values and beliefs of that culture. Do you agree with this viewpoint? Give good reasons to support this claim; or give good reasons to denounce it.

Suggestions for Extended Thinking and Research

1. Write an essay in which you define one of the following terms: honesty, courage, integrity, identity. Use Rich's essay for support, and use illustrations and specific examples from your life and those you know.

2. Read several of Rich's poems. Choose three of your favorites, and write an essay in which you compare and contrast these three poems in terms of themes and values. Use any themes and values from this essay whenever appropriate.

MARK MATHABANE

The African Contribution

> *Born in South Africa in 1960, Mark Mathabane grew up under the harsh strictures of the apartheid system. His first book,* Kaffir Boy *(1986), explains and evaluates his childhood experiences. Explaining his title, Mathabane notes that* Kaffir *is a slang term used by some South African whites to degrade blacks. This selection comes from his second book,* Kaffir Boy in America *(1989), written to describe his life as a student who came to the United States on a tennis scholarship.*

Prereading/Journal-Writing Suggestions

1. Explain your experience with a book you read that you couldn't put down — one that engulfed you, kept you reading, made you hope that the last page would never come.
2. Explain your process as you study something new. (This need not be formal study in school but might instead relate to work, family life, a hobby, or the like. You might think of a past learning experience as well as a more recent experience to use as examples as you explain your process.)

In the library one afternoon, having completed my homework, I began browsing among the bookshelves. I came upon a paperback copy of *Black Boy,* Richard Wright's searing autobiography. My attention was arrested by the title and by the following defiant words on the back cover of the book: "The white South said that it knew 'niggers,' and I was what the white South called 'nigger.' Well, the white South had never known me — never known what I thought, what I felt."

I mentally replaced "white South" with "white South Africa," and "nigger" with "Kaffir," and was intrigued by how Richard Wright's feelings mirrored my own. I immediately sat down in a chair by the window and began reading the book. I was overwhelmed; I could not put the book down. I even missed my economics class because I was so engrossed. When the library closed I was three-quarters of the way through the book. Bleary-eyed, I went back to my room and read the rest.

The next day I went back to the library and asked the head librarian — a good-natured Franciscan priest with white hair and a charming smile — if the library had more books by black authors. He guided me to the treasure. I checked out Richard Wright's *Native Son,* Eldridge Cleaver's *Soul on Ice,* W. E. B. Du Bois's *Souls of Black Folks, The Autobiography of Malcolm X,* Franz Fanon's *The Wretched of the Earth,* Claude Brown's *Manchild of the Promised Land,* James Baldwin's *The Fire Next Time* and *Notes of a Native Son,* Maya

Angelou's *I Know Why the Caged Bird Sings,* James Weldon Johnson's *The Autobiography of an Ex-Colored Man,* and the autobiography and incendiary speeches of Frederick Douglass. I devoured the books with relish.

After this momentous discovery I knew that my life would never be the same. Here were black men and women, rebels in their own right, who had felt, thought, and suffered deeply, who had grown up under conditions that had threatened to destroy their very souls; here they were, baring their bleeding hearts on paper, using words as weapons, plunging into realms of experience I had never before thought reachable, and wrestling with fate itself in an heroic attempt to make the incomprehensible — man's inhumanity to man — comprehensible. Most astonishing was that these men and women had written about what I felt and thought, what I had been through as a black man, what I desired, what I dreamed about, and what I refused to compromise.

"These are soul mates," I said to myself, "these are my true brothers 5 and sisters." Where had they been all those years when I was lost in the wilderness, feeling so alone, wondering why I was being misunderstood by the world, why I seemed so at odds with complacent reality? I had to learn to write like them, to purge myself of what they had purged themselves of so eloquently. Here was a way through which I could finally understand myself, perform the duty I'd pledged to my countrymen and to my mother.

Inspired by these black writers, I bought myself a pair of notebooks and sat down one evening and began to write. I chose as a topic an issue of which I had only superficial knowledge, but one which appealed to my fancy. Words came very easily to the pen, but when I paused to evaluate what I had written and compared it to the masters I was determined to emulate, I found my effort ridiculous. The language was verbose, the ideas vague and incoherent. What was I doing wrong? Maybe I needed some expert advice. One day Mr. Allan, my English teacher, asked us to write a short story.

My story — a vivid, fictional description of Africa — was considered the best by Mr. Allan, who was a hard-to-please but excellent critic and teacher of English. He was stingy with A's, no matter how well the job was done. I received an A for my essay; my previous assignments had merited C's and B-minuses.

I carefully analyzed the essay to determine what exactly had so impressed the scrupulous teacher. I came up with the following answer: to write well, write about what you know, for experience is the best teacher, and writing is a means of self-expression.

Flushed with confidence from writing the essay, I jotted down ideas for more essays and possibly novels. I filled notebooks with descriptions and characters and plots. Maybe writing is my calling in life, I thought. Determined to hone my skills, I went back to my favorite writers for tips on how to go about the arduous task of learning how to move the world with the right word and the right accent. Every one of the writers I admired had been a voracious reader of books. I was already one. They had felt deeply. I felt deeply, too. They possessed an inborn obsession to share with the rest of humanity, through the written word, their innermost feelings, their vision of life, its agony and ecstasy, its manifold pains and sorrows and joys, its loves and hatreds — all of which they had extracted by looking deeply and with compassion into the human heart.

Such a temperament I believed I still lacked because I had yet to acquire 10 a sound liberal arts education. The college library had an impressive record collection of Shakespeare's plays; the dramas of Sophocles, Euripides, and Aristophanes; the *Dialogues* of Plato; the poems of Milton; and the plays of Dryden and Goldsmith, read by such giants of the stage as Paul Robeson, Claire Bloom, Sir Laurence Olivier, Anthony Quayle, Richard Burton, Sir John Gielgud, and Paul Schofield, among others. I checked out these records at the rate of three a day, and listened to them over and over again. The head librarian expressed pleasure at seeing me madly in love with Shakespeare and soon I was being talked about.

I took an English course with Professor Ann Klein. She instantly detected my enthusiastic love for poetry and helped me improve my taste and understanding of Keats, Shelley, Wordsworth, Coleridge, and Byron. Whereas heretofore my enjoyment of classical music had been visceral, I enrolled in a piano class out of a belief that the best way to understand classical music was to play an instrument.

Other subjects I now enjoyed were economics and philosophy. In the latter, taught by the easygoing, amiable Father Lucan, I was introduced to the brilliant ideas and provocative arguments for greater liberty, toleration, and individuality by Locke, Rousseau, and John Stuart Mill. The notably eclectic course Personal and Moral Life merely mentioned in passing their great ideas, but I went out in search of the complete works and read them avidly. I was fascinated by Rousseau's *The Social Contract,* especially his famous assertion "Man is born free, and everywhere he is in chains. One thinks himself the master of others and still remains a greater slave than they." But I found some of his arguments elliptical and contradictory. Mill and Locke became my favorite philosophers. I was amazed to discover, with repeated readings of their seminal works, that they basically confirmed what I had believed instinctively about the nature of freedom, individuality, and natural and civil rights. Locke's "Treatise on Toleration," his "Second Essay on Government," and Mill's *On Liberty* and *The Subjection of Women* left a decisive influence on my mind. This immersion in books alleviated the stress of constantly worrying about the condition of my mother and family.

Once again my love affair with the world of books landed me in trouble. I now walked about with a mind pregnant with thoughts inspired by reading. I longed to live only in the world of the imagination and ideas because physical reality suddenly seemed artificial, cold, dead. I became absentminded. Some of the black students on campus wondered why I no longer came to their parties, why I occasionally sat alone in the cafeteria, deep in thought.

"He's too proud," someone said.

"He's trying to be white," another said.   15

"He thinks he is better than us."

"He's stir-crazy."

They never understood my need for solitude, that "to fly from, need not be to hate, mankind." They never understood why I found great pleasure in watching squirrels racing up and down trees, in walking down to the Mississippi River and spending the afternoon staring at its murky waters, at the falling autumn leaves along its banks, at clouds sailing across the sky, and at the sleepy town of Hannibal on the other side, where Mark Twain was born. They never understood why I loved memorizing poetry, why I used quotations from books to illustrate a point, or why I urged them to become more politically active on campus so they could better protect their interests and make their presence felt as blacks. I tried establishing ties of solidarity with them, given our common experiences growing up in the ghetto, but we kept drifting apart because of our divergent attitudes. I was eager to fight, to protest, as black Americans had done in the 1960s, during those unforgettable days of Martin Luther King, Jr., Malcolm X, and Stokely Carmichael's misunderstood credo of Black Power. They were eager to accommodate, to live for the moment, to make their peace with the status quo, to wallow in apathy and self-pity. At times it appeared that I had come to America a generation too late. In fairness to many of these black students, they were concerned that an activist attitude might lose them their athletic scholarships or financial aid.

In celebration of black history month, in February 1980, I wrote the following poem, entitled "Longing for My Roots." It was a nostalgic poem, inspired by thoughts of home and of my ailing mother.

when I was a little child
living amidst innocence among
the chaste hills
and the pure forests and purer
streams
i never for a single moment paused
to think
that there might come a
time
when all i would have to live with
was to be just a memory

all the enchanting silhouettes of
the africa
i used to so lovingly know
all the natural beauty of her
beasts
the magnificent plumage of her
wild birds
the blithesomeness of her

black people
the eternal feeling of freedom
among singing titihoyes
the rivers that seem to eddy whirl
their courses
through hills and plains

all the everlasting elegance of
the springbok
the gentle tip-tappering of
summer's rain
the haunting murmur of
the windsong
the thundering of hooves
upon the serengeti

all that i am now without
all that boundless joy
i once so much cherished
i have prematurely left behind
to die and to decay

yet an african still am i
a proud man as such
i am black (soot black)
a handsome black warrior as such
i am still the proud possessor
of that undaunted spirit
reminiscent of endless freedom
among the misty hills
where the zebra used to cry
with ecstatic joy

i still remember the kraal
the grassy citadel of
my forefathers
i still can smell
the scent of fresh cowdung
and in hours of solitude
i still can hear
the bewitching sound of cowhide drums
and see through the haze of time
valiant, plumed warriors
as they leap and fall
while others

fall
never to leap again

even now
far, far away from home
oceans of water away
i still can see the misty hills
i can still hear mama's voice
echoing through the valley of
a thousand hills
calling me to come home
for supper around the fireside

I showed the poem to several black students. Some of them, apparently 20
ignorant or ashamed of their heritage as African-Americans, regarded it as
confirmation of Africa's primitiveness. But I was proud of it. I knew that
Africa, despite its many and serious problems, despite the Western tendency
to stereotype it, remained a place of immense natural and cultural beauty, and
that its diverse, proud, brave, resilient, and beautiful peoples are descended
from some of the oldest civilizations on earth, which have made valuable
contributions to literature, art, music, dance, science, religion, and other
fields of human endeavor.

Suggestions for Writing and Discussion

1. From this piece, describe Mark Mathabane's personality — his view toward learning, toward himself, toward life, toward others. How do you
   evaluate the values these views suggest? Do you share the same values? Or
   do you see Mathabane's goals and ideals as distinctly different from your
   own?
2. Can you explain why Mathabane was so overwhelmed with the writings
   of black American authors?
3. Why does Mathabane set himself on a pilgrimage to learn how to write
   more effectively? Can you explain the source of his inspiration? Can you
   relate to this type of zealous quest?
4. As Mathabane sees it, what was the major difference between his past
   writing assignments (on which he earned B's and C's) and his story about
   Africa (on which he earned an A). Have you ever made similar evaluations
   of your own writing? Choose a piece of your own writing that you particularly like and explain its strengths.
5. What commonalities did Mathabane discover among his favorite writers?
   What didn't he find in their backgrounds that he, perhaps, had experienced
   in his own?
6. What does Mathabane mean when he says that his "love affair with the
   world of books" got him in trouble? Would you define his experiences as

trouble? Why or why not? In what ways does a book's power differ from a visual or real-world experience? Can one be valued over the other?

7. What might Mathabane mean by "At times it appeared that I had come to America a generation too late." What had happened in this past generation? Why might Mathabane just now be recognizing this new way of thinking?

8. Read Mathabane's poem slowly, out loud. Then silently, to yourself, re-read this poem. Jot down (or annotate) the images that move you the most. What do you now know about Africa that you didn't know before? What do you know about Mathabane? What do you know about yourself?

Suggestions for Extended Thinking and Research

1. Research the politics of South Africa in the 1950s and early 1960s. Compare the workings of the government and its rules and policies with those in the United States during the same period of time. How have those policies changed in South Africa? In the United States? Explain why you do or do not think additional changes are needed.

2. List your five favorite authors. Research each one of their lives in order to discover their approaches to writing. Search for any of their early failings as well as their successes to give you an accurate picture about the writer's life.

3. Read three books, essays, short stories, or poems by black authors whose works you have never read before. (The list in paragraph 3 provides some possibilities; consider also the writings of Alice Walker, Toni Morrison, Toni Cade Bambara, Paule Marshall, June Jordan, and Gloria Naylor.) While reading the selections you choose, keep a reaction journal, a place to respond to anything you wish. At the end of your readings, review your response journal. Write an essay in which you synthesize and analyze your responses to these three works.

4. Read three books, essays, short stories, or poems by authors who are rooted in your own family's culture. For example, if your ancestors are from Poland, find three Polish writers to study and read; if your ancestors are Puerto Rican, find three Puerto Rican authors to read. As in suggestion 3, keep a response journal for these readings. Write an essay, perhaps along the lines of Mathabane's piece, in which you analyze what you have learned and explain in what ways the readings have affected you.

JAY FORD

20/20 Hindsight

Born in 1969, Jay Ford grew up in New York City, where he completed his elementary and secondary schooling. He graduated from Wesleyan University with a major in African-American history. To complete his major, Ford studied in Kenya for part of his junior year. In this essay, Ford explains the insights he gained during his stay in Kenya, an African nation that won independence from Great Britain in 1963.

Prereading/Journal-Writing Suggestions

1. Imagine you win a six-month excursion to Africa. Explain where you would like to visit and what you would like to see on this trip.
2. List every image and/or fact that comes to mind when you think of Africa. (For instance, list countries, cities, languages.)
3. Write about a time you were a minority in a crowd. How did you feel? How did you think others would react to you? How did your expectations compare with the actual reactions you observed?

Born into a middle class African–American family on the upper west side of Manhattan, I have spent most of my life chasing the (white) American dream. Absorbing the rhetoric brewed by the media, school curricula, and, more important, my teachers, I was graduated from high school with the goal of travelling to Europe, achieving a college degree, becoming a corporate lawyer and, eventually, marrying a spouse who would be most likely white or a light-skinned black. We would have two homes and probably three children. This was my rough sketch of my future, one with which I was satisfied. I would be a success and this was very important because I clearly represent what W. E. B. DuBois coined as the "talented tenth." Therefore, I had a responsibility to my people to succeed, to vanquish the disabilities associated with my color and earn my place in white America, my America.

In starting off on my journey to success, I met my first obstacle as I neared the end of my sophomore year in college. The student body had taken over the administration building in hopes of persuading the University to divest monies invested in corporations in South Africa. A meeting between the students and the administration had been arranged during which the administration had thoroughly explained its position on divestment. Now it was the students' turn to respond. As student after student approached the microphone, explaining what he/she believed to be the most important reasons for disinvesting, an unsettling feeling began to overwhelm me. Although all of the explanations were more than legitimate reasons to disinvest, none of them had touched my personal reasons for protesting the University's position on divestment.

When it was my turn, I did not actually know what I wanted to say, but I was determined to say something. "My name is Julius J. Ford. I am an Afro-American. Inherent in my title is the word African, meaning 'of Africa.'" My ancestry is from Africa. Africans are therefore my people, my history. So as long as you continue to oppress my people through violence or investment or silence, you oppress me. And as long as you oppress me, I will fight you! I will fight you!" As I returned to my seat, my friend leaned over, patted me on the back and said, "That was great, I never really knew you felt that way." I turned to him and said, "Neither did I."

It was this event that made me question myself. How could I be satisfied with my sketch of success when it had no background or depth? Why had I not felt this strongly about Africa or Africans before? Why was I more attracted to women who possessed European features (straight hair, light skin, thin nose) than those who possessed African features? Why did I feel that Europe was so great and Africa so primitive? Why did I choose to call myself an African-American when I knew virtually nothing about Africa? These questions would trouble my soul for the remainder of the year. In fact, they would push me to apply to a student exchange program in East Africa, Kenya.

Called "An Experiment in International Living," the program would 5 offer me travel throughout the country, during which time I would live in both rural and urban areas, in both huts and hotels, for approximately four months from February through mid-May, 1989. I would be equipped with two academic directors with numerous university and government contacts and ensured a variety of learning opportunities, as I would stay with native families and be allowed to venture off on my own.

Even though this program seemingly presented an optimum opportunity to find answers to all my pending questions, I was still apprehensive about my decision to go. But, perhaps if there was one specific incident that canceled any wavering on my part, it was that Friday afternoon at drama class. On Fridays, I taught drama to about twenty 9–14-year-old kids from predominantly black families with low incomes at a community center about twenty minutes from my college. On this particular day I had decided to ask the class what they thought about my taking a trip to Africa. They shot off these responses: "Why would you want to go to Africa to get even blacker than you are now?", "Why don't you take a trip somewhere nice like Paris, London, Rome?", "But they say in Africa every one is backwards, they can't teach you anything," "People are so black and ugly there." And, although some of the comments from the children were said specifically to make the other children laugh, many of them were exemplifications of how our educational system and other forms of external social propaganda affect a black child's mind.

When I first arrived in Kenya, we stayed in its capital city, Nairobi. Surprisingly enough, my first impression of Nairobi was that it was just like any American city: skyscrapers, movie theatres, discos, and crime. In fact, I was a bit disappointed, feeling that I had travelled fifteen hours in a Pan Am jet just to come back to New York City. But upon more detailed observation, I realized that this city was quite different from any other I had visited before. This city was black and, when I say black, I'm not talking your coffee-colored Atlanta, Oakland, Harlem black people. I mean black! I mean when you were small and used to play games and chose to embarrass the darkest kid on the block by calling him "midnight," "shadow," and "teeth black."

But the lesson to be learned in Nairobi was that all shades of black were equally attractive and the small children did not penalize attractiveness according to shade of skin, or length of hair, or size of nose. Furthermore, being in a black city, knowing I was in a mostly black country that sits on a predominantly black continent, enhanced my confidence and hence my actions. For the first time in my life I felt as though I could do anything, fit in anywhere, be welcomed by everyone because of my color. This was the feeling I had often assumed blacks felt during the Twenties, the period of the Harlem Renaissance. It was wonderful! I would go for days without being aware of my color. It did not seem to matter.

It was only a few weeks into the program, however, when I began to notice racial insecurities developing within my peer group (of twenty-four I was the only black). As many as half a dozen of the other students declared that they had begun to view black children as more beautiful than white, that black women and black features were more pleasing to the eye than white ones. Others simply segregated themselves from the black society as much as possible, refusing to stay with families without another white person present. Perhaps, then, inherent in the role of minority come feelings of inferiority, a certain lack of confidence, insecurity.

Because there is much tribalism in Kenya, the first title I had to drop 10 was African-American. When people around me refer to themselves as Masai or Kikuyu as opposed to Kenyan or East African, then how could I refer to myself as an African? Furthermore, the language I spoke, my values, morals and education were not African. So this put me in an awkward position. No one could question my ancestry as African because of my color, so I enjoyed most benefits of majority status. Yet, to many Kenyans, I was much more similar to a white American than an African so there was a wide gap between us.

It was here I realized that to be an accepted descendant of Africa I had a lot of work to do. I needed to learn a new language and a new culture. I needed to assimilate, and I figured that that shouldn't be too hard as I had twenty years of experience in that in the United States. But, the difference between my American and Kenyan assimilations is that in Kenya it seemed to be welcomed if not encouraged by the majority. The more knowledge I attained of Kenya and the more I left my English at home and spoke Swahili or another tribal language, the more cultural doors opened to me. For example, as I became increasingly familiar with Gidiam tribal customs and my use of Kiswahili improved, I was able to travel along the coast for days never worrying about food or lodging. I was often given the opportunity to sit and discuss with elders, and take part in tribal ceremonies and had responsibilities bestowed on me by elder men, *Mzees,* or my temporary *Mama.* In fact, toward the end of my trip, when travelling alone, it was often difficult for me to convince people that I was African-American. They would tell me, *"Una toka Africa qwa sababo una weza kusema Kiswahili na una famhamu Africa life"* (You are from Africa because you are able to speak Kiswahili and you understand African life). The more I learned, the more comfortable I was with the title African-American.

I also took more pride in myself. Here it was important to learn that the black empowerment was not from sheer numbers, it was from the fact that the blacks in Africa possess a communal sense of self, a shared past that is to never be forgotten, that has passed through generations, and is used as a reference for modern-day experiences. An exemplification of this concept is the way in which Kenyans and Africans in general treat their elderly. In Kenya you are told that you never grow to equal your parents' authority or knowledge. Your elders will forever be your elders and respected as such. In Kenya, elderly people are cherished not forgotten.

As we visited small villages in the areas of Kisumu, Nakru, and on the coast, villages which by American standards were far below the poverty line, we were welcomed with feasts of foods, drinks, people and music. To them we were guests paying them the honor of visitation. Even on a more individual level, most Kenyan families were extraordinarily hospitable. To be welcomed into a stranger's home and be offered food, wine, and a bed for an unlimited number of days is shocking to Americans and even more so to a New Yorker.

This humanistic view was very difficult to adapt to because it affected every level of Kenyan society. For example, Kenyans have a very limited concept of personal space (but in a country with a population growth rate of 4.3 percent that is quite understandable). So it was often difficult for me to discover that my four newly acquired brothers were also my newly acquired bedmates, to change money at the bank while the people behind me were looking over my shoulder examining my passport and money exchange papers, and to learn not to tell your family that you would like to be left alone because crazy people stay by themselves.

Also, Americans are lost outside of a linear society. We are taught from 15 kindergarten to stay in line. Order for us is symbolically represented by the line, and we therefore choose to see all other forms of non-linear collective activity as chaotic. Kenyans, however, do not have this same view of order. They choose to mass together, aggressively seeking out their desires and bringing new meaning to the words "organized chaos." Mobs catch buses, herds are seen at ticket counters, and, unfortunately, until your adjustment period is complete, you stand apart from the chaos, "jaw dropped," staring at the stampede of people. As a result, you do not obtain a ticket or get on the bus.

This conception of order plus the Kenyan view of personal space make for exciting moments in the public sphere. For example, there is a type of

Kenyan public transportation called *matatus*. Matatus are small privately owned minivans that serve as buses for local citizens. To ride a matatu is like taking the most crowded New York City subway car during rush hour, placing that car on Broadway, and allowing a taxicab driver to control the wheel. Matatus do not actually stop at designated bus stops; in fact, they do not actually stop at all. Instead, they simply slow down and those who need to get off push and shove their way to the front of the van and jump out. And as for those who wish to board, they simply chase the matatu down and shove and push their way onto the van. As with circus clown cars, there is always room for one more.

Another linear concept I was introduced to was time. In rural areas there would sometimes be days when we would have no activities planned. It was at these moments when I would curse my directors for poor planning. But I was soon to learn that doing nothing was not necessarily wasted time. This time to think, relax, conversationalize was most important for a peaceful state of mind. I finally understood that it is not imperative even in America to eat breakfast, read the paper in the street while you are running to the subway, or to work two jobs just to pay off your life insurance bill. Here there was not "so much to do and so little time"; here there was a great deal to do but also the belief that that which is supposed to get done will get done in time.

For example, during the last month of my stay in Kenya I visited a small farm in Kisumu Kaubu, Uganda, with a woman and her three sons. I was only to stay for a day and one night. I had come to visit just prior to the time the rains were expected, so I had assumed that the family was going to spend very little time relaxing with me because it was imperative that the soil and seeds for the year be prepared for the rains which could come at any moment.

However, once I arrived, we did very little field work. We talked instead — about the history of her people, about America, and about American perceptions of Kenya. Of course this was hard work since their English was very limited and my Swahili is fair at best. And as the day crept on to the night, I asked her how she could afford to give her attentions to me when the threat of the rains could come at any day now. *"Pole Pole, bwana,"* she replied (We have not neglected our work to the fields. We have only delayed our work so to welcome our new son, who by joining us will ease our workload). I then asked her, "But, Mama, it is already 11:00 and I leave tomorrow at 9:00." She replied, "Don't worry, bwana, we start to work the cattle (plow) at 2:00 A.M. Good night."

It seemed as though Kenyan culture chose to be humanistic rather than materialistic. The value placed on human life and interaction is much greater than in the States. To shake hands, to share a meal or even your home with a foreigner is an honor, not a burden. And, for you as a guest to turn down that hand, meal, or bed is an insult. How wonderfully strange to travel to a foreign land where people who can hardly understand what language you speak are ready to take you home and make you part of the family. They wouldn't last too long in New York, I thought.

In most places in Kenya, it was common knowledge for one to know his/her environment. People could name the types of trees along the roads, tell you animals indigenous to the area, and explain which types of soil were best for growing specific crops. They could tell you the staple foods of different parts of Kenya *or* even the U.S. In fact, their world geography was superior to that of most American college students. Access to information, whether at home or in schools, was a privilege to be appreciated by those involved and then passed down to younger generations orally. I wonder why I did not feel this way. My country offers more educational opportunities than any other in the world and yet seldom are these opportunities fully exploited. American students go to school, but they do not go to learn. They go to get A's and move up economically. They go to play the game, the educational game of success that I like to refer to as DT (Diploma Training), a process that verifies one's intelligence by certificate as opposed to action or common sense.

Furthermore, along with this overwhelming appreciation for knowledge, Kenyans show reverence for everyday simplicities which we in America take for granted: the appreciation for candlelight, running water, a toilet with a seat cover, a long hot shower every day. Learning to live is to stay in Kenya and survive with twenty-three other people living mostly off rain water, sleeping in huts, and eating many fruits and vegetables with only the occasional beef meal. I felt as though Kenya taught me a new dimension of life, a rebirth of sorts. It put objectives, time, goals, values into a new perspective. It did not tell me, "Please be aware of how much water you use because a drought warning is in effect." It gave me a gallon of water and told me to drink and bathe for an undetermined period. It did not tell me of the beauties of nature, rather it revealed them to me by greeting me in the morning with the sights of Mt. Kenya, Kilimanjaro, and Lake Victoria. I saw no need for National Geographic or wildlife television, for when it wanted to introduce me to animals, a monkey, leopard, or family of raccoons would become my fellow pedestrians. There was no urge to tell me of the paradox of zoos when it could show me national parks with hundreds of acres of land.

In Kenya I felt more free than I have ever felt before. The only thing holding me captive was the earth which would grow the food, the sky which would quench the earth of its thirst, and the sun which would warm and help all things to grow. But these masters were sure to give back all that you have put in. When you worked hard, your rewards were great, and if you chose to relax so would your crop and cattle. And with a give-and-take relationship like this, one learns that it is okay to take time, time for others, for oneself, time to enjoy and appreciate all that life and earth offer. Some choose to call this type of relationship religion, a covenant with the Lord and her divinity (sky, earth, and animals, and I will not deny that there was a strong sense of God or Allah or Sa or Buddha).

A forest burning to the ground germinates the soil, allowing new life to grow. The omnipotence of nature — floods, lightning, hurricanes, earthquakes, the beauty of a cheetah or giraffe running, an open field, the sky, the mountains, the sea — is overwhelming and foreign to me living so long in a concrete jungle. When all of this engulfed me and I took the time to embrace it, I became convinced that there exists a master craftsperson of this creation, that there exists a God.

Kenya has more than (just) given me a new perception of the world; Kenya has widened my world view. I now realize that there are other significant cultures in the world besides a western one. I no longer think of the world in First, Second, and Third World terms. There are aspects of Kenyan values which should be regarded as more First World than American: humanistic sentiments, importance of family, pride of ancestry, appreciation and respect for other peoples' differences.

Also, whereas I ventured off to Kenya to learn about a new culture and its new people, I found that most of the more important discoveries and evaluations were about myself. Upon leaving Kenya I feel that I have grown more confident about my African-Americanness, my perceptions of the world around me, and my expectation of 21/21 vision and beyond. I do not believe I could have gone anywhere else on earth and been as personally challenged.

Suggestions for Writing and Discussion

1. On the basis of his very first impressions, explain what lessons you believe Ford learned, not only about Kenya but also about himself.
2. After the first few weeks, what changes does Ford notice in the group? Do you agree with his thought that "in the role of minority come feelings of inferiority, a certain lack of confidence, insecurity"? Support your answer by giving details and examples from personal experience or observation.
3. What does Ford have to do in order to be accepted into this new culture? Would a foreigner in America have to adjust in a similar manner? Explain your answer with specific examples.
4. Compare how native Kenyans entertain foreigners with how Americans treat foreigners. What similarities do you find? What differences? Obviously, there is not one simple answer to this question. Explore as many possibilities as you can, based on experience, observation, reading, or watching television documentaries and news programs.
5. What does Ford mean when he says "Americans are lost outside of a linear society"? How would you define a "linear society"? Explain why you do or do not agree with this perception.
6. Compare Ford's concept of "linear time" to the Kenyans' view of order. Which concept does Ford prefer? Which one do you prefer? Explain your reasons.
7. According to Ford, Kenyan culture is more concerned with people than with material goods. He writes that "the value placed on human life . . . is much greater than in the States." After analyzing the facts and examples he has provided to support this contention, explain whether you agree with this observation.
8. Ford makes a comparison between American schools and schools in

Kenya. He concludes, "American students go to school, but they do not go to learn." From your own experience and observations and from what you have read, evaluate the American education system. Then explain why you agree or disagree with Ford's observation.

9. What is Ford's purpose in making such comparisons throughout this essay? Do you believe he achieves his purpose? Does he suggest any possibilities for synthesis between the two cultures? Do you see such possibilities?

Suggestions for Extended Thinking and Research

1. Find several current, reliable sources concerning Kenya and research one or more of the topics that Ford addresses: family, education, philosophies, traditions, acceptance of other cultures. Write an analysis of your findings, explaining why and how they support, enhance, or challenge Ford's perceptions.

2. Explain why you disagree or agree strongly with a statement Ford has made about Americans and their culture. You might write this explanation as a letter directed to Ford.

3. Write an essay evaluating the discoveries you made when you visited a new culture. (This new culture does not have to be a different country. Instead, it could be the culture of a family that is very different from your own, or the culture of a university or college, or the culture of a region of the United States you had not previously visited.) Avoid writing a simple travel log. Instead, aim to reveal the deeper workings of the culture you encountered, as Ford did; in addition, explain how these discoveries changed or affected you.

DAVID MORRIS

Rootlessness

> *David Morris is the author of* The New City States *(1983) and coauthor, with Karl Hess, of* Neighborhood Power: The New Localism *(1975). Morris currently serves as codirector of the Institute for Local Self-Reliance in Washington, D.C., writes an editorial column for the* St. Paul Pioneer Press-Dispatch, *and contributes frequently to other magazines and journals, particularly those concerned with social issues. "Rootlessness" was first published in the* Utne Reader *in the May/June 1990 issue.*

Prereading/Journal-Writing Suggestions

1. What was your hometown like when you were growing up? What is it like today? Have the changes been for the better or for the worse?
2. Could you survive without a car? Write a piece in which you imagine what today would be like if the automobile had never been invented.
3. Most Americans feel as if they know television celebrities better than their own next-door neighbors. Do you fit into this category? What explanations do you have for this phenomenon, in general?

Americans are a rootless people. Each year one in six of us changes residences; one in four changes jobs. We see nothing troubling in these statistics. For most of us, they merely reflect the restless energy that made America great. A nation of immigrants, unsurprisingly, celebrates those willing to pick up stakes and move on: the frontiersman, the cowboy, the entrepreneur, the corporate raider.

Rootedness has never been a goal of public policy in the United States. In the 1950s and 1960s local governments bulldozed hundreds of inner city neighborhoods, all in the name of urban renewal. In the 1960s and 1970s court-ordered busing forced tens of thousands of children to abandon their neighborhood schools, all in the interest of racial harmony. In the 1980s a wave of hostile takeovers shuffled hundreds of billions of dollars of corporate assets, all in the pursuit of economic efficiency.

Hundreds of thousands of informal gathering spots that once nurtured community across the country have disappeared. The soda fountain and lunch counter are gone. The branch library is an endangered species. Even the number of neighborhood taverns is declining. In the 1940s, 90 percent of beer and spirits was consumed in public places. Today only 30 percent is.

This privatization of American public life is most apparent to overseas visitors. "After four years here, I still feel more of a foreigner than in any other place in the world I have been," one well-traveled woman told Ray

Oldenburg, the author of the marvelous new book about public gathering spots, *The Great Good Place* (1990, Paragon House). "There is no contact between the various households, we rarely see the neighbors and certainly do not know any of them."

The woman contrasts this with her life in Europe. "In Luxembourg,   5 however, we would frequently stroll down to one of the local cafés in the evening and there pass a very congenial few hours in the company of the local fireman, dentist, bank employee, or whoever happened to be there at the time."

In most American cities, zoning laws prohibit mixing commerce and residence. The result is an overreliance on the car. Oldenburg cites the experience of a couple who had lived in a small house in Vienna and a large one in Los Angeles: "In Los Angeles we are hesitant to leave our sheltered home in order to visit friends or to participate in cultural or entertainment events because every such outing involves a major investment of time and nervous strain in driving long distances. In Vienna everything, opera, theaters, shops, cafés, are within easy walking distance."

Shallow roots weaken our ties in the neighborhood and workplace. The average blue-collar worker receives only seven days' notice before losing his or her job, only two days when not backed by a union. The *Whole Earth Review* unthinkingly echoes this lack of connectedness when it advises its readers to "first visit an electronics store near you and get familiar with the features — then compare price and shop mail order via [an] 800 number."

This lack of connectedness breeds a costly instability in American life. In business, when owners have no loyalty to workers, workers have no loyalty to owners. Quality of work suffers. Visiting Japanese management specialists point to our labor turnover rate as a key factor in our relative economic decline. In the pivotal electronics industry, for example, our turnover rate is four times that of Japan's.

American employers respond to declining sales and profit margins by cutting what they regard as their most expendable resource: employees. In Japan, corporate accounting systems consider labor a fixed asset. Japanese companies spend enormous amounts of money training workers. "They view that training as an investment, and they don't want to let the investment slip away," Martin K. Starr of Columbia University recently told *Business Week.* Twenty percent of the work force, the core workers in major industrial companies, have lifetime job security in Japan.

Rootlessness in the neighborhood also costs us dearly. Neighborliness 10 saves money, a fact we often overlook because the transactions of strong, rooted neighborhoods take place outside of the money economy.

- Neighborliness reduces crime. People watch the streets where children play and know who the strangers are.
- Neighborliness saves energy. In the late 1970s Portland, Oregon, discovered it could save 5 percent of its energy consumption simply by reviving the corner grocery store. No longer would residents in

need of a carton of milk or a loaf of bread have to drive to a shopping mall.

• Neighborliness lowers the cost of health care. "It is cruel and unusual punishment to send someone to a nursing home when they are not sick," says Dick Ladd, head of Oregon's Senior Services. But when we don't know our neighbors we can't rely on them. Society picks up the tab. In 1987 home-based care cost $230 a month in Oregon compared to $962 per month for nursing home care.

Psychoanalyst and author Erich Fromm saw a direct correlation between the decline in the number of neighborhood bartenders and the rise in the number of psychiatrists. "Sometimes you want to go where everybody knows your name," goes the apt refrain of the popular TV show *Cheers*. Once you poured out your troubles over a nickel beer to someone who knew you and your family. And if you got drunk, well, you could walk home. Now you drive cross town and pay $100 an hour to a stranger for emotional relief.

The breakdown of community life may explain, in part, why the three 15 best-selling drugs in America treat stress: ulcer medication (Tagamet), hypertension (Inderal), tranquilizer (Valium).

American society has evolved into a cultural environment where it is ever harder for deep roots to take hold. What can we do to change this?

• **Rebuild walking communities**. Teach urban planners that overdependence on transportation is a sign of failure in a social system. Impose the true costs of the car on its owners. Recent studies indicate that to do so would raise the cost of gasoline by as much as $2 a gallon. Recently Stockholm declared war on cars by imposing a $50 a month fee for car owners, promising to increase the fee until the city was given back to pedestrians and mass transit.

• **Equip every neighborhood with a library, a coffeehouse, a diversified shopping district, and a park**.

• **Make rootedness a goal of public policy**. In the 1970s a Vermont land use law, for example, required an economic component to environmental impact statements. In at least one case, a suburban shopping mall was denied approval because it would undermine existing city businesses. In Berkeley, citizens voted two to one to permit commercial rent control in neighborhoods whose independently owned businesses were threatened by gentrification.

• **Reward stability and continuity**. Today, if a government seizes 20 property it pays the owner the market price. Identical homes have identical value, even if one is home to a third-generation family, while the other is occupied by a new tenant. Why not pay a premium, say 50 percent above the current market price, for every 10 years the occupant has lived there? Forty years of residence would be rewarded with compensation four times greater than the market price. The increment above the market price should go not to the owner but to the occupant, if the two are not the same. By favoring occupants over owners, this policy not only rewards neighborliness, but promotes social justice. By raising the overall costs of dislocation, it also discourages development that undermines rootedness.

- **Prohibit hostile takeovers**. Japanese, German, and Swedish corporations are among the most competitive and innovative in the world. But in these countries hostile takeovers are considered unethical business practices or are outlawed entirely.
- **Encourage local and employee ownership**. Protecting existing management is not the answer if that management is not locally rooted. Very few cities have an ongoing economic campaign to promote local ownership despite the obvious advantages to the community. Employee ownership exists in some form in more than 5,000 U.S. companies, but in only a handful is that ownership significant.
- **And above all, correct our history books**. America did not become a wealthy nation because of rootlessness, but in spite of it. A multitude of natural resources across an expansive continent and the arrival of tens of millions of skilled immigrants furnished us enormous advantages. We could overlook the high social costs of rootlessness. This is no longer true.

Instability is not the price we must pay for progress. Loyalty, in the plant and the neighborhood, does not stifle innovation. These are lessons we've ignored too long. More rooted cultures such as Japan and Germany are now outcompeting us in the marketplace, and in the neighborhood. We would do well to learn the value of community.

Suggestions for Writing and Discussion

1. Morris begins this piece by calling Americans a "rootless people." What reasons does he give for this restless condition? Can you supply any others?
2. As a result of this rootlessness, Morris sees Americans as becoming a disconnected people as well. What is your evaluation? Do you agree with the effects Morris believes result from this disconnection? Do you see other effects? Explain.
3. Why does Morris believe so strongly in neighborhood and community unity? What difference does it make to the average person? Compare his view of neighborhood and community unity with your own view.
4. According to Erich Fromm, bartenders work just as well as psychiatrists to calm people's fears and release them from their anxieties. This comparison implies that it is easy for people to pour out their troubles as long as they are talking to professionals or to friendly acquaintances rather than to intimate friends or family. Do you subscribe to this view that it's easier to talk about problems with someone who doesn't know you well than with someone who does? Explain, using examples to illustrate your ideas.
5. Evaluate Morris's suggestions for rebuilding community closeness. Which one do you feel is most important? Which is most feasible? Are any of his ideas unrealistic? Idealistic? Explain.

6. What is Morris's main purpose in writing this piece? Who is his intended audience? What details from the article might appeal particularly to the audience you have defined? What type of reader might not be receptive to this piece? Explain your answer.

Suggestions for Extended Thinking and Research

1. In the last paragraph, Morris states that we should learn about community and the success it breeds from countries such as Japan and Germany. Research either one of these countries, focusing specifically on communities and work opportunities. After doing this research, write an essay in which you explain why you do or do not support Morris's claim.
2. Research the roots of your hometown. Find out what life was like before 1950 by conducting interviews with several of the town's oldest residents. Your purpose is to find out what once existed. Then in an objective essay, synthesize all of your primary sources and come to some conclusion: How have progress and change affected your town's sense of unity?
3. Morris doesn't analyze how malls changed the downtown shopping districts in many small towns and cities. Write an essay based on one of these two options.
   A. Compare the atmosphere of an older established shopping area downtown with that of a mall. Use direct observations and interviews for your sources.
   B. Explain why a mall, as a life source all its own, can or cannot serve as a community that encourages a sense of connection and unity among those who shop and work there.

AMY TAN

Two Kinds

> *In 1952, two and a half years after her parents arrived from China and settled in Oakland, California, Amy Tan was born. She earned both undergraduate and graduate degrees from San Jose State University; following graduation, she worked for several years as a language consultant and free-lance technical writer. After returning from a visit to China with her mother, she published her first novel,* The Joy Luck Club *(1989), from which this story is taken.*

Prereading/Journal-Writing Suggestions

1. When you were a small child, what did you imagine you'd be when you grew up? Have those dreams changed or stayed the same? Explain.
2. Write about a time when you came up against something that was difficult for you to do — perhaps some type of lessons you had to take when you were young. How did you approach this difficulty? Did anyone help you or encourage you? Did you give up easily or after a struggle? Did you persevere until you got it? Did you learn anything about yourself from this experience?
3. In what ways is your inner self different from the self that your family or friends see?
4. Write about a childhood fight you had with a parent. What was this fight about? What happened? Did anybody win the fight?

My mother believed you could be anything you wanted to be in America. You could open a restaurant. You could work for the government and get good retirement. You could buy a house with almost no money down. You could become rich. You could become instantly famous.

"Of course, you can be prodigy, too," my mother told me when I was nine. "You can be best anything. What does Auntie Lindo know? Her daughter, she is only best tricky."

America was where all my mother's hopes lay. She had come to San Francisco in 1949 after losing everything in China: her mother and father, her family home, her first husband, and two daughters, twin baby girls. But she never looked back with regret. Things could get better in so many ways.

We didn't immediately pick the right kind of prodigy. At first my mother thought I could be a Chinese Shirley Temple. We'd watch Shirley's old movies on TV as though they were training films. My mother would poke my arm and say, "*Ni kan.* You watch." And I would see Shirley tapping her feet, or singing a sailor song, or pursing her lips into a very round O while saying "Oh, my goodness."

"*Ni kan,*" my mother said, as Shirley's eyes flooded with tears. "You already know how. Don't need talent for crying!"

Soon after my mother got this idea about Shirley Temple, she took me to the beauty training school in the Mission District and put me in the hands of a student who could barely hold the scissors without shaking. Instead of getting big fat curls, I emerged with an uneven mass of crinkly black fuzz. My mother dragged me off to the bathroom and tried to wet down my hair.

"You look like Negro Chinese," she lamented, as if I had done this on purpose.

The instructor of the beauty training school had to lop off these soggy clumps to make my hair even again. "Peter Pan is very popular these days," the instructor assured my mother. I now had hair the length of a boy's, with curly bangs that hung at a slant two inches above my eyebrows. I liked the haircut, and it made me actually look forward to my future fame.

In fact, in the beginning I was just as excited as my mother, maybe even more so. I pictured this prodigy part of me as many different images, and I tried each one on for size. I was a dainty ballerina girl standing by the curtain, waiting to hear the music that would send me floating on my tiptoes. I was like the Christ child lifted out of the straw manger, crying with holy indignity. I was Cinderella stepping from her pumpkin carriage with sparkly cartoon music filling the air.

In all of my imaginings I was filled with a sense that I would soon become perfect. My mother and father would adore me. I would be beyond reproach. I would never feel the need to sulk, or to clamor for anything.

But sometimes the prodigy in me became impatient. "If you don't hurry up and get me out of here, I'm disappearing for good," it warned. "And then you'll always be nothing."

Every night after dinner my mother and I would sit at the Formica-topped kitchen table. She would present new tests, taking her examples from stories of amazing children that she read in *Ripley's Believe It or Not* or *Good Housekeeping, Reader's Digest,* or any of a dozen other magazines she kept in a pile in our bathroom. My mother got these magazines from people whose houses she cleaned. And since she cleaned many houses each week, we had a great assortment. She would look through them all, searching for stories about remarkable children.

The first night she brought out a story about a three-year-old boy who knew the capitals of all the states and even of most of the European countries. A teacher was quoted as saying that the little boy could also pronounce the names of the foreign cities correctly. "What's the capital of Finland?" my mother asked me, looking at the story.

All I knew was the capital of California, because Sacramento was the name of the street we lived on in Chinatown. "Nairobi!" I guessed, saying the most foreign word I could think of. She checked to see if that might be one way to pronounce *Helsinki* before showing me the answer.

The tests got harder — multiplying numbers in my head, finding the queen of hearts in a deck of cards, trying to stand on my head without using my hands, predicting the daily temperatures in Los Angeles, New York, and London. One night I had to look at a page from the Bible for three minutes and then report everything I could remember. "Now Jehoshaphat had riches and honor in abundance and . . . that's all I remember, Ma," I said.

And after seeing, once again, my mother's disappointed face, something inside me began to die. I hated the tests, the raised hopes and failed expectations. Before going to bed that night I looked in the mirror above the bathroom sink, and when I saw only my face staring back — and understood that it would always be this ordinary face — I began to cry. Such a sad, ugly girl! I made high-pitched noises like a crazed animal, trying to scratch out the face in the mirror.

And then I saw what seemed to be the prodigy side of me — a face I had never seen before. I looked at my reflection, blinking so that I could see more clearly. The girl staring back at me was angry, powerful. She and I were the same. I had new thoughts, willful thoughts — or, rather, thoughts filled with lots of won'ts. I won't let her change me, I promised myself. I won't be what I'm not.

So now when my mother presented her tests, I performed listlessly, my head propped on one arm. I pretended to be bored. And I was. I got so bored that I started counting the bellows of the foghorns out on the bay while my mother drilled me in other areas. The sound was comforting and reminded me of the cow jumping over the moon. And the next day I played a game with myself, seeing if my mother would give up on me before eight bellows. After a while I usually counted only one bellow, maybe two at most. At last she was beginning to give up hope.

Two or three months went by without any mention of my being a prodigy. And then one day my mother was watching the *Ed Sullivan Show* on TV. The TV was old and the sound kept shorting out. Every time my mother got halfway up from the sofa to adjust the set, the sound would come back on and Sullivan would be talking. As soon as she sat down, Sullivan would go silent again. She got up — the TV broke into loud piano music. She sat down — silence. Up and down, back and forth, quiet and loud. It was like a stiff, embraceless dance between her and the TV set. Finally, she stood by the set with her hand on the sound dial.

She seemed entranced by the music, a frenzied little piano piece with a mesmerizing quality, which alternated between quick, playful passages and teasing, lilting ones.

"*Ni kan,*" my mother said, calling me over with hurried hand gestures. "Look here."

I could see why my mother was fascinated by the music. It was being pounded out by a little Chinese girl, about nine years old, with a Peter Pan haircut. The girl had the sauciness of a Shirley Temple. She was proudly modest, like a proper Chinese child. And she also did a fancy sweep of a curtsy, so that the fluffy skirt of her white dress cascaded to the floor like the petals of a large carnation.

In spite of these warning signs, I wasn't worried. Our family had no piano and we couldn't afford to buy one, let alone reams of sheet music and piano lessons. So I could be generous in my comments when my mother bad-mouthed the little girl on TV.

"Play note right, but doesn't sound good!" my mother complained. "No singing sound."

"What are you picking on her for?" I said carelessly. "She's pretty good. 25 Maybe she's not the best, but she's trying hard." I knew almost immediately that I would be sorry I had said that.

"Just like you," she said. "Not the best. Because you not trying." She gave a little huff as she let go of the sound dial and sat down on the sofa.

The little Chinese girl sat down also, to play an encore of "Anitra's Tanz," by Grieg. I remember the song, because later on I had to learn how to play it.

Three days after watching the *Ed Sullivan Show* my mother told me what my schedule would be for piano lessons and piano practice. She had talked to Mr. Chong, who lived on the first floor of our apartment building. Mr. Chong was a retired piano teacher, and my mother had traded house-cleaning services for weekly lessons and a piano for me to practice on every day, two hours a day, from four until six.

When my mother told me this, I felt as though I had been sent to hell. I whined, and then kicked my foot a little when I couldn't stand it anymore.

"Why don't you like me the way I am?" I cried. "I'm *not* a genius! I can't 30 play the piano. And even if I could, I wouldn't go on TV if you paid me a million dollars!"

My mother slapped me. "Who ask you to be genius?" she shouted. "Only ask you be your best. For you sake. You think I want you to be genius? Hnnh! What for! Who ask you!"

"So ungrateful," I heard her mutter in Chinese. "If she had as much talent as she has temper, she'd be famous now."

Mr. Chong, whom I secretly nicknamed Old Chong, was very strange, always tapping his fingers to the silent music of an invisible orchestra. He looked ancient in my eyes. He had lost most of the hair on the top of his head, and he wore thick glasses and had eyes that always looked tired. But he must have been younger than I thought, since he lived with his mother and was not yet married.

I met Old Lady Chong once, and that was enough. She had a peculiar smell, like a baby that had done something in its pants, and her fingers felt like a dead person's, like an old peach I once found in the back of the refrigerator; its skin just slid off the flesh when I picked it up.

I soon found out why Old Chong had retired from teaching piano. He 35 was deaf. "Like Beethoven!" he shouted to me. "We're both listening only in our head!" And he would start to conduct his frantic silent sonatas.

Our lessons went like this. He would open the book and point to different things, explaining their purpose: "Key! Treble! Bass! No sharps or flats! So this is C major! Listen now and play after me!"

And then he would play the C scale a few times, a simple chord, and then, as if inspired by an old unreachable itch, he would gradually add more notes and running trills and a pounding bass until the music was really something quite grand.

I would play after him, the simple scale, the simple chord, and then just play some nonsense that sounded like a cat running up and down on top of garbage cans. Old Chong would smile and applaud and say, "Very good! But now you must learn to keep time!"

So that's how I discovered that Old Chong's eyes were too slow to keep up with the wrong notes I was playing. He went through the motions in half time. To help me keep rhythm, he stood behind me and pushed down on my right shoulder for every beat. He balanced pennies on top of my wrists so that I would keep them still as I slowly played scales and arpeggios. He had me curve my hand around an apple and keep that shape when playing chords. He marched stiffly to show me how to make each finger dance up and down, staccato, like an obedient little soldier.

He taught me all these things, and that was how I also learned I could be 40 lazy and get away with mistakes, lots of mistakes. If I hit the wrong notes because I hadn't practiced enough, I never corrected myself. I just kept playing in rhythm. And Old Chong kept conducting his own private reverie.

So maybe I never really gave myself a fair chance. I did pick up the basics pretty quickly, and I might have become a good pianist at that young age. But I was so determined not to try, not to be anybody different, and I learned to play only the most ear-splitting preludes, the most discordant hymns.

Over the next year I practiced like this, dutifully in my own way. And then one day I heard my mother and her friend Lindo Jong both talking in a loud, bragging tone of voice so that others could hear. It was after church, and I was leaning against a brick wall, wearing a dress with stiff white petticoats. Auntie Lindo's daughter, Waverly, who was my age, was standing farther down the wall, about five feet away. We had grown up together and shared all the closeness of two sisters, squabbling over crayons and dolls. In other words, for the most part, we hated each other. I thought she was snotty. Waverly Jong had gained a certain amount of fame as "Chinatown's Littlest Chinese Chess Champion."

"She bring home too many trophy," Auntie Lindo lamented that Sunday. "All day she play chess. All day I have no time do nothing but dust off her winnings." She threw a scolding look at Waverly, who pretended not to see her.

"You lucky you don't have this problem," Auntie Lindo said with a sigh to my mother.

And my mother squared her shoulders and bragged: "Our problem 45 worser than yours. If we ask Jing-mei wash dish, she hear nothing but music. It's like you can't stop this natural talent."

And right then I was determined to put a stop to her foolish pride.

A few weeks later Old Chong and my mother conspired to have me play in a talent show that was to be held in the church hall. By then my parents had saved up enough to buy me a secondhand piano, a black Wurlitzer spinet with a scarred bench. It was the showpiece of our living room.

For the talent show I was to play a piece called "Pleading Child," from Schumann's *Scenes From Childhood*. It was a simple, moody piece that sounded more difficult than it was. I was supposed to memorize the whole thing. But I dawdled over it, playing a few bars and then cheating, looking up to see what notes followed. I never really listened to what I was playing. I daydreamed about being somewhere else, about being someone else.

The part I liked to practice best was the fancy curtsy: right foot out, touch the rose on the carpet with a pointed foot, sweep to the side, bend left leg, look up, and smile.

My parents invited all the couples from their social club to witness my 50 debut. Auntie Lindo and Uncle Tin were there. Waverly and her two older brothers had also come. The first two rows were filled with children either younger or older than I was. The littlest ones got to go first. They recited simple nursery rhymes, squawked out tunes on miniature violins, and twirled hula hoops in pink ballet tutus, and when they bowed or curtsied, the audience would sigh in unison, *"Awww,"* and then clap enthusiastically.

When my turn came, I was very confident. I remember my childish excitement. It was as if I knew, without a doubt, that the prodigy side of me really did exist. I had no fear whatsoever, no nervousness. I remember thinking, This is it! This is it! I looked out over the audience, at my mother's blank face, my father's yawn, Auntie Lindo's stiff-lipped smile, Waverly's sulky expression. I had on a white dress, layered with sheets of lace, and a pink bow in my Peter Pan haircut. As I sat down, I envisioned people jumping to their feet and Ed Sullivan rushing up to introduce me to everyone on TV.

And I started to play. Everything was so beautiful. I was so caught up in how lovely I looked that I wasn't worried about how I would sound. So I was surprised when I hit the first wrong note. And then I hit another, and another. A chill started at the top of my head and began to trickle down. Yet I couldn't stop playing, as though my hands were bewitched. I kept thinking my fingers would adjust themselves back, like a train switching to the right track. I played this strange jumble through to the end, the sour notes staying with me all the way.

When I stood up, I discovered my legs were shaking. Maybe I had just been nervous, and the audience, like Old Chong, had seen me go through the right motions and had not heard anything wrong at all. I swept my right foot out, went down on my knee, looked up, and smiled. The room was quiet, except for Old Chong, who was beaming and shouting, "Bravo! Bravo! Well done!" But then I saw my mother's face, her stricken face. The audience clapped weakly, and as I walked back to my chair, with my whole face quivering as I tried not to cry, I heard a little boy whisper loudly to his mother, "That was awful," and the mother whispered, "Well, she certainly tried."

And now I realized how many people were in the audience — the whole world, it seemed. I was aware of eyes burning into my back. I felt the shame of my mother and father as they sat stiffly through the rest of the show.

We could have escaped during intermission. Pride and some strange 55 sense of honor must have anchored my parents to their chairs. And so we watched it all: The eighteen-year-old boy with a fake moustache who did a magic show and juggled flaming hoops while riding a unicycle. The breasted girl with white makeup who sang an aria from *Madame Butterfly* and got an honorable mention. And the eleven-year-old boy who won first prize playing a tricky violin song that sounded like a busy bee.

After the show the Hsus, the Jongs, and the St. Clairs, from the Joy Luck Club, came up to my mother and father.

"Lots of talented kids," Auntie Lindo said vaguely, smiling broadly.

"That was somethin' else," my father said, and I wondered if he was referring to me in a humorous way, or whether he even remembered what I had done.

Waverly looked at me and shrugged her shoulders. "You aren't a genius like me," she said matter-of-factly. And if I hadn't felt so bad, I would have pulled her braids and punched her stomach.

But my mother's expression was what devastated me: a quiet, blank 60 look that said she had lost everything. I felt the same way, and everybody seemed now to be coming up, like gawkers at the scene of an accident, to see what parts were actually missing.

When we got on the bus to go home, my father was humming the busy-bee tune and my mother was silent. I kept thinking she wanted to wait until we got home before shouting at me. But when my father unlocked the door to our apartment, my mother walked in and went straight to the back, into the bedroom. No accusations. No blame. And in a way, I felt disappointed. I had been waiting for her to start shouting, so that I could shout back and cry and blame her for all my misery.

I had assumed that my talent-show fiasco meant that I would never have to play the piano again. But two days later, after school, my mother came out of the kitchen and saw me watching TV.

"Four clock," she reminded me, as if it were any other day. I was stunned, as though she were asking me to go through the talent-show torture again. I planted myself more squarely in front of the TV.

"Turn off TV," she called from the kitchen five minutes later.

I didn't budge. And then I decided. I didn't have to do what my mother 65 said anymore. I wasn't her slave. This wasn't China. I had listened to her before, and look what happened. She was the stupid one.

She came out of the kitchen and stood in the arched entryway of the living room. "Four clock," she said once again, louder.

"I'm not going to play anymore," I said nonchalantly. "Why should I? I'm not a genius."

She stood in front of the TV. I saw that her chest was heaving up and down in an angry way.

"No!" I said, and I now felt stronger, as if my true self had finally emerged. So this was what had been inside me all along.

"No! I won't!" I screamed. 70

She snapped off the TV, yanked me by the arm and pulled me off the floor. She was frighteningly strong, half pulling, half carrying me toward the piano as I kicked the throw rugs under my feet. She lifted me up and onto the hard bench. I was sobbing by now, looking at her bitterly. Her chest was heaving even more and her mouth was open, smiling crazily as if she were pleased that I was crying.

"You want me to be someone that I'm not!" I sobbed. "I'll never be the kind of daughter you want me to be!"

"Only two kinds of daughters," she shouted in Chinese. "Those who are obedient and those who follow their own mind! Only one kind of daughter can live in this house. Obedient daughter!"

"Then I wish I weren't your daughter. I wish you weren't my mother," I shouted. As I said these things I got scared. It felt like worms and toads and slimy things crawling out of my chest, but it also felt good, that this awful side of me had surfaced, at last.

"Too late change this," my mother said shrilly. 75

And I could sense her anger rising to its breaking point. I wanted to see it spill over. And that's when I remembered the babies she had lost in China, the ones we never talked about. "Then I wish I'd never been born!" I shouted. "I wish I were dead! Like them."

It was as if I had said magic words. Alakazam! — her face went blank, her mouth closed, her arms went slack, and she backed out of the room, stunned, as if she were blowing away like a small brown leaf, thin, brittle, lifeless.

It was not the only disappointment my mother felt in me. In the years that followed, I failed her many times, each time asserting my will, my right to fall short of expectations. I didn't get straight As. I didn't become class president. I didn't get into Stanford. I dropped out of college.

Unlike my mother, I did not believe I could be anything I wanted to be. I could only be me.

And for all those years we never talked about the disaster at the recital 80 or my terrible declarations afterward at the piano bench. Neither of us talked about it again, as if it were a betrayal that was now unspeakable. So I never found a way to ask her why she had hoped for something so large that failure was inevitable.

And even worse, I never asked her about what frightened me the most: Why had she given up hope? For after our struggle at the piano, she never mentioned my playing again. The lessons stopped. The lid to the piano was closed, shutting out the dust, my misery, and her dreams.

So she surprised me. A few years ago she offered to give me the piano, for my thirtieth birthday. I had not played in all those years. I saw the offer as a sign of forgiveness, a tremendous burden removed.

"Are you sure?" I asked shyly. "I mean, won't you and Dad miss it?"

"No, this your piano," she said firmly. "Always your piano. You only one can play."

"Well, I probably can't play anymore," I said. "It's been years." 85

"You pick up fast," my mother said, as if she knew this was certain. "You have natural talent. You could be genius if you want to."

"No, I couldn't."

"You just not trying," my mother said. And she was neither angry nor sad. She said it as if announcing a fact that could never be disproved. "Take it," she said.

But I didn't at first. It was enough that she had offered it to me. And after that, every time I saw it in my parents' living room, standing in front of the bay window, it made me feel proud, as if it were a shiny trophy that I had won back.

Last week I sent a tuner over to my parents' apartment and had the piano 90 reconditioned, for purely sentimental reasons. My mother had died a few months before, and I had been getting things in order for my father, a little bit at a time. I put the jewelry in special silk pouches. The sweaters she had knitted in yellow, pink, bright orange — all the colors I hated — I put in moth-proof boxes. I found some old Chinese silk dresses, the kind with little slits up the sides. I rubbed the old silk against my skin, and then wrapped them in tissue and decided to take them home with me.

After I had the piano tuned, I opened the lid and touched the keys. It sounded even richer than I remembered. Really, it was a very good piano. Inside the bench were the same exercise notes with handwritten scales, the same secondhand music books with their covers held together with yellow tape.

I opened up the Schumann book to the dark little piece I had played at the recital. It was on the left-hand page, "Pleading Child." It looked more difficult than I remembered. I played a few bars, surprised at how easily the notes came back to me.

And for the first time, or so it seemed, I noticed the piece on the right-hand side. It was called "Perfectly Contented." I tried to play this one as well. It had a lighter melody but with the same flowing rhythm and turned out to be quite easy. "Pleading Child" was shorter but slower; "Perfectly Contented" was longer but faster. And after I had played them both a few times, I realized they were two halves of the same song.

Suggestions for Writing and Discussion

1. From this story, how would you characterize Jing-mei's mother? What are her strengths? What are her weaknesses?
2. How would you characterize Jing-mei as a child? What are her strengths? Her weaknesses?
3. Describe the relationship between mother and daughter in the beginning of this story. When does it begin to change? Why does it change?
4. Make a list of the words, phrases, and events you responded to most strongly in this story. From this list, how would you characterize Tan's approach as a storyteller?
5. Choose one quotation from this story — one that you may have noticed on your first reading. Write a brief response, explaining why this quote caught your fancy.
6. In what ways does Old Chong fit into the themes in this story? What's his main contribution to this piece?
7. The conflict between mother and daughter reaches a climax when Jing-mei shouts out at her mother, "I wish I were dead! Like them." What's your initial reaction to this confrontation? Do you think Jing-mei is being exceptionally cruel? Why or why not? In the end, who wins this battle of the wills?
8. Explain and analyze the insights Jing-mei, the adult, has as she reenters her parents' apartment.
9. The title of this piece, "Two Kinds," can be interpreted in a number of ways. Certainly on a literal level it refers to the "two kinds" of daughters Jing-mei's mother mentions. But what might this title refer to on a deeper, less obvious level? As you respond, consider especially the story's final paragraph.

Suggestions for Extended Thinking and Research

1. Read Amy Tan's *Joy Luck Club* and write an essay evaluating one aspect of this novel. For example, did you like the structure of the interwoven stories? Were there any characters you found particularly believable (or unbelievable)? How did you relate to the conflicts between generations?
2. Research traditional Chinese traditions, beliefs, and philosophies. Choose just one item from these categories and compare it with a tradition, belief, or philosophy that is part of the American mainstream.
3. Write an essay in which you attempt to persuade your audience of classmates that (a) Jing-mei's mother was much too demanding of her daughter;

(b) Jing-mei was much too stubborn and rebellious as a daughter; (c) Jing-mei's mother was right in her perception of her daughter — Jing-mei didn't try her best; or (d) Jing-mei's mother didn't know her daughter — Jing-mei did try her best. Make sure to provide evidence from the story to support your ideas.

————————————

LORNA DEE CERVANTES

Refugee Ship

> *Born in the Mission District of San Francisco in 1954, Lorna Dee Cervantes was raised in San Jose, California, where she published her first poem in her high school newspaper. In 1974, she founded Mango Publications, which features the works of Chicano writers. Cervantes received a fellowship from the National Endowment for the Arts in 1978, and in 1981 she published* Emplumada, *a collection of poems. She wrote "Refugee Ship" when she was twenty years old; she first read and published the poem in Mexico City.*

Prereading/Journal-Writing Suggestion

Think about a time when you were in the middle — a time in between, when you didn't fit into any place comfortably. Freewrite about your emotions and your state of mind at this time.

like wet cornstarch
I slide past *mi abuelita's* eyes
bible placed by her side
she removes her glasses
the pudding thickens   5

mamá raised me with no language
I am an orphan to my spanish name
the words are foreign, stumbling on my tongue
I stare at my reflection in the mirror
brown skin, black hair   10

I feel I am a captive
aboard the refugee ship
a ship that will never dock
a ship that will never dock

Suggestions for Writing and Discussion

1. If you were to sketch an illustration for this short poem, what would you include in this picture? What would you put as a central focus? Why?
2. What is your response to the simile "like wet cornstarch"? How does the image work with the rest of the stanza and the rest of the poem?
3. The speaker only notices two details in the mirror. What does this recognition suggest? What does the absence of other features suggest?

4. The speaker's life is much like "a ship that will never dock/a ship that will never dock." What kind of life does this image suggest? What is the effect of the repetition of this line at the end of the poem?
5. In line 7, the author fails to capitalize the word *spanish*. Why do you think she made this choice?

TOPICS FOR MAKING CONNECTIONS: ROOTS AND MEMORIES

1. Several of the writings in this thematic section deal with culture and how it affects the relationship between a child and a parent. Analyze the inner conflicts, the discoveries, and the resolutions that occur within this framework.
2. Use at least three of the selections in this section in order to analyze the different processes by which we come to know who we are.
3. To what extent should one's identity — sense of self — relate to and draw upon the past (including ethnic and religious traditions and beliefs)? In addition to using several sources from this section, draw upon your own experiences and observations to answer this question.
4. Compare the differences between being rooted and being uprooted. Examine both the positive and the negative aspects of each, and come to some conclusion about how each state of being contributes to what we know and who we are.
5. Analyze the effects of being caught between two identities. Besides using the sources in this section for references, rely on your own experiences and observations. What happens when we are caught in a struggle of who we know we might be with who we used to be or with who someone else wants us to be?
6. Write an essay in which you show that loss of one identity is just a natural stage in the evolution of becoming a whole person.
7. Many of the writings in this section deal with the struggle to learn about one's self and one's place in the world. Examine several of these processes and come to some conclusions about the best ways to address such complex issues. What do we need to do? Where do we need to go? Who has the answers? How can we find them?
8. Review the selections in this section that you have read. Select the piece that you enjoyed the most and the one that you liked the least. Now try to analyze why you enjoyed the piece you did: Was it the topic? The theme? The style? The language? Also, analyze why you didn't favor the other piece. In other words, what are the major differences between these two pieces as far as you, the reader, are concerned?
9. From all of these readings, choose the person or character you most admired and the character or person you least admired. Compare these two and demonstrate the reasons for your evaluation.

10. List several questions and issues raised by selections in this section. Evaluate these questions and issues, and explain which one is the most important to you. Write an essay in which you try to convince others that this issue is of great importance. Use contemporary examples and your own experience as major support in this essay.

American Dreams
and Creations

Previews: AMERICAN DREAMS AND CREATIONS

"Please imagine that the drum method of speech is so exquisite that Africans can, without recourse to words, recite proverbs, record history, and send long messages. The drum is to West African society what the book is to literate society."

From: *Shanghai Blues,* WILLIAM ZINSSER

The Civil Rights Movement changed my view of music. It was after my first march. I began to sing a song and in the course of singing changed the song so that it made sense for that particular moment. Although I was not consciously aware of it, this was one of my earliest experiences with how my music was supposed to *function*. This music was to be integrative of and consistent with everything I was doing at that time; it was to be tied to activities that went beyond artistic affairs such as concerts, dances, and church meetings.

From: *Black Music in Our Hands,* BERNICE REAGON

The legendary spider woman insisted white shell woman learn to spin before learning to weave. Tiana Bighorse advised me similarly. However, as it turned out, I so loved spinning and dyeing that six months later I was still caught in its web. I walked all elevations of the reservation, seeking native plants and learning to evoke their muted hues. A hundred and twenty colored skeins later my weaving mentor, in a tone suggesting the honeymoon was over asked when I was going to learn to weave.

So I made a loom of cedar and began my first weaving.

From: *Halo of the Sun,* NOËL BENNETT

Yet, if "Dances With Wolves" had been about *people* who happen to be Indians, rather than about *Indians* (uniformly stoic, brave, nasty to their enemies, nice to their friends), it might have stood a better chance of acting as a bridge between societies that have for too long woodenly characterized each other.

From: *Indians in Aspic,* MICHAEL DORRIS

"Everyone seemed to have some communal knowledge when I did not have — and then I realized that the metaphor of *house* was totally wrong for me. Suddenly I was homeless. There were not attics and cellars and crannies. I had no such house in my memories. As a child I read of such things in books, and my family had promised such a house, but the best they could do was offer the miserable bungalow I was embarrassed with all my life."

From: *Sandra Cisneros: Sneaking Past the Guards,* JIM SAGEL

NITAYA KANCHANAWAN

Elvis, Thailand, and I

Born and raised in Thailand, Nitaya Kanchanawan came to the United States as a graduate student, where she earned a doctorate degree at the University of Texas, Austin. Currently, she serves as assistant dean of planning and development at Ramkhamhaeng University in Bangkok. This essay first appeared in The Southern Quarterly, *a journal published by the University Press of Mississippi. In it, Kanchanawan analyzes and evaluates the impact of American rock singer Elvis Presley and his music on her native country.*

Prereading/Journal-Writing Suggestions

1. Reflect on your memories of your first musical idol–either a person or a group. How old were you when this artist or group affected you most? What first attracted you — the words, the artist, the melody, the rhythm? What did your friends think of your idol? What did your parents think? How long was this artist or group popular?
2. Nearly everyone has heard of Elvis Presley and has heard at least a few of his songs. What's your reaction to Elvis? To his music? If you are a fan of his, explain why you like him. If you are not a particular fan, explain why you think Elvis has such a following.

The South first knew Elvis Presley when it heard "That's All Right, Mama"; and America became familiar with his name when "Heartbreak Hotel" came out. But to the world, especially Thailand, the name Elvis Presley was heard for the first time when *Love Me Tender* was released about the end of 1956 or the beginning of 1957.

My family went to see *Love Me Tender* not because of Elvis but because the film was shown in our favorite theater. After the show what all of us and presumably all the audience did was to scan the cast's names and guess — "Who was that 'cute singing star'?" We knew Richard Egan and Debra Paget, so he must be Elvis Presley. What a strange name! It was very hard to pronounce since there is neither "v" nor "r" in Thai. Anyway, we practiced pronouncing his name all the way home. That was the first time I saw and heard Elvis Presley. I was in elementary school and barely understood English.

He has been very popular since then in both the music and movie fields. He was the biggest foreign star in Thailand. During the late fifties and the early sixties he appeared on the cover of every movie magazine and song book. Some song books had him on the cover continuously for a couple of years. His songs were the most requested, and all the DJs fought to be the first who played Elvis's new releases. A wealthy girl paid a radio station to broadcast his songs every Sunday morning for over ten years. This was to help other fans who could not afford the records. And of course, there were a lot of Elvis imitators. It seemed that every string band had its own Elvis.

There were some reactions from the parents, but not as violent as those in the United States. The main difference was that American parents first saw Elvis on TV, while Thai parents first saw him in *Love Me Tender*. Some parents objected to his movement, partly because it seemed proper to object and partly because it was a patriotic deed to reject anything that was not Thai.

Elvis did not change Thailand as he changed America musically and culturally. He, however, provoked more interest in American popular music. As an oriental country, Thailand is drastically different from the United States. Since World War II Thailand has been known as one of the pro-American countries, but that is mainly political. We have our own culture — our own music that is much different from any American music — not to mention rock and roll. It may be said that American music — whatever type it is — has been appreciated by a minority of the population: those in big cities and those who study English. There has always been a silent conflict between those American (and British) music followers and Thai music followers. Thai music followers almost intentionally ignore foreign artists. They, however, knew Elvis and were amazed at his popularity.

Before Elvis, Thai singers in all fields rarely moved their bodies when they sang. Some even hardly moved the mouth — not to mention the expression of their feeling towards the songs. Elvis's movement and expression shocked the conservative minds. They were shocked even by his movement in the movies, which was almost nothing compared to his on-stage gyration. Every Thai singer who sang American songs started to move. Thai teenagers started to imitate Elvis — his hairdo and his clothes. The reaction of young people to Elvis was unprecedented.

In the late fifties and sixties when Elvis's popularity was at its height, he was known everywhere in Thailand. Wherever people knew of Coke they knew of Elvis. I went to help a poor hill tribe and could easily find Coca-Cola there. It was unusual for a Thai to express love, excitement, and devotion openly. This may be another reason for some objection from Thai parents. In the fifties if American parents thought that Elvis introduced "vulgar" things to their children, you can be sure what Thai parents thought — Elvis did destroy Thai culture!

In the sixties, things were different. Elvis fans in Thailand were as excited as those in the United States when he got out of the army. They were waiting for his first movie, "G.I. Blues." Elvis was big in the news again when Their Majesties the King and Queen of Thailand visited a set of "G.I. Blues" during their state visit to the United States in 1960. It was surprising to see Elvis sit side by side with the Queen. No one in Thailand was allowed to be that close to her. Elvis's fans treasured that picture. The Queen herself was reported to have said that she was also an Elvis admirer.

The sixties were the best time for Elvis in Thailand. His kind of movies fit the idea of Thai entertainment — they were strictly to entertain. People were happy when they left the theater. The Thais love to see "beautiful things" and listen to "beautiful sounds." Elvis was universally accepted by that time.

What impressed the Thais most was his personality—his personal life 10 and behavior. It was a pleasant surprise to learn that Elvis was a polite, generous, honest young man. His love and devotion to his family touched the Thai heart. This is crucial to his appeal to the Thais. We always have an unpleasant picture of Americans who never care. We always think of Americans as having so much freedom that they never listen to or respect their elders and don't support their parents. Elvis presented one of the best pictures of American people. We always said that "He did just like a Thai." Even when he divorced his wife, there were no hard words—"He still supports her, just like a Thai."

Elvis's singing ability also appeals to the Thais. My father, who appreciates Thai music, pays no attention to Elvis's "fast" and "noisy" numbers. Once he heard an Elvis ballad and asked me: "Are you sure that is Elvis? That is wonderful. He must have various voices."

When Elvis stopped making movies in the seventies, he was almost out of the current scene, because the only contact we have was through his movies and his songs over the radio. Not every fan acquires his records, because they are really expensive for people in a developing country. We never witnessed any of his TV shows except "Aloha From Hawaii," which was a tape from Japan. The TV station decided at the very last moment that we were too poor to receive the program directly by satellite.

The seventies were a quiet time for Elvis in Thailand. He was, however, remembered and was always there. For the fans he was always number one. There are, however, many kinds of fans: Among them are those who remember him in connection with his movies and early songs, but are unaware of the later kinds of music Elvis heavily leaned towards—country, inspiration, and current hits; and those who followed his career until the end of his life. Those who are not Elvis fans admit that he was one of the great American singers, but they never understand the impact he had and still has on his fans. From time to time in the seventies, there were newspaper articles from people who had just come back from the United States describing how wonderful and beautiful Elvis was in his live concerts. These writers unanimously praised him for his singing and performing abilities. They even advised that Elvis was one of the best examples for any entertainer to follow.

When Elvis died on August 16, 1977, the silent love for him broke out. He was in the headlines of all the Thai newspapers for almost a week. He was mentioned in every column, even in the political one. Writers who had never touched his name wrote about him. All of them praised him and referred to him as an example of a "good man." The entertainment fields paid respect and expressed their love for him. Radio, TV stations, and movie houses arranged special programs on him, and dozens of tribute books have been released mourning his passing. One of the editors stated that "He was the King of Rock and Roll—a great singer, a millionaire. But the greatest thing about him is that he loved, respected, and was devoted to his parents, and he was generous. . . . It is appropriate to call him 'The Great Singer of the World.' . . . I feel obliged to make this special issue. I do not hope and I am not sure that it will be a best seller because it is not aimed at the youth market. Those who love and are interested in Elvis must be at least twenty-five years of age now. But I must do it and willingly do it. . . . I have done my duty — paid tribute to the singer who is always on our mind. When he was alive he did so much for us. . . ." There was a warning for some dishonest people — "When you die, would you have half of the mourning people have for Elvis?" While NBC here broadcast "Nashville Remembers Elvis" on his forty-third birthday, a TV station in Thailand broadcast "Remembering Elvis," featuring an Elvis imitator, every Sunday from January 8 to March. No one was quicker than a Thai movie producer who, a few months after Elvis's death, released a movie about a Thai country singer. Thai country song followers, the majority of the country, may not be familiar with Elvis. But those of us in the cities, including the media, recognized immediately that the singing star in that movie dressed and posed just like Elvis — in a famous white jumpsuit and in a familiar Elvis pose.

We have to admit that after the Vietnam War, American popularity in the East declined. Elvis was perhaps the only American who was unanimously praised, even by those anti-American persons. 15

My personal interest in Elvis began long ago. Our family are not serious music lovers. But whenever there is music in the air, my mother prefers classical or traditional Thai and my father likes popular Thai. Those have always been the kinds of music in our home. I am the only one in the family who listens to all kinds of music — any kind of Thai, including country, and any kind of Western music. No one objects to my taste. Actually I was introduced to Elvis's music almost at the same time I started studying classical piano in elementary school. Elvis, Bach, Mozart, Beethoven, Brahms, and Tschaikovsky were exposed to me during my childhood, and it was Elvis I preferred. It was Elvis who led me to the study of various kinds of American music during my graduate-student years in the United States.

When I first listened to Elvis's songs I did not understand most of his words, but it was a pleasure to hear him sing. I did not know why, but I started to "follow" him. When I was young I did not have enough money to buy his records, but I managed to keep all the clippings about him — both positive and negative. For me it started as a hobby to study his life and career. Now more than twenty years have passed, and I realize that Elvis Presley was a very special person — and also a decent human being.

Elvis was special in that when you talked about Elvis you never realized that he was an American or a Christian or that he spoke English — he was just Elvis. Legally he may belong to America, but spiritually he belongs to the world. Let me emphasize here that most of his international admirers have never fully understood what he sang or said. The sound and sight of him made them happy — and that was enough.

Elvis had an amazing influence on his fans. This fact may differentiate him from other artists. There is no race, no religion, no politics, no class, no age among Elvis's fans. They became friends because of Elvis. I have quite a few good friends — both Thai and American — who started the friendship through a mutual interest in Elvis. I was in Texas on August 16, 1977. There were quite a few phone calls from my "Elvis friends" from as far away as New York. We had to talk and cry with someone who really understood our feeling. We have lost not an entertainer, but ELVIS. At an Elvis convention held after his death, I met a lot more Elvis fans — all sexes and all ages. The most marvelous thing was that there were no boring questions like "How do you like this country?" "What is Buddhism?" "Tell me about your country." We spoke the same language — Elvis. There was only one person who realized some difference at the very last moment before the party was over and asked: "By the way, where did you come from?"

Elvis was just a human being in that he was not perfect. He was happy   20 and unhappy; he did right and wrong like the rest of us. Five years as a student in the United States gave me more insight to his life. The incidents after August 16, 1977, told me more about Elvis and the world.

When I was young I liked him as a star. Now I love and respect him as a human being and would like to thank him for the happiness he brought to my life.

In June 1979, nearly two years after his death, Elvis records, tribute books, and posters are on the markets. Recently, an article entitled "War" appeared in the newspaper. The author had interviewed people in the street, and one person said, "America could bring peace to the world only when Elvis Presley was still alive. Just as they cannot bring that poor boy back, they can't bring peace to this part of the world." Radio stations still play his songs, and his movies are still shown on television and privately for guests in some elite clubs. Some Elvis imitators still have their acts in night clubs, and some Thai country singers are touring the country in white jumpsuits.

This week I discussed current American (and some European) books on Elvis over our university educational radio program. It was a surprise to see that people were impressed and wanted to know more about Elvis and to hear more of his music. The Thais have no idea what has been going on about Elvis since his death. On the first anniversary of his death some newspapers carried articles that expressed surprise about the unusual activity in Memphis. They were surprised to know that Elvis was still "big" in America.

Suggestions for Writing and Discussion

1. According to Kanchanawan, why was Elvis so popular in Thailand? Was he popular in America for these same reasons?
2. Most Americans have little in-depth knowledge of Thailand and its culture. From this short essay, what have you learned about Thailand, its people, and their values?
3. In what ways did Elvis affect the Thais' culture? Compare what you see as his effect on the Thai culture with the effect he had here in America.

4. Kanchanawan writes (paragraph 7) that it was unusual for people in her country to "express love, excitement, and devotion openly." Are these emotions typically expressed openly by most Americans? Use specific examples from your observations and experiences to respond.

5. Why do you think people in Thailand would be surprised to find that Elvis was "a polite, generous, honest young man"?

6. Kanchanawan states that "Elvis presented one of the best pictures of American people," and notes he was a "decent human being." First of all, what evidence does Kanchanawan give to support that evaluation of Elvis? Second, do you think most popular singers and groups today fit into these same categories? Support your answer with specific examples.

7. Explain the implications of the following quotation: "America could bring peace to the world only when Elvis Presley was still alive. Just as they cannot bring that poor boy back, they can't bring peace to this part of the world" (paragraph 22).

8. Why, as Kanchanawan notes at the conclusion of her essay, would Thais be surprised to know that years after his death, Elvis was still remembered in our own country? What impression must the Thai people have of Americans? Do you think this impression is justified?

Suggestions for Extended Thinking and Research

1. What American personality today would you nominate for "Superstar of the World"? Write an essay in which you explain what a person needs in order to be acclaimed worldwide, and give specific evidence about why your superstar should hold this title.

2. Research the life and career of Elvis Presley by using several credible, unbiased sources. Write an essay in which you convince Kanchanawan that her impression of Elvis is incorrect, or write an essay in which you add even more credence to her claims.

3. Research the life and career of an internationally acclaimed singer outside the United States. In what ways does this person reflect his or her native culture? How is this culture reflected in his or her music? How can you account for this person's worldwide appeal?

WILLIAM ZINSSER

Shanghai Blues

Born in New York in 1922 and educated at Princeton University, William Zinsser worked for the New York Herald Tribune *from 1947 to 1959 as a features editor, drama editor, film critic, and editorialist. From 1971 to 1979, Zinsser taught at Yale University. Drawing on both his teaching and writing experiences, he has written, among other books,* On Writing Well *and* Writing with a Word Processor. *Currently a free-lance writer, Zinsser contributes regularly to numerous publications.*

Prereading/Journal-Writing Suggestions

1. Most of us have at least one area in which we have talent (or would very much like to have talent). Imagine that you have become a world-renowned celebrity in the art of your choice. Write a mini-autobiography of yourself, concentrating on how you became so accomplished in this area. What factors influenced and motivated you? Did you ever get discouraged? Did anyone serve as your inspiration? What advice do you have for others who may want to follow in your footsteps?

2. What internal qualities does a person need in order to be outstanding at something? What external factors contribute to a person's success? Use specific examples to accompany your explanation.

3. If you could have dinner with three famous artists (from the field or fields of your choice), who would you invite and why? What might you learn from each of these people?

Jazz came to China for the first time on the afternoon of June 2nd, when the American bassist and French-horn player Willie Ruff introduced himself and his partner, the pianist Dwike Mitchell, to several hundred students and professors who were crowded into a large room at the Shanghai Conservatory of Music. The professors and the students were all expectant, without knowing quite what to expect. They knew only that they were about to hear the first American jazz concert ever presented to the Chinese. Probably they were not surprised to find that the two musicians were black, though black Americans are a rarity in the People's Republic. What they undoubtedly didn't expect was that Ruff would talk to them in Chinese, and when he began they murmured with delight.

Ruff is a lithe, dapper man of fifty who takes visible pleasure in sharing his enthusiasms, and it was obvious that there was no place he would rather have been than in China's oldest conservatory, bringing the music of his people to still another country deprived of that commodity. In 1959, he and

Mitchell — who have played together as the Mitchell-Ruff Duo for twenty-six years — introduced jazz to the Soviet Union, and for that occasion Ruff taught himself Russian, his seventh language. In 1979, he hit on the idea of making a similar trip to China, and he began taking intensive courses in Chinese at Yale, where he is a professor of both music and Afro-American studies. By last winter, he felt he was fluent enough in Mandarin to make the trip.

Now Ruff stood at the front of the room, holding several sheets of paper on which he had written, in Chinese characters, what he wanted to tell his listeners about the origins of jazz. He looked somewhat like an Oriental sage himself. "In the last three hundred and fifty years, black people in America have created a music that is a rich contribution to Western culture," he began. "Of course, three hundred and fifty years, compared to the long and distinguished history of Chinese music seems like only a moment. But please remember that the music of American black people is an amalgam whose roots are deep in African history, and that it has also taken many characteristics from the music of Europe." Ruff has an amiable voice, and as he spoke the men and women in the room were attentive but relaxed — not an audience straining to decipher a foreigner's accent. "In Africa, the drum is the most important musical instrument," Ruff went on. "But to me the fascinating thing is that the people also use their drums to talk. Please imagine that the drum method of speech is so exquisite that Africans can, without recourse to words, recite proverbs, record history, and send long messages. The drum is to West African society what the book is to literate society."

I wondered what the audience would make of that. Not only was China the oldest of literate societies; we were in the one Asian city that was encrusted with Western thought as transmitted in books, in journals, and in musical notation. Even the architecture of Shanghai was a patchwork of Western shapes — a residue of the days when the city had a huge foreign population and was divided into districts that were controlled by different European countries. At the conservatory, we were in the former French concession, and its main building was in a red brick French Provincial style, with a sloping red tile roof and a porte cochère. Another French-style building housed the conservatory's library of a hundred thousand books about music. Newer buildings served as classrooms and practice rooms, and the music that eddied out of the windows was the dreary fare of Western academic rigor: vocal scales endlessly rising, piano arpeggios repeated until they were mastered, chamber groups starting and stopping and starting again. We could have been in Vienna of the nineties or Paris of the twenties. In any case, we were a long way from Africa. And we were farther still from music created spontaneously.

"In the seventeenth century, when West Africans were captured and 5 brought to America as slaves, they brought their drums with them," Ruff continued. "But the slave-owners were afraid of the drum because it was so potent; it could be used to incite the slaves to revolt. So they outlawed the drum. This very shrewd law had a tremendous effect on the development of black people's music. Our ancestors had to develop a variety of drum substitutes. One of them, for example, was tap dancing — I'm sure you've all heard of that. Now I'd like to show you another drum substitute that you probably don't know about — one that uses the hands and the body to make rhythm. It's called hambone." There was no translating "hambone" into Mandarin, but Ruff quickly had an intricate rhythm going to demonstrate, slapping himself with the palms of his hands and smacking his open mouth to create a series of resonating pops. Applause greeted this proof that the body could be its own drum.

"By the time jazz started to develop, all African instruments in America had disappeared," Ruff went on. "So jazz borrowed the instruments of Western music, like the ones that we're playing here today." He went over to his bass and showed how he used it as a percussion instrument by picking the strings with his fingers instead of playing them with a bow. "Only this morning," he said, "I gave a lesson to your distinguished professor of bass, and he is already *very good*."

Moving on from rhythm to terrain more familiar to his listeners, Ruff pointed out that jazz took its structural elements from European harmony. "Mr. Mitchell will now give you an example of the music that American slaves found in the Christian churches — Protestant hymns that had been brought from Europe," he said. "Slaves were encouraged to embrace Christianity and to use its music. Please listen." Mitchell played an old Protestant hymn. "The slaves adopted these harmonized melodies and transformed them into their own, very emotional spirituals," Ruff said when Mitchell had finished. "Mr. Mitchell and I will sing you a famous Negro spiritual from the days of slavery. It's called 'My Lord, What a Morning.'" With Mitchell playing a joyful accompaniment, the two men sang five or six choruses of the lovely old song, Mitchell carrying the melody in his deep voice, Ruff taking the higher, second part. The moment, musically beautiful, had an edge of faraway sadness. I couldn't help thinking of another alien culture onto which the Protestant hymns of Europe had once been strenuously grafted. It was just beyond the conservatory gates.

"Mr. Mitchell will now show you how the piano can be used as a substitute for the instruments of the orchestra," Ruff said. "Please notice that he uses his left hand to play the bass and also to make his rhythm section. Later, he will use his right hand to play the main melody and to fill in the harmony. This style is called ragtime." Mitchell struck up a jaunty rag. The students perked up at the playful pattern of notes. Ruff looked out at his class and beamed. The teacher in him was beginning to slip away; the musician in him was telling him to start the concert.

Mitchell and Ruff met in 1947, when they were servicemen at Lockbourne Air Force Base, outside Columbus, Ohio. Mitchell, then seventeen and a pianist in the unit band, needed an accompanist, and he gave the newly arrived Ruff, a sixteen-year-old French-horn player, a crash course in playing the bass. Thus the duo was unofficially born. When they were discharged, they followed separate paths and lost contact. Mitchell went to the Philadelphia Musical Academy. Ruff went to the Yale School of Music, where he studied with Paul Hindemith. Venturing out with his master's degree in 1954, he was told that no American symphony orchestra would hire a black musician, and he accepted an offer to join the Tel Aviv Symphony as first French horn. Shortly before he was to leave, he happened to turn his television set on to "The Ed Sullivan Show." Lionel Hampton's orchestra was playing, and as the camera panned over to the piano Ruff saw a familiar figure at the keyboard. Mitchell, it turned out, had been Hampton's pianist for the past two years. Ruff telephoned him backstage at the CBS studio. Mitchell hinted of imminent vacancies in the brass section. A few days later, Israel lost — and Hampton got — a superb French horn.

The Mitchell-Ruff Duo — "the oldest continuous group in jazz without   10 personnel changes," Ruff says — was formed in 1955, when the two men left Hampton and struck out on their own. They were booked regularly by the major night clubs as the second act with the great bands of the day: Louis Armstrong, Duke Ellington, Dizzy Gillespie, Miles Davis. "They were our mentors," Ruff recalls. "They'd play a set and then we'd play a set and they'd hang around and tell us what we could be doing better. We learned everything from those men. Count Basie's band raised us. In 1956, they were the hottest band in the country — they were the most expensive band and we were the cheapest — and we sold out Birdland every night. One evening, Miles Davis brought Billie Holiday in to hear us, and we just about fell through the floor. We were still just kids."

Meanwhile, they caught the attention of another set of patrons — a group of older women in New York who had formed an organization called Young Audiences to introduce elementary- and high-school students to chamber music. For teachers, the women chose young professionals who could communicate with words as well as with music, and Mitchell and Ruff were the first people they selected to teach jazz. Ruff recalls, "It was done under the supervision of the founders — Mrs. Lionello Perera, a great patron of music, and Mrs. Edgar Leventritt, who started the Leventritt Competition — and Nina Collier and several other ladies who sat on the board. They taught us definite techniques, such as how to catch the attention of children, and they also gave us lessons in grooming and enunciation and conduct. They were very stern and really quite unpleasant, but instructive. Everything they told us turned out to be true."

Armed with these graces, Mitchell and Ruff hit the road for Young Audiences, often giving seven or eight performances a day, going from school to school, first in New York and later in Boston, Baltimore, and San Francisco. They did a tour of Indian schools in New Mexico. The duo alternated these forays with its stands in Manhattan clubs. Then, in 1959, it went to Russia. Ruff himself arranged the trip with Soviet officials after the State Department, which had been trying for two years to get Louis Armstrong into the Soviet Union, declined to help. In Russia, the two Americans found

still a creature of the West. But that era would soon come to an end. During the Second World War, the Japanese occupied Shanghai, foreigners were interned in concentration camps, and the colonizing grip of the West was finally broken.

It was no time or place for a musician to make a living — "One month's salary would buy one shoe," Professor Tan recalled — and, seeking a more practical trade, he went to architecture school and earned his degree. He returned to music after the war, however, joining the Shanghai Conservatory in 1947, and becoming its deputy director in 1949, when the Communists came to power in China. The school then began its biggest era of growth. The student body and the faculty were greatly expanded, and European music regained its hold. But the older students were also required to go away and work for three months every year on farms and in factories. "The peasants and workers disliked Western music because it belonged to the rich people," Professor Tan recalled. "And our students couldn't practice much, because they met so much criticism. At the conservatory, we never knew where we stood. Periods of criticism would alternate with periods of relaxation. It was an uneasy time. In fact, just before the Cultural Revolution I was thinking of retiring from teaching. I had a sense of a coming storm. We are like animals — we can feel that."

The storm broke on June 5, 1966. The first winds of the Cultural Revolution hit the conservatory from within. "On the first day, posters were put up and meetings were held denouncing the director, Professor Ho Lu-ting," Professor Tan said. "The next day, the attack was aimed at me. I was accused of poisoning the minds of the students. My crime was that I was teaching Mozart. I happen to be a blind admirer of European and American people and music and culture, so everything I had been teaching was poison. Bach and Beethoven were poison. And Brahms. And Paganini.

"At first, it was only posters and meetings. Then the conservatory was closed, and much of our music was destroyed. We were beaten every day by students and by young people who came in from outside. Boys of ten or eleven would throw stones at us. They really believed we were bad people — especially any professor who was over forty. The older you were, the worse you were. For a year, more than a hundred of us older teachers were beaten and forced to spend every day shut up together in a closed shed. Then there was a year when we had to do hard labor. Ten professors died from the strain; one of them had a heart attack when a young guard made him run after him for a mile. He just dropped dead at the end. Then came the solitary confinement. Our director was kept in prison, in chains, for five years. I was put in the worst room they could find here — a very small room in the basement, hardly any bigger than my bed. It had no light and no windows, and it was smelly because it was next to a septic tank, and there was nothing to do to pass the time. I was kept there for fourteen months."

In 1971, Professor Tan was allowed to go home to live with his family pending the verdict on his "crimes," but he still had to do physical labor at the conservatory during the day. Needless to say, no Western music was played there. Finally, in 1976, the Gang of Four was overthrown, the professors were declared innocent, and the conservatory was reopened. Professor Tan told me that among the students he readmitted were some who had beaten and tormented him. I said that I could hardly imagine such forbearance. "I didn't think about that," he said. "The past is the past."

Professor Tan is a small, gentle man with white hair and a modest manner. He dresses in the informal work clothes that everybody wears in Shanghai; nobody would take him for one of the city's cultural eminences. He moves somewhat slowly and wears fairly strong glasses — marks, perhaps, of his long captivity. "The students have made astonishing progress since 1976, because now they can play wholeheartedly," he told me. "I love being able to teach the violin again. It's such an enjoyment to hear people who are truly talented. Yesterday, a girl played the 'Scottish Fantasy' of Max Bruch, and although I was supposed to be teaching her, I only sat and listened and never said a word. It was just right." He was equally pleased by the thought of bringing jazz to his students. "I've never seen any jazz musicians in China," he said. "Nobody here knows anything about jazz. When I heard Mr. Ruff and Mr. Mitchell play at Yale, I realized that it was very important music. I wanted my teachers and my students to hear it. I wanted them to know what real American jazz is like."

When Mitchell finished his ragtime tune, the audience clapped — apparently glad to hear some of the converging elements that Ruff had talked about earlier. "Now we're going to give you an example of blues," Ruff said. "Blues" was another word that didn't lend itself to Mandarin, and it sounded unusually strung out: "blooooooze." Ruff continued, "One of the fundamental principles of jazz is form, and blues are a perfect illustration. Blues almost always have a twelve-bar form. This twelve-bar form never changes. It wouldn't change even if we stayed here and played it all night." He paused to let this sink in. "But you don't have to worry — we aren't going to play it that long." It was his first joke in Chinese, and it went over well. Mitchell then played an easygoing blues — a classic sample of what came up the river from New Orleans, with a strong left hand ornamented by graceful runs in the right hand. Ruff joined in on bass, and they played several twelve-bar choruses.

After that number, Ruff brought up the matter of improvisation, which he called "the lifeblood of jazz." He said that when he was young he had worried because his people hadn't developed from their experience in America a written tradition of opera, like Chinese opera, that chronicled great or romantic events. "But later I stopped worrying, because I saw that the master performers of our musical story — Louis Armstrong, Ella Fitzgerald, and so many others — have enriched our culture with the beauty of what they created spontaneously. Now please listen one more time to the blues form, and count the measures along with me." He wanted his listeners to count, he said, because the rules of jazz require the improviser, however wild his melodic journeys, to repeat the harmonic changes that went into the first statement of the theme. "After you count with me a few times through, Mr. Mitchell will begin one of his famous improvisations," Ruff said.

Mitchell played a simple blues theme, emphasizing the chord changes, and Ruff counted the twelve bars aloud in English. Mitchell then restated the theme, embroidering it slightly, and this time Ruff counted in Chinese: "*Yi, cr, san, si, wu, liu, qi, ba* . . ." This so delighted the students that they forgot to join him. "I can't hear you," Ruff said, teacher-fashion, but they kept quiet and enjoyed his climb up the numerical ladder. Afterward, Mitchell embarked on a series of dazzling improvisations, some constructed of runs like those played by Art Tatum, some built on strong chord progressions (he can move immense chord clusters up and down the keyboard with incredible speed); next, Ruff took a chorus on the bass; then they alternated their improvised flights, moving in twelve-bar segments to an ending that seemed inevitable— as if they had played it a hundred times before.

Changing the mood, Ruff announced that Mitchell would play "Yester- 30 days." Jerome Kern's plaintive melody is hardly the stuff of traditional jazz, nor was Mitchell's rendition of it—a treatment of classical intricacy, closer to Rachmaninoff (one of his heroes) than to any jazz pianist. The students applauded with fervor. Staying in a relatively classical vein, Ruff switched to the French horn, and the two men played Billy Strayhorn's "Lush Life" in a vein that was slow and lyrical, almost like a German lied, and that perhaps surprised the students with its lack of an obvious rhythm.

The next number was one that I didn't recognize. It moved at a bright tempo and had several engaging themes that were brought back by the piano or the French horn—the usual jazzmen's game of statement and response. Twice, Mitchell briefly introduced a contrapuntal motif that was a deliberate imitation of Bach, and each time it drew a ripple of amusement from the professors and the students. It was the first time they had heard a kind of music that they recognized from their own studies.

"That number is called 'Shanghai Blues,'" Ruff said at the end. "We just made it up." The audience buzzed with amazement and pleasure.

I had been watching the professors and the students closely during the concert. Their faces had the look of people watching the slow approach of some great natural force—a tornado or a tidal wave. They had been listening to music that their experience had not prepared them to understand. Two black men were playing long stretches of music without resorting to any printed notes. Yet they obviously hadn't memorized what they were playing; their music took unexpected turns, seemingly at the whim of the musicians, straying all over the keyboard and all over the landscape of Western tonality. Nevertheless, there was order. Themes that had been abandoned came back in different clothes. If the key changed, as it frequently did, the two men were always in the same key. Often there was a playfulness between the two instruments, and always there was rapport. But if the two players were exchanging any signals, the message was too quick for the untrained eye.

I could tell that the music was holding the Chinese listeners in a strong grip. Their minds seemed to be fully engaged. Their bodies, however, were not. Only three pairs of feet in the whole room were tapping — Ruff's, Mitchell's, and mine. Perhaps this was a Chinese characteristic, this stillness of listening. Moreover, the music wasn't easy. It never again approached the overt syncopation of the ragtime that Mitchell had played early in the program; that was where the essential gaiety of jazz had been most accessible. Nor did it have the flat-out gusto that an earlier generation of black musicians might have brought to China — the thumping rhythms and simpler harmonies of a James P. Johnson or a Fats Waller. It was not that Mitchell and Ruff were playing jazz that was pedantic or sedate. On the contrary, I have seldom heard Mitchell play with more exuberant shifts of energy and mood. But the music was full of subtleties; even a Westerner accustomed to jazz would have been charmed by its intelligence and wit. I had to remind myself that the Chinese had heard no Western music of any kind from 1966 to 1976. A twenty-one-year-old student in the audience, for instance, would have begun to listen to composers like Mozart and Brahms only within the past five years. The jazz that he was hearing now was not so different as to be a whole new branch of music. Mitchell was clearly grounded in Bach and Chopin; Ruff's French horn had echoes of all the classical works — Debussy's "Rêverie," Ravel's "Pavane" — in which that instrument has such uncanny power to move us.

After "Shanghai Blues," Ruff asked for questions.   35

"Where do people go to study jazz in America?" a student wanted to know. "What kind of courses do they take?"

Ruff explained that jazz courses, where they existed at all, would be part of a broad college curriculum that included, say, languages and history and physics. "But, really, jazz isn't learned in universities or conservatories," he said. "It's music that is passed on by older musicians to those of us who are younger."

It was not a helpful answer. What kind of subject didn't have its own academy? A shyness settled over the room, though the students seemed full of curiosity. Professor Tan got up and stood next to Ruff. "I urge you to ask questions," he said. "I can assure you that jazz has many principles that apply to your studies here. In fact, I have many questions myself."

An old professor stood up and asked, "When you created the 'Shanghai Blues' just now, did you have a form for it, or a logical plan?"

"I just started tapping my foot," Ruff replied, tapping his foot to recon-   40 struct the moment. "And then I started to play the first thought that came into my mind with the horn. And Mitchell heard it. And he answered. And after that we heard and answered, heard and answered, heard and answered."

The old professor said, "But how can you ever play it again?"

"We never can," Ruff replied.

"That is beyond our imagination," the professor said. "Our students here play a piece a hundred times, or two hundred times, to get it exactly right. You play something once — something very beautiful — and then you just throw it away."

Now the questions tumbled out. What was most on the students' minds quickly became clear: it was the mystery of improvisation. (The Chinese don't even have a word for improvisation of this kind; Ruff translated it as "something created during the process of delivery.") All the questions poked at this central riddle — "Could a Chinese person improvise?" and "Could two strangers improvise together?" and "How can you compose at such speed?" — and during this period Ruff took one question and turned it into a moment that stood us all on our ear.

Was it really possible, a student wanted to know, to improvise on any 45 tune at all — even one that the musicians had never heard before?

Ruff's reply was casual. "I would like to invite one of the pianists here to play a short traditional Chinese melody that I'm sure we would not know, and we will make a new piece based on that," he said.

The room erupted in oohs and cheers. I caught a look on Mitchell's face that said, "This time you've gone too far." The students began to call the name of the young man they wanted to have play. When they found him in the crowd, he was so diffident that he got down on the floor to keep from being dragged out. But his friends dragged him out anyway, and, regaining his aplomb, he walked to the piano and sat down with the formality of a concert artist. He was about twenty-two. Mitchell stood to one side, looking grave.

The young man played his melody beautifully and with great feeling. It seemed to be his own composition, unknown to the other people. It began with four chords of distinctively Chinese structure, moved down the scale in a stately progression, paused, turned itself around with a transitional figure of lighter weight, and then started back up, never repeating itself and finally resolving the theme with a suspended chord that was satisfying because it was so unexpected. It was a perfect small piece, about fourteen bars long. The student walked back to his seat, and Mitchell went back to the piano. The room grew quiet.

Mitchell's huge hands hovered briefly over the keys, and then the young man's melody came back to him. It was in the same key; it had the same chords, slightly embellished near the end; and, best of all, it had the same mood. Having stated the theme, Mitchell broadened it the second time, giving it a certain majesty, coloring the student's chords with dissonances that were entirely apt. He gave the Chinese chords a jazz texture but still preserved their mood. Then Ruff joined him on his bass, and they took the melody through a number of variations, Mitchell giving it a whole series of new lives but never losing its integrity. I listened to his feat with growing excitement. For me, it was the climax of years of marvelling at his ear and at his sensitivity to the material at hand. The students were equally elated and astonished. For them, it was the ultimate proof — because it touched their own heritage — that for a jazz improviser no point of departure is alien.

After that number, a few more questions were asked, and Mitchell and 50 Ruff concluded with a Gershwin medley from "Porgy and Bess" and a genial rendition of "My Old Flame." Professor Tan thanked the two men and formally ended the concert. Then he went over to Mitchell and took his hands in his own. "You are an artist," he said.

Later, I told Mitchell that I thought Ruff had given him an unduly nervous moment when he invited the students to supply a melody.

"Well, naturally I was nervous, because I didn't have any idea what to expect," he said. "But, you know, that boy phrased his piece *perfectly*. The minute he started to play, I got his emotions. I understood exactly what he was feeling, and the rest was easy. The notes and the chords just fell into place."

Suggestions for Writing and Discussion

1. Reread Ruff's opening speech to his Chinese audience (paragraph 3). What do you learn that you never knew before? If you were a member of the audience, would you want Ruff to continue on? Why or why not?
2. Ruff explains that in America, so powerful was the drum believed to be that its use was actually banned by whites who feared their slaves' responses to the drumbeat. What did masters fear from the drum? In your opinion, were their fears justified? Can music inspire people to act in ways they would not act if the music were absent? Explain.
3. Zinsser gives a solid explanation of how Mitchell and Ruff learned jazz. Who were their teachers, and what influences were instrumental in their success as artists?
4. Zinsser also explains that besides being gifted musicians, both Ruff and Mitchell were excellent teachers of music. What do you think — should a teacher in a certain discipline also be an accomplished practitioner in that field?
5. Why does Ruff decide to go to Shanghai in the first place? What does this reveal about his character? When Tan decides to invite the jazz musicians to the conservatory, what does this action reveal about him?
6. Examine Professor Tan's education and his subsequent experience as a teacher and a musician. Can you see any similarities between any of his experiences and those of Mitchell and Ruff? Explain.
7. Argue that the Chinese practice of sending students to farms and factories for three months out of the year is either beneficial or detrimental to an educational experience. Do you think a similar program would work here in the United States? Explain.
8. In being denied Western music of any kind from 1966 to 1976, what types of music and what musicians had the Chinese students never heard? How might this omission have contributed to the "stillness of listening" on the part of the audience?
9. Work on your own definition of *improvisation*. As you develop this definition, explain how Mitchell can invent a song based on the Chinese student's original composition, which he has heard only moments before.
10. Compare the traditional ways of learning a musical composition with the jazz improvisational method. Can a person be a true artist while only

mastering one of these ways of learning? Explain your answer, relying on the essay and your own experience.

_____

Suggestions for Extended Thinking and Research

1. Research one of the great jazz artists who influenced Mitchell and Ruff: Louis Armstrong, Duke Ellington, Dizzy Gillespie, Miles Davis. Besides reading several sources about your artist, listen and respond to several of his works.
2. Research traditional Chinese music in order to discover its traditional musical instruments, its composers, and its philosophies.

_____

BERNICE REAGON

Black Music in Our Hands

> *Bernice Reagon, who grew up in Albany, Georgia, demonstrated her commitment to civil rights when she was a student at Albany State College. She joined the Student Nonviolent Coordinating Committee and was expelled because of her activism with this group. She then transferred to Spelman College, earning a degree in black history and music; in 1975, she received a doctorate in these fields from Howard University. Currently, Reagon serves as oral director of the D.C. Black Repertory Company and, in addition, works for the Smithsonian Institution as a consultant in black music.*

Prereading/Journal-Writing Suggestions

1. Think about a hobby you enjoy: reading, singing, jogging, playing an instrument, dancing, drawing. Write about your experience when you do this hobby alone. Now write about how this experience changes (or might change) when you share it with another person. For example, what's the difference between playing a flute alone in your room and playing with another person? With a small group? With a large orchestra? What are the benefits of being alone? Of being part of a group?

2. What songs, composers, or specific types of music move your spirit? Think back to an early memory that involves one of your specific choices. How important were the events surrounding this memory to your love of this type of music today?

3. Would the world be any different if people went through life, day after day, without any music, any singing, any melodies, any whistling, any harmony whatsoever? Write about a world in which music has yet to be discovered or a world in which music is banned on the basis that it is a powerful, dangerous force.

In the early 1960's, I was in college at Albany State. My major interests were music and biology. In music I was a contralto soloist with the choir, studying Italian arias and German lieder. The black music I sang was of three types:

1) Spirituals sung by the college choir. These were arranged by such people as Nathaniel Dett and William Dawson and had major injections of European musical harmony and composition. 2) Rhythm'n'Blues, music done by and for Blacks in social settings. This included the music of bands at proms, juke boxes, and football game songs. 3) Church music; gospel was a major part of Black church music by the time I was in college. I was a soloist with the gospel choir.

Prior to the gospel choir, introduced in my church when I was twelve, was many years' experience with unaccompanied music — Black choral singing, hymns, lined out by strong song leaders with full, powerful, richly ornate congregational responses. These hymns were offset by upbeat, clapping call-and-response songs.

I saw people in church sing and pray until they shouted. I knew *that* music as a part of a cultural expression that was powerful enough to take people from their conscious selves to a place where the physical and intellectual being worked in harmony with the spirit. I enjoyed and needed that experience. The music of the church was an integral part of the cultural world into which I was born.

Outside of church, I saw music as good, powerful sounds you made or   5
listened to. Rhythm and blues — you danced to; music of the college choir — you clapped after the number was finished.

The Civil Rights Movement changed my view of music. It was after my first march. I began to sing a song and in the course of singing changed the song so that it made sense for that particular moment. Although I was not consciously aware of it, this was one of my earliest experiences with how my music was supposed to *function*. This music was to be integrative of and consistent with everything I was doing at that time; it was to be tied to activities that went beyond artistic affairs such as concerts, dances, and church meetings.

The next level of awareness came while in jail. I had grown up in a rural area outside the city limits, riding a bus to public school or driving to college. My life had been a pretty consistent, balanced blend of church, school, and proper upbringing. I was aware of a Black educated class that taught me in high school and college, of taxi cabs I never rode in, and of people who used buses I never boarded. I went to school with their children.

In jail with me were all these people. All ages. In my section were women from about thirteen to eighty years old. Ministers' wives and teachers and teachers' wives who had only nodded at me or clapped at a concert or spoken to my mother. A few people from my classes. A large number of people who rode segregated city buses. One or two women who had been drinking along the two-block stretch of Little Harlem as the march went by. Very quickly, clashes arose: around age, who would have authority, what was proper behavior?

The Albany Movement was already a singing movement, and we took the songs to jail. There the songs I had sung because they made me feel good or because they said what I thought about a specific issue did something. I would start a song and everybody would join in. After the song, the differences among us would not be as great. Somehow, making a song required an expression of that which was common to us all. The songs did not feel like the same songs I had sung in college. This music was like an instrument, like holding a tool in your hand.

I found that although I was younger than many of the women in my section of the jail, I was asked to take on leadership roles. First as a song leader and then in most other matters concerning the group, especially in discussions, or when speaking with prison officials. 10

I fell in love with that kind of music. I saw that to define music as something you listen to, something that pleases you, is very different from defining it as an instrument with which you can drive a point. In both instances, you can have the same song. But using it as an instrument makes it a different kind of music.

The next level of awareness occurred during the first mass meeting after my release from jail. I was asked to lead the song that I had changed after the first march. When I opened my mouth and began to sing, there was a force and power within myself I had never heard before. Somehow this music — music I could use as an instrument to do things with, music that was mine to shape and change so that it made the statement I needed to make — released a kind of power and required a level of concentrated energy I did not know I had. I liked the feeling.

For several years, I worked with the Movement eventually doing Civil Rights songs with the Freedom Singers. The Freedom Singers used the songs, interspersed with narrative, to convey the story of the Civil Rights Movement's struggles. The songs were more powerful than spoken conversation. They became a major way of making people who were not on the scene feel the intensity of what was happening in the south. Hopefully, they would move the people to take a stand, to organize support groups or participate in various projects.

The Georgia Sea Island Singers, whom I first heard at the Newport Festival, were a major link. Bessie Jones, coming from within twenty miles of Albany, Georgia, had a repertoire and song-leading style I recognized from the churches I had grown up in. She, along with John Davis, would talk about songs that Black people had sung as slaves and what those songs meant in terms of their struggle to be free. The songs did not sound like the spirituals I had sung in college choirs; they sounded like the songs I had grown up with in church. There I had been told the songs had to do with worship of Jesus Christ.

The next few years I spent focusing on three components: 1) The music I had found in the Civil Rights Movement. 2) Songs of the Georgia Sea Island Singers and other traditional groups, and the ways in which those songs were linked to the struggles of Black peoples at earlier times. 3) Songs of the church that now sounded like those traditional songs and came close to having, for many people, the same kind of freeing power. 15

There was another experience that helped to shape my present-day use of music. After getting out of jail, the mother of the church my father pastored was at the mass meeting. She prayed, a prayer I had heard hundreds of times. I had focused on its sound, tune, rhythm, chant, whether the moans came at the proper pace and intensity. That morning I heard every word that she said.

She did not have to change one word of prayer she had been praying for much of her Christian life for me to know she was addressing the issues we were facing at that moment. More than her personal prayer, it felt like an analysis of the Albany, Georgia, Black community.

My collection, study, and creation of Black music has been, to a large extent, about freeing the sounds and the words and the messages from casings in which they have been put, about hearing clearly what the music has to say about Black people and their struggle.

When I first began to search, I looked for what was then being called folk music, rather than for other Black forms, such as jazz, rhythm and blues, or gospel. It slowly dawned on me that during the Movement we had used all those forms. When we were relaxing in the office, we made up songs using popular rhythm and blues tunes; songs based in rhythm and blues also came out of jails, especially from the sit-in movement and the march to Selma, Alabama. "Oh Wallace, You Never Can Jail Us All" is an example from Selma. "You Better Leave Segregation Alone" came out of the Nashville Freedom Rides and was based on a bit by Little Willie John, "You Better Leave My Kitten Alone." Gospel choirs became the major musical vehicle in the urban center of Birmingham, with the choir led by Carlton Reese. There was also a gospel choir in the Chicago work, as well as an instrumental ensemble led by Ben Branch.

Jazz had not been a strong part of my musical life. I began to hear it as I traveled north. Thelonious Monk and Charlie Mingus played on the first SNCC benefit at Carnegie Hall. I heard of and then heard Coltrane. Then I began to pick up the pieces that had been laid by Charlie Parker and Coleman Hawkins and whole lifetimes of music. This music had no words. But, it had power, intensity, and movement under various degrees of pressure; it had vocal texture and color. I could feel that the music knew how it felt to be Black and Angry, Black and Down, Black and Loved, Black and Fighting.

I now believe that Black music exists in every place where Black people 20 run, every corner where they live, every level on which they struggle. We have been here a long while, in many situations. It takes all that we have created to sing our song. I believe that Black musicians/artists have a responsibility to be conscious of their world and to let their consciousness be heard in their songs.

And we need it all—blues, gospel, ballads, children's games, dance, rhythms, jazz, lovesongs, topical songs—doing what it has always done. We need Black music that functions in relation to the people and community who provide the nurturing compost that makes its creation and continuation possible.

Suggestions for Writing and Discussion

1. In this piece, Reagon describes the different roles that music has played in

her life. Identify these roles and explain what her interaction with music on these different levels reveals about her character.

2. In paragraph 9, Reagon writes that "this music was like an instrument, like holding a tool in your hand." She repeats this analogy throughout the essay. Find several other references to music as an instrument, and analyze what this comparison implies about music as well as the musician.

3. Why, in paragraph 10, do the women in jail ask Reagon to take on the role of leader, even though she was one of the youngest women there?

4. According to Reagon, music is a powerful, moving force within the black community. How does Reagon define black music? Do you agree with her definition? Analyze some of the various forces within black music in order to come to some conclusion about what distinguishes this music from other types of music: country/western, classical, pop/rock, Muzak.

5. As Reagon implies, music can be used for several purposes. After you identify some of these purposes, consider another artistic expression that shares these same levels of purpose.

6. What might be Reagon's purpose in writing this piece? For what specific audience, if any, is this essay intended? Explain your answers.

Suggestions for Extended Thinking and Research

1. Research the historical roots of a specific type of black music: gospel, jazz, spirituals, rhythm and blues, rap. Applying Reagon's theme that music is a powerful, moving force, decide what specific issues or values within the historical context are being "moved." In other words, what part does music play as far as the problems, conflicts, issues, and conquests of the times are concerned?

2. Research the life, times, influences, and artistic achievements of a specific black musician, either living or in the past. Besides using a strict library approach to this topic, list and respond to several works by this artist. In addition, conduct several interviews or survey a number of your fellow students, friends, and relatives to discover their responses to this musician and his or her music. Analyze and explain what you have discovered through your research.

3. John Ciardi, a noted poet and teacher, believed that if students wanted to understand poetry, they only had to know one great poem well. Applying this same principle to music, choose one musical selection that represents the kind of music you love best. Learn this piece well—inside and out. Your learning process may involve playing an instrument, or you may choose simply to listen (and relisten) to the music. In an oral presentation (or a brief paper accompanied by a tape), teach an appreciation of this music to your peers and your instructor and explain why you chose this selection.

NOËL BENNETT
Halo of the Sun

> *Noël Bennett is a free-lance writer who spent several years on a Navajo reservation where her husband served as a physician in the clinic. In this essay, excerpted from her book* Halo of the Sun: Stories Told and Retold *(1987), she explains and compares her own approach to weaving with the approaches she encountered among the Native American craftswomen. She traces her own discovery that Navajo weaving is not only an art form but also a symbol of the Navajo way of life.*

Prereading/Journal-Writing Suggestions

1. If you could choose one art form, one craft, or even one commercial product that symbolizes the American culture you know, what would it be and why would you choose it?
2. Everyone is an authority on something. Imagine that someone comes to you for advice on the one thing you know well. Write about what you know, and include what advice you would give to someone who also wants to be an authority on this subject. Where should they start? What will they have to do? How long will it take?
3. Every culture holds its share of superstitions. Brainstorm for superstitions that you have "inherited" from your family, those that you have learned from your friends, and those that perhaps have no specific origin. Have you ever been a victim of one of these superstitions? Write about a specific event in your life in which a superstition played a part.

Gusts picked at the edges of the silted earth, first gently, then with growing vigor, until a mauve haze obscured the flat sageland before me. I urged my son to hurry. In his small hand he clenched a worn food card. On the back a young Navajo man two days before had drawn an intricate map to his mother's hogan. His mother, a weaver.

Shawn, six, was my moral support, a help in countering my failing resolve. I had been on reservation less than a week. There were at least two years ahead during which to leisurely find a weaver. Learning Navajo weaving couldn't require two years of motivated, concerted effort. I could go next week. . . .

I headed the car down the road.

Finding a weaver had not been easy. The terse traders, Navajo rugs piled about them, knew of none. The urbane doctors' wives, unventuring in their year of stay, knew of none. My husband Jack, home from his first day at the new hospital, had encountered none.

As we turned onto the rutted road at the trading post, the cards to comb 5 the wool bounced beside me and I steadied them. Already they were looking used. Two days before, Jack, home for lunch amidst packing boxes, had listened sympathetically to my frustration in finding a weaver. When he left for the hospital, I lay down for a nap, but no sooner had I closed my eyes when I heard him open the door again.

"I know you need a rest. But I know you'll like it even less if I go to work without telling you. There's a lady sitting in the brush herding sheep — and she's combing her wool!"

I hurried across sand and sage toward a distant figure bleached in noon-day glare. With mild curiosity she watched me. At close range her dark, bright eyes and rutted skin caused me to hesitate. I didn't speak Navajo; she probably didn't speak English. I settled beside her in the sun.

"Hello."

She spoke in Navajo and continued carding: wool on the left card, just the right amount; right card on top; a series of long combing motions; a quick double sliding push-pull.

She was carding with her back to her flock. Behind her I could see sheep 10 grazing contentedly in prime Tuba City pasturage — Anglo doctors' lawns. Approximately every half-hour she glanced about. "Surprised" at seeing the sheep nibbling in gardens, she jumped up and herded them back to the barren sagebrush and then resumed carding. While I watched, the sheep made their way back to greener grass. After two hours, she suddenly got up, flung a word melodically into the silence, and left. Her sheep with her.

Within minutes I was on my way to the trading post to buy my own cards. Back home I positioned wool and cards precisely as I had seen her do. Comb. Grate. Mesh. She had turned her wool to silk, mine was now matted. I continued to practice. At the end of the day, sitting by a pile of jumbled wool rolls, I resolved to find a weaver to teach me.

Years before, as a foreign exchange student in Germany, I had sat on cobblestones and painted village scenes. Soon the local children discovered the "artista." Not long afterwards parents came to get their kids — and peek at the painting. A conversation was initiated. Then a lunch invitation. Suddenly, there we were eating. . . .

So maybe if I sat in the middle of town carding, someone would help me learn. All I needed was a good location and enough courage. Tuba City options were limited: two trading posts, an elementary school, a Dairy Queen, one gas station and the laundromat.

The women do the laundry and the women do the weaving. I piled dirty clothes into the jeep, cards and wool on top. Half an hour later, laundry turning inside machines, I sat on the ground outside and began to card. Women and children took notice and stood near, forming a circle. No one said a word. Time went by. I began to realize Tuba City wasn't Beutelsbach.

No one pitied my clumsiness with the cards. No matter how much 15 difficulty I encountered, no one offered help. No advice. No words at all. Just a soft easy giggle occasionally rippling around the growing circle. There was nothing to do but continue. Intently. Completely. With singleness of mind.

Perhaps fifteen minutes later I looked up to face the silence. Women were now three deep about me. A black pick-up was pulling to a stop at the edge of the crowd, a young man and woman were getting out. Slowly the woman came over and knelt beside me.

"What are you doing?" It wasn't a positive, inquisitive — "What are you doing?" Nor was it a negative, derogatory — "What are you doing!" The inflection was neutral. Flat. Balanced just in between.

"I'm trying to card wool."

Dead silence.

Wrong answer! Could have said anything but that.   20

An inner dialogue filled in the unnerving space. I desperately wished someone would help me, so I said aloud,

"I'm having a hard time."

Silence.

Self-evident. Words wasted on the obvious. Don't talk now till she *does.*

I began a new batch of wool, intent on matching her reserve. I came to 25 the end. Still she hadn't spoken. I laid another wool roll on the pile.

"Can you help me?"

Silence.

"Just keep carding."

I know, now, her answer was the best that could have been given — my mind knew the method; my hands had yet to refine pressure and rhythm. But that was not what I wanted to hear. I wanted real help: "You're holding the cards wrong. You're using too much pressure. Too much wool."

But the silence had been broken. And questions now bobbed up in 30 various parts of the circle, then traveled in Navajo around the perimeter. When they came to the young woman, she translated.

"They want to know where you get your wool."

"It's my mother's sheep," I answered, knowing that with the Navajo, sheep belong to the women. "From California." Translation into Navajo. Hands reaching to feel "California wool." Again, indistinguishable clicks and stops coming the course of the circle.

"What color is it?" Lips pointed toward the dirty wool before me. The question was odd to me. I answered the obvious.

"It's white." Then clarified, "I haven't washed it yet." The translation went around but quickly came back.

"They think it's grey; they can't believe it's white."   35

I looked at my dirty white wool. Mixed with black California soil, it was grey. Maybe the Navajo white wool, mixed with red Arizona soil, would be pink. I shared the thought. Many hands reached in the bag and my mother's sheep disappeared into the circle.

The next question came quickly. "They want to know who's training you."

The wording was strange to me, but the question was in the right place. I took my time with the answer. There was a beauty in not having to blurt out the first thing that came to mind. "Nobody. . . . Yesterday I watched an old lady carding in the sagebrush. . . . I'd like to learn more."

Stillness. Stillness. Unrelenting stillness. "Do you know anyone who could teach me?"

As soon as I heard my own words, I chided myself. I had now asked 40 twice. I returned to carding. In the time it took to process three more wool rolls, the woman from the pick-up began to speak.

"My mother-in-law weaves." My heart pounded hopefully. "She's a good weaver." Another wool-roll later. "She sells her rugs at the Cameron Trading Post."

"Would she teach me?"

"You ask her. She speaks good English."

Her husband drew the map on the back of a food card. The woman, Clara, assured me I could come any time. I loaded the now very clean, wet clothes, the worn food card, and what was left of Mom's wool in the back of the jeep. I drove off with one of the first headaches of my life.

Here we were now — past the trading post, past the fork, taking the road 45 behind the mountain, past the turn to the right we were not supposed to take and now we were heading down the road to her hogan.

The night before I had attended a lecture on patient etiquette given by a Navajo man to new doctors at the hospital. Afterward, I told him I would be visiting a weaver the next morning. Was there anything I should know?

> Don't park right in front of the hogan door. The hogan is one room. If you stop right in front and the door is open, you can see inside the hogan and you will know if somebody's in there. If they're there and don't want to come out, they just stay inside. So it's better you don't know if they're there. That way everybody saves face. And don't get right out. Just wait awhile. Someone will come out if they want to see you; not if they don't.

So Shawn and I waited together. Children emerged, circling the car, peering in windows. I was uncertain how they counted in the etiquette; if children acknowledged our presence, was it all right to get out? Or did we need to wait for an adult to welcome us? After five minutes, we got out and slowly walked across the camp toward the black pick-up we had first seen at the laundry.

"What do you want?"

A handsome young man had come out of the hogan. Perfect English; unreadable expression. Not a cordial "Can-I-help-you-What-do-you-want?"

Nor a hostile "What-are-you-doing-here-What-do-you-want?" Just between. I asked for Clara. He looked away, then gestured toward the hogan. "She's brushing her hair."

Clara paused in the hogan doorway, brush in hand, shiny black hair 50 hanging long and free. She eyed me uncertainly. . . .

"I just came to see about weaving." Her expression didn't change. "Did you ask your mother-in-law?"

She went back to brushing her hair. I felt the ticking of seconds and then minutes. Then she stopped.

"Yes."

Silence.

"What did she say?" I felt a growing impatience as I rephrased the 55 obvious. These silences were grating on me, underscoring my position as an outsider. I considered leaving.

"She hasn't answered yet."

I almost laughed aloud at her reply. I felt the tension leave. They weren't treating me, the Anglo, differently. Long silence was the Navajo way.

I began to look about me, in no hurry now to talk. There was time to savor colors and textures. The children's bare feet and the red dark earth blended as one; a pile of untanned sheep skins lay over a smooth rail fence. Adults had joined the circle, their faces neither friendly nor unfriendly.

"You ask her. She speaks good English."

I looked at Clara and saw her gesture toward a woman standing in 60 shadow to my left. Clothed in long traditional satin skirt and velvet blouse, she looked about fifty and yet seemed ageless. Her feet were solidly together, arms folded before her. How long had she been there? Could it be she did speak English? *If* she understood English, *if* Clara had asked her, or even if she had heard Clara and me talking, she would know why I had come. I had, in effect, already asked. So I simply smiled.

There was no response. But then her expression began to change. She shifted her weight, and slowly crossed the packed earth to the sheep corral. In one clean motion she pulled a goat skin off the rail. Tufted white was swept aside to reveal shimmering golds and rusts. A rug in progress. And color enough to fill all sound and space.

I stepped forward. My fingertips scanned the surface: soft, earthy lanolin; rhythmic joints possible only through years of repetition.

"It's beautiful. Clara said you were a good weaver and you are." Words blurted forth against the silence I meant to keep. I couldn't help it. It was a statement of truth, the kind that needs no answer.

One came anyway — a clear voice seeking seldom-used words.

"I should be. I've been weaving since I was seven." 65

That was my meeting with Tiana Bighorse. Later, when I did formally ask if she would teach me, her reply was equally to the point.

"How long do you have to learn?"

I would be in Tuba City two years. There seemed no better answer. But I waited for what I thought to be an appropriate time then confidently said:

"Two years." Her expression clouded and I hastily added, "Will that be enough?"

She shifted her eyes. Downward, then back at me. "Perhaps." 70

It has been twenty years since that meeting day. Many times I have recalled the economical words of a woman who had been weaving almost half a century spoken to a young stranger wanting to undertake the craft. And with the passing of time I have come to further understand. Two years was not nearly enough. . . .

The legendary spiderwoman insisted white shell woman learn to spin before learning to weave. Tiana Bighorse advised me similarly. However, as it turned out, I so loved spinning and dyeing that six months later I was still caught in its web. I walked all elevations of the reservation, seeking native plants and learning to evoke their muted hues. A hundred and twenty colored skeins later my weaving mentor, in a tone suggesting the honeymoon was over, asked when I was going to learn to weave.

So I made a loom of cedar and began my weaving. If I had continued following tradition, the rug would have been striped. But, having not been long on reservations, my Anglo eagerness set the design and I began instead a sampler rug — one to combine all my dyed yarns with as many techniques as possible. It was to become a sampler of challenges.

I was just beginning my first design in colors from wild carrot and cedar bark, when son Shawn came to sit on my lap mid-row. Wanting to bring him into the experience, I asked him what design should follow: "A snake, a stick, and the sun," he said.

The serpent from San Ildefonso offered itself as a prototype for the 75 snake. Another Navajo friend, Helen Tsinnie, — "Philosophic Weaver" — helped me begin. We used an especially difficult technique including repetitive triangles for tail and tongue spears, ornate horning for the head. Weaving it in, unraveling, weaving it right . . . through time and persistence the snake came into being.

The stick and tufted sun were next followed by a design in two-face, where both sides of the weaving are different. Again the complexity was absorbing and I felt proud and relieved getting through this really difficult part. Vowing never again to weave another two-face, I unknowingly began my greatest test.

It started quietly one morning when a Navajo family came to visit. Grandmother. Mother. Daughter. Like most Navajo visitors, they walked about the house, looking at everything, interested in how the Anglo family lived. I understood, for I enjoyed being in Navajo hogans. I took my visitors for a tour of the livingroom, showing them the Navajo loom with its growing sampler, proud of the two-face band I had just completed. Next I demonstrated the Anglo treadle loom on the far side of the room. Like these visitors, Navajo weavers were always fascinated by the heddles and pedals. But, sometime during the demonstration, I noticed Grandmother had not moved from the Navajo loom and was now speaking loudly in Navajo. Her gestures were agitated. I asked Mother what Grandmother was saying.

"It is nothing," she shrugged.

I continued on, showing the three women my many skeins of dyed yarns. I used the Navajo names of specific dyeplants, hoping Grandmother would be able to understand and perhaps feel more included. Grandmother didn't move. She was still by the loom, talking. Clearly she was upset. This time I turned to Granddaughter. What was bothering Grandmother? Again a laughing, off-hand remark — something old-fashioned Grandmother was rattling on about. Speaking quietly again to Mother, I told her I cared very much about old-time beliefs. I would like to hear what Grandmother wanted me to know. With this gentle urging the Mother began.

Grandmother was talking about a worry, an old-time belief. It was bad 80 luck to weave a snake in a rug. Violating the taboo could bring harmful consequences. I was taken aback. What could I do to right my mistake. Take the rug off the loom and not finish it?

"No. The rug would still be there."

"Take it off and burn it?" I offered. I thought about hours of painstaking work, and my attachment to each of the difficult designs.

"No, it would still exist."

The only solution, Grandmother said, was to unravel the piece. . . .

After my guests had left, I sat gazing at my weaving. I could not bring 85 myself to begin the unraveling. So much of myself had been woven into it; taking it out would be a personal loss. I stopped weaving.

Unaware of what had happened since her last visit, Helen Tsinnie stopped by. She said I had made good progress. During a quiet moment, I told her about Grandmother's visit. I asked if she had ever heard of such a taboo. Yes, she admitted after a pause. Her mother had done it once — woven a big, black snake from bottom to top. Everyone who had seen it had told her not to do it. They said it would bring danger. They told her it would make her blind. But she did it anyway.

The night she was finishing her rug, it was stormy. Thunder and lightning came close together, again and again. As she untied the rug from the loom, the night loosed its anger. Lightning struck and killed two horses: one she used to herd the sheep, one she used to tighten the loom. It was only then she understood: Snake and Lightning are one. They work together for harm.

"How come I wasn't told of this taboo before starting the snake?"

My friend thought for a long time, then said, "It isn't bad luck if you don't believe in it."

Helen had thought it would be all right for an Anglo to weave a snake. 90

She had not foreseen I would take in Navajo weaving in such depth — technique *and* belief.

There was a further pause, then, "I think I made a mistake. If something happens to you — maybe not till next week, or next month or next year — if something happens to you they'll say it's because you put a snake in the rug. And," she added, "if nothing happens, they'll say it's because you're a witch."

I put away my weaving tools.

Six months later I was in a trading post, looking at pawn jewelry about to be sold. While I was admiring the pieces, a Navajo lady came up behind me and pointed to three specific items: "That's mine, that's mine, and that's mine." Turning, I recognized Tiana Bighorse. As she had no money to redeem her pieces, I offered what little I had to buy one back for her. Which did she like best? A Zuni inlaid bracelet that her daughter had given her for Mothers Day. I examined it closely. The design was of a beautiful big eagle, with wings outstretched. And between beak and both talons stretched a snake.

"Isn't it bad luck to have a snake in a bracelet?" I asked quietly.

She looked at me pointedly. "Why should it be bad luck?"   95

I moved on to the cashier, also a friend. While paying, I again asked the question.

"Of course not." She eyed me curiously. I began to think I had the strange beliefs.

Then on the way to the car, as Tiana Bighorse was putting the bracelet back on her wrist, she paused.

"You buy this back for me so I tell you. It *is* bad luck to put a snake in a bracelet. My son try to get it off. He don't have the right tools." She pointed to hack marks outside the beak and beside both talons. "But it's O.K. The Snake is about to be food for the Eagle."

There it was! When I got home later that afternoon, I excitedly ran 100 inside yelling to my family, "What bird eats more snakes than any other?"

"Roadrunner," Shawn and Jack yelled back simultaneously from different parts of the house.

Right then I sat down and wove two roadrunners into the top of my rug.

From that day on, if any traditional Navajo weavers even started to look at the serpent, I'd say quickly, "Hey, it's O.K. If that snake makes a move, those roadrunners will be down to get him in a moment."

Years later, I gave a lecture at the Denver Museum of Natural History and told this story of my first weaving. Bertha Stevens, Navajo weaver, was in the audience. Through the years, she and her medicineman-sandpainter husband, Fred Stevens, had traveled and demonstrated extensively throughout the world.

Bertha is of the culture that holds the snake taboo. But she has broken 105 with Navajo tradition by excelling openly as an individual. When the lecture was over, Bertha waited until the entire crowd had left. Then she came to talk with me. She had listened with understanding to my story and wanted to give me something.

"I want you to remember," she told me.

"You have always walked in Beauty. All you have to do is keep going."

Suggestions for Writing and Discussion

1. Why doesn't Bennett just come out and ask someone in the area to show her the art of weaving? What stands in her way? Analyze and evaluate her approach. Do you think she used the best possible approach? Or do you think another approach might have been more effective? Explain.

2. Retrace the steps Bennett takes in order to learn this art form. What does this challenging process reveal about Bennett herself?

3. Compare the Navajo way of teaching with, say, a typical approach to teaching in the classrooms where you have been a student. What traits must a Navajo possess in order to be an effective teacher? What traits do you believe characterized the effective teachers in your schools? What values are suggested by each of the approaches you have explained?

4. Reread the Navajo customs (paragraph 47) regarding visiting another's hogan. What values are inherent in such manners? How does this approach differ from a neighborly visit in your town or city?

5. If long silences are the Navajo way, what is the Anglo way, as far as communication goes? Evaluate what can be gained in long silences as well as what can be lost.

6. Why, exactly, did Bennett stop weaving for six months? Was she superstitious? Was she lazy? Was she discouraged? What prompts her eventually to finish her piece? What do both of these points — the stopping and the starting again — tell us about Bennett and perhaps about artists in general?

Suggestions for Extended Thinking and Research

1. Research in greater detail the Navajo art of weaving or any other Native American art. Find out about the beginnings of this art and its general process. Explain how beliefs and values within the culture are a part of this artistic process, as well as the product itself.

2. All of us are artists in the general sense that we have the ability to create something new from our inner thoughts and ideas and from the resources of the world around us. Research your own process in art — be it in music, words, physical expression, cooking, colors, materials, or the like. Write an essay in which you "watch" yourself at work as an artist. Where do you get an idea? When do you start? What do you use? When do you get discouraged? How do others enter into this process with you? When are you satisfied that your work of art is complete?

3. Choose three other areas of Navajo life: rituals, family life, male/female relationships, celebrations, home settings, activities, education, language, religious beliefs, nature, politics. Compare and contrast these three areas with the same areas in mainstream American culture in order to answer these questions: In what ways are these cultures the same? In what ways are these cultures different? And what is significant — if anything — about these similarities and differences?

MICHAEL DORRIS

Indians in Aspic

> *Michael Dorris contributes frequently to the* New York Times, *where this essay first appeared in February 1991. He is the author of* The Broken Cord *and, with his wife, Louise Erdrich,* The Crown of Columbus. *Both Dorris and Erdrich are actively involved in issues and concerns related to Native American communities.*

Prereading/Journal-Writing Suggestions

1. Think back on your earliest impressions of American Indians. What did you think Indians were like? Where did you get this impression — from a book, a story you heard, a television show, a movie, something else? Try to remember the specific source that shaped your views on Indians. Did this source present you with what you would now consider a fair picture? Explain.

2. Use your imagination: You get the chance to star in a Hollywood movie hit. You can be either a member of a group of early settlers or a member of an Indian tribe. Which do you choose to be and why?

CORNISH, N.H. The Sioux and Lieut. John Dunbar, the character enthusiastically played by Kevin Costner in "Dances With Wolves," meet auspiciously: He's naked, and that so disconcerts a group of mounted warriors that the naïve young soldier lives to tell the tale, a sort of Boy Scout Order of the Arrow ritual carried to the nth power.

Dunbar, renamed Dances With Wolves, quickly earns merit badges in Pawnee-bashing and animal telepathy, and marries Stands With a Fist (Mary McDonnell), a passionate young widow who just happens to be a white captive cum Campfire Girl of impressive cross-cultural accomplishments. Eventually the "With" family strikes out on their own — the nucleus of a handsome new Anglo tribe — sadder, wiser and certainly more sensitive as a result of their native American immersion.

Mr. Costner follows in a long tradition of literary and cinematic heroes who have discovered Indians. Robinson Crusoe did it off the coast of Brazil, Natty Bumppo did it in New York State and everyone from Debra Paget ("Broken Arrow," 1950) and Natalie Wood ("The Searchers," 1956) to Dustin Hoffman ("Little Big Man," 1970) and Richard Harris ("A Man Called Horse," 1970) has done it in Hollywood.

Usually these visits do not bode well for the aboriginal hosts — just ask the Mohicans. Appreciative white folks always seem to show up shortly before the cavalry (who are often looking for them) or Manifest Destiny, and record the final days of peace before the tribe is annihilated. Readers and viewers of such sagas are left with a predominant emotion of regret for a golden age now but a faint memory. In the imaginary mass media world of neat beginnings, middles and ends, American Indian society, whatever its virtues and fascinations as an arena for Euro-American consciousness-raising, is definitely past tense.

Thematically virtually all of these works share a subtle or not so subtle message: Indians may be poor, they may at first seem strange or forbidding or primitive, but by golly once you get to know them they have a thing or two to teach us about The Meaning of Life.

The tradition goes back a long way. Europeans like Jean-Jacques Rousseau and Karl May (the turn-of-this-century novelist whose books, a mixture of Louis L'Amour and the Hardy Boys, have been a rite of passage for generations of German youth) laid out a single range for Indians to inhabit: savage-savage to noble-savage. Indians embody the concept of "the other" — a foreign, exotic, even cartoonish panorama against which "modern" (that is, white) men can measure and test themselves, and eventually, having proved their mettle in battle, be dubbed as natural leaders by their hosts.

Placed within the genre, "Dances With Wolves" shows some signs of evolution. Kevin Costner obviously spared no expense to achieve a sense of authenticity in his production. He filmed on the Pine Ridge reservation in South Dakota and defied conventional Hollywood wisdom to assemble a large and talented native American supporting cast. Great attention was paid to ethnographically correct costumes, and if the streets in the native camp seem a tad too spotless to be believed, at least the tepees are museum quality.

Impressively, large segments of the film are spoken in Lakota, the language of the western Sioux, and though the subtitles are stilted — Indians in the movies seem incapable of using contractions — they at least convey the impression that native Americans had an intellectual life.

When I saw "Dances With Wolves" at an advance screening, I predicted that it would be less than a box-office smash. Though spectacular to look at, it struck me as too long, too predictable, too didactic to attract a large audience. Twelve Academy Award nominations and $100 million in revenue later, was I ever wrong. In fact, the movie probably sells tickets precisely *because* it delivers the old-fashioned Indians that the ticket-buying audience expects to find. Dunbar is our national myth's everyman — handsome, sensitive, flexible, right-thinking. He passes the test of the frontier, out-Indians the Indians, achieves a pure soul by encountering and surmounting the wilderness.

Yet, if "Dances With Wolves" had been about *people* who happen to be Indians, rather than about *Indians* (uniformly stoic, brave, nasty to their enemies, nice to their friends), it might have stood a better chance of acting as a bridge between societies that have for too long woodenly characterized each other.

With such tremendous popularity, the film is sure to generate a bubble of sympathy for the Sioux, but hard questions remain: Will this sentiment be

practical, translating into public support for native American religious freedom cases before the Supreme Court, for restoration of Lakota sacred lands
(the Black Hills) or water rights, for tribal sovereignty, for providing the
money desperately needed by reservation health clinics? Pine Ridge is the
most economically impoverished corner of America today, the Census Bureau
says, but will its modern Indian advocates in business suits, men and women
with lap-top computers and perfect English, be the recipients of a tidal wave
of good will?

Or will it turn out, once again, that the only good Indians — the only
Indians whose causes and needs we can embrace — are lodged safely in the
past, wrapped neatly in the blankets of history, magnets for our sympathy
because they require nothing of us but tears in a dark theater?

Suggestions for Writing and Discussion

1. Let's start right off with the title of this piece: What exactly *is* aspic? How
   might it connect to the author's point in this piece?
2. From the first two paragraphs alone, what clues can you pick up on the
   author's tone (his attitude toward his subject and toward his readers)? What
   might be Dorris's purpose in using this tone? As a reader, does this tone/
   approach appeal to you? Why or why not?
3. Why, in paragraph 5, does Dorris capitalize "The Meaning of Life"? Does
   this technique add to or detract from his critique? Explain your answer.
4. In what ways does Dorris believe *Dances With Wolves* is different from most
   Indian genre films? In what ways is it typical? From your own television-
   and film-viewing experiences, do you agree or disagree with his evaluation? Explain.
5. Overall, what is Dorris's main point in this piece? To whom is he addressing this message — Hollywood filmmakers or those of us in the audience?
   Does he seem to be suggesting changes he would like to see or simply
   explaining problems? Explain your answer.
6. Should a movie or a television show aim for realism and truth? Explain the
   reasons for your response by referring to specific films or programs that
   you have found either highly praiseworthy or extremely lacking in those
   qualities you admire.

Suggestions for Extended Thinking and Research

1. If you have seen *Dances With Wolves,* write your own critique of this film
   and the issues it deals with. Refer to several points that Dorris makes in his
   essay. Do you agree or disagree with him on these points? Support your
   stance with specific examples from the movie itself and other films related
   to the early American West.
2. Search for several other reviews of *Dances With Wolves,* as well as written
   interviews with Kevin Costner regarding this film. (You might try the

New York Times Index as a place to begin looking for such reviews.) Write an analysis in which you synthesize these reviews and interviews and the Dorris essay.

3. Argue that general audiences should or should not trust the evaluation of a film to a movie critic, such as Siskel or Ebert (or Dorris!). Use as your support at least two other specific movies you have seen and subsequent reviews on these films.

JIM SAGEL

Sandra Cisneros: Sneaking Past the Guards

> *Jim Sagel writes poems both in English and in Spanish. He is the winner of the Casa de las Americas literary award. In this essay, which first appeared in* Publisher's Weekly, March 1991, *he analyzes the challenges faced by writers such as Sandra Cisneros who come from a culture different from mainstream America and whose works strive to "startle the jaded reader" and "poetically unravel stereotypes."*

Prereading/Journal-Writing Suggestions

1. Each one of us has at least one book within us. What is your great book about? List the events, people, and the conflicts that you could write about. Analyze as well what your purpose and your audience might be for this book.
2. List all of the different cultures represented by any writers you have read. Are any Hispanic American authors on this list? If so, who are they? If not, why do you think you've never read anything by a Hispanic American author?

Taped to her word processor is a prayer card to San Judas, a gift from a Mexico City cabdriver. Her two indispensable literary sources are mail order catalogues and the San Antonio (Tex.) phone book. She lights candles and reads the *Popul Vuh* before sitting down to write long into the night, becoming so immersed in her characters that she dreams their dialogue: once she awoke momentarily convinced she was Inés, bride of the Mexican revolutionary Emiliano Zapata.

Such identification with her characters and her culture is altogether natural for Sandra Cisneros, a writer who has always found her literary voice in the real voices of her people, her immediate family and the extended *famiulis* of Latino society.

"I'm trying to write the stories that haven't been written. I feel like a cartographer; I'm determined to fill a literary void," Cisneros says. With the Random House publication of her new collection of stories, *Woman Hollering Creek* (Fiction Forecasts, Feb. 15), and the simultaneous reissuing of her earlier collection of short fiction, *The House on Mango Street,* in a Vintage edition, Cisneros finds herself in a position to chart those barrio ditches and borderland arroyos that have not appeared on most copies of the American literary map but which, nonetheless, also flow into the "mainstream."

The 36-year-old daughter of a Mexican father and a Chicana mother, Cisneros is well aware of the additional pressure to succeed with this pair of books that represent the opportunity for a wider readership, not only for herself but for scores of other Latina and Latino writers right behind the door that she is cracking open.

"One of the most frightening pressures I faced as I wrote this book was   5 the fear that I would blow it," Cisneros says, sweeping a lock of her closely cropped black hair from her forehead as she sips a midmorning cup of coffee. "I kept asking myself, What have I taken on here? That's why I was so obsessed with getting everybody's stories out. I didn't have the luxury of doing my own."

Coupled with that "responsibility to do a collective good job," is Cisneros's anxiety about how her work will be perceived by the general reading public. Universal as her themes are, Cisneros knows her characters live in an America very different from that of her potential readers. From her friend Lucy, "who smells like corn," to Salvador, whose essence resides "inside that wrinkled shirt, inside the throat that must clear itself and apologize each time it speaks," Cisneros's literary landscape teems with characters who live, love and laugh in the flowing cadences of the Spanish language.

Yet, unlike her character Salvador, Cisneros offers no apologies when she speaks. Energetic and abounding with *gusto* — only the Spanish word will do to describe her engaging humor — Cisneros relishes the opportunity to startle the jaded reader and poetically unravel stereotypes, especially those that relate to Latinas.

"I'm the mouse who puts a thorn in the lion's paw," she says, with an arch smile reminiscent of the red-lipped *sonrisa* on the cover of *My Wicked Wicked Ways* (Third Woman Press, 1987), a collection of poetry celebrating the "bad girl" with her "lopsided symmetry of sin / and virtue."

"An unlucky fate is mine / to be born woman in a family of men," Cisneros writes in one of her "wicked" poems, yet it is that very "fate" that laid the groundwork for the literary career of this writer, whose name derives from the Spanish word for "swan."

Born in Chicago in 1954, Cisneros grew up in a family of six brothers   10 and a father, or "seven fathers," as she puts it. She recalls spending much of her early childhood moving from place to place. Because her paternal grandmother was so attached to her favorite son, the Cisneros family returned to Mexico City "like the tides."

"The moving back and forth, the new schools, were very upsetting to me as a child. They caused me to be very introverted and shy. I do not remember making friends easily, and I was terribly self-conscious due to the cruelty of the nuns, who were majestic at making one feel little. Because we moved so much, and always in neighborhoods that appeared like France after World War II — empty lots and burned-out buildings — I retreated inside myself."

It was that "retreat" that transformed Cisneros into an observer, a role she feels she still plays today. "When I'm washing sheets at the laundromat, people still see me as just a girl. I take advantage of that idea. The little voice I used to hate I now see as an asset. It helps me get past the guards."

Among the first "guards" that Cisneros sneaked past were the literary sentinels at the University of Iowa's Writer's Workshop, which she attended in the late '70s. Her "breakthrough" occurred during a seminar discussion of archetypal memories in Bachelard's *Poetics of Space*. As her classmates spoke about the house of the imagination, the attics, stairways and cellars of childhood, Cisneros felt foreign and out of place.

"Everyone seemed to have some communal knowledge which I did not have — and then I realized that the metaphor of *house* was totally wrong for me. Suddenly I was homeless. There were no attics and cellars and crannies. I had no such house in my memories. As a child I had read of such things in books, and my family had promised such a house, but the best they could do was offer the miserable bungalow I was embarrassed with all my life. This caused me to question myself, to become defensive. What did I, Sandra Cisneros, know? What *could* I know? My classmates were from the best schools in the country. They had been bred as fine hothouse flowers. I was a yellow weed among the city's cracks.

"It was not until this moment when I separated myself, when I consid- 15 ered myself truly distinct, that my writing acquired a voice. I knew I was a Mexican woman, but I didn't think it had anything to do with why I felt so much imbalance in my life, whereas it had everything to do with it! My race, my gender, my class! That's when I decided I would write about something my classmates couldn't write about."

Thus it was that *The House on Mango Street* was born and Cisneros discovered what she terms her "first love," a fascination with speech and voices. Writing in the voice of the adolescent Esperanza, Cisneros created a series of interlocking stories, alternately classified as a novel and as a collection of prose poems because of the vivid and poignant nature of the language. Since its first publication in 1984 by Arte Público Press, *Mango Street* has sold some 30,000 copies. The book is used in classes from junior high school through graduate school in subjects ranging from Chicano studies to psychology to culture, ideas and values at Stanford University, where it has been adopted as part of the "new curriculum."

Mango Street was also the catalyst that drew Cisneros to her literary agent or, to be more accurate, that led Susan Bergholz to Cisneros. Bergholz was so moved after reading the book that she did something she had never done before: she set out to track down the writer. "It was a delightful chase," Bergholz recalls, in spite of the fact that it took some three to four years to accomplish.

Ironically, even while Bergholz was enlisting the aid of Richard Bray of Guild Books to contact Cisneros, the writer was going through what she calls the worst year of her life, 1987. She had spent the previous year in Texas through the auspices of a Dobie-Paisano fellowship. Though the experience had convinced her to make Texas her permanent home, the writer found herself unable to make a living once the fellowship expired.

While her boyfriend waited tables, Cisneros handed out fliers in local supermarkets and laundromats, trying to scrape together enough students to teach a private writing workshop. At last, she was forced to leave her newly adopted home, her confidence shaken and her outlook on life darkened.

The depression she sank into followed her to California, where she accepted a guest lectureship at California State University in Chico. "I thought I couldn't teach. I found myself becoming suicidal. Richard Bray had told me Susan was looking for me, but I was drowning, beyond help. I had the number for months, but I didn't call. It was frightening because it was such a calm depression." 20

An NEA fellowship in fiction revitalized Cisneros and helped her get on her feet again, both financially and spiritually. Finally calling that Manhattan phone number stuffed in her pocket, Cisneros sent Bergholz a small group of new stories. With only 39 pages in hand, Bergholz sold *Woman Hollering Creek* to Joni Evans and Erroll McDonald at Random House/Vintage; Julie Grau became the book's enthusiastic editor.

Then, of course, the real work began for Cisneros, whose previous output had been about one story every six months. "There's nothing like a deadline to teach you discipline, especially when you've already spent your advance. *Susto* helps," Cisneros says, explaining that fear motivated her to put in eight-to-12 hour days. Though exhausting, the experience was genuinely empowering.

"Before, I'd be scratching my *nalgas,* waiting for inspiration. Now I know I can work this hard. I know I did the best I could."

That's not to say Cisneros believes she's done the best work of her career. "I'm looking forward to the books I'll write when I'm 60," she observes. She's also looking forward to the contributions other Latina and Latino writers will be making in the future. "There's a lot of good writing in the mainstream press that has nothing to say. Chicano writers have a lot to say. The influence of our two languages is profound. The Spanish language is going to contribute something very rich to American literature."

Meanwhile, this self-described "migrant professor" plans to continue her personal and literary search for the "home in the heart," as Elenita the Witch Woman describes it in *Mango Street.* As "nobody's mother and nobody's wife," Cisneros most resembles Inés Alfaro, the powerful central character in "Eyes of Zapata," the story Cisneros considers her finest achievement. 25

Small, but "bigger" than the general himself, Inés is the woman warrior, the *Soldadera* who understands what the men will never comprehend, that "the wars begin here, in our hearts and in our beds." She is the *bruja,* the *nagual* who flies through the night, the fierce and tender lover who risks all, the eater of black things that make her hard and strong.

She is, in short, a symbol of the Latina herself, the Mexican woman whose story is at last being told, a story of life and blood and grief and "all the flower colors of joy." It is a story at once intimate and universal, guaranteed to shove a bittersweet thorn into the paws of literary lions everywhere.

Suggestions for Writing and Discussion

1. Cisneros admits to being concerned about how a general audience might respond to the characters she creates. As she says, her characters "live in an America very different from" that of most readers. As a reader, do you think Cisneros's concern is justified? Do most readers shy away from books in which main characters are of different nationalities/ethnic backgrounds? Explain with your own experience as a reader.

    If you do not read many novels, consider, instead, the films you see. Do you prefer to watch movies where the characters are culturally similar to you? Culturally different? Or does culture make no difference when you choose which film to see? Explain, making references to specific movies.

2. What components of Cisneros's early childhood might have contributed to her eventual life as a writer? What aspects of her education may also have contributed to this career?

3. Explain the levels of meaning found in Cisneros's metaphor comparing herself and her classmates: "They had been bred as fine hothouse flowers. I was a yellow weed among the city's cracks." Create a metaphor to compare yourself with your classmates in elementary or high school. Will your metaphor reflect similarity to your colleagues or differences? Explain.

4. What does Cisneros seem to have in common with most aspiring writers? What does this "writer's life" imply about the status of writers in our country?

5. Cisneros admits that she wrote eight to twelve hours a day not because she was inspired by a higher muse but out of fear of her impending deadlines. Do you think less of her as an artist after this admission? Explain. Do you think you write (or study, or work in general) more productively when you are under pressure or when you are able to set your own deadlines? Explain.

6. Analyze Sagel's closing comment on Cisneros's life: "It is a story at once intimate and universal, guaranteed to shove a bittersweet thorn into the paws of literary lions everywhere." Do you see this metaphor as positive, negative, or a combination of both? Explain.

Suggestions for Extended Thinking and Research

1. Practice using a writer's greatest tool—that of being a good observer. Recall a significant person or place in your life, and write a descriptive narrative as if you were seeing this person or place for the last time.

2. Write an extended metaphor that explains your cultural experiences compared with those of the majority of students in the classes you are currently taking.

3. Read Cisneros's *House on Mango Street* and write a review that addresses the depth of theme, wholeness of characters, significance of place, pertinence of events, and author's use of language.

ELAINE HEDGES
Quilts and Women's Culture

> *Elaine Hedges has supported herself as a student and writer by working in post offices, restaurants, libraries, and offices. She earned a doctorate in the history of American civilization from Harvard University and has taught at Harvard, Wellesley, San Francisco State College, and the University of California, Berkeley. Currently, she is professor of English and director of women's studies at Towson State University, Baltimore. Her publications include* Women Writing and Teaching, Land and Imagination: The American Rural Dream, *and* In Her Own Image: Women Working in the Arts, *from which this essay is taken.*

Prereading/Journal-Writing Suggestions

1. In the nineteenth century, quilting was a common activity that brought many women together. What activity today do women participate in together? What equivalent activity do men today participate in together? From your answers, can you draw any conclusions about male and female group interactions?

2. Most cultures hold the tradition of passing items down from generation to generation. If you could have just one item from your grandparents' past (or your parents'), what one item would you choose and why?

3. If you were living in nineteenth-century America, what do you think your life would be like? Describe one day, from morning until night. What do you like most about living in this time period? What do you miss most about the twentieth century?

Women's needlework has been a universal form of activity, uniting women of different classes, races, and nations. Until the era of manufactured textiles — very recent, in the long span of history — it has always been necessary for women to sew, to provide the clothing, linens and blankets for their families. And wherever and whenever extra time and energy have allowed, sewing has become "esthetic," has been an outlet for creativity. Often this has been a creativity which a patriarchal society has officially stifled. Where women have been denied literacy, let alone access to higher education and the professions, their creative aspiration and need might find expression, as it often did for Black women in the pre–Civil War South, for instance, in the making of gardens, or blues songs, or quilts. Alice Walker has eloquently discussed these creative energies and frustrations of Black women in her article "In Search of Our Mothers' Gardens," and she comments on a quilt made one hundred years ago by an anonymous Black woman in Alabama and now hanging in the Smithsonian Museum in Washington. Its maker, as she says, was "an artist who left her mark in the only materials she could afford, and in the only medium her position in society allowed her to use."

The origins of quilting are ancient: both the Egyptians and the Chinese quilted, as did the Persians, from whom it was introduced into Europe by the Crusaders. In the United States, from the colonial period through the nineteenth century, quilt making or what is known as "patchwork," became a highly developed art, a unique female art, and *the* major creative outlet for women. Patchwork, like so much of women's original art, arose out of necessity: in this case the necessity for warmth, in clothing (which was sometimes quilted) and in bed covers, the form the quilt most commonly took. And it arose out of scarcity: there was little cloth in the American colonies in the seventeenth and early eighteenth centuries; what was imported from England and the continent was expensive; and so all scraps and fragments were saved, salvaged from worn-out items, and reused. The activity of quilting consisted of two main stages: designing and sewing the quilt top, which would be exposed on the bed; and doing the actual "quilting," which consisted of binding or stitching this finished top layer to a plain bottom layer, with filling or wadding in between. It was this triple thickness which gave warmth.

From the beginning, however, women expended time and care on the making of quilts beyond their utilitarian purpose. Artistry was possible, and was pursued in two areas. First, the quilt top offered nearly limitless possibilities of design and color as one pieced and sewed together small, straightedged bits of fabric to create an overall patterned top known as a "pieced" quilt; or as one "appliquéd," that is, sewed small pieces or patches of fabric according to some design on to a larger ground fabric. These were the two main kinds of "patchwork." Second, in the quilting or stitching together of the three layers, fine sewing could be practiced. Small stitches and different, highly complex kinds of stitches were employed, often to create intricate designs of scrolls, flowers or feathers. In Emily Dickinson's words (Poem 617), "I'll do seams — a Queen's endeavor/Would not blush to own."

The results, as one looks at hundreds and hundreds of quilts, are varied and dazzling — truly a visual feast. There is an esthetic indigenous to quilts, and the more one knows about the craft and the techniques — the possibilities and limitations of various fabrics and ways of cutting them, the geometric intricacies of various designs, the various stitch patterns and color combinations — the more one can appreciate and even marvel at the skill, the sophistication, the inventiveness, the visual daring that quilts display. That women responded to the technical challenge implicit in quilt making, just as a painter might set and solve a technical problem of shading or perspective or design, is apparent when one learns, for instance, of a pieced quilt that contains 30,000 pieces, each ½ inch by ¾ inch in size.

The quilt involved both individual and collective artistry. Usually, an individual woman designed and executed the top layer. The work of quilting together the three layers, however, was a large collective effort. To the "quilt-

5

ing bee" would be invited the best sewers from the community. Quilting bees were usually festive occasions, opportunities to renew and cement friendships, to reestablish social bonds among women otherwise isolated, especially on the western frontier, to exchange news and ideas and to express feelings. Under the stimulus of friendly competition, women vied to do their best sewing, creating art within a context that had a broadly nourishing social function. Where men had the tavern or saloon, the marketplace or the courthouse square for bonding together, women had the quilting bee.

The origins of many quilt stitches and patterns go far back in time, and as an art form, therefore, much of it remains anonymous. It is, in its overall distinguishing features, more representative of a culture or a society than of an individual or any series of individuals. As such, it asserted and conveyed values of continuity, stability and tradition — all useful values in a country of immigrants and of geographic mobility.

Within its broad traditionalism and anonymity, however, variations and distinctions developed. There were regional variations, ethnic or religious variations, and finally, individual variations, in the works of specific quilt makers whose names are known to us. Regional variations would include, for example, what is known as the Baltimore quilt, an appliquéd Friendship quilt of the early nineteenth century with distinctive, recognizable designs, which reached an extremely high level of skill. Ethnic or religious variations would include the quilts of the Amish and of the Moravians; similar to and yet distinguishable from each other in their color ranges and patterns, these quilts are significantly different from those of other groups.

Regionally, too, distinctions were introduced into quilt making through the interesting process of renaming. Ordinarily quilts were given names, usually the name of the basic pattern chosen for the top layer. In the course of time, and with geographical movement within the United States, name changes and small design variations were introduced in response to local needs and to both sectional and national events. Thus, during the Civil War a traditional rose pattern (of which there were many) was modified by the addition of a black patch at its center and renamed the *Radical Rose,* in recognition of the slavery controversy. A chain or loop pattern originally called *Job's Tears* — one of many early pattern names taken from the Bible — was renamed the *Slave Chain* in the early 1820s; by 1840 the same pattern was being called *Texas Tears* in response to new political developments; and after the Civil War it was used to describe *The Rocky Road to Kansas.* Indeed, quilt names provide a capsule version of much nineteenth-century American history, not least the hardships of the western journey. A pattern made of rectangles inside diagonal bands, and known in pre-Revolutionary New England as *Jacob's Ladder,* from the Bible, became in western Kentucky *The Underground Railroad,* and in Mississippi and the prairie states *Wagon Tracks* or the *Trail of the Covered Wagon.*

With equal inventiveness women renamed traditional patterns to accommodate them to the local landscape. Thus a pattern called *Duck's Foot in the Mud* on Long Island became *Bear's Paw* in western Pennsylvania and Ohio.

Quilt names, indeed, give us insight into many aspects of the lives of the women who made them and their families. There are names of occupations, from farming to carpentry and mechanics, names (although fewer) of recreations and amusements, and names expressing moral beliefs and hopes and dreams. *Hens and Chickens* to *Trip around the World* encompass the polarities, real and ideal, of many women's lives. Whereas it has been estimated that the total of distinctively different quilt patterns is probably not more than three hundred, the names run into the thousands.

Finally, out of such regional and other variations come individual, 10 signed achievements. Many women did sign their quilts: their skill was recognized; they responded with pride and aspiration; they aimed to create a work of art for posterity.

Quilts, then, were an outlet for creative energy, a source and emblem of sisterhood and solidarity, and a graphic response to historical and political change. The quilt could also serve as inspiration and imaginative stimulus. At the beginning of her semiautobiographical novel, *Daughter of Earth,* Agnes Smedley describes her impoverished childhood:

> I recall a crazy-quilt my mother once had. She made it from the remnants of gay and beautiful cotton materials. . . . [The] crazy-quilt held me for hours. It was an adventure.

It was also, of course, what Smedley and other working-class women had instead of books and paintings.

Finally, quilts, or women's sewing in general, can be seen as sometimes providing opportunities for political discussion and statement. Susan B. Anthony's first talk on equal rights for women was at a quilting bee, and she and Elizabeth Cady Stanton frequently used such gatherings to advocate political action and change. Earlier, Sarah Grimké advised women to embroider anti-slavery slogans and images on domestic artifacts, urging "May the point of our needles prick the slave-owner's conscience." And there is the delightful story of the subversive wife who had her husband sleep under a quilt that bore, unknown to him, a pattern named after the political party he opposed.

But such freedoms or assertions must be ultimately interpreted in the larger context of women's work and oppression within a patriarchal society — an oppression of which needlework was not only symbol but actuality. Before the days of machine-made clothing and blankets, little girls were forced to learn to sew; and learning to sew often took precedence over, or was the female substitute for, learning to read and write. Sewing is thus used by Emily Dickinson in one of her poems (Number 508) as a symbol of the childhood and female bondage she rejects as she arrives at her own achieved status of poet. Sewing, for instance, of samplers with moral messages, was intended to inculcate in little girls their class or gender virtues of neatness, submissiveness, docility and patience. One learned quilting by working on one small square, sewing it, ripping out the stitching, sewing it again, over and over and over, until proficiency had been achieved. Many women learned to hate the work. In other countries, various kinds of needlework have amounted and still amount to sheer exploitation of girls and women: young girls painstakingly tieing the innumerable fine knots in Persian rugs because their fingers are small enough to do the work; young girls seated in rows in convents in Belgium, making lace for hours on end, not allowed to raise their eyes from their work; Italian women going blind after a lifetime of lace making.

To return to this country, one must ask to what extent needlework had to substitute, for women, for what might have been more freely chosen work, or for various forms of political activism. *Does* one respond with admiration, or dismay, to that quilt of 30,000 pieces? One may admire the dexterity of Pennsylvania Dutch women, who challenged themselves with the sewing of convex and concave, rather than merely straight, edges. Their quilts show a higher degree of exacting sewing than do the quilts of New England women, and may therefore receive higher accolades as art. But one realizes it was an art born of oppression: the Pennsylvania Dutch women were among the most severely confined, almost never allowed to learn to read, rarely venturing beyond the home.

In the Victorian era, when middle-class women lost the productive role 15 they had held in an earlier agricultural economy, quilts became more and more decorative, more and more examples of conspicuous waste in their use of expensive fabrics such as satin, lace, brocade and velvet. They became an inadvertently ironic sign of women as consumer rather than producer, and of her confinement to a narrowed and less functional domestic sphere. They became a badge of her oppression and even an unfortunate safety valve that could delay rebellion by diverting energy.

Our response to quilts as an art form rooted both in meaningful work and in cultural oppression will therefore inevitably be complex: a combination of admiration and awe at limitations overcome and of sorrow and anger at limitations imposed.

Suggestions for Writing and Discussion

1. Hedges argues that when a patriarchal society stifles women's outlets for creativity, women will find ways of making everyday activities creative, for instance "in the making of gardens, or blues songs, or quilts." Do you see any ways in which the twentieth century is still stifling for women? As you respond, consider the ways women creatively express themselves, and compare these creative avenues with those followed by men. Explain the significance you see in the similarities and differences.

2. What social factors contributed to quilt making as a creative art form? What changes occurred so that quilt making, for the most part, moved from a necessity to a hobby?

3. In paragraph 5, Hedges describes quilting bees and saloons or the marketplace as places that provided social functions for women and for men. Comparing the two types of social outlets, what conclusions can you draw

about relationships between women and relationships between men in the nineteenth century? Have these relationships changed today? Explain.

4. Quilts, Hedges writes, were more distinguishing of the culture than of any one individual. What visual art today is most distinguishing of twentieth-century American culture? Explain your answer.

5. Not only were quilts visually pleasing, but the patterns were also indicative of the social problems of the times. Analyze the titles that Hedges provides in paragraphs 8–9, and explain whether—and why—you believe these titles reflect such social concerns.

6. Because quilting was an activity undertaken solely by women, sometimes under inhumane conditions (paragraph 13), Hedges raises the question: "*Does* one respond with admiration, or dismay, to that quilt of 30,000 pieces?" Respond to her question and give justification for your response.

Suggestions for Extended Thinking and Research

1. Research another craft from nineteenth-century America. As Hedges does, look to the roots of this craft and the subsequent reflection of this craft in the culture.

2. Choose one specific section of the United States and research in detail the quilts from this location (the Amish in Pennsylvania, Appalachian quilts, prerevolutionary New England, for example).

3. A possible collaborative project: Each class member will design and decorate one patch, which may become part of a larger quilt. Keep a process notebook on each step of your own participation in this activity. How did you come up with the design? What changes did you make? How did you choose colors? Materials? When did you work on this patch? How long did it take you? Did you enjoy it, or did you find it tedious? As you were working on this one patch, were you thinking what others would think of your work? How does your response to your own work change as you view it combined with the work of other class members?

ALICE WALKER

Everyday Use
For Your Grandmama

> *The youngest of eight children born in Eatonton, Georgia, in 1944 to share-croppers Minnie and Willie Lee Walker, Alice Walker's early life was shaped by a number of contradictory forces. On the one hand, she suffered from economic deprivation and the hardships imposed by segregation. On the other hand, she grew strong within her closely knit family and the extended black church congregation and community. She began her college education at Spelman in Atlanta but transferred to Sarah Lawrence in New York. Her first publications came shortly after her graduation in 1965. She is best known for her novel* The Color Purple, *which was awarded both the Pulitzer Prize and the American Book Award in 1983 and was later made into a highly acclaimed film.*

Prereading/Journal-Writing Suggestions

1. In what ways are members of your family like one another? In what ways is each member's personality unique? Give a short description of the main characteristics of each family member.
2. If you could have just one item from your family's past heritage, what would you choose and why?
3. As people mature and move out into the world, do you believe most of them become quite different from their old "family selves"? Or do most stay more or less the same, with only minor, unimportant changes? Use specific examples from your own experiences and observations to explain your beliefs.

I will wait for her in the yard that Maggie and I made so clean and wavy yesterday afternoon. A yard like this is more comfortable than most people know. It is not just a yard. It is like an extended living room. When the hard clay is swept clean as a floor and the fine sand around the edges lined with tiny, irregular grooves anyone can come and sit and look up into the elm tree and wait for the breezes that never come inside the house.

Maggie will be nervous until after her sister goes: she will stand hopelessly in corners homely and ashamed of the burn scars down her arms and legs, eyeing her sister with a mixture of envy and awe. She thinks her sister has held life always in the palm of one hand, that "no" is a word the world never learned to say to her.

You've no doubt seen those TV shows where the child who has "made it" is confronted, as a surprise, by her own mother and father, tottering in weakly from backstage. (A pleasant surprise, of course: What would they do if parent and child came on the show only to curse out and insult each other?)

On TV mother and child embrace and smile into each other's faces. Sometimes the mother and father weep, the child wraps them in her arms and leans across the table to tell how she would not have made it without their help. I have seen these programs.

Sometimes I dream a dream in which Dee and I are suddenly brought together on a TV program of this sort. Out of a dark and soft-seated limousine I am ushered into a bright room filled with many people. There I meet a smiling, gray, sporty man like Johnny Carson who shakes my hand and tells me what a fine girl I have. Then we are on the stage and Dee is embracing me with tears in her eyes. She pins on my dress a large orchid, even though she has told me once that she thinks orchids are tacky flowers.

In real life I am a large, big-boned woman with rough, man-working hands. In the winter I wear flannel nightgowns to bed and overalls during the day. I can kill and clean a hog as mercilessly as a man. My fat keeps me hot in zero weather. I can work outside all day, breaking ice to get water for washing; I can eat pork liver cooked over the open fire minutes after it comes steaming from the hog. One winter I knocked a bull calf straight in the brain between the eyes with a sledge hammer and had the meat hung up to chill before nightfall. But of course all this does not show on television. I am the way my daughter would want me to be: a hundred pounds lighter, my skin like an uncooked barley pancake. My hair glistens in the hot bright lights. Johnny Carson has much to do to keep up with my quick and witty tongue.

But that is a mistake. I know even before I wake up. Who ever knew a Johnson with a quick tongue? Who can even imagine me looking a strange white man in the eye? It seems to me I have talked to them always with one foot raised in flight, with my head turned in whichever way is farthest from them. Dee, though. She would always look anyone in the eye. Hesitation was no part of her nature.

"How do I look, Mama?" Maggie says, showing just enough of her thin body enveloped in pink skirt and red blouse for me to know she's there, almost hidden by the door.

"Come out into the yard," I say.

Have you ever seen a lame animal, perhaps a dog run over by some careless person rich enough to own a car, sidle up to someone who is ignorant enough to be kind to him? That is the way my Maggie walks. She has been like this, chin on chest, eyes on ground, feet in shuffle, ever since the fire that burned the other house to the ground.

Dee is lighter than Maggie, with nicer hair and a fuller figure. She's a woman now, though sometimes I forget. How long ago was it that the other house burned? Ten, twelve years? Sometimes I can still hear the flames and feel Maggie's arms sticking to me, her hair smoking and her dress falling off her in little black papery flakes. Her eyes seemed stretched open, blazed open by the flames reflected in them. And Dee. I see her standing off under the sweet gum tree she used to dig gum out of; a look of concentration on her face as she watched the last dingy gray board of the house fall in toward the red-hot brick chimney. Why don't you do a dance around the ashes? I'd wanted to ask her. She had hated the house that much.

I used to think she hated Maggie, too. But that was before we raised the money, the church and me, to send her to Augusta to school. She used to read to us without pity; forcing words, lies, other folks' habits, whole lives upon us two, sitting trapped and ignorant underneath her voice. She washed us in a river of make-believe, burned us with a lot of knowledge we didn't necessarily need to know. Pressed us to her with the serious way she read, to shove us away at just the moment, like dimwits, we seemed about to understand.

Dee wanted nice things. A yellow organdy dress to wear to her graduation from high school; black pumps to match a green suit she'd made from an old suit somebody gave me. She was determined to stare down any disaster in her efforts. Her eyelids would not flicker for minutes at a time. Often I fought off the temptation to shake her. At sixteen she had a style of her own: and knew what style was.

I never had an education myself. After second grade the school was closed down. Don't ask me why: in 1927 colored asked fewer questions than they do now. Sometimes Maggie reads to me. She stumbles along good-naturedly but can't see well. She knows she is not bright. Like good looks and money, quickness passed her by. She will marry John Thomas (who has mossy teeth in an earnest face) and then I'll be free to sit here and I guess just sing church songs to myself. Although I never was a good singer. Never could carry a tune. I was always better at a man's job. I used to love to milk till I was hooked in the side in '49. Cows are soothing and slow and don't bother you, unless you try to milk them the wrong way.

I have deliberately turned my back on the house. It is three rooms, just like the one that burned, except the roof is tin; they don't make shingle roofs any more. There are no real windows, just some holes cut in the sides, like the portholes in a ship, but not round and not square, with rawhide holding the shutters up on the outside. This house is in a pasture, too, like the other one. No doubt when Dee sees it she will want to tear it down. She wrote me once that no matter where we "choose" to live, she will manage to come see us. But she will never bring her friends. Maggie and I thought about this and Maggie asked me, "Mama, when did Dee ever *have* any friends?"

She had a few. Furtive boys in pink shirts hanging about on washday 15 after school. Nervous girls who never laughed. Impressed with her they worshiped the well-turned phrase, the cute shape, the scalding humor that erupted like bubbles in lye. She read to them.

When she was courting Jimmy T she didn't have much time to pay to us, but turned all her faultfinding power on him. He *flew* to marry a cheap gal from a family of ignorant flashy people. She hardly had time to recompose herself.

When she comes I will meet — but there they are!
Maggie attempts to make a dash for the house, in her shuffling way, but

I stay her with my hand. "Come back here," I say. And she stops and tries to dig a well in the sand with her toe.

It is hard to see them clearly through the strong sun. But even the first glimpse of leg out of the car tells me it is Dee. Her feet were always neat-looking, as if God himself had shaped them with a certain style. From the other side of the car comes a short, stocky man. Hair is all over his head a foot long and hanging from his chin like a kinky mule tail. I hear Maggie suck in her breath. "Uhnnnh," is what it sounds like. Like when you see the wriggling end of a snake just in front of your foot on the road. "Uhnnnh."

Dee next. A dress down to the ground, in this hot weather. A dress so 20 loud it hurts my eyes. There are yellows and oranges enough to throw back the light of the sun. I feel my whole face warming from the heat waves it throws out. Earrings gold, too, and hanging down to her shoulders. Bracelets dangling and making noises when she moves her arm up to shake the folds of the dress out of her armpits. The dress is loose and flows, and as she walks closer, I like it. I hear Maggie go "Uhnnnh" again. It is her sister's hair. It stands straight up like the wool on a sheep. It is black as night and around the edges are two long pigtails that rope about like small lizards disappearing behind her ears.

"Wa-su-zo-Tean-o!" she says, coming on in that gliding way the dress makes her move. The short stocky fellow with the hair to his navel is all grinning and he follows up with "Asalamalakim, my mother and sister!" He moves to hug Maggie but she falls back, right up against the back of my chair. I feel her trembling there and when I look up I see the perspiration falling off her chin.

"Don't get up," says Dee. Since I am stout it takes something of a push. You can see me trying to move a second or two before I make it. She turns, showing white heels through her sandals, and goes back to the car. Out she peeks next with a Polaroid. She stoops down quickly and lines up picture after picture of me sitting there in front of the house with Maggie cowering behind me. She never takes a shot without making sure the house is included. When a cow comes nibbling around the edge of the yard she snaps it and me and Maggie *and* the house. Then she puts the Polaroid in the back seat of the car, and comes up and kisses me on the forehead.

Meanwhile Asalamalakim is going through the motions with Maggie's hand. Maggie's hand is as limp as a fish, and probably as cold, despite the sweat, and she keeps trying to pull it back. It looks like Asalamalakim wants to shake hands but wants to do it fancy. Or maybe he don't know how people shake hands. Anyhow, he soon gives up on Maggie.

"Well," I say. "Dee."

"No, Mama," she says. "Not 'Dee,' Wangero Leewanika Kemanjo!" 25

"What happened to 'Dee'?" I wanted to know.

"She's dead," Wangero said. "I couldn't bear it any longer being named after the people who oppress me."

"You know as well as me you was named after your aunt Dicie," I said. Dicie is my sister. She named Dee. We called her "Big Dee" after Dee was born.

"But who was *she* named after?" asked Wangero.

"I guess after Grandma Dee," I said.   30

"And who was she named after?" asked Wangero.

"Her mother," I said, and saw Wangero was getting tired. "That's about as far back as I can trace it," I said. Though, in fact, I probably could have carried it back beyond the Civil War through the branches.

"Well," said Asalamalakim, "there you are."

"Uhnnnh," I heard Maggie say.

"There I was not," I said, "before 'Dicie' cropped up in our family, so 35 why should I try to trace it that far back?"

He just stood there grinning, looking down on me like somebody inspecting a Model A car. Every once in a while he and Wangero sent eye signals over my head.

"How do you pronounce this name?" I asked.

"You don't have to call me by it if you don't want to," said Wangero.

"Why shouldn't I?" I asked. "If that's what you want us to call you, we'll call you."

"I know it might sound awkward at first," said Wangero.   40

"I'll get used to it," I said. "Ream it out again."

Well, soon we got the name out of the way. Asalamalakim had a name twice as long and three times as hard. After I tripped over it two or three times he told me to just call him Hakim-a-barber. I wanted to ask him was he a barber, but I didn't really think he was, so I didn't ask.

"You must belong to those beef-cattle peoples down the road," I said. They said "Asalamalakim" when they met you, too, but they didn't shake hands. Always too busy: feeding the cattle, fixing the fences, putting up salt-lick shelters, throwing down hay. When the white folks poisoned some of the herd the men stayed up all night with rifles in their hands. I walked a mile and a half just to see the sight.

Hakim-a-barber said, "I accept some of their doctrines, but farming and raising cattle is not my style." (They didn't tell me, and I didn't ask, whether Wangero [Dee] had really gone and married him.)

We sat down to eat and right away he said he didn't eat collards and pork 45 was unclean. Wangero, though, went on through the chitlins and corn bread, the greens and everything else. She talked a blue streak over the sweet potatoes. Everything delighted her. Even the fact that we still used the benches her daddy made for the table when we couldn't afford to buy chairs.

"Oh, Mama!" she cried. Then turned to Hakim-a-barber. "I never knew how lovely these benches are. You can feel the rump prints," she said, running her hands underneath her and along the bench. Then she gave a sigh and her hand closed over Grandma Dee's butter dish. "That's it!" she said. "I knew there was something I wanted to ask you if I could have." She jumped up from the table and went over in the corner where the churn stood, the milk in it clabber by now. She looked at the churn and looked at it.

"This churn top is what I need," she said. "Didn't Uncle Buddy whittle it out of a tree you all used to have?"

"Yes," I said.

"Uh huh," she said happily. "And I want the dasher, too."

"Uncle Buddy whittle that, too?" asked the barber.   50

Dee (Wangero) looked up at me.

"Aunt Dee's first husband whittled the dash," said Maggie so low you almost couldn't hear her. "His name was Henry, but they called him Stash."

"Maggie's brain is like an elephant's," Wangero said, laughing. "I can use the churn top as a centerpiece for the alcove table," she said, sliding a plate over the churn, "and I'll think of something artistic to do with the dasher."

When she finished wrapping the dasher the handle stuck out. I took it for a moment in my hands. You didn't even have to look close to see where hands pushing the dasher up and down to make butter had left a kind of sink in the wood. In fact, there were a lot of small sinks; you could see where thumbs and fingers had sunk into the wood. It was beautiful light yellow wood, from a tree that grew in the yard where Big Dee and Stash had lived.

After dinner Dee (Wangero) went to the trunk at the foot of my bed and   55 started rifling through it. Maggie hung back in the kitchen over the dishpan. Out came Wangero with two quilts. They had been pieced by Grandma Dee and then Big Dee and me had hung them on the quilt frames on the front porch and quilted them. One was in the Lone Star pattern. The other was Walk Around the Mountain. In both of them were scraps of dresses Grandma Dee had worn fifty and more years ago. Bits and pieces of Grandpa Jarrell's paisley shirts. And one teeny faded blue piece, about the size of a penny matchbox, that was from Great Grandpa Ezra's uniform that he wore in the Civil War.

"Mama," Wangero said sweet as a bird. "Can I have these old quilts?"

I heard something fall in the kitchen, and a minute later the kitchen door slammed.

"Why don't you take one or two of the others?" I asked. "These old things was just done by me and Big Dee from some tops your grandma pieced before she died."

"No," said Wangero. "I don't want those. They are stitched around the borders by machine."

"That'll make them last better," I said.   60

"That's not the point," said Wangero. "These are all pieces of dresses Grandma used to wear. She did all this stitching by hand. Imagine!" She held the quilts securely in her arms, stroking them.

"Some of the pieces, like those lavender ones, come from old clothes her mother handed down to her," I said, moving up to touch the quilts. Dee (Wangero) moved back just enough so that I couldn't reach the quilts. They already belonged to her.

"Imagine!" she breathed again, clutching them closely to her bosom.

"The truth is," I said, "I promised to give them quilts to Maggie, for when she marries John Thomas."

She gasped like a bee had stung her.   65

"Maggie can't appreciate these quilts!" she said. "She'd probably be backward enough to put them to everyday use."

"I reckon she would," I said. "God knows I been saving 'em for long enough with nobody using 'em. I hope she will!" I didn't want to bring up how I had offered Dee (Wangero) a quilt when she went away to college. Then she had told me they were old-fashioned, out of style.

"But they're *priceless!*" she was saying now, furiously; for she has a temper. "Maggie would put them on the bed and in five years they'd be in rags. Less than that!"

"She can always make some more," I said. "Maggie knows how to quilt."

Dee (Wangero) looked at me with hatred. "You just will not understand.   70 The point is these quilts, *these* quilts!"

"Well," I said, stumped. "What would *you* do with them?"

"Hang them," she said. As if that was the only thing you *could* do with quilts.

Maggie by now was standing in the door. I could almost hear the sound her feet made as they scraped over each other.

"She can have them, Mama," she said, like somebody used to never winning anything, or having anything reserved for her. "I can 'member Grandma Dee without the quilts."

I looked at her hard. She had filled her bottom lip with checkerberry   75 snuff and it gave her face a kind of dopey, hangdog look. It was Grandma Dee and Big Dee who taught her how to quilt herself. She stood there with her scarred hands hidden in the folds of her skirt. She looked at her sister with something like fear but she wasn't mad at her. This was Maggie's portion. This was the way she knew God to work.

When I looked at her like that something hit me in the top of my head and ran down to the soles of my feet. Just like when I'm in church and the spirit of God touches me and I get happy and shout. I did something I never had done before: hugged Maggie to me, then dragged her on into the room, snatched the quilts out of Miss Wangero's hands and dumped them into Maggie's lap. Maggie just sat there on my bed with her mouth open.

"Take one or two of the others," I said to Dee.

But she turned without a word and went out to Hakim-a-barber.

"You just don't understand," she said, as Maggie and I came out to the car.

"What don't I understand?" I wanted to know.   80

"Your heritage," she said. And then she turned to Maggie, kissed her, and said, "You ought to try to make something of yourself, too, Maggie. It's really a new day for us. But from the way you and Mama still live you'd never know it."

She put on some sunglasses that hid everything above the tip of her nose and her chin.

Maggie smiled; maybe at the sunglasses. But a real smile, not scared. After we watched the car dust settle I asked Maggie to bring me a dip of snuff. And then the two of us sat there just enjoying, until it was time to go in the house and go to bed.

Suggestions for Writing and Discussion

1. Describe the main personality and character traits of the three women in this story. Do they share any qualities or are they entirely different? Explain, with specific references to details, examples, and conversations in "Everyday Use."
2. One theme in this story deals with appearance versus reality. Find several examples that demonstrate this theme. What main idea or ideas does this theme suggest?
3. How does education — or lack of education — contribute to the relationships in this story? Consider how education unites characters or separates them from each other.
4. Speculate on Dee's (Wangero's) motives for coming home with her friend when she'd told her mother that she would never bring friends to her family's house. What is it that she now values about her past? Why, for example, does she want the churn top and the quilts? What is it that Maggie and her mother value about their past and the objects that reflect that past?
5. Evaluate the changes (or lack of change) you see in these characters. In your opinion, does anyone change for the better? For the worse? Explain.
6. Analyze the implications of the title. For example, consider Dee's statement that if Maggie got the quilts, "she'd probably be backward enough to put them to everyday use." If you were asked to arbitrate this disagreement, whose side would you be on? Should the quilts be put to "everyday use"? Why or why not?

Suggestions for Extended Thinking and Research

1. Read several other short stories or novels by Alice Walker, and then write a paper evaluating the characters she presents. Note which characters she presents as admirable and which she portrays as pompous, mean-spirited, or even evil. Then describe and explain the values she most supports and admires.
2. Imagine that each character in this story is to be represented as a piece of the same patchwork quilt. Describe the fabrics, patterns, colors, and images you would choose for each character's patch. How would you place these patches in relation to each other? Explain your reasons.

VICTOR HERNÁNDEZ-CRUZ

urban dream

> Victor Hernández-Cruz was born in 1949 in Aguas Buenas, a small village in Puerto Rico. When he was five, he and his family moved to New York, where he attended Benjamin Franklin High School and was associated with The Gut Theater. He has published four collections of poetry and, since the early 1970s, has lived in San Francisco, where he continues to write and give readings. Combining English and Spanish in his poetry, Hernández-Cruz sees Hispanic culture as it is defined in the United States through three main images: visual, musical, and lingual.

Prereading/Journal-Writing Suggestion

From your imagination or from your own experience, what images do you have of life in a large urban city? What colors do you see? What else catches your eye? What sounds do you hear? What smells do you smell? What do you taste? What do you feel? Write these images as quickly as they come into your mind. Jot them down, one after another, with each image on a separate line. When the images fail to come quickly, stop. What title do you give this piece, your poem?

1

there was fire & the people were yelling.   running crazing.
screaming & falling.   moving up side down.   there was fire.
fires.   & more fires.   & walls caving to the ground.   & mercy
mercy.   death.   bodies falling down.   under bottles flying in the
air. garbage cans going up against windows.   a car singing   5
brightly a blue flame.   a snatch. a snag.   sounds of bombs.   &
other things blowing up.
times square
electrified.   burned.   smashed. stomped
hey over here   10
hey you.   where you going.
no walking.   no running.   no standing.
STOP
you crazy.   running.   stick
this stick up your eyes.   pull your heart out.   15
hey.

2

after noise.   comes silence.   after brightness (or great big flames)
comes darkness.   goes with whispering.   (even soft music can be heard)
even lips smacking.   foots stepping all over bones & ashes, all over
blood & broken lips that left their head somewhere else, all over   20
livers, & bright white skulls with hair on them. standing over a river
watching hamburgers floating by.   steak with teeth in them.
flags.   & chairs.   & beds.   & golf sets.   & mickeymouse broken in
half.
governors & mayors step out the show.   they split.   25

3

dancing arrives.

Suggestions for Writing and Discussion

1. Read "urban dream" all the way through without stopping to ask questions. What is your initial reaction to this piece? How does it make you feel?
2. After writing your reaction to this piece, write three questions you have about this poem. Reread the poem. Talk about it with someone else. Then go back and see what responses you may now have to your own questions.
3. Go back to the poem again. This time, imagine that the words to this poem are actually lyrics to a song. What kind of music would be fitting for this piece? Why?
4. What are the main images in part 1? What is happening here? What are the main images in part 2? What has happened here? What is the image in the last part? How does this fit or connect to the action in the first two parts?

TOPICS FOR MAKING CONNECTIONS: AMERICAN DREAMS AND CREATIONS

Draw on as many sources in this chapter as you need and also rely on your own experiences in order to write answers for the following questions regarding the connections between art, culture, and one's dreams.

1. Analyze the various ways in which art can be conceived, delivered, and nourished within certain cultures.
2. To what extent does an artist's culture affect his or her approach to art?
3. How can art be specific to one's culture and yet universal at the same time? Refer to several culturally based artistic expressions in this section in order to come to some satisfying answer.

4. Compare and contrast the artistic processes from at least three of the essays in this section.
5. Referring to several selections from this section, analyze art's contribution to people's daily lives.
6. Analyze the importance of a mentor in the process of learning an art.
7. Where do artists get their ideas? Analyze several of the essays in the section in order to discover a variety of possibilities for the beginnings of an artistic idea.
8. Compare and contrast the values and beliefs inherent in three different cultures that are represented in this section.
9. Argue that someone born outside a culture can or cannot come to a deeper understanding of the values and beliefs within a certain culture just by observing its popular works of art.
10. Considering selections in this section as well as your own observations, which do you believe is greater — culture's influence on art and the artist, or the artist's influence on culture?

Men and Women

Previews: MEN AND WOMEN

In no country has such constant care been taken as in America to trace two clearly distinct lines of action for the two sexes and to make them keep pace one with the other, but in two pathways that are always different.

From: *How the Americans Understand the Equality of the Sexes*, ALEXIS DE TOCQUEVILLE

I will remove myself as an obstacle in the path that your children, against all odds, are making toward the light. I will not assassinate them for dreaming dreams and offering new visions of how to live. I will cease trying to lead your children, for I can see I have never understood where I was going. I will agree to sit quietly for a century or so, and meditate on this.

That is what the white man can say to the black woman.
We are listening.

From: *The Right to Life: What Can the White Man Say to the Black Woman?*, ALICE WALKER

The definitions of woman's roles are as diverse as [American Indian] tribal cultures in the Americas. In some she is devalued, in others she wields considerable power. In some she is a familial/clan adjunct, in some she is as close to autonomous as her economic circumstances and psychological traits permit. But in no tribal definitions is she perceived in the same way as are women in western industrial and postindustrial cultures.

From: *Where I Come from Is Like This*, PAULA GUNN ALLEN

These are hard times for men. Machismo is going out of style among the middle class, and any man who dares to play that role is likely to be snubbed, ridiculed, or karate-punched for his sexist foolishness. Hollywood heroes betray what's happening.

From: *Between a Rock and a Soft Place: A Century of American Manhood*, PETER FILENE

Just so, I recall the points at which some of my boyhood friends were finally seduced by the perception of themselves as tough guys. When a mark cowered and surrendered his money without resistance, myth and reality merged — and paid off. It is, after all, only manly to embrace the power to frighten and intimidate. We, as men, are not supposed to give an inch of our lane on the highway; we are to seize the fighter's edge in work and in play and even in love; we are to be valiant in the face of hostile forces.

From: *Just Walk on By: A Black Man Ponders His Power to Alter Public Space*, BRENT STAPLES

PAULA GUNN ALLEN
Where I Come from Is Like This

> *Paula Gunn Allen comes from roots that include both the Laguna Pueblo and Sioux cultures. An acclaimed essayist, poet, and fiction writer, Allen's best-known novel is* The Woman Who Owned the Shadows *(1983). Currently, she teaches at the University of California, Berkeley, where she is professor of Native American and ethnic studies. This selection comes from her collection of nonfiction essays,* The Sacred Hoop *(1986).*

Prereading/Journal-Writing Suggestions

1. In your journal, freewrite for twenty minutes by completing the following statement: "Where I come from is like. . . ."
2. Set a timer for three minutes; then look at yourself in a mirror until the timer rings. Next, sit down and describe who you saw in that mirror and what you thought about as you studied your physical image.

I

Modern American Indian women, like their non-Indian sisters, are deeply engaged in the struggle to redefine themselves. In their struggle they must reconcile traditional tribal definitions of women with industrial and postindustrial non-Indian definitions. Yet while these definitions seem to be more or less mutually exclusive, Indian women must somehow harmonize and integrate both in their own lives.

An American Indian woman is primarily defined by her tribal identity. In her eyes, her destiny is necessarily that of her people, and her sense of herself as a woman is first and foremost prescribed by her tribe. The definitions of woman's roles are as diverse as tribal cultures in the Americas. In some she is devalued, in others she wields considerable power. In some she is a familial/clan adjunct, in some she is as close to autonomous as her economic circumstances and psychological traits permit. But in no tribal definitions is she perceived in the same way as are women in western industrial and post-industrial cultures.

In the west, few images of women form part of the cultural mythos, and these are largely sexually charged. Among Christians, the madonna is the female prototype, and she is portrayed as essentially passive: her contribution is simply that of birthing. Little else is attributed to her and she certainly possesses few of the characteristics that are attributed to mythic figures among Indian tribes. This image is countered (rather than balanced) by the witch-goddess/whore characteristics designed to reinforce cultural beliefs about women, as well as western adversarial and dualistic perceptions of reality.

The tribes see women variously, but they do not question the power of femininity. Sometimes they see women as fearful, sometimes peaceful, sometimes omnipotent and omniscient, but they never portray women as mindless, helpless, simple, or oppressed. And while the women in a given tribe, clan, or band may be all these things, the individual woman is provided with a variety of images of women from the interconnected supernatural, natural, and social worlds she lives in.

As a half-breed American Indian woman, I cast about in my mind for negative images of Indian women, and I find none that are directed to Indian women alone. The negative images I do have are of Indians in general and in fact are more often of males than of females. All these images come to me from non-Indian sources, and they are always balanced by a positive image. My ideas of womanhood, passed on largely by my mother and grandmothers, Laguna Pueblo women, are about practicality, strength, reasonableness, intelligence, wit, and competence. I also remember vividly the women who came to my father's store, the women who held me and sang to me, the women at Feast Day, at Grab Days, the women in the kitchen of my Cubero home, the women I grew up with; none of them appeared weak or helpless, none of them presented herself tentatively. I remember a certain reserve on those lovely brown faces; I remember the direct gaze of eyes framed by bright-colored shawls draped over their heads and cascading down their backs. I remember the clean cotton dresses and carefully pressed hand–embroidered aprons they always wore; I remember laughter and good food, especially the sweet bread and the oven bread they gave us. Nowhere in my mind is there a foolish woman, a dumb woman, a vain woman, or a plastic woman, though the Indian women I have known have shown a wide range of personal style and demeanor.

My memory includes the Navajo woman who was badly beaten by her Sioux husband; but I also remember that my grandmother abandoned her Sioux husband long ago. I recall the stories about the Laguna woman beaten regularly by her husband in the presence of her children so that the children would not believe in the strength and power of femininity. And I remember the women who drank, who got into fights with other women and with the men, and who often won those battles. I have memories of tired women, partying women, stubborn women, sullen women, amicable women, selfish women, shy women, and aggressive women. Most of all I remember the women who laugh and scold and sit uncomplaining in the long sun on feast days and who cook wonderful food on wood stoves, in beehive mud ovens, and over open fires outdoors.

Among the images of women that come to me from various tribes as well as my own are White Buffalo Woman, who came to the Lakota long ago and brought them the religion of the Sacred Pipe which they still practice; Tinotzin the goddess who came to Juan Diego to remind him that she still walked the hills of her people and sent him with her message, her demand and her proof to the Catholic bishop in the city nearby. And from Laguna I take the images of Yellow Woman, Coyote Woman, Grandmother Spider (Spider Old Woman), who brought the light, who gave us weaving and medicine, who gave us life. Among the Keres she is known as Thought Woman who created us all and who keeps us in creation even now. I remember Iyatiku, Earth Woman, Corn Woman, who guides and counsels the people to peace and who welcomes us home when we cast off this coil of flesh as huskers cast off the leaves that wrap the corn. I remember Iyatiku's sister, Sun Woman, who held metals and cattle, pigs and sheep, highways and engines and so many things in her bundle, who went away to the east saying that one day she would return.

II

Since the coming of the Anglo-Europeans beginning in the fifteenth century, the fragile web of identity that long held tribal people secure has gradually been weakened and torn. But the oral tradition has prevented the complete destruction of the web, the ultimate disruption of tribal ways. The oral tradition is vital; it heals itself and the tribal web by adapting to the flow of the present while never relinquishing its connection to the past. Its adaptability has always been required, as many generations have experienced. Certainly the modern American Indian woman bears slight resemblance to her forebears — at least on superficial examination — but she is still a tribal woman in her deepest being. Her tribal sense of relationship to all that is continues to flourish. And though she is at times beset by her knowledge of the enormous gap between the life she lives and the life she was raised to live, and while she adapts her mind and being to the circumstances of her present life, she does so in tribal ways, mending the tears in the web of being from which she takes her existence as she goes.

My mother told me stories all the time, though I often did not recognize them as that. My mother told me stories about cooking and childbearing; she told me stories about menstruation and pregnancy; she told me stories about gods and heroes, about fairies and elves, about goddesses and spirits; she told me stories about the land and the sky, about cats and dogs, about snakes and spiders; she told me stories about climbing trees and exploring the mesas; she told me stories about going to dances and getting married; she told me stories about dressing and undressing, about sleeping and waking; she told me stories about herself, about her mother, about her grandmother. She told me stories about grieving and laughing, about thinking and doing; she told me stories about school and about people; about darning and mending; she told me stories about turquoise and about gold; she told me European stories and Laguna stories; she told me Catholic stories and Presbyterian stories; she told me city stories and country stories; she told me political stories and religious stories. She told me stories about living and stories about dying. And in all of those stories she told me who I was, who I was supposed to be, whom I came from, and who would follow me. In this way she taught me the meaning of the words she said, that all life is a circle and everything has a place within it. That's what she said and what she showed me in the things she did and the way she lives.

Of course, through my formal, white, Christian education, I discovered 10 that other people had stories of their own — about women, about Indians, about fact, about reality — and I was amazed by a number of startling suppositions that others made about tribal customs and beliefs. According to the un-Indian, non-Indian view, for instance, Indians barred menstruating women from ceremonies and indeed segregated them from the rest of the people, consigning them to some space specially designed for them. This showed that Indians considered menstruating women unclean and not fit to enjoy the company of decent (nonmenstruating) people, that is, men. I was surprised and confused to hear this because my mother had taught me that white people had strange attitudes toward menstruation: they thought something was bad about it, that it meant you were sick, cursed, sinful, and weak and that you had to be very careful during that time. She taught me that menstruation was a normal occurrence, that I could go swimming or hiking or whatever else I wanted to do during my period. She actively scorned women who took to their beds, who were incapacitated by cramps, who "got the blues."

As I struggled to reconcile these very contradictory interpretations of American Indians' traditional beliefs concerning menstruation, I realized that the menstrual taboos were about power, not about sin or filth. My conclusion was later borne out by some tribes' own explanations, which, as you may well imagine, came as quite a relief to me.

The truth of the matter as many Indians see it is that women who are at the peak of their fecundity are believed to possess power that throws male power totally out of kilter. They emit such force that, in their presence, any male-owned or -dominated ritual or sacred object cannot do its usual task. For instance, the Lakota say that a menstruating woman anywhere near a yuwipi man, who is a special sort of psychic, spirit-empowered healer, for a day or so before he is to do his ceremony will effectively disempower him. Conversely, among many, if not most, tribes, important ceremonies cannot be held without the presence of women. Sometimes the ritual woman who empowers the ceremony must be unmarried and virginal so that the power she channels is unalloyed, unweakened by sexual arousal and penetration by a male. Other ceremonies require tumescent women, others the presence of mature women who have borne children, and still others depend for empowerment on postmenopausal women. Women may be segregated from the company of the whole band or village on certain occasions, but on certain occasions men are also segregated. In short, each ritual depends on a certain balance of power, and the positions of women within the phases of womanhood are used by tribal people to empower certain rites. This does not derive from a male-dominant view; it is not a ritual observance imposed on women by men. It derives from a tribal view of reality that distinguishes tribal people from feudal and industrial people.

Among the tribes, the occult power of women, inextricably bound to our hormonal life, is thought to be very great; many hold that we possess innately the blood-given power to kill — with a glance, with a step, or with a judicious mixing of menstrual blood into somebody's soup. Medicine women among the Pomo of California cannot practice until they are sufficiently mature; when they are immature, their power is diffuse and is likely to interfere with their practice until time and experience have it under control. So women of the tribes are not especially inclined to see themselves as poor helpless victims of male domination. Even in those tribes where something akin to male domination was present, women are perceived as powerful, socially, physically, and metaphysically. In times past, as in times present, women carried enormous burdens with aplomb. We were far indeed from the "weaker sex," the designation that white aristocratic sisters unhappily earned for us all.

I remember my mother moving furniture all over the house when she wanted it changed. She didn't wait for my father to come home and help — she just went ahead and moved the piano, a huge upright from the old days, the couch, the refrigerator. Nobody had told her she was too weak to do such things. In imitation of her, I would delight in loading trucks at my father's store with cases of pop or fifty-pound sacks of flour. Even when I was quite small I could do it, and it gave me a belief in my own physical strength that advancing middle age can't quite erase. My mother used to tell me about the Acoma Pueblo women she had seen as a child carrying huge ollas (water pots) on their heads as they wound their way up the tortuous stairwell carved into the face of the "Sky City" mesa, a feat I tried to imitate with books and tin buckets. ("Sky City" is the term used by the Chamber of Commerce for the mother village of Acoma, which is situated atop a high sandstone table mountain.) I was never very successful, but even the attempt reminded me that I was supposed to be strong and balanced to be a proper girl.

Of course, my mother's Laguna people are Keres Indian, reputed to be 15 the last extreme mother-right people on earth. So it is no wonder that I got notably nonwhite notions about the natural strength and prowess of women. Indeed, it is only when I am trying to get non-Indian approval, recognition, or acknowledgment that my "weak sister" emotional and intellectual ploys get the better of my tribal woman's good sense. At such times I forget that I just moved the piano or just wrote a competent paper or just completed a financial transaction satisfactorily or have supported myself and my children for most of my adult life.

Nor is my contradictory behavior atypical. Most Indian women I know are in the same bicultural bind: we vacillate between being dependent and strong, self-reliant and powerless, strongly motivated and hopelessly insecure. We resolve the dilemma in various ways: some of us party all the time;

some of us drink to excess; some of us travel and move around a lot; some of us land good jobs and then quit them; some of us engage in violent exchanges; some of us blow our brains out. We act in these destructive ways because we suffer from the societal conflicts caused by having to identify with two hopelessly opposed cultural definitions of women. Through this destructive dissonance we are unhappy prey to the self-disparagement common to, indeed demanded of, Indians living in the United States today. Our situation is caused by the exigencies of a history of invasion, conquest, and colonization whose searing marks are probably ineradicable. A popular bumper sticker on many Indian cars proclaims: "If You're Indian You're In," to which I always find myself adding under my breath, "Trouble."

III

No Indian can grow to any age without being informed that her people were "savages" who interfered with the march of progress pursued by respectable, loving, civilized white people. We are the villains of the scenario when we are mentioned at all. We are absent from much of white history except when we are calmly, rationally, succinctly, and systematically dehumanized. On the few occasions we are noticed in any way other than as howling, bloodthirsty beings, we are acclaimed for our noble quaintness. In this definition, we are exotic curios. Our ancient arts and customs are used to draw tourist money to state coffers, into the pocketbooks and bank accounts of scholars, and into support of the American-in-Disneyland promoters' dream.

As a Roman Catholic child I was treated to bloody tales of how the savage Indians martyred the hapless priests and missionaries who went among them in an attempt to lead them to the one true path. By the time I was through high school I had the idea that Indians were people who had benefited mightily from the advanced knowledge and superior morality of the Anglo-Europeans. At least I had, perforce, that idea to lay beside the other one that derived from my daily experience of Indian life, an idea less dehumanizing and more accurate because it came from my mother and the other Indian people who raised me. That idea was that Indians are a people who don't tell lies, who care for their children and their old people. You never see an Indian orphan, they said. You always know when you're old that someone will take care of you—one of your children will. Then they'd list the old folks who were being taken care of by this child or that. No child is ever considered illegitimate among the Indians, they said. If a girl gets pregnant, the baby is still part of the family, and the mother is too. That's what they said, and they showed me real people who lived according to those principles.

Of course the ravages of colonization have taken their toll; there are orphans in Indian country now, and abandoned, brutalized old folks; there are even illegitimate children, though the very concept still strikes me as absurd. There are battered children and neglected children, and there are battered wives and women who have been raped by Indian men. Proximity to the "civilizing" effects of white Christians has not improved the moral quality of life in Indian country, though each group, Indian and white, explains the situation differently. Nor is there much yet in the oral tradition that can enable us to adapt to these inhuman changes. But a force is growing in that direction, and it is helping Indian women reclaim their lives. Their power, their sense of direction and of self will soon be visible. It is the force of the women who speak and work and write, and it is formidable.

Through all the centuries of war and death and cultural and psychic 20 destruction have endured the women who raise the children and tend the fires, who pass along the tales and the traditions, who weep and bury the dead, who are the dead, and who never forget. There are always the women, who make pots and weave baskets, who fashion clothes and cheer their children on at powwow, who make fry bread and piki bread, and corn soup and chili stew, who dance and sing and remember and hold within their hearts the dream of their ancient peoples — that one day the woman who thinks will speak to us again, and everywhere there will be peace. Meanwhile we tell the stories and write the books and trade tales of anger and woe and stories of fun and scandal and laugh over all manner of things that happen every day. We watch and we wait.

My great-grandmother told my mother: Never forget you are Indian. And my mother told me the same thing. This, then, is how I have gone about remembering, so that my children will remember too.

Suggestions for Writing and Discussion

1. Allen believes that Indian women, like other women, must strive for harmony between traditional roles and those of modern-day society. What part of the traditional Indian role does Allen want to embrace? What new characteristics does she suggest the Indian women's role incorporate?

2. In paragraph 5, Allen writes that she formed her ideas of womanhood from her female relatives. Although each woman was unique, Allen writes that they all had one thing in common: "none of them presented herself tentatively." What do you think Allen means by this phrase? Write a sentence that explains what your female or male relatives had in common. How does your phrase compare with Allen's? Use your phrase to develop an essay that explains male/female relationships "where you come from."

3. Allen goes on to write that in her past, she remembers no woman who was "foolish," "dumb," "vain," or "plastic." Looking back on your own past, can you make the same claim? Can you make this claim about the men you know? Explain your responses.

4. Throughout this piece, Allen uses personal as well as historical examples to support her ideas. Analyze the effects of this dual perspective on the reader, using your own responses to her explanations to show what you mean.

5. Look closely at the topics that Allen's mother dealt with in her stories (paragraph 9). Categorize these various topics and then synthesize your findings to suggest the skills, knowledge, emotions, and values that are important to a Native American woman.

6. According to Allen, how does a Native American woman view her "hormonal life," and how does this view differ from that of her white, middle-class counterpart? What cultural values does each view reflect?

7. Allen writes that a Native American woman's goal in life is to become "strong and balanced." What two goals do you think the mothers in your own cultural community wish for their daughters today? What two goals do you think mothers in your own cultural community wish for their sons?

8. Allen lists various ways in which Native American women deal with the conflicts inherent in womanhood (paragraph 16). Compare her list with the ways you believe women in your community deal with conflicts in their own lives. Do you see these coping strategies as different from those of the men in your community? Explain.

9. Someone once wrote that you can tell the values of a culture by how it treats its young and its aged. How did the Native Americans care for these groups of people, and how do people in your community today care for these same groups? What conclusions can you draw about these two cultures on the basis of your answers?

10. Allen's great-grandmother gave her the following advice: "Never forget you are an Indian." Suppose that you had one last piece of advice to give to your children, and complete the following sentence: Never forget _____. Why would you choose this advice for your children?

Suggestions for Extended Thinking and Research

1. Choose a popular television show or movie today in which women assume the key roles. What role do these media characters portray, and in what ways does a woman's real-life role differ from the media's version?

2. Research the roles of women in another American Indian tribe, such as Hopi, Sioux, Iroquois, or Algonquin. Compare the rituals, roles, and values of these Indian women with those of the Laguna Pueblo women.

3. Are gender roles determined by nature or nurture? Use this essay and your own experience, as well as the findings from three modern-day sociologists or psychologists, in order to answer this question in an extended essay.

PETER FILENE

Between a Rock and a Soft Place: A Century of American Manhood

> *Born in New York City in 1941, Peter Filene teaches history at the University of North Carolina, Chapel Hill. Long interested in gender issues, Filene is the author of* Him/Her/Self: Sex Roles in Modern America. *"Between a Rock and a Soft Place" first appeared in* South Atlantic Quarterly *(Duke University Press, 1985).*

Prereading/Journal-Writing Suggestions

1. From your experiences and observations, create a verbal portrait describing your image of the American male. What does he look like? How does he act? What's important to him? What does he need? What does he want? What does he believe? Reflecting on your "portrait," do you really know anyone who fits this image exactly?
2. For women: Imagine you are a man, the same age and in the same circumstances that you are in now. What advantages do you have being a man? What disadvantages do you have?

    For men: Imagine you are a woman, the same age and in the same circumstances that you are in now. What advantages do you have being a woman? What disadvantages do you have?

In middle-class circles these days, one can hardly drop into a conversation or pick up a magazine or skim through a book without encountering sentences that begin: "The trouble with men is . . ." These are not exclusively women's sentences; this is not a sexual class war, with Amazonian feminists launching guerrilla raids upon men. More and more, the accusations also come from men themselves.

"We've been accused of everything from racism to sexism to warmaking to being generally responsible for trying to destroy the planet," a male freelance writer told readers of the *New York Times Magazine* in 1978. "Since the 50's, we've been forced to get to know ourselves a little better and some of us haven't liked what we've learned." Five years later, things had not improved. "I don't know what it's like on the East Coast," a thirty-seven-year-old California psychotherapist said, "but out here for the past twenty years, 'male' has been equivalent to 'negative.'" Back on the East Coast, meanwhile, arts commentator Lucy Lippard said it was like this: "While I'm only too glad to see men or anyone else 'working on themselves,' if I were completely honest I'd have to say it isn't working, or rather that there's something missing." Progressive-thinking men, she claimed, were trying to be "more like women . . . — in touch with themselves, fluid, emotional, vulnerable, and able to cry, as well as to fuck authentically with affectionate passion." But Lippard concluded sadly that so far, the heart of male-female relationships contained only numbness or even less than that, a void.[1]

These are hard times for men. Machismo is going out of style among the middle class, and any man who dares to play that role is likely to be snubbed, ridiculed, or karate-punched for his sexist foolishness. Hollywood heroes betray what's happening. To be sure, James Bond continues to juggle glossy weapons and breathless blondes, but John Wayne has died, Superman giggles and blushes, and E. T. wants to go home. Even *Playboy*, that manual of robust self-indulgence, is showing signs of exhaustion. After twenty years of popularity among prosperous young men, its circulation has slumped. A new generation, both male and female, is coming on the scene, to whom Hugh Hefner's ideals of huge tits and anonymous sex acts seem less appetizing. In one of *Playboy*'s own cartoons a few years ago, you could hear the future arriving. There are the familiar ninety-pound weakling and his girl and the bully on the beach. But this time the weakling (in sandals) is kicking the sand, saying, "Get lost, creep! There's a new man on the beach and your macho bullshit doesn't cut it anymore!" And the bully replies: "That man is the biggest nuisance on the beach! Why can't he learn that real men today are gentle and sensitive and . . . ?" Meanwhile the girlfriend murmurs to herself: "This is getting a little weird . . ."[2]

Not only a little weird, but also a lot confusing. In the face of such outcries against men and among them, one is tempted to make either of two quick steps of diagnosis. The crisis of masculinity is new, one is tempted to think, and the women's movement is responsible for it. Or the crisis is as old as Adam, and the women's movement is finally calling it out into the open. Neither of these diagnoses contains the whole truth, however. Contrary to appearances, feminism is not entirely to blame for the trouble with men, nor are men themselves. The truth is more complex than villainy lying on one side of the war between the sexes. Even had there been no women's movement, men would be struggling against the push and pull of their social roles. For the masculine dilemma has to do only partly with women. On the other hand, the fault lies not entirely in ourselves, that we are men, but also in our circumstances.

Diagnosis becomes clearer if we take the long view — a century-long view. In this historical perspective we see that the trouble with American men has existed for more than a hundred years, but until our own century it was disguised or mitigated by three kinds of circumstances. As those circumstances gave way, the trouble emerged into the open and became unavoidable. As modernity developed around him, it became harder and harder for a boy to grow up into a man.

The first circumstance involves expectations. A middle-class boy grew up in Victorian America with much clearer prescriptions of how he was supposed to "be a man" than his modern-day grandson would be given. The ideal of "manly character" laid heavy demands upon the body, mind, and soul, but at least one knew what he was up against. When character dissolved into "self-fulfillment," however, the strictly masculine commandments gave way and the trouble began.

Along with the shift in expectations came changes in the opportunities for men to test those expectations. Rural America turned urban, work involved brain more than brawn, individualism melted into corporate bureaucracy. While the content of ideal manhood was relaxing, the conditions of proving it were disintegrating. Ambiguity doubled.

And it tripled when the roles of women began altering in drastic ways. As the domestic angel entered college and career, as the deferential lady demanded equal rights in politics and law and bed, the traditional gender arrangement fell apart. Men had depended upon women to perform one half of the division of labor, economic as well as emotional labor. Men had depended upon women's dependency. So when women stepped out of their role, men were left flailing inside their own.

Men's troubles are old troubles, at least a century old. But they have become so noticeable and bedeviling only as the supportive props of traditional manhood splintered. We look back to Victorian America, then, not to lament a golden age, but to explain how men have entered their recent dilemma and how they can get out of it.

Expectations

The words of Victorian fathers fell upon their sons like rain — cold, 10 serious, and clear. To help nine-year-old Stanley "be a good man if God lets you grow up," Granville Bascom Hall in 1853 laid down six rules of conduct: "In the first place then, ask the advice of your parents. . . . 2nd, Hear all they have to say and remember it all. 3rd — Never reject their advice because *you cannot see* it to be wise. . . . 4th — Never . . ." But we need not read on through 4th and 5th and 6th, because they follow the same line of filial obedience in equally implacable words.[3]

Theodore Roosevelt, Senior, issued his asthmatic young son a manly prescription that was more varied but no less strict. "You have the mind but you have not the body, and without the help of the body the mind cannot go as far as it should. You must *make* your body." Ten years later, as Teddy went off to Harvard with well-developed body and mind, his father offered further advice: "Take care of your morals first, your health next, and finally your studies."[4]

Obedience, work, strength of body and mind, and then add to these ingredients a heavy dose of self-reliance and religion. In 1878 the Reverend Joseph Wilson wrote to "My Dearest Son" when Woodrow was a junior at Princeton:

> It is not now my purpose to preach to you upon the subject of "ambition. . . ." To attain distinction is commendable. But, to *deserve* distinction is a far worthier aim than distinction itself. . . . You *have* talents — you have *character* — you have manly bearing. You have

almost every advantage coupled I trust with genuine love for God.
Do not allow yourself, then, to feed on dreams. . . . The roast beef
of hard industry gives blood for climbing the hills of life. It is genius
that usually gets to the highest tops — but, what is the secret heart of
genius? the ability to work with painstaking self-denial.[5]

And when a son forgot these manly lessons, a father took pains to
remind him. Twenty-six-year-old Lincoln Steffens landed in New York City,
completing three carefree years of European study, and was handed an envelope containing one hundred dollars and a letter. "My dear son," it began, and
then went on to tell Lennie that his father was finally cutting the purse strings.
"By now you must know about all there is to know of the theory of life, but
there's a practical side as well. It's worth knowing. I suggest that you learn it,
and the way to study it, I think, is to stay in New York and hustle."[6]

Eugene Debs escaped this sort of reprimand by leaving home and school
at age fifteen to work on the railroad. Self-reliance, he soon discovered, was a
frightening business. "Sometimes I am all alone and I am so homesick, I
hardly know what to do," he confessed to his parents. Moreover, jobs were
scarce in the depression of the 1870s, and poverty hovered menacingly around
him. But he was determined "to prove that I can act manly when must be."[7]

One way or another, each boy grew up to be a man, a "true man." They 15
pursued different occupations: Hall was a psychologist, Roosevelt a writer,
cowboy, soldier, and politician; Wilson a scholar and politician; Steffens a
journalist; and Debs a trade unionist and socialist. But all climbed the hills of
life dutifully, piously, industriously, self-reliantly, and self-denyingly, all hearing the same paternal adverbs tolling in their consciences as they proved their
manly character. They waged furious ideological quarrels with one another:
Hall denounced Rooseveltian imperialism in 1898 and praised the Wilsonian
crusade in 1917; Wilson and Roosevelt competed against each other twice for
the presidency; Wilson jailed Debs for antiwar activity; Steffens denounced
Wilson's peace treaty and embraced Lenin instead. Nevertheless, all five men
acted out the same basic script of Victorian masculinity.

A century later, the style of that script seems as quaint as detachable
collars and spats. But once you deflate the pompous pieties and straighten out
the baroque syntax, the expectations heaped upon Victorian boys sound remarkably similar to the ones heaped upon modern boys. Be tough, be cou-
rageous, take risks; don't cry or show weakness; work, achieve, succeed;
depend upon yourself.[8] Although twentieth-century middle-class fathers
tended to be more affectionate and supportive than their own fathers had
been, in their children's memory they still were the background parent. Mom
played the leading role on childhood's stage, making meals, nursing hurt
knees and feelings, saying yes or no. More to the point, when modern Dad
did become involved, he tended to treat sons and daughters differently. On
the would-be man he concentrated more directiveness, support, and strict
discipline — an active posture; on the would-be woman he was content with
affection and protection.[9]

Boys should learn not to be sissies, in other words, and girls not to be tomboys. When modern children left parental laps and went to school, they met up with the same teachings. In eighty percent of grade-school books of the 1960s, and almost as large a majority of books in the 1970s, boys outnumbered and "out-did" girls. Boys stood, climbed, and rode bikes, performed chemistry experiments and helped Dad build things, rescued people from cattle stampedes, and never cried. Girls sat and watched and daydreamed, cared for pets or siblings, helped Mom make cookies, rode as passengers on boys' bikes, and cried frequently.[10] If we advance the plot from childhood to adolescence, it was *Sports Illustrated* versus *Seventeen*.

Traditional stereotyping of the two sexes governs more strongly than we may have believed. That contrast should not blind us, however, to significant evolution within the masculine ideal. Brother Jack and sister Jill may be steered in very different directions, but Jack is not looking toward the same ideals as his grandfather. Instead of unquestioning obedience to his parents, a modern middle-class son expects to negotiate and reason because his parents (long before Dr. Spock, by the way) have prized a "democratic" family. Amid this new sort of domestic political system, self-reliance and rugged competition become obstreperous traits. Children of both sexes are encouraged to be more pliable citizens. Be true to yourself, think for yourself, but also be tolerant of others. Work hard, strive for success, but also get along with other people, be a good member of the team. In the course of a century, "character" has evolved into "personality." As part of that transformed sense of self, the notion of masculinity has softened and expanded, still bearing many Victorian inheritances but also turning increasingly "feminine."[11]

From one perspective, this broadened repertoire of expectations has made things easier for boys. Instead of the narrow identity permitted by all those "thou shalt not" commandments of nineteenth-century parents, boys are permitted a more spacious self. But there is a less happy perspective. If one sees this space as sheer vacancy, offering too few guidelines and asking too much self-direction, then spaciousness makes things harder. Is the identity bottle half-full or half-empty? A man's perspective ultimately depends on his temperament. But I suspect that the balance these days is tipping toward "empty"—toward hardship, toward "the trouble with men" that both sexes have been grumbling about. Even in the best of circumstances, ambiguity of expectations can be troubling. When the two other once-supportive circumstances of masculinity are no longer giving support, then ambiguity will be very troubling indeed. And that is what has occurred. The prescriptions of masculinity may be wider, but the opportunities for proving it are narrower. And modern masculinity—like Victorian manliness—requires proof.

Opportunities

You must make your body, Theodore Roosevelt, Senior, insisted; you 20 must make your mind. A hundred years later, manhood remains a matter of "making" rather than becoming. It is not a phase into which a boy inevitably graduates over time, but a status which he must achieve by struggle. A girl grows into womanhood, translating childhood nurturance into wifely and motherly nurturance. A boy, by contrast, must prove himself a man, earning mastery over his inner weaknesses and the outer challenges of the world.[12]

When the world was rural, the challenges were harsh but at least they were tangible, and so the proof was just as tangible. At Harvard, Theodore Roosevelt showed manliness by diligent study and moral purity. But how much more emphatically he could show it in the Dakota Bad Lands! Hunting buffalo, elk, and bear, rounding up boat thieves and cattle, riding horseback for twelve or twenty-four hours through subzero weather, Theodore left no doubt in anyone's mind that he was a "true man" and, eventually, the emblematic man of his era.[13] A smelly buffalo hide declared graduation from boyhood far better than any sheepskin diploma.

Coming from patrician New York City, Roosevelt never fully escaped the status of dude (which is perhaps why he tried so hard and boasted so much). His future friend Lincoln Steffens, by contrast, was a westerner by birth, galloping through his California youth as "the boy on horseback." No asthma for Lennie, nor much early schooling except in the school of hard knocks. But not much conventional success either, and Steffens eventually went to New York to show his father and himself that he could succeed in some career or other. Business was his father's recommendation, literary writing was his own hope. In the end, the job market settled the argument, and Steffens became a newspaper journalist covering the rough-and-tumble "beat" of the Lower East Side. "Will it make a man of me?" Steffens asked himself.[14] In a remarkably short time it did. As a muckraker fighting with his pen against urban outlaws, Steffens became nationally famous.

As his story suggests, however, the circumstances of success were changing at the turn of the century. In modernizing America, the message was "Go east, young man." The prairies were being crisscrossed by railroad tracks and asphalt sidewalks. Buffalo Bill worked in Barnum and Bailey's Circus. People were crowding into cities, businesses were growing into corporations and corporations into multimillion-dollar trusts, John Henry was losing to the inexhaustible machine. In 1870, two of three men were self-employed; in 1920, only one of three (and today only one of ten). By 1910, six of ten wage-earners in manufacturing were working for companies of more than 100 employees; by 1929, seven of ten. (Today, 30 percent of the entire nonagricultural labor force works for businesses with more than five hundred employees.) Amid such "progress," men yearned desperately for tangible proofs of manly character.[15]

In 1917, Harvard senior John Dos Passos complained to a friend: "I think we are all of us a pretty milky lot, — don't you? — with our tea-table convictions and our radicalism that keeps so consistently within the bounds of decorum. . . . And what are we fit for when they turn us out of Harvard? We're too intelligent to be successful businessmen and we haven't the sand or the energy to be anything else."[16] Thirty years earlier, Roosevelt had set out for the Bad Lands. But twenty-four years earlier, historian Frederick Jackson

Turner had declared the frontier was gone. As the open land closed, where was an aspiring youth to test his manliness?

Well, there was still the battlefield. War offered a more genuine red 25 badge of courage than any fight against corruption or monopolies. When William James's father refused to let him fight in the Civil War, but younger brother Wilky managed to enlist and be wounded, nineteen-year-old William felt "one of the very lightest of featherweights," lacking "the grip and energy" of other men. When Stanley Hall's father secured him an army exemption rather than let him wage war against the Confederacy, he inflicted on his son "the very sorest of all memories." Dos Passos was luckier. In 1917 he went to France, crouched beneath the blood-red explosions of a German bombardment, and exclaimed:

> But gosh I want to be able to express, later, all of this, all the tragedy and hideous excitement of it . . . the grey crooked fingers of the dead, the dark look of dirty mangled bodies . . . , the vast tom-tom of the guns, the ripping tear shells make when they explode. . . . When one shell comes I want another, nearer, nearer. . . . I want to throw the dice at every turn with the old roisterer Death . . . and through it all I feel more alive than ever before.[17]

Wars served as crucibles of manhood, but they interrupted rather than reversed the inexorable socioeconomic trends. The heroic world was vanishing. War itself was fought by tanks and then planes and then missiles as much as by men. After 1865 the wilderness steadily retreated before cities and highways, until the only frontier hung in the transatlantic air for Lindbergh and other pioneers to fly and then — higher yet, beyond gravity and the reach of anyone but a few astronauts — the frontier became outer space. Meanwhile the occupational world was modernizing. Middle-class work became segmented by specialization, depersonalized by bureaucracies, abstracted by computers, muffled by fringe benefits and pension plans.

In this setting, what place is there for "the roast beef of hard industry"? Old-fashioned ambition continues in new-fashioned modes. Up-and-coming professional men of the twentieth century work as many hours as they would have worked in the nineteenth: more than fifty-five hours per week for one fourth of them, more than sixty hours for one sixth. They live the strenuous life of the court room, the operating room, or the corporate board room. For more physical proof of themselves they turn, not to battlefields, but to the racquet ball court, the jogging track, or the Nautilus-equipped gym in their office building. Like their sons hunched for hours in front of Star War video games, repelling Darth Vader armies with their thumbs, their fathers enjoy the recreational equivalent of war.

In short, middle-class men have adapted their behavior to modern circumstances. They have sublimated, displaced, replaced — call it what you will, they have in any case learned how to update traditional manly activity. But the satisfaction is not what it once was.

"I work hard and take a full briefcase home most nights," says Chuck Powell, a forty-one-year-old comptroller with a Big Board company. "My life in the past five years has . . . become frenetic. . . . I feel a lot of pressure and I get more tired than I'm willing to admit, even to myself." His biggest dissatisfaction, he says, comes from lack of recognition by his employers. But the dilemma embraces more than the part of himself he brings to the office. "I guess I've got a puritanical streak in me that says profit and all that jazz aren't the be-all and end-all of my life. At sixty what am I going to tell my kids I did with my life? . . . I guess my personal and business values just don't click at times. And that's really frustrating."[18]

There are many Chuck Powells out there in the skyscraper heights of 30 the corporate economy. According to repeated surveys by the University of Michigan in 1969, 1973, and 1977, job satisfaction has declined significantly, most of all among college graduates. Men's discontent is directed not at inadequate pay or hours, but at inadequate meaning. They want to be able to say: "My work is important and gives me a feeling of accomplishment."

The issue is not simply work, however, but work as a part of the rest of their lives. According to those same surveys, one third of married workers feel that their jobs interfere with family life "somewhat" or "a lot." And family matters to them. "What are the important things to you?" a sociologist asked two hundred executives in a large company. Sixty percent said "family," fewer than 20 percent said "career." Even more troubled testimony emerges from an American Management Association poll in 1973, which reported that four of five businessmen placed their major aspirations not in the firms that employed them, but in their home life. Likewise, a Louis Harris poll in 1979 of men aged eighteen to fifty found that the vast majority rated health, love, peace of mind, and family as being personally "very important"; work came in a distant fifth. In other words, Superman wants more time off from fighting Lex Luther and stopping runaway express trains. He wants more opportunity to shed his blue tights and become good old Clark Kent playing at home with Lois Lane and Superbaby.[19]

So how do men resolve this conflict between the way they spend most of their waking hours (on the job) and the way they would like to spend some of them (with family and self)? One resolution is a midlife crisis. According to social psychologists like Daniel Levinson (*The Seasons of a Man's Life*), our lives move through a cycle. The thirties are the time when a man settles down, works hard to make his niche, and enters the "Boom" phase of "Becoming One's Own Man." Near the age of forty, however, a typical man enters midlife transition, a period of renewed questions and fresh tasks. Now that "the returns are in" from his youthful dreams of money, fame, and power, he must look at the options he chose against, the desires he postponed, the other voices in the other rooms of his self. In particular, a middle-aged man becomes aware of his inclination toward creativity and human attachment (what Erik Erikson calls "generativity"). He cultivates imagination, sensitivity to others' needs, and loving friendships. It is time, at last, for the "feminine" side of his personality to be given life.[20]

Modern social psychologists have popularized the concept of midlife transition, but it is not simply a modern story. Looking back a century, we see the same cycle among Victorian men. At first it is easy to overlook, because they rode into middle age without the label of "midlife crisis" and with less of a jolt. But we should not mistake what was happening. During their late thirties came the same troubled turn of life, although it made less trouble for them than for us because Victorian circumstances were more supportive of conventional manliness.

Consider, for example, Lincoln Steffens at the age of thirty-six. When he was offered the chance to become managing editor of *McClure's,* the most prestigious American magazine of the day, it should have been a jubilant moment. But not at all. "I am home—sick today," he told his father. "Some symptoms of nervous prostration. . . . All signs are pointing to a temporary retirement." The months-long breakdown occurred because, on the verge of occupational triumph, Steffens realized—first subconsciously and later consciously—that he was failing in other realms. His novel was unwritten, his marriage was loveless and childless. In conventional public terms he was a successful man, but those terms did not cover the private man. He finally took the *McClure's* job, crisscrossed the nation on research and speaking tours, winning extraordinary acclaim. But in the process he drifted farther and farther from his wife. He became a husband who slept alone in hotel rooms as he rode the circuit of celebrity. Only in his fifties, after his first wife died and he remarried, did Steffens fulfill "one of the deepest desires of my life"—fatherhood. Radiant fatherhood is what he called it. "The best rectification I have ever had is (my son) Pete, who lets me love him more and more and ever more."[21]

Eugene Debs suffered the same bittersweet blend of public celebrity and private regret. As the charismatic spokesman of socialism, he journeyed from crowd to ardent crowd, interview upon interview, one presidential candidacy after another. The personal price, however, was high. Like Steffens, Debs was evading a loveless, childless marriage, collapsing under periodic psychosomatic illnesses, and harboring an inner hollowness. He too fell in love with another woman. But here the two biographies part company. Katherine Debs had not died and Mabel Curry was married. During the last decade of his life, Debs slid into depression and despair, but it is hard to say whether his wartime sentence to the federal penitentiary or his prison of unrequited love was more responsible.[22]

"No man can be a good citizen who is not a good husband and a good father," Theodore Roosevelt proclaimed.[23] Roosevelt himself, as you would expect, was better than good: an ardent husband to one wife and then, after she died, to a second wife, while also a devoted father of five children. Few Victorian men matched his overachievement. In fact, many seemed unaware of their domestic needs before entering middle age. They put up with indifferent marriages, or rationalized them, or turned their backs on them, investing their primary hopes in successful careers. Only during their forties did they stop, look homeward, and reckon the emotional gains and losses.

Midlife crisis may be part of an innate sequence (a "season") or it may be caused by external events. Social psychologists are arguing hotly about this issue, and it is too soon to say where the truth lies. Either way, it seems that men of a century ago and men of our own time have tended to go through a common pattern. Both groups have struggled to "live up to" the script of manliness, only to discover — in the second act of their lives — that they must struggle to rewrite the script along gentler, more vulnerable, less masculine lines. *"Plus ça change,"* one is tempted to say, wryly. Play it again, Sam, and yet again, this same old story, the quest for fame and glory, a case of do or die, as a century of time goes by.

But it is not quite the same old story. It has turned more difficult and more uncertain. For one thing, the modern manly script has been liberalized, permitting more interpretation by the actors, emphasizing personality more than character. At the same time the opportunities for proving one's manliness have become less tangible and physical. Together these trends produce an unsettling vagueness. "What exactly does it mean to be a man, and how will I know that I have made myself into one?" Victorians provided answers that were rigid but also clear-cut, so that a man could measure how much he had succeeded or failed. Modern men, by contrast, pursue the plastic goals of "growth" and "happiness." And they pursue it in a plastic world of bureaucratic organizations that produce services or ideas rather than tangible goods. Little wonder, then, that modern men — at midlife or even earlier — seek gratification less in their careers than in their families. A sales account or a computer does not hug, kiss, and whisper "I love you."

But here enters the third and most troubling change of circumstance. Women no longer are acting out their old-fashioned script of domesticity and deference. While the modern male script resembles the Victorian version, the modern female script has been radically rewritten. As a result, the drama of the genders has turned chaotic. Actor and actress are talking past each other, singing a duet of different songs, as the director angrily shouts: "The trouble with men is . . ."

Women

Until recently, marriage was presumed to be a woman's career. In 1885, [40] for example, Woodrow Wilson wrote to his fiancée Ellen Axson, while she was taking art courses in New York City. He felt "guiltily selfish" in reminding her, he said, but "of course there's that fact that marriage will take away almost all your chance to work" in art. "Ah, sweetheart, this thing has torn my heart more than once," Wilson went on. "And yet that is what is involved in becoming a wife; we shall want to go to house-keeping as soon as possible." How did Ellen respond to this selfish fact? She said yes, and yes, and yes. Ten years and three daughters later, she continued to say yes: "How I thank God for you my darling — noble man, perfect husband that you are — my own true love, so absolutely *all* that a woman could desire the man to be to whom she gives her heart and life."[24]

It is hard for us today to take such gush at face value. We suspect Mrs. Wilson of self-delusion, brainwashing, or masochism to be so happily dedicating herself to husband and family. Where she sees love, we see exploitation; where she talks of giving, we mutter of giving away. Higher education for women, two feminist movements, and more relaxed attitudes towards religious duty and divorce have made the traditional division of labor seem obsolete. As a result, Woodrow Wilson's grandson cannot depend on his fiancée today to respond the way Ellen did. Modern women give drastically different answers.

In 1982 George Gallup asked a national sample of women: "Which one of the alternatives on this list do you feel would provide the most interesting and satisfying life for you personally?" Eight of ten told him that their ideal lifestyle is to be married with children, but half of these hopeful mothers wanted to combine motherhood with a full-time job (10 percent more than in 1975). Among younger women the choice was more emphatic; by a two-to-one margin they voted for "doing it all."[25] Female equality of roles, rights, and power remains more an ideal than a reality, of course. Nevertheless, the egalitarian principle has decisively displaced nineteenth-century notions of a wife's relationship to her husband. She will be neither the better half nor the subordinate half, only the other half.

A house divided cannot stand. As women revise their part of the division of economic and emotional labor, men have been left holding their own part in bewilderment. Knowingly or unknowingly, selfishly or generously, in weakness or strength, they had depended upon their wives for support in the symbiosis of marriage. "My own darling," twenty-seven-year-old Woodrow Wilson wrote to Ellen shortly after she agreed to marry him, "I suppose there never was a man more dependent than I on love and sympathy, more devoted to home and home life; and, my darling, my heart is overflowing with gratitude and gladness because of the assurance that it now has a new love to lean upon — a love which will some day be the centre of a new home and the joy of new home life. I shall not begin to live a complete life, my love, until you are my wife."[26]

He meant every word of it. During their thirty years of marriage Wilson's devotion flowed unwaveringly, unabashedly, in pages of purple prose when they were apart and presumably in oratory and whispers when they were together. Without a wife, his life was not complete — *he* was not complete. He meant it. When Ellen died of Bright's disease at the age of fifty-four, he remarried within a year and a half.

If marriage was a Victorian woman's career, it was no less presumed by men for themselves. By a melancholy coincidence, Steffens, Roosevelt, and Hall each suffered the premature death of his first wife, and each remarried (Roosevelt within a year, Hall within nine years, and Steffens first living with one woman until, ten years later, he married another). All of them thus rejoined the ranks of the other 70 percent of their gender in 1900 who were married.[27] "Spinster" had derisory connotations, but "bachelor" — whatever gay-doggish image it carried — meant for most men what Wilson said it meant for him: less than a fully happy life.

Much has changed in middle-class marriages since 1900: the average number of children; attitudes toward the practice of sexuality, especially women's sexuality; the frequency and the acceptability of divorce; and wives' employment. But men continue to want — to need — to be married. The persistently high rates of marriage and remarriage testify to that. So does the rate of mental illness, physical illness, and suicide among unmarried men — a rate significantly higher than among married men and also among unmarried women.[28] *Playboy* may preach the swinging single life, and singles bars may welcome the playboys, and Andy Capp may complain on the comics page every morning about his henpecked fate. But the truth is that the happiest, healthiest men are husbands.

And the probability is that they have found health and happiness in a symbiotic relationship. Her softness complements his toughness, her attention to people complements his attention to things, her feeling complements his doing, and together they make him whole. This arrangement worked well so long as both partners played their parts. But as women have begun to step out of role, reclaiming the rest of their possibilities, the arrangement has collapsed. The men who are left behind in their half of the old symbiosis are left wanting, almost as incomplete as if they were unmarried.

Is it any surprise, then, that they have had trouble with the women's movement? At first they went through a stage of self-defense against feminists: (angrily) "How dare you accuse me, you bitch, after all I've done for you?" or (plaintively) "What have I done to deserve this, my darling?" As they learned that they would survive female independence, however, growing numbers of liberal middle-class males in the 1970s turned from defensiveness to support: "If you want a career and a baby, I'll help you, dear." When they did attack, they attacked themselves: "The trouble with men is . . ." And that seems to be as far as liberated men have come: between a rock and a soft place.

From Here On

What is the way out of this trap? One way is for men to stop reacting and to begin acting — in other words, to learn the lessons of their history and to take a hand in shaping their future. Although the feminist movement has forced men to change their traditional attitudes and practices, their troubles did not begin with feminism nor will they end with men becoming feminists. Men sidestep the truth when they blame women for their dilemma. But they take only half a step forward when they placate or imitate women. At a time when injustices to women remain flagrant, they deserve to occupy center stage in the drama we call "sexual inequality." But the gender problem will not end if women win equality of rights and opportunities. Even if that idealistic day should arrive, men would still be left with their century-old dilemma of trying to define their own roles in the face of drastically altered "manly" expectations and opportunities. Feminism has taught us that women deserve to be asked, in the words of Gallup's pollsters, "Which one of the alternatives on this list do you feel would provide the most interesting and satisfying life for you personally?" The past century of history teaches us that the same question needs to be asked of men, too.

A few men have, in effect, been doing exactly that. Beyond supporting 50 women and rejecting machoism, they have been widening the social space for both genders. That is what gay men have done, occupying a part of the sexual and emotional spectrum previously restricted to women. That is what straight men have done who are staying home as househusbands or taking custody of their children after divorce. But we need not resort to such exceptional cases to find examples of egalitarianism.

A survey asked a national sample of Americans in 1977 whether they preferred the idea of shared marriage roles or a traditional marriage. Among the general public, shared roles emerged the slight but surprising winner, 48 to 43 percent. Among persons aged eighteen to twenty-nine, however, that preference won by a resounding margin of three to one. For more exciting portents, listen to the 28,000 readers of *Psychology Today* who responded in 1977 to a lengthy questionnaire about masculinity. Most of the men wanted to be warmer, gentler, and more loving, and they disdained competition, aggressiveness, or sexual conquest (although they still had trouble asking for directions when they became lost while driving). Most of the women, in turn, shared these same ideals for men as well as for themselves.[29] To be sure, *Psychology Today* readers are younger, more educated, and more affluent than most Americans, but people like them usually point which way the cultural wind is blowing.

Opinions are one thing, but behavior is more convincing. Consider the behavior of those innumerable husbands who stand beside their wives under the hot lights of the operating room, coaching their wives breath by breath, push by pelvic push, toward the moment of birth.[30] These men of Lamaze are not extirpating some awful macho part of themselves, nor trying to be "like a woman." They are becoming full partners in parenthood—no longer content with simply having planted that sperm nine months earlier and then sitting off-stage in the waiting room. By accompanying their wives throughout pregnancy, labor, and delivery, they have enhanced their own power without subtracting from women's. One gender's gain does not necessarily mean the other gender's loss. On the contrary, beyond stereotypes lies more space for people to move about. Out there, beyond stereotypes, a man coaches his wife and also coaches his son's (or daughter's) Little League team.

Even the most forward-looking Americans have not arrived there, not by a long shot. In fact, we still are groping to find words for what is happening—"househusband," "parenting," "dual-career families," all clumsy efforts to articulate half-formed ideas. But slowness and clumsiness are hardly surprising, because we are talking about a profound cultural realignment. The winds of change blew for years before women won the vote, another half-century before the modern feminist movement began. They will have to blow far into the next century, no doubt, before men will have outgrown their troubles. In the meantime, we can nurture ourselves with images of a future when a man is free to weep and wear cowboy boots, to bathe his children and then watch the Pittsburgh Steelers, to bake bread on Thursday and play poker with the guys on Friday, to ask for a hug from a male friend or a female friend, whoever happens to be there when you need it.

Notes

1. Stephen Singular, "Moving On: Reaping the Rewards of the Women's Movement," *New York Times Magazine,* 30 April 1978, 18; John Skow, "In California: Roar, Lion, Roar," *Time,* 7 November 1983, 17; Lucy Lippard, "Coming Soon: The Fall and Rise of the New Man," *Village Voice,* 1 November 1983, 96.

2. *Playboy,* September 1974, 147. For background, see Joe L. Dubbert, *A Man's Place: Masculinity in Transition* (Englewood Cliffs, N.J., 1979), 267–69.

3. "St. Nicholas" (G. B. Hall) to G. Stanley Hall, 1 January 1853, quoted in Dorothy Ross, *G. Stanley Hall: The Psychologist as Prophet* (Chicago, 1972), 5. Let me take a moment and a footnote to talk about methodology. I have chosen five middle-class men as the spokes by which the Victorian half of this essay evolves:

	Birthplace	Occupation	Political Ideology	Father's Occupation
G. Stanley Hall (1844–1924)	Mass.	psychologist	?	farmer
Eugene V. Debs (1855–1926)	Ind.	unionist	socialist	merchant
Woodrow Wilson (1856–1924)	Va.	teacher, politician	liberal Democrat	minister
Theodore Roosevelt (1858–1919)	N.Y.	politician	liberal Republican	banker
Lincoln Steffens (1886–1936)	Calif.	journalist	liberal, then radical	banker

They do not qualify as a social-scientific "sample." But they are geographically, occupationally, and ideologically diverse, while concentric in time, class, and (as the essay will show) attitudes toward masculinity. Therefore I claim them as representative men.

4. Quoted in Edmund Morris, *The Rise of Theodore Roosevelt* (New York, 1979), 60; and quoted in Carleton Putnam, *Theodore Roosevelt: The Formative Years, 1858–1886* (New York, 1958), 1:141.

5. Joseph Ruggles Wilson to Woodrow Wilson, 25 January 1878, in *The Papers of Woodrow Wilson,* ed. Arthur S. Link (Princeton, N.J., 1966), 1:345–46.

6. Quoted in Lincoln Steffens, *Autobiography* (New York, 1931), 169.

7. Debs to "Dear Parents," 29 September 1874, and to Louise Debs, 3 and 8 October 1874, quoted in Nick Salvatore, *Eugene V. Debs: Citizen and Socialist* (Urbana, Ill., 1982), 18–19.

8. Deborah David and Robert Brannon, eds., *The Forty-nine Percent Majority: The Male Sex Role* (Reading, Mass., 1976), 11–36.

9. Wanda C. Bronson, Edith S. Katten, and Norman Livson, "Patterns of Authority and Affection in Two Generations," *Journal of Abnormal and Social Psychology* 58 (March 1959): 148–50; Leonard Benson, *Fatherhood: A Sociological Perspective* (New York, 1968), 192–95, 234–37; Melvin L. Kohn, *Class and Conformity: A Study in Values* (Homewood, Ill., 1969), 112–15, 123, 125; Robert A. Fein, "Research on Fathering: Social Policy and an Emergent Perspective," in *Family in Transition: Rethinking Marriage, Child Rearing, and Family Organization,* ed. Arlene and Jerome H. Skolnick, 3rd ed. (Boston, 1980), 399.

10. Elizabeth Fisher, "Children's Books: the Second Sex, Junior Division," in *And Jill Came Tumbling After: Sexism in American Education,* ed. Judith Stacey, Susan Bereaud, and Joan Daniels (New York, 1974), 116–22; Women on Words & Images, *Dick and Jane as Victims: Sex Stereotyping in Children's Readers,* 2nd ed. (Princeton, N.J., 1975), chs. 4, 7, and passim.

11. On the family, see Peter G. Filene, *Him/Her/Self: Sex Roles in Modern America* (New York, 1975), 162–66, 197–99. On character versus personality, I am indebted to Warren Susman's lecture at the University of North Carolina in 1975. See also Daniel R. Miller and Guy E. Swanson, *The Changing American Parent: A Study in the Detroit Area* (New York, 1958), 52–54.

12. Benson, *Fatherhood,* 188–92; Ruth E. Hartley, "Sex-Role Pressures in the Socialization of the Male Child," *Psychological Reports,* 5 (1959): 457–68, reprinted in *Men and Masculinity,* ed. Joseph Pleck and Jack Sawyer (Englewood Cliffs, N.J., 1974).

13. Morris, *Roosevelt,* chs. 8, 11, esp. pp. 285–95, 301–03, 322–31.

14. Steffens to his father, 3 November 1893, Steffens Papers, Columbia University.

15. Rosabeth Moss Kanter, *Men and Women of the Corporation* (New York, 1977), 15–16; U.S. Bureau of the Census, *Statistical Abstract of the United States: 1982–1983.*

16. Dos Passos to Arthur K. McComb, 3 July 1917, quoted in Melvin Landsberg, *Dos Passos' Path to U.S.A.: A Political Biography, 1912–1936* (Boulder, Colo., 1972), 56.

17. Jean Strouse, *Alice James: A Biography* (Boston, 1980), 70–72; Ross, *Hall,* 10; Dos Passos, "Notebook," 26 August (1917), reprinted in introduction to Dos Passos, *One Man's Initiation: 1917* (Ithaca, N.Y., 1969), 22.

18. Quoted in Barrie S. Greiff and Preston K. Munter, "Tradeoffs," *Harvard Magazine,* May-June 1980, 48C. See also Peter M. Grath, "Faster than a Speeding Bullet . . . ," *The Washingtonian,* September 1981, 150–55. For an insightful general interpretation, based on national polls in 1957 and repeated in 1976, see Joseph Veroff, Elizabeth Douvan, and Richard Kulka, *The Inner American: A Self Portrait from 1957 to 1976* (New York, 1981), esp. 17–25, 292–97.

19. *New Ways to Work Newsletter* (Palo Alto, Calif.), Spring 1979; U.S. Department of Commerce, *Social Indicators: 1976 — Selected Data on Social Conditions and Trends in the United States* (Washington, D.C., 1976), 389; the executive poll is in Kanter, *Men and Women,* 105; the AMA poll is in *The New York Times,* 3 June 1973, 4:12; Louis Harris and Associates, "The Playboy Report on American Men: A Study of the Values, Attitudes, and Goals of U.S. Males 18–49 Years Old" (Chicago, 1979).

20. Daniel J. Levinson et al., *The Seasons of a Man's Life* (New York, 1978), chs. 9, 13, 15, esp. 196–200 and 228–39; Erik Erikson, *Childhood and Society,* 2nd ed. (New York, 1963), 266–68.

21. Steffens to his father, 4 May 1901, to Laura Suggett, 16 April 1924, and to Marie Howe, 8 February 1926, in *The Letters of Lincoln Steffens*, 2 vols., ed. Ella Winter and Granville Hicks (New York, 1938), 1:137, 2:64, and 2:734. Also Steffens, "Radiant Fatherhood: An Old Father's Confession of Superiority," (1925), reprinted in *Lincoln Steffens Speaking* (New York, 1936), 5–6.

22. Salvatore, *Debs,* 277–80, 288, 339–40, and ch. 10 passim.

23. Quoted in *Theodore Roosevelt,* ed. Dewey Grantham (Englewood Cliffs, N.J., 1971), 41.

24. Wilson to Ellen Axson, 27 March 1885, and Ellen to Woodrow Wilson, 6 February 1894, in *The Priceless Gift: The Love Letters of Woodrow Wilson and Ellen Axson Wilson,* ed. Eleanor Wilson McAdoo (New York, 1962), 126–27, 185.

25. *The Gallup Report,* no. 203, August 1982, 27.

26. Wilson to Axson, 2 October 1883, in *Priceless Gift,* ed. McAdoo, 19.

27. U.S. Bureau of the Census, *Historical Statistics of the United States, Colonial Times to 1970,* Bicentennial Ed., pt. 2 (Washington, D.C., 1975), 21.

28. Jessie Bernard. *The Future of Marriage* (New Haven, Conn., 1982), 17, 21, 31–32.

29. *New York Times,* 27 November 1977, p. 75; Carol Tavris, "Men and Women Report Their Views on Masculinity," *Psychology Today,* January 1977, 35–42, 87.

30. "New Science of Birth," *Newsweek,* 15 November 1976, 60; "A New Kind of Life with Father," ibid., 30 November 1981, 93.

Suggestions for Writing and Discussion

1. In a sentence, what is Filene's main point in this piece? What specific sources does he rely on to support this point?
2. Evaluate the various sources that Filene uses in this piece. Are these sources fair, unbiased, credible, representative of a total population of men, sufficient, and varied?
3. What three circumstances, according to Filene, have made men's roles so complicated today? What specifics for each circumstance does Filene mention?
4. Compare fathers of today with fathers in the Victorian period as suggested by this essay. What characteristics do these two groups share? What characteristics are different?
5. In what ways, according to Filene, has the husband/wife relationship changed from the days of early America to the present day? Do you agree or disagree with his contentions?
6. In the end, what does Filene propose as a goal for American men today? What specifics does he propose as the means for reaching these goals? Can you provide any other specifics that might assist men in reaching this goal?

Suggestions for Extended Thinking and Research

1. Complete the following title and write an essay that supports it: A Century of American Womanhood: Between a _____ and a
   _____ .

2. Examine a specific gender role in your own culture during this past century from another country's cultural viewpoint.

ALEXIS DE TOCQUEVILLE
How the Americans Understand the Equality of the Sexes

> Born in France in 1805 to an aristocratic family, Alexis de Tocqueville first visited the United States in 1831. Sent by the French government to study the American prison and penal system, he also spent many hours of his own time meeting and talking with Americans whose political and social lives fascinated him. In 1835 and 1840, he published his observations about American society in his two-volume study Democracy in America, from which the following selection is taken.

Prereading/Journal Writing Suggestions

1. From your experience and your observations, are men and women treated as equals in this country? Write about a specific instance in your life that supports your answer to this question.
2. List the top ten qualities that you think most men value in a woman. List the top ten qualities that you think most women value in a man. Compare your two lists and write a journal entry about the differences between these two lists.

I have shown how democracy destroys or modifies the different inequalities that originate in society; but is this all, or does it not ultimately affect that great inequality of man and woman which has seemed, up to the present day, to be eternally based in human nature? I believe that the social changes that bring nearer to the same level the father and son, the master and servant, and, in general, superiors and inferiors will raise woman and make her more and more the equal of man. But here, more than ever, I feel the necessity of making myself clearly understood; for there is no subject on which the coarse and lawless fancies of our age have taken a freer range.

There are people in Europe who, confounding together the different characteristics of the sexes, would make man and woman into beings not only equal but alike. They would give to both the same functions, impose on both the same duties, and grant to both the same rights; they would mix them in all things — their occupations, their pleasures, their business. It may readily be conceived that by thus attempting to make one sex equal to the other, both are degraded, and from so preposterous a medley of the works of nature nothing could ever result but weak men and disorderly women.

It is not thus that the Americans understand that species of democratic equality which may be established between the sexes. They admit that as nature has appointed such wide differences between the physical and moral constitution of man and woman, her manifest design was to give a distinct employment to their various faculties; and they hold that improvement does not consist in making beings so dissimilar do pretty nearly the same things, but in causing each of them to fulfill their respective tasks in the best possible manner. The Americans have applied to the sexes the great principle of political economy which governs the manufacturers of our age, by carefully dividing the duties of man from those of woman in order that the great work of society may be the better carried on.

In no country has such constant care been taken as in America to trace two clearly distinct lines of action for the two sexes and to make them keep pace one with the other, but in two pathways that are always different. American women never manage the outward concerns of the family or conduct a business or take a part in political life; nor are they, on the other hand, ever compelled to perform the rough labor of the fields or to make any of those laborious efforts which demand the exertion of physical strength. No families are so poor as to form an exception to this rule. If, on the one hand, an American woman cannot escape from the quiet circle of domestic employments, she is never forced, on the other, to go beyond it. Hence it is that the women of America, who often exhibit a masculine strength of understanding and a manly energy, generally preserve great delicacy of personal appearance and always retain the manners of women although they sometimes show that they have the hearts and minds of men.

Nor have the Americans ever supposed that one consequence of democratic principles is the subversion of marital power or the confusion of the natural authorities in families. They hold that every association must have a head in order to accomplish its object, and that the natural head of the conjugal association is man. They do not therefore deny him the right of directing his partner, and they maintain that in the smaller association of husband and wife as well as in the great social community the object of democracy is to regulate and legalize the powers that are necessary, and not to subvert all power.

This opinion is not peculiar to one sex and contested by the other; I never observed that the women of America consider conjugal authority as a fortunate usurpation of their rights, or that they thought themselves degraded by submitting to it. It appeared to me, on the contrary, that they attach a sort of pride to the voluntary surrender of their own will and make it their boast to bend themselves to the yoke, not to shake it off. Such, at least, is the feeling expressed by the most virtuous of their sex; the others are silent; and in the United States it is not the practice for a guilty wife to clamor for the rights of women while she is trampling on her own holiest duties.

It has often been remarked that in Europe a certain degree of contempt lurks even in the flattery which men lavish upon women; although a European frequently affects to be the slave of woman, it may be seen that he never sincerely thinks her his equal. In the United States men seldom compliment women, but they daily show how much they esteem them. They constantly display an entire confidence in the understanding of a wife and a profound respect for her freedom; they have decided that her mind is just as fitted as that of a man to discover the plain truth, and her heart as firm to embrace it; and they have never sought to place her virtue, any more than his, under the shelter of prejudice, ignorance, and fear.

It would seem in Europe, where man so easily submits to the despotic sway of women, that they are nevertheless deprived of some of the greatest attributes of the human species and considered as seductive but imperfect beings; and (what may well provoke astonishment) women ultimately look upon themselves in the same light and almost consider it as a privilege that they are entitled to show themselves futile, feeble, and timid. The women of America claim no such privileges.

Again, it may be said that in our morals we have reserved strange immunities to man, so that there is, as it were, one virtue for his use and another for the guidance of his partner, and that, according to the opinion of the public, the very same act may be punished alternately as a crime or only as a fault. The Americans do not know this iniquitous division of duties and rights; among them the seducer is as much dishonored as his victim.

It is true that the Americans rarely lavish upon women those eager   10 attentions which are commonly paid them in Europe, but their conduct to women always implies that they suppose them to be virtuous and refined; and such is the respect entertained for the moral freedom of the sex that in the presence of a woman the most guarded language is used lest her ear should be offended by an expression. In America a young unmarried woman may alone and without fear undertake a long journey.

The legislators of the United States, who have mitigated almost all the penalties of criminal law, still make rape a capital offense, and no crime is visited with more inexorable severity by public opinion. This may be accounted for; as the Americans can conceive nothing more precious than a woman's honor and nothing which ought so much to be respected as her independence, they hold that no punishment is too severe for the man who deprives her of them against her will. In France, where the same offense is visited with far milder penalties, it is frequently difficult to get a verdict from a jury against the prisoner. Is this a consequence of contempt of decency or contempt of women? I cannot but believe that it is a contempt of both.

Thus the Americans do not think that man and woman have either the duty or the right to perform the same offices, but they show an equal regard for both their respective parts; and though their lot is different, they consider both of them as beings of equal value. They do not give to the courage of woman the same form or the same direction as to that of man, but they never doubt her courage; and if they hold that man and his partner ought not always to exercise their intellect and understanding in the same manner, they at least believe the understanding of the one to be as sound as that of the other, and her intellect to be as clear. Thus, then, while they have allowed the social inferiority of woman to continue, they have done all they could to raise her morally and intellectually to the level of man; and in this respect they appear to me to have excellently understood the true principle of democratic improvement.

As for myself, I do not hesitate to avow that although the women of the United States are confined within the narrow circle of domestic life, and their situation is in some respects one of extreme dependence, I have nowhere seen woman occupying a loftier position; and if I were asked, now that I am drawing to the close of this work, in which I have spoken of so many important things done by the Americans, to what the singular prosperity and growing strength of that people ought mainly to be attributed, I should reply: To the superiority of their women.

Suggestions for Writing and Discussion

1. In your own words, describe Alexis de Tocqueville's impression of American women in the nineteenth century. What does he observe as the woman's role in marriage at this time in American history?
2. Compare de Tocqueville's impression of American women living in a democracy with their counterparts in Europe. What are the greatest distinctions between these two groups of women and the relationships between the sexes in America and abroad, as he describes them?
3. On the issue of sexual indiscretions, de Tocqueville claims that men and women are seen as being equally at fault. Similarly, on the issue of rape, he claims that "no punishment is too severe for the man who deprives her of [honor and independence] against her will." Accepting these tenets as truth, are these same standards upheld in today's American society? Support your answer with specific examples or evidence.
4. De Tocqueville writes that "the object of democracy is to regulate and legalize the powers that are necessary, and not to subvert all power." Thus, he says, women in America consider their subservient wifely duties as a privilege, which they view as doing their part to help America as a whole. Argue for or against the concept that one sex should play a particular role primarily for the good of a country.
5. In this piece, nineteenth-century American women are seen as extremely dependent on men, and yet, de Tocqueville claims, women occupy "a loftier position." To whom might de Tocqueville be comparing American women, and further, how might he define this "loftier position"?
6. De Tocqueville was a French historian who believed that democracy would eventually sweep most countries of the world. In this piece, what does he see as the strengths and weaknesses for men and women living under such a form of government?

Suggestions for Extended Thinking and Research

1. Read one of de Tocqueville's famous works, *Democracy in America* or *The*

Old Regime and the Revolution. Write an essay in which you explore, explain, and evaluate one or more of the author's basic philosophical beliefs.

2. Choose three different observations that de Tocqueville makes in this piece, and compare them with present-day observations. What has changed over the past 160 years? Come to some conclusion: Are men and women better off today? Is American society better off today?

BRENT STAPLES

Just Walk on By: A Black Man Ponders His Power to Alter Public Space

> *Educated at Widener University and the University of Chicago, where he earned a doctorate in psychology in 1982, Brent Staples is a journalist who has served on the editorial board of the* New York Times *since 1990. A prolific writer, he has been published in such magazines and journals as* Down Beat, Harper's, New York Woman, *and the* New York Times Magazine. *"Just Walk on By" was first published in* Ms. *magazine in 1986.*

Prereading/Journal-Writing Suggestions

1. To people who don't know you, in what ways is your personal appearance misleading about the person deep inside, the person who you really are?
2. Write about a time in which your initial impression of someone else was wrong. On what facts did you make your initial judgment? What caused you to change your mind? What, if anything, did you learn from this event?
3. If you are walking all alone at night and a black man in jeans and a beard is following close behind you, what thoughts might go through your head? If you are alone at night and a black man in a conservative suit is walking behind you, do you have the same thoughts? What if each of these men were white? What if each were a black woman (minus the beard, of course)? A white woman? Explain the differences and similarities in the responses you describe.

My first victim was a woman — white, well dressed, probably in her early twenties. I came upon her late one evening on a deserted street in Hyde Park, a relatively affluent neighborhood in an otherwise mean, impoverished section of Chicago. As I swung onto the avenue behind her, there seemed to be a discreet, uninflammatory distance between us. Not so. She cast back a worried glance. To her, the youngish black man — a broad six feet two inches with a beard and billowing hair, both hands shoved into the pockets of a bulky military jacket — seemed menacingly close. After a few more quick glimpses, she picked up her pace and was soon running in earnest. Within seconds she disappeared into a cross street.

That was more than a decade ago. I was twenty-two years old, a graduate student newly arrived at the University of Chicago. It was in the echo of that terrified woman's footfalls that I first began to know the unwieldy inheritance I'd come into — the ability to alter public space in ugly ways. It was clear that she thought herself the quarry of a mugger, a rapist, or worse.

Suffering a bout of insomnia, however, I was stalking sleep, not defenseless wayfarers. As a softy who is scarcely able to take a knife to a raw chicken — let alone hold it to a person's throat — I was surprised, embarrassed, and dismayed all at once. Her flight made me feel like an accomplice in tyranny. It also made it clear that I was indistinguishable from the muggers who occasionally seeped into the area from the surrounding ghetto. That first encounter, and those that followed, signified that a vast, unnerving gulf lay between nighttime pedestrians — particularly women — and me. And I soon gathered that being perceived as dangerous is a hazard in itself. I only needed to turn a corner into a dicey situation, or crowd some frightened, armed person in a foyer somewhere, or make an errant move after being pulled over by a policeman. Where fear and weapons meet — and they often do in urban America — there is always the possibility of death.

In that first year, my first away from my hometown, I was to become thoroughly familiar with the language of fear. At dark, shadowy intersections in Chicago, I could cross in front of a car stopped at a traffic light and elicit the *thunk, thunk, thunk, thunk* of the driver — black, white, male, or female — hammering down the door locks. On less traveled streets after dark, I grew accustomed to but never comfortable with people who crossed to the other side of the street rather than pass me. Then there were the standard unpleasantries with police, doormen, bouncers, cabdrivers, and others whose business is to screen out troublesome individuals *before* there is any nastiness.

I moved to New York nearly two years ago and I have remained an avid night walker. In central Manhattan, the near-constant crowd cover minimizes tense one-on-one street encounters. Elsewhere — visiting friends in SoHo, where sidewalks are narrow and tightly spaced buildings shut out the sky — things can get very taut indeed.

Black men have a firm place in New York mugging literature. Norman 5 Podhoretz in his famed (or infamous) 1963 essay, "My Negro Problem — And Ours," recalls growing up in terror of black males; they "were tougher than we were, more ruthless," he writes — and as an adult on the Upper West Side of Manhattan, he continues, he cannot constrain his nervousness when he meets black men on certain streets. Similarly, a decade later, the essayist and novelist Edward Hoagland extols a New York where once "Negro bitterness bore down mainly on other Negroes." Where some see mere panhandlers, Hoagland sees "a mugger who is clearly screwing up his nerve to do more than just *ask* for money." But Hoagland has "the New Yorker's quick-hunch posture for broken-field maneuvering," and the bad guy swerves away.

I often witness that "hunch posture," from women after dark on the warrenlike streets of Brooklyn where I live. They seem to set their faces on neutral and, with their purse straps strung across their chests bandolier style, they forge ahead as though bracing themselves against being tackled. I understand, of course, that the danger they perceive is not a hallucination. Women are particularly vulnerable to street violence, and young black males are drastically overrepresented among the perpetrators of that violence. Yet these truths are no solace against the kind of alienation that comes of being ever the suspect, against being set apart, a fearsome entity with whom pedestrians avoid making eye contact.

It is not altogether clear to me how I reached the ripe old age of twenty-two without being conscious of the lethality nighttime pedestrians attributed to me. Perhaps it was because in Chester, Pennsylvania, the small, angry industrial town where I came of age in the 1960s, I was scarcely noticeable against a backdrop of gang warfare, street knifings, and murders. I grew up one of the good boys, had perhaps a half-dozen fistfights. In retrospect, my shyness of combat has clear sources.

Many things go into the making of a young thug. One of those things is the consummation of the male romance with the power to intimidate. An infant discovers that random flailings send the baby bottle flying out of the crib and crashing to the floor. Delighted, the joyful babe repeats those motions again and again, seeking to duplicate the feat. Just so, I recall the points at which some of my boyhood friends were finally seduced by the perception of themselves as tough guys. When a mark cowered and surrendered his money without resistance, myth and reality merged — and paid off. It is, after all, only manly to embrace the power to frighten and intimidate. We, as men, are not supposed to give an inch of our lane on the highway; we are to seize the fighter's edge in work and in play and even in love; we are to be valiant in the face of hostile forces.

Unfortunately, poor and powerless young men seem to take all this nonsense literally. As a boy, I saw countless tough guys locked away; I have since buried several, too. They were babies, really — a teenage cousin, a brother of twenty-two, a childhood friend in his midtwenties — all gone down in episodes of bravado played out in the streets. I came to doubt the virtues of intimidation early on. I chose, perhaps even unconsciously, to remain a shadow — timid, but a survivor.

The fearsomeness mistakenly attributed to me in public places often has 10 a perilous flavor. The most frightening of these confusions occurred in the late 1970s and early 1980s when I worked as a journalist in Chicago. One day, rushing into the office of a magazine I was writing for with a deadline story in hand, I was mistaken for a burglar. The office manager called security and, with an ad hoc posse, pursued me through the labyrinthine halls, nearly to my editor's door. I had no way of proving who I was. I could only move briskly toward the company of someone who knew me.

Another time I was on assignment for a local paper and killing time before an interview. I entered a jewelry store on the city's affluent Near North Side. The proprietor excused herself and returned with an enormous red Doberman pinscher straining at the end of a leash. She stood, the dog extended toward me, silent to my questions, her eyes bulging nearly out of her head. I took a cursory look around, nodded, and bade her good night. Relatively speaking, however, I never fared as badly as another black male journalist. He went to nearby Waukegan, Illinois, a couple of summers ago to work on a story about a murderer who was born there. Mistaking the reporter for the killer, police hauled him from his car at gunpoint and but for his press credentials would probably have tried to book him. Such episodes are not uncommon. Black men trade tales like this all the time.

In "My Negro Problem — And Ours," Podhoretz writes that the hatred he feels for blacks makes itself known to him through a variety of avenues — one being his discomfort with that "special brand of paranoid touchiness" to which he says blacks are prone. No doubt he is speaking here of black men. In time, I learned to smother the rage I felt at so often being taken for a criminal. Not to do so would surely have led to madness — via that special "paranoid touchiness" that so annoyed Podhoretz at the time he wrote the essay.

I began to take precautions to make myself less threatening. I move about with care, particularly late in the evening. I give a wide berth to nervous people on subway platforms during the wee hours, particularly when I have exchanged business clothes for jeans. If I happen to be entering a building behind some people who appear skittish, I may walk by, letting them clear the lobby before I return, so as not to seem to be following them. I have been calm and extremely congenial on those rare occasions when I've been pulled over by the police.

And on late-evening constitutionals along streets less traveled by, I employ what has proved to be an excellent tension-reducing measure: I whistle melodies from Beethoven and Vivaldi and the more popular classical composers. Even steely New Yorkers hunching toward nighttime destinations seem to relax, and occasionally they even join in the tune. Virtually everybody seems to sense that a mugger wouldn't be warbling bright, sunny selections from Vivaldi's *Four Seasons*. It is my equivalent of the cowbell that hikers wear when they know they are in bear country.

Suggestions for Writing and Discussion

1. In his opening paragraph, Staples describes a woman who was so nervous because a black man was walking behind her that she took off running. Do you think her reaction is a common one? Is it justified? Explain your answers.
2. Why, at the age of twenty-two, is Staples, a black man, surprised at the reaction that people have toward him on his nightly walks? Besides the reaction of surprise, what other feelings might he have when people avoid him or hurry away from him, simply because he is a black man?
3. In paragraph 5, Staples cites two pieces of literature that convey the image of black man as mugger. When people fear someone because he is a black male, where does their concept of "black as dangerous" come from?
4. Staples admits that women are "particularly vulnerable to street violence, and young black males are drastically overrepresented among the perpetrators of that violence." So what is his point in this essay? Does he seek to

place blame or analyze causes? Or does he have another purpose for writing?

5. According to Staples, in what ways do the concepts of being male and having power connect? Do you agree with his point that men are supposed to be tough?

6. Briefly summarize Staples's solution to walking at night without intimidating other pedestrians. Explain why this tactic apparently works to ease a stranger's fear. What does this solution say about Staples himself? Consider, for example, the implications in Staples's final comparison between the purpose of his whistling on his nightly walks and the purpose of hikers' cowbells.

Suggestions for Extended Thinking and Research

1. Watch prime-time television for several weeks. Notice how many shows and commercials include black male characters, and note the types of roles these characters play. From your observations, what categories do these characters fall into? Are any of the roles stereotypes? Are any of the characters "real" people? Come to some conclusion about how black men are portrayed on television.

2. Staples explains why he did not get pulled into the life of a street mugger. Research the reasons why many youths today join street gangs. By using a variety of reliable sources (concentrate on interviews and current journal articles), come to some conclusions about why a young person today might be drawn to a life of crime and violence.

ALICE WALKER

The Right to Life: What Can the White Man Say to the Black Woman?

> *Best known for her works of fiction (see, for example, "Everyday Use," pp. 337–344), Alice Walker has also been active for many years in civil rights actions. During her time at Spelman College in Georgia, she worked for the voter registration movement; later, she became involved in welfare rights issues in Mississippi and New York. This selection appears in Walker's anthology* Her Blue Body Everything We Know; *it originated as a speech she made at a prochoice rally in Washington, D.C., on April 8, 1989.*

Prereading/Journal-Writing Suggestions

1. Write about a significant event in your life when you felt you had little or no control. How did you react in this situation? Were you completely helpless? Did you have anyone else who was in this same situation with you? What happened in the end?
2. A sense of injustice is fine fuel for journal writing. Write about a time in your life when you were either a witness to or a victim of injustice.

> *What is of use in these words I offer in memory and recognition of our common mother. And to my daughter.*

What can the white man say to the black woman?

For four hundred years he ruled over the black woman's womb.

Let us be clear. In the barracoons and along the slave shipping coasts of Africa, for more than twenty generations, it was he who dashed our babies' brains out against the rocks.

What can the white man say to the black woman?   5

For four hundred years he determined which black woman's children would live or die.

Let it be remembered. It was he who placed our children on the auction block in cities all across the Eastern half of what is now the United States, and listened to and watched them beg for their mothers' arms, before being sold to the highest bidder and dragged away.

What can the white man say to the black woman?

We remember that Fannie Lou Hamer, a poor sharecropper on a Mississippi plantation, was one of twenty-one children; and that on plantations across the South black women often had twelve, fifteen, twenty children. Like their enslaved mothers and grandmothers before them, these black women were sacrificed to the profit the white man could make from harnessing their bodies and their children's bodies to the cotton gin.

What can the white man say to the black woman?   10

We see him lined up, on Saturday nights, century after century, to make the black mother, who must sell her body to feed her children, go down on her knees to him.

Let us take note:

He has not cared for a single one of the dark children in his midst, over hundreds of years.

Where are the children of the Cherokee, my great-grandmother's people?
    Gone.   15
Where are the children of the Blackfoot?
    Gone.
Where are the children of the Lakota?
    Gone.

Of the Cheyenne?   20
Of the Chippewa?
Of the Iroquois?
Of the Sioux?
Of the Akan?
Of the Ibo?   25
Of the Ashanti?
Of the Maori and the Aborigine?[1]

Where are the children of "the slave coast" and Wounded Knee?

We do not forget the forced sterilizations and forced starvations on the reservations, here as in South Africa. Nor do we forget the smallpox-infested blankets Indian children were given by the Great White Fathers of the United States Government.

What has the white man to say to the black woman?   30

---

[1] Tribal, indigenous children destroyed during the white "settlement" of the West.

When we have children you do everything in your power to make them feel unwanted from the moment they are born. You send them to fight and kill other dark mothers' children around the world. You shove them onto public highways into the path of oncoming cars. You shove their heads through plate glass windows. You string them up and you string them out.

What has the white man to say to the black woman?

From the beginning, you have treated all dark children with absolute hatred.

30,000,000 African children died on the way to the Americas, where nothing awaited them but endless toil and the crack of a bullwhip. They died of a lack of food, of lack of movement in the holds of ships. Of lack of friends and relatives. They died of depression, bewilderment and fear.

What has the white man to say to the black woman?   35

Let us look around us: Let us look at the world the white man has made for the black woman and her children.

It is a world in which the black woman is still forced to provide cheap labor, in the form of children, for the factory farms and on the assembly lines of the white man.

It is a world into which the white man dumps every foul, person-annulling drug he smuggles into Creation.

It is a world where many of our babies die at birth, or later of malnutrition, and where many more grow up to live lives of such misery they are forced to choose death by their own hands.

What has the white man to say to the black woman, and to all women 40 and children everywhere?

Let us consider the depletion of the ozone; let us consider homelessness and the nuclear peril; let us consider the destruction of the rainforests — in the name of the almighty hamburger. Let us consider the poisoned apples and the poisoned water and the poisoned air, and the poisoned earth.

And that all of our children, because of the white man's assault on the planet, have a possibility of death by cancer in their almost immediate future.

What has the white male lawgiver to say to any of us? Those of us who love life too much to willingly bring more children into a world saturated with death.

Abortion, for many women, is more than an experience of suffering beyond anything most men will ever know, it is an act of mercy, and an act of self-defense.

To make abortion illegal, again, is to sentence millions of women and 45 children to miserable lives and even more miserable deaths.

Given his history, in relation to us, I think the white man should be ashamed to attempt to speak for the unborn children of the black woman. To force us to have children for him to ridicule, drug, turn into killers and homeless wanderers is a testament to his hypocrisy.

What can the white man say to the black woman?

Only one thing that the black woman might hear.

Yes, indeed, the white man can say, your children have the right to life. Therefore I will call back from the dead those 30,000,000 who were tossed overboard during the centuries of the slave trade. And the other millions who died in my cotton fields and hanging from my trees.

I will recall all those who died of broken hearts and broken spirits, under 50 the insult of segregation.

I will raise up all the mothers who died exhausted after birthing twenty-one children to work sunup to sundown on my plantation. I will restore to full health all those who perished for lack of food, shelter, sunlight, and love; and from my inability to recognize them as human beings.

But I will go even further:

I will tell you, black woman, that I wish to be forgiven the sins I commit daily against you and your children. For I know that until I treat your children with love, I can never be trusted by my own. Nor can I respect myself.

And I will free your children from insultingly high infant mortality rates, short life spans, horrible housing, lack of food, rampant ill health. I will liberate them from the ghetto. I will open wide the doors of all the schools and the hospitals and businesses of society to your children. I will look at your children and see, not a threat, but a joy.

I will remove myself as an obstacle in the path that your children, against 55 all odds, are making toward the light. I will not assassinate them for dreaming dreams and offering new visions of how to live. I will cease trying to lead your children, for I can see I have never understood where I was going. I will agree to sit quietly for a century or so, and meditate on this.

That is what the white man can say to the black woman.

We are listening.

Suggestions for Writing and Discussion

1. Read this piece all the way through, annotating the passages and images that strike you most strongly (obviously, individual responses to these images will differ widely and may include affirmation, horror, anger, and inspiration). What images have you chosen on this initial reading? What is your reaction to these images and to this piece in general?
2. As noted in the introduction, this piece originated as a speech at a prochoice rally in Washington, D.C., April 1989. Given the meeting, the location, and the date of events, what effect do you think this speech might have had on the audience? Explain your answer with specific reasons.
3. What, if anything, surprised you as you were reading this piece?
4. Consider Walker's choice of language and the way she organizes her information. What might be the advantages of adopting this repetitive format of raising the same question and then moving on to graphic statements? What might be the disadvantages?
5. This piece focuses primarily on white men and black women, yet many in Walker's audience saw these two groups as representative of many groups of people. What other specific groups could you place under "white men"? What other specific groups are characterized by "black women"?
6. Here is a line from this piece:

   From the beginning, you have treated all dark children with absolute hatred.

   Is this statement fair? Is it true? Why would the author choose such strong rhetoric here?
7. Comment on the effectiveness of the ending of this piece.

Suggestions for Extended Thinking and Research

1. This piece moves chronologically, from the capture of African slaves to present treatment of minorities. Choose one specific historic wrong mentioned here (slave shipping, sharecropping, cotton picking, Indian conflicts) and research in depth the conditions of this time, the white community's part in the wrong, and the immediate effects felt by the minorities.
2. Write a speech that you intend to give at either a prochoice rally or a prolife rally or at a rally dedicated to some other controversial issue. Model the organization of this piece by choosing one central question to ask throughout your speech.

JOANNA RUSS

When It Changed

Born and raised in New York City, Joanna Russ has written plays, essays, novels, and short stories, many in the fantasy–science fiction genre and most related to gender issues. Her best-known novels include The Female Man *(1975) and* The Two of Them *(1978). In addition, she is the author of a book of feminist criticism, whose title —* How to Suppress Women's Writing *— suggests the witty, ironic tone characteristic of all her writing, both fiction and nonfiction. This story first appeared in the anthology* Again, Dangerous Visions *(1972).*

Prereading/Journal-Writing Suggestion

Imagine a world in which the species is either all men or all women, and reproduction is possible due to innovative scientific discoveries. First of all, which group would have the easiest time surviving, men or women? Second, what might this homogeneous group be able to achieve that it couldn't in a heterosexual situation? Lastly, what might be the greatest problem this group would have to deal with?

Katy drives like a maniac; we must have been doing over 120 kilometers per hour on those turns. She's good, though, extremely good, and I've seen her take the whole car apart and put it together again in a day. My birthplace on Whileaway was largely given to farm machinery and I refuse to wrestle with a five-gear shift at unholy speeds, not having been brought up to it, but even on those turns in the middle of the night, on a country road as bad as only our district can make them, Katy's driving didn't scare me. The funny thing about my wife, though: she will not handle guns. She has even gone hiking in the forests above the forty-eighth parallel without firearms, for days at a time. And that *does* scare me.

Katy and I have three children between us, one of hers and two of mine. Yuriko, my eldest, was asleep in the back seat, dreaming twelve-year-old dreams of love and war: running away to sea, hunting in the North, dreams of strangely beautiful people in strangely beautiful places, all the wonderful guff you think up when you're turning twelve and the glands start going. Some day soon, like all of them, she will disappear for weeks on end to come back grimy and proud, having knifed her first cougar or shot her first bear, dragging some abominably dangerous dead beastie behind her, which I will never forgive for what it might have done to my daughter. Yuriko says Katy's driving puts her to sleep.

For someone who has fought three duels, I am afraid of far, far too much. I'm getting old. I told this to my wife.

"You're thirty-four," she said. Laconic to the point of silence, that one. She flipped the lights on, on the dash — three kilometers to go and the road getting worse all the time. Far out in the country. Electric-green trees rushed into our headlights and around the car. I reached down next to me where we bolt the carrier panel to the door and eased my rifle into my lap. Yuriko stirred in the back. My height but Katy's eyes, Katy's face. The car engine is so quiet, Katy says, that you can hear breathing in the back seat. Yuki had been alone in the car when the message came, enthusiastically decoding her dot-dashes (silly to mount a wide-frequency transceiver near an I.C. engine, but most of Whileaway is on steam). She had thrown herself out of the car, my gangly and gaudy offspring, shouting at the top of her lungs, so of course she had had to come along. We've been intellectually prepared for this ever since the Colony was founded, ever since it was abandoned, but this is different. This is awful.

"Men!" Yuki had screamed, leaping over the car door. "They've come   5 back! Real Earth men!"

We met them in the kitchen of the farmhouse near the place where they had landed; the windows were open, the night air very mild. We had passed all sorts of transportation when we parked outside — steam tractors, trucks, an I.C. flatbed, even a bicycle. Lydia, the district biologist, had come out of her Northern taciturnity long enough to take blood and urine samples and was sitting in a corner of the kitchen shaking her head in astonishment over the results; she even forced herself (very big, very fair, very shy, always painfully blushing) to dig up the old language manuals — though I can talk the old tongues in my sleep. And do. Lydia is uneasy with us; we're Southerners and too flamboyant. I counted twenty people in that kitchen, all the brains of North Continent. Phyllis Spet, I think, had come in by glider. Yuki was the only child there.

Then I saw the four of them.

They are bigger than we are. They are bigger and broader. Two were taller than I, and I am extremely tall, one meter eighty centimeters in my bare feet. They are obviously of our species but *off*, indescribably off, and as my eyes could not and still cannot quite comprehend the lines of those alien bodies, I could not, then, bring myself to touch them, though the one who spoke Russian — what voices they have — wanted to "shake hands," a custom from the past, I imagine. I can only say they were apes with human faces. He seemed to mean well, but I found myself shuddering back almost the length of the kitchen — and then I laughed apologetically — and then to set a good example (*interstellar amity,* I thought) did "shake hands" finally. A hard, hard hand. They are heavy as draft horses. Blurred, deep voices. Yuriko had sneaked in between the adults and was gazing at *the men* with her mouth open.

He turned *his* head — those words have not been in our language for six hundred years — and said, in bad Russian:

"Who's that?"   10

"My daughter," I said, and added (with that irrational attention to good manners we sometimes employ in moments of insanity), "My daughter, Yuriko Janeston. We use the patronymic. You would say matronymic."

He laughed, involuntarily. Yuki exclaimed, "I thought they would be *good-looking!*" greatly disappointed at this reception of herself. Phyllis Helgason Spet, whom someday I shall kill, gave me across the room a cold, level venomous look, as if to say: *Watch what you say. You know what I can do.* It's true that I have little formal status, but Madam President will get herself in serious trouble with both me and her own staff if she continues to consider industrial espionage good clean fun. Wars and rumors of wars, as it says in one of our ancestors' books. I translated Yuki's words into *the man's* dog-Russian, once our *lingua franca,* and *the man* laughed again.

"Where are all your people?" he said conversationally.

I translated again and watched the faces around the room; Lydia embarrassed (as usual), Spet narrowing her eyes with some damned scheme, Katy very pale.

"This is Whileaway," I said.   15

He continued to look unenlightened.

"Whileaway," I said. "Do you remember? Do you have records? There was a plague on Whileaway."

He looked moderately interested. Heads turned in the back of the room, and I caught a glimpse of the local professions-parliament delegate; by morning every town meeting, every district caucus, would be in full session.

"Plague?" he said. "That's most unfortunate."

"Yes," I said. "Most unfortunate. We lost half our population in one 20 generation."

He looked properly impressed.

"Whileaway was lucky," I said. "We had a big initial gene pool, we had been chosen for extreme intelligence, we had a high technology and a large remaining population in which every adult was two-or-three experts in one. The soil is good. The climate is blessedly easy. There are thirty millions of us now. Things are beginning to snowball in industry — do you understand? — give us seventy years and we'll have more than one real city, more than a few industrial centers, full-time professions, full-time radio operators, full-time machinists, give us seventy years and not everyone will have to spend three-quarters of a lifetime on the farm." And I tried to explain how hard it is when artists can practice full-time only in old age, when there are so few, so very few who can be free, like Katy and myself. I tried also to outline our government, the two houses, the one by professions and the geographic one; I told him the district caucuses handled problems too big for the individual towns. And that population control was not a political issue, not yet, though give us time and it would be. This was a delicate point in our history; give us time. There was no need to sacrifice the quality of life for an insane rush into industrialization. Let us go our own pace. Give us time.

"Where are all the people?" said that monomaniac.

I realized then that he did not mean people, he meant *men,* and he was giving the word the meaning it had not had on Whileaway for six centuries.

"They died," I said. "Thirty generations ago."

25

I thought we had poleaxed him. He caught his breath. He made as if to get out of the chair he was sitting in; he put his hand to his chest; he looked around at us with the strangest blend of awe and sentimental tenderness. Then he said, solemnly and earnestly:

"A great tragedy."

I waited, not quite understanding.

"Yes," he said, catching his breath again with that queer smile, that adult-to-child smile that tells you something is being hidden and will be presently produced with cries of encouragement and joy, "a great tragedy. But it's over." And again he looked around at all of us with the strangest deference. As if we were invalids.

"You've adapted amazingly," he said.

30

"To what?" I said. He looked embarrassed. He looked inane. Finally he said, "Where I come from, the women don't dress so plainly."

"Like you?" I said. "Like a bride?" for the men were wearing silver from head to foot. I had never seen anything so gaudy. He made as if to answer and then apparently thought better of it; he laughed at me again. With an odd exhilaration — as if we were something childish and something wonderful, as if he were doing us an enormous favor — he took one shaky breath and said, "Well, we're here."

I looked at Spet, Spet looked at Lydia, Lydia looked at Amalia, who is the head of the local town meeting, Amalia looked at I don't know whom. My throat was raw. I cannot stand local beer, which the farmers swill as if their stomachs had iridium linings but I took it anyway, from Amalia (it was her bicycle we had seen outside as we parked), and swallowed it all. This was going to take a long time. I said, "Yes, here you are," and smiled (feeling like a fool), and wondered seriously if male-Earth-people's minds worked so very differently from female-Earth-people's minds, but that couldn't be so or the race would have died out long ago. The radio network had got the news around planet by now and we had another Russian speaker, flown in from Varna; I decided to cut out when *the man* passed around pictures of his wife, who looked like the priestess of some arcane cult. He proposed to question Yuki, so I barreled her into a back room in spite of her furious protests, and went out on the front porch. As I left, Lydia was explaining the difference between parthenogenesis (which is so easy that anyone can practice it) and what we do, which is the merging of ova. That is why Katy's baby looks like me. Lydia went on to the Ansky Process and Katy Ansky, our one full-polymath genius and the great-great- I don't know how many times great-grandmother of my own Katharina.

A dot-dash transmitter in one of the outbuildings chattered faintly to itself: operators flirting and passing jokes down the line.

There was a man on the porch. The other tall man. I watched him for a 35

few minutes—I can move very quietly when I want to—and when I allowed
him to see me, he stopped talking into the little machine hung around his
neck. Then he said calmly, in excellent Russian, "Did you know that sexual
equality has been reestablished on Earth?"

"You're the real one," I said, "aren't you? The other one's for show." It
was a great relief to get things cleared up. He nodded affably.

"As a people, we are not very bright," he said. "There's been too much
genetic damage in the last few centuries. Radiation. Drugs. We can use Whileaway's genes, Janet." Strangers do not call strangers by the first name.

"You can have cells enough to drown in," I said. "Breed your own."

He smiled. "That's not the way we want to do it." Behind him I saw
Katy come into the square of light that was the screened-in door. He went on,
low and urbane, not mocking me, I think, but with the self-confidence of
someone who has always had money and strength to spare, who doesn't know
what it is to be second-class or provincial. Which is very odd, because the day
before, I would have said that was an exact description of me.

"I'm talking to you, Janet," he said, "because I suspect you have more 40
popular influence than anyone else here. You know as well as I do that par-
thenogenetic culture has all sorts of inherent defects, and we do not—if we
can help it—mean to use you for anything of the sort. Pardon me; I should
not have said 'use.' But surely you can see that this kind of society is
unnatural."

"Humanity is unnatural," said Katy. She had my rifle under her left
arm. The top of that silky head does not quite come up to my collarbone, but
she is as tough as steel; he began to move, again with that queer smiling
deference (which his fellow had showed to me but he had not), and the gun
slid into Katy's grip as if she had shot with it all her life.

"I agree," said the man. "Humanity is unnatural. I should know. I have
metal in my teeth and metal pins here." He touched his shoulder. "Seals are
harem animals," he added, "and so are men; apes are promiscuous and so are
men; doves are monogamous and so are men; there are even celibate men and
homosexual men. There are homosexual cows, I believe. But Whileaway is
still missing something." He gave a dry chuckle. I will give him the credit of
believing that it had something to do with nerves.

"I miss nothing," said Katy, "except that life isn't endless."

"You are—?" said the man, nodding from me to her.

"Wives," said Katy. "We're married." Again the dry chuckle. 45

"A good economic arrangement," he said, "for working and taking care
of the children. And as good an arrangement as any for randomizing heredity,
if your reproduction is made to follow the same pattern. But think, Katharina
Michaelason, if there isn't something better that you might secure for your
daughters. I believe in instincts, even in Man, and I can't think that the two of
you—a machinist, are you? and I gather you are some sort of chief of police—
don't feel somehow what even you must miss. You know it intellectually, of
course. There is only half a species here. Men must come back to Whileaway."

Katy said nothing.

"I should think, Katharina Michaelason," said the man gently "that you, of all people, would benefit most from such a change," and he walked past Katy's rifle into the square of light coming from the door. I think it was then that he noticed my scar, which really does not show unless the light is from the side: a fine line that runs from temple to chin. Most people don't even know about it.

"Where did you get that?" he said, and I answered with an involuntary grin. "In my last duel." We stood there bristling at each other for several seconds (this is absurd but true) until he went inside and shut the screen door behind him. Katy said in a brittle voice, "You damned fool, don't you know when we've been insulted?" and swung up the rifle to shoot him through the screen, but I got to her before she could fire and knocked the rifle out of aim; it burned a hole through the porch floor. Katy was shaking. She kept whispering over and over, "That's why I never touched it, because I knew I'd kill someone. I knew I'd kill someone." The first man — the one I'd spoken with first — was still talking inside the house, something about the grand movement to recolonize and rediscover all that Earth had lost. He stressed the advantages to Whileaway: trade, exchange of ideas, education. He, too, said that sexual equality had been reestablished on Earth.

Katy was right, of course; we should have burned them down where 50 they stood. Men are coming to Whileaway. When one culture has the big guns and the other has none, there is a certain predictability about the outcome. Maybe men would have come eventually in any case, I like to think that a hundred years from now my great-grandchildren could have stood them off or fought them to a standstill, but even that's no odds; I will remember all my life those four people I first met who were muscled like bulls and who made me — if only for a moment — feel small. A neurotic reaction, Katy says. I remember everything that happened that night; I remember Yuki's excitement in the car, I remember Katy's sobbing when we got home as if her heart would break, I remember her lovemaking, a little peremptory as always, but wonderfully soothing and comforting. I remember prowling restlessly around the house after Katy fell asleep with one bare arm flung into a patch of light from the hall. The muscles of her forearms are like metal bars from all that driving and testing of her machines. Sometimes I dream about Katy's arms. I remember wandering into the nursery and picking up my wife's baby, dozing for a while with the poignant, amazing warmth of an infant in my lap, and finally returning to the kitchen to find Yuriko fixing herself a late snack. My daughter eats like a Great Dane.

"Yuki," I said, "do you think you could fall in love with a man?" and she whooped derisively. "With a ten-foot toad!" said my tactful child.

But men are coming to Whileaway. Lately I sit up nights and worry about the men who will come to this planet, about my two daughters and Betta Katharinason, about what will happen to Katy, to me, to my life. Our ancestors' journals are one long cry of pain and I suppose I ought to be glad now, but one can't throw away six centuries, or even (as I have lately discovered) thirty-four years. Sometimes I laugh at the question those four men hedged about all evening and never quite dared to ask, looking at the lot of us, hicks in overalls, farmers in canvas pants and plain shirts: *Which of you plays the role of the man?* As if we had to produce a carbon copy of their mistakes! I doubt very much that sexual equality has been reestablished on Earth. I do not like to think of myself mocked, of Katy deferred to as if she were weak, of Yuki made to feel unimportant or silly, of my other children cheated of their full humanity or turned into strangers. And I'm afraid that my own achievements will dwindle from what they were — or what I thought they were — to the not-very-interesting curiosa of the human race, the oddities you read about in the back of the book, things to laugh at sometimes because they are so exotic, quaint but not impressive, charming but not useful. I find this more painful than I can say. You will agree that for a woman who has fought three duels, all of them kills, indulging in such fears is ludicrous. But what's around the corner now is a duel so big that I don't think I have the guts for it; in Faust's words: *Verweile doch, du bist so schoen!* Keep it as it is. Don't change.

Sometimes at night I remember the original name of this planet, changed by the first generation of our ancestors, those curious women for whom, I suppose, the real name was too painful a reminder after the men died. I find it amusing, in a grim way, to see it all so completely turned around. This, too, shall pass. All good things must come to an end.

Take my life but don't take away the meaning of my life.

For-A-While.   55

Suggestions for Writing and Discussion

1. What could be the different meanings of *it* in the title of this piece?
2. Compare the relationship that Katy and the speaker, Janet, have with a typical man–woman marriage relationship with which you are familiar.
3. Examine the various reactions that the women have to the appearance of the four men. Which of these reactions do you feel are similar to those women might have today if men they do not know should unexpectedly arrive at an all-female meeting? Which reactions do you see as different?
4. Examine the reactions of the second man to the women in Whileaway. What do you think motivates his responses? Explain.
5. When the women try to explain how self-sufficient their lives are, the alien man says, "Whileaway is still missing something." Besides the actual presence of men, what is Whileaway missing?
6. Analyze and evaluate the statement that in Katy and Janet's marriage, the man can't tell "which one plays the role of the man."

Suggestions for Extended Thinking and Research

1. Review a movie, book, or television show in which women assume the heroic, central role. How realistic are these roles, and what are the central messages in this piece?

2. Choose one of the following creative approaches to this story.
   - Assume that this short story is really only the first chapter in Russ's book. Write the final chapter.
   - Rewrite this story from the four men's point of view.
   - Write your own version of this story, showing a Whileaway that has been occupied for 600 years by men only, and where the aliens who appear are four women.

3. Write an essay in which you analyze the relationships between men and women as presented by several sources in this section. Feel free to synthesize your own personal knowledge on this topic into the essay as well.

4. Which sex really has the upper hand in America today? Write an essay in which you argue effectively for either the men or the women.

5. In what ways does a black man's life differ from a white man's life? Write an essay in which you compare these two groups and draw some conclusions about what traits these men share, as well as what, if anything, keeps them distinct and apart.

6. In what ways do you see white women's lives in the United States as different from the lives of minority women? Write an essay in which you analyze these two groups in order to find the similarities and the differences among women according to their culture.

7. "Am I really my brother's or sister's keeper?" Write an essay in which you explore whether or not each human has a moral responsibility to aid fellow humans. Explore your own philosophy on this question and refer as well to several sources in this section.

8. Write a possible solution to one of the social problems mentioned in this section. First, set the scope of the problem, and explore several possibilities. Then settle on what you feel may be the best solution.

9. Working as a group with several other students in your class, design a questionnaire that raises questions about how men view women on your college campus or how women view men. Distribute the questionnaire among faculty, staff, and students. After studying the data you gather, write an essay in which you draw conclusions from the information you received and from the discussions with your group about these data. Do your conclusions coincide or contradict any of the writers in this section?

10. Compare the power that men have with the power that women possess. Are these two groups equally "strong," or does one group have an advantage over the other? Make sure you document your findings with sources from this section and any outside sources you wish to consult.

11. Write a dialogue between the speaker in "The Right to Life" and author Peter Filene. How might Filene answer the speaker's questions, and what might her reactions be?

12. You have the choice of being born a white man, a black man, a Native American man, a white woman, a black woman, or a Native American woman. From the opinions and facts offered in this section, make a decision. Support your answer not from a personal standpoint but from the standpoint that you are "unborn" and have only these sources to guide you.

13. Working with a group of your fellow students, interview professional women to discover how the feminist movement has affected their career, their roles, and the quality of their lives. Interview professional men for the same purpose. Then write a report explaining and evaluating your findings. Do these findings contradict or confirm the beliefs of any author in this section? Do they contradict or confirm your own?

4

Writing to Persuade

In Section 2, the selections tell stories and offer descriptions that re-create for the reader people, events, and emotions important to the writers' lives. The selections in Section 3 include descriptions and stories yet aim primarily to explain ideas, processes, or concepts. In Section 4, the readings describe, tell stories, and explain; but the main goal of each selection is to persuade readers to see a particular point of view as important and valid.

In the first thematic section, "Rights and Responsibilities," each piece offers a persuasive argument related to the laws, privileges, obligations, and moral principles on which we base our lives. Elizabeth Cady Stanton provides a historical perspective in her 1892 speech "The Solitude of Self," which demands that women be regarded as self-reliant and fully capable of taking responsibility for their own lives. In "Equal Opportunity, Not Equal Results," William Bradford Reynolds argues that affirmative action programs create more problems than they solve. In contrast, Jesse Jackson urges readers to consider instead "Why Blacks Need Affirmative Action." Judith Jarvis Thompson offers "A Defense of Abortion," but Greg Keath calls for a different point of view in "Abortion Is Not a Civil Right." Andrew Sullivan raises the provocative question of legalizing marriages for gay couples in "Here Comes the Groom." Leonard Kriegel, in "A Loaded Question," makes a moving plea for gun control. Finally, in "Multiculturalism: E Pluribus Plures," Diane Ravitch urges a broad perspective for multicultural education.

The second theme addresses "Questions of Language." Arguments in this section relate to the way we judge and react to speech patterns that are the same as or different from our own. Angelo Gonzalez claims that bilingual education is "The Key to Basic Skills," while Richard Rodriguez counters that educating children in two languages is "Outdated and Unrealistic." In "Four-Letter Words Can Hurt You," Barbara Lawrence asks readers to see that the four-letter words many people use without thinking are, in fact, "implicitly sadistic" and "degrading to women." Peter Farb, in "Linguistic Chauvinism," argues that black English should be recognized as a separate language and should be studied and preserved to ensure linguistic diversity. But Rachel Jones, in "What's Wrong with Black English," asserts that speaking a "dialect" excludes people "from full participation in the world we live in." In "A Question of Language," Gloria Naylor offers examples to convince her audience that the ugliest racial epithet can be turned into a powerful word of praise, depending on the context in which it is used. Robin Lakoff, in "Talking Like a Lady," argues that many language choices made by English speakers are related to their gender and to the strikingly different ways she believes young girls and young boys are taught to speak.

The section "Crossing Borders" provides persuasive writing related to issues that arise when citizens of the United States encounter the cultures of other nations. Alice Bloom's "On a Greek Holiday" argues that it is extremely difficult to discover the complexity of another country while visiting as a tourist. In "Pornography Here and Abroad," Aryeh Neier maintains that the absence of pornography in many repressive and violent countries suggests that pornography may not be causally related to hostility toward women. Martin Esslin's article, "Beyond the Wasteland," asks American television viewers to take a careful look at what might be learned from British public television programming. The United States war on drugs is the subject of Lester C. Thurow's essay, "U.S. Drug Policy: Colossal Ignorance"; Thurow urges that we stop focusing on foreign countries and their contribution to our drug problems and, instead, work more effectively "on the streets of New York and Los Angeles." Mustafa Nabil, in "The Arabs' Image," claims that Americans must change their stereotyped views of Arab nations to serve the cause of world peace. Finally, in "Should Hiroshima Have Been Bombed?" and "Hiroshima: An Act of Terrorism," Paul Fussell and Michael Walzer, respectively, present their opposing beliefs regarding the United States decision to bomb Hiroshima at the end of World War II.

READING AND UNDERSTANDING PERSUASIVE WRITING

Whenever you read, you pay attention to the writer's main ideas and to the way he or she supports and develops those ideas. However, when you are reading thoughtfully and critically, once you are aware of these literally stated points, you also need to consider what is being implied. It is particularly important to be aware of the power of implications when you read essays or articles that aim to persuade.

To make inferences — that is, to "read between the lines" — you need to pay special attention to the distinction between fact and the author's opinion. In addition, note carefully the author's *tone* (the author's attitude toward the subject and toward the audience), which often reflects biases, beliefs, and values.

Rational Appeals

As you read persuasive writing, notice the way the writer seeks to convince you that a particular point of view is worthy of your consideration — and, ultimately, of your adoption. Most writers use a combination of facts and opinions. There's certainly nothing wrong with giving your attention to another's opinion — but do not be lulled into thinking that because an idea is stated in print, it has to be the truth. *Facts* are statements or statistics that can be verified through a source (or sources) that most knowledgeable people believe to be reliable. For instance, a writer may state that American journalist Harriet Quimby was the second woman to be a licensed pilot and, in 1912, the first woman to fly across the English Channel, citing the *1992 Information Please Almanac* as the source. You could easily check to verify these details, so accepting them as facts is certainly reasonable. On the other hand, if the writer then stated that Quimby contributed more to the advancement of women in aviation than did Amelia Earhart, that would be an opinion. For you, as a reader, to be convinced that this opinion was worthy of consideration would require much more evidence than a simple statement.

In judging the evidence you expect the writer to provide, you should ask yourself the following questions.

1. *Has the writer provided sufficient evidence?* In the example just given, for instance, providing just one or two comparisons between Quimby and Earhart would not be enough. Instead, the writer might list significant contributions made by Quimby and significant contributions made by Earhart, pointing out the reasons that Quimby's list shows her influence to have been greater than Earhart's. In addition, the writer might cite the views of scholars who are well respected in such fields as women's studies or aviation history and whose evaluations corroborated the writer's contention.

2. *Has the writer used only relevant evidence?* For example, it may be interesting to know the high school or college backgrounds of these two aviators. But their grade point averages or extracurricular activities could hardly be used to persuade an intelligent reader that one or the other had made more significant contributions to the field of women in aviation.

3. *Has the writer qualified the evidence, where needed?* Very seldom can words such as *all, every,* and *never* be used accurately. To be believable, statements often require such qualifying words as *some, most,* or *in many cases.* For example, "Everyone agrees that Quimby's flight across the English Channel marked the beginning of women's history in aviation" is subject to challenge if even one dissenting example can be found. A more careful writer would, instead, say something like this: "Many aviation buffs agree that Quimby's flight across the English Channel marked the beginning of women's history in aviation."

4. *Has the writer successfully avoided* logical fallacies *(flaws in reasoning)?* Logical fallacies often sound reasonable, but critical reading shows

that the writer's thinking has gone astray. Sometimes, fallacies result from a writer's carelessness; other times, a writer may purposely use fallacious reasoning, hoping to manipulate the unwary reader. Logical fallacies include — but are not limited to — the following types.

A. *Begging the question* — using circular statements to claim that something is true. For instance, "Amelia Earhart is well known as a woman pilot only because she has gained much publicity as a female aviator" begs the question. This statement says that Earhart is well known only because she is well known and does not make a sensible point.

B. *Hasty generalization* — making a generalization from only one or two examples. *Stereotyping* — making broad claims about all members of a particular group on the basis of the actions or beliefs of some of that group — is a type of hasty generalization that is particularly relevant to reading and writing about cross-cultural issues. For example, if someone were to say that because Earhart and Quimby were both United States citizens, American women must have a natural talent for flying, that would be a hasty generalization that stereotyped American women. Note that stereotyping can identify either a positive trait or a negative trait. It's just as illogical — and potentially damaging — to assume that all members of one race, religion, or social group share a particular talent as it is to suggest that they all share a specific weakness or lack.

C. *Ad hominem (Latin for "to the man")* — claiming that irrelevant personal qualities should be considered reason to qualify or disqualify an individual for a particular office, position, honor, or roll. For example, noting that a candidate for mayor fails to keep her house neatly painted has nothing to do with how she might lead the city.

D. *Post hoc, ergo propter hoc (Latin for "after this, therefore because of this)* — assuming that because one action or event preceded another, the first event or action caused the second to happen. For instance, noting that Harriet Quimby received her pilot's license shortly before ratification of the Nineteenth Amendment, which gave women in the United States the right to vote, is accurate. However, to suggest that Quimby's licensing somehow caused the Nineteenth Amendment to be passed would be illogical.

E. *Red herring* — introducing an irrelevant issue that sidetracks the audience from the main argument. For instance, in the Quimby versus Earhart issue, a red herring might be a question like "Why worry about Quimby's and Earhart's contributions when so many men have made more significant contributions?" Whether men have made more significant contributions is an entirely different issue and not relevant to the Quimby-Earhart topic.

F. *False dilemma (either-or fallacy)* — offering only two possibilities when other alternatives clearly exist. For instance, suppose someone said that women who want to have careers in aviation should either devote themselves to full-time flying or should work at desk jobs. This statement ignores the many other options that are available (part-time work, work in maintenance, work related to building aircraft, for example).

G. *Bandwagon* — stating or implying that because many people are doing something, it is justified. For example, someone might say that since many people still prefer to fly with a male pilot than to fly with a female pilot, male pilots must be better at their work than female pilots. This statement suggests that simply because a biased action is supported by a large number of people, that action should be respected and emulated.

Emotional Appeals

Differentiating fact and opinion and evaluating the various rational appeals a writer uses are two things you do when you read a persuasive piece of writing. In addition, you should pay close attention to the way the writer appeals to your emotions.

Criteria for evaluating emotional appeals cannot be defined as easily as criteria for judging rational appeals. Traditional discussions of argument and persuasion often suggest that any appeal to the emotions is somehow dishonest and suspect. Yet as humans, we make most of the decisions in our lives — including choosing the values we live by — not only from what our minds know to be true but also from what our emotions lead us to see as valid. Most of us agree that a balance between intellect and emotion is desirable; few of us would want to live in a world controlled solely by thought or solely by feelings.

The problem, then, is to recognize how a writer appeals to our feelings and to reject false manipulation while not ignoring the claims of emotions we see as genuine and worthy of our response. An example of an argument based primarily on emotional appeals is the "I Have a Dream" speech that television stations throughout the United States replay on each anniversary of Martin Luther King's birthday. While King does use rational appeals in this speech, what most of us remember most keenly are the perfectly chosen words, the effective repetition, and the moving examples of men, women, and children who have been denied their dreams. Is this use of emotional appeals valid? Each person has to decide for herself or himself. Those who disagree with King and refuse to see any reason to entertain his dream would probably argue that his appeal to emotions is not valid. Those in the audience who agree with King — or who listen with a mind open to possibilities — would almost certainly say that the plea for equality *must* be made at least in part through emotional means. For it is in one's heart as well as in one's mind that the commitment to such an ideal must be affirmed. In this book, persuasive essays that depend strongly on emotional appeals include "A Loaded Question" (pp. 461–470), "A Question of Language" (pp. 518–521), and "Should Hiroshima Have Been Bombed?" (pp. 587–595).

Appeals to the emotions are made in many ways. Consider these points as you evaluate such appeals.

1. *Word choice.* Remember that words have both literal *(denotative)* and emotional *(connotative)* meanings. For instance, while *clever* and *cunning* both describe a person as skillful and talented, most people would prefer to be called clever, because *cunning* also implies a crafty slyness. As you read persuasive writing, watch carefully for the connotations of words. Decide whether the other evidence offered convinces you that the word chosen truly describes the person or situation or whether, instead, it has been used primarily to divert your attention from making a fair assessment.

2. *Figurative language.* An extension of word choice is the use of figurative language. A writer or speaker may use startling or unusual metaphors or similes to gain the attention and sympathy of the audience. For example, in the "I Have a Dream" Speech, Martin Luther King compares the Emancipation Proclamation to "a great beacon light of hope to millions of Negro slaves who had been seared in the flames of withering injustice."

3. *Sentence patterns.* Certain sentence patterns — for example, repetition of a key word or phrase — can fire the emotions in either a positive or a negative way. Repetition can lead, and has led, to terrifying mob violence; yet in other instances, it has inspired selfless and idealistic actions. Once again, as a responsible listener/reader, you need to be aware of the way these devices are used and decide for yourself whether you consider the argument worthy of your emotional response.

4. *Imitative language patterns.* A writer or speaker may use language patterns familiar from other respected sources, thus tacitly asking the audience to give to this argument the same emotional responses that would have been given to the original source. Martin Luther King begins "I Have a Dream" with this sentence: "Five score years ago, a great American, in whose symbolic shadow we stand, signed the Emancipation Proclamation." Not only does he refer directly to President Abraham Lincoln, but also, with his opening phrase, he recalls Lincoln's Gettysburg Address. In other places in the speech, King echoes the cadences of the King James Bible, with sentences such as "one day every valley shall be exalted, every hill and mountain shall be made low, . . . and the glory of the Lord shall be revealed. . . ." Through these imitative language choices, King associates his message both with a highly revered political figure and with religious doctrine. For many in his audience, these two associations arouse powerful positive responses.

WRITING TO PERSUADE

Understanding both rational and emotional appeals provides a strong base for writing persuasively. In addition, it's helpful to consider topics that are worthy of argument and topics that are not. Keep in mind these guidelines.

1. *Matters of fact* are not worthy of argument. If you know that Ingrid Bergman and Yul Brynner won the Oscars for best actress and best actor in 1956 but your friend insists these awards went, instead, to Joanne Woodward and Alec Guinness, you can easily prove that you are right by consulting an almanac or entertainment encyclopedia. There's no sense wasting time and energy trying to convince someone to believe a fact that can be verified through a source you both consider accurate and reliable.

2. *Matters of taste* are not worthy of argument. While you might reasonably argue that your co-worker should at least try the salad you have made of fiddlehead ferns and dandelion greens, you can't reasonably expect to persuade her that she likes the concoction. Our tastes (in food, pleasure reading, style of dressing, and so on) do change, of course, but not through the process of someone else arguing that we should, for a given list of reasons, make such a change.

A reasonable subject for a persuasive argument, then, is a subject that raises questions that are controversial. Usually, such a subject has many aspects. For instance, if the subject relates to the solution for a problem, ordinarily no one answer shows itself as the only correct answer. In addition, most controversial issues are extremely broad and complex. When you choose to write about them, you need to narrow your topic to suit the time and space you have to devote to writing the argument. For instance, to try to write a three- to five-page paper arguing for or against legalized abortion or capital punishment would be extremely difficult. Instead, you would narrow the topic so that you were arguing, say, about the use of tax money to pay for abortions for welfare patients or about the rights of those convicted of a capital crime to appeal their sentences.

SAMPLE ESSAY: WRITING TO PERSUADE

As an example of an essay that persuades, we will consider Dave Harris's process as he responded to the following assignment.

After reading several of the selections from the section "Rights and Responsibilities," write an essay arguing for a right or responsibility that you believe needs our society's attention. As you develop your argument, keep in mind the audience you are trying to persuade. Make certain that whatever evidence and appeals you use (rational or emotional) will be convincing to this audience.

Before you read Dave's response to this assignment, you may want to read two or three selections from the section "Rights and Responsibilities." Especially recommended are "The Solitude of Self" (pp. 421–426), "Equal Opportunity, Not Equal Results" (pp. 446–452), "Why Blacks Need Affirmative Action" (pp. 453–455), and "A Loaded Question" (pp. 461–470).

Exploring Ideas: Mapping

After reading several selections from the section, Dave thought about what he saw as important rights and responsibilities. To consider his ideas, he used a strategy called *mapping* (or *webbing*). This process is similar to listing and freewriting demonstrated in Sections 2 (p. 27) and 3 (p. 203), but it encourages a visual — rather than a linear — exploration. There are no hard-and-fast rules for mapping. But usually, you start out with a general subject — perhaps a word or a phrase — in the middle of a blank sheet of paper. From there, you try to come up with several possible subdivisions of that idea, circling these new possibilities and attaching them to the original circled idea with lines. Mapping helps you to discover what you know about a topic and, in addition, serves as a rough outline for planning and writing the first draft.

After spending a semester at the University of London, Dave had returned to school in the United States with a profoundly changed view of the relationship between the United States and other countries. He saw the views he had previously held — and the views he believed many of his friends still held — as cause for concern. To explore this concern and to shape it into an argument, Dave began by writing the subject that interested him — American views of other countries — in the center of the paper. After that, he identified three main categories related to this subject: (1) areas of concern, (2) problems for the United States caused by this view, and (3) solutions for the problems. Finally, he worked at seeing the issues related to each of these categories. Dave did not complete this map all at one sitting. He began with the main topic and the three subtopics; then he added a few points to each subtopic. He then put the map away, keeping his thoughts in his mind and pondering them whenever he had a few moments free (a strategy called *incubation*). After a few days had passed, he found time to sit down with his map and add several new possibilities.

Planning and Writing a Draft

As Dave looked at his map, he realized that in his paper he would try to persuade his fellow classmates that American views of other countries and their citizens are often extremely narrow and sometimes dangerously limited. To convince his audience, he knew that he would have to provide examples to show that the limited view did exist and to show that this limited view posed problems.

GATHERING EVIDENCE To evaluate his thesis, Dave took several steps. First, he wrote a survey with questions relating to knowledge of countries other than the United States and asked fifty students, all of whom were born and raised in the United States and who came from various age, ethnic,

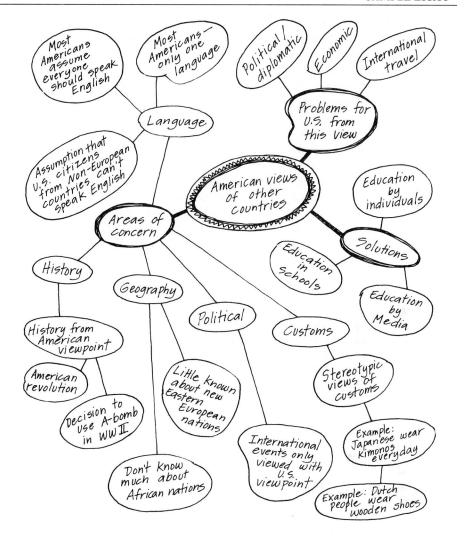

Most Americans assume everyone should speak English

Most Americans—only one language

Political/diplomatic

Economic

International travel

Language

Problems for U.S. from this view

Assumption that U.S. citizens from Non-European countries can't speak English

American views of other countries

Education by individuals

Areas of concern

Solutions

History

Education in schools

Geography

Education by Media

Political

History from American viewpoint

Customs

American revolution

Little known about new Eastern European nations

Stereotypic views of customs

Decision to use A-bomb in WW II

Example: Japanese wear kimonos everyday

Don't know much about African nations

International events only viewed with U.S. viewpoint

Example: Dutch people wear wooden shoes

religious, and socioeconomic groups, to respond to the survey. Thirty-eight students responded; and as Dave read what they had written, he saw that the data supported his thesis.

Dave also read several issues of newspapers and newsmagazines from the past three years to see how the American news media reported stories relating to other countries. He noticed that in most of the stories he read, only the American point of view was given much attention or emphasis. He decided to use stories on the Gulf War as an example.

Finally, Dave asked the principals of seven schools (from elementary to secondary level) if he could look at their social studies and literature textbooks. As he had expected, he found that most of the textbooks were seriously out of date and that little attention was paid to historic figures or writers who were not part of the Western cultural tradition. For instance, ancient history textbooks focused on Egypt, Greece, and Rome, with little or no mention of early Oriental, Native American, or African (other than Egyptian) civilizations.

CONSIDERING TONE AND VOICE After evaluating the data he had gathered and seeing that it did support his thesis, Dave considered his audience and how readers would respond to the tone and voice he would use as he wrote. *Tone* means the attitude of the writer toward the audience and the subject. *Voice* is closely connected with tone, because the writer's voice establishes his or her image in the reader's mind. While tone and voice are always significant considerations during the composing process, they deserve particular attention when the writer's aim is persuasion.

Most often, when you are writing to persuade, you establish a voice that encourages your readers to see you as a fair, thoughtful, and reasonable person. You avoid heated accusations, snide observations, and defensive comments, because most readers immediately raise their guard when they are addressed by a writer's voice filled with unbridled anger, bitterness, sarcasm, or bias. In addition to choosing your words carefully, you also provide as much solid evidence as possible to establish a voice that enables the reader to trust your expertise about the subject you are addressing.

The voice you convey to your audience also indicates your tone. When you take the time and effort to write in a way that establishes common ground — connections — between you and your readers, you show them that your attitude toward them is respectful rather than adversarial. You show your commitment to your subject, and to your position on that subject, by choosing language that conveys the depth of your concern and yet also shows that you are not narrow minded and have not ignored objections that may be raised to the points you are making.

Dave realized that the students he hoped to convince were, on the whole, as sincerely concerned as he was with being fair-minded citizens of the world in which they lived. He knew he would have to take care as he wrote not to sound like someone who had become instantly wise and who was now trying to force his views on others. He also recognized that he would need more evidence than just his own observations and experiences to convince his readers that his ideas about American views of other countries were valid.

Keeping these points in mind, and using the categories and subcategories from his mapping, Dave wrote this draft.

SEEING WITH NEW EYES

When I began classes at the University of London, I expected my British classmates to be as curious about the United States as I was about England. I had so many questions about everything, from the relationship between Parliament and the royal family to the way the subway system (called "the tube") worked. What surprised me was that most of my friends from Great Britain or other European countries knew as much, or sometimes more, about government, politics, film stars, and even sports in the United States as I did. During the four months I lived in London, and since I have returned to the United States, I have been thinking about this observation, and I have become convinced that many of us in this country have a very limited view of the world we live in. Furthermore, I believe that this narrow view can lead to and has led to problems that we need to address.

To test my belief that many of my fellow students here in the United States shared the lack of knowledge I brought with me to England, I wrote a survey asking several questions — some of which I could not have answered when I left for my semester at the University of London. I asked fifty students who were born and raised in the United States to answer these questions; thirty-eight students responded. While I realize that thirty-eight students at one college cannot be considered conclusive evidence of a problem, I think their responses do suggest that questions need to be raised. Most of them could not name the heads of foreign governments, many were unaware of geographical data, and some retained outdated, stereotypical views of the daily lives of people who live in other countries. Again, I emphasize that these responses do not constitute conclusive proof that all or even a majority of college students lack knowledge of other countries. Certainly, however, these answers indicate the need to consider the possibility that we Americans have a narrow view of the world, to investigate where that narrow view comes from, and to understand why it might cause problems.

There are no doubt many causes for the limited view we often take of the world outside the United States. I investigated only two of them. First, I read several newspaper and newsmagazine accounts of one important event relating to the United States and some other country or countries. One event that impressed me most during the past few years was the Gulf War, so I decided to focus on that. As I read the accounts of the end of the war, I noticed one thing that seemed to me representative of the way stories about other countries are reported by the American press. Many, many of the stories looked at the suffering of American civilians, such as people whose family members had to leave their jobs because they were called up to be sent to the Gulf. On the other hand, very few of the stories told much about what was going on for Iraqi civilians.

Another cause of narrow thinking comes from what we learn in our schools. Public schools, in particular, have a problem, because in these schools books are bought with public funds, not purchased by the individual student. Limited public funding means that old books are often not replaced. I looked at the social studies texts (history, geography, and political science) in seven schools in this city. From elementary school to high school, I found the same thing. The textbooks were seriously out of date. While teachers may give supplementary information to fill in the gaps, the out-of-date textbooks remain in students' hands, giving them ideas about other countries that are now incorrect.

How can we begin to address this problem of the narrow view many Americans have of the world? By identifying two of the places where the problem originates, I have also identified where changes can begin. First, we should all be aware when reading or listening to mass media that the stories may be slanted only toward the American viewpoint. We should ask ourselves the question: How would other countries see this issue? We can also write letters to newspapers, newsmagazines, and television stations asking for more balanced coverage. On the local level, we can check textbooks and other teaching materials in public schools and lobby for the purchase of more up-to-date materials — or at least for the removal of texts that contain incorrect and misleading information.

Revising: Providing Specific Details and Examples

When Dave reread his essay, he realized that although he had talked about the survey he had done, about the articles he had read in newspapers and magazines, and about his visits to local schools, he had not provided enough specific details and examples to be convincing. He then reviewed the notes he had taken as he gathered his data and rewrote the body of his essay to include the evidence the first draft lacked. Here are the revised paragraphs.

To test my belief that many of my fellow students shared the lack of knowledge I brought with me to England, I wrote a survey asking several questions — some of which I could not have answered when I left for my semester at the University of London. I asked fifty students who were born and raised in the United States to answer these questions; thirty-eight students responded. While I realize that thirty-eight students at one college cannot be considered conclusive evidence of a problem, I think their responses do suggest that questions need to be raised. Most of them could not name the heads of foreign governments, many were unaware of geographical data, and some retained outdated, stereotypical views of the daily lives of people who live in other countries. Consider, for example, these points:

1. Only five of the thirty-eight students could name the prime minister of England.
2. Only seven knew who Boris Yeltsin was, and only one knew the name of the group of countries he currently leads.
3. No one knew the name of the premiere of France.
4. Only three could name more than three countries in Africa.
5. Six answered "true" to the following statement: "Most people in Japan wear kimonos as their regular, daily form of dress."

Again, I emphasize that these responses do not constitute conclusive proof that all or even a majority of college students lack knowledge of other countries. Certainly, however, they indicate the need to consider the possibility that we Americans have a narrow view of the world, to investigate where that narrow view comes from, and why it might cause problems.

There are no doubt many causes for the limited view we often take of the world outside the United States. I investigated only two of them. First, I read several newspaper and newsmagazine accounts of one important event relating to the United States and some other country or countries (I chose *Newsweek, Time,* and the *New York Times.*) One event that impressed me greatly during the past few years was the Gulf War, so I decided to focus on that. As I read the accounts of the end of the war, I noticed one thing that seemed to me representative of the way stories about other countries are reported by the American press. Many, many of the stories stressed that the loss of life was "amazingly light" (*Time,* March 23, 1991, p. 56) or that casualties were "almost miraculously low" (*New York Times,* March 27, 1991, p. 1). Of course, these stories were talking about American lives lost — not about the thousands of Iraqis (many of them civilians) who were killed. While many of us may not have much sympathy with the government of Iraq, I don't think most Americans would just discount the deaths of thousands of people (including old people, children, and babies). Yet the media reports encouraged us not to think beyond the effects on our own lives.

Another cause of narrow thinking comes from what we learn in our schools. Public schools, in particular, have a problem, because in these schools books are bought with public funds, not purchased by the individual student. Because public funds are limited, old books are often not replaced. I looked at the social studies texts (history, geography, and political science) in seven schools in this city. From elementary school to high school, I found the same thing. The textbooks were seriously out of date. Not one book I looked at had a publication date later than 1985; many had publication dates in the early 1980s; one history text was published in 1975. That means that none of these books could contain any information about the reunification of Germany, the end of the Cold War, or the breakdown of the Soviet Union. While teachers may give supplementary information to address these problems, the out-of-date textbooks remain in students' hands, giving them ideas about other countries that are now incorrect.

Suggestions for Writing to Persuade

1. Determine the main idea you will argue for or against. For example, you might try to persuade readers to question a previously accepted point of view. You might try to convince your audience to accept a proposal for solving a problem. Or you might challenge a law or rule you see as unjust.
2. Gather data related to your main idea. Make certain that you have enough evidence to support your idea before you begin to write. Remember that as you gather evidence, you may change your mind and see that you

cannot, in fact, support the idea you began with. Then you will have to begin again with a revised thesis idea.

3. Evaluate your audience carefully and then consider the voice and tone you will use.

4. Consider points that might be made against your argument, and plan ways to address these points.

5. Plan and write your draft(s) so that the evidence you offer moves smoothly and logically from one point to the next.

6. Revise your draft(s), paying particular attention to the evidence you have offered and to your use of rational and emotional appeals.

7. Consider your word choice, making certain you have established a convincing, reasonable, and reliable voice.

8. Evaluate your conclusion to make sure that it does more than summarize what you have already said. For example, you might provide a solution for a problem or suggest related issues worthy of further exploration.

Rights and
Responsibilities

Previews: RIGHTS AND RESPONSIBILITIES

The strongest reason why we ask for woman a voice in the government under which she lives; in the religion she is asked to believe; equality in social life, where she is the chief factor; a place in the trades and professions, where she may earn her bread, is because of her birthright to self-sovereignty; because as an individual she must rely on herself.

From: *The Solitude of Self,* ELIZABETH CADY STANTON

If someone threatens you with death unless you torture someone else to death, I think you have not the right, even to save your life, to do so. But the case under consideration here is very different. In our case there are only two people involved, one whose life is threatened, and one who threatens it. Both are innocent: the one who is threatened is not threatened because of any fault, the one who threatens does not threaten because of any fault. For this reason we may feel that we bystanders cannot intervene. But the person threatened can.

From: *A Defense of Abortion,* JUDITH JARVIS THOMSON

Blacks must no longer keep silent on this issue. We cannot permit the public to continue to imagine that we are obediently following our national leaders in endorsing abortion on demand and we must resist the forces that drive black women to seek abortion. . . . We are already besieged by homicide, drugs, AIDS, and an alarmingly high infant mortality rate. We do not need to reenact the sterilization programs of the 1930s and 1940s.

From: *Abortion Is Not a Civil Right,* GREG KEATH

There is one white attorney for every 680 whites, but only one black attorney for every 4,000 blacks; one white physician for every 659 whites, but only one black physician for every 5,000 blacks; and one white dentist for every 1,900 whites, but only one black dentist for every 8,400 blacks. Less than 1 percent of all engineers — or of all practicing chemists — is black. Cruel and uncompassionate injustice created gaps like these. We need creative justice and compassion to help us close them.

From: *Why Blacks Need Affirmative Action,* JESSE JACKSON

A confession, then: I may be as fascinated by guns as my gun-owning and gun-loving friend in Maine, but were it up to me, I would rid America of its guns. I would be less verbally self-righteous about gun control than I was in the past, for I think I have begun to understand those who, like my friend in Maine, have arguments of their own in defense of guns. They are formidable arguments.

From: *A Loaded Question: What Is It about Americans and Guns?,* LEONARD KRIEGAL

ELIZABETH CADY STANTON
The Solitude of Self

> *Born in 1815, Elizabeth Cady was educated by her parents at home and, later, at the Troy, New York, Female Seminary. As a young woman, she became deeply committed to the antislavery movement, and through this work she met and married Henry Brewster Stanton, who was also an activist in early civil rights actions. While raising their seven children, the Stantons continued to be involved in issues of freedom and equality, including rights for women. In 1851, Elizabeth Cady Stanton met Susan B. Anthony, who for fifty years was to be her collaborator for feminist causes. In 1892, when she was seventy-six years old, Stanton delivered the speech presented here, which is generally considered the strongest statement of her feminist beliefs.*

Prereading/Journal-Writing Suggestions

1. What is your definition or impression of someone who is a "feminist"? According to your definition, what feminist ideas do you strongly believe in? What feminist ideas do you disagree with?
2. Complete the following analogy, and then freewrite for ten minutes in order to explain your philosophy of life: "For me, life is like. . . ."
3. Using examples from your own life (from even today, perhaps), explain the difference between loneliness and solitude.

The point I wish plainly to bring before you on this occasion is the individuality of each human soul; our Protestant idea, the right of individual conscience and judgment; our republican idea, individual citizenship. In discussing the rights of woman, we are to consider, first, what belongs to her as an individual, in a world of her own, the arbiter of her own destiny, an imaginary Robinson Crusoe, with her woman, Friday, on a solitary island. Her rights under such circumstances are to use all her faculties for her own safety and happiness.

Secondly, if we consider her as a citizen, as a member of a great nation, she must have the same rights as all other members, according to the fundamental principles of our Government.

Thirdly, viewed as a woman, an equal factor in civilization, her rights and duties are still the same — individual happiness and development.

Fourthly, it is only the incidental relations of life, such as mother, wife, sister, daughter, which may involve some special duties and training. . . .

The strongest reason for giving woman all the opportunities for higher education, for the full development of her faculties, her forces of mind and body; for giving her the most enlarged freedom of thought and action; a complete emancipation from all forms of bondage, of custom, dependence, superstition; from all the crippling influences of fear — is the solitude and personal responsibility of her own individual life. The strongest reason why we ask for woman a voice in the government under which she lives; in the religion she is asked to believe; equality in social life, where she is the chief factor; a place in the trades and professions, where she may earn her bread, is because of her birthright to self-sovereignty; because, as an individual, she must rely on herself. No matter how much women prefer to lean, to be protected and supported, nor how much men desire to have them do so, they must make the voyage of life alone, and for safety in an emergency, they must know something of the laws of navigation. To guide our own craft, we must be captain, pilot, engineer; with chart and compass to stand at the wheel; to watch the winds and waves, and know when to take in the sail, and to read the signs in the firmament over all. It matters not whether the solitary voyager is man or woman; nature, having endowed them equally, leaves them to their own skill and judgment in the hour of danger, and, if not equal to the occasion, alike they perish.

To appreciate the importance of fitting every human soul for independent action, think for a moment of the immeasurable solitude of self. We come into the world alone, unlike all who have gone before us, we leave it alone, under circumstances peculiar to ourselves. No mortal ever has been, no mortal ever will be like the soul just launched on the sea of life. There can never again be just such a combination of prenatal influences; never again just such environments as make up the infancy, youth and manhood of this one. Nature never repeats herself, and the possibilities of one human soul will never be found in another. No one has ever found two blades of ribbon grass alike, and no one will ever find two human beings alike. Seeing, then, that what must be the infinite diversity in human character, we can in a measure appreciate the loss to a nation when any class of the people is uneducated and unrepresented in the government.

We ask for the complete development of every individual, first, for his own benefit and happiness. In fitting out an army, we give each soldier his own knapsack, arms, powder, his blanket, cup, knife, fork and spoon. We provide alike for all their individual necessities; then each man bears his own burden.

Again, we ask complete individual development for the general good; for the consensus of the competent on the whole round of human interests, on all questions of national life; and here each man must bear his share of the general burden. It is sad to see how soon friendless children are left to bear their own burdens, before they can analyze their feelings; before they can even tell their joys and sorrows, they are thrown on their own resources. The great lesson that nature seems to teach us at all ages is self-dependence, self-protection, self-support. . . .

We ask no sympathy from others in the anxiety and agony of a broken friendship or shattered love. When death sunders our nearest ties, alone we sit in the shadow of our affliction. Alike amid the greatest triumphs and darkest tragedies of life, we walk alone. On the divine heights of human attainment, eulogized and worshipped as a hero or saint, we stand alone. In ignorance, poverty and vice, as a pauper or criminal, alone we starve or steal; alone we suffer the sneers and rebuffs of our fellows; alone we are hunted and hounded through dark courts and alleys, in by-ways and high-ways; alone we stand in the judgment seat; alone in the prison cell we lament our crimes and misfortunes; alone we expiate them on the gallows. In hours like these we realize the awful solitude of individual life, its pains, its penalties, its responsibilities, hours in which the youngest and most helpless are thrown on their own resources for guidance and consolation. Seeing, then, that life must ever be a march and a battle that each soldier must be equipped for his own protection, it is the height of cruelty to rob the individual of a single natural right.

To throw obstacles in the way of a complete education is like putting 10 out the eyes; to deny the rights of poverty is like cutting off the hands. To refuse political equality is to rob the ostracized of all self-respect; of credit in the market place; of recompense in the world of work, of a voice in choosing those who make and administer the law, a choice in the jury before whom they are tried, and in the judge who decides their punishment. [Think of] . . . woman's position! Robbed of her natural rights, handicapped by law and custom at every turn, yet compelled to fight her own battles, and in the emergencies of life to fall back on herself for protection. . . .

The young wife and mother, at the head of some establishment, with a kind husband to shield her from the adverse winds of life, with wealth, fortune and position, has a certain harbor of safety, secure against the ordinary ills of life. But to manage a household, have a desirable influence in society, keep her friends and the affections of her husband, train her children and servants well, she must have rare common sense, wisdom, diplomacy, and a knowledge of human nature. To do all this, she needs the cardinal virtues and the strong points of character that the most successful statesman possesses. An uneducated woman trained to dependence, with no resources in herself, must make a failure of any position in life. But society says women do not need a knowledge of the world, the liberal training that experience in public life must give, all the advantages of collegiate education; but when for the lack of all this, the woman's happiness is wrecked, alone she bears her humiliation; and the solitude of the weak and ignorant is indeed pitiable. In the wild chase for the prizes of life, they are ground to powder.

In age, when the pleasures of youth are passed, children grown up, married and gone, the hurry and bustle of life in a measure over, when the hands are weary of active service, when the old arm chair and the fireside are the chosen resorts, then men and women alike must fall back on their own resources. If they cannot find companionship in books, if they have no interest in the vital questions of the hour, no interest in watching the consummation of reforms with which they might have been identified, they soon pass into their dotage. The more fully the faculties of the mind are developed and kept in use, the longer the period of vigor and active interests in all around us continues. If, from a life-long participation in public affairs, a woman feels responsible for the laws regulating our system of education, the discipline of our jails and prisons, the sanitary condition of our private homes, public building and thoroughfares, an interest in commerce, finance, our foreign relations, in any or all these questions, her solitude will at least be respectable, and she will not be driven to gossip or scandal for entertainment.

The chief reason for opening to every soul the doors to the whole round of human duties and pleasures is the individual development thus attained, the resources thus provided under all circumstances to mitigate the solitude that at times must come to everyone. . . .

Inasmuch, then, as woman shares equally the joys and sorrows of time and eternity, is it not the height of presumption in man to propose to represent her at the ballot box and the throne of grace, to do her voting in the state, her praying in the church, and to assume the position of high priest at the family altar?

Nothing strengthens the judgment and quickens the conscience like individual responsibility. Nothing adds such dignity to character as the rec- 15 ognition of one's self-sovereignty; the right to an equal place, everywhere conceded — a place earned by personal merit, not an artificial attainment by inheritance, wealth, family and position. Conceding, then, that the responsibilities of life rest equally on man and woman, that their destiny is the same, they need the same preparation for time and eternity. The talk of sheltering woman from the fierce storms of life is the sheerest mockery, for they beat on her from every point of the compass, just as they do on man, and with more fatal results, for he has been trained to protect himself, to resist, and to conquer. Such are the facts in human experience, the responsibilities of individual sovereignty. Rich and poor, intelligent and ignorant, wise and foolish, virtuous and vicious, man and woman; it is ever the same, each soul must depend wholly on itself.

Whatever the theories may be of woman's dependence on man, in the supreme moments of her life, he cannot bear her burdens. Alone she goes to the gates of death to give life to every man that is born into the world; no one can share her fears, no one can mitigate her pangs; and if her sorrow is greater than she can bear, alone she passes beyond the gates into the vast unknown. . . .

So it ever must be in the conflicting scenes of life, in the long, weary march, each one walks alone. We may have many friends, love, kindness, sympathy and charity, to smooth our pathway in everyday life, but in the tragedies and triumphs of human experience, each mortal stands alone. . . .

Women are already the equals of men in the whole realm of thought, in art, science, literature and government. . . . The poetry and novels of the century are theirs, and they have touched the keynote of reform, in religion, politics and social life. They fill the editor's and professor's chair, plead at the bar of justice, walk the wards of the hospital, speak from the pulpit and the

platform. Such is the type of womanhood that an enlightened public sentiment welcomes today, and such the triumph of the facts of life over the false
theories of the past.

Is it, then, consistent to hold the developed woman of this day within
the same narrow political limits as the dame with the spinning wheel and
knitting needles occupied in the past? No, no! Machinery has taken the labors
of woman as well as man on its tireless shoulders; the loom and the spinning
wheel are but dreams of the past; the pen, the brush, the easel, the chisel, have
taken their places, while the hopes and ambitions of women are essentially
changed.

We see reason sufficient in the outer conditions of human beings for in- 20
dividual liberty and development, but when we consider the self-dependence
of every human soul, we see the need of courage, judgment and the exercise
of every faculty of mind and body, strengthened and developed by use, in
woman as well as man.

Whatever may be said of man's protecting power in ordinary conditions,
amid all the terrible disasters by land and sea, in the supreme moments of
danger, alone woman must ever meet the horrors of the situation. The Angel
of Death even makes no royal pathway for her. Man's love and sympathy
enter only into the sunshine of our lives. In that solemn solitude of self,
that links us with the immeasurable and the eternal, each soul lives alone
forever. . . .

And yet, there is a solitude which each and every one of us has always
carried with him, more inaccessible than the ice-cold mountains, more profound than the midnight sea; the solitude of self. Our inner being which we
call ourself, no eye nor touch of man or angel has ever pierced. It is more
hidden than the caves of the gnome; the sacred adytum of the oracle; the
hidden chamber of Eleusinian mystery, for to it only omniscience is permitted
to enter.

Such is individual life. Who, I ask you, can take, dare take on himself
the rights, the duties, the responsibilities of another human soul?

Suggestions for Writing and Discussion

1. From reading this essay, what portrait would you create of Elizabeth Cady
   Stanton? What gestures might she make? What would be the expression
   on her face? Where would she be? Who, if anyone, would be with her?
   What might she be doing?
2. On what single basic belief does Stanton base this entire argument? Is this
   a belief that most people today would support? Explain.
3. In this piece, Stanton appeals to reason, to moral beliefs, and to emotions.
   Find examples from the text that appeal to the audience's sense of logic,
   sense of right, and sense of feeling. What appeal does she primarily use in
   this piece? Why does she emphasize this appeal?

4. From this piece, can you tell whether or not Stanton is a devout believer in God? In America? Do you think these issues would have made any difference to her audience at the time?
5. In your own words, write a sentence for each category listed, explaining the benefits Stanton believes each derives from a woman's right to be educated and to be free.
   A. The individual woman
   B. The family
   C. The community
   D. The country
6. Throughout this speech, Stanton compares women to two occupations traditionally held by men. What are these occupations, and what does Stanton gain by using these specific comparisons?
7. In one sentence and in your own words, state what you believe Stanton's philosophy of life might be.

Suggestions for Extended Thinking and Research

1. Research several sources (primary, if possible) to discover a good picture of what America was like in 1892. What were the dominant issues? What were the new inventions? What conflicts were taking place? After doing this research, analyze how various groups of Americans you have read about might have reacted to Stanton's speech.
2. Research one other American woman from this same era who worked for women's right to vote. Find one of her speeches or a piece of her writing, and analyze this piece in comparison with Stanton's.

JUDITH JARVIS THOMSON
A Defense of Abortion

> *Born in 1929, Judith Jarvis Thomson was educated at Barnard, Columbia, and Cambridge University, England. She is Professor of Philosophy at Massachusetts Institute of Technology and is the author of* Rights, Restitution, and Risk *(1986), a highly regarded book of essays defining philosophical questions related to legal, moral, and political issues. "A Defense of Abortion" was written two years before the* Roe v. Wade *Supreme Court ruling in 1973 that declared many legal restrictions on abortions to be unconstitutional. In this argument, Thomson raises many issues sure to become increasingly relevant as the controversy surrounding the legalization of abortion continues to grow.*

Prereading/Journal-Writing Suggestions

1. What is your impression or definition of people who are "pro-choice" advocates? What is your impression or definition of those who are "pro-life" advocates? What do you think is the basic division between these two groups?
2. Is it possible to legislate morality? Freewrite on this question for ten minutes.

Most opposition to abortion relies on the premise that the fetus is a human being, a person, from the moment of conception. The premise is argued for, but, as I think, not well. Take, for example, the most common argument. We are asked to notice that the development of a human being from conception through birth into childhood is continuous; then it is said that to draw a line, to choose a point in this development and say "before this point the thing is not a person, after this point it is a person" is to make an arbitrary choice, a choice for which in the nature of things no good reason can be given. It is concluded that the fetus is, or anyway that we had better say it is, a person from the moment of conception. But this conclusion does not follow. Similar things might be said about the development of an acorn into an oak tree, and it does not follow that acorns are oak trees, or that we had better say they are. Arguments of this form are sometimes called "slippery slope arguments"—the phrase is perhaps self-explanatory— and it is dismaying that opponents of abortion rely on them so heavily and uncritically.[1]

I am inclined to agree, however, that the prospects for "drawing a line" in the development of the fetus look dim. I am inclined to think also that we

---

[1] I am very much indebted to James Thomson for discussion, criticism, and many helpful suggestions.

shall probably have to agree that the fetus has already become a human person well before birth. Indeed, it comes as a surprise when one first learns how early in its life it begins to acquire human characteristics. By the tenth week, for example, it already has a face, arms and legs, fingers and toes; it has internal organs, and brain activity is detectable.[2] On the other hand, I think that the premise is false, that the fetus is not a person from the moment of conception. A newly fertilized ovum, a newly implanted clump of cells, is no more a person than an acorn is an oak tree. But I shall not discuss any of this. For it seems to me to be of great interest to ask what happens if, for the sake of argument, we allow the premise. How, precisely, are we supposed to get from there to the conclusion that abortion is morally impermissible? Opponents of abortion commonly spend most of their time establishing that the fetus is a person, and hardly any time explaining the step from there to the impermissibility of abortion. Perhaps they think the step too simple and obvious to require much comment. Or perhaps instead they are simply being economical in argument. Many of those who defend abortion rely on the premise that the fetus is not a person, but only a bit of tissue that will become a person at birth; and why pay out more arguments than you have to? Whatever the explanation, I suggest that the step they take is neither easy nor obvious, that it calls for closer examination than it is commonly given, and that when we do give it this closer examination we shall feel inclined to reject it.

I propose, then, that we grant that the fetus is a person from the moment of conception. How does the argument go from here? Something like this, I take it. Every person has a right to life. So the fetus has a right to life. No doubt the mother has a right to decide what shall happen in and to her body; everyone would grant that. But surely a person's right to life is stronger and more stringent than the mother's right to decide what happens in and to her body, and so outweighs it. So the fetus may not be killed; an abortion may not be performed.

It sounds plausible. But now let me ask you to imagine this. You wake up in the morning and find yourself back to back in bed with an unconscious violinist. A famous unconscious violinist. He has been found to have a fatal kidney ailment, and the Society of Music Lovers has canvassed all the available medical records and found that you alone have the right blood type to help. They have therefore kidnapped you, and last night the violinist's circulatory system was plugged into yours, so that your kidneys can be used to extract poisons from his blood as well as your own. The director of the hospital now tells you, "Look, we're sorry the Society of Music Lovers did this to you —

[2]Daniel Callahan, *Abortion: Law, Choice and Morality* (New York, 1970), p. 373. This book gives a fascinating survey of the available information on abortion. The Jewish tradition is surveyed in David M. Feldman, *Birth Control in Jewish Law* (New York, 1968), Part 5; the Catholic tradition in John T. Noonan, Jr., "An Almost Absolute Value in History," in *The Morality of Abortion,* ed. John T. Noonan, Jr. (Cambridge, Mass., 1970).

we would never have permitted it if we had known. But still, they did it, and the violinist now is plugged into you. To unplug you would be to kill him. But never mind, it's only for nine months. By then he will have recovered from his ailment, and can safely be unplugged from you." Is it morally incumbent on you to accede to this situation? No doubt it would be very nice of you if you did, a great kindness. But do you *have* to accede to it? What if it were not nine months, but nine years? Or longer still? What if the director of the hospital says, "Tough luck, I agree, but you've now got to stay in bed, with the violinist plugged into you, for the rest of your life. Because remember this. All persons have a right to life, and violinists are persons. Granted you have a right to decide what happens in and to your body, but a person's right to life outweighs your right to decide what happens in and to your body. So you cannot ever be unplugged from him." I imagine you would regard this as outrageous, which suggests that something really is wrong with the plausible-sounding argument I mentioned a moment ago.

In this case, of course, you were kidnapped; you didn't volunteer for 5 the operation that plugged the violinist into your kidneys. Can those who oppose abortion on the ground I mentioned make an exception for a pregnancy due to rape? Certainly. They can say that persons have a right to life only if they didn't come into existence because of rape; or they can say that all persons have a right to life, but that some have less of a right to life than others, in particular, that those who came into existence because of rape have less. But these statements have a rather unpleasant sound. Surely the question of whether you have a right to life at all, or how much of it you have, shouldn't turn on the question of whether or not you are the product of a rape. And in fact the people who oppose abortion on the ground I mentioned do not make this distinction, and hence do not make an exception in case of rape.

Nor do they make an exception for a case in which the mother has to spend the nine months of her pregnancy in bed. They would agree that would be a great pity, and hard on the mother; but all the same, all persons have a right to life, the fetus is a person, and so on. I suspect, in fact, that they would not make an exception for a case in which, miraculously enough, the pregnancy went on for nine years, or even the rest of the mother's life.

Some won't even make an exception for a case in which continuation of the pregnancy is likely to shorten the mother's life; they regard abortion as impermissible even to save the mother's life. Such cases are nowadays very rare, and many opponents of abortion do not accept this extreme view. All the same, it is a good place to begin; a number of points of interest come out in respect to it.

1. Let us call the view that abortion is impermissible even to save the mother's life "the extreme view." I want to suggest first that it does not issue from the argument I mentioned earlier without the addition of some fairly powerful premises. Suppose a woman has become pregnant, and now learns that she has a cardiac condition such that she will die if she carries the baby to

term. What may be done for her? The fetus, being a person, has a right to life, but as the mother is a person too, so has she a right to life. Presumably they have an equal right to life. How is it supposed to come out that an abortion may not be performed? If mother and child have an equal right to life, shouldn't we perhaps flip a coin? Or should we add to the mother's right to life her right to decide what happens in and to her body, which everybody seems to be ready to grant — the sum of her rights now outweighing the fetus' right to life?

The most familiar argument here is the following. We are told that performing the abortion would be directly killing[3] the child, whereas doing nothing would not be killing the mother, but only letting her die. Moreover, in killing the child, one would be killing an innocent person, for the child has committed no crime, and is not aiming at his mother's death. And then there are a variety of ways in which this might be continued. (1) But as directly killing an innocent person is always and absolutely impermissible, an abortion may not be performed. Or, (2) as directly killing an innocent person is murder, and murder is always and absolutely impermissible, an abortion may not be performed.[4] Or, (3) as one's duty to refrain from directly killing an innocent person is more stringent than one's duty to keep a person from dying, an abortion may not be performed. Or, (4) if one's only options are directly killing an innocent person or letting a person die, one must prefer letting the person die, and thus an abortion may not be performed.[5]

Some people seem to have thought that these are not further premises which must be added if the conclusion is to be reached, but that they follow from the very fact that an innocent person has a right to life.[6] But this seems

[3]The term "direct" in the arguments I refer to is a technical one. Roughly, what is meant by *direct killing* is either killing as an end in itself, or killing as a means to some end; for example, the end of saving someone else's life. See note 6, below, for an example of its use.

[4]Cf. *Encyclical Letter of Pope Pius XI on Christian Marriage,* St. Paul Editions (Boston, n.d.), p. 32: "however much we may pity the mother whose health and even life is gravely imperiled in the performance of the duty allotted to her by nature, nevertheless what could ever be a sufficient reason for excusing in any way the direct murder of the innocent? This is precisely what we are dealing with here." Noonan (*The Morality of Abortion,* p. 43) reads this as follows: "What cause can ever avail to excuse in any way the direct killing of the innocent? For it is a question of that."

[5]The thesis in (4) is in an interesting way weaker than those in (1), (2), and (3): they rule out abortion even in cases in which both mother *and* child will die if the abortion is not performed. By contrast, one who held the view expressed in (4) could consistently say that one needn't prefer letting two persons die to killing one.

[6]Cf. the following passage from Pius XII, *Address to the Italian Catholic Society of Midwives:* "The baby in the maternal breast has the right to life immediately from God — Hence there is no man, no human authority, no science, no medical, eugenic, social, economic or moral 'indication' which can establish or grant a valid juridical ground for a direct deliberate disposition of an innocent human life, that is a disposition which looks to its destruction either as an end or as a means to another end perhaps in itself not illicit. — The baby, still not born, is a man in the same degree and for the same reason as the mother" (quoted in Noonan, *The Morality of Abortion,* p. 45).

to me to be a mistake, and perhaps the simplest way to show this is to bring out that while we must certainly grant that innocent persons have a right to life, the theses in (1) through (4) are all false. Take (2), for example. If directly killing an innocent person is murder, and thus is impermissible, then the mother's directly killing the innocent person inside her is murder, and thus is impermissible. But it cannot seriously be thought to be murder if the mother performs an abortion on herself to save her life. It cannot seriously be said that she *must* refrain, that she *must* sit passively by and wait for her death. Let us look again at the case of you and the violinist. There you are, in bed with the violinist, and the director of the hospital says to you, "It's all most distressing, and I deeply sympathize, but you see this is putting an additional strain on your kidneys, and you'll be dead within the month. But you have to stay where you are all the same. Because unplugging you would be directly killing an innocent violinist, and that's murder, and that's impermissible." If anything in the world is true, it is that you do not commit murder, you do not do what is impermissible, if you reach around to your back and unplug yourself from that violinist to save your life.

The main focus of attention in writings on abortion has been on what a third party may or may not do in answer to a request from a woman for an abortion. This is in a way understandable. Things being as they are, there isn't much a woman can safely do to abort herself. So the question asked is what a third party may do, and what the mother may do, if it is mentioned at all, is deduced, almost as an afterthought, from what it is concluded that third parties may do. But it seems to me that to treat the matter in this way is to refuse to grant to the mother that very status of person which is so firmly insisted on for the fetus. For we cannot simply read off what a person may do from what a third party may do. Suppose you find yourself trapped in a tiny house with a growing child. I mean a very tiny house, and a rapidly growing child — you are already up against the wall of the house and in a few minutes you'll be crushed to death. The child on the other hand won't be crushed to death; if nothing is done to stop him from growing he'll be hurt, but in the end he'll simply burst open the house and walk out a free man. Now I could well understand it if a bystander were to say, "There's nothing we can do for you. We cannot choose between your life and his, we cannot be the ones to decide who is to live, we cannot intervene." But it cannot be concluded that you too can do nothing, that you cannot attack it to save your life. However innocent the child may be, you do not have to wait passively while it crushes you to death. Perhaps a pregnant woman is vaguely felt to have the status of house, to which we don't allow the right of self-defense. But if the woman houses the child, it should be remembered that she is a person who houses it.

I should perhaps stop to say explicitly that I am not claiming that people have a right to do anything whatever to save their lives. I think, rather, that there are drastic limits to the right of self-defense. If someone threatens you with death unless you torture someone else to death, I think you have not the right, even to save your life, to do so. But the case under consideration here is very different. In our case there are only two people involved, one whose life is threatened, and one who threatens it. Both are innocent: the one who is threatened is not threatened because of any fault, the one who threatens does not threaten because of any fault. For this reason we may feel that we bystanders cannot intervene. But the person threatened can.

In sum, a woman surely can defend her life against the threat to it posed by the unborn child, even if doing so involves its death. And this shows not merely that the theses in (1) through (4) are false; it shows also that the extreme view of abortion is false, and so we need not canvass any other possible ways of arriving at it from the argument I mentioned at the outset.

2. The extreme view would of course be weakened to say that while abortion is permissible to save the mother's life, it may not be performed by a third party, but only by the mother herself. But this cannot be right, either. For what we have to keep in mind is that the mother and the unborn child are not like two tenants in a small house which has, by an unfortunate mistake, been rented to both: the mother *owns* the house. The fact that she does adds to the offensiveness of deducing that the mother can do nothing from the supposition that third parties can do nothing. But it does more than this: it casts a bright light on the supposition that third parties can do nothing. Certainly it lets us see that a third party who says "I cannot choose between you" is fooling himself if he thinks this is impartiality. If Jones has found and fastened on a certain coat, which he needs to keep him from freezing, but which Smith also needs to keep him from freezing, then it is not impartiality that says "I cannot choose between you" when Smith owns the coat. Women have said again and again "This body is *my* body!" and they have reason to feel angry, reason to feel that it has been like shouting into the wind. Smith, after all, is hardly likely to bless us if we say to him, "Of course it's your coat, anybody would grant that it is. But no one may choose between you and Jones who is to have it."

We should really ask what it is that says "no one may choose" in the face 15 of the fact that the body that houses the child is the mother's body. It may be simply a failure to appreciate this fact. But it may be something more interesting, namely the sense that one has a right to refuse to lay hands on people, even where it would be just and fair to do so, even where justice seems to require that somebody do so. Thus justice might call for somebody to get Smith's coat back from Jones, and yet you have a right to refuse to be the one to lay hands on Jones, a right to refuse to do physical violence to him. This, I think, must be granted. But then what should be said is not "no one may choose," but only "*I* cannot choose," and indeed not even this, but "*I* will not *act*," leaving it open that somebody else can or should, and in particular that anyone in a position of authority, with the job of securing people rights, both can and should. So this is no difficulty. I have not been arguing that any given third party must accede to the mother's request that he perform an abortion to save her life, but only that he may.

I suppose that in some views of human life the mother's body is only on loan to her, the loan not being one which gives her any prior claim to it. One who held this view might well think it impartiality to say "I cannot choose." But I shall simply ignore this possibility. My own view is that if a human being has any just, prior claim to anything at all, he has a just, prior claim to his own body. And perhaps this needn't be argued for here anyway, since, as I mentioned, the arguments against abortion we are looking at do grant that the woman has a right to decide what happens in and to her body.

But although they do grant it, I have tried to show that they do not take seriously what is done in granting it. I suggest the same thing will reappear even more clearly when we turn away from cases in which the mother's life is at stake, and attend, as I propose we now do, to the vastly more common cases in which a woman wants an abortion for some less weighty reason than preserving her own life.

3. Where the mother's life is not at stake, the argument I mentioned at the outset seems to have a much stronger pull. "Everyone has a right to life, so the unborn person has a right to life." And isn't the child's right to life weightier than anything other than the mother's own right to life, which she might put forward as ground for an abortion?

This argument treats the right to life as if it were unproblematic. It is not, and this seems to me to be precisely the source of the mistake.

For we should now, at long last, ask what it comes to, to have a right to life. In some views having a right to life includes having a right to be given at least the bare minimum one needs for continued life. But suppose that what in fact *is* the bare minimum a man needs for continued life is something he has no right at all to be given? If I am sick unto death, and the only thing that will save my life is the touch of Henry Fonda's cool hand on my fevered brow, then all the same, I have no right to be given the touch of Henry Fonda's cool hand on my fevered brow. It would be frightfully nice of him to fly in from the West Coast to provide it. It would be less nice, though no doubt well meant, if my friends flew out to the West Coast and carried Henry Fonda back with them. But I have no right at all against anybody that he should do this for me. Or again, to return to the story I told earlier, the fact that for continued life that violinist needs the continued use of your kidneys does not establish that he has a right to be given the continued use of your kidneys. He certainly has no right against you that *you* should give him continued use of your kidneys. For nobody has any right to use your kidneys unless you give him such a right; and nobody has the right against you that you shall give him this right — if you do allow him to go on using your kidneys, this is a kindness on your part, and not something he can claim from you as his due. Nor has he any right against anybody else that *they* should give him continued use of your kidneys. Certainly he had no right against the Society of Music Lovers that they should plug him into you in the first place. And if you now start to unplug yourself, having learned that you will otherwise have to spend nine years in bed with him, there is nobody in the world who must try to prevent you, in order to see to it that he is given something he has a right to be given.

Some people are rather stricter about the right to life. In their view, it does not include the right to be given anything, but amounts to, and only to, the right not to be killed by anybody. But here a related difficulty arises. If everybody is to refrain from killing that violinist, then everybody must refrain from doing a great many different sorts of things. Everybody must refrain from slitting his throat, everybody must refrain from shooting him — and everybody must refrain from unplugging you from him. But does he have a right against everybody that they shall refrain from unplugging you from him? To refrain from doing this is to allow him to continue to use your kidneys. It could be argued that he has a right against us that *we* should allow him to continue to use your kidneys. That is, while he had no right against us that we should give him the use of your kidneys, it might be argued that he anyway has a right against us that we shall not now intervene and deprive him of the use of your kidneys. I shall come back to third-party interventions later. But certainly the violinist has no right against you that *you* shall allow him to continue to use your kidneys. As I said, if you do allow him to use them, it is a kindness on your part, and not something you owe him.

The difficulty I point to here is not peculiar to the right to life. It reappears in connection with all the other natural rights; and it is something which an adequate account of rights must deal with. For present purposes it is enough just to draw attention to it. But I would stress that I am not arguing that people do not have a right to life — quite to the contrary, it seems to me that the primary control we must place on the acceptability of an account of rights is that it should turn out in that account to be a truth that all persons have a right to life. I am arguing only that having a right to life does not guarantee having either a right to be given the use of or a right to be allowed continued use of another person's body — even if one needs it for life itself. So the right to life will not serve the opponents of abortion in the very simple and clear way in which they seem to have thought it would.

4. There is another way to bring out the difficulty. In the most ordinary sort of case, to deprive someone of what he has a right to is to treat him unjustly. Suppose a boy and his small brother are jointly given a box of chocolates for Christmas. If the older boy takes the box and refuses to give his brother any of the chocolates, he is unjust to him, for the brother has been given a right to half of them. But suppose that, having learned that otherwise it means nine years in bed with that violinist, you unplug yourself from him. You surely are not being unjust to him, for you gave him no right to use your kidneys, and no one else can have given him any such right. But we have to notice that in unplugging yourself, you are killing him; and violinists, like everybody else, have a right to life, and thus in the view we are considering just now, the right not to be killed. So here you do what he supposedly has a right you shall not do, but you do not act unjustly to him in doing it.

The emendation which may be made at this point is this: the right to life consists not in the right not to be killed, but rather in the right not to be killed unjustly. This runs a risk of circularity, but never mind: it would enable us to square the fact that the violinist has a right to life with the fact that you do not act unjustly toward him in unplugging yourself, thereby killing him. For if you do not kill him unjustly, you do not violate his right to life, and so it is no wonder you do him no injustice.

But if this emendation is accepted, the gap in the argument against   25 abortion stares us plainly in the face: it is by no means enough to show that the fetus is a person, and to remind us that all persons have a right to life — we need to be shown also that killing the fetus violates its right to life, i.e., that abortion is unjust killing. And is it?

I suppose we may take it as a datum that in a case of pregnancy due to rape the mother has not given the unborn person a right to the use of her body for food and shelter. Indeed, in what pregnancy could it be supposed that the mother has given the unborn person such a right? It is not as if there were unborn persons drifting about the world, to whom a woman who wants a child says "I invite you in."

But it might be argued that there are other ways one can have acquired a right to the use of another person's body than by having been invited to use it by that person. Suppose a woman voluntarily indulges in intercourse, knowing of the chance it will issue in pregnancy, and then she does become pregnant; is she not in part responsible for the presence, in fact the very existence, of the unborn person inside her? No doubt she did not invite it in. But doesn't her partial responsibility for its being there itself give it a right to the use of her body?[7] If so, then her aborting it would be more like the boy's taking away the chocolates, and less like your unplugging yourself from the violinist — doing so would be depriving it of what it does have a right to, and thus would be doing it an injustice.

And then, too, it might be asked whether or not she can kill it even to save her own life: If she voluntarily called it into existence, how can she now kill it, even in self-defense?

The first thing to be said about this is that it is something new. Opponents of abortion have been so concerned to make out the independence of the fetus, in order to establish that it has a right to life, just as its mother does, that they have tended to overlook the possible support they might gain from making out that the fetus is *dependent* on the mother, in order to establish that she has a special kind of responsibility for it, a responsibility that gives it rights against her which are not possessed by any independent person — such as an ailing violinist who is a stranger to her.

On the other hand, this argument would give the unborn person a right   30 to its mother's body only if her pregnancy resulted from a voluntary act, undertaken in full knowledge of the chance a pregnancy might result from it. It would leave out entirely the unborn person whose existence is due to rape.

---

[7]The need for a discussion of this argument was brought home to me by members of the Society for Ethical and Legal Philosophy, to whom this paper was originally presented.

Pending the availability of some further argument, then, we would be left with the conclusion that unborn persons whose existence is due to rape have no right to the use of their mothers' bodies, and thus that aborting them is not depriving them of anything they have a right to and hence is not unjust killing.

And we should also notice that it is not at all plain that this argument really does go even as far as it purports to. For there are cases and cases, and the details make a difference. If the room is stuffy, and I therefore open a window to air it, and a burglar climbs in, it would be absurd to say, "Ah, now he can stay, she's given him a right to the use of her house — for she is partially responsible for his presence there, having voluntarily done what enabled him to get in, in full knowledge that there are such things as burglars, and that burglars burgle." It would be still more absurd to say this if I had had bars installed outside my windows, precisely to prevent burglars from getting in, and a burglar got in only because of a defect in the bars. It remains equally absurd if we imagine it is not a burglar who climbs in, but an innocent person who blunders or falls in. Again, suppose it were like this: people-seeds drift about in the air like pollen, and if you open your windows, one may drift in and take root in your carpets or upholstery. You don't want children, so you fix up your windows with fine mesh screens, the very best you can buy. As can happen, however, and on very, very rare occasions does happen, one of the screens is defective; and a seed drifts in and takes root. Does the person-plant who now develops have a right to the use of your house? Surely not — despite the fact that you voluntarily opened your windows, you knowingly kept carpets and upholstered furniture, and you knew that screens were sometimes defective. Someone may argue that you are responsible for its rooting, that it does have a right to your house, because after all you *could* have lived out your life with bare floors and furniture, or with sealed windows and doors. But this won't do — for by the same token anyone can avoid a pregnancy due to rape by having a hysterectomy, or anyway by never leaving home without a (reliable!) army.

It seems to me that the argument we are looking at can establish at most that there are *some* cases in which the unborn person has a right to the use of its mother's body, and therefore some cases in which abortion is unjust killing. There is room for much discussion and argument as to precisely which, if any. But I think we should sidestep this issue and leave it open, for at any rate the argument certainly does not establish that all abortion is unjust killing.

5. There is room for yet another argument here, however. We surely must all grant that there may be cases in which it would be morally indecent to detach a person from your body at the cost of his life. Suppose you learn that what the violinist needs is not nine years of your life, but only one hour: all you need do to save his life is to spend one hour in that bed with him. Suppose also that letting him use your kidneys for that one hour would not affect your health in the slightest. Admittedly you were kidnapped. Admittedly you did not give anyone permission to plug him into you. Nevertheless

it seems to me plain you *ought* to allow him to use your kidneys for that hour — it would be indecent to refuse.

Again, suppose pregnancy lasted only an hour, and constituted no threat to life or health. And suppose that a woman becomes pregnant as a result of rape. Admittedly she did not voluntarily do anything to bring about the existence of a child. Admittedly she did nothing at all which would give the unborn person a right to the use of her body. All the same it might well be said, as in the newly emended violinist story, that she ought to allow it to remain for that hour — that it would be indecent in her to refuse.

Now some people are inclined to use the term "right" in such a way that 35 it follows from the fact that you ought to allow a person to use your body for the hour he needs, that he has a right to use your body for the hour he needs, even though he has not been given that right by any person or act. They may say that it follows also that if you refuse, you act unjustly toward him. This use of the term is perhaps so common that it cannot be called wrong; nevertheless it seems to me to be an unfortunate loosening of what we would do better to keep a tight rein on. Suppose that box of chocolates I mentioned earlier had not been given to both boys jointly, but was given only to the older boy. There he sits, stolidly eating his way through the box, his small brother watching enviously. Here we are likely to say "You ought not to be so mean. You ought to give your brother some of those chocolates." My own view is that it just does not follow from the truth of this that the brother has any right to any of the chocolates. If the boy refuses to give his brother any, he is greedy, stingy, callous — but not unjust. I suppose that the people I have in mind will say it does follow that the brother has a right to some of the chocolates, and thus that the boy does act unjustly if he refuses to give his brother any. But the effect of saying this is to obscure what we should keep distinct, namely the difference between the boy's refusal in this case and the boy's refusal in the earlier case, in which the box was given to both boys jointly, and in which the small brother thus had what was from any point of view clear title to half.

A further objection to so using the term "right" that from the fact that A ought to do a thing for B, it follows that B has a right against A that A do it for him, is that it is going to make the question of whether or not a man has a right to a thing turn on how easy it is to provide him with it; and this seems not merely unfortunate, but morally unacceptable. Take the case of Henry Fonda again. I said earlier that I had no right to the touch of his cool hand on my fevered brow, even though I needed it to save my life. I said it would be frightfully nice of him to fly in from the West Coast to provide me with it, but that I had no right against him that he should do so. But suppose he isn't on the West Coast. Suppose he has only to walk across the room, place a hand briefly on my brow — and lo, my life is saved. Then surely he ought to do it, it would be indecent to refuse. Is it to be said "Ah, well, it follows that in this case she has a right to the touch of his hand on her brow, and so it would be an injustice in him to refuse?" So that I have a right to it when it is easy for him to provide it, though no right when it's hard? It's rather a shocking idea that anyone's rights should fade away and disappear as it gets harder and harder to accord them to him.

So my own view is that even though you ought to let the violinist use your kidneys for the one hour he needs, we should not conclude that he has a right to do so — we would say that if you refuse, you are, like the boy who owns all the chocolates and will give none away, self-centered and callous, indecent in fact, but not unjust. And similarly, that even supposing a case in which a woman pregnant due to rape ought to allow the unborn person to use her body for the hour he needs, we should not conclude that he has a right to do so; we should conclude that she is self-centered, callous, indecent, but not unjust, if she refuses. The complaints are no less grave; they are just different. However, there is no need to insist on this point. If anyone does wish to deduce "he has a right" from "you ought," then all the same he must surely grant that there are cases in which it is not morally required of you that you allow that violinist to use your kidneys, and in which he does not have a right to use them, and in which you do not do him an injustice if you refuse. And so also for mother and unborn child. Except in such cases as the unborn person has a right to demand it — and we were leaving open the possibility that there may be such cases — nobody is morally *required* to make large sacrifices, of health, of all other interests and concerns, of all other duties and commitments, for nine years, or even for nine months, in order to keep another person alive.

6. We have in fact to distinguish between two kinds of Samaritan: the Good Samaritan and what we might call the Minimally Decent Samaritan. The story of the Good Samaritan, you will remember, goes like this:

> A certain man went down from Jerusalem to Jericho, and fell among thieves, which stripped him of his raiment, and wounded him, and departed, leaving him half dead.
>
> And by chance there came down a certain priest that way; and when he saw him, he passed by on the other side.
>
> And likewise a Levite, when he was at the place, came and looked on him, and passed by on the other side.
>
> But a certain Samaritan, as he journeyed, came where he was; and when he saw him he had compassion on him.
>
> And went to him, and bound up his wounds, pouring in oil and wine, and set him on his own beast, and brought him to an inn, and took care of him.
>
> And on the morrow, when he departed, he took out two pence, and gave them to the host, and said unto him, "Take care of him; and whatsoever thou spendest more, when I come again, I will repay thee."
>
> (Luke 10:30–35)

The Good Samaritan went out of his way, at some cost to himself, to help one in need of it. We are not told what the options were, that is, whether or not the priest and the Levite could have helped by doing less than the Good Samaritan did, but assuming they could have, then the fact they did nothing at all shows they were not even Minimally Decent Samaritans, not because they were not Samaritans, but because they were not even minimally decent.

These things are a matter of degree, of course, but there is a difference, and it comes out perhaps most clearly in the story of Kitty Genovese, who, as you will remember, was murdered while thirty-eight people watched or listened, and did nothing at all to help her. A Good Samaritan would have rushed out to give direct assistance against the murderer. Or perhaps we had better allow that it would have been a Splendid Samaritan who did this, on the ground that it would have involved a risk of death for himself. But the thirty-eight not only did not do this, they did not even trouble to pick up a phone to call the police. Minimally Decent Samaritanism would call for doing at least that, and their not having done it was monstrous.

After telling the story of the Good Samaritan, Jesus said "Go, and do 40 thou likewise." Perhaps he meant that we are morally required to act as the Good Samaritan did. Perhaps he was urging people to do more than is morally required of them. At all events it seems plain that it was not morally required of any of the thirty-eight that he rush out to give direct assistance at the risk of his own life, and that it is not morally required of anyone that he give long stretches of his life — nine years or nine months — to sustaining the life of a person who has no special right (we were leaving open the possibility of this) to demand it.

Indeed, with one rather striking class of exceptions, no one in any country in the world is *legally* required to do anywhere near as much as this for anyone else. The class of exceptions is obvious. My main concern here is not the state of the law in respect to abortion, but it is worth drawing attention to the fact that in no state in this country is any man compelled by law to be even a Minimally Decent Samaritan to any person; there is no law under which charges could be brought against the thirty-eight who stood by while Kitty Genovese died. By contrast, in most states in this country women are compelled by law to be not merely Minimally Decent Samaritans, but Good Samaritans to unborn persons inside them. This doesn't by itself settle anything one way or the other, because it may well be argued that there should be laws in this country — as there are in many European countries — compelling at least Minimally Decent Samaritanism.[8] But it does show that there is a gross injustice in the existing state of the law. And it shows also that the groups currently working against liberalization of abortion laws, in fact

---

[8]For a discussion of the difficulties involved and a survey of the European experience with such laws, see *The Good Samaritan and the Law,* ed. James M. Ratcliffe (New York, 1966).

working toward having it declared unconstitutional for a state to permit abortion, had better start working for the adoption of Good Samaritan laws generally, or earn the charge that they are acting in bad faith.

I should think, myself, that Minimally Decent Samaritan laws would be one thing, Good Samaritan laws quite another, and in fact highly improper. But we are not here concerned with the law. What we should ask is not whether anybody should be compelled by law to be a Good Samaritan, but whether we must accede to a situation in which somebody is being compelled — by nature, perhaps — to be a Good Samaritan. We have, in other words, to look now at third-party interventions. I have been arguing that no person is morally required to make large sacrifices to sustain the life of another who has no right to demand them, and this even where the sacrifices do not include life itself; we are not morally required to be Good Samaritans or anyway Very Good Samaritans to one another. But what if a man cannot extricate himself from such a situation? What if he appeals to us to extricate him? It seems to me plain that there are cases in which we can, cases in which a Good Samaritan would extricate him. There you are, you were kidnapped, and nine years in bed with that violinist lie ahead of you. You have your own life to lead. You are sorry, but you simply cannot see giving up so much of your life to the sustaining of his. You cannot extricate yourself, and ask us to do so. I should have thought that — in light of his having no right to the use of your body — it was obvious that we do not have to accede to your being forced to give up so much. We can do what you ask. There is no injustice to the violinist in our doing so.

7. Following the lead of the opponents of abortion, I have throughout been speaking of the fetus merely as a person, and what I have been asking is whether or not the argument we began with, which proceeds only from the fetus's being a person, really does establish its conclusion. I have argued that it does not.

But of course there are arguments and arguments, and it may be said that I have simply fastened on the wrong one. It may be said that what is important is not merely the fact that the fetus is a person, but that it is a person for whom the woman has a special kind of responsibility issuing from the fact that she is its mother. And it might be argued that all my analogies are therefore irrelevant — for you do not have that special kind of responsibility for that violinist, Henry Fonda does not have that special kind of responsibility for me. And our attention might be drawn to the fact that men and women both *are* compelled by law to provide support for their children.

I have in effect dealt (briefly) with this argument in section 4 above; but a (still briefer) recapitulation now may be in order. Surely we do not have any such "special responsibility" for a person unless we have assumed it, explicitly or implicitly. If a set of parents do not try to prevent pregnancy, do not obtain an abortion, and then at the time of birth of the child do not put it out for adoption, but rather take it home with them, then they have assumed responsibility for it, they have given it rights, and they cannot *now* withdraw support from it at the cost of its life because they now find it difficult to go on providing for it. But if they have taken all reasonable precautions against having a child, they do not simply by virtue of their biological relationship to the child who comes into existence have a special responsibility for it. They may wish to assume responsibility for it, or they may not wish to. And I am suggesting that if assuming responsibility for it would require large sacrifices, then they may refuse. A Good Samaritan would not refuse — or anyway, a Splendid Samaritan, if the sacrifices that had to be made were enormous. But then so would a Good Samaritan assume responsibility for that violinist; so would Henry Fonda, if he is a Good Samaritan, fly in from the West Coast and assume responsibility for me.

8. My argument will be found unsatisfactory on two counts by many of those who want to regard abortion as morally permissible. First, while I do argue that abortion is not impermissible, I do not argue that it is always permissible. There may well be cases in which carrying the child to term requires only Minimally Decent Samaritanism of the mother, and this is a standard we must not fall below. I am inclined to think it a merit of my account precisely that it does *not* give a general yes or a general no. It allows for and supports our sense that, for example, a sick and desperately frightened fourteen-year-old schoolgirl, pregnant due to rape, may *of course* choose abortion, and that any law which rules this out is an insane law. And it also allows for and supports our sense that in other cases resort to abortion is even positively indecent. It would be indecent in the woman to request an abortion, and indecent in a doctor to perform it, if she is in her seventh month, and wants the abortion just to avoid the nuisance of postponing a trip abroad. The very fact that the arguments I have been drawing attention to treat all cases of abortion, or even all cases of abortion in which the mother's life is not at stake, as morally on a par ought to have made them suspect at the outset.

Secondly, while I am arguing for the permissibility of abortion in some cases, I am not arguing for the right to secure the death of the unborn child. It is easy to confuse these two things in that up to a certain point in the life of the fetus it is not able to survive outside the mother's body; hence removing it from her body guarantees its death. But they are importantly different. I have argued that you are not morally required to spend nine months in bed, sustaining the life of that violinist; but to say this is by no means to say that if, when you unplug yourself, there is a miracle and he survives, you then have a right to turn around and slit his throat. You may detach yourself even if this costs him his life; you have no right to be guaranteed his death, by some other means, if unplugging yourself does not kill him. There are some people who will feel dissatisfied by this feature of my argument. A woman may be utterly devastated by the thought of a child, a bit of herself, put out for adoption and never seen or heard of again. She may therefore want not merely that the child be detached from her, but more, that it die. Some opponents of abortion are inclined to regard this as beneath contempt — thereby showing insensitivity to what is surely a powerful source of despair. All the same, I agree that the desire for the child's death is not one which anybody may gratify, should it turn out to be possible to detach the child alive.

At this place, however, it should be remembered that we have only been pretending throughout that the fetus is a human being from the moment of conception. A very early abortion is surely not the killing of a person, and so is not dealt with by anything I have said here.

Suggestions for Writing and Discussion

1. Imagine that you are Thomson, getting ready to draft this piece in 1971. What is the primary appeal you choose to use in this argument, and why do you make this choice?
2. In your own words, what is Thomson saying by using the analogy of the violin player? By using the boys' box of candy? By using the mother as a house? Which one of these analogies do you find most effective? Which one do you find least effective? Explain the reasons for your choices.
3. Why, when she maintains a legal perspective for almost the entire argument, does Thomson include the story of the Good Samaritan from the Bible? What does she hope to gain by using this? In your opinion, is the inclusion of this parable effective or not?
4. Would you say Thomson's personal beliefs toward abortion are amoral, immoral, or moral? Explain.
5. According to Thomson, what's the difference between illegal, immoral, and indecent? Do you agree with her definitions? Explain.
6. As Thomson writes, in this country, no one is legally obligated to help another person in need. In your opinion, should the United States consider adopting "Good Samaritan" laws? Can you foresee any resistance to these laws? Explain.
7. In summary, one might say that while Thomson believes that having a child is a noble act, she sees giving birth neither as a responsibility of nor as a requirement for women. Do you think Elizabeth Cady Stanton would agree with this statement? Explain what you think her position on abortion might be in relation to Thomson's.

Suggestions for Extended Thinking and Research

1. Research the basic rulings in the *Roe v. Wade* case. Research as well more recent rulings and render a prediction: Will future laws regarding abortion become more or less restrictive?
2. Write an effective argument against a woman's right to abortion.
3. Write an essay in which you analyze any rights and responsibilities that men have as far as their unborn fetuses are concerned.

GREG KEATH

Abortion Is Not a Civil Right

> *Founder and president of the Black Alliance for Family, Greg Keath writes and speaks frequently on issues related to black families. This argument first appeared in the* Wall Street Journal *on September 27, 1989.*

Prereading/Journal-Writing Suggestions

1. What group of people in this country do you think has more abortions than the rest? What reasons can you offer? What resources could you use to check your projections in order to confirm or revise them?
2. Is poverty a good reason for an abortion? Explain your response.

The battle around the abortion issue has raged for years with the understanding that the major combatants involved are either white liberals, white evangelical Protestants, or white Catholics. Meanwhile, black America — which is affected more profoundly by abortion than is any other group in society — has experienced its own sharp internal division. While most black leaders have favored abortion rights, opinion surveys have found mainstream blacks to be among those most strongly opposed to abortion on demand.

Where does black America really stand on the issue? Statistics from the Department of Health and Human Services suggest that black women are more than twice as likely to abort their children as white women. For every three black babies born, two are aborted. Forty-three percent of all abortions in the United States are performed on black women. From figures supplied by the federal government and the Alan Guttmacher Institute, Richard D. Glasow of National Right to Life has estimated that some 400,000 black pregnancies are aborted each year. At the same time, according to a 1988 poll taken by the National Opinion Research Center, 62 percent of blacks said abortion should be illegal under all circumstances.

How can blacks consistently tell pollsters they oppose abortion while we exercise that right proportionately more than any other group in America? In part, black abortion rates reflect the pressure of social service and private welfare agencies in our communities. A black teenager told me she had asked Planned Parenthood in Detroit for help in carrying her baby to term and putting it up for adoption. But because the baby's father was white, a clinician advised her to abort the baby because, "No one wants to adopt a zebra." Better-educated black women are pushed toward abortion by different forces: the threat to educational hopes or aspirations to economic independence.

As these women struggle with their profound moral choices, many national black leaders have ceased to look at abortion as a moral problem with moral consequences, and have come to see it instead as an opportunity for forging political alliances. At the March for Life rally in 1977 Jesse Jackson said, "The solution to a [crisis pregnancy] is not to kill the innocent baby but to deal with [the mother's] values and her attitudes toward life." Twelve years later, he spoke to the enormous April 1989 abortion rights march in Washington.

The black leadership has succumbed to the temptation to present abor- 5 tion as a civil-rights issue. By this reasoning, abortion is to women in the 1980s what desegregation was to blacks in the 1960s. Any erosion of abortion rights would accelerate the "move to the right" that black leaders say threatens black progress. At a news conference earlier this year sponsored by Planned Parenthood, Jesse Jackson, Andrew Young, and Julian Bond issued a statement denouncing Operation Rescue, comparing those who participate in abortion clinic sit-ins to "the segregationists who fought desperately to block black Americans from access to their rights."

But many blacks wonder whether black civil rights and abortion fit so neatly together. Black pregnancies have historically been the target of social engineers such as Margaret Sanger, founder of Planned Parenthood. Sanger was convinced that blacks, Jews, Eastern Europeans, and other non-Aryan groups were detracting from the creative intellectual and social potential of America, and she wanted those groups' numbers reduced. In her first book, *Pivot of Civilization,* she warned of free maternity care for the poor: "Instead of decreasing and aiming to eliminate the stocks that are most detrimental to the future of the race and the world it tends to render them to a menacing degree dominant."

In the late 1930s Sanger instituted the Negro Project, a program to gain the backing of black ministers, physicians, and political leaders for birth control and sterilization in the black community. Sanger wrote, "The most successful education approach to the Negro is through a religious appeal. We do not want word to go out that we want to exterminate the Negro population, and the minister is the man who can straighten out that idea if it ever occurs to any of their more rebellious members."

There are disturbing indications that this state of mind has not vanished. Even now, 70 percent of the clinics operated by Planned Parenthood—the operator of the largest chain of abortion facilities in the nation—are in black and Hispanic neighborhoods. The schools in which their school-based clinics are located are substantially nonwhite. In a March 1939 letter, Sanger explained why clinics had to be located where the "dysgenic" races lived: "The birth control clinics all over the country are doing their utmost to reach the lower strata of our population . . . but we must realize that there are hundreds of thousands of women who never leave their own vicinity."

Blacks must no longer keep silent on this issue. We cannot permit the public to continue to imagine that we are obediently following our national leaders in endorsing abortion on demand and we must resist the forces that drive black women to seek abortion. The black community in cities such as

Baltimore, Chicago, Detroit, and Washington, D.C., has started crisis pregnancy centers to help these women. We are already besieged by homicide, drugs, AIDS, and an alarmingly high infant mortality rate. We do not need to reenact the sterilization programs of the 1930s and 1940s.

___

Suggestions for Writing and Discussion

1. Summarize Greg Keath's main point in this article. What may have prompted him to write this piece in the first place?
2. What does Keath believe are the causes for the black abortion rate in this country? What other causes might you add to this list?
3. If Jesse Jackson were running for president, do you think Keath would campaign for or against him? Explain your answer with inferences drawn from the text.
4. Keath writes that "black pregnancies have historically been the target of social engineers such as Margaret Sanger, founder of Planned Parenthood." What does he believe was Sanger's main purpose for targeting the black community? What evidence does he offer to support his idea that Sanger was mainly concerned with the black community? Why doesn't Keath cite any other social engineers?
5. What does Keath gain, or lose, by using Sanger as the sole example for one-third of this article? What might his purpose be in doing this?
6. Keath gives possible reasons why blacks have so many abortions, but he does not give reasons why they should not. How can you tell what his position is on this issue? In your opinion, why doesn't Keath give positive reasons for black women to avoid abortions?
7. On what issues might Keath agree with Elizabeth Cady Stanton? With Judith Thomson? On what points might he argue with either one or both of these women?

___

Suggestions for Extended Thinking and Research

1. Do your own research on Margaret Sanger. According to your findings, what was her personal philosophy with regard to women's rights, the poor, and minorities? Do your findings support or contradict the charges that Keath made in his article?
2. Read Sanger's book *Pivot of Civilization*. From reading this book, how would you describe her philosophy of life? Does she call for the reduction of the non-Aryan race, or is this belief exaggerated or taken out of context by Keath?
3. Read current speeches made by black leaders today. What is the primary message that they seem to be giving to the black American community? In your opinion, are they simply "playing politics"? Explain your response.

___

WILLIAM BRADFORD REYNOLDS
Equal Opportunity, Not Equal Results

> *During the Reagan administration, William Bradford Reynolds served as assistant attorney general for civil rights. This argument first appeared in* The Moral Foundations of Civil Rights *(1986).*

Prereading/Journal-Writing Suggestions

1. Imagine that you are a white male and a recent college graduate looking for a job. You and a member of a minority race are applying for the same position. You are both equally qualified for the position, but the minority applicant gets the position because the company believes in fostering diversity among its employees. Do you have a right to complain about this procedure? What would you do?

2. Imagine that you are a woman with three years' experience in management in your company. Your boss hires a younger white male, who just graduated from college, for a position in which he will earn substantially more than you presently do. What do you do? Complain? Grin and bear it? Take legal action? Explain!

3. Do you think that individuals in this country are granted equal opportunities in education? Use experiences in your own life in answering this question.

No one disputes that "affirmative action" is a subject of vital significance for our society. The character of our country is determined in large measure by the manner in which we treat our individual citizens — whether we treat them fairly or unfairly, whether we ensure equal opportunity to all individuals, or guarantee equal results to selected groups. As assistant attorney general, I am faced daily with what seem to have emerged on the civil rights horizon as the two predominant competing values that drive the debate on this issue — that is, the value of equal opportunity and the value of equal results. I have devoted a great deal of time and attention to the very different meanings these concepts lend to the phrase "affirmative action."

Typically, to the understandable confusion of almost everyone, "affirmative action" is the term used to refer to both of these contrasting values. There is, however, a world of difference between "affirmative action" as a measure for ensuring equality of opportunity and "affirmative action" as a tool for achieving equality of results.

In the former instance, affirmative steps are taken so that all individuals (whatever their race, color, sex, or national origin) will be given the chance to compete with all others on equal terms; each is to be given his or her place at the starting line without advantage or disadvantage. In the latter, by contrast, the promise of affirmative action is that those who participate will arrive at the finish line in prearranged places — places allocated by race or sex.

I have expressed on a number of occasions my conviction that the promise of equal results is a false one. We can never assure equal results in a world in which individuals differ greatly in motivation and ability; nor, in my view, is such a promise morally or constitutionally acceptable. In fact, this was well understood at the time that the concept of "affirmative action" was first introduced as a remedial technique in the civil rights arena. In its original formulation, that concept embraced only nonpreferential affirmative efforts, such as training programs and enhanced recruitment activities, aimed at opening wide the doors of opportunity to all Americans who cared to enter. Thus, President Kennedy's Executive Order 10925, one of the earliest to speak to the subject, stated that federal contractors should "take affirmative action to ensure that the applicants are employed, and that employees are treated during employment, without regard to their race, creed, color, or national origin."

This principle was understood by all at that time to mean simply that 5 individuals previously neglected in the search for talent must be allowed to apply and be considered along with all others for available jobs or contracting opportunities, but that the hiring and selection decisions would be made from the pool of applicants without regard to race, creed, color, or national origin — and later sex. No one was to be afforded a preference, or special treatment, because of group membership; rather, all were to be treated equally as individuals based on personal ability and worth.

This administration's commitment is to what Vice Chairman of the Civil Rights Commission Morris Abram calls the "original and undefiled meaning" of "affirmative action." Where unlawful discrimination exists, we see that it is brought to an abrupt and uncompromising halt; where that discrimination has harmed any individual, we ensure that every victim of the wrongdoing receives "make-whole" relief; and, where affirmative steps in the nature of training programs and enhanced recruitment efforts are needed, we require such steps to be taken to force open the doors of opportunity that have too long remained closed to far too many.

The criticism, of course, is that we do not go far enough. The remedial use of goals and timetables, quotas, or other such numerical devices, designed to achieve a particular balance in race or sex in the work force, has been accepted by the lower federal courts as an available instrument of relief, and therefore, it is argued, such an approach should not be abandoned. There are several responses to this sort of argumentation.

The first is a strictly legal one and rests on the Supreme Court's recent decision in *Firefighters Local Union No. 1784 v. Stotts,* 104 S. Ct. 2576 (1984). The Supreme Court in *Stotts* did not merely hold that federal courts are prohibited from ordering racially preferential layoffs to maintain a certain racial percentage, or that courts cannot disrupt bona fide seniority systems. To be sure, it did so rule, but the Court said much more, and in unmistakably forceful terms. As Justice Stevens remarked during his August 4, 1984, commencement address at Northwestern University, the decision represents "a far-reaching pronouncement concerning the limits on a court's power to prescribe affirmative action as a remedy for proven violations of Title VII of the Civil Rights Act." For the *Stotts* majority grounded the decision, at bottom, on the holding that federal courts are without *any* authority under Section 706(g) — the remedial provision of Title VII — to order a remedy, either by consent decree or after full litigation, that goes beyond enjoining the unlawful conduct and awarding "make-whole" relief for actual victims of the discrimination. Thus, quotas or other preferential techniques that, by design, benefit nonvictims because of race or sex cannot be a part of Title VII relief ordered in a court case, whether the context is hiring, promotion, or layoffs.

A brief review of the opinion's language is particularly useful to understanding the sweep of the decision. At issue in *Stotts* was a district court injunction ordering that certain white firefighters with greater seniority be laid off before blacks with less seniority in order to preserve a certain percentage of black representation in the fire department's work force. The Supreme Court held that this order was improper because "there was no finding that any of the blacks protected from layoff had been a victim of discrimination." Relying explicitly on Section 706(g) of Title VII, the Court held that Congress intended to "provide make-whole relief only to those who have been actual victims of illegal discrimination."

Specific portions of the legislative history of the act were cited in support 10 of this interpretation. For example, Hubert Humphrey, the principal force behind passage of Title VII in the Senate, had assured his colleagues during consideration of the statute that:

> [t]here is nothing in [the proposed bill] that will give any power to the Commission *or to any court* to require hiring, firing or promotion of employees in order to meet a racial "quota" or to achieve a certain racial balance. That bugaboo has been brought up a dozen times; but it is nonexistent.

Moreover, the Court recognized that the interpretive memorandum of the bill entered into the Congressional Record by Senators Clark and Case stated unambiguously that "Title VII does not permit the ordering of racial quotas in business or unions."

After *Stotts,* it is, I think, abundantly clear that Section 706(g) of Title VII does not tolerate remedial action by courts that would grant to nonvictims of discrimination — at the expense of wholly innocent employees or potential employees — an employment preference based solely on the fact that they are members of a particular race or gender. Quotas, or any other numerical device based on color or sex, are by definition victim-blind: they embrace without distinction, and accord preferential treatment to, persons having no claim to "make-whole" relief. Accordingly, whether such formulas are employed for hiring, promotion, or layoffs, they must fail under any reading of the statute's remedial provision.

There are equally strong policy reasons for coming to this conclusion. The remedial use of preferences had been justified by the courts primarily on the theory that they are necessary to cure "the effects of past discrimination" and thus, in the words of one Supreme Court Justice, to "get beyond racism." This reasoning is twice-flawed.

First, it is premised on the proposition that any racial imbalance in the employer's work force is explainable only as a lingering effect of past racial discrimination. The analysis is no different where gender-based discrimination is involved. Yet, in either instance, equating "underrepresentation" of certain groups with discrimination against those groups ignores the fact that occupation selection in a free society is determined by a host of factors, principally individual interest, industry, and ability. It simply is not the case that applicants for any given job come proportionally qualified by race, gender, and ethnic origin in accordance with U.S. population statistics. Nor do the career interests of individuals break down proportionally among racial or gender groups. Accordingly, a selection process free of discrimination is no more likely to produce "proportional representation" along race or sex lines than it is to ensure proportionality among persons grouped according to hair color, shoe size, or any other irrelevant personal characteristic. No human endeavor, since the beginning of time, has attracted persons sharing a common physical characteristic in numbers proportional to the representation of such persons in the community. "Affirmative action" assumptions that one might expect otherwise in the absence of race or gender discrimination are ill-conceived.

Second, and more important, there is nothing *remedial* — let alone *equitable* — about a court order that *requires* the hiring, promotion, or retention of a person who has not suffered discrimination solely because that person is a member of the same racial or gender group as other persons who were victimized by the discriminatory employment practices. The rights protected under Title VII belong to individuals, not to groups. The Supreme Court made clear some years ago that "the basic policy of Title VII requires that courts focus on fairness to individuals rather than fairness to classes." The same message was again delivered in *Stotts*. As indicated, remedying a violation of Title VII requires that the individual victimized by the unlawful discrimination be restored to his or her "rightful place." It almost goes without saying, however, that a person who is *not* victimized by the employer's discriminatory practices has no claim to a "rightful place" in the employer's work force. And according preferential treatment to *nonvictims* in no way remedies the injury suffered by persons who have in fact been discriminated against in violation of Title VII.

Moreover, racial quotas and other forms of preferential treatment unjus- 15
tifiably infringe on the legitimate employment interests and expectations of third parties, such as incumbent employees, who are free of any involvement

in the employer's wrongdoing. To be sure, awarding retroactive seniority and other forms of "rightful place" relief to individual victims of discrimination also unavoidably infringes upon the employment interests and expectations of innocent third parties. Indeed, this fact has compelled some, including Chief Justice Burger, to charge that granting rightful place relief to victims of racial discrimination is on the order of "robbing Peter to pay Paul."

The legitimate "rightful place" claims of identifiable victims of discrimination, however, warrant imposition of a remedy that calls for a sharing of the burden by those innocent incumbent employees whose "places" in the work force are the product of, or at least enhanced by, the employer's unlawful discrimination. Restoring the victim of discrimination to the position he or she would have occupied but for the discrimination merely requires incumbent employees to surrender some of the largesse discriminatorily conferred upon them. In other words, there is justice in requiring Peter, as a kind of third-party beneficiary of the employer's discriminatory conduct, to share in the burden of making good on the debt to Paul created by that conduct. But an incumbent employee should not be called upon as well to sacrifice or otherwise compromise his legitimate employment interests in order to accommodate persons *never wronged* by the employer's unlawful conduct. An order directing Peter to pay Paul in the absence of any proof of a debt owing to Paul is without remedial justification and cannot be squared with basic notions of fairness.

Proponents of the so-called remedial use of class-based preferences often counter this point with a twofold response. First, they note that the effort to identify and make whole all victims of the employer's discriminatory practices will never be 100 percent successful. While no one can dispute the validity of this unfortunate point, race- and gender-conscious preferences simply do not answer this problem. The injury suffered by a discriminatee who cannot be located is in no way ameliorated — much less remedied — by conferring preferential treatment on other randomly selected members of his or her race or sex. A person suffering from an appendicitis is not relieved of the pain by an appendectomy performed on the patient in the next room.

Second, proponents of judicially imposed numerical preferences argue that preferences are necessary to ensure that the employer does not return to his or her discriminatory ways. The fallacy in this reasoning is self-evident. Far from *preventing* future discrimination, imposition of such remedial devices *guarantees* future discrimination. Only the color or gender of the ox being gored is changed.

It is against this backdrop that the Court's decision in *Stotts* assumes so much significance in the "affirmative action" debate. The inescapable consequence of *Stotts* is to move government at the federal, state, and local levels noticeably closer to the overriding objective of providing all citizens with a truly equal opportunity to compete on merit for the benefits that our society has to offer — an opportunity that allows an individual to go as far as the person's energy, ability, enthusiasm, imagination, and effort will allow — and not be hemmed in by the artificial allotment given to his or her group in the form of a numerical preference. The promise is that we might now be able to bring an end to that stifling process by which government and society view their citizens as possessors of racial or gender characteristics, not as the unique individuals they are; where advancements are viewed not as hard-won achievements, but as conferred "benefits."

The use of race or sex, in an effort to restructure society along lines that 20 better represent someone's preconceived notions of how our limited educational and economic resources should be allocated among the many groups in our pluralistic society, necessarily forecloses opportunities to those having the misfortune—solely by reason of gender or skin color—to be members of a group whose allotment has already been filled. Those so denied, such as the more senior white Memphis firefighters laid off to achieve a more perfect racial balance in the fire department, are discriminated against every bit as much as the black Memphis firefighters excluded from employment. In our zeal to eradicate discrimination from society, we must be ever vigilant not to allow considerations of race or sex to intrude upon the decisional process of government. That was precisely the directive handed down by Congress in the Civil Rights Act of 1964 and, as *Stotts* made clear, the command has full application to the courts. Plainly, "affirmative action" remedies must be guided by no different principle. For the simple fact remains that wherever it occurs, and however explained, "no discrimination based on race [or sex] is benign. . . . no action disadvantaging a person because of color [or gender] is affirmative."

Suggestions for Writing and Discussion

1. According to Reynolds, what are the meanings given to "affirmative action," and which one does he uphold? Do you agree with his definition? Explain.
2. Why, according to Reynolds, can't employers be expected to promise equal results to employees? What is your response to this point?
3. What reasons does Reynolds give to counter his opponents' main criticism toward affirmative action legislation? How do you think his critics might respond to these reasons?
4. Explain the significance of Title VII in relation to the discussion on affirmative action.
5. As noted in the introduction, Reynolds was assistant attorney general for civil rights during the Reagan administration. What might have prompted him to write this piece in 1986?
6. If Elizabeth Cady Stanton and William Bradford Reynolds were both running for vice president of the United States, who do you think, on the basis of their essays, minority voters would be most apt to choose? Who do you think you would be most apt to vote for? Explain your answers.

Suggestions for Extended Thinking and Research

1. Research current cases or allegations relating to affirmative action. Analyze one or several cases in order to determine the major complaints in these cases today. Report on any outcomes you find.
2. Do a survey on your campus or in your hometown focusing on the difference between equal opportunities and equal results. What do most people feel about this issue? Do you find that this topic is one that most people have definite feelings about one way or another?

JESSE JACKSON

Why Blacks Need Affirmative Action

> *Born in South Carolina in 1941, Jesse Jackson became a Baptist minister who actively followed in the footsteps of Martin Luther King, Jr. Jackson served as director of Project Breadbasket and headed the 1968 Poor People's Campaign. In 1971, he founded PUSH (People United to Save Humanity). In addition, Jackson has been active in national politics, including campaigns for the Democratic presidential nomination. This argument first appeared in* Regulation *in September/October 1978.*

Prereading/Journal-Writing Suggestions

1. Write about a time when you were a victim of discrimination or an instance when you observed discrimination. Describe the circumstances, feelings, and outcomes of this event.
2. Write about a time in your life when you or someone you know received "preferential treatment" over someone else. Looking back on this now, would you say that, as a result of the preferential treatment, some other person was a victim of discrimination? Explain your answer.

According to a recent publication of the Equal Employment Opportunity Commission, at the present rate of "progress" it will take forty-three years to end job discrimination — hardly a reasonable timetable.

If our goal is educational and economic equity and parity — and it is — then we need affirmative action to catch up. We are behind as a result of discrimination and denial of opportunity. There is one white attorney for every 680 whites, but only one black attorney for every 4,000 blacks; one white physician for every 659 whites, but only one black physician for every 5,000 blacks; and one white dentist for every 1,900 whites, but only one black dentist for every 8,400 blacks. Less than 1 percent of all engineers — or of all practicing chemists — is black. Cruel and uncompassionate injustice created gaps like these. We need creative justice and compassion to help us close them.

Actually, in the U.S. context, "reverse discrimination" is illogical and a contradiction in terms. Never in the history of mankind has a majority, with power, engaged in programs and written laws that discriminate against itself. The only thing whites are giving up because of affirmative action is unfair advantage — something that was unnecessary in the first place.

Blacks are not making progress at the expense of whites, as news accounts make it seem. There are 49 percent more whites in medical school today and 64 percent more whites in law school than there were when affirmative action programs began some eight years ago.

In a recent column, William Raspberry raised an interesting question.   5
Commenting on the *Bakke* case, he asked, "What if, instead of setting aside
16 of 100 slots, we added 16 slots to the 100?" That, he suggested, would allow
blacks to make progress and would not interfere with what whites already
have. He then went on to point out that this, in fact, is exactly what has
happened in law and medical schools. In 1968, the year before affirmative
action programs began to get under way, 9,571 whites and 282 members of
minority groups entered U.S. medical schools. In 1976, the figures were
14,213 and 1,400 respectively. Thus, under affirmative action, the number of
"white places" actually rose by 49 percent: white access to medical training
was not diminished, but substantially increased. The trend was even more
marked in law schools. In 1969, the first year for which reliable figures are
available, 2,933 minority-group members were enrolled; in 1976, the number
was up to 8,484. But during the same period, law school enrollment for
whites rose from 65,453 to 107,064 — an increase of 64 percent. In short, it is
a myth that blacks are making progress at white expense.

Allan Bakke did not really challenge preferential treatment in general,
for he made no challenge to the preferential treatment accorded to the children
of the rich, the alumni and the faculty, or to athletes or the very talented —
only to minorities.

Suggestions for Writing and Discussion

1. What is Jackson's main point in this argument? How might Reynolds
   (pp. 446–451) respond to this point? How might Jackson respond to Reynolds's main point?
2. Both Jackson and Reynolds address the issue of "reverse discrimination."
   What exactly does this phrase mean according to Reynolds, and what
   exactly does it mean according to Jackson? Which version are you most
   apt to agree with? Explain.
3. Jackson claims that a gap between blacks and whites in different occupations exists primarily because of discrimination and lack of opportunity
   for black people. In the area of medicine, for example, he states that there
   is only one black physician for every 5,000 blacks, but one white physician
   for every 659 whites. Explain what specific discriminatory practices and
   what lack of opportunities might, indeed, contribute to this gap. Can you
   think of other factors that might be involved?
4. How convincing is Jackson's argument to you? What sections of this piece
   are especially convincing? What sections or comments do you find yourself
   arguing against?
5. Analyze Jackson's use of statistics in this piece. Does he misuse or skew
   any information here? Do you find any examples in which statistics are
   missing?
6. Describe Jackson's tone and voice in this piece. Do you feel that Jackson is
   initiating an idea in this argument or counterattacking a criticism? Explain
   your response.

7. What would Jackson say is the employer's responsibility in hiring practices? What would Reynolds say is the responsibility of the person in charge of hiring?

Suggestions for Extended Thinking and Research

1. Research articles in the *New York Times* regarding the Bakke case. Find out what this case was about: Who was Bakke, what were the circumstances in this case, what was the major complaint, what was the outcome and the reaction to this outcome?
2. Research any current case regarding discrimination of any kind. What are the circumstances regarding this case? What is the major complaint? In what way is this case like others you've read about? After carrying out this research, write an argument related to some aspect of the issues it raises.
3. Write an argument showing why you agree or disagree with either Jackson or Reynolds (or why you take yet another point of view).

ANDREW SULLIVAN

Here Comes the Groom

> *Andrew Sullivan earned a doctoral degree in government at Harvard University. He has written widely on gay issues and has worked as associate editor at the* New Republic, *which published this essay in August 1989.*

Prereading/Journal-Writing Suggestions

1. What differences do you see between living together and being married? Do you believe those differences are significant? Explain.
2. Freewrite for ten minutes on your initial reaction to allowing gay and lesbian couples the right to marriage.

A (Conservative) Case for Gay Marriage

Last month in New York, a court ruled that a gay lover had the right to stay in his deceased partner's rent-control apartment because the lover qualified as a member of the deceased's family. The ruling deftly annoyed almost everybody. Conservatives saw judicial activism in favor of gay rent control: three reasons to be appalled. Chastened liberals (such as the *New York Times* editorial page), while endorsing the recognition of gay relationships, also worried about the abuse of already stretched entitlements that the ruling threatened. What neither side quite contemplated is that they both might be right, and that the way to tackle the issue of unconventional relationships in conventional society is to try something both more radical and more conservative than putting courts in the business of deciding what is and is not a family. That alternative is the legalization of civil gay marriage.

The New York rent-control case did not go anywhere near that far, which is the problem. The rent-control regulations merely stipulated that a "family" member had the right to remain in the apartment. The judge ruled that to all intents and purposes a gay lover is part of his lover's family, inasmuch as a "family" merely means an interwoven social life, emotional commitment, and some level of financial interdependence.

It's a principle now well established around the country. Several cities have "domestic partnership" laws, which allow relationships that do not fit into the category of heterosexual marriage to be registered with the city and qualify for benefits that up till now have been reserved for straight married couples. San Francisco, Berkeley, Madison, and Los Angeles all have legislation, as does the politically correct Washington, D.C. suburb, Takoma Park. In these cities, a variety of interpersonal arrangements qualify for health insurance, bereavement leave, insurance, annuity and pension rights, housing rights (such as rent-control apartments), adoption and inheritance rights.

Eventually, according to gay lobby groups, the aim is to include federal income tax and veterans' benefits as well. A recent case even involved the right to use a family member's accumulated frequent-flier points. Gays are not the only beneficiaries; heterosexual "live-togethers" also qualify.

There's an argument, of course, that the current legal advantages extended to married people unfairly discriminate against people who've shaped their lives in less conventional arrangements. But it doesn't take a genius to see that enshrining in the law a vague principle like "domestic partnership" is an invitation to qualify at little personal cost for a vast array of entitlements otherwise kept crudely under control.

To be sure, potential DPs have to prove financial interdependence, 5 shared living arrangements, and a commitment to mutual caring. But they don't need to have a sexual relationship or even closely mirror old-style marriage. In principle, an elderly woman and her live-in nurse could qualify. A couple of uneuphemistically confirmed bachelors could be DPs. So could two close college students, a pair of seminarians, or a couple of frat buddies. Left as it is, the concept of domestic partnership could open a Pandora's box of litigation and subjective judicial decision-making about who qualifies. You either are or are not married; it's not a complex question. Whether you are in a "domestic partnership" is not so clear.

More important, the concept of domestic partnership chips away at the prestige of traditional relationships and undermines the priority we give them. This priority is not necessarily a product of heterosexism. Consider heterosexual couples. Society has good reason to extend legal advantages to heterosexuals who choose the formal sanction of marriage over simply living together. They make a deeper commitment to one another and to society; in exchange, society extends certain benefits to them. Marriage provides an anchor, if an arbitrary and weak one, in the chaos of sex and relationships to which we are all prone. It provides a mechanism for emotional stability, economic security, and the healthy rearing of the next generation. We rig the law in its favor not because we disparage all forms of relationships other than the nuclear family, but because we recognize that not to promote marriage would be to ask too much of human virtue. In the context of the weakened family's effect upon the poor, it might also invite social disintegration. One of the worst products of the New Right's "family values" campaign is that its extremism and hatred of diversity has disguised this more measured and more convincing case for the importance of the marital bond.

The concept of domestic partnership ignores these concerns, indeed directly attacks them. This is a pity, since one of its most important objectives — providing some civil recognition for gay relationships — is a noble cause and one completely compatible with the defense of the family. But the way to go about it is not to undermine straight marriage; it is to legalize old-style marriage for gays.

The gay movement has ducked this issue primarily out of fear of division. Much of the gay leadership clings to notions of gay life as essentially outsider, antibourgeois, radical. Marriage, for them, is co-optation into straight society. For the Stonewall generation, it is hard to see how this vision of conflict will ever fundamentally change. But for many other gays — my guess, a majority — while they don't deny the importance of rebellion twenty years ago and are grateful for what was done, there's now the sense of a new opportunity. A need to rebel has quietly ceded to a desire to belong. To be gay and to be bourgeois no longer seems such an absurd proposition. Certainly since AIDS, to be gay and to be responsible has become a necessity.

Gay marriage squares several circles at the heart of the domestic partnership debate. Unlike domestic partnership, it allows for recognition of gay relationships, while casting no aspersions on traditional marriage. It merely asks that gays be allowed to join in. Unlike domestic partnership, it doesn't open up avenues for heterosexuals to get benefits without the responsibilities of marriage, or a nightmare of definitional litigation. And unlike domestic partnership, it harnesses to an already established social convention the yearnings for stability and acceptance among a fast-maturing gay community.

Gay marriage also places more responsibilities upon gays: It says for the first time that gay relationships are not better or worse than straight relationships, and that the same is expected of them. And it's clear and dignified. There's a legal benefit to a clear, common symbol of commitment. There's also a personal benefit. One of the ironies of domestic partnership is that it's not only more complicated than marriage, it's more demanding, requiring an elaborate statement of intent to qualify. It amounts to a substantial invasion of privacy. Why, after all, should gays be required to prove commitment before they get married in a way we would never dream of asking of straights? 10

Legalizing gay marriage would offer homosexuals the same deal society now offers heterosexuals: general social approval and specific legal advantages in exchange for a deeper and harder-to-extract-yourself-from commitment to another human being. Like straight marriage, it would foster social cohesion, emotional security, and economic prudence. Since there's no reason gays should not be allowed to adopt or be foster parents, it could also help nurture children. And its introduction would not be some sort of radical break with social custom. As it has become more acceptable for gay people to acknowledge their loves publicly, more and more have committed themselves to one another for life in full view of their families and their friends. A law institutionalizing gay marriage would merely reinforce a healthy social trend. It would also, in the wake of AIDS, qualify as a genuine public health measure. Those conservatives who deplore promiscuity among some homosexuals should be among the first to support it. Burke could have written a powerful case for it.

The argument that gay marriage would subtly undermine the unique legitimacy of straight marriage is based upon a fallacy. For heterosexuals, straight marriage would remain the most significant — and only legal — social bond. Gay marriage could only delegitimize straight marriage if it were a real alternative to it, and this is clearly not true. To put it bluntly, there's precious little evidence that straights could be persuaded by any law to have sex with —

let alone marry — someone of their own sex. The only possible effect of this sort would be to persuade gay men and women who force themselves into heterosexual marriage (often at appalling cost to themselves and their families) to find a focus for their family instincts in a more personally positive environment. But this is clearly a plus, not a minus: Gay marriage could both avoid a lot of tortured families and create the possibility for many happier ones. It is not, in short, a denial of family values. It's an extension of them.

Of course, some would claim that any legal recognition of homosexuality is a de facto attack upon heterosexuality. But even the most hardened conservatives recognize that gays are a permanent minority and aren't likely to go away. Since persecution is not an option in a civilized society, why not coax gays into traditional values rather than rail incoherently against them?

There's a less elaborate argument for gay marriage: It's good for gays. It provides role models for young gay people who, after the exhilaration of coming out, can easily lapse into short-term relationships and insecurity with no tangible goal in sight. My own guess is that most gays would embrace such a goal with as much (if not more) commitment as straights. Even in our society as it is, many lesbian relationships are virtual textbook cases of monogamous commitment. Legal gay marriage could also help bridge the gulf often found between gays and their parents. It could bring the essence of gay life — a gay couple — into the heart of the traditional straight family in a way the family can most understand and the gay offspring can most easily acknowledge. It could do as much to heal the gay-straight rift as any amount of gay rights legislation.

If these arguments sound socially conservative, that's no accident. It's   15 one of the richest ironies of our society's blind spot toward gays that essentially conservative social goals should have the appearance of being so radical. But gay marriage is not a radical step. It avoids the mess of domestic partnership; it is humane; it is conservative in the best sense of the word. It's also practical. Given the fact that we already allow legal gay relationships, what possible social goal is advanced by framing the law to encourage those relationships to be unfaithful, undeveloped, and insecure?

Suggestions for Writing and Discussion

1. Why does Sullivan consider his proposal for allowing gays and lesbians to engage in civil marriage a "conservative" solution?
2. What are the problems inherent in "domestic partnership" laws? Who, really, is protected under these laws?
3. Why, according to Sullivan, is marriage a better arrangement for gay people than simply living together?
4. Do you think Sullivan is right? Would family members be more apt to accept a gay relationship if the couple were married? Predict your own family's reactions about such an arrangement.

5. One of Sullivan's underlying points is that marriage, as an institution, places more responsibility upon couples. What's your reaction or response to this statement?
6. What might be some opposing viewpoints to gay marriages that Sullivan fails to address? How would you address those viewpoints?
7. Carefully read Sullivan's last sentence in this piece. Respond to his question as well as to the word choices he makes to conclude his piece.

Suggestions for Extended Thinking and Research
1. Research the laws in your state to discover what legal issues relate to gay rights. Report on your findings to the class.
2. Read articles by gay activists on the issues with which they are concerned. Do any advocate marriage for gays? Do their reasons coincide with Sullivan's? Would any of them disagree with Sullivan's proposal?

LEONARD KRIEGEL

A Loaded Question: What Is It about Americans and Guns?

Leonard Kriegel's most recent book is a collection of essays, Falling into Life. *He is currently working on a novel and, in addition, writes essays for journals and magazines such as* Harper's, *where this essay first appeared in May 1992.*

Prereading/Journal-Writing Suggestions

1. Think back in your own life to your first exposure to or awareness of guns. Under what circumstances do you remember being aware of guns? What was your reaction to guns? What is your reaction today to guns?
2. Freewrite for ten minutes on the following statement: "Guns don't kill; people do."

I have fired a gun only once in my life, hardly experience enough to qualify one as an expert on firearms. As limited as my exposure to guns has been, however, my failure to broaden that experience had nothing at all to do with moral disapproval or with the kind of righteous indignation that views an eight-year-old boy playing cops and robbers with a cap pistol as a preview of the life of a serial killer. None of us can speak with surety about alternative lives, but had circumstances been different I suspect I not only would have hunted but very probably would have enjoyed it. I might even have gone in for target shooting, a "sport" increasingly popular in New York City, where I live (like bowling, it is practiced indoors in alleys). To be truthful, I have my doubts that target shooting would really have appealed to me. But in a country in which grown men feel passionately about a game as visibly ludicrous as golf, anything is possible.

The single shot I fired didn't leave me with a traumatic hatred of or distaste for guns. Quite the opposite. I liked not only the sense of incipient skill firing that shot gave me but also the knowledge that a true marksman, like a good hitter in baseball, had to practice — and practice with a real gun. Boys on the cusp of adolescence are not usually disciplined, but they do pay attention to the demands of skill. Because I immediately recognized how difficult it would be for me to practice marksmanship, I was brought face to face with the fact that my career as a hunter was over even before it had started.

Like my aborted prospects as a major league ballplayer, my short but happy life as a hunter could be laid at the metaphorical feet of the polio virus which left me crippled at the age of eleven. Yet the one thing that continues to amaze me as I look back to that gray February afternoon when I discovered the temptation of being shooter and hunter is that I did not shoot one or the other of the two most visible targets — myself or my friend Jackie, the boy who owned the .22.

Each of us managed to fire one shot that afternoon. And when we returned to the ward in which we lived along with twenty other crippled boys between the ages of nine and thirteen, we regaled our peers with a story unashamedly embellished in the telling. As the afternoon chill faded and the narrow winter light in which we had hunted drifted toward darkness, Jackie managed to hide the .22 from ward nurses and doctors on the prowl. What neither of us attempted to hide from the other boys was our brief baptism in the world of guns.

Like me, Jackie was a Bronx boy, as ignorant about guns as I was. Both 5 of us had been taken down with polio in the summer of '44. We had each lost the use of our legs. We were currently in wheelchairs. And we had each already spent a year and a half in the aptly named New York State Reconstruction Home, a state hospital for long-term physical rehabilitation. Neither of us had ever fired anything more lethal than a Daisy air rifle, popularly known as a BB gun — and even that, in my case at least, had been fired under adult supervision. But Jackie and I were also American claimants, our imaginations molded as much by Hollywood westerns as by New York streets. At twelve, I was a true Jeffersonian who looked upon the ownership of a six-shooter as every American's "natural" right.

To this day I don't know how Jackie got hold of that .22. He refused to tell me. And I still don't know how he got rid of it after our wheelchair hunt in the woods. For months afterward I would try to get him to promise that he and I would go hunting again, but, as if our afternoon hunt had enabled him to come to terms with his own illusions about the future (something that would take me many more years), Jackie simply shook his head and said, "That's over." I begged, wheedled, cajoled, threatened. Jackie remained obdurate. A single shot for a single hunt. It would have to be sufficient.

I never did find out whether or not I hit the raccoon. On the ride back to the ward, Jackie claimed I had. After he fired his shot, he dropped from his wheelchair and slid backward on his rump to the abandoned water pipe off the side of the dirt road into which the raccoon had leaped at the slashing crack of the .22. His hand came down on something red — a bloodstain, he excitedly suggested, as he lifted himself into his wheelchair and we turned to push ourselves back to the ward. It looked like a rust stain to me, but I didn't protest. I was quite willing to take whatever credit I could. That was around an hour after the two of us, fresh from lunch, had pushed our wheelchairs across the hospital grounds, turning west at the old road that cut through the woods and led to another state home, this one ministering to the retarded. The .22, which lay on Jackie's lap, had bounced and jostled as we maneuvered our wheelchairs across that rutted road in search of an animal — any animal would do — to shoot. The early February sky hung above us like a charcoal drawing, striations of gray slate shadings feeding our nervous expectation.

It was Jackie who first spotted the raccoon. Excited, he handed the .22

to me, a gesture spurred, I then thought, by friendship. Now I wonder whether his generosity wasn't simply self-protection. Until that moment, the .22 lying across Jackie's dead legs had been an abstraction, as much an imitation gun as the "weapons" boys in New York City constructed out of the wood frames and wood slats of fruit and vegetable crates, nails, and rubber bands — cutting up pieces of discarded linoleum and stiff cardboard to use as ammunition. I remember the feel of the .22 across my own lifeless legs, the weight of it surprisingly light, as I stared at the raccoon who eyed us curiously from in front of the broken pipe. Then I picked up the gun, aimed, and squeezed the trigger, startled not so much by the noise nor by the slight pull, but by the fact that I had actually fired at something. The sound of the shot was crisp and clean. I felt as if I had done something significant.

Jackie took the gun from me. "Okay," he said eagerly. "My turn now." The raccoon was nowhere in sight, but he aimed in the direction of the water pipe into which it had disappeared and squeezed the trigger. I heard the crack again, a freedom of music now, perhaps because we two boys had suddenly been bound to each other and had escaped, for this single winter afternoon moment, the necessary but mundane courage which dominates the everyday lives of crippled children. "Okay," I heard him cry out happily, "we're goddamn killers now."

A formidable enough hail and farewell to shooting. And certainly better 10 than being shot at. God knows what happened to that raccoon. Probably nothing; but for me, firing that single shot was both the beginning and the end of my life as a marksman. The raccoon may have been wounded, as Jackie claimed. Perhaps it had crawled away, bleeding, to die somewhere in the woods. I doubt it. And I certainly hope I didn't hit it, although in February 1946, six months before I returned to the city and to life among the "normals," I would have taken its death as a symbolic triumph. For that was a time I needed any triumph I could find, no matter how minor. Back then it seemed natural to begin an uncertain future with a kill — even if one sensed, as I did, that my career as a hunter was already over. The future was hinting at certain demands it would make. And I was just beginning to bend into myself, to protect my inner man from being crushed by the knowledge of all I would never be able to do. Hunting would be just another deferred dream.

But guns were not a dream. Guns were real, definitive, stamped on the imagination by their functional beauty. A gun was not a phallic symbol; a gun didn't offer me revenge on polio; a gun would not bring to life dead legs or endow deferred dreams with substance. I am as willing as the next man to quarantine reality within psychology. But if a rose is no more than a rose, then tell me why a gun can't simply be a gun? Guns are not monuments to fear and aspiration any more than flowers are.

I was already fascinated by the way guns looked. I was even more fascinated by what they did and by what made people use them. Like any other twelve-year-old boy, I was absorbed by talk about guns. Six months after the end of the Second World War, boys in our ward were still engrossed by the way talking about guns entangled us in the dense underbrush of the national psyche. And no one in that ward was more immersed in weaponry than I. On the verge of adolescence, forced to seek and find adventure in my own imagination, I was captivated by guns.

It was a fascination that would never altogether die. A few weeks ago I found myself nostalgically drifting through the arms and armor galleries of the Metropolitan Museum of Art. Years ago I had often taken my young sons there. A good part of my pleasure now derived from memories pinned to the leisurely innocence of those earlier visits. As I wandered among those rich cabinets displaying ornate pistols and rifles whose carved wood stocks were embossed with gold and silver and ivory and brass, I was struck by how incredibly lovely many of these weapons were. It was almost impossible to conceive of them as serving the function they had been designed to serve. These were not machines designed to kill and maim. Created with an eye to beauty, their sense of decorative purpose was as singular as a well-designed eighteenth-century silver drinking cup. These guns in their solid display cases evoked a sense of the disciplined craftsmanship to which a man might dedicate his life.

Flintlocks, wheel locks, a magnificent pair of ivory pistols owned by Catherine the Great — all of them as beckoning to the touch of fingers, had they not been securely locked behind glass doors, as one of those small nineteenth-century engraved cameos that seem to force time itself to surrender its pleasures. I gazed longingly at a seventeenth-century wheel lock carbine, coveting it the way I might covet a drinking cup by Cellini or a small bronze horse and rider by Bologna. Its beautifully carved wooden stock had been inlaid with ivory, brass, silver, and mother-of-pearl, its pride of artisanship embossed with the name of its creator, Caspar Spät. I smiled with pleasure. Then I wandered through the galleries until I found myself in front of a case displaying eighteenth-century American flintlock rifles, all expressing the democratic spirit one finds in Louis Sullivan's buildings or Whitman's poetry or New York City playgrounds built by the WPA during the Great Depression. Their polished woods were balanced by ornately carved stag-antler powder horns, which hung like Christmas decorations beneath them. To the right was another display case devoted to long-barreled Colt revolvers; beyond that, a splendidly engraved 1894 Winchester rifle and a series of Smith & Wesson revolvers, all of them decorated by Tiffany.

And yet they were weapons, designed ultimately to do what weapons 15 have always done — destroy. Only in those childlike posters of the 1970s did flower stems grow out of the barrel of a gun. People who shoot, like people who cook, understandably choose the best tools available. And if it is easier to hit a target with an Uzi than a homemade zip gun, chances are those who want to hit the target will feel few qualms about choosing the Uzi.

Nonetheless, these galleries are a remarkable testimony to the functional beauty of guns. Nor am I the only person who has been touched by their beauty. The problem is to define where the killing ceases and the beauty begins. At what point does a young boy's sense of adventure transform itself into the terror of blood and destruction and pain and death? I remember my sons' excitement when they toured these splendid galleries with me. (Yes, doctor, I did permit them to enjoy guns. And neither became a serial killer.) These weapons helped bring us together, bound father and sons, just as going to baseball games or viewing old Chaplin movies had.

Geography may not be the sole father of morality, but one would have to be remarkably naive to ignore its claims altogether. As I write this, I can see on the table in front of me a newspaper headlining the most recent killings inflicted on New York City's anarchic populace. Firearms now rule street and schoolyard, even as the rhetoric of politicians demanding strict gun control escalates — along with the body count.

And yet I recognize that one man's fear and suffering is another man's freedom and pleasure. Here is the true morality of geography. Like it or not, we see the world against a landscape of accommodation. Guns may be displayed behind glass cases in that magnificent museum, but in the splendid park in which that museum has been set down like a crowning jewel, guns have been known to create not art but terror. Functional beauty, it turns out, does not alter purpose.

I have a friend who has lived his entire life in small towns in Maine. My friend is both a hunter and a connoisseur of guns. City streets and guns may be a volatile mix, but the Maine woods and guns apparently aren't. Rifles and pistols hang on my friend's living room wall like old family portraits. They are lived with as comfortably as a family heirloom. My friend speaks knowingly of their shape, describes each weapon lovingly, as if it possessed its own substance. He is both literate and civilized, but he would never deny that these guns are more than a possession to him. They are an altar before which he bends the knee, a right of ownership he considers inviolable, even sacrosanct. And yet my friend is not a violent man.

I, too, am not a violent man. But I am a New Yorker. And like most 20 people who live in this city, I make certain assumptions about the value of the very indignities one faces by choosing to live here. If I didn't, I probably couldn't remain in New York. For with all of the problems it forces one to face, the moral geography of New York also breeds a determination not to give in to the daily indignities the city imposes.

During the summer of 1977, I lived within a different moral geography. I was teaching a graduate seminar on Manhood and American Culture at the University of New Mexico in Albuquerque, tracing the evolution of the American man from Ben Franklin's sturdy, middle-class acolyte to the rugged John Wayne of *Stagecoach*. Enchanted by the New Mexico landscape, I would frequently drive off to explore the small towns and brilliant canyons in whose silences ghosts still lingered. One day a friend volunteered to drive with me into the Manzano Mountains. I had announced my desire to look at the ruins of a seventeenth-century mission fort at Gran Quivira, while he wanted me to meet a man who had, by himself, built a house in those haunting, lovely mountains.

Tension between Anglos and Hispanics was strong in New Mexico in the summer of 1977. Even a stranger could feel a palpable, almost physical, struggle for political and cultural hegemony. Coming from a New York in which the growing separation of black and white was already threatening to transform everyday life into a racial battlefield, I did not feel particularly intimidated by this. Instead of black and white, New Mexico's ethnic and racial warfare would be between Anglo, Hispanic, and Indian. Mountainair, where we were to visit my friend's friend, was considered an Anglo town. Chilili, some miles up the road, was Hispanic.

My friend's friend had built his house on the outskirts of Mountainair, with a magnificent view of ponderosa pine. He was a man in his early sixties and had come to New Mexico from Virginia soon after World War II to take a job as a technical writer in a nuclear research laboratory in Albuquerque. Before the war he had done graduate work in literature at the University of Virginia, but the demands of fatherhood had decided him against finishing his doctorate. Like so many Americans before him, he had taken wife and young children to start over in the West.

In the warmth and generosity of his hospitality, however, he remained a true Southerner. As we sat and talked and laughed in the huge sun-drenched living room that opened onto that magnificent view of mountains and pines and long New Mexico sky, I could not help but feel that here was the very best of this nation — a man secure in himself, a man of liberal sympathies and a broad understanding of human behavior and a love of children and grand-children and wife, a man who spoke perceptively of Jane Austen's novels and spoke sadly of the savage threat of drugs (his oldest son, a veteran of the war in Vietnam, was living with him, along with wife and three-year-old daugh-ter, trying to purge the heroin addiction that threatened to wreck his life).

I remember him happily holding forth on Jane Austen's *Persuasion* when   25 his body suddenly seemed to freeze in mid-sentence. I could hear a motor in the distance. Without another word, he turned and crossed the room. Twin double-barreled shotguns hung on the wall above the fireplace. He took one, his right hand scooping shells from a canvas bag hanging from a thong looped around a horseshoe nail banged shoulder-high into the wall. His son, the ex-Marine, grabbed the other gun and scooped shells from the same bag. Through the glassed-in cathedral living room leading to the porch, I watched the two of them stand side by side, shotguns pointed at a pickup truck already out of range. "Those bastards!" I heard my host snarl.

"We'll get 'em yet, Pop," his son said. "I swear it."

After we left to drive on to the ruins at Gran Quivira, I asked the friend who had accompanied me to explain what had happened. "A pickup truck from Chilili. Hispanics driving up the mountain to cut trees. It's illegal. But they do it anyway."

"Do the trees belong to your friend?"

"Not his trees. Not his mountain." Then he shrugged.
"But it's his gun."   30

I angrily cast my eyes at the man and find myself staring into the twin
barrels of a shotgun loosely held but pointed directly at me. It is that same
summer in Albuquerque, three weeks later, and I am sitting in the driver's
seat of my car, my ten-year-old son, Bruce, directly behind me. Alongside
him is the eleven-year-old daughter of the man who had invited me to teach
at the University of New Mexico. I have just backed my car away from a
gasoline pump to allow another car to move out of the garage into the road.
As the other car came out of the gas station, the man with the shotgun adroitly
cut me off and maneuvered his rust-pocked yellow pickup ahead of me in line
before I could get back to the gas pump.

My first reaction is irritation with my car, as if the steel and chrome
were sentient and responsible. It is the same ugly gold 1971 Buick in which,
five summers earlier, I had driven through a Spanish landscape remarkably
similar to the New Mexico in which I now find myself. Bruce had been with
me then, too, along with his older brother and mother. But it is not the Buick
that attracts men with guns. Nor is it that mythical violence of American life
in which European intellectuals believe so fervently. In Spain we had been
stopped at a roadblock, a sandbagged machine gun aimed by one of Franco's
troops perusing traffic like a farmer counting chickens in a henhouse. The
soldiers had asked for passports, scowled at the children, examined the Buick
as if it were an armored tank, inspecting glove compartment and trunk and
wedging their hands into the spaces between seat and back. At the hotel
restaurant at which we stopped for lunch twenty minutes later, we learned
that two *guardia civil* had been ambushed and killed by Basque guerrillas.
During Franco's last years, such acts grew more and more frequent. Spain was
filled with guns and soldiers. One was always aware of the presence of soldiers
patrolling the vacation beaches of the Costa del Sol — and particularly aware
of their guns.

As I am aware of the shotgun now. And as I am growing aware of that
same enraged sense of humiliation and helplessness that seized me as those
Spanish soldiers examined car and sons and wife, their guns casually pointed
at all I loved most in the world, these other lives that made my life significantly mine. "Guns don't kill, people do!" Offer that mind-deadening cliché
to a man at a roadblock watching the faces of soldiers for whom the power of
a gun is simply that it permits them to feel contempt for those without guns.
Tell that to a man sitting in a car with two young children, contemplating
doing what he knows he cannot do because the gun is in another man's hands.
Both in Spain and in this New Mexico that Spain had planted in the New
World like a genetic acorn breeding prerogatives of power, guns endowed
men with a way to settle all questions of responsibility.

The man with the shotgun says nothing. He simply holds the weapon
in his beefy hand, its muzzle casually pointed in my direction. I toy with the
notion of getting out of the car and confronting him. I am angry, enraged. I

don't want to give in to his rude power. Only my son and my colleague's daughter are in the back of the car. Defensively, I turn to look at them. My colleague's daughter is wide-eyed and frightened. Bruce is equally frightened, but his eyes are on me. I am his father and he expects me to do something, to say something, to alter the balance of expectation and reality. Our car was on line for gas first. To a ten-year-old, justice is a simple arithmetic.

To that ten-year-old's father it is not necessarily more complex. I could   35 tell myself that it was insane to tell a man pointing a shotgun at me and these two children that he has broken the rules. Chances are he wouldn't have fired, would probably have responded with a shrug of the shoulders no more threatening than a confession of ignorance.

Obviously, none of this mattered. My growing sense of humiliation and rage had nothing to do with having to wait an extra minute or two while the station attendant filled the tank of the pickup. I was in no particular rush. I was simply returning home from a day-long excursion to a state park, where my son and his new friend had crawled through caves and climbed rocks splashed by a warm spring. But I was facing a man with a shotgun, a man who understood that people with guns define options for themselves.

The man with the gun decides whether or not to shoot, just as he chooses where to point his gun. It is not political power that stems from the barrel of a gun, as Maoists used to proclaim so ritualistically. It is individual power, the ability to impose one's presence on the world, simply because guns always do what language only sometimes does: Guns command! Guns command attention, guns command discipline, guns command fear.

And guns bestow rights and prerogatives, even to those who have read Jane Austen and engaged the world in their own comedy of manners. There is a conditional nature to all rights. And there are obligations that should not be shunted aside. Guns are many things, some symbolic, some all too real. But in real life they are always personal and rarely playful. They measure not capacity but the obligation the bearer of the gun has to believe that power belongs not to the gun but to him. And yet were I to tell this to my friend in Maine — that sophisticated, literate, humane man — I suspect he would turn to me and say, "That's right. There's always got to be somebody's finger on the trigger."

A confession, then: I may be as fascinated by guns as my gun-owning and gun-loving friend in Maine, but were it up to me, I would rid America of its guns. I would be less verbally self-righteous about gun control than I was in the past, for I think I have begun to understand those who, like my friend in Maine, have arguments of their own in defense of guns. They are formidable arguments. Their fear matches mine, and I assume that their anguish over the safety of their children is also equal to mine. I, too, know the statistics. I can repeat, as easily as he can, that in Switzerland, where an armed citizenry is the norm, the homicide rate is far lower than in many countries that carefully control the distribution of guns to their populace. Laws are simply words on paper — unless they embody what a population wants.

There is no logic with which I can convince my gun-owning friend in 40
Maine. But there are images I wish I could get him to focus on. Like me, he
is a writer. Only I write about cities, and my friend writes about the Maine
woods. He is knowledgeable about animals and rocks and trees and silence,
and I am knowledgeable about stubs of grass growing between cracks in a
concrete sidewalk and the pitch and pull of conflicting voices demanding
recognition. I wish I could explain to him the precise configuration of that
double-barreled shotgun pointing at me and those two children. Maybe then
I could convince him that truth is not merely a matter of geography. Yes, guns
don't kill and people do—but in the America he and I share, those people
usually kill with guns.

Four years after that incident at the gas station, I was sitting with Bruce
in a brasserie in Paris. It was a sunny July afternoon and we were eating lunch
at a small outside table, the walls of the magisterial Invalides beckoning to us
from across the street. Bruce was fourteen, and fifteen minutes earlier he had
returned from his first trip alone on the Paris Metro. Suddenly a man approached, eyes menacing and bloodshot. He was short and thick, his body
seemingly caked by the muscularity of a beaten-down club fighter or an
unemployed stevedore. He stared at us, eyes filled with the rage of the insane.
Then he flexed his muscles as if he were on exhibit as a circus strong man,
cried out something—a sound I remember as a cross between gargling and
choking—and disappeared just as suddenly down the street.

The incident still haunts me. The French, I suspect, are as violent as they
like to claim we Americans are. But in Paris it is difficult for a man filled with
rage and craziness to get hold of a gun. Not impossible, mind you, just
difficult. Somewhere along the line, the French have learned not that guns
don't kill and people do but that people with guns can kill. And they know
what we have yet to acknowledge—that when the Furies dance in the head
it's best to keep the weapons in display cases in the museum. For that, at least,
I wish my friend in Maine could learn to be grateful. As I was, eating lunch
with my son in Paris.

Suggestions for Writing and Discussion

1. After reading this piece all the way through, stop for a minute and think
   about one specific section that affected you most. What part comes to
   mind? Why do you think that particular section affected you?
2. If you had to categorize this piece, would you classify it as an argument, a
   personal narrative, or an essay that explains? Give your reasons for your
   choice.
3. When do you think Kriegel solidified his position on gun control? Why
   did this event have such an impact on him?
4. Do you think this piece would convince Kriegel's friend in Maine to put
   away his guns? Why or why not? Write a dialogue between the two men,
   showing how each would counter the arguments of the other.
5. What does Kriegel accomplish with the detailed explanation of his first

exposure to guns in this piece? How does this experience relate to Kriegel's main point about guns? How does Kriegel's inability to walk relate to his early response to guns?

6. Although Kriegel's main question is, "What is it about Americans and guns?" in this piece he only refers to one specific group of Americans and their fascination with guns: American males. Why does Kriegel exclude women in his discussion of Americans and guns? Is his approach blatantly sexist?

7. Concerning handling guns, Kriegel writes that "one man's fear and suffering is another man's freedom and pleasure." Can you think of any other material possessions that also fit this statement? Are these possessions also legal?

8. Explain what Kriegel means by the following statement: "When the Furies dance in the head it's best to keep the weapons in display cases in the museum."

Suggestions for Extended Thinking and Research

1. Write a letter to Kriegel in response to this piece — you are the best friend, living in Maine, whom he mentions in the article.

2. If you have had a firsthand experience with guns, write a personal narrative about this experience. However, do not come out and state your personal belief about guns — let the story reveal your thesis.

3. Research the correlation between guns and killings in our country. Present your findings and recommendations to the class.

DIANE RAVITCH
Multiculturalism: E Pluribus Plures

> *Noted educator and author Diane Ravitch has been widely praised for her book* The Troubled Crusade: American Education, 1945–1980, *which analyzes and evaluates the history of education in the United States. Ravitch teaches history and education at Teachers College, Columbia University. The following selection is excerpted from her essay by the same title, which first appeared in the* American Scholar *(summer 1990).*

Prereading/Journal-Writing Suggestions

1. How would you define the word *multiculturalism*? What examples can you offer to support your definition? Do you see the connotations of this word as primarily positive or primarily negative? Explain.
2. Describe in detail a learning experience that you would call "multicultural." This experience may have occurred in school, but consider also encounters with multiculturalism (as you define it) at work, in your community, or in relation to a hobby or leisure activity.

Questions of race, ethnicity, and religion have been a perennial source of conflict in American education. The schools have often attracted the zealous attention of those who wish to influence the future, as well as those who wish to change the way we view the past. In our history, the schools have been not only an institution in which to teach young people skills and knowledge, but an arena where interest groups fight to preserve their values, or to revise the judgments of history, or to bring about fundamental social change. In the nineteenth century, Protestants and Catholics battled over which version of the Bible should be used in school, or whether the Bible should be used at all. In recent decades, bitter racial disputes — provoked by policies of racial segregation and discrimination — have generated turmoil in the streets and in the schools. The secularization of the schools during the past century has prompted attacks on the curricula and textbooks and library books by fundamentalist Christians, who object to whatever challenges their faith-based views of history, literature, and science.

Given the diversity of American society, it has been impossible to insulate the schools from pressures that result from differences and tensions among groups. When people differ about basic values, sooner or later those disagreements turn up in battles about how schools are organized or what the schools should teach. Sometimes these battles remove a terrible injustice, like racial segregation. Sometimes, however, interest groups politicize the curriculum and attempt to impose their views on teachers, school officials, and textbook publishers. Across the country, even now, interest groups are pressuring local school boards to remove myths and fables and other imaginative literature from children's readers and to inject the teaching of creationism in biology. When groups cross the line into extremism, advancing their own agenda without regard to reason or to others, they threaten public education itself, making it difficult to teach any issues honestly and making the entire curriculum vulnerable to political campaigns.

For many years, the public schools attempted to neutralize controversies over race, religion, and ethnicity by ignoring them. Educators believed, or hoped, that the schools could remain outside politics; this was, of course, a vain hope since the schools were pursuing policies based on race, religion, and ethnicity. Nonetheless, such divisive questions were usually excluded from the curriculum. The textbooks minimized problems among groups and taught a sanitized version of history. Race, religion, and ethnicity were presented as minor elements in the American saga; slavery was treated as an episode, immigration as a sidebar, and women were largely absent. The textbooks concentrated on presidents, wars, national politics, and issues of state. An occasional "great black" or "great woman" received mention, but the main narrative paid little attention to minority groups and women.

With the ethnic revival of the 1960s, this approach to the teaching of history came under fire, because the history of national leaders — virtually all of whom were white, Anglo-Saxon, and male — ignored the place in American history of those who were none of the above. The traditional history of elites had been complemented by an assimilationist view of American society, which presumed that everyone in the American melting pot would eventually lose or abandon those ethnic characteristics that distinguished them from mainstream Americans. The ethnic revival demonstrated that many groups did not want to be assimilated or melted. Ethnic studies programs popped up on campuses to teach not only that "black is beautiful," but also that every other variety of ethnicity is "beautiful" as well; everyone who had "roots" began to look for them so that they too could recover that ancestral part of themselves that had not been homogenized.

As ethnicity became an accepted subject for study in the late 1960s, 5 textbooks were assailed for their failure to portray blacks accurately; within a few years, the textbooks in wide use were carefully screened to eliminate bias against minority groups and women. At the same time, new scholarship about the history of women, blacks, and various ethnic minorities found its way into the textbooks. At first, the multicultural content was awkwardly incorporated as little boxes on the side of the main narrative. Then some of the new social historians (like Stephan Thernstrom, Mary Beth Norton, Gary Nash, Winthrop Jordan, and Leon Litwack) themselves wrote textbooks, and the main narrative itself began to reflect a broadened historical understanding of race, ethnicity, and class in the American past. Consequently, today's history textbooks routinely incorporate the experiences of women, blacks, American Indians, and various immigrant groups.

Although most high school textbooks are deeply unsatisfactory (they still largely neglect religion, they are too long, too encyclopedic, too superficial, and lacking in narrative flow), they are far more sensitive to pluralism than their predecessors. For example, the latest edition of Todd and Curti's *Triumph of the American Nation,* the most popular high school history text, has significantly increased its coverage of blacks in America, including profiles of Phillis Wheatley, the poet; James Armistead, a revolutionary war spy for Lafayette; Benjamin Banneker, a self-taught scientist and mathematician; Hiram Revels, the first black to serve in the Congress; and Ida B. Wells-Barnett, a tireless crusader against lynching and racism. Even better as a textbook treatment is Jordan and Litwack's *The United States,* which skillfully synthesizes the historical experiences of blacks, Indians, immigrants, women, and other groups into the mainstream of American social and political history. The latest generation of textbooks bluntly acknowledges the racism of the past, describing the struggle for equality by racial minorities while identifying individuals who achieved success as political leaders, doctors, lawyers, scholars, entrepreneurs, teachers, and scientists.

As a result of the political and social changes of recent decades, cultural pluralism is now generally recognized as an organizing principle of this society. In contrast to the idea of the melting pot, which promised to erase ethnic and group differences, children now learn that variety is the spice of life. They learn that America has provided a haven for many different groups and has allowed them to maintain their cultural heritage or to assimilate, or — as is often the case — to do both; the choice is theirs, not the state's. They learn that cultural pluralism is one of the norms of a free society; that differences among groups are a national resource rather than a problem to be solved. Indeed, the unique feature of the United States is that its common culture has been formed by the interaction of its subsidiary cultures. It is a culture that has been influenced over time by immigrants, American Indians, Africans (slave and free) and by their descendants. American music, art, literature, language, food, clothing, sports, holidays, and customs all show the effects of the commingling of diverse cultures in one nation. Paradoxical though it may seem, the United States has a common culture that is multicultural.

Our schools and our institutions of higher learning have in recent years begun to embrace what Catherine R. Stimpson of Rutgers University has called "cultural democracy," a recognition that we must listen to a "diversity of voices" in order to understand our culture, past and present. This understanding of the pluralistic nature of American culture has taken a long time to forge. It is based on sound scholarship and has led to major revisions in what children are taught and what they read in school. The new history is — indeed, must be — a warts-and-all history; it demands an unflinching examination of racism and discrimination in our history. Making these changes is difficult, raises tempers, and ignites controversies, but gives a more interesting and accurate account of American history. Accomplishing these changes is valuable, because there is also a useful lesson for the rest of the world in America's relatively successful experience as a pluralistic society. Throughout human history, the clash of different cultures, races, ethnic groups, and religions has often been the cause of bitter hatred, civil conflict, and international war. The ethnic tensions that now are tearing apart Lebanon, Sri Lanka, Kashmir, and various republics of the Soviet Union remind us of the costs of unfettered group rivalry. Thus, it is a matter of more than domestic importance that we closely examine and try to understand that part of our national history in which different groups competed, fought, suffered, but ultimately learned to live together in relative peace and even achieved a sense of common nationhood.

Alas, these painstaking efforts to expand the understanding of American culture into a richer and more varied tapestry have taken a new turn, and not for the better. Almost any idea, carried to its extreme, can be made pernicious, and this is what is happening now to multiculturalism. Today, pluralistic multiculturalism must contend with a new, particularistic multiculturalism. The pluralists seek a richer common culture; the particularists insist that no common culture is possible or desirable. The new particularism is entering the curriculum in a number of school systems across the country. Advocates of particularism propose an ethnocentric curriculum to raise the self-esteem and academic achievement of children from racial and ethnic minority backgrounds. Without any evidence, they claim that children from minority backgrounds will do well in school *only* if they are immersed in a positive, prideful version of their ancestral culture. If children are of, for example, Fredonian ancestry, they must hear that Fredonians were important in mathematics, science, history, and literature. If they learn about great Fredonians and if their studies use Fredonian examples and Fredonian concepts, they will do well in school. If they do not, they will have low self-esteem and will do badly.

At first glance, this appears akin to the celebratory activities associated   10 with Black History Month or Women's History Month, when schoolchildren learn about the achievements of blacks and women. But the point of those celebrations is to demonstrate that neither race nor gender is an obstacle to high achievement. They teach all children that everyone, regardless of their race, religion, gender, ethnicity, or family origin, can achieve self-fulfillment, honor, and dignity in society if they aim high and work hard.

By contrast, the particularistic version of multiculturalism is unabashedly filiopietistic and deterministic. It teaches children that their identity is determined by their "cultural genes." That something in their blood or their race memory or their cultural DNA defines who they are and what they may achieve. That the culture in which they live is not their own culture, even though they were born here. That American culture is "Eurocentric," and therefore hostile to anyone whose ancestors are not European. Perhaps the most invidious implication of particularism is that racial and ethnic minorities are not and should not try to be part of American culture; it implies that American culture belongs only to those who are white and European; it implies that those who are neither white nor European are alienated from

American culture by virtue of their race or ethnicity; it implies that the only culture they do belong to or can ever belong to is the culture of their ancestors, even if their families have lived in this country for generations.

The war on so-called Eurocentrism is intended to foster self-esteem among those who are not of European descent. But how, in fact, is self-esteem developed? How is the sense of one's own possibilities, one's potential choices, developed? Certainly, the school curriculum plays a relatively small role as compared to the influence of family, community, mass media, and society. But to the extent that curriculum influences what children think of themselves, it should encourage children of all racial and ethnic groups to believe that they are part of this society and that they should develop their talents and minds to the fullest. It is enormously inspiring, for example, to learn about men and women from diverse backgrounds who overcame poverty, discrimination, physical handicaps, and other obstacles to achieve success in a variety of fields. Behind every such biography of accomplishment is a story of heroism, perseverance, and self-discipline. Learning these stories will encourage a healthy spirit of pluralism, of mutual respect, and of self-respect among children of different backgrounds. The children of American society today will live their lives in a racially and culturally diverse nation, and their education should prepare them to do so.

The pluralist approach to multiculturalism promotes a broader interpretation of the common American culture and seeks due recognition for the ways that the nation's many racial, ethnic, and cultural groups have transformed the national culture. The pluralists say, in effect, "American culture belongs to us, all of us; the U.S. is us, and we remake it in every generation." But particularists have no interest in extending or revising American culture; indeed, they deny that a common culture exists. Particularists reject any accommodation among groups, any interactions that blur the distinct lines between them. The brand of history that they espouse is one in which everyone is either a descendant of victims or oppressors. By doing so, ancient hatreds are fanned and re-created in each new generation. Particularism has its intellectual roots in the ideology of ethnic separatism and in the black nationalist movement. In the particularist analysis, the nation has five cultures: African American, Asian American, European American, Latino/Hispanic, and Native American. The huge cultural, historical, religious, and linguistic differences within these categories are ignored, as is the considerable intermarriage among these groups, as are the linkages (like gender, class, sexual orientation, and religion) that cut across these five groups. No serious scholar would claim that all Europeans and white Americans are part of the same culture, or that all Asians are part of the same culture, or that all people of Latin-American descent are of the same culture, or that all people of African descent are of the same culture. Any categorization this broad is essentially meaningless and useless.

Several districts — including Detroit, Atlanta, and Washington, D.C. — are developing an Afrocentric curriculum. *Afrocentricity* has been described in a book of the same name by Molefi Kete Asante of Temple University. The Afrocentric curriculum puts Africa at the center of the student's universe. African Americans must "move away from an [*sic*] Eurocentric framework" because "it is difficult to create freely when you use someone else's motifs, styles, images, and perspectives." Because they are not Africans, "white teachers cannot inspire in our children the visions necessary for them to overcome limitations." Asante recommends that African Americans choose an African name (as he did), reject European dress, embrace African religion (not Islam or Christianity) and love "their own" culture. He scorns the idea of universality as a form of Eurocentric arrogance. The Eurocentrist, he says, thinks of Beethoven or Bach as classical, but the Afrocentrist thinks of Ellington or Coltrane as classical; the Eurocentrist lauds Shakespeare or Twain, while the Afrocentrist prefers Baraka, Shange, or Abiola. Asante is critical of black artists like Arthur Mitchell and Alvin Ailey who ignore Afrocentricity. Likewise, he speaks contemptuously of a group of black university students who spurned the Afrocentrism of the local Black Student Union and formed an organization called Inter-race: "Such madness is the direct consequence of self-hatred, obligatory attitudes, false assumptions about society, and stupidity."

The conflict between pluralism and particularism turns on the issue of universalism. Professor Asante warns his readers against the lure of universalism: "Do not be captured by a sense of universality given to you by the Eurocentric viewpoint; such a viewpoint is contradictory to your own ultimate reality." He insists that there is no alternative to Eurocentrism, Afrocentrism, and other ethnocentrisms. In contrast, the pluralist says, with the Roman playwright Terence, "I am a man: nothing human is alien to me." A contemporary Terence would say "I am a person" or might be a woman, but the point remains the same: You don't have to be black to love Zora Neale Hurston's fiction or Langston Hughes's poetry or Duke Ellington's music. In a pluralist curriculum, we expect children to learn a broad and humane culture, to learn about the ideas and art and animating spirit of many cultures. We expect that children, whatever their color, will be inspired by the courage of people like Helen Keller, Vaclav Havel, Harriet Tubman, and Feng Lizhe. We expect that their response to literature will be determined by the ideas and images it evokes, not by the skin color of the writer. But particularists insist that children can learn only from the experiences of people from the same race.

Particularism is a bad idea whose time has come. It is also a fashion spreading like wildfire through the education system, actively promoted by organizations and individuals with a political and professional interest in strengthening ethnic power bases in the university, in the education profession, and in society itself. One can scarcely pick up an educational journal without learning about a school district that is converting to an ethnocentric curriculum in an attempt to give "self-esteem" to children from racial minorities. A state-funded project in a Sacramento high school is teaching young black males to think like Africans and to develop the "African Mind Model

Technique," in order to free themselves of the racism of American culture. A popular black rap singer, KRS-One, complained in an op-ed article in the *New York Times* that the schools should be teaching blacks about their cultural heritage, instead of trying to make everyone Americans. "It's like trying to teach a dog to be a cat," he wrote. KRS-One railed about having to learn about Thomas Jefferson and the Civil War, which had nothing to do (he said) with black history.

Pluralism can easily be transformed into particularism, as may be seen in the potential uses in the classroom of the Mayan contribution to mathematics. The Mayan example was popularized in a movie called *Stand and Deliver*, about a charismatic Bolivian-born mathematics teacher in Los Angeles who inspired his students (who are Hispanic) to learn calculus. He told them that their ancestors invented the concept of zero; but that wasn't all he did. He used imagination to put across mathematical concepts. He required them to do homework and to go to school on Saturdays and during the Christmas holidays, so that they might pass the Advanced Placement mathematics examination for college entry. The teacher's reference to the Mayans' mathematical genius was a valid instructional device: It was an attention-getter and would have interested even students who were not Hispanic. But the Mayan example would have had little effect without the teacher's insistence that the class study hard for a difficult examination.

Ethnic educators have seized upon the Mayan contribution to mathematics as the key to simultaneously boosting the ethnic pride of Hispanic children and attacking Eurocentrism. One proposal claims that Mexican-American children will be attracted to science and mathematics if they study Mayan mathematics, the Mayan calendar, and Mayan astronomy. Children in primary grades are to be taught that the Mayans were first to discover the zero and that Europeans learned it long afterwards from the Arabs, who had learned it in India. This will help them see that Europeans were latecomers in the discovery of great ideas. Botany is to be learned by study of the agricultural techniques of the Aztecs, a subject of somewhat limited relevance to children in urban areas. Furthermore, "ethnobotanical" classifications of plants are to be substituted for the Eurocentric Linnaean system. At first glance, it may seem curious that Hispanic children are deemed to have no cultural affinity with Spain; but to acknowledge the cultural tie would confuse the ideological assault on Eurocentrism.

This proposal suggests some questions: Is there any evidence that the teaching of "culturally relevant" science and mathematics will draw Mexican-American children to the study of these subjects? Will Mexican-American children lose interest or self-esteem if they discover that their ancestors were Aztecs or Spaniards, rather than Mayans? Are children who learn in this way prepared to study the science and mathematics that are taught in American colleges and universities and that are needed for advanced study in these fields? Are they even prepared to study the science and mathematics taught in *Mexican* universities? If the class is half Mexican-American and half something else, will only the Mexican-American children study in a Mayan and Aztec

mode or will all the children? But shouldn't all children study what is culturally relevant for them? How will we train teachers who have command of so
many different systems of mathematics and science?

Particularism is akin to cultural Lysenkoism, for it takes as its premise 20
the spurious notion that cultural traits are inherited. It implies a dubious,
dangerous form of cultural predestination. Children are taught that if their
ancestors could do it, so could they. But what happens if a child is from a
cultural group that made no significant contribution to science or mathematics? Does this mean that children from that background must find a culturally
appropriate field in which to strive? How does a teacher find the right cultural
buttons for children of mixed heritage? And how in the world will teachers
use this technique when the children in their classes are drawn from many
different cultures, as is usually the case? By the time that every culture gets its
due, there may be no time left to teach the subject itself. This explosion of
filiopietism (which, we should remember, comes from adults, not from students) is reminiscent of the period some years ago when the Russians claimed
that they had invented everything first; as we now know, this nationalistic
braggadocio did little for their self-esteem and nothing for their economic
development. We might reflect, too, on how little social prestige has been
accorded in this country to immigrants from Greece and Italy, even though
the achievements of their ancestors were at the heart of the classical
curriculum.

Particularism can easily be carried to extremes. Students of Fredonian
descent must hear that their ancestors were seminal in the development of all
human civilization and that without the Fredonian contribution, we would
all be living in caves or trees, bereft of art, technology, and culture. To explain
why Fredonians today are in modest circumstances, given their historic em-
inence, children are taught that somewhere, long ago, another culture stole
the Fredonians' achievements, palmed them off as their own, and then oppressed the Fredonians.

I first encountered this argument almost twenty years ago, when I was
a graduate student. I shared a small office with a young professor, and I
listened as she patiently explained to a student why she had given him a D on
a term paper. In his paper, he argued that the Arabs had stolen mathematics
from the Nubians in the desert long ago (I forget in which century this theft
allegedly occurred). She tried to explain to him about the necessity of historical evidence. He was unconvinced, since he believed that he had uncovered a
great truth that was beyond proof. The part I couldn't understand was how
anyone could lose knowledge by sharing it. After all, cultures are constantly
influencing one another, exchanging ideas and art and technology, and the
exchange usually is enriching, not depleting.

Today, there are a number of books and articles advancing controversial
theories about the origins of civilization. An important work, *The African
Origin of Civilization: Myth or Reality,* by Senegalese scholar Cheikh Anta

Diop, argues that ancient Egypt was a black civilization, that all races are descended from the black race, and that the achievements of "western" civilization originated in Egypt. The views of Diop and other Africanists have been condensed into an everyman's paperback titled *What They Never Told You in History Class* by Indus Khamit Kush. This latter book claims that Moses, Jesus, Buddha, Mohammed, and Vishnu were Africans: that the first Indians, Chinese, Hebrews, Greeks, Romans, Britains, and Americans were Africans; and that the first mathematicians, scientists, astronomers, and physicians were Africans. A debate currently raging among some classicists is whether the Greeks "stole" the philosophy, art, and religion of the ancient Egyptians and whether the ancient Egyptians were black Africans. George G. M. James's *Stolen Legacy* insists that the Greeks "stole the Legacy of the African Continent and called it their own." James argues that the civilization of Greece, the vaunted foundation of European culture, owed everything it knew and did to its African predecessors. Thus, the roots of western civilization lie not in Greece and Rome, but in Egypt and, ultimately, in black Africa.

In school districts where most children are black and Hispanic, there has been a growing tendency to embrace particularism rather than pluralism. Many of the children in these districts perform poorly in academic classes and leave school without graduating. They would fare better in school if they had well-educated and well-paid teachers, small classes, good materials, encouragement at home and school, summer academic programs, protection from the drugs and crime that ravage their neighborhoods, and higher expectations of satisfying careers upon graduation. These are expensive and time-consuming remedies that must also engage the larger society beyond the school. The lure of particularism is that it offers a less complicated anodyne, one in which the children's academic deficiencies may be addressed — or set aside — by inflating their racial pride. The danger of this remedy is that it will detract attention from the real needs of schools and the real interests of children, while simultaneously arousing distorted race pride in children of all races, increasing racial antagonism and producing fresh recruits for white and black racist groups.

The rising tide of particularism encourages the politicization of all curricula in the schools. If education bureaucrats bend to the political and ideological winds, as is their wont, we can anticipate a generation of struggle over the content of the curriculum in mathematics, science, literature, and history. Demands for "culturally relevant" studies, for ethnostudies of all kinds, will open the classroom to unending battles over whose version is taught, who gets credit for what, and which ethno-interpretation is appropriate. Only recently have districts begun to resist the demands of fundamentalist groups to censor textbooks and library books (and some have not yet begun to do so).

The spread of particularism throws into question the very idea of American public education. Public schools exist to teach children the general skills and knowledge that they need to succeed in American society, and the specific skills and knowledge that they need in order to function as American citizens. They receive public support because they have a public function. Historically, the public schools were known as "common schools" because they were schools for all, even if the children of all the people did not attend them. Over the years, the courts have found that it was unconstitutional to teach religion in the common schools, or to separate children on the basis of their race in the common schools. In their curriculum, their hiring practices, and their general philosophy, the public schools must not discriminate against or give preference to any racial or ethnic group. Yet they are permitted to accommodate cultural diversity by, for example, serving food that is culturally appropriate or providing library collections that emphasize the interests of the local community. However, they should not be expected to teach children to view the world through an ethnocentric perspective that rejects or ignores the common culture. For generations, those groups that wanted to inculcate their religion or their ethnic heritage have instituted private schools — after school, on weekends, or on a full-time basis. There, children learn with others of the same group — Greeks, Poles, Germans, Japanese, Chinese, Jews, Lutherans, Catholics, and so on — and are taught by people from the same group. Valuable as this exclusive experience has been for those who choose it, this has not been the role of public education. One of the primary purposes of public education has been to create a national community, a definition of citizenship and culture that is both expansive and *inclusive*.

The curriculum in public schools must be based on whatever knowledge and practices have been determined to be best by professionals — experienced teachers and scholars — who are competent to make these judgments. Professional societies must be prepared to defend the integrity of their disciplines. When called upon, they should establish review committees to examine disputes over curriculum and to render judgment, in order to help school officials fend off improper political pressure. Where genuine controversies exist, they should be taught and debated in the classroom. Was Egypt a black civilization? Why not raise the question, read the arguments of the different sides in the debate, show slides of Egyptian pharaohs and queens, read books about life in ancient Egypt, invite guest scholars from the local university, and visit museums with Egyptian collections? If scholars disagree, students should know it. One great advantage of this approach is that students will see that history is a lively study, that textbooks are fallible, that historians disagree, that the writing of history is influenced by the historian's politics and ideology, that history is written by people who make choices among alternative facts and interpretations, and that history changes as new facts are uncovered and new interpretations win adherents. They will also learn that cultures and civilizations constantly interact, exchange ideas, and influence one another, and that the idea of racial or ethnic purity is a myth. Another advantage is that students might once again study ancient history, which has all but disappeared from the curricula of American schools. (California recently introduced a required sixth grade course in ancient civilizations, but ancient history is otherwise *terra incognita* in American education.)

The multicultural controversy may do wonders for the study of history, which has been neglected for years in American schools. At this time, only half of our high school graduates ever study any world history. Any serious attempt to broaden students' knowledge of Africa, Europe, Asia, and Latin America will require at least two, and possibly three years of world history (a requirement thus far only in California). American history, too, will need more time than the one-year high-school survey course. Those of us who have insisted for years on the importance of history in the curriculum may not be ready to assent to its redemptive power, but hope that our new allies will ultimately join a constructive dialogue that strengthens the place of history in the schools.

As cultural controversies arise, educators must adhere to the principle of "E Pluribus Unum." That is, they must maintain a balance between the demands of the one — the nation of which we are common citizens — and the many — the varied histories of the American people. It is not necessary to denigrate either the one or the many. Pluralism is a positive value, but it is also important that we preserve a sense of an American community — a society and a culture to which we all belong. If there is no overall community with an agreed-upon vision of liberty and justice, if all we have is a collection of racial and ethnic cultures, lacking any common bonds, then we have no means to mobilize public opinion on behalf of people who are not members of our particular group. We have, for example, no reason to support public education. If there is no larger community, then each group will want to teach its own children in its own way, and public education ceases to exist.

History should not be confused with filiopietism. History gives no 30 grounds for race pride. No race has a monopoly on virtue. If anything, a study of history should inspire humility, rather than pride. People of every racial group have committed terrible crimes, often against others of the same group. Whether one looks at the history of Europe or Africa or Latin America or Asia, every continent offers examples of inhumanity. Slavery has existed in civilizations around the world for centuries. Examples of genocide can be found around the world, throughout history, from ancient times right through to our own day. Governments and cultures, sometimes by edict, sometimes simply following tradition, have practiced not only slavery, but human sacrifice, infanticide, cliterodectomy, and mass murder. If we teach children this, they might recognize how absurd both racial hatred and racial chauvinism are.

What must be preserved in the study of history is the spirit of inquiry, the readiness to open new questions and to pursue new understandings. History, at its best, is a search for truth. The best way to portray this search is through debate and controversy, rather than through imposition of fixed beliefs and immutable facts. Perhaps the most dangerous aspect of school history is its tendency to become Official History, a sanctified version of the Truth taught by the state to captive audiences and embedded in beautiful mass-market textbooks as holy writ. When Official History is written by committees responding to political pressures, rather than by scholars synthesizing the best available research, then the errors of the past are replaced by the politically fashionable errors of the present. It may be difficult to teach children that history is both important and uncertain, and that even the best historians never have all the pieces of the jigsaw puzzle, but it is necessary to do so. If state education departments permit the revision of their history courses and textbooks to become an exercise in power politics, then the entire process of state-level curriculum-making becomes suspect, as does public education itself.

The question of self-esteem is extraordinarily complex, and it goes well beyond the content of the curriculum. Most of what we call self-esteem is formed in the home and in a variety of life experiences, not only in school. Nonetheless, it has been important for blacks — and for other racial groups — to learn about the history of slavery and of the civil rights movement; it has been important for blacks to know that their ancestors actively resisted enslavement and actively pursued equality; and it has been important for blacks and others to learn about black men and women who fought courageously against racism and who provide models of courage, persistence, and intellect. These are instances where the content of the curriculum reflects sound scholarship, and at the same time probably lessens racial prejudice and provides inspiration for those who are descendants of slaves. But knowing about the travails and triumphs of one's forebears does not necessarily translate into either self-esteem or personal accomplishment. For most children, self-esteem — the self-confidence that grows out of having reached a goal — comes not from hearing about the monuments of their ancestors but as a consequence of what they are able to do and accomplish through their own efforts.

As I reflected on these issues, I recalled reading an interview a few years ago with a talented black runner. She said that her model is Mikhail Baryshnikov. She admires him because he is a magnificent athlete. He is not black; he is not female; he is not American-born; he is not even a runner. But he inspires her because of the way he trained and used his body. When I read this, I thought how narrow-minded it is to believe that people can be inspired *only* by those who are exactly like them in race and ethnicity.

Suggestions for Writing and Discussion

1. Consider the definition of *multiculturalism* that you wrote or discussed in response to prereading suggestion 1. After reading what Ravitch has written, would you make any changes to your original definition? Explain.
2. Explain the distinction Ravitch makes between the terms *pluralistic multiculturalism* and *particularistic multiculturalism*. Then evaluate the argument she builds by using these two terms. What is your response to this argument?
3. Take the position of a person who believes in particularistic multiculturalism (as defined by Ravitch). How might this person refute her arguments?
4. In the third paragraph, Ravitch notes, "For many years, the public schools attempted to neutralize controversies over race, religion, and ethnicity by

ignoring them." Take the position of a person who still believes this approach to be justified. How might such a person argue against the case Ravitch makes for pluralistic multiculturalism?

5. After reading Ravitch's argument, and after planning the counterarguments called for in suggestions 3 and 4, decide on your own views regarding multicultural education. Describe your ideal program for students at a particular academic level (kindergarten, elementary school, middle school, high school, or college), and argue for the implementation of this program.

Suggestions for Extended Thinking and Research

1. Do research on the multicultural education issue. Read essays reflecting many different points of view. Consider, for instance, Arthur Schlesinger, Jr.'s essay "The American Creed: From Dilemma to Decomposition" (*New Perspectives Quarterly,* Summer 1991) as well as Diane Ravitch's response to that essay (*New Perspectives Quarterly,* Fall 1991). After discovering several different perspectives, explain whether and how your initial response to "Multiculturalism: E Pluribus Plures" has changed.

2. After reading "Multiculturalism: E Pluribus Plures," design a questionnaire intended to discover views of multicultural education on your campus. Interview several professors who teach courses considered to take a multicultural approach, asking them to suggest colleagues who hold different views on multicultural education. After gathering as many diverse views as possible, write a paper explaining what you have discovered. Conclude by arguing for the view of multicultural education that you have developed in response to the ideas and opinions you heard during the interviews.

LESLIE MARMON SILKO

Lullaby

> *Leslie Marmon Silko was born in Albuquerque, New Mexico, in 1948 and grew up on the Laguna Pueblo Reservation. After graduating from the University of New Mexico and attending law school, she returned to the Laguna Pueblo, where she currently lives and writes. She has published many short stories and poems, including a volume of poetry,* Laguna Woman: Poems *(1974), and a novel,* Ceremony *(1977). In 1974 she received the Award for Poetry from the* Chicago Review, *and in 1975, this story, "Lullaby," was chosen to appear in Martha Foley's* Best Short Stories *of 1975.*

Prereading/Journal-Writing Suggestions

1. Think about events that you've read about in the newspapers or seen on television this past year. What story (or types of stories) have moved you strongly? Write about one of these stories and describe your response to it.
2. Under what circumstances should authorities take children away from their family? Explain.
3. If you are a parent, what was the most difficult situation that you and your children faced? As a child, what was the most difficult situation that you and your parents faced?

The sun had gone down but the snow in the wind gave off its own light. It came in thick tufts like new wool — washed before the weaver spins it. Ayah reached out for it like her own babies had, and she smiled when she remembered how she had laughed at them. She was an old woman now, and her life had become memories. She sat down with her back against the wide cottonwood tree, feeling the rough bark on her back bones; she faced east and listened to the wind and snow sing a high-pitched Yeibechei song. Out of the wind she felt warmer, and she could watch the wide, fluffy snow fill in her tracks, steadily, until the direction she had come from was gone. By the light of the snow she could see the dark outline of the big arroyo a few feet away. She was sitting on the edge of Cebolleta Creek, where in the springtime the thin cows would graze on grass already chewed flat to the ground. In the wide, deep creek bed where only a trickle of water flowed in the summer, the skinny cows would wander, looking for new grass along winding paths splashed with manure.

Ayah pulled the old Army blanket over her head like a shawl. Jimmie's blanket — the one he had sent to her. That was a long time ago and the green wool was faded, and it was unraveling on the edges. She did not want to think about Jimmie. So she thought about the weaving and the way her mother had done it. On the tall wooden loom set into the sand under a tamarack tree for shade. She could see it clearly. She had been only a little girl when her grandma gave her the wooden combs to pull the twigs and burrs from the raw, freshly washed wool. And while she combed the wool, her grandma sat beside her spinning a silvery strand of yarn around the smooth cedar spindle. Her mother worked at the loom with yarns dyed bright yellow and red and gold. She watched them dye the yarn in boiling black pots full of beeweed petals, juniper berries, and sage. The blankets her mother made were soft and woven so tight that rain rolled off them like birds' feathers. Ayah remembered sleeping warmly on cold windy nights, wrapped in her mother's blankets on the hogan's sandy floor.

The snow drifted now, with the northwest wind hurling it in gusts. It drifted up around her black overshoes—old ones with little metal buckles. She smiled at the snow which was trying to cover her little by little. She could remember when they had no black rubber overshoes; only the high buckskin leggings that they wrapped over their elkhide moccasins. If the snow was dry or frozen, a person could walk all day and not get wet; and in the evenings the beams of the ceiling would hang with lengths of pale buckskin leggings drying out slowly.

She felt peaceful remembering. She didn't feel cold any more. Jimmie's blanket seemed warmer than it had ever been. And she could remember the morning he was born. She could remember whispering to her mother, who was sleeping on the other side of the hogan, to tell her it was time now. She did not want to wake the others. The second time she called to her, her mother stood up and pulled on her shoes; she knew. They walked to the old stone hogan together, Ayah walking a step behind her mother. She waited alone learning the rhythms of the pains while her mother went to call the old woman to help them. The morning was already warm even before dawn and Ayah smelled the bee flowers blooming and the young willow growing at the springs. She could remember that so clearly, but his birth merged into the births of the other children and to her it became all the same birth. They named him for the summer morning and in English they called him Jimmie.

It wasn't like Jimmie died. He just never came back, and one day a dark blue sedan with white writing on its doors pulled up in front of the boxcar shack where the rancher let the Indians live. A man in a khaki uniform trimmed in gold gave them a yellow piece of paper and told them that Jimmie was dead. He said the Army would try to get the body back and then it would be shipped to them; but it wasn't likely because the helicopter had burned after it crashed. All of this was told to Chato because he could understand English. She stood inside the doorway holding the baby while Chato listened. Chato spoke English like a white man and he spoke Spanish too. He was taller than the white man and he stood straighter too. Chato didn't explain why; he just told the military man they could keep the body if they found it. The white man looked bewildered; he nodded his head and left. Then Chato looked at her and shook his head, and then he told her, "Jimmie isn't coming home anymore," and when he spoke, he used the words to speak of the dead. She didn't cry then, but she hurt inside with anger. And she mourned him as the years passed, when a horse fell with Chato and broke his leg, and the white rancher told them he wouldn't pay Chato until he could work again. She mourned Jimmie because he would have worked for his father then; he would have saddled the big bay horse and ridden the fence lines each day, with wire cutters and heavy gloves, fixing the breaks in the barbed wire and putting the stray cattle back inside again.

She mourned him after the white doctors came to take Danny and Ella away. She was at the shack alone that day they came. It was back in the days before they hired Navajo women to go with them as interpreters. She recognized one of the doctors. She had seen him at the children's clinic at Cañoncito about a month ago. They were wearing khaki uniforms and they waved papers at her and a black ball-point pen, trying to make her understand their English words. She was frightened by the way they looked at the children, like the lizard watches the fly. Danny was swinging on the tire swing on the elm tree behind the rancher's house, and Ella was toddling around the front door, dragging the broomstick horse Chato made for her. Ayah could see they wanted her to sign the papers, and Chato had taught her to sign her name. It was something she was proud of. She only wanted them to go, and to take their eyes away from her children.

She took the pen from the man without looking at his face and she signed the papers in three different places he pointed to. She stared at the ground by their feet and waited for them to leave. But they stood there and began to point and gesture at the children. Danny stopped swinging. Ayah could see his fear. She moved suddenly and grabbed Ella into her arms; the child squirmed, trying to get back to her toys. Ayah ran with the baby toward Danny; she screamed for him to run and then she grabbed him around his chest and carried him too. She ran south into the foothills of juniper trees and black lava rock. Behind her she heard the doctors running, but they had been taken by surprise, and as the hills became steeper and the cholla cactus were thicker, they stopped. When she reached the top of the hill, she stopped to listen in case they were circling around her. But in a few minutes she heard a car engine start and they drove away. The children had been too surprised to cry while she ran with them. Danny was shaking and Ella's little fingers were gripping Ayah's blouse.

She stayed up in the hills for the rest of the day, sitting on a black lava boulder in the sunshine where she could see for miles all around her. The sky was light blue and cloudless, and it was warm for late April. The sun warmth relaxed her and took the fear and anger away. She lay back on the rock and watched the sky. It seemed to her that she could walk into the sky, stepping through clouds endlessly. Danny played with little pebbles and stones, pretending they were birds' eggs and then little rabbits. Ella sat at her feet and dropped fistfuls of dirt into the breeze, watching the dust and particles of sand intently. Ayah watched a hawk soar high above them, dark wings gliding;

hunting or only watching, she did not know. The hawk was patient and he circled all afternoon before he disappeared around the high volcanic peak the Mexicans called Guadalupe.

Late in the afternoon, Ayah looked down at the gray boxcar shack with the paint all peeled from the wood: the stove pipe on the roof was rusted and crooked. The fire she had built that morning in the oil drum stove had burned out. Ella was asleep in her lap now and Danny sat close to her, complaining that he was hungry; he asked when they would go to the house. "We will stay up here until your father comes," she told him, "because those white men were chasing us." The boy remembered then and he nodded at her silently.

If Jimmie had been there he could have read those papers and explained 10 to her what they said. Ayah would have known then, never to sign them. The doctors came back the next day and they brought a BIA policeman with them. They told Chato they had her signature and that was all they needed. Except for the kids. She listened to Chato sullenly; she hated him when he told her it was the old woman who died in the winter, spitting blood; it was her old grandma who have given the children this disease. "They don't spit blood," she said coldly. "The whites lie." She held Ella and Danny close to her, ready to run to the hills again. "I want a medicine man first," she said to Chato, not looking at him. He shook his head. "It's too late now. The policeman is with them. You signed the paper." His voice was gentle.

It was worse than if they had died: to lose the children and to know that somewhere, in a place called Colorado, in a place full of sick and dying strangers, her children were without her. There had been babies that died soon after they were born, and one that died before he could walk. She had carried them herself, up to the boulders and great pieces of the cliff that long ago crashed down from Long Mesa; she laid them in the crevices of sandstone and buried them in fine brown sand with round quartz pebbles that washed down the hills in the rain. She had endured it because they had been with her. But she could not bear this pain. She did not sleep for a long time after they took her children. She stayed on the hill where they had fled the first time, and she slept rolled up in the blanket Jimmie had sent her. She carried the pain in her belly and it was fed by everything she saw: the blue sky of their last day together and the dust and pebbles they played with; the swing in the elm tree and broomstick horse choked life from her. The pain filled her stomach and there was no room for food or for her lungs to fill with air. The air and the food would have been theirs.

She hated Chato, not because he let the policeman and doctors put the screaming children in the government car, but because he had taught her to sign her name. Because it was like the old ones always told her about learning their language or any of their ways: It endangers you. She slept alone on the hill until the middle of November when the first snows came. Then she made a bed for herself where the children had slept. She did not lie down beside Chato again until many years later, when he was sick and shivering and only her body could keep him warm. The illness came after the white rancher told

Chato he was too old to work for him anymore, and Chato and his old woman should be out of the shack by the next afternoon because the rancher had hired new people to work there. That had satisfied her. To see how the white man repaid Chato's years of loyalty and work. All of Chato's fine-sounding English talk didn't change things.

It snowed steadily and the luminous light from the snow gradually diminished into the darkness. Somewhere in Ceboletta a dog barked and other village dogs joined with it. Ayah looked in the direction she had come, from the bar where Chato was buying the wine. Sometimes he told her to go on ahead and wait; and then he never came. And when she finally went back looking for him, she would find him passed out at the bottom of the wooden steps to Azzie's Bar. All the wine would be gone and most of the money too, from the pale blue check that came to them once a month in a government envelope. It was then that she would look at his face and his hands, scarred by ropes and the barbed wire of all those years, and she would think, this man is a stranger; for forty years she had smiled at him and cooked his food, but he remained a stranger. She stood up again, with the snow almost to her knees, and she walked back to find Chato.

It was hard to walk in the deep snow and she felt the air burn in her lungs. She stopped a short distance from the bar to rest and readjust the blanket. But this time he wasn't waiting for her at the bottom step with his old Stetson hat pulled down and his shoulders hunched up in his long wool overcoat.

She was careful not to slip on the wooden steps. When she pushed the 15 door open, warm air and cigarette smoke hit her face. She looked around slowly and deliberately, in every corner, in every dark place that the old man might find to sleep. The bar owner didn't like Indians in there, especially Navajos, but he let Chato come in because he could talk Spanish like he was one of them. The men at the bar stared at her, and the bartender saw that she left the door open wide. Snowflakes were flying inside like moths and melting into a puddle on the oiled wood floor. He motioned to her to close the door, but she did not see him. She held herself straight and walked across the room slowly, searching the room with every step. The snow in her hair melted and she could feel it on her forehead. At the far corner of the room, she saw red flames at the mica window of the old stove door; she looked behind the stove just to make sure. The bar got quiet except for the Spanish polka music playing on the jukebox. She stood by the stove and shook the snow from her blanket and held it near the stove to dry. The wet wool smell reminded her of newborn goats in early March, brought inside to warm near the fire. She felt calm.

In past years they would have told her to get out. But her hair was white now and her face was wrinkled. They looked at her like she was a spider crawling slowly across the room. They were afraid; she could feel the fear. She looked at their faces steadily. They reminded her of the first time the white people brought her children back to her that winter. Danny had been shy and hid behind the thin white woman who brought them. And the baby had not known her until Ayah took her into her arms, and then Ella had nuzzled close to her as she had when she was nursing. The blonde woman was nervous and kept looking at a dainty gold watch on her wrist. She sat on the bench near the small window and watched the dark snow clouds gather around the mountains; she was worrying about the unpaved road. She was frightened by what she saw inside too: the strips of venison drying on a rope across the ceiling and the children jabbering excitedly in a language she did not know. So they stayed for only a few hours. Ayah watched the government car disappear down the road and she knew they were already being weaned from these lava hills and from this sky. The last time they came was in early June, and Ella stared at her the way the men in the bar were now staring. Ayah did not try to pick her up; she smiled at her instead and spoke cheerfully to Danny. When he tried to answer her, he could not seem to remember and he spoke English words with the Navajo. But he gave her a scrap of paper that he had found somewhere and carried in his pocket; it was folded in half, and he shyly looked up at her and said it was a bird. She asked Chato if they were home for good this time. He spoke to the white woman and she shook her head. "How much longer?" he asked, and she said she didn't know; but Chato saw how she stared at the boxcar shack. Ayah turned away then. She did not say good-bye.

She felt satisfied that the men in the bar feared her. Maybe it was her face and the way she held her mouth with teeth clenched tight, like there was nothing anyone could do to her now. She walked north down the road, searching for the old man. She did this because she had the blanket, and there would be no place for him except with her and the blanket in the old adobe barn near the arroyo. They always slept there when they came to Cebolleta. If the money and the wine were gone, she would be relieved because then they could go home again; back to the old hogan with a dirt roof and rock walls where she herself had been born. And the next day the old man could go back to the few sheep they still had, to follow along behind them, guiding them, into dry sandy arroyos where sparse grass grew. She knew he did not like walking behind old ewes when for so many years he rode big quarter horses and worked with cattle. But she wasn't sorry for him; he should have known all along what would happen.

There had not been enough rain for their garden in five years; and that was when Chato finally hitched a ride into the town and brought back brown boxes of rice and sugar and big tin cans of welfare peaches. After that, at the first of the month they went to Cebolleta to ask the postmaster for the check; and then Chato would go to the bar and cash it. They did this as they planted the garden every May, not because anything would survive the summer dust, but because it was time to do this. The journey passed the days that smelled silent and dry like the caves above the canyon with yellow painted buffaloes on their walls.

He was walking along the pavement when she found him. He did not stop or turn around when he heard her behind him. She walked beside him and she noticed how slowly he moved now. He smelled strong of woodsmoke and urine. Lately he had been forgetting. Sometimes he called her by his sister's name and she had been gone for a long time. Once she had found him wandering on the road to the white man's ranch, and she asked him why he was going that way; he laughed at her and said, "You know they can't run that ranch without me," and he walked on determined, limping on the leg that had been crushed many years before. Now he looked at her curiously, as if for the first time, but he kept shuffling along, moving slowly along the side of the highway. His gray hair had grown long and spread out on the shoulders of the long overcoat. He wore the old felt hat pulled down over his ears. His boots were worn out at the toes and he had stuffed pieces of an old red shirt in the holes. The rags made his feet look like little animals up to their ears in snow. She laughed at his feet; the snow muffled the sound of her laugh. He stopped and looked at her again. The wind had quit blowing and the snow was falling straight down; the southeast sky was beginning to clear and Ayah could see a star.

"Let's rest awhile," she said to him. They walked away from the road and up the slope to the giant boulders that had tumbled down from the red sandrock mesa throughout the centuries of rainstorms and earth tremors. In a place where the boulders shut out the wind, they sat down with their backs against the rock. She offered half of the blanket to him and they sat wrapped together.

The storm passed swiftly. The clouds moved east. They were massive and full, crowding together across the sky. She watched them with the feeling of horses — steely blue-gray horses startled across the sky. The powerful haunches pushed into the distances and the tail hairs streamed white mist behind them. The sky cleared. Ayah saw that there was nothing between her and the stars. The light was crystalline. There was no shimmer, no distortion through earth haze. She breathed the clarity of the night sky; she smelled the purity of the half moon and the stars. He was lying on his side with his knees pulled up near his belly for warmth. His eyes were closed now, and in the light from the stars and the moon, he looked young again.

She could see it descend out of the night sky: an icy stillness from the edge of the thin moon. She recognized the freezing. It came gradually, sinking snowflake by snowflake until the crust was heavy and deep. It had the strength of the stars in Orion, and its journey was endless. Ayah knew that with the wine he would sleep. He would not feel it. She tucked the blanket around him, remembering how it was when Ella had been with her; and she felt the rush so big inside her heart for the babies. And she sang the only song she knew to sing for babies. She could not remember if she had ever sung it to her children, but she knew that her grandmother had sung it and her mother had sung it:

The earth is your mother,
*   she holds you.*
The sky is your father,
*   he protects you.*
Sleep,
sleep.
Rainbow is your sister,
*   she loves you.*
The winds are your brothers,
*   they sing to you.*
Sleep,
sleep.
We are together always
We are together always
There never was a time
when this
was not so.

Suggestions for Writing and Discussion

1. In "Lullaby," Silko writes that Ayah "was an old woman now, and her life had become memories." What are the most joyful memories Ayah recalls? What are the most painful? Are there many in between?

2. As she sits against the cottonwood tree, what would Ayah say she has learned during her lifetime? How might Ayah complete the following? "For me, life has been like. . . ."

3. In what ways did the world change between the time of Jimmie's birth and the time the story ends? What, if any, changes did Ayah make during this time?

4. Silko writes that even though Ayah knew Chato for over forty years, he "remained a stranger to her." Why do you think this is?

5. When Ayah's children come for a visit the last time, why doesn't she say good-bye to them? Who has changed in this scene? Why?

6. How does this piece relate to the section theme "Rights and Responsibilities"? Explain.

7. Although this is a fictional short story, can you imagine any parts that might be true? What parts reveal the knowledge of the writer? How were you affected by this piece?

8. If Hollywood were to produce this story, who would be depicted as the hero (or heroes), and who would be depicted as the villain (or villains)?

Suggestions for Extended Thinking and Research

1. Research what happened to the Navajos once the American government took over their lives. How many Navajos are living today? What are their lives like? Where do they live? What work do they do? What are their average wages or salaries? How many receive higher educations?

2. Read and analyze one of Silko's poems from her collection *Laguna Woman: Poems*.

3. Write a poem based on your reactions to "Lullaby."

GWENDOLYN BROOKS

The Mother

> *Born in Chicago in 1917, Gwendolyn Brooks has been writing poetry since she was seven years old. She has worked actively with many writers' and poets' workshops, and her work has been particularly influenced by the young black poets she met at the Second Black Writers' Conference held at Fiske University in 1967. These young poets persuaded her to make a strong commitment in her work to addressing racial issues. In addition, although Brooks does not define herself as a feminist, her poetry has also been strongly sympathetic to the problems and concerns of women.*

Prereading/Journal-Writing Suggestions

1. What painful memory have you carried with you for a long, long time? Can you ever imagine a time when you will no longer feel this pain? Explain.
2. If you could change any one thing you've done in your past, what would it be and why?
3. Write about a painful event in your life that you wouldn't change even if you could go back. Explain why you would keep that event in your life.

Abortions will not let you forget.
You remember the children you got that you did not get,
The damp small pulps with a little or with no hair,
The singers and workers that never handled the air.
You will never neglect or beat   5
Them, or silence or buy with a sweet.
You will never wind up the sucking-thumb
Or scuttle off ghosts that come.
You will never leave them, controlling your luscious sigh,
Return for a snack of them, with gobbling mother-eye.   10

I have heard in the voices of the wind the voices of my dim killed children.
I have contracted. I have eased
My dim dears at the breasts they could never suck.
I have said, Sweets, if I sinned, if I seized
Your luck   15
And your lives from your unfinished reach,
If I stole your births and your names,
Your straight baby tears and your games,

Your stilted or lovely loves, your tumults, your marriages, aches, and your
   deaths,
If I poisoned the beginnings of your breaths,   20
Believe that even in my deliberateness I was not deliberate.
Though why should I whine,
Whine that the crime was other than mine? —
Since anyhow you are dead.
Or rather, or instead,   25
You were never made.
But that too, I am afraid,
Is faulty: oh, what shall I say, how is the truth to be said?
You were born, you had body, you died.
It is just that you never giggled or planned or cried.   30

Believe me, I loved you all.
Believe me, I knew you, though faintly, and I loved,
   I loved you all.

Suggestions for Writing and Discussion

1. Obviously, the topic of this poem is abortion. Why, then, is it entitled "The Mother"?
2. In the first stanza, the speaker talks about abortion in terms of the second person, *you*. Why do you think Brooks chooses to begin this way?
3. As a reader and responder, what do you consider to be the most painful images in this piece? Why?
4. What might the speaker mean in the phrase "Believe that even in my deliberateness I was not deliberate (line 21)?
5. Explain what the speaker means by saying (lines 22–23), "Though why should I whine/Whine that the crime was other than mine?"
6. What is the truth (line 27) that Brooks strives for in this poem? What's your reaction to this truth?
7. The "you" in the last stanza now refers to the speaker's unborn children. Why does the speaker shift from addressing others, to addressing herself, to addressing her children?
8. Keeping in mind the theme of rights and responsibilities, whose rights are addressed in this piece? Whose responsibilities?
9. Compare the mother in this poem with the mother in Silko's story. Analyze each one of them in terms of her strengths and her weaknesses. Come to some conclusion about which one is the better mother.

Suggestions for Extended Thinking and Research

1. In one or two sentences, describe what you see as the central idea of this poem. Then write an essay in which you support or disagree with the mother in this piece.

2. Is the mother in this piece a good mother? Write an essay in which you answer this question. Begin by defining what a good mother is and by giving examples (firsthand and otherwise) of those you consider to be model mothers. Then analyze the mother in this poem, compare her with your model mother, and, in your conclusion, argue that she is — or is not — a good mother.

TOPICS FOR MAKING CONNECTIONS: RIGHTS AND RESPONSIBILITIES

1. Choose four characters from the selections in this section to participate in a conversation regarding the following statement: "We don't need any laws in this country and we don't need the Constitution. All we need to do is treat people with respect."
2. Write a conversation among Stanton, Keath, and Kriegel about a person's basic rights.
3. Imagine that the speaker in the poem "The Mother" or Ayah, as a young mother in "Lullaby," has written you a letter asking for your advice. What encouragement or advice do you give her, considering her situation? Who can you advise her to turn to for help? What do you tell her to believe in? What action can she possibly take to help herself?
4. What makes an effective argument? Compare and contrast one piece that moved or convinced you the most and one that had little or no effect on you; Analyze what elements of writing appeal to you as a reader.
5. Imagine a meeting between Elizabeth Cady Stanton and Ayah, the Indian woman in "Lullaby." What advice would Stanton give to Ayah? What could Ayah offer as her philosophy on life? What questions would Ayah ask of Stanton regarding the progress women have made? How might Stanton respond?
6. Write an essay in which you argue that democracy can or cannot work in a country in which capitalism, by its very nature, fosters class and economic inequalities.
7. Working in a small group, research the hiring and promotion policies of several large corporations to discover how many positions of power are held by women and minorities. Argue for or against the continuation (or institution) of affirmative action policies in these companies.
8. Make a guess about what three of the following people would say is wrong with American government today: Jesse Jackson, Gwendolyn Brooks, Elizabeth Cady Stanton, Greg Keath, Andrew Sullivan, Leonard Kriegel. Write the argument they, as a committee, would formulate to support their contentions.
9. Argue for or against the following proposition: Education is essential if all humans are to achieve equal rights. Refer to several sources in this section as you write your argument.

Questions of Language

Previews: QUESTIONS OF LANGUAGE

Reading programs taught in English to children with Spanish as a first language wastes their acquired linguistic attributes and also impedes learning by forcing them to absorb skills of reading simultaneously with a new language.

From: *Bilingual Education: The Key to Basic Skills,* ANGELO GONZALEZ

Foreign-language acquisition is one thing for the upper-class child in a convent school learning to curtsy. Language acquisition can only seem a loss for the ghetto child, for the new language is psychologically awesome, being, as it is, the language of the bus driver and Papa's employer. The child's difficulty will turn out to be psychological more than linguistic because what he gives up are symbols of home.

From: *Bilingual Education: Outdated and Unrealistic,* RICHARD RODRIGUEZ

Why should any words be called obscene? Don't they all describe natural human functions? Am I trying to tell them, my students demand, that the "strong, earthy, gut-honest" — or, if they are fans of Norman Mailer, the "rich, liberating, existential" — language they use to describe sexual activity isn't preferable to "phony-sounding, middle-class words like 'intercourse' and 'copulate'?" "Cop You Late!" they say with fancy inflections and gagging grimaces. "Now, what is *that* supposed to mean?

From: *Four-Letter Words Can Hurt You,* BARBARA LAWRENCE

The first time it happened to me I was nine years old. Cornered in the school bathroom by the class bully and her sidekick, I was offered the opportunity to swallow a few of my teeth unless I satisfactorily explained why I always got good grades, why I talked "proper" or "white."

From: *What's Wrong with Black English?,* RACHEL L. JONES

I remember the first time I heard the word *nigger.* In my third-grade class, our math tests were being passed down the rows, and as I handed the papers to a little boy in back of me, I remarked that once again he had received a much lower mark than I did. He snatched his test from me and spit out that word. Had he called me a nymphomaniac or a necrophiliac, I couldn't have been more puzzled. I didn't know what a nigger was, but I knew that whatever it meant, it was something he shouldn't have called me.

From: *A Question of Language,* GLORIA NAYLOR

ANGELO GONZALEZ

Bilingual Education: The Key to Basic Skills

> *Angelo Gonzalez serves as educational director of ASPIRA, an organization that promotes awareness and advocacy of issues related to Hispanic Americans. This essay and the essay by Richard Rodriguez that follows it appeared as companion pieces in the* New York Times *"Educational Supplement." Together, these essays suggest the complexity of the bilingual education question.*

Prereading/Journal-Writing Suggestions

1. If you moved to a foreign country and had the choice of attending either a school where classes were taught in your native language or one where classes were conducted in the foreign language, which one would you choose? What problems might you encounter in the school of your choice? What might you learn (or fail to learn)?

2. Write about a particular class in your educational experience in which you didn't learn as much as you wanted to. What factors came into play in this experience? How might you have learned more in this situation?

If we accept that a child cannot learn unless taught through the language he speaks and understands; that a child who does not speak or understand English must fall behind when English is the dominant medium of instruction; that one needs to learn English so as to be able to participate in an English-speaking society; that self-esteem and motivation are necessary for effective learning; that rejection of a child's native language and culture is detrimental to the learning process: then any necessary effective educational program for limited or no English-speaking ability must incorporate the following:

- Language arts and comprehensive reading programs taught in the child's native language.
- Curriculum content areas taught in the native language to further comprehension and academic achievement.
- Intensive instruction in English.
- Use of materials sensitive to and reflecting the culture of children within the program.

Most Important Goal

The mastery of basic reading skills is the most important goal in primary education since reading is the basis for much of all subsequent learning. Ordinarily, these skills are learned at home. But where beginning reading is taught in English, only the English-speaking child profits from these early acquired skills that are prerequisites to successful reading development. Reading programs taught in English to children with Spanish as a first language waste their acquired linguistic attributes and also impede learning by forcing them to absorb skills of reading simultaneously with a new language.

Both local and national research data provide ample evidence for the efficacy of well-implemented programs. The New York City Board of Education Report on Bilingual Pupil Services for 1982–83 indicated that in all areas of the curriculum — English, Spanish and mathematics — and at all grade levels, students demonstrated statistically significant gains in tests of reading in English and Spanish and in math. In all but two of the programs reviewed, the attendance rates of students in the program, ranging from 86 to 94 percent, were higher than those of the general school population. Similar higher attendance rates were found among students in high school bilingual programs.

At Yale University, Kenji Hakuta, a linguist, reported recently on a study of working-class Hispanic students in the New Haven bilingual program. He found that children who were the most bilingual, that is, who developed English without the loss of Spanish, were brighter in both verbal and nonverbal tests. Over time, there was an increasing correlation between English and Spanish — a finding that clearly contradicts the charge that teaching in the home language is detrimental to English. Rather the two languages are interdependent within the bilingual child, reinforcing each other.

Essential Contribution

As Jim Cummins of the Ontario Institute for Studies in Education has argued, the use and development of the native language makes an essential contribution to the development of minority children's subject-matter knowledge and academic learning potential. In fact, at least three national data bases — the National Assessment of Educational Progress, National Center for Educational Statistics–High School and Beyond Studies, and the Survey of Income and Education — suggest that there are long-term positive effects among high school students who have participated in bilingual-education programs. These students are achieving higher scores on tests of verbal and mathematics skills.

These and similar findings buttress the argument stated persuasively in the recent joint recommendation of the Academy for Educational Development and the Hazen Foundation, namely, that America needs to become a more multilingual nation and children who speak a non-English language are a national resource to be nurtured in school.

Unfortunately, the present Administration's educational policies would seem to be leading us in the opposite direction. Under the guise of protecting the common language of public life in the United States, William J. Bennett, the Secretary of Education, unleashed a frontal attack on bilingual education. In a major policy address, he engaged in rhetorical distortions about the nature and effectiveness of bilingual programs, pointing only to unnamed negative research findings to justify the Administration's retrenchment efforts.

Arguing for the need to give local school districts greater flexibility in determining appropriate methodologies in serving limited-English-proficient students, Mr. Bennett fails to realize that, in fact, districts serving large numbers of language-minority students, as is the case in New York City, do have that flexibility. Left to their own devices in implementing legal mandates, many school districts have performed poorly at providing services to all entitled language-minority students.

A Harsh Reality

The harsh reality in New York City for language-minority students was documented comprehensively last month by the Educational Priorities Panel. The panel's findings revealed that of the 113,831 students identified as being limited in English proficiency, as many as 44,000 entitled students are not receiving any bilingual services. The issue at hand is, therefore, not one of choice but rather violation of the rights of almost 40 percent of language-minority children to equal educational opportunity. In light of these findings the Reagan Administration's recent statements only serve to exacerbate existing inequities in the American educational system for linguistic-minority children. Rather than adding fuel to a misguided debate, the Administration would serve these children best by insuring the full funding of the 1984 Bilingual Education Reauthorization Act as passed by the Congress.

Suggestions for Writing and Discussion

1. In your own words and in one sentence only, what is Gonzalez's central point in this essay?
2. List and evaluate the specific sources Gonzalez uses in order to support his thesis. How credible are these sources? How reliable are they? How varied and up to date are they?
3. In this essay, Gonzalez chooses to appeal to the reader's sense of logic, for the most part. First of all, why do you think he adopts this rhetorical approach? Second, for what specific readers might this approach be most effective? Explain your answers.
4. Gonzalez claims that "children who speak a non-English language are a national resource to be nurtured in school." However, he does not provide specifics as to how this should be done. If you were an elementary school teacher, what specifically could you do in order to nurture these children?
5. Gonzalez writes that bilingual education is not a matter of choice: It is a matter of rights. On what principle does he make this claim? Do you agree or disagree with his position here? Explain your answer.

Suggestion for Extended Thinking and Research

Call several schools in your area to learn whether bilingual education is a concern. If it is, discover how they approach this issue. Talk with a variety of people in the schools: teachers, principals, even students. Also, research your state and local school offices in order to discover what the existing policy is on bilingual education. Write a report on your findings and share it with your class.

RICHARD RODRIGUEZ

Bilingual Education: Outdated and Unrealistic

> *Born to Mexican immigrant parents in 1944, Richard Rodriguez experienced painful conflicts between speaking Spanish — his "home" language — and speaking English — the "public" language expected from him at school. He resolved these conflicts by speaking, reading, and writing English nearly exclusively from his elementary school years onward. After graduating from Stanford University, he earned a graduate degree from the University of California at Berkeley and later became a professor of Renaissance literature at Berkeley. Best known for his autobiography,* Hunger of Memory *(1982), Rodriguez has written extensively about issues related to bilingual learning.*

Prereading/Journal-Writing Suggestions

1. Have you ever experienced a conflict between what you learned at home and what you encountered in the classroom at school? If so, describe the conflict and explain how you resolved it, or discuss why you believe the conflict remains unresolved.
2. If you are bilingual (or multilingual), explain the benefits as well as any drawbacks you see in knowing more than one language. If you are not bilingual (or multilingual), talk with someone who is, asking this person about the advantages and disadvantages of knowing two or more languages. Then explain your response to what you have learned.

How shall we teach the dark-eyed child *ingles*? The debate continues much as it did two decades ago.

Bilingual education belongs to the 1960's, the years of the black civil rights movement. Bilingual education became the official Hispanic demand; as a symbol, the English-only classroom was intended to be analogous to the segregated lunch counter; the locked school door. Bilingual education was endorsed by judges and, of course, by politicians well before anyone knew the answer to the question: Does bilingual education work?

Who knows? *Quien sabe?*

The official drone over bilingual education is conducted by educationalists with numbers and charts. Because bilingual education was never simply a matter of pedagogy, it is too much to expect educators to resolve the matter. Proclamations concerning bilingual education are weighted at bottom with Hispanic political grievances and, too, with middle-class romanticism.

No one will say it in public; in private, Hispanics argue with me about 5
bilingual education and every time it comes down to memory. Everyone remembers going to that grammar school where students were slapped for speaking Spanish. Childhood memory is offered as parable; the memory is

meant to compress the gringo's long history of offenses against Spanish, Hispanic culture, Hispanics.

It is no coincidence that, although all of America's ethnic groups are implicated in the policy of bilingual education, Hispanics, particularly Mexican-Americans, have been its chief advocates. The English words used by Hispanics in support of bilingual education are words such as "dignity," "heritage," "culture." Bilingualism becomes a way of exacting from gringos a grudging admission of contrition — for the 19th-century theft of the Southwest, the relegation of Spanish to a foreign tongue, the injustice of history. At the extreme, Hispanic bilingual enthusiasts demand that public schools "maintain" a student's sense of separateness.

Hispanics may be among the last groups of Americans who still believe in the 1960's. Bilingual-education proposals still serve the romance of that decade, especially of the late 60's, when the heroic black civil rights movement grew paradoxically wedded to its opposite — the ethnic revival movement. Integration and separatism merged into twin, possible goals.

With integration, the black movement inspired middle-class Americans to imitations — the Hispanic movement; the Gray Panthers; feminism; gay rights. Then there was withdrawal, with black glamour leading a romantic retreat from the anonymous crowd.

Americans came to want it both ways. They wanted in and they wanted out. Hispanics took to celebrating their diversity, joined other Americans in dancing rings around the melting pot.

Mythic Metaphors

More intently than most, Hispanics wanted the romance of their dual 10 cultural allegiance backed up by law. Bilingualism became proof that one could have it both ways, could be a full member of public America and yet also separate, privately Hispanic. "Spanish" and "English" became mythic metaphors like country and city, describing separate islands of private and public life.

Ballots, billboards, and, of course, classrooms in Spanish. For nearly two decades now, middle-class Hispanics have had it their way. They have foisted a neat ideological scheme on working-class children. What they want to believe about themselves, they wait for the child to prove, that it is possible to be two, that one can assume the public language (the public life) of America, even while remaining what one was, existentially separate.

Adulthood is not so neatly balanced. The tension between public and private life is intrinsic to adulthood — certainly middle-class adulthood. Usually the city wins because the city pays. We are mass people for more of the day than we are with our intimates. No Congressional mandate or Supreme Court decision can diminish the loss.

I was talking the other day to a carpenter from Riga, in the Soviet Republic of Latvia. He has been here six years. He told me of his having to force himself to relinquish the "luxury" of reading books in Russian or Latvian so he could begin to read books in English. And the books he was able to read in English were not of a complexity to satisfy him. But he was not going back to Riga.

Beyond any question of pedagogy there is the simple fact that a language gets learned as it gets used, fills one's mouth, one's mind, with the new names for things.

The civil rights movement of the 1960's taught Americans to deal with 15 forms of discrimination other than economic — racial, sexual. We forget class. We talk about bilingual education as an ethnic issue; we forget to notice that the program mainly touches the lives of working-class immigrant children. Foreign-language acquisition is one thing for the upper-class child in a convent school learning to curtsy. Language acquisition can only seem a loss for the ghetto child, for the new language is psychologically awesome, being, as it is, the language of the bus driver and Papa's employer. The child's difficulty will turn out to be psychological more than linguistic because what he gives up are symbols of home.

Pain and Guilt

I was that child! I faced the stranger's English with pain and guilt and fear. Baptized to English in school, at first I felt myself drowning — the ugly sounds forced down my throat — until slowly, slowly (held in the tender grip of my teachers), suddenly the conviction took; English was my language to use.

What I yearn for is some candor from those who speak about bilingual education. Which of its supporters dares speak of the price a child pays — the price of adulthood — to make the journey from a working-class home into a middle-class schoolroom? The real story, the silent story of the immigrant child's journey is one of embarrassments in public; betrayal of all that is private; silence at home; and at school the hand tentatively raised.

Bilingual enthusiasts bespeak an easier world. They seek a linguistic solution to a social dilemma. They seem to want to believe that there is an easy way for the child to balance private and public, in order to believe that there is some easy way for themselves.

Ten years ago, I started writing about the ideological implications of bilingual education. Ten years from now some newspaper may well invite me to contribute another Sunday supplement essay on the subject. The debate is going to continue. The bilingual establishment is now inside the door. Jobs are at stake. Politicians can only count heads; growing numbers of Hispanics will insure the compliance of politicians.

Publicly, we will continue the fiction. We will solemnly address this 20 issue as an educational question, a matter of pedagogy. But privately, Hispanics will still seek from bilingual education an admission from the gringo that Spanish has value and presence. Hispanics of middle class will continue to seek the romantic assurance of separateness. Experts will argue. Dark-eyed children will sit in the classroom. Mute.

Suggestions for Writing and Discussion

1. How does Rodriguez's basic contention differ from Gonzalez's main point (see "Bilingual Education, pp. 499–502)?
2. Gonzalez appeals primarily to the reader's reason. What appeal(s) does Rodriguez choose in this piece? Find five specific words, phrases, or passages that support your answer; and go on to explain how each phrase affected you as a reader.
3. Gonzalez's use of local and national test results seems convincing, and yet Rodriguez claims that we still don't know whether or not bilingual education works. Why isn't he convinced by these statistics? Do you agree with him? Explain.
4. Although both Rodriguez and Gonzalez are descendants of Hispanic culture, their goals for the education of Hispanic children differ. Explain the goals that each writer promotes in his piece, and draw some inferences about what is at the core of their disagreement.
5. In a public school, should a child be entitled to his or her native language in the classroom? Support your position with three convincing reasons, and address opposing viewpoints as part of your argument.
6. After reading both Rodriguez's and Gonzalez's essays, which approach do you feel would be most effective for residents in your community or in a community nearby that has a significant bilingual population? In your answer, explain how several specific points the author makes might connect with the characteristics specific to your community.

Suggestion for Extended Thinking and Research

Many countries—for example, Belgium, Holland, and Switzerland—have more than one official language. In addition, in many countries students learn at least one other language (often English) in addition to their country's official language(s). Do research on the language education in these countries and then argue for or against the following proposition: "Every student in the United States should be required to become fluent both in English and in at least one other language."

BARBARA LAWRENCE

Four-Letter Words Can Hurt You

> *Barbara Lawrence is Professor of Language and Literature at the State University of New York, Old Westbury. She has written extensively on questions of language, particularly from a feminist perspective. This essay first appeared as an Op Ed piece in the* New York Times *in 1973.*

Prereading/Journal-Writing Suggestions

1. List all of the terms you can think of that men use in referring to women. Similarly, list all of the terms you can think of that women use when referring to men. Compare these two lists and come to some conclusions: What do men who use certain terms really think of women, and what do women who use certain terms think of men?

2. What five words in the English language do you find most offensive? Can you think of a situation in which these words would not be offensive to you? Explain.

Why should any words be called obscene? Don't they all describe natural human functions? Am I trying to tell them, my students demand, that the "strong, earthy, gut-honest" — or, if they are fans of Norman Mailer, the "rich, liberating, existential" — language they use to describe sexual activity isn't preferable to "phony-sounding, middle-class words like 'intercourse' and 'copulate'?" "Cop You Late!" they say with fancy inflections and gagging grimaces. "Now, what is *that* supposed to mean?"

Well, what is it supposed to mean? And why indeed should one group of words describing human functions and human organs be acceptable in ordinary conversation and another, describing presumably the same organs and functions, be tabooed — so much so, in fact, that some of these words still cannot appear in print in many parts of the English-speaking world?

The argument that these taboos exist only because of "sexual hangups" (middle-class, middle-age, feminist), or even that they are a result of class oppression (the contempt of the Norman conquerors for the language of their Anglo-Saxon serfs), ignores a much more likely explanation, it seems to me, and that is the sources and functions of the words themselves.

The best known of the tabooed sexual verbs, for example, comes from the German *ficken,* meaning "to strike"; combined, according to Partridge's etymological dictionary *Origins,* with the Latin sexual verb *futuere;* associated in turn with the Latin *fustis,* "a staff or cudgel"; the Celtic *buc,* "a point, hence to pierce"; the Irish *bot,* "the male member"; the Latin *battuere,* "to beat"; the Gaelic *batair,* "a cudgeller"; the Early Irish *bualaim,* "I strike"; and so forth. It is one of what etymologists sometimes call "the sadistic group of words for the man's part in copulation."

The brutality of this word, then, and its equivalents ("screw," "bang," etc.), is not an illusion of the middle class or a crotchet of Women's Liberation. In their origins and imagery these words carry undeniably painful, if not sadistic, implications, the object of which is almost always female. Consider, for example, what a "screw" actually does to the wood it penetrates; what a painful, even mutilating, activity this kind of analogy suggests. "Screw" is particularly interesting in this context, since the noun, according to Partridge, comes from words meaning "groove," "nut," "ditch," "breeding sow," "scrofula" and "swelling," while the verb, besides its explicit imagery, has antecedent associations to "write on," "scratch," "scarify," and so forth — a revealing fusion of a mechanical or painful action with an obviously denigrated object.

Not all obscene words, of course, are as implicitly sadistic or denigrating to women as these, but all that I know seem to serve a similar purpose: to reduce the human organism (especially the female organism) and human functions (especially sexual and procreative) to their least organic, most mechanical dimension; to substitute a trivializing or deforming resemblance for the complex human reality of what is being described.

Tabooed male descriptives, when they are not openly denigrating to women, often serve to divorce a male organ or function from any significant interaction with the female. Take the word "testes," for example, suggesting "witnesses" (from the Latin *testis*) to the sexual and procreative strengths of the male organ; and the obscene counterpart of this word, which suggests little more than a mechanical shape. Or compare almost any of the "rich," "liberating" sexual verbs, so fashionable today among male writers, with that much-derided Latin word "copulate" ("to bind or join together") or even that Anglo-Saxon phrase (which seems to have had no trouble surviving the Norman Conquest) "make love."

How arrogantly self-involved the tabooed words seem in comparison to either of the other terms, and how contemptuous of the female partner. Understandably so, of course, if she is only a "skirt," a "broad," a "chick," a "pussycat" or a "piece." If she is, in other words, no more than her skirt, or what her skirt conceals; no more than a breeder, or the broadest part of her; no more than a piece of human being or a "piece of tail."

The most severely tabooed of all the female descriptives, incidentally, are those like a "piece of tail," which suggest (either explicitly or through antecedents) that there is no significant difference between the female channel through which we are all conceived and born and the anal outlet common to both sexes — a distinction that pornographers have always enjoyed obscuring.

This effort to deny women their biological identity, their individuality, their humanness, is such an important aspect of obscene language that one can only marvel at how seldom, in an era preoccupied with definitions of obscenity, this fact is brought to our attention. One problem, of course, is that many of the people in the best position to do this (critics, teachers, writers) are so reluctant today to admit that they are angered or shocked by obscenity. Bored, maybe, unimpressed, aesthetically displeased, but—no matter how brutal or denigrating the material—never angered, never shocked.

And yet how eloquently angered, how piously shocked many of these same people become if denigrating language is used about any minority group other than women; if the obscenities are racial or ethnic, that is, rather than sexual. Words like "coon," "kike," "spic," "wop," after all, deform identity, deny individuality and humanness in almost exactly the same way that sexual vulgarisms and obscenities do.

No one that I know, least of all my students, would fail to question the values of a society whose literature and entertainment rested heavily on racial or ethnic pejoratives. Are the values of a society whose literature and entertainment rest as heavily as ours on sexual pejoratives any less questionable?

Suggestions for Writing and Discussion

1. Barbara Lawrence's piece was first published in 1973. Is this topic more or less relevant in terms of life in the 1990s? Explain your answer with specifics.
2. Lawrence argues that words should be considered obscene on the basis of their original sources and their functions. First, explain what she means by "source" and "function." Second, does she convince you that these aspects of words should be taken into consideration to determine whether or not a word should be deemed obscene?
3. Why does Lawrence so clearly include derogatory ethnic terms like *kike, coon,* and *wop* (paragraph 11), whereas she fails to list the taboo sexual terms?
4. Even if you totally agree with Lawrence on this issue, come up with an argument that counterattacks one of her main points. Can you further predict how she might respond to this debate?
5. Do you agree with Lawrence on her point that people today are not shocked when they hear "obscene" language? If you agree, what factors in our society may serve to desensitize people to these words? If you disagree, offer specific examples as support for your position.

Suggestion for Extended Thinking and Research

Get acquainted with the *Oxford English Dictionary* by researching the origin, use, changes, and meanings of three of your favorite words (brainstorm on this first!). What did you learn about these words by using this source?

ROBIN LAKOFF

Talking Like a Lady

> *Born and raised in Brooklyn, New York, Robin Lakoff is a professor of linguistics at the University of California, Berkeley. She is coauthor of* Face Value: The Politics of Beauty *(1984) and* When Talk Is Not Cheap: Or, How to Find the Right Therapist When You Don't Know Where to Begin *(1985). "Talking Like a Lady" is excerpted from her book* Language and a Woman's Place *(1975).*

Prereading/Journal-Writing Suggestion

According to some studies, when men and women talk with one another, the following things happen: Women ask 70 percent of the questions, and men interrupt 96 percent of the time. From your own experience, do you follow these patterns? Do most of the people you talk with follow these patterns? Explain, also, your own responses to people who ask questions or who interrupt while you are having conversations with them.

"Women's language" shows up in all levels of the grammar of English. We find differences in the choice and frequency of lexical items; in the situations in which certain syntactic rules are performed; in intonational and other supersegmental patterns. As an example of lexical differences, imagine a man and a woman both looking at the same wall, painted a pinkish shade of purple. The woman may say:

(1) The wall is mauve,

with no one consequently forming any special impression of her as a result of the words alone; but if the man should say (1), one might well conclude he was imitating a woman sarcastically or was a homosexual or an interior decorator. Women, then, make far more precise discriminations in naming colors than do men; words like *beige, ecru, aquamarine, lavender,* and so on are unremarkable in a woman's active vocabulary, but absent from that of most men. I have seen a man helpless with suppressed laughter at a discussion between two other people as to whether a book jacket was to be described as "lavender" or "mauve." Men find such discussion amusing because they consider such a question trivial, irrelevant to the real world.

We might ask why fine discrimination of color is relevant for women, but not for men. A clue is contained in the way many men in our society view other "unworldly" topics, such as high culture and the Church, as outside the world of men's work, relegated to women and men whose masculinity is not unquestionable. Men tend to relegate to women things that are not of concern to them, or do not involve their egos. Among these are problems of fine color discrimination. We might rephrase this point by saying that since women are not expected to make decisions on important matters, such as what kind of job to hold, they are relegated the noncrucial decisions as a sop. Deciding whether to name a color "lavender" or "mauve" is one such sop.

If it is agreed that this lexical disparity reflects a social inequity in the position of women, one may ask how to remedy it. Obviously, no one could seriously recommend legislating against the use of the terms "mauve" and "lavender" by women, or forcing men to learn to use them. All we can do is give women the opportunity to participate in the real decisions of life.

Aside from specific lexical items like color names, we find differences between the speech of women and that of men in the use of particles that grammarians often describe as "meaningless." There may be no referent for them, but they are far from meaningless: they define the social context of an utterance, indicate the relationship the speaker feels between himself and his addressee, between himself and what he is talking about.

As an experiment, one might present native speakers of standard Amer-   5
ican English with pairs of sentences, identical syntactically and in terms of referential lexical items, and differing merely in the choice of "meaningless" particles, and ask them which was spoken by a man, which a woman. Consider:

> (2) (a) Oh dear, you've put the peanut butter in the refrigerator again.
>   (b) Shit, you've put the peanut butter in the refrigerator again.

It is safe to predict that people would classify the first sentence as part of "women's language," the second as "men's language." It is true that many self-respecting women are becoming able to use sentences like (2)(b) publicly without flinching, but this is a relatively recent development, and while perhaps the majority of Middle America might condone the use of (b) for men, they would still disapprove of its use by women. (It is of interest, by the way, to note that men's language is increasingly being used by women, but women's language is not being adopted by men, apart from those who reject the American masculine image [for example, homosexuals]. This is analogous to the fact that men's jobs are being sought by women, but few men are rushing to become housewives or secretaries. The language of the favored group, the group that holds the power, along with its nonlinguistic behavior, is generally adopted by the other group, not vice versa. In any event, it is a truism to state that the "stronger" expletives are reserved for men, and the "weaker" ones for women.)

Now we may ask what we mean by "stronger" and "weaker" expletives. (If these particles were indeed meaningless, none would be stronger than any other.) The difference between using "shit" (or "damn," or one of many others) as opposed to "oh dear," or "goodness," or "oh fudge" lies in how forcefully one says how one feels — perhaps, one might say, choice of particle is a function of how strongly one allows oneself to feel about something, so that the strength of an emotion conveyed in a sentence corresponds to the strength of the particle. Hence in a really serious situation, the use of "trivializing" (that is, "women's") particles constitutes a joke, or at any rate, is highly inappropriate. (In conformity with current linguistic practice, throughout this work an asterisk [*] will be used to mark a sentence that is inappropriate in some sense, either because it is syntactically deviant or used in the wrong social context.)

(3) (a) *Oh fudge, my hair is on fire.
    (b) *Dear me, did he kidnap the baby?

As children, women are encouraged to be "little ladies." Little ladies don't scream as vociferously as little boys, and they are chastised more severely for throwing tantrums or showing temper: "high spirits" are expected and therefore tolerated in little boys; docility and resignation are the corresponding traits expected of little girls. Now, we tend to excuse a show of temper by a man where we would not excuse an identical tirade from a woman: women are allowed to fuss and complain, but only a man can bellow in rage. It is sometimes claimed that there is a biological basis for this behavior difference, though I don't believe conclusive evidence exists that the early differences in behavior that have been observed are not the results of very different treatment of babies of the two sexes from the beginning; but surely the use of different particles by men and women is a learned trait, merely mirroring nonlinguistic differences again, and again pointing out an inequity that exists between the treatment of men, and society's expectations of them, and the treatment of women. Allowing men stronger means of expression than are open to women further reinforces men's position of strength in the real world: for surely we listen with more attention the more strongly and forcefully someone expresses opinions, and a speaker unable — for whatever reason — to be forceful in stating his views is much less likely to be taken seriously. Ability to use strong particles like "shit" and "hell" is, of course, only incidental to the inequity that exists rather than its cause. But once again, apparently accidental linguistic usage suggests that women are denied equality partially for linguistic reasons, and that an examination of language points up precisely an area in which inequity exists. Further, if someone is allowed to show emotions, and consequently does, others may well be able to view him as a real individual in his own right, as they could not if he never showed emotion. Here again, then, the behavior a woman learns as "correct" prevents her from being taken seriously as an individual, and further is considered "correct" and necessary for a woman precisely because society does *not* consider her seriously as an individual.

Similar sorts of disparities exist elsewhere in the vocabulary. There is, for instance, a group of adjectives which have, besides their specific and literal meanings, another use, that of indicating the speaker's approbation or admiration for something. Some of these adjectives are neutral as to sex of speaker: either men or women may use them. But another set seems, in its figurative use, to be largely confined to women's speech. Representative lists of both types are below:

neutral	*women only*
great	adorable
terrific	charming
cool	sweet
neat	lovely
	divine

As with the color words and swear words already discussed, for a man 10 to stray into the "women's" column is apt to be damaging to his reputation, though here a woman may freely use the neutral words. But it should not be inferred from this that a woman's use of the "women's" words is without its risks. Where a woman has a choice between the neutral words and the women's words, as a man has not, she may be suggesting very different things about her own personality and her view of the subject matter by her choice of words of the first set or words of the second.

(4) (a) What a terrific idea!
    (b) What a divine idea!

It seems to me that (a) might be used under any appropriate conditions by a female speaker. But (b) is more restricted. Probably it is used appropriately (even by the sort of speaker for whom it was normal) only in case the speaker feels the idea referred to be essentially frivolous, trivial, or unimportant to the world at large—only an amusement for the speaker herself. Consider, then, a woman advertising executive at an advertising conference. However feminine an advertising executive she is, she is much more likely to express her approval with (4)(a) than with (b), which might cause raised eyebrows, and the reaction: "That's what we get for putting a woman in charge of this company."

On the other hand, suppose a friend suggests to the same woman that she should dye her French poodles to match her cigarette lighter. In this case, the suggestion really concerns only her, and the impression she will make on people. In this case, she may use (b), from the "women's language." So the choice is not really free: words restricted to "women's language" suggest that concepts to which they are applied are not relevant to the real world of (male) influence and power.

One may ask whether there really are no analogous terms that are available to men — terms that denote approval of the trivial, the personal; that express approbation in terms of one's own personal emotional reaction, rather than by gauging the likely general reaction. There does in fact seem to be one such word: it is the hippie invention "groovy," which seems to have most of the connotations that separate "lovely" and "divine" from "great" and "terrific" excepting only that it does not mark the speaker as feminine or effeminate.

(5) (a) What a terrific steel mill!
    (b) *What a lovely steel mill! (male speaking)
    (c) What a groovy steel mill!

I think it is significant that this word was introduced by the hippies, and, when used seriously rather than sarcastically, used principally by people who have accepted the hippies' values. Principal among these is the denial of the Protestant work ethic: to a hippie, something can be worth thinking about even if it isn't influential in the power structure, or moneymaking. Hippies are separated from the activities of the real world just as women are — though in the former case it is due to a decision on their parts, while this is not uncontroversially true in the case of women. For both these groups, it is possible to express approval of things in a personal way — though one does so at the risk of losing one's credibility with members of the power structure. It is also true, according to some speakers, that upper-class British men may use the words listed in the "women's" column, as well as the specific color words and others we have categorized as specifically feminine, without raising doubts as to their masculinity among other speakers of the same dialect. (This is not true for lower-class Britons, however.) The reason may be that commitment to the work ethic need not necessarily be displayed: one may be or appear to be a gentleman of leisure, interested in various pursuits, but not involved in mundane (business or political) affairs, in such a culture, without incurring disgrace. This is rather analogous to the position of a woman in American middle-class society, so we should not be surprised if these special lexical items are usable by both groups. This fact points indeed to a more general conclusion. These words aren't, basically, "feminine"; rather, they signal "uninvolved," or "out of power." Any group in a society to which these labels are applicable may presumably use these words; they are often considered "feminine," "unmasculine," because women are the "uninvolved," "out-of-power" group par excellence.

Another group that has, ostensibly at least, taken itself out of the search for power and money is that of academic men. They are frequently viewed by other groups as analogous in some ways to women — they don't really work, they are supported in their frivolous pursuits by others, what they do doesn't really count in the real world, and so on. The suburban home finds its counterpart in the ivory tower: one is supposedly shielded from harsh realities in both. Therefore it is not too surprising that many academic men (especially those who emulate British norms) may violate many of these sacrosanct rules I have just laid down: they often use "women's language." Among themselves, this does not occasion ridicule. But to a truck driver, a professor saying, "What a lovely hat!" is undoubtedly laughable, all the more so as it reinforces his stereotype of professors as effete snobs.

When we leave the lexicon and venture into syntax, we find that syntactically too women's speech is peculiar. To my knowledge, there is no syntactic rule in English that only women may use. But there is at least one rule that a woman will use in more conversational situations than a man. (This fact indicates, of course, that the applicability of syntactic rules is governed partly by social context — the positions in society of the speaker and addressee, with respect to each other, and the impression one seeks to make on the other.) This is the rule of tag-question formation.[1]

A tag, in its usage as well as its syntactic shape (in English) is midway 15 between an outright statement and a yes-no question: it is less assertive than the former, but more confident than the latter. Therefore it is usable under certain contextual situations: not those in which a statement would be appropriate, nor those in which a yes-no question is generally used, but in situations intermediate between these.

One makes a statement when one has confidence in his knowledge and is pretty certain that his statement will be believed; one asks a question when one lacks knowledge on some point and has reason to believe that this gap can and will be remedied by an answer by the addressee. A tag question, being

---

[1]Within the lexicon itself, there seems to be a parallel phenomenon to tag-question usage, which I refrain from discussing in the body of the text because the facts are controversial and I do not understand them fully. The intensive *so,* used where purists would insist upon an absolute superlative, heavily stressed, seems more characteristic of women's language than of men's, though it is found in the latter, particularly in the speech of male academics. Consider, for instance, the following sentences:

(a) I feel *so* unhappy!
(b) That movie made me *so* sick!

Men seem to have the least difficulty using this construction when the sentence is unemotional, or nonsubjective — without reference to the speaker himself:

(c) That sunset is *so* beautiful!
(d) Fred is *so* dumb!

Substituting an equative like *so* for absolute superlatives (like *very, really, utterly*) seems to be a way of backing out of committing oneself strongly to an opinion, rather like tag questions (cf. discussion below, in the text). One might hedge in this way with perfect right in making aesthetic judgments, as in (c), or intellectual judgments, as in (d). But it is somewhat odd to hedge in describing one's own mental or emotional state: who, after all, is qualified to contradict one on this? To hedge in this situation is to seek to avoid making any strong statement: a characteristic, as we have noted already and shall note further, of women's speech.

intermediate between these, is used when the speaker is stating a claim, but lacks full confidence in the truth of that claim. So if I say:

(6) Is John here?

I will probably not be surprised if my respondent answers "no"; but if I say

(7) John is here, isn't he?

instead, chances are I am already biased in favor of a positive answer, wanting only confirmation by the addressee. I still want a response from him, as I do with a yes-no question; but I have enough knowledge (or think I have) to predict that response, much as with a declarative statement. A tag question, then, might be thought of as a declarative statement without the assumption that the statement is to be believed by the addressee: one has an out, as with a question. A tag gives the addressee leeway, not forcing him to go along with the views of the speaker.

There are situations in which a tag is legitimate, in fact the only legitimate sentence form. So, for example, if I have seen something only indistinctly, and have reason to believe my addressee had a better view, I can say:

(8) I had my glasses off. He was out at third, wasn't he?

Sometimes we find a tag question used in cases in which the speaker knows as well as the addressee what the answer must be, and doesn't need confirmation. One such situation is when the speaker is making "small talk," trying to elicit conversation from the addressee:

(9) Sure is hot here, isn't it?

In discussing personal feelings or opinions, only the speaker normally has any way of knowing the correct answer. Strictly speaking, questioning one's own opinions is futile. Sentences like (10) are usually ridiculous.

(10) *I have a headache, don't I?

But similar cases do, apparently, exist, in which it is the speaker's opinions, rather than perceptions, for which corroboration is sought, as in (11):

(11) The way prices are rising is horrendous, isn't it?

While there are of course other possible interpretations of a sentence like this, one possibility is that the speaker has a particular answer in mind — "yes" or "no" — but is reluctant to state it baldly. It is my impression, though I do not have precise statistical evidence, that this sort of tag question is much more apt to be used by women than by men. If this is indeed true, why is it true? 20

These sentence types provide a means whereby a speaker can avoid committing himself, and thereby avoid coming into conflict with the addressee. The problem is that, by so doing, a speaker may also give the impression of not being really sure of himself, of looking to the addressee for confirmation, even of having no views of his own. This last criticism is, of course, one often leveled at women. One wonders how much of it reflects a use of language that has been imposed on women from their earliest years.

Related to this special use of a syntactic rule is a widespread difference perceptible in women's intonational patterns.[2] There is a peculiar sentence intonation pattern, found in English as far as I know only among women, which has the form of a declarative answer to a question, and is used as such, but has the rising inflection typical of a yes-no question, as well as being especially hesitant. The effect is as though one were seeking confirmation, though at the same time the speaker may be the only one who has the requisite information.

(12) (a) When will dinner be ready?
     (b) Oh . . . around six o'clock . . .?

It is as though (b) were saying, "Six o'clock, if that's OK with you, if you agree." (a) is put in the position of having to provide confirmation, and (b) sounds unsure. Here we find unwillingness to assert an opinion carried to an extreme. One likely consequence is that these sorts of speech patterns are taken to reflect something real about character and play a part in not taking a woman seriously or trusting her with any real responsibilities, since "she can't make up her mind" and "isn't sure of herself." And here again we see that people form judgments about other people on the basis of superficial linguistic behavior that may have nothing to do with inner character, but has been imposed upon the speaker, on pain of worse punishment than not being taken seriously.

Such features are probably part of the general fact that women's speech sounds much more "polite" than men's. One aspect of politeness is as we have just described: leaving a decision open, not imposing your mind, or views, or claims on anyone else. Thus a tag question is a kind of polite statement, in that it does not force agreement or belief on the addressee. A request may be in the same sense a polite command, in that it does not overtly require obedience, but rather suggests something be done as a favor to the speaker. An overt order (as in an imperative) expresses the (often impolite) assumption of the speaker's superior position to the addressee, carrying with it the right to enforce compliance, whereas with a request the decision on the face of it is left up to the addressee. (The same is true of suggestions: here, the implication is not that the addressee is in danger if he does not comply — merely that he will be glad if he does. Once again, the decision is up to the addressee, and a

---

[2]For analogues outside of English to these uses of tag questions and special intonation patterns, cf. my discussion of Japanese particles in "Language in Context," *Language,* 48 (1972), pp. 907–927. It is to be expected that similar cases will be found in many other languages as well. See, for example, M. R. Haas's very interesting discussion of differences between men's and women's speech mostly involving lexical dissimilarities in many languages, in D. Hymes, ed., *Language in Culture and Society* (New York: Harper & Row, 1964).

suggestion therefore is politer than an order.) The more particles in a sentence that reinforce the notion that it is a request, rather than an order, the politer the result. The sentences of (13) illustrate these points: (a) is a direct order, (b) and (c) simple requests, and (d) and (e) compound requests.[3]

(13) (a) Close the door.
     (b) Please close the door.
     (c) Will you close the door?
     (d) Will you please close the door?
     (e) Won't you close the door?

Let me first explain why (e) has been classified as a compound request. (A sentence like *Won't you please close the door* would then count as a doubly compound request.) A sentence like (13)(c) is close in sense to "Are you willing to close the door?" According to the normal rules of polite conversation, to agree that you are willing is to agree to do the thing asked of you. Hence this apparent inquiry functions as a request, leaving the decision up to the willingness of the addressee. Phrasing it as a positive question makes the (implicit) assumption that a "yes" answer will be forthcoming. Sentence (13)(d) is more polite than (b) or (c) because it combines them: *please* indicating that to accede will be to do something for the speaker, and *will you,* as noted suggesting that the addressee has the final decision. If, now, the question is phrased with a negative, as in (13)(e), the speaker seems to suggest the stronger likelihood of a negative response from the addressee. Since the assumption is then that the addressee is that much freer to refuse, (13)(e) acts as a more polite request than (13)(c) or (d); (c) and (d) put the burden of refusal on the addressee, as (e) does not.

Given these facts, one can see the connection between tag questions and 25 tag orders and other requests. In all these cases, the speaker is not committed as with a simple declarative or affirmative. And the more one compounds a request, the more characteristic it is of women's speech, the less of men's. A sentence that begins *Won't you please* (without special emphasis on *please*) seems to me at least to have a distinctly unmasculine sound. Little girls are indeed taught to talk like little ladies, in that their speech is in many ways more polite than that of boys or men, and the reason for this is that politeness involves an absence of a strong statement, and women's speech is devised to prevent the expression of strong statements.

Suggestions for Writing and Discussion

1. Explain Lakoff's main point regarding the contrast in language between men and women. What is your response to this point?
2. Throughout this piece, many statements sound as if they are "begging the question" (a statement presented as factual and true, although it still "begs"

---

[3]For more detailed discussion of these problems, see Lakoff, "Language in Context."

for supporting evidence). Examine each of the following examples, and determine whether or not the statement needs further evidence in order to be true:

    A. "Men tend to relegate to women things that are not of concern to them, or do not involve their egos."

    B. "As children, women are encouraged to be 'little ladies.'"

    C. "For surely we listen with more attention the more strongly and forcefully someone expresses opinions."

    D. "The suburban home finds its counterpart in the ivory tower: one is supposedly shielded from harsh realities in both."

    E. "One asks a question when one lacks knowledge on some point and has reason to believe that this gap can and will be remedied by an answer by the addressee."

3. By showing the commonality of language between women and hippies, women and British aristocrats, and women and male academics, what is Lakoff implying?

4. Although Lakoff doesn't come out and state what she advocates for women, what do you think she might like to see happen as far as women's language is concerned?

5. Choose just one paragraph from this piece and evaluate it in terms of word choice, tone, sentence structure, and syntax. What can you conclude regarding Lakoff's tone and interaction with the audience in this section? Would you say that this paragraph is reflective of the overall tone of this piece?

6. What type of audience might be most receptive to this essay? Explain your answer.

Suggestions for Extended Thinking and Research

1. Write an essay in which you argue that instead of women becoming more assertive, society would be better served if men adopted women's patterns in language.

2. Record several observations of the interactions of men and women in one specific setting: a college classroom, a singles' bar, a library, a supermarket, a sporting match, a restaurant, a living room. After taking careful notes, write an essay in which you draw conclusions on the way each group uses language. Do your findings support Lakoff's work, contrast to her main points, or reveal something new?

GLORIA NAYLOR

A Question of Language

> *After earning a graduate degree in Afro-American Studies from Yale University, Gloria Naylor worked as a columnist for the* New York Times. *In addition, she has been visiting professor and writer in residence at Princeton University, New York University, the University of Pennsylvania, Boston University, and Brandeis. Her first novel,* The Women of Brewster Place *(1982), won an American Book award. "A Question of Language" was first published in the* New York Times *in 1986.*

Prereading/Journal-Writing Suggestions

1. What do you think has had more influence in your life — the spoken word or the written word? Explain by using specific incidents from your past that support your answer.
2. In your household, what topics were or are taboo as far as children are concerned? Explain.

Language is the subject. It is the written form with which I've managed to keep the wolf away from the door and, in diaries, to keep my sanity. In spite of this, I consider the written word inferior to the spoken, and much of the frustration experienced by novelists is the awareness that whatever we manage to capture in even the most transcendent passages falls far short of the richness of life. Dialogue achieves its power in the dynamics of a fleeting moment of sight, sound, smell, and touch.

I'm not going to enter the debate here about whether it is language that shapes reality or vice versa. That battle is doomed to be waged whenever we seek intermittent reprieve from the chicken and egg dispute. I will simply take the position that the spoken word, like the written word, amounts to a nonsensical arrangement of sounds or letters without a consensus that assigns "meaning." And building from the meanings of what we hear, we order reality. Words themselves are innocuous; it is the consensus that gives them true power.

I remember the first time I heard the word *nigger*. In my third-grade class, our math tests were being passed down the rows, and as I handed the papers to a little boy in back of me, I remarked that once again he had received a much lower mark than I did. He snatched his test from me and spit out that word. Had he called me a nymphomaniac or a necrophiliac, I couldn't have been more puzzled. I didn't know what a nigger was, but I knew that whatever it meant, it was something he shouldn't have called me. This was verified when I raised my hand, and in a loud voice repeated what he had said and watched the teacher scold him for using a "bad" word. I was later to go home and ask the inevitable question that every black parent must face — "Mommy, what does 'nigger' mean?"

And what exactly did it mean? Thinking back, I realize that this could not have been the first time the word was used in my presence. I was part of a large extended family that had migrated from the rural South after World War II and formed a close-knit network that gravitated around my maternal grandparents. Their ground-floor apartment in one of the buildings they owned in Harlem was a weekend mecca for my immediate family, along with countless aunts, uncles, and cousins who brought along assorted friends. It was a bustling and open house with assorted neighbors and tenants popping in and out to exchange bits of gossip, pick up an old quarrel or referee the ongoing checkers game in which my grandmother cheated shamelessly. They were all there to let down their hair and put up their feet after a week of labor in the factories, laundries, and shipyards of New York.

Amid the clamor, which could reach deafening proportions — two or   5
three conversations going on simultaneously, punctuated by the sound of a baby's crying somewhere in the back rooms or out on the street — there was still a rigid set of rules about what was said and how. Older children were sent out of the living room when it was time to get into the juicy details about "you-know-who" up on the third floor who had gone and gotten herself "p-r-e-g-n-a-n-t!" But my parents, knowing that I could spell well beyond my years, always demanded that I follow the others out to play. Beyond sexual misconduct and death, everything else was considered harmless for our young ears. And so among the anecdotes of the triumphs and disappointments in the various workings of their lives, the word *nigger* was used in my presence, but it was set within contexts and inflections that caused it to register in my mind as something else.

In the singular, the word was always applied to a man who had distinguished himself in some situation that brought their approval for his strength, intelligence, or drive:

"Did Johnny really do that?"

"I'm telling you, that nigger pulled in $6,000 of overtime last year. Said he got enough for a down payment on a house."

When used with a possessive adjective by a woman — "my nigger" — it became a term of endearment for husband or boyfriend. But it could be more than just a term applied to a man. In their mouths it became the pure essence of manhood — a disembodied force that channeled their past history of struggle and present survival against the odds into a victorious statement of being: "Yeah, that old foreman found out quick enough — you don't mess with a nigger."

In the plural, it became a description of some group within the com-   10
munity that had overstepped the bounds of decency as my family defined it: Parents who neglected their children, a drunken couple who fought in public,

people who simply refused to look for work, those with excessively dirty mouths or unkempt households were all "trifling niggers." This particular circle could forgive hard times, unemployment, the occasional bout of depression — they had gone through all of that themselves — but the unforgivable sin was lack of self-respect.

A woman could never be a *nigger* in the singular, with its connotation of confirming worth. The noun *girl* was its closest equivalent in that sense, but only when used in direct address and regardless of the gender doing the addressing. *Girl* was a token of respect for a woman. The one-syllable word was drawn out to sound like three in recognition of the extra ounce of wit, nerve or daring that the woman had shown in the situation under discussion.

"G-i-r-l, stop. You mean you said that to his face?"

But if the word was used in a third-person reference or shortened so that it almost snapped out of the mouth, it always involved some element of communal disapproval. And age became an important factor in these exchanges. It was only between individuals of the same generation, or from an older person to a younger (but never the other way around), that "girl" would be considered a compliment.

I don't agree with the argument that use of the word *nigger* at this social stratum of the black community was an internalization of racism. The dynamics were the exact opposite: the people in my grandmother's living room took a word that whites used to signify "worthlessness or degradation and rendered it impotent. Gathering there together, they transformed *nigger* to signify the varied and complex human beings they knew themselves to be. If the word was to disappear totally from the mouths of even the most liberal of white society, no one in that room was naïve enough to believe it would disappear from white minds. Meeting the word head-on, they proved it had absolutely nothing to do with the way they were determined to live their lives.

So there must have been dozens of times that the word *nigger* was spoken 15 in front of me before I reached the third grade. But I didn't "hear" it until it was said by a small pair of lips that had already learned it could be a way to humiliate me. That was the word I went home and asked my mother about. And since she knew that I had to grow up in America, she took me in her lap and explained.

Suggestions for Writing and Discussion

1. Naylor begins this piece by stating, "Language is the subject." What, then, is the major problem that this subject confronts? What is Naylor's main point about this subject?
2. When, according to Naylor, can language be powerfully effective? When can it be powerfully destructive?
3. In your own words, what are the different connotations of the word *nigger* when Naylor heard it used among her own people, in her own household? Why wasn't she puzzled by the meaning of *nigger* at these times in her life?

4. Why does Naylor condone black people using the word *nigger* but finds it derogatory when used by people outside of this race? What gives one group a "right" to a word, while the use of it by an outside group is considered "wrong"?

5. At the end of this piece, when Naylor's mother takes her on her lap to explain what the white boy meant by the term *nigger*, what do you think she says? Consider writing your response in the form of a dialogue between mother and daughter.

Suggestion for Extended Thinking and Research

Each of the words in the following list contains various levels of meaning. Choose one word from this list and interview fifteen people, asking each for his or her definition of the word. Have those you are interviewing use each word in a sentence to clarify its meaning, and feel free to ask any questions based on the meaning they've assigned to this word. Take careful notes during each interview, and then write an essay in which you synthesize the various meanings people associate with this word.

Foreign	Polite
Dominance	Duty
Clever	Politician
Ambition	Glamorous
Culture	Habit
Feminist	Masculine
Feminine	Progress

PETER FARB
Linguistic Chauvinism

> *Peter Farb has served as curator for American Indian Cultures at Riverside Museum in New York City. "Linguistic Chauvinism" is an excerpt from his widely acclaimed book* Word Play: What Happens When People Talk, *published in 1974.*

Prereading/Journal-Writing Suggestions

1. *Part I:* How does an audience affect the way we write? In order to find out, think about the most disturbing thing that happened to you this past week. Then write three different letters about this event to three different audiences from the following list.

Your best friend	The mail carrier
Your mother or father	A casual acquaintance or
Your teacher	co-worker
Your preacher	An intimate friend or your spouse
	Your son or daughter

   Part II: After writing these three versions, describe how considering audience changes or affects the way you communicate.
2. Every family or generation has its share of peculiar sayings or slang expressions. Write about some of the expressions common in your family or generation, and explain to an outsider exactly what these terms mean.

What we hear today as Black English is probably the result of five major influences: African languages; West African pidgin; a Plantation Creole once spoken by slaves in the southern United States as well as by blacks as far north as Canada; Standard English; and, finally, urbanization in the northern ghettos. The influence of African languages on black speech was long denied, until in 1949 Lorenzo Dow Turner published the results of his fifteen-year study of Gullah, a black dialect spoken in the coastal region around Charleston, South Carolina, and Savannah, Georgia. Gullah is important in the history of Black English because this region continued to receive slaves direct from Africa as late as 1858 — and so any influence from Africa would be expected to survive there longer. Turner accumulated compelling evidence of resemblances in pronunciation, vocabulary, and grammar between Gullah and various West African languages. He listed some 4,000 Gullah words for personal names, numbers, and objects that are derived directly from African languages. Some of these words — such as *tote, chigger, yam,* and *tater* ("potato") — eventually entered Standard English.

The second influence, pidginization, is more apparent because the languages spoken today by the descendants of slaves almost everywhere in the New World — regardless of whether these languages were based on English, French, Dutch, Spanish, or Portuguese — share similarities in sound patterns and in grammar. For example, the common Black English construction *He done close the door* has no direct equivalent in Standard English, but it is similar to structures found in Portuguese Pidgin, Weskos of West Africa, French Creole of Haiti, the Shanan Creole of Surinam, and so on. An analysis of the speech of slaves — as recorded in eighteenth-century letters, histories, and books of travel — indicates that the great majority of them in the continental United States spoke pidgin English, as much in the North as in the South. This was to be expected since blacks speaking many languages were thrown together in the West African slave factories and they had to develop some means of communication. No matter what their mother tongues were, they had been forced to learn a second language, an African Pidgin English that at least as early as 1719 had been spread around the world by the slave trade. We can be certain of that year because it marked the publication of Daniel Defoe's *Robinson Crusoe,* which contains numerous examples of this pidgin and also uses, in the character Friday, the West African and slave tradition of bestowing personal names based on the days of the week.

Therefore most slaves must have arrived in the New World speaking a pidgin that enabled them to communicate with each other and eventually also with their overseers. In the succeeding generations a small number of blacks were taught Standard English. But the great majority apparently expanded their pidgin into a creole language — called Plantation Creole by some linguists even though it was also spoken in the North — by grafting an English vocabulary onto the structures of their native languages and pidgins. This creole probably began to develop as soon as the first generation of slaves was born in the New World. Cotton Mather and other writers record its use in Massachusetts: the writings of T. C. Haliburton (creator of the humorous Yankee character Sam Slick) show that it reached as far north as Halifax, Nova Scotia; Harriet Beecher Stowe attests to its use in New York and Benjamin Franklin to its presence in Philadelphia. Emancipation did not do away with Plantation Creole. In fact, it spread its use to the offspring of the former house slaves who had been taught Standard English. That is because segregated schools and racial isolation after the Civil War caused the great number of speakers of Plantation Creole to linguistically overwhelm the small number of black speakers of Standard English. Nevertheless, the fourth step — a process known as decreolization — has been constantly at work as blacks tend to move closer in speech to the Standard English they hear all around them. The final step in the creation of the Black English known today was the surge of blacks into northern ghettos. The ghetto experience placed the final stamp on

Black English by mixing various kinds of Plantation Creole, filtering out some features and emphasizing others. Variations are apparent in the Black English spoken locally in such cities as Baltimore, New York, Detroit, Chicago, and Los Angeles, but these variations are minor in comparison to the major differences between Black English in general and Standard English.

I would need an entire volume to discuss these differences adequately, but let me at least point out a few of them. Black English does not sound like Standard English because it often uses different sounds. In the case of vowels, groups of words like *find-found-fond* and *pen-pin* are pronounced almost exactly alike. The distinctive sounds of Black English, though, result more from the pronunciation of the consonants. *Th* at the beginning of a word is often pronounced either *d*, as in *dey*, or *t*, as in *tink;* in the middle of a word or at the end, *th* often becomes *v* or *f,* with the result that *father* is pronounced *faver* and *mouth* is pronounced *mouf.* Black English dispenses with *r* to an even greater extent than the Standard speech heard along the eastern coast of North America. It not only loses the *r* after vowels and at the end of words, as do some Standard dialects which pronounce *sore* and *saw* in the same way, but in addition it dispenses with *r* between vowels, thus making *Paris* and *pass* sound alike. *L* also is almost completely lost except when it begins a word, with the result that no distinction is made between such pairs of words as *help-hep* and *toll-toe.* Final clusters of consonants are nearly always simplified by the loss of one of the consonants, usually *t* or *d* but often *s* or *z* as well, with the result that *meant-mend-men, start-started,* and *give-gives* are pronounced in the same way.

Some linguists have stated that Black English grammar resulted simply 5 from the loss of the consonant sounds that carry much of the burden of forming suffixes in Standard English. The absence of verb tenses, for example, was attributed to the loss of *d* (as when *burned* becomes *burn'*) or *l* (as when *I'll go* becomes *I go*). The statement in Black English *He workin'* was long thought to be the same as the Standard *He's working,* except that black pronunciation dropped the *s* in the contraction of the verb *is.* But it now appears that the structure of Black English is much more complicated than the mere loss of suffixes due to a failure to pronounce them.

The black speaker is apparently using a different grammar, which disregards *is* in the Standard *He's working* and instead chooses to emphasize the auxiliary verb *be. He be workin'* means that the person referred to has been working continuously for a long time; but *He workin',* without the *be,* means that the person is working now, at this very moment. A speaker of Black English would no more say *He be workin' right now* (that is, use the habitual *be* to tell about something happening only at this moment) than a speaker of Standard English would say *He is sleeping tomorrow* (that is, ignore the tense of the verb). The use and non-use of the auxiliary *be* is clearly seen in the Black English sentence *You makin' sense, but you don't be makin' sense* — which in Standard English means "You just said something smart, but you don't habitually say anything smart." The speaker of Black English, therefore, is obliged by his language to mark certain kinds of verbs as describing either momentary action or habitual action. In contrast, the speaker of Standard English is not obliged to make this distinction — although he must make others which speakers of Black English ignore, such as the tense of the verb.

Black English also differs considerably from Standard English in the various ways in which negative statements are structured. The Black English *He ain't go* is not simply the equivalent of the Standard *He didn't go*. The speaker of Black English is not using *ain't* as a past tense, but rather to express the negative for the momentary act of going, whether it happened in the past or is happening right now. If the Black English speaker, on the other hand, wants to speak of someone who is habitually the kind of person who does not go, he would say *He ain't goin'*. *Ain't* also serves several other functions in Black English. *Dey ain't like dat* might be thought by speakers of Standard to mean "They aren't like that" — but it actually means "They didn't like that," because in this usage *ain't* is the negative of the auxiliary verb *to do*. *Ain't* can also emphasize a negation by doubling it, as in *He ain't no rich*. And in what would be a negative *if*-clause in Standard English, the rules of Black English eliminate the *if* and invert the verb — with the result that the equivalent of the Standard *He doesn't know if she can go* is the Black English *He don't know can she go*.

I have touched on merely a few of the obvious differences between the rules of Black English and the rules of Standard English in regard to verbs. Numerous other aspects of Black English verbs could be discussed — such as *I done go, I done gone, I been done gone,* and *I done been gone*. Or I could mention other constructions, such as the possessive case, in which I could demonstrate that *John book* in Black English is a different kind of possessive than *John's book* is in Standard English. But by now it should be apparent that important differences exist between the two dialects.

The wonder is that it took people so long to realize that Black English is neither a mispronunciation of Standard English nor an accumulation of random errors made in the grammar of Standard. Utterances in Black English are grammatically consistent and they are generated by rules in the same way that utterances in Standard English are generated by rules. Miss Fidditch may not regard utterances in Black English to be "good English" — but that is beside the point, because Black English is using a different set of rules than those of Standard English.

In addition to pronunciation and grammatical distinctions, Black English differs from Standard in the way language is used in the speech community. Black speakers generally place much more emphasis on effective talking than do white speakers, and they are immersed in verbal stimulation throughout the day to a considerably greater extent than middle-class whites. Playing the dozens is only one of the numerous speech events which depend upon the competitive exhibition of verbal skills in the ghetto. Rapping, jiving, rifting, louding, and toasting are other verbal ways in which the black achieves status in his community. Whereas a white is apt to feel embarrassed 10 when he repeats himself, a black feels he has the license to repeat whatever he is saying, sometimes from the very beginning. And he expects to evoke a feedback from his audience that not only permits him to continue talking but also urges him to do so by such expressions of audience approval as *right on* or *amen*. Status within the black community is sometimes determined by one's material or spiritual attributes, but it is almost always determined by a speaker's ability to demonstrate his command over the different uses of language. Speech is, in fact, regarded as a performance in which the speaker is continually on stage. His verbal behavior is appraised by the standards of performance as being either *cool* or *lame* — and not by the white standards of tactful conversation.

The sharing of much the same vocabulary camouflages basic differences between Black and Standard English. And that is why most school systems are unaware that lower-class black children enter the first grade speaking a mother dialect that is not Standard English. The exasperated white teacher, who knows little about Black English, usually concludes that the black child is unteachable because he refuses to learn to read the simple English of his mother tongue. The teacher reprimands the black child for saying *they toys* and *He work* when he clearly sees printed in his reader *their toys* and *He's working*. Actually, the black child should be commended for his quickness in translating Standard English symbols on the printed page into his own dialect, Black English.

The black child's ability to read Black English, even though he may fail in reading Standard, is supported by an incident that happened to William A. Stewart, of the Center for Applied Linguistics in Washington, D.C. He was in the process of translating "The Night Before Christmas" into Black English, ignoring Black English pronunciation but otherwise using Black English grammar:

> It's the night before Christmas, and all through the house
> Ain't nobody moving, not even a mouse.
> There go them stocking, hanging up on the wall.
> So Santa Claus can full them up, if he pay our house a call.

While he was working on the translation, a ten-year-old black girl, who was regarded in her school as having a reading problem, glanced over his shoulder. With great speed and accuracy, she read aloud what Stewart had written. But when he asked her to read the same lines in the original Standard English form, she failed miserably. Clearly, the girl could read perfectly well — not Standard English, but the language of her mother dialect, Black English.

Experiences such as this one have led some linguists to advocate teaching ghetto children the rules of Standard English as if they were learning a foreign language. But Stewart would go even further. He wants black children to be taught to read Black English first, so that the words and structures they see on the printed page would correspond directly to the daily speech they hear in their community. He argues that once the child has mastered the principle of reading the tongue in which he is fluent, he will find it comparatively easy to make the transition to the Standard. To that end he has produced several readers in parallel Black and Standard versions, one of which, *Ollie,* contains such sentences as:

> Ollie big sister, she name La Verne. La Verne grown up now, and she ain't scared of nobody. But that don't mean she don't never be scared. The other day when she in the house, La Verne she start to screaming and hollering. Didn't nobody know what was the matter.

If the black child survives the trauma of school — and most black children do not, because of the problem in the early years of learning to read that strange dialect, Standard English — he will have become, in effect, bilingual in two dialects that use English words. And, like most bilinguals, he will have to employ the strategy of language-switching. But whereas someone in Paraguay has to know only when to speak either Spanish or Guarani, the black must know the two extremes of Black English and Standard English, as well as the many gradations in between. The expert dialect-switcher can quickly place his speech somewhere along the spectrum ranging from Black English to Standard English, depending upon whom he is talking to: upper-class white, lower-class white, educated black, lower-class black, recent black migrant from the South, family and close friends, and so on. It is a formidable linguistic accomplishment.

The problems faced by the bilingual black speaker are the same as those faced by American-born children of immigrant parents who enter school knowing Spanish, Italian, Greek, Yiddish, Polish, Hungarian, or other foreign languages — with one important difference. Teachers feel that the white children speak real languages, languages with their own dictionaries and literature, and therefore the teachers are likely to be patient in starting at the beginning when teaching these children English. But few teachers display the same sympathy toward the black child who speaks a language that they believe is the same as their own, the only difference being that the black child speaks it carelessly and stubbornly refuses to be grammatical. Often black teachers themselves are the worst offenders in stigmatizing Black English. They struggled for an education and put tremendous effort into learning to speak Standard English. Obviously, they view as inferior that speech which they worked so hard to unlearn in themselves.

The native languages of Africa were suppressed long ago, in the slave factories and on the plantations, but pressure against the numerous foreign languages spoken by immigrants to the United States did not begin until after the First World War. That was when many native-born Americans considered "Americanization" and "the melting-pot philosophy" to be the alchemy that would transmute the "baser" languages of immigrants into the golden American tongue. Americanization placed a special emphasis on extirpating the languages of the immigrants, for the obvious reason that language carries the culture of its speakers. Get rid of the language — and the nation has also rid itself of the alien's instrument of perception, his means of expressing foreign values, his maintenance of a culture transported from another continent. Theodore Roosevelt's statement in 1919 is typical of the Americanization position:

> We have room for but one language here and that is the English language, for we intend to see that the crucible turns our people out as Americans and not as dwellers in a polyglot boarding house.

The Americanization movement reached its height in the 1930s, but its effects continue to be felt. Every census since then has revealed that fewer Americans claim a non-English mother tongue. And even those who acknowledge their bilingualism do so with a feeling that they have traitorously maintained an alien way of life. The crime of Americanization is that it convinced those whose tongues were stigmatized that they were deserving of the stigma.

Other people, though, regard the maintenance of a diversity of languages as a source of strength for the nation. They recall that English is not an indigenous language of America, that it was merely one of the languages exported to the New World by colonial powers. Opponents of Americanization also point out that no nation in the world speaks only one language. Even France, which comes closest to the uniformity of a single national language, has German speakers in Alsace-Lorraine, Breton speakers in Brittany, Basque speakers in the Pyrenees, and Provençal speakers in the south.

The simple truth is that a culturally diversified society is a vital one and affords maximum freedom for creativity and achievement. But if a practical benefit of linguistic diversity is needed, then it can be found in the fact that non-English speakers in America provide a natural resource that both in war and in peace has met national needs. Millions of Americans were shamed into losing their foreign-language competence at the very time that the federal and local governments spent vast amounts of money to increase the teaching of foreign languages in schools.

It is as dispiriting to hear a language die as it is to stand idly by and watch the bald eagle, the whooping crane, or any other form of life disappear from the face of the earth. The supporters of linguistic diversity do not propose a return to the curse of Babel; they do not urge a world fragmented into groups that are unable to communicate. Instead, linguistic sciences can possibly achieve the best of two worlds.

Suggestions for Writing and Discussion

1. What, exactly, is the meaning of *chauvinism*? How does this word connect to Farb's main point in this piece? Use a dictionary as you work on your response to this question.
2. According to Farb, how do the structures and purposes of black language differ from that of standard American?
3. As a linguistic scholar, Farb's insights into the black language far exceed

that of the average person. What did you learn by reading this piece? What information surprised you? What questions would you like to be able to ask Farb in person?

4. From a linguist's standpoint, Farb contends that many black children do not survive the "trauma of school" because of their difficulty reading and using standard English. Other than language difficulties, can you see any factors that may contribute to the trauma of school for some of these black children? Are any of these factors more important than Farb's language issue? Explain your answer.

5. Farb concludes that unless a language is acknowledged in its own right, it will not survive. What evidence does Farb give to support this claim? Do you agree or disagree with him on this point? Explain your position.

6. Evaluate the general appeal that Farb adopts in this piece. Find five specific words, phrases, or passages that support your claim. As a writer, why might Farb choose this approach over any other? Explain your answer.

7. Do you agree with Farb? Should public schools accommodate the language of black students? If so, explain what points were most convincing in this piece. If not, explain what points you disagree with, and give your counterargument in its place.

Suggestions for Extended Thinking and Research

1. Research in greater depth the languages of Gullah, Pidgin, or Creole. Write an essay in which you further explain one or two of the basic points Farb makes in this piece.

2. Analyze a popular rap song in terms of the major points Farb makes in this piece.

RACHEL L. JONES

What's Wrong with Black English?

> *When Rachel Jones was a sophomore at Southern Illinois University, she wrote this essay, which originally appeared in* Newsweek's *"My Turn" column. She offers a view of black English that is very different from Peter Farb's (pp. 524–531).*

Prereading/Journal-Writing Suggestions

1. As far as your choices for speaking are concerned, explain how you alter your way of speaking depending on the audience, the place, and the circumstance. Try to write about a specific incident that happened this past week.

2. Are there any words or phrases in standard English that you usually refrain from using? Why do you exclude these words from your everyday vocabulary? What conclusions can you draw about the ways in which you use language?

William Labov, a noted linguist, once said about the use of black English, "It is the goal of most black Americans to acquire full control of the standard language without giving up their own culture." He also suggested that there are certain advantages to having two ways to express one's feelings. I wonder if the good doctor might also consider the goals of those black Americans who have full control of standard English but who are every now and then troubled by that colorful, grammar-to-the-winds patois that is black English. Case in point—me.

I'm a 21-year-old black born to a family that would probably be considered lower-middle class—which in my mind is a polite way of describing a condition only slightly better than poverty. Let's just say we rarely if ever did the winter-vacation thing in the Caribbean. I've often had to defend my humble beginnings to a most unlikely group of people for an even less likely reason. Because of the way I talk, some of my black peers look at me sideways and ask, "Why do you talk like you're white?"

The first time it happened to me I was nine years old. Cornered in the school bathroom by the class bully and her sidekick, I was offered the opportunity to swallow a few of my teeth unless I satisfactorily explained why I always got good grades, why I talked "proper" or "white." I had no ready answer for her, save the fact that my mother had from the time I was old enough to talk stressed the importance of reading and learning, or that L. Frank Baum and Ray Bradbury were my closest companions. I read all my older brothers' and sisters' literature textbooks more faithfully than they did, and even lightweights like the Bobbsey Twins and Trixie Belden were allowed into my bookish inner circle. I don't remember exactly what I told those girls, but I somehow talked my way out of a beating.

"White Pipes"

I was reminded once again of my "white pipes" problem while apartment hunting in Evanston, Ill., last winter. I doggedly made out lists of available places and called all around. I would immediately be invited over — and immediately turned down. The thinly concealed looks of shock when the front door opened clued me in, along with the flustered instances of "just getting off the phone with the girl who was ahead of you and she wants the rooms." When I finally found a place to live, my roommate stirred up old memories when she remarked a few months later, "You know, I was surprised when I first saw you. You sounded white over the phone." Tell me another one, sister.

I should've asked her a question I've wanted an answer to for years: how 5 does one "talk white"? The silly side of me pictures a rabid white foam spewing forth when I speak. I don't use Valley Girl jargon, so that's not what's meant in my case. Actually, I've pretty much deduced what people mean when they say that to me, and the implications are really frightening.

It means that I'm articulate and well-versed. It means that I can talk as freely about John Steinbeck as I can about Rick James. It means that "ain't" and "he be" are not staples of my vocabulary and are only used around family and friends. (It is almost Jekyll and Hyde-ish the way I can slip out of academic abstractions into a long, lean, double-negative-filled dialogue, but I've come to terms with that aspect of my personality.) As a child, I found it hard to believe that's what people meant by "talking proper"; that would've meant that good grades and standard English were equated with white skin, and that went against everything I'd ever been taught. Running into the same type of mentality as an adult has confirmed the depressing reality that for many blacks, standard English is not only unfamiliar, it is socially unacceptable.

James Baldwin once defended black English by saying it had added "vitality to the language," and even went so far as to label it a language in its own right, saying, "Language [i.e., black English] is a political instrument" and a "vivid and crucial key to identity." But did Malcolm X urge blacks to take power in this country "any way y'all can"? Did Martin Luther King Jr. say to blacks, "I has been to the mountaintop, and I done seed the Promised Land"? Toni Morrison, Alice Walker and James Baldwin did not achieve their eloquence, grace and stature by using only black English in their writing. Andrew Young, Tom Bradley and Barbara Jordan did not acquire political power by saying, "Y'all crazy if you ain't gon vote for me." They all have full command of standard English, and I don't think that knowledge takes away from their blackness or commitment to black people.

Soulful

I know from experience that it's important for black people, stripped of culture and heritage, to have something they can point to and say, "This is ours, *we* can comprehend it, *we* alone can speak it with a soulful flourish." I'd be lying if I said that the rhythms of my people caught up in "some serious rap" don't sound natural and right to me sometimes. But how heartwarming is it for those same brothers when they hit the pavement searching for employment? Studies have proven that the use of ethnic dialects decreases power in the marketplace. "I be" is acceptable on the corner, but not with the boss.

Am I letting capitalistic, European-oriented thinking fog the issue? Am I selling out blacks to an ideal of assimilating, being as much like white as possible? I have not formed a personal political ideology, but I do know this: it hurts me to hear black children use black English, knowing that they will be at yet another disadvantage in an educational system already full of stumbling blocks. It hurts me to sit in lecture halls and hear fellow black students complain that the professor "be tripping dem out using big words dey can't understand." And what hurts most is to be stripped of my own blackness simply because I know my way around the English language.

I would have to disagree with Labov in one respect. My goal is not so 10 much to acquire full control of both standard and black English, but to one day see more black people less dependent on a dialect that excludes them from full participation in the world we live in. I don't think I talk white, I think I talk right.

Suggestions for Writing and Discussion

1. What, exactly, is Jones's viewpoint as far as black English is concerned? How does she support this claim?
2. In what ways might Jones's position as a college student affect the way readers view her main premises? If she was a student in a class taught by Peter Farb (author of "Linguistic Chauvinism," pp. 524–531), on what specific points might she disagree with her instructor?
3. Why does Jones include her family background in this piece? How would the essay be changed if this information was excluded? Explain your answer.
4. How does Jones's preferred choice of dialect connect her to or disconnect her from other cultures?
5. Jones indicates that her literacy stems from white writers only. Explain why she may have only read popular white fiction. If she had also read black writers, might her ideas on language be any different? Explain your answer.
6. Why does Jones include the language used by famous black leaders and writers in America, past and present? What does she gain by using these

specific people as examples? Can you think of any influential black people
who do not fit into her category?
7. Do you think Jones's piece would be convincing to black students today?
What points might be more convincing than others? Why?

Suggestion for Extended Thinking and Research

Observe the portrayal of language on a popular television sitcom in
which the main characters are black. Do these characters conform to Jones's
white English dialect, or do they use the black English she describes? If you
were Jones, how would you react to the way language is used in this show?

GISH JEN

What Means Switch

> *An American with Chinese roots, Gish Jen grew up in Scarsdale, New York, and was educated at Harvard, Stanford, and the Iowa Writers Workshop. She has received grants from the National Endowment for the Arts, the James Michener/ Copernicus Society, the Bunting Institute, and the Massachusetts Artists' Foundation. Her work has appeared in many magazines and collections, including the* New Yorker, *the* Atlantic Monthly, *and* The Best American Short Stories 1988. *She is the author of a widely acclaimed novel depicting the life of contemporary Chinese immigrants,* Typical Americans *(1991). The story "What Means Switch" first appeared in the* Atlantic *in 1990.*

Prereading/Journal-Writing Suggestions

1. When you were an adolescent, what kinds of things did you do in order to fit in with a particular group? Were you successful? Try to freewrite about one time in which you changed (or refused to change) in some way in order to be accepted.
2. If you had to choose one of the following to be the most important relationship in your life, which one would it be and why?
   A. You and your friends
   B. You and your family
   C. You and your community

There we are, nice Chinese family—father, mother, two born-here girls. Where should we live next? My parents slide the question back and forth like a cup of ginseng neither one wants to drink. Until finally it comes to them, what they really want is a milkshake (chocolate) and to go with it a house in Scarsdale. What else? The broker tries to hint: the neighborhood, she says. Moneyed. Many delis. Meaning rich and Jewish. But someone has sent my parents a list of the top ten schools nation-wide (based on the opinion of selected educators and others) and so *many-deli* or not we nestle into a Dutch colonial on the Bronx River Parkway. The road's windy where we are, very charming; drivers miss their turns, plough up our flower beds, then want to use our telephone. "Of course," my mom tells them, like it's no big deal, we can replant. We're the type to adjust. You know—the lady drivers weep, my mom gets out the Kleenex for them. We're a bit down the hill from the private plane set, in other words. Only in our dreams do our jacket zippers jam, what with all the lift tickets we have stapled to them, Killington on top of Sugarbush on top of Stowe, and we don't even know where the Virgin Islands are— although certain of us do know that virgins are like priests and nuns, which there were a lot more of in Yonkers, where we just moved from, than there are here.

This is my first understanding of class. In our old neighborhood everybody knew everything about virgins and non-virgins, not to say the technicalities of staying in-between. Or almost everybody, I should say; in Yonkers I was the laugh-along type. Here I'm an expert.

"You mean the man . . .?" Pig-tailed Barbara Gugelstein spits a mouthful of coke back into her can. "That is *so* gross!"

Pretty soon I'm getting popular for a new girl, the only problem is Danielle Meyers, who wears blue mascara and has gone steady with two boys. "How do *you* know," she starts to ask, proceeding to edify us all with how she French-kissed one boyfriend and just regular kissed another. ("Because, you know, he had braces.") We hear about his rubber bands, how once one popped right into her mouth. I begin to realize I need to find somebody to kiss too. But how?

Luckily, I just about then happen to tell Barbara Gugelstein I know   5
karate. I don't know why I tell her this. My sister Callie's, is the liar in the family; ask anybody. I'm the one who doesn't see why we should have to hold our heads up. But for some reason I tell Barbara Gugelstein I can make my hands like steel by thinking hard. "I'm not supposed to tell anyone," I say.

The way she backs away, blinking, I could be the burning bush.

"I can't do bricks," I say — a bit of expectation management. "But I can do your arm if you want." I set my hand in chop position.

"Uhh, it's okay," she says. "I know you can, I saw it on TV last night."

That's when I recall that I too saw it on TV last night — in fact, at her house. I rush on to tell her I know how to get pregnant with tea.

"With *tea?*"   10

"That's how they do it in China."

She agrees that China is an ancient and great civilization that ought to be known for more than spaghetti and gunpowder. I tell her I know Chinese. *"Be-yeh fa-foon,"* I say. *"Shee-veh. Ji nu."* Meaning, "Stop acting crazy. Rice gruel. Soy sauce." She's impressed. At lunch the next day, Danielle Meyers and Amy Weinstein and Barbara's crush, Andy Kaplan, are all impressed too. Scarsdale is a liberal town, not like Yonkers, where the Whitman Road Gang used to throw crabapple mash at my sister Callie and me and tell us it would make our eyes stick shut. Here we're like permanent exchange students. In another ten years, there'll be so many Orientals we'll turn into Asians; a Japanese grocery will buy out that one deli too many. But for now, the midsixties, what with civil rights on TV, we're not so much accepted as embraced. Especially by the Jewish part of town — which, it turns out, is not all of town at all. That's just an idea people have, Callie says, and lots of them could take us or leave us same as the Christians, who are nice too; I shouldn't generalize. So let me not generalize except to say that pretty soon I've been to so many bar and bas mitzvahs, I can almost say myself whether the kid chants like an angel or like a train conductor, maybe they could use him on the commuter line. At seder I know to forget the bricks, get a good pile of that mortar. Also I know what is schmaltz. I know that I am a goy. This is not why people like me, though. People like me because I do not need to use deodorant, as I demonstrate in the locker room before and after gym. Also, I can explain to them, for example, what is tofu (der-voo, we say at home). Their mothers invite me to taste-test their Chinese cooking.

"Very authentic." I try to be reassuring. After all, they're nice people, I like them. "De-lish." I have seconds. On the question of what we eat, though, I have to admit, "Well, no, it's different than that." I have thirds. "What my mom makes is home style, it's not in the cookbooks."

Not in the cookbooks! Everyone's jealous. Meanwhile, the big deal at home is when we have turkey pot pie. My sister Callie's the one introduced them — Mrs. Wilder's, they come in this green-and-brown box — and when we have them, we both get suddenly interested in helping out in the kitchen. You know, we stand in front of the oven and help them bake. Twenty-five minutes. She and I have a deal, though, to keep it secret from school, as everybody else thinks they're gross. We think they're a big improvement over authentic Chinese home cooking. Ox-tail soup — now that's gross. Stir-fried beef with tomatoes. One day I say, "You know Ma, I have never seen a stir-fried tomato in any Chinese restaurant we have ever been in, ever."

"In China," she says, real lofty, "we consider tomatoes are a delicacy."   15

"Ma," I say. "Tomatoes are *Italian*."

"No respect for elders." She wags her finger at me, but I can tell it's just to try and shame me into believing her. "I'm tell you, tomatoes *invented* in China."

"*Ma.*"

"Is true. Like noodles. Invented in China."

"That's not what they said in *school*."   20

"In *China*," my mother counters, "we also eat tomatoes uncooked, like apple. And in summertime we slice them, and put some sugar on top."

"Are you sure?"

My mom says of course she's sure, and in the end I give in, even though she once told me that China was such a long time ago, a lot of things she can hardly remember. She said sometimes she has trouble remembering her characters, that sometimes she'll be writing a letter, just writing along, and all of sudden she won't be sure if she should put four dots or three.

"So what do you do then?"

"Oh, I just make a little sloppy."   25

"You mean you *fudge?*"

She laughed then, but another time, when she was showing me how to write my name, and I said, just kidding, "Are you sure that's the right number of dots now?" she was hurt.

"I mean, of course you know," I said. "I mean, *oy.*"

Meanwhile, what *I* know is that in the eighth grade, what people want to hear does not include how Chinese people eat sliced tomatoes with sugar on top. For a gross fact, it just isn't gross enough. On the other hand, the fact that somewhere in China somebody eats or has eaten or once ate living monkey brains—now that's conversation.

"They have these special tables," I say, "kind of like a giant collar. With a hole in the middle, for the monkey's neck. They put the monkey in the collar, and then they cut off the top of its head."

"Whadda they use for cutting?"

I think. "Scalpels."

"Scalpels?" says Andy Kaplan.

"Kaplan, don't be dense," Barbara Gugelstein says. "The Chinese *invented* scalpels."

Once a friend said to me, You know, everybody is valued for something. She explained how some people resented being valued for their looks; others resented being valued for their money. Wasn't it still better to be beautiful and rich than ugly and poor, though? You should be just glad, she said, that you have something people value. It's like having a special talent, like being good at ice-skating, or opera-singing. She said, You could probably make a career out if it.

Here's the irony: I am.

*

Anyway. I am ad-libbing my way through eighth grade, as I've described. Until one bloomy spring day, I come in late to homeroom, and to my chagrin discover there's a new kid in class.

Chinese.

So what should I do, pretend to have to go to the girls' room, like Barbara Gugelstein the day Andy Kaplan took his ID back? I sit down; I am so cool I remind myself of Paul Newman. First thing I realize, though, is that no one looking at me is thinking of Paul Newman. The notes fly:

"*I* think he's cute."

"Who?" I write back. (I am still at an age, understand, when I believe a person can be saved by aplomb.)

"I don't think he talks English too good. Writes it either."

"Who?"

"They might have to put him behind a grade, so don't worry."

"He has a crush on you already, you could tell as soon as you walked in, he turned kind of orangish."

I hope I'm not turning orangish as I deal with my mail, I could use a secretary. The second round starts:

"What do you mean who? Don't be weird. Didn't you *see* him??? Straight back over your right shoulder!!!!"

I have to look; what else can I do? I think of certain tips I learned in Girl Scouts about poise. I cross my ankles. I hold a pen in my hand. I sit up as though I have a crown on my head. I swivel my head slowly, repeating to myself, *I* could be Miss America.

"Miss Mona Chang."

Horror raises its hoary head.   50

"Notes, please."

Mrs. Mandeville's policy is to read all notes aloud.

I try to consider what Miss America would do, and see myself, back straight, knees together, crying. Some inspiration. Cool Hand Luke, on the other hand, would, quick, eat the evidence. And why not? I should yawn as I stand up, and boom, the notes are gone. All that's left is to explain that it's an old Chinese reflex.

I shuffle up to the front of the room.

"One minute please," Mrs. Mandeville says.   55

I wait, noticing how large and plastic her mouth is.

She unfolds a piece of paper.

And I, Miss Mona Chang, who got almost straight A's her whole life except in math and conduct, am about to start crying in front of everyone.

I am delivered out of hot Egypt by the bell. General pandemonium. Mrs. Mandeville still has her hand clamped on my shoulder, though. And the next thing I know, I'm holding the new boy's schedule. He's standing next to me like a big blank piece of paper. "This is Sherman," Mrs. Mandeville says.

"Hello," I say.   60

"Non how a," I say.

I'm glad Barbara Gugelstein isn't there to see my Chinese in action.

"Ji nu," I say. *"Shee veh."*

Later I find out that his mother asked if there were any other Orientals in our grade. She had him put in my class on purpose. For now, though, he looks at me as though I'm much stranger than anything else he's seen so far. Is this because he understands I'm saying "soy sauce rice gruel" to him or because he doesn't?

"Sher-man," he says finally.   65

I look at his schedule card. Sherman Matsumoto. What kind of name is that for a nice Chinese boy?

                                    *

(Later on, people ask me how I can tell Chinese from Japanese. I shrug. You just kind of know, I say. *Oy!*)

                                    *

Sherman's got the sort of looks I think of as pretty-boy. Monsignor-black hair (not monk brown like mine), bouncy. Crayola eyebrows, one with a round bald spot in the middle of it, like a golf hole. I don't know how anybody can think of him as orangish; his skin looks white to me, with pink triangles hanging down the front of his cheeks like flags. Kind of delicate-looking, but the only truly uncool thing about him is that his spiral notebook has a picture of a kitty cat on it. A big white fluffy one, with a blue ribbon above each perky little ear. I get much opportunity to view this, as all the poor kid understands about life in junior high school is that he should follow me everywhere. It's embarrassing. On the other hand, he's obviously even more miserable than I am, so I try not to say anything. Give him a chance to adjust. We communicate by sign language, and by drawing pictures, which he's better at than I am; he puts in every last detail, even if it takes forever. I try to be patient.

A week of this. Finally I enlighten him. "You should get a new notebook."

His cheeks turn a shade of pink you mostly only see in hyacinths.   70

"Notebook." I point to his. I show him mine, which is psychedelic, with big purple and yellow stick-on flowers. I try to explain he should have one like this, only without the flowers. He nods enigmatically, and the next day brings me a notebook just like his, except that this cat sports pink bows instead of blue.

"Pret-ty," he says. "You."

He speaks English! I'm dumbfounded. Has he spoken it all this time? I consider: Pretty. You. What does that mean? Plus actually, he's said *plit-ty,* much as my parents would; I'm assuming he means pretty, but maybe he means pity. Pity. You.

"Jeez," I say finally.

"You are wel-come," he says.   75

I decorate the back of the notebook with stick-on flowers, and hold it so that these show when I walk through the halls. In class I mostly keep my book open. After all, the kid's so new; I think I really ought to have a heart. And for a livelong day nobody notices.

Then Barbara Gugelstein sidles up. "Matching notebooks, huh?"

I'm speechless.

"First comes love, then comes marriage, and then come chappies in a baby carriage."

"Barbara!"   80

"Get it?" she says. "Chinese Japs."

"Bar-*bra,*" I say to get even.

"Just make sure he doesn't give you any *tea,*" she says.

Are Sherman and I in love? Three days later, I hazard that we are. My thinking proceeds this way: I think he's cute, and I think he thinks I'm cute. On the other hand, we don't kiss and we don't exactly have fantastic conversations. Our talks *are* getting better, though. We started out, "This is a book." "Book." "This is a chair." "Chair." Advancing to, "What is this?" "This is a book." Now, for fun, he tests me.

"What is this?" he says.   85

"This is a book," I say, as if I'm the one who has to learn how to talk. He claps. "Good!"

Meanwhile, people ask me all about him, I could be his press agent.

"No, he doesn't eat raw fish."

"No, his father wasn't a kamikaze pilot."   90

"No, he can't do karate."

"Are you sure?" somebody asks.

*

Indeed he doesn't know karate, but judo he does. I am hurt I'm not the one to find this out; the guys know from gym class. They line up to be flipped, he flips them all onto the floor, and after that he doesn't eat lunch at the girls' table with me anymore. I'm more or less glad. Meaning, when he was there, I never knew what to say. Now that he's gone, though, I seem to be stuck at the "This is a chair" level of conversation. Ancient Chinese eating habits have lost their cachet; all I get are more and more questions about me and Sherman. "I dunno," I'm saying all the time. *Are* we going out? We do stuff, it's true. For example, I take him to the department stores, explain to him who shops in Alexander's, who shops in Saks. I tell him my family's the type that shops in Alexander's. He says he's sorry. In Saks he gets lost; either that, or else I'm the lost one. (It's true I find him calmly waiting at the front door, hands behind his back, like a guard.) I take him to the candy store. I take him to the bagel store. Sherman is crazy about bagels. I explain to him that Lender's is gross, he should get his bagels from the bagel store. He says thank you.

"Are you going steady?" people want to know.

How can we go steady when he doesn't have an ID bracelet? On the 95 other hand, he brings me more presents than I think any girl's ever gotten before. Oranges. Flowers. A little bag of bagels. But what do they mean? Do they mean thank you, I enjoyed our trip; do they mean I like you; do they mean I decided I liked the Lender's better even if they are gross, you can have these? Sometimes I think he's acting on his mother's instructions. Also I know at least a couple of the presents were supposed to go to our teachers. He told me that once and turned red. I figured it still might mean something that he didn't throw them out.

More and more now, we joke. Like, instead of "I'm thinking," he always says, "I'm sinking," which we both think is so funny, that all either one of us has to do is pretend to be drowning and the other one cracks up. And he tells me things — for example, that there are electric lights everywhere in Tokyo now.

"You mean you didn't have them before?"

"Everywhere now!" He's amazed too. "Since Olympics!"

"Olympics?"

"1960," he says proudly, and as proof, hums for me the Olympic theme 100 song. "You know?"

"Sure," I say, and hum with him happily. We could be a picture on a UNICEF poster. The only problem is that I don't really understand what the Olympics have to do with the modernization of Japan, any more than I get this other story he tells me, about that hole in his left eyebrow, which is from some time his father accidentally hit him with a lit cigarette. When Sherman was a baby. His father was drunk, having been out carousing; his mother was very mad but didn't say anything, just cleaned the whole house. Then his father was so ashamed he bowed to ask her forgiveness.

"Your mother cleaned the house?"

Sherman nods solemnly.

"And your father *bowed?*" I find this more astounding than anything I ever thought to make up. "That is so weird," I tell him.

"Weird," he agrees. "This I no forget, forever. *Father* bow to *mother!*" 105

We shake our heads.

As for the things he asks me, they're not topics I ever discussed before. Do I like it here? Of course I like it here, I was born here, I say. Am I Jewish? Jewish! I laugh. *Oy!* Am I American? "Sure I'm American," I say. "Everybody who's born here is American, and also some people who convert from what they were before. You could become American." But he says no, he could never. "Sure you could," I say. "You only have to learn some rules and speeches."

"But I Japanese," he says.

"You could become American anyway," I say. "Like I *could* become Jewish, if I wanted to. I'd just have to switch, that's all."

"But you Catholic," he says. 110

I think maybe he doesn't get what means switch.

I introduce him to Mrs. Wilder's turkey pot pies. "Gross?" he asks. I say they are, but we like them anyway. "Don't tell anybody." He promises. We bake them, eat them. While we're eating, he's drawing me pictures.

"This American," he says, and he draws something that looks like John Wayne. "This Jewish," he says, and draws something that looks like the Wicked Witch of the West, only male.

"I don't think so," I say.

He's undeterred. "This Japanese," he says, and draws a fair rendition of 115 himself. "This Chinese," he says, and draws what looks to be another fair rendition of himself.

"How can you tell them apart?" 120

"This way," he says, and he puts the picture of the Chinese so that it is looking at the pictures of the American and the Jew. The Japanese faces the wall. Then he draws another picture, of a Japanese flag, so that the Japanese has that to contemplate. "Chinese lost in department store," he says. "Japanese know how go." For fun, he then takes the Japanese flag and fastens it to the refrigerator door with magnets. "In school, in ceremony, we this way," he explains, and bows to the picture.

When my mother comes in, her face is so red that with the white wall behind her she looks a bit like the Japanese flag herself. Yet I get the feeling I better not say so. First she doesn't move. Then she snatches the flag off the refrigerator, so fast the magnets go flying. Two of them land on the stove. She crumples up the paper. She hisses at Sherman, *"This is the U.S. of A., do you hear me!"*

Sherman hears her.

"You call your mother right now, tell her come pick you up."   120

He understands perfectly. *I,* on the other hand, am stymied. How can two people who don't really speak English understand each other better than I can understand them? "But Ma," I say.

"Don't *Ma* me," she says.

Later on she explains that World War II was in China, too. "Hitler," I say. "Nazis. Volkswagens." I know the Japanese were on the wrong side, because they bombed Pearl Harbor. My mother explains about before that. The Napkin Massacre. "*Nan*-king," she corrects me.

"Are you sure?" I say. "In school, they said the war was about putting the Jews in ovens."

"Also about ovens."   125

"About both?"

"Both."

"That's not what they said in school."

"Just forget about school."

Forget about school? "I thought we moved here for the schools."   130

"We moved here," she says, "for your education."

Sometimes I have no idea what she's talking about.

"I like Sherman," I say after a while.

"He's nice boy," she agrees.

Meaning what? I would ask, except that my dad's just come home, 135 which means it's time to start talking about whether we should build a brick wall across the front of the lawn. Recently a car made it almost into our livingroom, which was so scary, the driver fainted and an ambulance had to come. "We should have discussion," my dad said after that. And so for about a week, every night we do.

*

"Are you just friends, or more than just friends?" Barbara Gugelstein is giving me the cross-ex.

"Maybe," I say.

"Come on," she says, "I told you *everything* about me and Andy."

I actually *am* trying to tell Barbara everything about Sherman, but everything turns out to be nothing. Meaning, I can't locate the conversation in what I have to say. Sherman and I go places, we talk, one time my mother threw him out of the house because of World War II.

"I think we're just friends," I say.   140

"You think or you're sure?"

Now that I do less of the talking at lunch, I notice more what other people talk about—cheerleading, who likes who, this place in White Plains to get earrings. On none of these topics am I an expert. Of course, I'm still friends with Barbara Gugelstein, but I notice Danielle Meyers has spun away to other groups.

Barbara's analysis goes this way: To be popular, you have to have big boobs, a note from your mother that lets you use her Lord & Taylor credit card, and a boyfriend. On the other hand, what's so wrong with being unpopular? "We'll get them in the end," she says. It's what her dad tells her. "Like they'll turn out too dumb to do their own investing, and then they'll get killed in fees and then they'll have to move to towns where the schools stink. And my dad should know," she winds up. "He's a broker."

"I guess," I say.

But the next thing I know, I have a true crush on Sherman Matsumoto. 145 *Mis*ter Judo, the guys call him now, with real respect; and the more they call him that, the more I don't care that he carries a notebook with a cat on it.

I sigh. "Sherman."

"I thought you were just friends," says Barbara Gugelstein

"We were," I say mysteriously. This, I've noticed, is how Danielle Meyers talks; everything's secret, she only lets out so much, it's like she didn't grow up with everybody telling her she had to share.

And here's the funny thing: The more I intimate that Sherman and I are more than just friends, the more it seems we actually are. It's the old imagination giving reality a nudge. When I start to blush, he starts to blush; we reach a point where we can hardly talk at all.

"Well, there's first base with tongue, and first base without," I tell 150 Barbara Gugelstein.

In fact, Sherman and I have brushed shoulders, which was equivalent to first base I was sure, maybe even second. I felt as though I'd turned into one huge shoulder; that's all I was, one huge shoulder. We not only didn't talk, we didn't breathe. But how can I tell Barbara Gugelstein that? So instead I say, "Well there's second base and second base."

Danielle Meyers is my friend again. She says, "I know exactly what you mean," just to make Barbara Gugelstein feel bad.

"Like *what* do I mean?" I say.

Danielle Meyers can't answer.

"You know what I think?" I tell Barbara the next day. "I think Danielle's 155 giving us a line."

Barbara pulls thoughtfully on one of her pigtails.

*

If Sherman Matsumoto is never going to give me an ID to wear, he should at least get up the nerve to hold my hand. I don't think he sees this. I think of the story he told me about his parents, and in a synaptic firestorm realize we don't see the same things at all.

So one day, when we happen to brush shoulders again, I don't move away. He doesn't move away either. There we are. Like a pair of bleachers, pushed together but not quite matched up. After a while, I have to breathe, I can't help it. I breathe in such a way that our elbows start to touch too. We are in a crowd, waiting for a bus. I crane my neck to look at the sign that says where the bus is going; now our wrists are touching. Then it happens: He links his pinky around mine.

Is that holding hands? Later, in bed, I wonder all night. One finger, and not even the biggest one.

*

Sherman is leaving in a month. Already! I think, well, I suppose he will 160 leave and we'll never even kiss. I guess that's all right. Just when I've resigned myself to it, though, we hold hands all five fingers. Once when we are at the bagel shop, then again in my parents' kitchen. Then, when we are at the playground, he kisses the back of my hand.

He does it again not too long after that, in White Plains.

I invest in a bottle of mouthwash.

Instead of moving on, though, he kisses the back of my hand again. And again. I try raising my hand, hoping he'll make the jump from my hand to my cheek. It's like trying to wheedle an inchworm out the window. You know, *This way, this way.*

All over the world people have their own cultures. That's what we learned in social studies.

If we never kiss, I'm not going to take it personally.   165

*

It is the end of the school year. We've had parties. We've turned in our textbooks. Hooray! Outside the asphalt already steams if you spit on it. Sherman isn't leaving for another couple of days, though, and he comes to visit every morning, staying until the afternoon, when Callie comes home from her big-deal job as a bank teller. We drink Kool-Aid in the backyard and hold hands until they are sweaty and make smacking noises coming apart. He tells me how busy his parents are, getting ready for the move. His mother, particularly, is very tired. Mostly we are mournful.

The very last day we hold hands and do not let go. Our palms fill up with water like a blister. We do not care. We talk more than usual. How much is airmail to Japan, that kind of thing. Then suddenly he asks, will I marry him?

I'm only thirteen.

But when old? Sixteen?

If you come back to get me.   170

I come. Or you can come to Japan, be Japanese.

How can I be Japanese?

Like you become American. Switch.

He kisses me on the cheek, again and again and again.

His mother calls to say she's coming to get him. I cry. I tell him how 175 I've saved every present he's ever given me — the ruler, the pencils, the bags from the bagels, all the flower petals. I even have the orange peels from the oranges.

All?

I put them in a jar.

I'd show him, except that we're not allowed to go upstairs to my room. Anyway, something about the orange peels seems to choke him up too. *Mi*ster Judo, but I've gotten him in a soft spot. We are going together to the bathroom to get some toilet paper to wipe our eyes when poor tired Mrs. Matsumoto, driving a shiny new station wagon, skids up onto our lawn.

"Very sorry!"

We race outside.   180

"Very sorry!"

Mrs. Matsumoto is so short that about all we can see of her is a green cotton sun hat, with a big brim. It's tied on. The brim is trembling.

I hope my mom's not going to start yelling about World War II.

"Is all right, no trouble," she says, materializing on the step behind me and Sherman. She's propped the screen door wide open; when I turn I see she's waving. "No trouble, no trouble!"

"No trouble, no trouble!" I echo, twirling a few times with relief.   185

Mrs. Matsumoto keeps apologizing; my mom keeps insisting she shouldn't feel bad, it was only some grass and a small tree. Crossing the lawn, she insists Mrs. Matsumoto get out of the car, even though it means trampling some lilies of the valley. She insists that Mrs. Matsumoto come in for a cup of tea. Then she will not talk about anything unless Mrs. Matsumoto sits down, and unless she lets my mom prepare her a small snack. The coming in and the tea and the sitting down are settled pretty quickly, but they negotiate ferociously over the small snack, which Mrs. Matsumoto will not eat unless she can call Mr. Matsumoto. She makes the mistake of linking Mr. Matsumoto with a reparation of some sort, which my mom will not hear of.

"Please!"

"No no no no."

Back and forth it goes. "No no no no." "No no no no." "No no no no." What kind of conversation is that? I look at Sherman, who shrugs. Finally Mr. Matsumoto calls on his own, wondering where his wife is. He comes over in a taxi. He's a heavy-browed businessman, friendly but brisk — not at all a type you could imagine bowing to a lady with a taste for tie-on sun hats. My mom invites him in as if it's an idea she just this moment thought of. And would he maybe have some tea and a small snack?

Sherman and I sneak back outside for another farewell, by the side of 190 the house, behind the forsythia bushes. We hold hands. He kisses me on the cheek again, and then — just when I think he's finally going to kiss me on the lips — he kisses me on the neck.

Is this first base?

He does it more. Up and down, up and down. First it tickles, and then it doesn't. He has his eyes closed. I close my eyes too. He's hugging me. Up and down. Then down.

He's at my collarbone.

Still at my collarbone. Now his hand's on my ribs. So much for first base. More ribs. The idea of second base would probably make me nervous if he weren't on his way back to Japan and if I really thought we were going to get there. As it is, though, I'm not in much danger of wrecking my life on the shoals of passion; his unmoving hand feels more like a growth than a boyfriend. He has his whole face pressed to my neck skin so I can't tell his mouth from his nose. I think he may be licking me.

From indoors, a burst of adult laughter. My eyelids flutter. I start to try 195 and wiggle such that his hand will maybe budge upward.

Do I mean for my top blouse button to come accidentally undone?

He clenches his jaw, and when he opens his eyes, they're fixed on that button like it's a gnat that's been bothering him for far too long. He mutters in Japanese. If later in life he were to describe this as a pivotal moment in his youth, I would not be surprised. Holding the material as far from my body as possible, he buttons the button. Somehow we've landed up too close to the bushes.

*

What to tell Barbara Gugelstein? She says, "Tell me what were his last words. He must have said something last."

"I don't want to talk about it."

"Maybe he said, Good-bye?" she suggests. " 'Sayonara?' " She means well. 200

"I don't want to talk about it."

"Aw, come on, I told you everything about . . ."

I say, "Because it's private, excuse me."

She stops, squints at me as though at a far-off face she's trying to make out. Then she nods and very lightly places her hand on my forearm.

*

The forsythia seemed to be stabbing us in the eyes. Sherman said, more 205 or less, *You will need to study how to switch.*

And I said, *I think you should switch. The way you do everything is weird.*

And he said, *You just want to tell everything to your friends. You just want to have boyfriend to become popular.*

Then he flipped me. Two swift moves, and I went sprawling through the air, a flailing confusion of soft human parts such as had no idea where the ground was.

*

It is the fall, and I am in high school, and still he hasn't written, so finally I write him.

I still have all your gifts, I write. *I don't talk so much as I used to. Although I* 210 *am not exactly a mouse either. I don't care about being popular anymore. I swear. Are you happy to be back in Japan? I know I ruined everything. I was just trying to be entertaining. I miss you with all my heart, and hope I didn't ruin everything.*

He writes back, *You will never be Japanese.*

I throw all the orange peels out that day. Some of them, it turns out, were moldy anyway. I tell my mother I want to move to Chinatown.

"Chinatown!" she says.

I don't know why I suggested it.

"What's the matter?" she says. "Still boy-crazy? That Sherman?" 215
"No."
"Too much homework?"
I don't answer.
"Forget about school."
Later she tells me if I don't like school, I don't have to go everyday. 220
Some days I can stay home.
"Stay home?" In Yonkers, Callie and I used to stay home all the time,
but that was because the schools there were *waste of time*.
"No good for a girl be too smart anyway."

*

For a long time I think about Sherman. But after a while I don't think
about him so much as I just keep seeing myself flipped onto the ground, lying
there shocked as the Matsumotos get ready to leave. My head has hit a rock;
my brain aches as though it's been shoved to some new place in my skull.
Otherwise I am okay. I see the forsythia, all those whippy branches, and can't
believe how many leaves there are on a bush — every one green and perky and
durably itself. And past them, real sky. I try to remember about why the sky's
blue, even though this one's gone the kind of indescribable grey you associate
with the insides of old shoes. I smell grass. Probably I have grass stains all
over my back. I hear my mother calling through the back door, "Mon-a!
Everyone leaving now," and "Not coming to say good-bye?" I hear Mr. and
Mrs. Matsumoto bowing as they leave — or at least I hear the embarrassment
in my mother's voice as they bow. I hear their car start. I hear Mrs. Matsumoto
directing Mr. Matsumoto how to back off the lawn so as not to rip any more
of it up. I feel the back of my head for blood — just a little. I hear their chug-
chug grow fainter and fainter, until it has faded into the whuzz-whuzz of all
the other cars. I hear my mom singing, "*Mon-a! Mon-a!*" until my dad comes
home. Doors open and shut. I see myself standing up, brushing myself off so
I'll have less explaining to do if she comes out to look for me. Grass stains —
just like I thought. I see myself walking around the house, going over to have
a look at our churned-up yard. It looks pretty sad, two big brown tracks,
right through the irises and the lilies of the valley, and that was a new dogwood
we'd just planted. Lying there like that. I hear myself thinking about my
father, having to go dig it up all over again. Adjusting. I think how we
probably ought to put up that brick wall. And sure enough, when I go inside,
no one's thinking about me, or that little bit of blood at the back of my head,
or the grass stains. That's what they're talking about — that wall. Again. My
mom doesn't think it'll do any good, but my dad thinks we should give it a
try. Should we or shouldn't we? How high? How thick? What will the neighbors say? I plop myself down on a hard chair. And all I can think is, we are the
complete only family that has to worry about this. If I could, I'd switch
everything to be different. But since I can't, I might as well sit here at the table
for a while, discussing what I know how to discuss. I nod and listen to the
rest.

Suggestions for Writing and Discussion

1. Read this piece all the way through for enjoyment. As soon as you are finished, write a five-minute response to the values you see as represented by one of the characters in this piece.
2. Does Mona predominantly belong to one culture? Explain your answer with three pieces of evidence from the text.
3. Compare and contrast Mona and her mother, Mona and her friends, and Mona and Sherman. From these comparisons, what conclusions can you draw about Mona's ideals, hopes, fears, and values? What are the major conflicts in this story?
4. In one conversation with Sherman, Mona tells him to simply "switch" cultures. She thinks it's possible; Sherman believes it isn't. Whom do you agree with on this issue and why?
5. What's Mona's first reaction when she notices Sherman? What's the main reason she begins to change her impression of him? What does this reveal about Mona?
6. What, besides the cultural differences, can explain the tensions in communication between Mona and Sherman?
7. What incidents in the story help explain how culture affects relationships within the Japanese family? Within the Chinese family? How do these relationships differ from those in the typical American family?
8. Analyze the images in the final paragraph in terms of their symbolic value in this piece. Why might the author choose to use these images at this point in the story?

Suggestions for Extended Thinking and Research

1. Research the roles of family members in Japan or China today. Compare these roles with those in your own family, and write an essay in which you draw a significant conclusion on the basis of your findings.
2. Interview a student from another country who is here to study in America. Set up open-ended questions so that you not only get to know more about this person's country but also get to know the values, concerns, and attitudes of the individual toward America. After this interview, write an essay that balances what you learned about the individual's insights and his or her country.

KITTY TSUI

Don't Let Them Chip Away at Our Language

> *Kitty Tsui was born in Kowloon, Hong Kong, in 1952. She grew up in England and Hong Kong and moved with her family to the United States in 1969. In addition to being an actress and competitive bodybuilder, Tsui is an acclaimed artist and is the author of a collection of poetry,* The Words of a Woman Who Breathes Fire *(1983).*

Prereading/Journal-Writing Suggestions

1. Complete the following statement, and freewrite for five or ten minutes: "The one thing about my community, state, or country that really makes me angry is . . . ."
2. Why do you (or why don't you) get involved in an active way in community, state, or national issues that make you angry?

---

haa-low, okay,
dank que, gut bye.

the only words
my grandmother knew.
the only words of english   5
she spoke
on a regular basis
in her rhythm of
city cantonese
mixed with   10
chinatown slang:
du pont guy,
low-see beef,
and, you good gel,
sic gee mah go,   15
sic apple pie
yum coca co-la.

a few proper nouns
were also part of
her vocabulary.   20
ny name, kit-ee
san fan-see,
pete gid-ding

her favorite
weatherman on tv,   25
say-fu-way
where she would
stock up on
rolls of toilet paper,
sponges and ajax.   30
on sale, of course.

in the spring of 1985
a republican assemblyman
proposed a bill
to make english   35
the official language
of the state.
his rationale:
we're no longer
going to let them   40
chip away at our language.
if they can't
understand english
they shouldn't be here
at all.   45

we first came
in 1785, three seamen
stranded in baltimore.
later we were
merchants and traders,   50
cooks and tailors,
contract laborers hired
to work in the mines,
in construction,
in the canneries,   55
hired to do what no man would:
hang from cliffs in a basket,
endure harsh winters
and blast through rock
to build the iron horse.   60

we became sharecroppers
growing peanuts,
strawberries,
cabbage and
chrysanthemums.   65

opened restaurants
and laundries,
worked in rich homes,
on ranches and farms
tending stock,   70
cleaning house,
cooking and ironing,
chopping firewood,
composing letters home
dreaming of a wife, a son.   75

we are tong yan,
american born
and immigrants
living in l.a., arizona,
brooklyn and the bronx,   80
san mateo and the sunset.
we eat burgers and baw,
custard tart and bubblegum.
we are doctors, actors,
artists, carpenters,   85
maids and teachers,
gay and straight.
we speak in many tongues:
sam yup, say yup, street talk,
the queen's english.   90

please don't let them
chip away at our language.

Suggestions for Writing and Discussion

1. In what way does the title of this piece reflect the conflict and the thesis of this poem?
2. Tsui chooses to use only lowercase letters in this poem. Why do you think she does that? Would the poem have been changed for you if she had used capital letters in the conventional places? Explain.
3. Analyze the English words of which the speaker's grandmother had command (lines 1–31). What parts of American culture does she have access to? From what parts is she excluded? Why does Tsui bother to include the specific products that the grandmother uses? What do these details add to the poem?
4. Compare the responsibilities of the first Chinese settlers (lines 46–60) with those in later years (lines 61–75). What conclusions can you draw about this group of people?

5. What exactly does the speaker mean in the last two lines of this poem? Compare the tone of these lines with that in lines 39–41.

Suggestions for Extended Thinking and Research

1. Research the contributions of your ancestors to America. Write an essay, or perhaps a poem, in which you trace these contributions during three separate time periods in America's history, including the present, as Tsui does.
2. Write a letter of thanks in which you acknowledge the specific ways in which past family members have contributed to making you who you are today.

TOPICS FOR MAKING CONNECTIONS: QUESTIONS OF LANGUAGE

1. Write an essay in which you argue that language should belong to the people who speak it. Use the experiences and insights you find in at least three sources in this section for your support. You may, of course, use other outside sources as well.
2. Write an essay in which you argue for or against the following proposition: "The rules of standard American English ought to be followed by all writers and speakers in our society." Again, use as many sources as you can from this section, as well as pertinent outside sources you find on your own.
3. In what ways can the language of one dominating culture affect the mental, physical, and psychological health of subordinate cultures? In order to answer this question, use three to five sources from this section. Feel free to use your own experiences with language as well.
4. Write a conversation that might take place between two of the authors in this section. The viewpoints do not necessarily have to be contrasting in order for this conversation to be effective. For example, you could pair up Gonzalez and Rodriguez. You could also pair up Farb and Gonzalez or Jones and Rodriguez.
5. Write an essay on sexism or racism in the language of advertising. Use examples from current ads and commercials, and point out the dangers of this language as several authors in this section would see it.
6. Compare the language in three different types of popular music today: perhaps a white country-western female singer, an urban black rapper, and a white rock idol. How do the lyrics, messages, and syntax relate to what the authors in this section have told us?
7. Evaluate one piece in this section from a rhetorical standpoint. What appeals does the writer use? What type of language does the writer use? What evidence is used? Does the writer address the opposing argument?

Is the organization effective? Is the writer fair-minded or biased to a certain degree? As a critic, what is your overall judgment of this piece from a rhetorical standpoint? Is the argument convincing? Explain.

8. Write an extended metaphor for how sexist or racist language affects those subjected to it. You may choose the format of an essay or a poem for this topic.

9. Considering your own observations and what you have discovered from the selections in this section, write a speech in which you convince local high school or college students that our language creates and maintains sexist myths. Propose several suggestions that may help alleviate this condition.

10. Examine several copies of local high school and college history texts. Are women and ethnic minorities denigrated in any way in these textbooks? Do the texts focus on the historical contributions and superiority of "white, Anglo-Saxon men"? Report on your findings.

11. Write an essay in which you examine, using the sources in this section, the power of a single word. In a cultural context, how powerful is language at the word level?

12. Write an essay in which you explore the various social pressures on children to conform to gender roles. By referring to sources in this section, discuss some of these outside forces and evaluate how they work. Feel free to include your own experiences as well.

13. Choose a racial, national, sexist, or religious insult and analyze the possible implications of this slur. See if you can discover where the term originated and how the term has changed in meaning today.

14. Can people from one culture ever really understand a person from a different culture? Rely on your own experience as well as the information in this section in order to answer this question.

15. Does what we say really reflect what we think? Write an essay in which you explore this question in terms of your own life and the lives of the authors you have met in this section.

16. Write a paper in which you examine how television comics and sitcom characters create humor from Jewish stereotypes. Is the humor harmless? What do you think about the humor? What would the authors in this section think?

17. Using the selections in this section, write an essay in which you synthesize what you have learned about language and prejudice.

Crossing Borders

Previews: CROSSING BORDERS

Since I left the American Civil Liberties Union six years ago I've worked for organizations that are concerned with human rights in various repressive countries. In these countries, whether they are in Central America or Africa or Eastern Europe or wherever, there is virtually no pornography; but there is a great deal of the same hostility toward women and the same violence against women that one finds in the United States.

From: *Pornography Here and Abroad*, ARYEH NEIER

The war on drugs is not going to be won on the streets of Karachi; Medellín, Colombia; or Mexico City. It can be won only on the streets of New York and Los Angeles. If we do not want to pay the costs of winning the war on drugs in America, there is no "there" where it can be won.

From: *U.S. Drug Policy; Colossal Ignorance*, LESTER C. THUROW

Americans see Arabs as desert bedouins in flowing robes. Such stereotypes do not make distinctions between rich and poor Arab countries, or between Arabs who have lived since the dawn of history on the banks of the rivers where they planted crops, and those who are desert nomads. American portrayals of Arabs take no account of the universities and research centers all over the Arab World, or of the programs of economic growth and social development there.

From: *The Arab's Image*, MUSTAFA NABIL

Experience whispers that the pity is not that we used the bomb to end the Japanese war but that it wasn't ready earlier to end the German one.

From: *Should Hiroshima Have Been Bombed?*, PAUL FUSSELL

The bombing of Hiroshima was an act of terrorism; its purpose was political, not military. The goal was to kill enough civilians to shake the Japanese government and force it to surrender. And this is the goal of every terrorist campaign.

From: *Hiroshima: An Act of Terrorism*, MICHAEL WALZER

ALICE BLOOM

On a Greek Holiday

> *Born in Belleville, Illinois, Alice Bloom now teaches English at the University of Maine, Farmington. This selection comes from her essay "On a Greek Holiday," which first appeared in* The Hudson Review *in 1983.*

Prereading/Journal-Writing Suggestions

1. If you could choose to go anywhere in the world for a three-week vacation, where would you go and how would you plan to spend those three weeks? Be as imaginative and as specific as you can be!
2. What's the difference between vacationing in another country and working there? Compare and contrast the possible benefits and experiences of these different approaches to being in a foreign country.

. . . I am unable to "go on a vacation." To borrow the parlance of travel ads, I don't go to "get away," I go to get into. In addition to following [one's] love — lovers of place being such a trustworthy sort, an enviable sort — one travels not to enjoy oneself, or to repeat oneself, or to cosset oneself, or — past a certain age — to find oneself, but to find the distinctly other. That other, that is there, and is loved. The only interesting question on a trip for me is — what sustains life elsewhere? How deep does it go? Can one see it? This hope, this anticipation, is forcibly blocked. Henry Miller, in 193–, stood in Epidaurus, alone, in a "weird solitude," and felt the "great heart of the world beat." We stand at Epidaurus with several thousand others, some of whom are being called "my chickens" by their tour guide who calls herself "your mother hen," whose counterpart, this time at Delphi, explains several times that what is being looked at is the "bellybutton of the world, okay? The Greeks thought, this is the bellybutton of the world, okay?" "These stones all look alike to me," someone grumbles. There is no help for it; we're there with guidebooks ourselves; but this fact — tourism is big business — and others, throw us back, unwilling, into contemplation of our own dull home-soul, our dull bodily comforts, our own dull dwindling purse, our own dull resentments; because the other — in this case, Greece — is either rapidly disappearing or else, self-protective, is retreating so far it has disappeared. You can get there, but you can't get at it.

For instance, a study of travel posters and brochures, which in the process of setting dates and buying tickets always precedes a trip, shows us, by projection into these pictured, toothy, tourist bodies, having some gorgeous piece of ingestion: the yellow beach, the mossy blue ruin, a dinner table laden with food and red wine of the region, dancing, skiing, golfing, shop-ping, waving to roadside natives as our rented car sails by, as though we only go to play, as though all we do here at home is work, as though, for two or four weeks abroad, we seek regression.

Also in the posters, but as part of the landscape, there are the natives — whether Spanish, Greek, Irish, etc. — costumed as attractions, performing in bouzouki or bag-pipe bands, or doing some picturesque and nonindustrial piece of work such as fishing, weaving, selling colorful cheap goods in open-air markets, herding sheep or goats. The journey promised by the posters and brochures is a trip into everyone's imaginary past: one's own, drained of the normal childhood content of fear, death, space, hurt, abandonment, perplex-ity, and so forth, now presented as the salesmen think we think it should have been: one in which we only ate, slept, and played in the eternal sun under the doting care of benevolent elders.

And we are shown the benevolent elders, the imaginary natives who also, for a handsome fee, exist now, in the present of the trip we are about to take. ("Take" is probably a more telling verb here than we think.) They exist in a past where they are pictured having grown cheerfully old and wise doing only harmless, enjoyable, pre-industrial, clean, self-employed, open-air work, in pink crinkled cheeks, merry eyes, and wonderful quaint clothes, with baskets, nets, toy-shaped boats, flower boxes, cottages, sheep crooks, country roads, whitewashed walls, tea shop signs, and other paraphernalia of the pastoral wish. I have never seen a travel poster showing natives of the country enjoying their own food or beaches or ski-jumps or hotel balconies; nor have I ever seen a travel poster showing the natives working the night-shift in the Citroën factory, either.

The natives in the posters (are they Swiss, Mexican, Chilean, Turkish 5 models?) are happy parent figures, or character dolls, and their faces, like the faces of the good parents we are supposed to have dreamed, show them pleased with their own lot, busy but not too busy with a job that they ob-viously like, content with each other, and warmly indulgent of our need to play, to be fed good, clean food on time, and to be tucked into a nice bed at the end of our little day. They are the childhood people that also existed in early grammar-school readers, and nowhere else: adults in your neighbor-hood, in the identifiable costumes of their humble tasks, transitional-object people, smiling milkman, friendly aproned store-owner in his small friendly store, happy mailman happy to bring your happy mail, happy mommy, icons who make up a six-year-old's school-enforced dream town, who enjoy doing their nonindustrial, unmysterious tasks: mail, milk, red apple, cooky, just for you, so you can learn to decipher: See, Jip, see.

A travel remark I have always savored came from someone surprised in love for a place, just returned from a month in the Far East (no longer tagged "the mysterious," I've noticed), and who was explaining this trip at a party. She said, "I just loved Japan. It was so authentic and Oriental." Few people would go quite so naked as that, but the charm of her feelings seemed just right. Perhaps she had expected Tokyo to be more or less a larger version of the Japanese Shop in the Tokyo Airport. It is somewhat surprising that she found it to be anything much more.

One of the hushed-tone moral superiority stories, the aren't-we-advanced stories told by those lucky enough to travel in Soviet Russia, has to do with that government's iron management of the trip. There are people who can't be met, buildings that can't be entered, upper story windows that can't be photographed, streets that can't be strolled, districts that can't be crossed, cities in which it is impossible to spend the night, and so on. However, our notions of who we are and what comforts we demand and what conditions we'll endure, plus any country's understandably garbled versions of who we are, what we want, and what we'll pay for, are far more rigid than the strictures of any politburo because such strictures don't say "This is you, this is what you must want," but "This is what you can't, under any circumstances, do." That, though it inhibits movement, and no doubt in some cases prevents a gathering of or understanding of some crucial or desired bit of information, has at least the large virtue of defining the tourist as potentially dangerous. What we meet most of the time, here and abroad, is a definition of ourselves as harmless, spoiled babies, of low endurance and little information, minimal curiosity, frozen in infancy, frozen in longing, terrified for our next square meal and clean bed, and whose only potential danger is that we might refuse to be separated from our money.

Suppose, for a moment, that tourism — the largest "industry" in Greece (it employs, even more than shipping, the most people) — were also the largest industry in America. Not just in Manhattan or Washington, D.C., or Disneyland or Disneyworld or at the Grand Canyon or Niagara Falls, but in every motel, hotel, restaurant, in every McDonald's and Colonel Sanders and Howard Johnson's and Mom & Pop's, in every bar and neighborhood hang-out, truck stop, gas station, pharmacy, department store, museum, church, historical site, battleground, in every taxi, bus, subway, train, plane, in every public building, in post offices and banks and public bathrooms, on every street in every city, town, village and hamlet from West Jonesport, Maine, to Centralia, Illinois, to Parachute, Colorado, and every stop in between and beyond, just as it is in Greece: tourists.

Suppose that every other business establishment across the country therefore found it in their best interest to become a souvenir shop, selling cheap, mass-produced "gifts" for the tourists to take back home that, back home, would announce that they had visited America. What images would we mass produce for them? Millions of little bronzed Liberty Bells? Tepees? St. Louis Arches? Streetcars named "Desire"? Statues of Babe Ruth? of Liberty? of Daniel Boone? In Greece we saw miniature bottles of ouzo encased in tiny plastic replicas of the temple of Athena Nike. Could we do something so clever, and immediately recognizable, with miniatures of bourbon? Encase them in tiny plastic Washington Monuments? Lincoln Memorials? Would we feel misrepresented?

Third, suppose that a sizable portion of these tourists wanting gifts, 10 toilets, rooms, baths, meals, dollars, film, drinks, stamps, directions, are Greek; or else, let us suppose that we assumed, that whether actually Greek or not, wherever they come from they speak Greek as a second language. Assume, therefore, that our map and traffic and road signs, postings of instruction and information, advertisements, timetables, directions — "stop," "go," "hot," "cold," "men," "women," "open," "closed," "yes," "no," — to name a few rudiments of life, plus all the menus in all those sandwich counters, truck stops, fast-food outlets, lunch rooms, and so forth, had to be in Greek as well as in English. We have never been, so far, an occupied country, whether by forces enemy or not. Undoubtedly, if we were, as an ongoing fact of our "in-season" summer months, we Americans, having to offer our multitudinous wares in Greek, would come up with items as hilarious as those we collected from the English side of Greek menus: baygon and egs. Xamberger steake. Veat. Orange juise. Rost beef. Shrimp carry. Potoes, Spaggeti. Morcoroni. And our favorite, Fried Smooth Hound. (This turned out to be a harmless local fish, much to the disappointment of our children, born surrealists.)

Suppose that we had to post Bar Harbor, Plum Island, Chincoteague, Key West, Bay St. Louis, Galveston, Big Sur and Seattle beaches with "No Nakedness Allowed" signs, but that the Greeks and other tourists, freed from the cocoons of air-conditioned tour buses, armed with sun-oil in every degree of protection, rushed beachwards past the signs and stripped to their altogether, anyway? Would our police sit quietly in the shade and drink with other men and turn, literally, their khaki-clad rumps to the beach, as did the Greek police?

And food. Suppose we had to contrive to feed them, these hungry hordes? They will come here, as we go there, entrenched in their habits and encumbered with fears of being cheated, fears of indigestion, of recurrent allergies, of breaking their diets, of catching American trots, of being poisoned by our water, fattened by our grease and starch, put off by our feeding schedules, sickened by something weird or local. Suppose we decided, out of some semiconscious, unorganized, but national canniness, that what these tourists really want is our cobbled version of their national foods. Whom will we please: the English who want their teas at four, or the Italians who want supper at nine at night? Or both? And what will we cook and serve, and how will we spell it?

Or suppose they want to eat "American" food. What tastes like us? What flavors contain our typicality, our history, our heroes, our dirt, our speeches, our poets, our battles, our national shames? The hot dog? Corn on the cob? I have eaten, barring picnics and occasional abstention, probably about 130 meals in Greece. And Greek food, I feel somewhat qualified to say, contains their history, and tastes of sorrow and triumph, of olive oil and blood, in about equal amounts. It is the most astounding and the most boring food that I, an eater, have ever eaten. . . .

Two women are walking towards us, at noon, across the nearly deserted rocks. Most of the other swimmers and sunbathers are up in the café, eating lunch under the fig trees, the grapevine. These two women are not together, they walk several feet apart, and they do not look at each other. One is tall and blond, dressed in a flowered bikini and clogs, a tourist, English or American or Scandinavian or German. The other woman, a Greek, is carrying a basket, walking quickly, and gives the impression of being on a neighborhood errand. She is probably from one of the small old farms — sheep, olive trees, hens, gardens, goats — that border this stretch of sea and climb a little way into the pine and cypress woods.

Both are smoking and both walk upright. Beyond that, there is so little 15 similarity they could belong to different planets, eras, species, sexes. The tourist looks young, the Greek looks old; actually, she looks as old as a village well and the blond looks like a drawn-out infant, but there could be as little as five or ten years difference between them.

The Greek woman is short and heavy, waistless, and is wearing a black dress, a black scarf pulled low around her eyes, a black sweater, thick black stockings, black shoes. She is stupendously there, black but for the walnut of her face, in the white sun, against the white space. She looks, at once, as if she could do everything she's ever done, anything needed, and also at once, she gives off an emanation of humor, powers, secrets, determinations, acts. She is moving straight ahead, like a moving church, a black peaked roof, a hot black hat, a dark tent, like a doom, a government, a force for good and evil, an ultimatum, a determined animal. She probably can't read, or write; she may never in her life have left this island; but she is beautiful, she could crush you, love you, mend you, deliver you of child or calf or lamb or illusion, bleed a pig, spear a fish, wring a supper's neck, till a field, coax an egg into life. Her sex is like a votive lamp flickering in a black, airless room. As she comes closer, she begins to crochet — that's what's in her basket, balls of cotton string and thick white lace coming off the hook and her brown fingers.

The blond tourist, struggling along the hot pebbles in her clogs, is coming back to her beach mat and friends. She looks as though she couldn't dress a doll without having a fit of sulks and throwing it down in a tantrum. It may not be the case, of course. She is on holiday, on this Greek island, which fact means both money and time. She is no doubt capable, well-meaning, and by the standards and expectations of most of the world's people, well-educated and very rich and very comfortable. She can undoubtedly read and write, most blond people can, and has, wherever she comes from, a vote, a voice, a degree of some kind, a job, a career perhaps, money certainly, opinions, friends, health, talents, habits, central heating, living relatives, personalized checks, a return ticket, a summer wardrobe, the usual bits and clamor we all, tourists, have. But presence, she has not. Nor authority, nor immediacy, nor joy for the eye, nor a look of adding to the world, not of strength nor humor nor excitement. Nearly naked, pretty, without discernible blemish, blond, tall, tan, firm, the product of red meat and whole milk, vitamins, orange juice, women's suffrage, freedom of religion, child labor laws, compulsory education, the anxious, dancing, lifelong attendance of uncounted numbers of furrow-browed adults, parents, teachers, pediatricians, orthodontists, counselors, hairdressers, diet and health and career and exercise and fashion consultants, still, she is not much to look at. She looks wonderful, but your eye, your heart, all in you that wants to look out on the substance of the people of the day, doesn't care, isn't interested long, is, in fact, diminished a little.

She could be anything — a professor of Romance Languages at a major university, a clerk in a Jermyn Street shop, a flight attendant, a Stockholm lawyer, but nothing shows of that life or luck or work or history, not world, not pain or freedom or sufficiency. What you think of, what her person walking towards you in the fierce noon light forces you to think of, after the momentary, automatic envy of her perfections, is that she looks as though she's never had enough — goods or rights or attention or half-decent days. Whether she is or not, she looks unutterably dissatisfied and peevish. And yet, in order to be here on this blue white beach on this July day, unless you are chasing your own stray goat across the rocks, requires a position of luxury, mobility, and privilege common to us but beyond any imagining of the Greek woman who walks here too with a basket of string and her hot, rusty clothes but who, however, and not at all paradoxically, exudes a deep, sustained bass note of slumbering, solid contentment.

Insofar as ignorance always makes a space, romance rushes in to people it. With so little fact at hand about either of these lives, fact which might make things plain and profound as only fact can do, there is little but romance, theories, guess work, and yet, it seems, this accidental conjunction of women in the sun, considered, says it is not a matter of the one, the blond, being discontent in spite of much and the other, the farm woman in black, being smugly, perhaps ignorantly content with little. That theory is too much the stuff of individual virtue, and of fairy tales: grateful peasant, happy with scraps and rags, and querulous, bitchy princess, untried, suffering every pea, pursued by frogs, awaiting a magic deliverance. Because in literal, daily fact, the Greek woman has more than the tourist, and the tourist, wherever she comes from and despite her list of equipment and privileges, is also, in literal daily fact, deprived. To see this as a possible deciphering of this scene means to stop thinking of the good life strictly in terms of goods, services, and various rights, and think instead, insofar as we can, of other, almost muted because so nearly lost to us, needs of life.

Beyond seeing that she has two arms, two good legs, a tanned skin, 20 blond hair and friends, I know nothing about this particular tourist. Beyond knowing that she has two arms, two good legs, a face that could stop or move an army, a black dress, and can crochet lace, I know nothing about this particular peasant woman. I don't even know, it's only a clumsy guess, that "peasant" should be the qualifying adjective. I can only talk about these women as they appeared, almost a mirage in the shimmer of beach heat, almost icons, for a moment and walked past; and as they are on an island where I, too, have spent a notch of time. Whatever the Greek woman, and her kind, has enjoyed or missed, has suffered or lost in war, under dictatorship, under occupation, from men, in poverty or plenty, I don't know. The other woman, I won't describe, won't further guess at, for she is familiar to us; she is us.

I don't know in what order of importance, should that order exist or be articulable, the Greek woman would place what occurs on the visible street of her life. For that is all I do see, all that we can see, and it wrings the heart, that visible street. For one thing, in most places, the street is not yet given over to the demands of the motor. The Greek is still a citizen and a large part of his day is given to whatever life goes on in public, and that life takes place on the street. Much of what we do in private, in isolation, in small personally chosen groups — eating, drinking, talking, staring into space — is, in Greece, done on the impersonal, random street. This habit of daily gathering, which is done for no particular reason, that is, there is no special occasion, lends to every day and night the feel of mild, but lively festival.

Second, among the other visible things that "underdeveloped" means, it means that — due either to a generous wisdom that has survived, or else funding that is not yet available — there is not enough money for the fit to invent shelters for the unfit. For whatever reasons, the Greek woman still lives in a culture where this has not yet happened. That is, not only are the streets used by and for people, but all sorts of people are on them, still privileged to their piece of the sun, the common bread, the work, the gossip, the ongoing parade. Our children are pitying and amazed. After several days on these streets they assume that in Greece there are more fat and slow and old, more crippled and maimed, more feeble of mind and body, more blind and begging, more, in general, outcast folks than we, Americans, have. They are especially amazed at how *old* people get to be in Greece. Being young and American, and not living in New York, the only city we have that approximates the fullness and variety of a village, they assume this is evidence of extreme longevity on the one hand, and evidence of extreme bad health on the other. It was as hard to explain about American nursing homes and other asylums and institutions as it was to explain about public nudity, how archaeologists find hidden ruins, and other questions that came up on the trip.

A "developed" country is seldom mysterious but always mystifying. Where do things come from and where do they go? Life can be looked at, but not often comprehended in any of its ordinary particulars: food, shelter, work, money, producing and buying and selling. The Greek woman on the beach, again for many reasons, does still live in a world that, in those particulars — food, shelter, work, product, etc. — is comprehensible. Outside the few urban, industrial areas in Greece, it is still possible to build and conduct life without the benefit of technicians, specialists, explainers, bureaucrats, middlemen, and other modern experts. This means that there is possible an understanding of, a connection with, and a lack of technological mystification to many of the elements, objects, and products commonly lived with in any day. A typical Greek house is so simple and cunning that it could be built, or destroyed, by almost anyone. This may mean less convenience, but it also means more comprehension. For the ordinary person, there is relatively little of the multiform, continual, hardly-much-thought-about incomprehensibility of daily things — where does this lamb chop come from? where does this wash water go? — that most people in developed countries live with, or manage to ignore, every day. Therefore, for this Greek woman on the beach and her kind, there is another mind possible, one which sees, and understands, and in most instances can control many details; and a mind in which, therefore, many mysteries can grow a deeper root.

Food, to take another example, is eaten in season and most of it is locally grown, harvested or butchered, processed, sold and consumed. There is no particular moral virtue in this fact, but this fact does signify the possibility of a sharper, more acute (it sees, it has to see and comprehend more details) and more satisfied intelligence. Having money means being able to buy the end product; therefore, money replaces the need for intricate knowledge of processes; therefore, money replaces knowledge. The understanding of a glass of water or wine, a melon, an onion, or a fried fish, from inception to end, does mean living with a different kind of mind than the one which results from having merely bought and consumed the wine or fish or onion at the end. In that sense, therefore, it is possible that the unhappy peevishness and dissatisfaction on the face of the pretty tourist comes in part from a life of being left out of knowledge of the intricate details of the complete cycle of any single thing she is able to consume.

Including the country of Greece.   25

There is a new world everywhere now that money will buy. It is a world without a nation, though it exists as an overlay of life, something on the order of the computer, in almost any country of the globe. It is an international accommodation, and wherever it exists — whether in Madrid, London, Istanbul, Athens, Cleveland — it resembles a large airport lounge. In this way, the new world specially constructed everywhere for tourists is something like the thousands of Greek churches, as alike as eggs, and no matter what their size all modeled on the single great discovered design of Constantine's Hagia Sophia.

Inside this international accommodation is allowed only so much of any specific country as lends itself as background, decor, and trinkets. In this sense, the travel posters are an accurate portrayal of exactly how little can happen on a well-engineered trip: scenery and "gifts." Because most of the world is still what would be termed "poor," the more money you can spend, nearly any place, the more you are removed from the rich, complex life of that place. It is possible to buy everything that puts an average American life — taps that mix hot and cold, flush toilets, heating and cooling systems, menus in English — on top of any other existing world. It is possible to pay for every familiar security and comfort and, as the posters show, still have been *there* having it. At the end of the trip, you can say that you were there.

However, the extent to which one buys familiarity, in most of the world today, is also the extent to which one will not see, smell, taste, feel, or in any way be subjected to, enlightened by, or entered by that piece of the world and its people. The world's people are not blind to this fear of the unfamiliar and uncomfortable, nor insensitive to the dollars that will be paid to ward it off. In the winter months, when life returns to normal, the friendly Greek "waiters" resume their lives as masons, carpenters, builders, mechanics, schoolteachers, and so forth, a fact unknown to or overlooked by many tourists who assume, for example, that many unfinished buildings, seen languishing in the summer season, are due to neglect, laziness, disinterest, or what have you.

We all assume, and usually safely, that the more money you have the more you can buy. In travel, however, the opposite is true. The less money you spend, the less money you have to spend, perhaps, the more your chances of getting a whiff, now and then, of what another place is like. There are the ideals: walking a country, living there, learning its language. Short of that, those conditions which most of us cannot meet, one can try spending as little as possible: class D hotels, public transportation, street meals. And then one must try to be as brave and patient and good-humored and healthy as possible because, without a doubt, the less money you spend the closer you come to partaking of very annoying, confusing, exhausting, foreign, debilitating, sometimes outrageous discomfort.

For instance, the two things one would most want to avoid in Greece in 30 the summer are the intense heat and the unworldly, unimaginable, unforeseeable amount of din. Pandemonium is, after all, a Greek idea, but in actual life, it is hardly confined to the hour of noon. Silence is a vacuum into which, like proverbial nature, a single Greek will rush with a pure love of noise. Two Greeks together produce more noise than 200 of any other Western nation. Greeks love above all else the human voice, raised in any emotion; next to that they love their actions with objects. One Greek with any object — a string of beads, a two-cylinder engine, preferably one on the eternal blink, a rug to beat, a single child to mind, a chair to be moved — will fill all time and space with his operation; it will be the Platonic scrape of metal chair leg on stone street; it will be the one explanation to last for all eternity why the child should not torture the cat in the garden. A generalization: Greeks love horns, bells, animal cries, arguments, dented fenders, lengthy explanations, soccer games, small motors, pots and pans, cases of empty bottles, vehicles without mufflers, cups against saucers, fireworks, political songs, metal awnings, loudspeakers, musical instruments, grandmothers, the Orthodox liturgy, traffic jams, the sound of breaking glass, and Mercedes taxi cabs that tootle "Mary Had A Little Lamb."

A further generalization: the above generalization is one that only *not* spending money will buy. That is, you have to be in a class F room, in a hotel on the harbor, one flight above a taverna frequented by fishermen, 120 degrees in the room, no screens, mosquito coils burning in the unmoving air through the night, and through the night—a donkey in heat tethered in the walled garden below your shuttered, only shuttered, window. In other words, it's quiet, and cool, at the Hilton; and there are, God and international capitalism be thanked, no donkeys.

Suggestions for Writing and Discussion

1. In this piece, what exactly is Bloom advocating? Would you say she is writing this piece to persuade others to her point of view or for some other reason? Explain your answer.

2. What might Bloom's reason be for dedicating so much of the beginning of this piece to the description of travel posters? What does this section accomplish?

3. In great detail, Bloom focuses on the Greek peasant woman and the young visiting beachcomber. What inferences can you draw about American values and behaviors from these comparisons?

4. At the end of this comparison section, Bloom surmises that the young blonde woman is really an image of Americans. As she says, "She is us." Do you believe that this conclusion and the implications inherent here are justified? Argue for or against Bloom's view, supporting your response with specific evidence from your own experiences and observations.

5. What exactly does Bloom mean by the "simple" life? What does she mean by the "complex" life? After defining these terms, explain which you would use to characterize your own life right now.

6. Although Bloom doesn't come out and state it directly, she does allude to a philosophy that defines the basic source of human happiness. In a sentence, state in your own words what Bloom believes this source of happiness to be. In another sentence, describe the source of happiness for your own life.

7. Why, according to Bloom, do so many people tend to search out "international accommodations" in foreign countries? Do you agree with her reasoning here? Can you supply any other possibilities to explain this tendency?

Suggestions for Extended Thinking and Research

1. Interview students on campus who have had the opportunity to visit another country. Ask questions that will clarify their preferences and be-

haviors in a foreign country. If you have traveled in other countries, include your perceptions about your own preferences and behaviors. Then write an essay, drawing your own conclusions about Americans and vacations in foreign lands. Certainly feel free to refer to any points Bloom makes in her piece as well.

2. As a variation of suggestion 1, interview several travel agents to discover what most people ask for when they are planning to vacation out of the country. Do their responses support Bloom's allegations?

3. Write an essay about your own experiences vacationing in a foreign country. What approach did you take? Why did you go there? What did you learn? In retrospect, what would you do differently? What conclusions can you draw about yourself as a "vacationer"? As Bloom does in this piece, concentrate on using rich and vivid details — take the reader back with you to this experience.

ARYEH NEIER

Pornography Here and Abroad

> *Aryeh Neier has served as national executive director of the American Civil Liberties Union and currently works on the Human Rights Watch. His observations on pornography first appeared as part of the* Harper's *magazine forum in November 1984.*

Prereading/Journal-Writing Suggestions

1. How would you define *pornography*? On the basis of this definition, what specifically, in America today, would you categorize as being "pornographic"?
2. Why do you think there is a market for pornographic materials in America today? Do you see this market as being harmful? Freewrite about your reactions to pornography in terms of American society.

For a good many years, I confronted the issue of pornography as a civil libertarian, defending the right of anyone to express himself in any way he chose as long as he did not directly infringe on the rights of others. Since I left the American Civil Liberties Union six years ago I've worked for organizations that are concerned with human rights in various repressive countries. In these countries, whether they are in Central America or Africa or Eastern Europe or wherever, there is virtually no pornography; but there is a great deal of the same hostility toward women and the same violence against women that one finds in the United States. In fact, in many of these countries sexual violence — mass rape or sexual torture or sexual humiliation — is one of the main forms political repression takes. I conclude from the astounding level of sexual violence in these countries and the absence of pornography that pornography is really not very important, that it is no more or less important than the great variety of images that dominates the media in the United States and other Western countries: images of sex and violence and melodrama and ugliness and beauty.

I suppose there is so much pornography because, like the nightly melodramas on television, pornography is not very satisfying stuff; one seeks satisfaction by exposing oneself to more and more and more of it. Obviously, improvements in the technology involved in producing and distributing pornography contribute to the growing quantity of it. But more important is the fact that no particular pornographic image in Mr. Goldstein's magazine, or 100 or 1,000 other magazines, or 1,000 movies or live shows or whatever, means a great deal to the viewer. Thus he needs more and more images. In much the same way, one exposes oneself to a vast number of violent images or a vast number of melodramatic plots because none of them amounts to a great deal. What is really important about the surfeit of pornographic images is that it reflects one side of a society that is spoiled by too much of everything, including violent images of all sorts.

Suggestions for Writing and Discussion

1. In a sentence, summarize Neier's main point regarding pornography.
2. Neier writes that "there is so much pornography because . . . [it] is not very satisfying stuff." What's your reaction to this logic? Do you agree or disagree? Or are you not sure? Explain.
3. Do you believe there is a connection between pornography and violence? What connection do you see between pornography and a society's attitude toward women? How might these connections suggest Neier's definition of pornography?
4. Neier writes that pornography "reflects one side of a society that is spoiled by too much of everything, including violent images of all sorts." What else might pornography reflect about a society, specifically, American society?
5. According to Neier, pornography does not cause violence to women because in many cultures where pornography does not exist, there is still a great deal of violence against women. Do you accept this reasoning? If so, why? If not, how would you respond to Neier's logic?

Suggestions for Extended Thinking and Research

1. Most of Neier's position is based on his experiences in Western cultures. Research the effects of pornography in Eastern countries such as Japan or China. Can you find any evidence to support or refute Neier's claims that pornography is "really not very important"?
2. Find an article that argues against Neier's views on American society and pornography. Write a dialogue between Neier and the author of this article.

MARTIN ESSLIN

Beyond the Wasteland: What American TV Can Learn from the BBC

> *A professor of drama at Stanford University, Martin Esslin has written widely on the role of television in modern society. Versions of this article appear both in Esslin's 1982 book* The Age of Television *and in the* Boston Review, *a journal sponsored by the National Endowment for the Humanities*

Prereading/Journal-Writing Suggestions

1. Freewrite about your principal television and radio viewing and listening patterns. In other words, consider when you watch television or listen to the radio, why you do these things, and what effects these media have on you. What conclusions can you draw about yourself in relation to these forms of communication?

2. Imagine that you are in charge of the television programs in your area for one entire week. You can pick whatever kinds of shows you want to be broadcast. What types of shows do you pick, and how do you think the general public will respond to this week of television?

The invention of the printing press greatly increased man's capacity to communicate: information, facts, ideas, and opinions could be made available to far larger numbers of people at far lower costs than in previous epochs, when books had to be produced by scribes laboriously copying old manuscripts. It took a long time for the principle of freedom of the press to become established, however. Once this right was won in the more advanced countries of the Western world, this freedom became virtually limitless: almost anyone could get his ideas printed and distributed at relatively little expense. When the electronic mass media came into existence, they further enhanced mankind's capacity to communicate to even greater numbers at even greater speed. But they also presented a new and complex problem: there were only a limited number of channels available on the airwaves. If their number were increased above a certain limit, or their range increased by additional power, they would inevitably interfere with one another, there would be chaos, and the media's capacity to spread information and entertainment would break down altogether.

From the outset, the necessity of government control of the distribution of wavelengths and strength of broadcasting stations and the limitation of the number of stations created a problem for free speech and expression over the open airwaves. There could be as many printed forms of communication as anyone wanted, but only a limited number of outlets for broadcast communication. To whom should that privilege be given? And once those fortunate enough to be allocated such a channel of communication began to broadcast, how were they to finance their programs? Broadcasts could be received at no charge by anyone with a set; they could not be sold individually to each recipient as could a newspaper, pamphlet, or book.

In the infancy of radio the manufacturers of radio sets provided the programs at their own expense. They could not hope to sell their product unless they supplied something to be heard on the wonderful new contraptions. But after a while, when the thrill of hearing someone play a piano a hundred miles away had worn off, the public demanded more elaborate programming. And fulfilling that demand became ever more expensive.

Ways had to be found to finance the running and programming of radio stations. It is here that different solutions were found in Europe and in America.

In the United States every radio and television station has to be licensed   5 by the Federal Communications Commission (FCC). Established by Congress in 1934, and headed by seven commissioners appointed by the president with the consent of the Senate, the FCC is empowered to regulate all interstate and foreign communication by wire and radio, including telegraph, telephone, and broadcast. In this respect radio and television are as much under government control in the United States as they are elsewhere.

In Britain the manufacturers of radio sets joined together to form the British Broadcasting Company, which began daily transmissions in November 1922. From the very beginning all listeners operating a radio set had to obtain a "broadcasting receiving license" (analogous to the license to operate a car in the United States and in most other countries). The license fee initially amounted to ten shillings (at that time two dollars) per annum. The general manager of the company was a young Scotsman, John Reith, the son of a clergyman, a brilliant administrator, and a person of the sternest moral fiber. Reith believed that this powerful new instrument for informing, educating, and entertaining the masses should be managed in the public interest, independent of interference from the state or business. To meet this requirement John (later Sir John, and later still Lord) Reith invented a new kind of public body: an organization established by the state but independent of it in its daily operation, and financed directly by its users through the license fee. On January 1, 1927, the new British Broadcasting *Corporation* was set up under a royal charter, originally designed to run for ten years and to be renewable by Parliament at regular intervals thereafter.

How was the BBC's independence from government interference to be achieved? The corporation is controlled by a board of governors who are appointed by the queen for five-year terms of office. Their number has varied over the years — it is twelve at present. The BBC's charter stipulates that there must be at least one governor for each of the three non-English nations of the United Kingdom: Scotland, Wales, and Northern Ireland; and it has also become a practice that among the rest of the board there are always governors representative of the trade unions, business, women, the academic world, and the arts. Once appointed, the board of governors, under its chairman, is sovereign in its responsibility over the corporation. It is empowered to use the license fee according to its own judgment and to appoint the chief executive of the corporation, the director general. The executive function of the board of governors stops here: it is not meant to interfere in the daily operation of the administration and of the programs on radio and television. The royal charter also forbids the BBC to raise any revenue by advertising.

The board of governors has to ensure that the BBC remains wholly impartial in political matters. A balance must be maintained in the presentation of all responsible political views. During periods of general election campaigns the BBC has to allocate an agreed number of time slots for election broadcasts, which are provided by the political parties themselves and remain strictly outside the editorial control of the corporation (which, however, can be asked to furnish technical assistance in the form of studios, microphones, cameras, etc.). Between elections, similarly, there is an agreed number of "party political broadcasts" determined in a meeting of representatives of all the political parties in Parliament and on the basis of their strength in that body.

The royal charter of the BBC expressly specifies that the objective of the corporation is to disseminate "information, education and entertainment" — in that very significant order. The BBC thus regards itself as a public service with an important cultural and social role to play in the society.

The fixed license fee, which provided an ever-increasing and secure 10 income while the number of radio sets continued to grow at leaps and bounds in the 1920s and 1930s, allowed the BBC to experiment not only in programming but also in technical innovation. It was the BBC that started the first regular daily television service in the world in 1936. To finance this fledgling TV service a television license fee was introduced. And as the number of television sets grew to saturation point, the radio license fee was abolished. Today some nineteen million British households pay a license fee amounting to some $90 for a color set, about $45 for a black-and-white set each year. That is to say, television costs the British household less than $2 per week for a color set, less than $1 for a black-and-white set. Compare this with the cost of television in the United States: in 1978 total revenues of all commercial stations in the United States amounted to some $7 billion; if one divides this sum by the roughly sixty million households in the country, the annual cost of television per household, which must come out of prices paid in the marketplace, also amounts to about $115 — roughly $2.20 per week. The difference is that the BBC provides a service free from advertising and offering a much wider spectrum of programs.

The BBC as created by Reith became the model for most broadcasting organizations in Europe. Although commercial stations have also been licensed in most European countries (in Britain, for example, commercial television was introduced in 1954) and although some of the public broadcasting corporations in countries like France or Germany take a limited amount of advertising, the bulk of broadcasting expenses in Europe is still borne by the public broadcasting services. (In the Soviet-controlled parts of Europe, of course, all broadcasting is strictly government-run and controlled and merely an instrument of state propaganda.)

In the United States the development of broadcasting followed a completely different pattern. It may well have been a mere accident of history that there happened to be no equivalent to John Reith in America and that the problem of who should pay for the programming on radio stations was solved — on the analogy of the daily press — by the sale of advertising time on the air.

The situation in the United States was also basically different from that in Europe in that the vast size of the United States made it much more difficult to develop a centralized broadcasting service for the whole country. The great distances between the major centers of population favored a much more localized approach. In the smaller countries of Europe there was less scope for local stations that would not interfere with one another (at least with the state of technology as it existed in the 1920s and 1930s, before the advent of FM). In the United States it was possible to allocate a large number of relatively low powered stations to each major center of population. Nevertheless in radio — and later in television — a system of networking of the more ambitious program material had to develop simply because of the immense costs involved with producing high-standard programming, particularly in television. The U.S. system that evolved thus incorporated a considerable amount of local autonomy within a basic structure of three commercial networks financed entirely by advertising revenues.

So it came about that television in America became, in effect, a branch of the advertising industry. Whatever other qualities TV programs possess, they contribute to one basic purpose: to fill the gaps between advertisements, to induce people to turn on their sets so that they will see the advertisements. In his *New Yorker* profile of Johnny Carson, written in 1979, Kenneth Tynan quoted Carson as saying: "If you are selling hard goods — like soap or dog food — you simply can't afford to put on culture." One cannot put it more clearly or succinctly than that.

American commercial television, in generating enormous sums of 15 money through advertising, has been immensely successful in producing programs of high technical quality and the widest popular appeal–not only within the United States but worldwide. However, it has effectively abdicated any positive cultural function. The FCC, under its charter, is charged with the responsibility of interpreting "the public interest" in broadcasting. It also is empowered to remove broadcasting licenses from stations that have "demonstrably failed to serve the public interest, convenience or necessity." But in practice these powers are hardly ever exercised. The concept of the public interest remains exceedingly vague and is rarely interpreted as meaning more than the provision of news, public announcements, or the granting of air time to spokesmen of various political bodies or pressure groups.

The deficiencies of this state of affairs, which in 1961 the then-chairman of the FCC, Newton Minow, described as "the vast wasteland" of commercial television, were recognized officially by the establishment of the Public Broadcasting Service (PBS) through the Public Broadcasting Act, which became law in 1967. The PBS evolved out of the educational broadcasting stations that had tried to fill the arid stretches of the cultural wasteland in the 1950s. The PBS is, in effect, an alliance of local community and educational stations financed by grants from the Corporation for Public Broadcasting, also established by the 1967 Act, and supplemented by grants from the National Endowments for the Humanities and the Arts, funds from university sources, public subscriptions, and donations from big corporations that regard sponsorship of culturally respectable programs as a form of discreet prestige advertising. Thus, while in theory there is no advertising on PBS, there is frequent mention of sponsoring corporations' names; and, in addition, the stations have to devote considerable time to soliciting voluntary subscriptions and gifts from their public. This necessitates frequent intrusions analogous to the commercials on the big networks, and emphasizes the dire financial straits public broadcasting has been in since its inception.

The congressional appropriation for public television through the Corporation for Public Broadcasting was set at $162 million for 1981. The appropriation proposed for the CPB in President Reagan's budget for 1982 was only about 75 percent of that sum. The total annual revenue of public broadcasting (television *and radio*) amounted to about $600 million in 1979. This compares with a total advertising revenue of commercial television and radio of more than *$12 billion* in the same year — that is to say, commercial broadcasting was more than twenty times richer than public sector broadcasting.

Paucity of financial resources — basically crippling as it is — is by no means the only organizational weakness of the PBS. Its decentralized structure makes genuine networking of programs very difficult and thus deprives public TV of the great advantages of national publicity. Under this decentralized method of programming, initiating a new series entails a lengthy and cumbersome process by which a sufficient number of stations must be convinced to support such projects in advance. In the big public television organizations of Europe decisions of this nature can be swiftly and efficiently taken at the center. There are considerable advantages in size and concentration in television — as, indeed, is the case in the closely related film industry.

What are the advantages and disadvantages of a public TV service as compared to a completely commercial system? One of the dangers inherent in a public service system is paternalism: some authority decides what the viewers should see and hear simply on the basis of what it arbitrarily feels would be good for them. Yet in countries where a highly developed public system exists alongside a commercial one, that danger is minimized because of the market pressure on the commercial system to give its audience what it wants. Indeed, in a dual system the danger is often that the public service may be tempted to ignore its stated purpose to serve the public interest and instead pander to mass preferences because of a sense of competition with the commercial networks.

Another problem that plagues public TV service is that it may run short [20] of money, which in turn can increase its dependence on the government. The extent of government dependence is intimately connected to how the public broadcasting service is financed. In West Germany and Italy, for example, the public broadcasting service takes advertising, but it is usually confined to a clearly delimited area of the network's programming. In Britain the BBC, as noted, relies entirely on its annual license fee, which guarantees it a steady income and allows long-term planning. In periods of severe inflation, the license-fee system leaves the BBC in a dangerous position vis-a-vis the government, and the network's income may decline in real terms. In countries where the public broadcasting service is financed by an annual allocation in the national budget, long-term planning becomes more difficult and the dependence on the government is far greater. Nevertheless public TV services financed on that pattern, such as the ABC in Australia and the CBC in Canada, provide programs of high quality that are genuine alternatives to the fare on the numerous popular and prosperous commercial networks. In Canada, this includes programs from the three commercial American networks.

One of the most important positive features of services under public control is their ability to provide planned, high-quality viewing alternatives. The BBC, for example, has two television channels, BBC 1 and BBC 2. The program planning on these two networks is closely coordinated so that highly popular material on one channel is regularly paired with more specialized or demanding fare on the other. And though the percentage of the audience that tunes in to the challenging programming may be small, the scale of magnitude operative in the mass media is such that even a small percentage of the viewing audience represents a very large number of people indeed. A popular dramatic series on BBC 1, for instance, may reach an audience of 20 percent of the adult population of Britain—about ten million people. A play by Shakespeare on BBC 2 that may attract an audience of only 5 percent nonetheless reaches about two-and-a-half million people—a substantial audience for a work of art. It would take a theater with a seating capacity of 1,000 about seven years, or 2,500 performances, to reach an equivalent number of people! Nor should it be overlooked that this audience will include people whose influence may be greater in the long run than that of the ten million who watched the entertainment program. In this system, no segment of the viewing public is forced to compromise with any other. In our example, not only did BBC 1 provide a popular entertainment program as an alternative to the

Shakespeare, but, in addition, the commercial network offered still another popular program. By careful — perhaps paternalistic — planning the general audience satisfaction was substantially increased.

One of the difficulties of the American situation is that the size of the United States favors decentralization and the fragmentation of initiatives for the more ambitious programming of the public service network. A revitalized PBS would need a strong central governing body that could allocate to local producing stations the substantial sums of money they require for ambitious projects — projects that could compete with the best offerings of the rich commercial competitors.

Using existing satellite technology, such a truly national network of public service television could be made available to the entire country. If a public service television organization was able to provide simultaneous, alternative programming along the lines of BBC 1 and BBC 2, the cultural role of television in the United States could be radically improved, and the most powerful communication medium in history could realize its positive potential to inform, educate, and provide exposure to diverse cultural ideas.

Is such a solution within the realm of practical possibility, or is it pure fantasy? To me, one of the most astonishing aspects of the American scene is its parochialism about its broadcasting system. Commercial television, with all its faults, is regarded by otherwise enlightened and responsible citizens almost as part of the natural order of things, so that the very idea of an alternative does not even surface. Yet just a glance across the borders of the United States into Canada reveals the possibility of a system that, though far from perfect, is in many ways preferable. British visitors to the United States are regularly surprised to be asked, and with great frequency, "Why is British TV so good?" This question almost seems to spring from a conviction that some undefinable sensibility is found on that little island that is beyond the grasp of the United States. Taking into account the great resources and talents of Americans, the reality is that a more rational method of financing programs that aim for artistic respectability would probably produce superior results equivalent to the best of British television. The American cinema, after all, has produced first-rate and highly artistic entertainment for decades.

There remains always this vexing question of financing such a public service: assuming that one advocates an annual TV license fee or an excise tax, why should people who don't want to watch certain types of programs be required to pay for them? Yet people who do not have children pay taxes that finance public schools and universities; people who do not visit museums pay for them through their taxes. The question, then, becomes: is a rationally structured mass communications service — radio as well as TV — as vital to the well-being of the nation as are libraries, museums, schools, and universities?

The answer to me seems beyond doubt. The absence of an adequately funded public television service in the United States in an age when other nations are in a position to make much fuller use of the positive potential of so powerful a medium amounts to no less than a national tragedy. To say that nothing can be done about the status quo and act as if it is a fact of life that television should continue to be geared to the intellectual level of a twelve-year-old child is a mixture of abject defeatism and dispirited complacency. In a democracy there are vast possibilities when enough people of intelligence and determination become convinced that changes are necessary — and take the initiative to make those changes.

And this is the crux of the matter: if it is realized that the present condition of the mass communication media in the United States constitutes a calamitous deficiency and might well entail very real dangers for the future economic well-being as well as cultural creativity and general standing of the nation, then surely there is a case for doing something about it. I find it deeply depressing that Lawrence Lichty, the author of a thoughtful and concerned article on the state of television in America, "Success Story," in the Winter 1981 issue of the prestigious *Wilson Quarterly,* can say about this matter:

> One still reads, from time to time, laments in the press or in academic journals about what television "could have been," as if it could have been any different than what it actually became. Its future, as a mass marketing tool, was determined well before its birth, in a very Darwinian sense. A fish cannot fly; it swims.

This strikes me not only as false because highly parochial — radio and television did become different elsewhere — but also as horrifyingly defeatist. Had the same attitude been taken about slavery, civil rights, the status of women, we would still have slaves, still have segregation in hotels, restaurants, and buses, still have women as chattels of their husbands or fathers. Surely the essence of a democracy lies in its ability to change conditions that have been recognized as immoral, harmful, or degrading. What is essential is the will to effect such a change and the determination to make the masses of the people — who are in the last analysis capable of intelligent and wise insights — realize the need for such change. The wasteland of television is not an unalterable feature of the American landscape. It is man-made and therefore not beyond the range of determined social and political action.

Suggestions for Writing and Discussion

1. List the new ideas and new information you gained from reading this piece. Then freewrite for ten minutes or so, describing your responses to what you discovered.
2. Explain in your own words the differences Esslin sees between American television networking and the BBC.
3. Analyze the first paragraph of this piece in terms of the author's tone, purpose, and audience. Then analyze the last paragraph for the same elements. How do you account for shifts in tone, purpose, or audience?
4. Some writers choose to save their strongest argument until last. Examine

Esslin's final point and comment on its effectiveness in terms of his audience. Has he, in your opinion, saved his most effective argument for his conclusion?

5. A good argument often considers the points of view from the opposing position. Find two places in this piece where Esslin raises the opposition's points, and analyze the effectiveness of his rebuttal.

6. In what ways might the American television system reflect cultural values within our country?

7. Esslin writes that the BBC's objectives are to give "information, education, and entertainment—in that very significant order." Choose two American television networks and describe what you see as the objectives of those networks. Do you see these networks as nearly the same, or do you see significant differences? What do your discoveries suggest about the priorities of these networks?

Suggestions for Extended Thinking and Research

1. Write an essay in which you argue for or against the premise that entertainment is—and should be—the main priority of American television.

2. Write an essay that evaluates the differences between a popular network sitcom and a weekly (or series) comedy program on your public television channel. Describe the differences you see, and explain what those differences suggest about the audience to whom these programs are intended to appeal.

3. Write an essay in which you attempt to persuade your audience to support public television programming (or the reverse—to support private network television).

LESTER C. THUROW

U.S. Drug Policy: Colossal Ignorance

> *Lester C. Thurow is Professor of Economics and dean of the Sloan School of Management at the Massachusetts Institute of Technology. "U.S. Drug Policy: Colossal Ignorance" was first published in the* New York Times *in 1988.*

Prereading/Journal-Writing Suggestions

1. Freewrite in your journal about several possible causes for the drug problem in America today. After ten minutes of writing on this topic, state what you think is at the heart of the problem with drugs in our country.
2. If you were in charge of ridding your local high school of drugs, where would you start and whose help would you enlist? Why do you believe these strategies would be effective?

The United States' war on drugs has recently led to the attempted ouster of Panama's military leader, the virtual kidnapping of a Honduran, new efforts to burn crops in Bolivia and a proposed Congressional resolution accusing Mexican officials of accepting bribes. Only a short time ago, similar actions were directed at Pakistan, Colombia, Peru, Turkey, and Thailand.

Before we further damage our foreign relations, we should admit the failure of efforts to interdict drug supplies abroad and focus instead on reducing demand for drugs at home.

The current approach has led us to demand actions of others that we would not for a moment tolerate if asked of us. Consider what we would do if a foreign government kidnapped one of our citizens or if its parliament passed a resolution accusing us of complicity with drug dealers.

Moreover, we reject mobilization of our police and armed forces to interdict drugs at American borders, because it would create too much of a temptation for American officials. Yet opportunities for corruption that are unacceptable here are apparently considered acceptable "over there."

Those running our war on drugs understand neither economics nor history nor foreign cultures. Their economic ignorance is colossal. Drug sellers face what in the jargon of the economics profession is known as an inelastic demand curve. This means that if supplies are cut back by 10 percent, prices rise by more than 10 percent, leaving the seller with higher profits than before the cutback.

If our goal is to deprive criminals of large profits from selling drugs, economic theory and history teach us that legalization is the only answer. When liquor sales were legalized after Prohibition, criminals left the bootleg liquor industry because the huge profits available while the government was attempting to stop liquor sales vanished.

We may not wish to legalize drug use. By making it illegal, we make a statement that society has concluded that drug use is not in the self-interest of the individual and the nation. But if we do not legalize products for which there is a huge demand, profits will remain enormous and suppliers will always come forward. Individual sellers can be arrested, but others will take their place.

Viewed from the perspective of a foreign country such as Pakistan, where I once worked as a development economist, United States antidrug policies are simply arrogant. In many places, local peasant families have grown marijuana, coca, or opium for hundreds of years. Suddenly they are ordered not to grow what they have always grown.

Americans would never accede to such a request. Suppose some foreign government asked us to suppress tobacco farmers (perhaps burn their fields) to improve public health?

Not surprisingly, foreign peasants, knowing nothing of our drug prob-   10
lem, expand their production. Sales of drug crops are the best and perhaps the only way to escape generations of poverty. Drug merchants even become local heroes, as seen in Honduras when Washington obtained the extradition of Juan Ramon Matta, a purported drug trafficker.

Americans cannot persuade fellow citizens to quit using drugs, yet we order foreign governments to stop their peasants from growing them. Not surprisingly, they cannot. Their peasants fight back. Military force must be used. Foreign governments either end up losing control of their own country-sides or must begin shooting at their own citizens.

When foreign governments crack down on drug suppliers at America's request, drug suppliers have to start bribing local officials to get their supplies out of the country. Without the enormous profits that have been generated in the United States, such bribes could not be paid.

Who is to be blamed — the Mexicans who take those bribes or the Amer-icans whose purchases make those bribes possible? What is needed is a demand-side solution in the United States, not a supply-side solution in the rest of the world.

Industries disappear only when the demand for their products disappear. The effort to stop drugs has to focus on the user, not the supplier. It involves education programs to prevent addiction, the arrest and incarceration of all users and changes in the social environment of the poor who buy heroin and the rich who buy cocaine. However difficult, all possible solutions lie on the demand side.

A demand-side solution would be expensive. Jailing buyers, educating   15
addicts, and changing the conditions that lead to pathological behavior — none of these are cheap. But effective interdiction of drugs at our borders would require an enormous army of guards. Foreign interdiction is often advocated as a cheap alternative to expensive, politically divisive policies at home, but that view is a mirage.

The war on drugs is not going to be won on the streets of Karachi; Medellín, Colombia; or Mexico City. It can be won only on the streets of

New York and Los Angeles. If we do not want to pay the costs of winning the war on drugs in America, there is no "there" where it can be won.

Suggestions for Writing and Discussion

1. Evaluate the tone and voice Thurow uses in this piece. From your evaluation of these elements, what is your impression of the author? What type of a person is he? As a reader, how do you see your relationship with him?
2. In your own words, describe Thurow's bottom-line rationale for legalizing drugs in this country.
3. Thurow compares Pakistan's crop growers to America's tobacco growers. How effective do you find this comparison? Can you come up with another comparison that might get the point across just as effectively?
4. Which of Thurow's points are most convincing to you, the reader? Evaluate why you think these points are so effective.
5. What points would you like the author to support more fully? What points would you like to argue with the author? Explain your reasons.
6. Analyze the three solutions that Thurow proposes in terms of focusing on the drug user. How practical do you find these solutions? Can you offer any better solutions in terms of the user?
7. If Thurow were running for the United States drug commissioner, would you support his candidacy wholeheartedly, campaign zealously against his appointment, or remain neutral? Explain your decision as clearly and precisely as you can.

Suggestions for Extended Thinking and Research

1. Find another essay on this same topic with the intent of comparing and contrasting not only the authors' positions but also the argumentative elements found within each: appeal, tone, voice, purpose, organization, style.
2. Write an essay in rebuttal to Thurow's. As a fair-minded person, be sure to acknowledge any strong points Thurow makes and give adequate support for your opposing points of argument.

MUSTAFA NABIL

The Arabs' Image

> *Mustafa Nabil's article was originally published in* Al Mussawar, *a weekly newsmagazine in Cairo, Egypt. This excerpt first appeared in* World Press Review *in June 1986.*

Prereading/Journal-Writing Suggestions

1. What images of Arab culture do you have from such sources as childhood stories, fictional films, and fictional television programs? If you were to visit a country in the Arab world today, which of these images do you believe you would find reinforced? Which do you believe you would find contradicted?
2. What memories do you have of your own responses and of the responses of people you know to Arab countries and Arab-Americans during the Gulf War and its aftermath?

Arab Americans are mounting a campaign against the anti-Arab bias of the American media and of American society at large. Leading the protest are the Society of Arab Americans, founded in 1972, and the American-Arab Anti-Discrimination Committee, formed in 1980. The Arab-Israeli conflict and the oil crisis of the 1970s have exacerbated an atmosphere of hostility toward Arabs who have chosen to make their home in the U.S.

There are more than one million Arab Americans, 90 percent of them Christian and 10 percent Moslem. Arab immigration to the U.S., which has increased over the past century, first occurred from Lebanon during the era of Ottoman rule. Most early immigrants were merchants and traders with little education.

More recently, many Arab students who were sent to the U.S. to study chose to stay after completing their education. The Arab "brain drain" reached its peak in 1968–71, when Egypt alone lost some 7,000 professionals, many of them doctors, to the United States.

All that the average American ever hears about Arab countries concerns their polygamy, the status of their women, and the Islamic movements behind the Iranian revolution. Americans see Arabs as desert bedouins in flowing robes. Such stereotypes do not make distinctions between rich and poor Arab countries, or between Arabs who have lived since the dawn of history on the banks of rivers where they planted crops, and those who are desert nomads. American portrayals of Arabs take no account of the universities and research centers all over the Arab World, or of the programs of economic growth and social development there.

The American media choose to ignore all of this, preferring the racist 5
caricatures that spring from Western chauvinism that holds the civilizations
of the East in contempt. In television, probably the medium that most
strongly influences U.S. public opinion, hardly a week goes by without its
portraying the Arabs in a negative and bigoted fashion on series like *Vegas* or
Hawaii Five-O.

On such programs — and on commercials — Arabs appear as bloodthirsty terrorists and dissolute tribal sheiks who squander their vast wealth
among the women of their harems. The scriptwriters apparently get their
information, more imaginary than real, straight from the *Arabian Nights* and
the tales of Ali Baba.

In a major American newspaper a political cartoon depicts a huddle of
obese emirs, surrounded by belly dancers, as they munch huge mutton chops
and toss a single dry bone to a starving boy — who symbolizes the plight of
Africa. The message: Arabs plunder the world and care for nothing but dancing girls.

The U.S. film industry also has played on the negative stereotypes of
Arabs. In American movies the Sahara is a mysterious and dangerous setting
where Americans fall into the clutches of evil bedouin sheiks.

U.S. research centers now are offering programs to spread knowledge
of other cultures and countries to the American public. These centers have
translated and published foreign works of literature. The Department of
Middle Eastern Studies at the University of Washington in Seattle conducts
seminars for teachers in the hope that public-school systems will expand their
study of foreign cultures and rectify anti-Arab stereotypes.

Los Angeles, where more than 250,000 Arabs live, has an Arab-American 10
television station. It is run by Wahib Baqtar, a young Egyptian trained as an
architectural engineer. Baqtar reports that the station avoids discussions of
political matters and Arab disputes. Its schedule does include programs on
places of historical and cultural significance to Arabs.

If the U.S. believes in the cause of truth and in the importance of peace
and brotherhood among peoples, it must attempt to change its image of
Arabs. That imagery takes root in U.S. classrooms, where the minds of a new
generation are shaped, and flourishes in its media.

Suggestions for Writing and Discussion

1. Read the first sentence of this piece. As a reader, what is your initial
   reaction? What do you expect to happen in the rest of this piece?
2. In paragraph 4, Nabil lists several images that Americans have of Arabs.
   Do you agree that these are the ideas that the average American probably
   has? Argue for or against his contention.
3. Comment on Nabil's charge against television and evaluate the subsequent
   support of this charge in paragraphs 5–8: "Hardly a week goes by without

its [television's] portraying the Arabs in a negative and bigoted fashion on series like *Vegas* or *Hawaii Five-O.*"

4. In your opinion, what is Nabil's strongest argument in this piece? Evaluate why this argument is so effective. What suggestions can you make to strengthen other parts of the argument?

5. What do you see as Nabil's main purpose for this piece? Is it to incite the audience to action, or something else? What specific audience might be most likely to applaud Nabil's ideas? What specific audience might react negatively to this piece? Explain why.

Suggestions for Extended Thinking and Research

1. Read a national newspaper like the *New York Times,* the *San Francisco Chronicle,* the *Boston Globe,* the *Washington Post,* or the *Chicago Tribune* for one or two weeks. Note any articles or references to Arab-Americans. Make sure to check advertisements as well as articles. Also, observe television shows and commercials for one to two weeks with the same purpose in mind. Write an essay in which you draw some conclusions about how Arab-Americans are portrayed in the media.

2. Interview people from several different age groups on how they perceive Arab-Americans. Compare the groups in terms of generalizations made and general attitudes toward this cultural group.

3. Write an essay, much like Nabil's, in which you note how another cultural group is portrayed in the media in a negative and stereotypical way.

PAUL FUSSELL

Should Hiroshima Have Been Bombed?

> *A professor of eighteenth-century English literature, Paul Fussell teaches at the University of Pennsylvania. During World War II, he served as a combat officer in Europe, and he has written a book about World War I. This essay first appeared in 1981 in the* New Republic, *a liberal weekly magazine.*

Prereading/Journal-Writing Suggestions

1. Most of us can see a situation more clearly when time has passed and we can look back, a bit older, a bit wiser. Look back now to a decision you made when you were younger, a decision that quite possibly has affected where you are today. From your wiser standpoint now, do you support the decision you made when you were younger? Why do you still see it as a good decision, or why do you now think that you perhaps made a mistake?
2. Respond freely to the following saying: "All is fair in love and war."

Many years ago in New York I saw on the side of a bus a whiskey ad which I've remembered all this time, for it's been for me a model of the brief poem. Indeed, I've come upon few short poems subsequently that evinced more genuine poetic talent. The ad consisted of two lines of "free verse," thus:

> In life, experience is the great teacher.
> In Scotch, Teacher's is the great experience.

For present purposes we can jettison the second line (licking our lips ruefully as it disappears), leaving the first to encapsulate a principle whose banality suggests that it enshrines a most useful truth. I bring up the matter this August, the thirty-sixth anniversary of the A-bombing of Hiroshima and Nagasaki, to focus on something suggested by the long debate about the ethics, if any, of that affair: namely, the importance of experience, sheer vulgar experience, in influencing, if not determining, one's views about the first use of the bomb. And the experience I'm talking about is that of having come to grips, face to face, with an enemy who designs your death. The experience is common to those in the infantry and the Marines and even the line Navy, to those, in short, who fought the Second World War mindful always that their mission was, as they were repeatedly told, "to close with the enemy and destroy him." I think there's something to be learned about that war, as well as about the tendency of historical memory unwittingly to resolve ambiguity, by considering some of the ways testimonies emanating from experience complicate attitudes about the cruel ending of that cruel war.

"What did you do in the Great War, Daddy?" The recruiting poster deserves ridicule and contempt, of course, but its question is embarrassingly relevant here. The problem is one that touches on the matter of social class in America. Most of those with firsthand experience of the war at its worst were relatively inarticulate and have remained silent. Few of those destined to be destroyed if the main islands had had to be invaded went on to become our most eloquent men of letters or our most impressive ethical theorists or professors of history or international jurists. The testimony of experience has come largely from rough diamonds like James Jones and William Manchester, who experienced the war in the infantry and the Marine Corps. Both would agree with the point, if not perhaps the tone, of a remark about Hiroshima made by a naval officer menaced by the kamikazes off Okinawa: "Those were the best burned women and children I ever saw." Anticipating objection from the inexperienced, Jones, in his book *WWII,* is careful to precede his chapter on Hiroshima with one detailing the plans already in motion for the infantry assaults on the home islands of Kyushu, scheduled for November 1945, and ultimately Honshu. The forthcoming invasion of Kyushu, he notes, "was well into its collecting and stockpiling stages before the war ended." (The island of Saipan was designated a main ammunition and supply base for the invasion, and if you visit it today you can see some of the assembled stuff still sitting there.) "The assault troops were chosen and already in training," Jones reminds us, and he illuminates the situation by the light of experience:

> What it must have been like to some old-timer buck sergeant or staff sergeant who had been through Guadalcanal or Bougainville or the Philippines, to stand on some beach and watch this huge war machine beginning to stir and move all around him and know that he very likely had survived this far only to fall dead on the dirt of Japan's home islands, hardly bears thinking about.

On the other hand, John Kenneth Galbraith is persuaded that the Japanese would have surrendered by November without an invasion. He thinks the atom bombs were not decisive in bringing about the surrender and he implies that their use was unjustified. What did he do in the war? He was in the Office of Price Administration in Washington, and then he was director of the United States Strategic Bombing Survey. He was thirty-seven in 1945, and I don't demand that he experience having his ass shot off. I just note that he didn't. In saying this I'm aware of its offensive implications ad hominem. But here I think that approach justified. What's at stake in an infantry assault is so entirely unthinkable to those without experience of one, even if they possess very wide-ranging imaginations and sympathies, that experience is crucial in this case.

A similar remoteness from experience, as well as a similar rationalistic abstraction, seems to lie behind the reaction of an anonymous reviewer of William Manchester's *Goodbye Darkness: A Memoir of the Pacific War* for the

New York Review of Books. First of all the reviewer dislikes Manchester's calling the enemy Nips and Japs, but what really shakes him (her?) is this passage:

> After Biak the enemy withdrew to deep caverns. Rooting them out became a bloody business which reached its ultimate horrors in the last months of the war. You think of the lives which would have been lost in an invasion of Japan's home islands — a staggering number of Americans but millions more of Japanese — and you thank God for the atomic bomb.

Thank God for the atomic bomb. From this, "one recoils," says the reviewer. One does, doesn't one?

In an interesting exchange last year in the *New York Review of Books,* Joseph Alsop and David Joravsky set forth the by now familiar arguments on both sides of the debate. You'll be able to guess which sides they chose once you know that Alsop experienced capture by the Japanese at Hong Kong in 1942 and that Joravsky made no mortal contact with the Japanese: a young soldier, he was on his way to the Pacific when the war ended. The editors of the *New York Review* have given their debate the tendentious title "Was the Hiroshima Bomb Necessary?" — surely an unanswerable question (unlike "Was It Effective?") and one suggesting the intellectual difficulties involved in imposing ex post facto a rational ethics on this event. Alsop focuses on the power and fanaticism of War Minister Anami, who insisted that Japan fight to the bitter end, defending the main islands with the same means and tenacity with which it had defended Iwo and Okinawa. He concludes: "Japanese surrender could never have been obtained, at any rate without the honor-satisfying bloodbath envisioned by . . . Anami, if the hideous destruction of Hiroshima and Nagasaki had not finally galvanized the peace advocates into tearing up the entire Japanese book of rules." The Japanese planned to deploy the undefeated bulk of their ground forces, over two million men, plus 10,000 kamikaze planes, in a suicidal defense. That fact, says Alsop, makes it absurd to "hold the common view, by now hardly challenged by anyone, that the decision to drop the two bombs on Japan was wicked in itself, and that President Truman and all others who joined in making or who [like Oppenheimer] assented to this decision shared in the wickedness." And in explanation of "the two bombs" Alsop adds: "The true, climactic, and successful effort of the Japanese peace advocates . . . did not begin in deadly earnest until *after* the second bomb had destroyed Nagasaki. The Nagasaki bomb was thus the trigger to all the developments that led to peace."

Joravsky, now a professor of history at Northwestern, argues on the 5 other hand that those who decided to use the bomb on cities betray defects of "reason and self-restraint." It all needn't have happened, he asserts, "if the U.S. government had been willing to take a few more days and to be a bit more thoughtful in opening the age of nuclear warfare." But of course in its view it wasn't doing that: that's a historian's tidy hindsight. The government was ending the war conclusively, as well as irrationally remembering Pearl Harbor with a vengeance. It didn't know then what everyone knows now about leukemia and carcinoma and birth defects. History, as Eliot's "Gerontion" notes,

> has many cunning passages, contrived corridors
> And issues, deceives with whispering ambitions,
> Guides us by vanities. . . .
> $\qquad\qquad\qquad$ Think
> Neither fear nor courage saves us. Unnatural vices
> Are fathered by our heroism. Virtues
> Are forced upon us by our impudent crimes.

Understanding the past means feeling its pressure on your pulses and that's harder than Joravsky thinks.

The Alsop–Joravsky debate, which can be seen as reducing finally to a collision between experience and theory, was conducted with a certain civilized respect for evidence. Not so the way the new scurrilous agitprop *New Statesman* conceives those favoring the bomb and those opposing. They are, on the one hand, says Bruce Page, "the imperialist class-forces acting through Harry Truman," and, on the other, those representing "the humane, democratic virtues" — in short, "fascists" opposed to "populists." But ironically the bomb saved the lives not of any imperialists but only of the low and humble, the quintessentially democratic huddled masses — the conscripted enlisted men manning the fated invasion divisions. Bruce Page was nine years old when the war ended. For a man of that experience, phrases like "imperialist class-forces" come easily, and the issues look perfectly clear.

He's not the only one to have forgotten, if he ever knew, the savagery of the Pacific war. The dramatic postwar Japanese success at hustling and merchandising and tourism has (happily, in many ways) effaced for most people important elements of the assault context in which Hiroshima should be viewed. It is easy to forget what Japan was like before it was first destroyed and then humiliated, tamed, and constitutionalized by the West. "Implacable, treacherous, barbaric" — those were Admiral Halsey's characterizations of the enemy, and at the time few facing the Japanese would deny that they fit to a T. One remembers the captured American airmen locked for years in packing crates, the prisoners decapitated, the gleeful use of bayonets on civilians. The degree to which Americans register shock and extraordinary shame about the Hiroshima bomb correlates closely with lack of information about the war.

And the savagery was not just on one side. There was much sadism and brutality — undeniably racist — on ours. No Marine was fully persuaded of his manly adequacy who didn't have a well-washed Japanese skull to caress and who didn't have a go at treating surrendering Japs as rifle targets. Herman Wouk remembers it correctly while analyzing Ensign Keith in *The Caine Mutiny:* "Like most of the naval executioners of Kwajalein, he seemed to regard the enemy as a species of animal pest." And the enemy felt the same way about us: "From the grim and desperate taciturnity with which the Japanese died, they seemed on their side to believe they were contending with an invasion of large armed ants." Hiroshima seems to follow in natural sequence: "This obliviousness on both sides to the fact that the opponents were human beings may perhaps be cited as the key to the many massacres of the Pacific war." Since the Japanese resisted so madly, let's pour gasoline into their emplacements and light it and shoot the people afire who try to get out. Why not? Why not blow them all up? Why not, indeed, drop a new kind of big bomb on them? Why allow one more American high school kid to see his intestines blown out of his body and spread before him in the dirt while he screams when we can end the whole thing just like that?

On Okinawa, only weeks before Hiroshima, 123,000 Japanese and Americans *killed* each other. "Just awful" was the comment not of some pacifist but of MacArthur. One million American casualties was his estimate of the cost of the forthcoming invasion. And that invasion was not just a hypothetical threat, as some theorists have argued. It was genuinely in train, as I know because I was to be in it. When the bomb ended the war I was in the 45th Infantry Division, which had been through the European war to the degree that it had needed to be reconstituted two or three times. We were in a staging area near Reims, ready to be shipped across the United States for final preparation in the Philippines. My division was to take part in the invasion of Honshu in March 1946. (The earlier invasion of Kyushu was to be carried out by 700,000 infantry already in the Pacific.) I was a twenty-one-year-old second lieutenant leading a rifle platoon. Although still officially in one piece, in the German war I had already been wounded in the leg and back severely enough to be adjudged, after the war, 40 percent disabled. But even if my legs buckled whenever I jumped out of the back of the truck, my condition was held to be satisfactory for whatever lay ahead. When the bombs dropped and news began to circulate that "Operation Olympic" would not, after all, take place, that we would not be obliged to run up the beaches near Tokyo assault-firing while being mortared and shelled, for all the fake manliness of our façades we cried with relief and joy. We were going to live. We were going to grow up to adulthood after all. When the *Enola Gay* dropped its package, "There were cheers," says John Toland, "over the intercom; it meant the end of the war."

Those who cried and cheered are very different from high-minded, 10 guilt-ridden GIs we're told about by the late J. Glenn Gray in *The Warriors* (1959). During the war in Europe Gray was an interrogator in the Counter Intelligence Corps, and in that capacity he underwent the war at division level. After the war he became a professor of philosophy at Colorado College (never, I've thought, the venue of very much reality) and a distinguished editor of Heidegger. There's no doubt that Gray's outlook on everything was noble and elevated. But *The Warriors,* his meditation on modern soldiering, gives every sign of remoteness from experience. Division headquarters is miles behind the places where the soldiers experience terror and madness and relieve these pressures by sadism. "When the news of the atomic bombing of Hiroshima and Nagasaki came," Gray asks us to believe, "many an American soldier felt shocked and ashamed." But why, we ask? Because we'd bombed civilians? We'd been doing that for years and, besides the two bombs, wiped out 10,000 Japanese troops, not now often mentioned, John Hersey's kindly physicians and Jesuit priests being more touching. Were Gray's soldiers shocked and ashamed because we'd obliterated whole towns? We'd done that plenty of times. If at division headquarters some felt shocked and ashamed, down in the rifle companies none did, although Gray says they did:

> The combat soldier knew better than did Americans at home what those bombs meant in suffering and injustice. The man of conscience realized intuitively that the vast majority of Japanese in both cities were no more, if no less, guilty of the war than were his own parents, sisters, or brothers.

I find this canting nonsense: the purpose of dropping the bombs was not to "punish" people but to stop the war. To intensify the shame he insists we feel, Gray seems willing to fiddle the facts. The Hiroshima bomb, he says, was dropped "without any warning." But actually, two days before, 720,000 leaflets were dropped on the city urging everyone to get out and indicating that the place was going to be obliterated. Of course few left.

Experience whispers that the pity is not that we used the bomb to end the Japanese war but that it wasn't ready earlier to end the German one. If only it could have been rushed into production faster and dropped at the right moment on the Reich chancellery or Berchtesgaden or Hitler's military headquarters in East Prussia or — Wagnerian *coup de théâtre* — at Rommel's phony state funeral, most of the Nazi hierarchy could have been pulverized immediately, saving not just the embarrassment of the Nuremburg trials but the lives of about four million Jews, Poles, Slavs, gypsies, and other "subhumans," not to mention the lives and limbs of millions of Allied and Axis soldiers. If the bomb could have been ready even as late as July 1944, it could have reinforced the Von Stauffenberg plot and ended the war then and there. If the bomb had only been ready in time, the men of my infantry platoon would not have been killed and maimed.

All this is not to deny that like the Russian revolution, the atomic bombing of Japan was a vast historical tragedy, and every passing year magnifies the dilemma into which it has thrown the contemporary world. As with the Russian revolution there are two sides — that's why it's a tragedy rather than a disaster — and unless we are simple-mindedly cruel, like Bruce Page, we need to be painfully aware of both at once. To observe that from the viewpoint of the war's victims-to-be the bomb was precisely the right thing to drop is to purchase no immunity from horror. See, for example, the new book *Unforgettable Fire: Pictures Drawn by Atomic Bomb Survivors,* issued by the Japan Broadcasting Corporation and distributed here by Pantheon Books. It presents a number of amateur colored-pencil, pastel, and water-color depictions of the scene of the Hiroshima bombing made by the middle-aged and elderly survivors for a peace exhibition in 1975. In addition to the heartrending pictures the book offers brief moments of memoir, not for the weak-stomached:

> While taking my severely wounded wife out to the riverbank . . . , I was horrified indeed at the sight of a stark naked man standing in the rain with his eyeball in his palm. He looked to be in great pain but there was nothing I could do for him. I wonder what became of him. Even today, I vividly remember the sight. It was simply miserable.

The drawings and paintings, whose often childish style makes them doubly touching, are of skin hanging down, breasts torn off, people bleeding and burning, dying mothers nursing dead babies. A bloody woman holds a bloody child in the ruins of a house, and the artist remembers her calling, "Please help this child! Someone, please help this child. Please help! Someone, please." As Samuel Johnson said of the smothering of the innocent Desdemona in another tragedy, "It is not to be endured." Nor, we should notice, is an infantryman's account of having his arm blown off in the Arno Valley in Italy in 1944:

> I wanted to die and die fast. I wanted to forget this miserable world. I cursed the war, I cursed the people who were responsible for it, I cursed God for putting me here . . . to suffer for something I never did or knew anything about. For this was hell, and I never imagined anything or anyone could suffer so bitterly. I screamed and cursed. Why? Why? What had I done to deserve this? But no answer came. I yelled for medics, because subconsciously I wanted to live. I tried to apply my right hand over my bleeding stump, but I didn't have the strength to hold it. I looked to the left of me and saw the bloody mess that was once my left arm; its fingers and palm were turned upward, like a flower looking to the sun for its strength.

The future scholar-critic of rhetoric who writes *The History of Canting in the Twentieth Century* will find much to study in the utterances of those who dilate on the wickedness of the bomb-droppers. He will realize that such utterance can perform for the speaker a valuable double function. First, it can display the fineness of his moral weave. And second, by implication it can also inform the audience that during the war he was not socially so unfortunate as to find himself at the cutting edge of the ground forces, where he might have had to compromise the pure clarity of his moral vision by the experience of weighing his own life against other people's. Down there, which is where the other people were in the war, is the place where coarse self-interest is the rule. When the young soldier with the wild eyes comes at you firing, do you shoot him in the foot, hoping he'll be hurt badly enough to drop or mis-aim the gun with which he is going to kill you, or do you shoot him in the chest and make certain he stops being your mortal enemy? It would be stupid to expect soldiers to be very sensitive humanitarians ("Moderation in war is imbecility" — Admiral of the Fleet Lord Fisher); actually, only the barest decencies can be expected of them. They didn't start the war, except in the terrible sense hinted in Frederic Manning's observation based on his experience in the Great War: "War is waged by men; not by beasts, or by gods. It is a peculiarly human activity. To call it a crime against mankind is to miss at least half its significance; it is also the punishment of a crime." Knowing that fact by experience, soldiers have every motive for wanting a war stopped, by any means.

The predictable stupidity, parochialism, and greed in the postwar international mismanagement of the whole nuclear problem should not tempt us to misimagine the circumstances of the bomb's first "use." Nor should our well-justified fears and suspicions occasioned by the capture of the nuclear business by the mendacious classes (cf. Three Mile Island) tempt us to infer retrospectively extraordinary corruption, cruelty, and swinishness in those who decided to drop the bomb. Times change. Harry Truman was not a fascist, but a democrat. He was as close to a real egalitarian as we've seen in high office for a very long time. He is the only president in my lifetime who ever had the experience of commanding a small unit of ground troops obliged to kill people. He knew better than his subsequent critics what he was doing. The past, which as always did not know the future, acted in ways that ask to be imagined before they are condemned. Or even before they are simplified.

Suggestions for Writing and Discussion

1. Even though Fussell was never actually in Japan during WWII, why does he still think his status as a veteran of this war qualifies him to judge the decision to bomb Hiroshima as an appropriate one? Do you find this reasoning convincing? Explain.

2. What does the interrupting clause "if any" signify in Fussell's following statement?

   > I bring up the matter this August, the thirty-sixth anniversary of the A-bombing of Hiroshima and Nagasaki, to focus on something suggested by the long debate about the ethics, *if any,* of that affair.

3. Why does Fussell include the graphic and repulsive quotations from fellow veterans who have previously supported the use of the A-bomb? What is your response to those quotations?

4. Throughout this piece, Fussell offers the viewpoints of several authorities on both sides of the issues and then he offers his own comments. What does he gain, or lose, by using this balancing strategy?

5. Take two paragraphs from this piece and analyze them carefully for Fussell's word choice and style. What part do these two elements play in terms of the overall effectiveness of the argument?

6. In paragraph 13, in order to argue that war "is the place where coarse self-interest is the rule," Fussell compares the dropping of the A-bomb to the reaction a soldier has when an enemy is attacking him, face to face. In what sense is this comparison justified, and at what point might it break down?

7. Do you think Fussell appeals primarily to emotions, to reason, to the reader's sense of ethics? Or does he balance these appeals? Cite specific examples to support your evaluation. In addition, explain whether and why you find these appeals effective.

Suggestions for Extended Thinking and Research

1. Using the *New York Times Index* for 1945, find and read several editorials from the *New York Times* on the days and weeks following the destruction of Hiroshima and Nagasaki. What were the sentiments of the columnists at that time? What conclusions can you draw about the reaction of writers at that time?

2. Interview several veterans of past wars about the use of the atomic bomb. How many of them think the bomb should have been dropped? What are their reasons? How many of them echo Fussell's sentiments? How many disagree? What conclusions can you draw about what experience teaches us about war?

MICHAEL WALZER

Hiroshima: An Act of Terrorism

> *Michael Walzer, who has served as a member of the Institute for Advanced Study at Princeton, is the author of several books on political morality, including* Obligations *(1970),* Just and Unjust Wars *(1977), and* Spheres of Justice *(1983). This piece originally appeared as a response to Paul Fussell's essay (pp. 587–594).*

Prereading/Journal-Writing Suggestion

After reading Paul Fussell's essay, what is your reaction? Have you changed your mind in any way? Do you see war in a different light? Do you see soldiers in a different light? At this point, how do you feel about the decision to drop the A-bomb?

Paul Fussell's defense of the bombing of Hiroshima (*TNR*, August 22 and 29) is written, as he tells us repeatedly, from the standpoint of the ordinary GI. And that standpoint is human, all too human: let anyone die but me! There are no humanitarians in the foxholes. I can almost believe that. But Fussell's recital does remind me a little uneasily of the speech of that Conradian villain Gentleman Brown (in *Lord Jim*): "When it came to saving one's life in the dark, one didn't care who else went — three, thirty, three hundred people. . . ." And Brown went on to boast, very much as Fussell wants to do, that he made Jim wince with this "despairing frankness": "He very soon left off coming the righteous over me. . . ."

But we shouldn't be intimidated, and we shouldn't leave off, but accept the risks of righteousness. After all, Fussell's argument isn't only the argument of ordinary soldiers. It is also and more importantly the argument of ordinary generals — best expressed, I think, by the Prussian general von Moltke in 1880: "The greatest kindness in war is to bring it to a speedy conclusion. It should be allowable, with that end in view, to employ all means save those that are absolutely objectionable." But von Moltke, a stolid professional, probably still believed that the wholesale slaughter of civilians was "absolutely objectionable." With Fussell, it seems, there are no limits at all; anything goes, so long as it helps to bring the boys home.

Nor is this the argument only of GIs and generals. The bombing of Hiroshima was an act of terrorism; its purpose was political, not military. The goal was to kill enough civilians to shake the Japanese government and force it to surrender. And this is the goal of every terrorist campaign. Happily, none of today's terrorist movements have yet been able to kill on the scale of the modern state, and so they have not enjoyed successes as dramatic as the one Fussell describes. But their ordinary members, the terrorists in the foxholes, as it were, must think much as he does: if only we could kill enough people, not a dozen here and there, in a pub, a bus station, or a supermarket, but a whole city full, we could end the struggle once and for all, liberate our land, get the British out of Ireland, force the Israelis to accept a PLO state, and so on. To the boys of the IRA, to young Palestinians in Lebanon, that argument is surely as attractive as it was to the young Paul Fussell on his way to the Pacific in 1945. It is the same argument.

What is wrong with it? If war is indeed a tragedy, if its suffering is inevitable, then nothing is wrong with it. War is war, and what happens, happens. In fact, however, war imposes choices on officers and enlisted men alike. "There wasn't a single soldier," says an Israeli officer who fought in the Six-Day War, "who didn't at some stage have to decide, to choose, to make a moral decision. . . ." Fussell, who has written so beautifully about the literature of war, must know this to be true. And he must also know that there is a moral argument, different from his own argument, that shapes these military choices. Perhaps that argument is most often expounded by those professors far from the battlefield for whom he has such contempt. But it is an argument as old as war itself and one that many soldiers have believed and struggled to live by. It holds, most simply, that combat should be a struggle between combatants, and that noncombatants — civilian men, women, and children — should be protected as far as possible against its cruelties. "The soldier, be he friend or foe," wrote Douglas MacArthur, "is charged with the protection of the weak and the unarmed. It is the very essence and reason of his being . . . a sacred trust." Like policemen, firemen, and sailors at sea, soldiers have a responsibility to accept risks themselves rather than impose risks on ordinary citizens. That is a hard requirement when the soldiers are conscripts. Still, they are trained and armed for war and ordinary citizens are not; and that is a practical difference that makes a moral difference.

Consider how the risks of police work might be reduced, and how many more criminals might be caught, if we permitted the police to ignore the rights of ordinary citizens, to fire indiscriminately into crowds, to punish the innocent relatives of criminals, and so on. But we don't grant such permissions. Nor are soldiers permitted comparable acts, even if they carry with them the promise of success.

There is a code. It is no doubt often broken, particularly in the heat of battle. But honorable men live by it while they can. Hiroshima was a violation of that code. So was the earlier terror bombing of cities — Hamburg, Dresden, Tokyo — but Hiroshima was worse because it was even more terrifying. Its long-term effects were literally unknowable by the men who decided to impose them. And the effects were not imposed, any more than those of the earlier bombing, in the heat of battle, face-to-face with enemy soldiers who aim to kill and have already killed comrades and friends. Though there were soldiers in Hiroshima, they were not the targets of the attack (or else we would have attacked a military base); the city was the target and all its inhabitants.

Fussell writes (again) as a democrat, on behalf of "the low and humble, the quintessentially democratic huddled masses — the conscripted enlisted men manning the fated invasion divisions." Given that standpoint, one might have expected him to question the U.S. demand for unconditional surrender that made the invasion of the Japanese islands seem absolutely necessary. There were people in the U.S. government in 1945 who thought a negotiated settlement possible without an invasion and without the use of the atomic bomb. Surely some attempt should have been made — not only for the sake of our own soldiers, but also for those other "huddled masses," the civilian inhabitants of Hiroshima (and Nagasaki too). Why don't they figure in Fussell's democratic reckoning! If Harry Truman's first responsibility was to American soldiers, he was not without responsibility elsewhere; no man is. And if one is reckoning, what about all the future victims of a politics and warfare from which restraint has been banished? Given the state of our political and moral order, with which Hiroshima probably has something to do, aren't we all more likely to be the victims than the beneficiaries of terrorist attacks?

Suggestions for Writing and Discussion

1. Michael Walzer begins his second paragraph by stating that "we shouldn't be intimidated" by the "boasting" of those who have been to war, such as Paul Fussell. From this statement, what is Walzer implying about Fussell's argument? Do you agree that Fussell is boasting? Cite specific examples to support your evaluation.

2. Do you think Fussell would agree that Walzer summarizes his main point adequately by saying that "there are no limits at all: anything goes, so long as it helps to bring the boys home" (paragraph 2)?

3. What do you think of Walzer's claim that the bombing of Hiroshima was a terrorist activity, much like PLO activities today? How is this analogy justified, and at any point does it break down?

4. In comparing Fussell's and Walzer's essays, which author do you feel presents himself as the most fair-minded? Support your choice with several examples from the text.

5. Walzer writes that "war imposes choices" on soldiers, while Fussell implies that during war, soldiers are obligated to follow orders. On this point alone, a huge gulf emerges between the two writers. One sees the bombing as a moral issue, the other as an action outside the moral landscape. Considering these two opposite philosophies, where do you fit best? Explain your choice as clearly as possible.

6. Overall, even if you do not agree with the author's stance, which essay do

you think most people would find most effective — Fussell's or Walzer's? Explain why.

Suggestion for Extended Thinking and Research

Read several other opinions on this topic in order to find evidence that neither Fussell nor Walzer uses in his argument. If both writers were confronted with this new evidence, what adjustments or concessions would each have to make in order to address these new points? Explain how these new points might strengthen or weaken Fussell's and Walzer's arguments.

ROBERT OLEN BUTLER

The Trip Back

Robert Olen Butler has published several novels, including The Alleys of Eden, Sun Dogs, Countrymen of Bones, On Distant Ground, *and* Wabash. *In addition, he is the author of many highly acclaimed short stories that have appeared in such journals as the* Hudson Review, *the* Sewanee Review, *and the* Gettysburg Review. *"The Trip Back" is an excerpt from a book of fourteen stories and a novella; each piece is told in the first person through the eyes of a different Vietnamese immigrant who has now become, in many ways, "American" and who lives in southern Louisiana. Drafted into the army during the Vietnam conflict, Butler received training in the Vietnamese language and served as a military intelligence operative and assistant to the American foreign service office in Saigon. "The Trip Back" is based, in part, on the people he met while serving in Vietnam.*

Prereading/Journal-Writing Suggestions

1. We think our most precious memories will be with us forever. In reality, however, significant moments fade and disappear with time. In your journal, write down descriptions of five specific people and five specific moments with those people that you never want to forget.

2. Old age is not a stage of life most of us anticipate with pleasure. Write about how you would want to spend your final days. Where do you want to live? What do you want to do? Do you want to live alone or be with others? What friends and relatives do you see yourself depending on?

3. How are the manners, customs, and values of your generation different from those of your grandparents' generation? What, if anything, has been lost? What, if anything, has been gained?

4. Write down three things that are most important in your life right now. How much of your day is dedicated to these things? How much of your day is a distraction from what is really important to you? Think only about how you've spent today thus far as an aid to answering these last two questions.

I am just a businessman, not a poet. It is the poet who is supposed to see things so clearly and to remember. Perhaps it is only the poets who can die well. Not the rest of us. I drove from my home in Lake Charles, Louisiana, to the airport in Houston, Texas, to pick up my wife's grandfather. And what is it that I experienced on that trip? What is it that struck me as I got off the interstate highway in Beaumont, knowing the quick route to the airport as I do? I was driving through real towns in Texas. One was named China, another Nome. One was Liberty. If I were a man who believed in symbols and omens, I would have smiled at this. I was passing through Liberty to pick up my wife's grandfather whose own liberty my wife and I and the man's nephew in San Francisco had finally won, after many years of trying. He was arriving this very day from the West Coast after living thirteen years under Communist rule in our home country of Vietnam. Perhaps a poet would think of those things — about Liberty, Texas, and my wife's grandfather — and write a memorable poem. Though maybe not. I am ignorant of these matters. Maybe it is only the bird taking flight or the frog jumping into the pond that the poet is interested in.

All I know is that for me I drove the two-lane highway across Texas and I just noticed the businesses — the little ones that seemed so Vietnamese to me in the way the people always looked for some new angle, some empty corner in the marketplace. I noticed the signs for stumpgrinding and for house leveling and for mud pumping, the different stands along the way — fireworks, fruit and vegetables, hubcaps, and antiques. The Paradise Club had a miniskirt contest, the Bait Barn had a nightcrawler special, and Texas Winners had a baseball trophy sale. There was a Donut Delight and a Future Star Twirling Academy and a hand-painted sign on a post saying that the finest porch swings were a mile down this dusty road. The Mattress Man said on his sign, right underneath his business name, "Jesus Is Lord."

I am a Catholic and I must say that this made me smile. The Lord of the Universe, the Man of Sorrows, turned into the Lord of the Mattress, the Mattress Man. But even so, I understood what this owner was trying to do, appealing specially to those of his own kind. This is good business practice, when you know your sales area. I have done very well for myself in Lake Charles in the laundry and dry cleaning business. It is very simple. People sweat a lot in the climate of southern Louisiana, and there was a place for a very good laundry and dry cleaner. I have two locations in Lake Charles, and I will soon open one in Sulphur. So it was this that interested me as I drove through Texas, as it always does. I am a businessman. It is my way.

And if I were a man who believed in symbols and omens, I would have been very interested toward the end of my journey when I came to a low highway bridge that took me across the wide converging of two rivers, for as I entered the bridge, the sign said, "Lost and Old Rivers." These two rivers were full of little islands and submerged trees, and it was hard to see how the two ran together, for they looked more like one sprawling thing, like perhaps a large lake, something that was bound in and not moving, not flowing. Lost and old.

I had not given much serious thought to Mr. Chinh, my wife's grandfather. I knew this: my wife loved him very much. We are all like that in Vietnam. We honor our families. My four children honor me very much, and I honor them. My wife is devoted to me, and I am devoted to her. I love her. We were very lucky in that our parents allowed us to marry for love. That is to say, my mother and father and my wife's mother allowed it. Her father was   5 dead. We still have a little shrine in our house and pray for him, which is the way of all Vietnamese, even if they are Catholic. As Catholics we understand this as the communion of saints. But my wife has no clear memory of her father. He died when she was very young. He drowned swimming in the South China Sea. And after that, Mr. Chinh became like a father for my wife.

She wept the night before my trip to the airport. She was very happy to have her grandfather again and very sorry that she missed all those years with him. I heard her muffling the sound of her crying in the pillow, and I touched her on the shoulder and felt her shaking, and then I switched on the light by the bed. She turned her face sharply away from me, as if I would reproach her for her tears, as if there was some shame in it. I said to her, "Mai, it is all right. I understand your feeling."

"I know," she said, but she did not turn back to me. So I switched the light off once more, and in the dark she came to me and I held her.

You must wait to understand why it is important, but at this point I must confess one thing. My wife came to me in the dark and I held her, and her crying slowed and stopped, and of course I was happy for that. I was happy to hold my wife in the dark in this moment of strong feeling for her and to be of help, but as I lay there, my mind could not focus on this woman that I love. My mind understood that she was feeling these things for a man of her own blood who had been very important to her and who then disappeared from her life for more than a decade and now was coming back into it. But these are merely bloodless words, things of the mind. And that was all they were to me even lying there in the dark. I made those words run in my head, but what was preoccupying me at that moment was an itching on my heel that I could not scratch and the prices of two different types of paint for the outer shop of the new dry cleaning store. My wife was a certain pressure, a warmth against me, but there was also a buzz in the electric alarm clock that I was just as conscious of.

Do not misjudge me. I am not a cold man. I drew my wife closer as she grew quieter, but it was a conscious decision, and even saying that, I have to work hard to remember the moment, and the memory that I have is more like a thought than a memory of my senses. And it's not as if the itching on my heel, the buzz of the clock, are any more vivid. I have to work extremely hard to reconstruct this very recent night so that I can even tell you with assurance that there was a clock in the room or that there was a foot at the end of my leg.

But you will see that it is Mr. Chinh who has put me in this present state 10 of agitation. After a time, as I held her in the bed, my wife said, "My tears are mostly happy. Don't worry for me, Khanh. I only wish I was small enough and his back was strong enough that I could ride upon it again."

At the airport gate I looked at the people filing through the door from the jetway. The faces were all white or Spanish, and they filed briskly through the door and rushed away, and then there were a long few moments when no one appeared. I began to think that Mr. Chinh had missed the plane. I thought of the meal that my wife was preparing at home. She and my children and our best friends in Lake Charles had been working since dawn on the house and on the food for this wonderful reuniting, and when the door to the jetway gaped there with no one coming through, that is the only thought I had, that the food would be ruined. I did not worry about Mr. Chinh or wonder what the matter could really be.

I looked over to the airline agents working behind their computers, checking in the passengers for the next flight. I was ready to seek their help when I glanced back to the door and there was Mr. Chinh. He was dressed in a red-and-black plaid sport shirt and chino pants, and he was hunched a little bit over a cane, but what surprised me was that he was not alone. A Vietnamese man about my age was holding him up on the side without the cane and bending close and talking into his ear. Then the younger man looked up and saw me, and I recognized a cousin of my wife, the son of Mr. Chinh's nephew. He smiled at me and nodded a hello, and he jiggled the old man into looking at me as well. Mr. Chinh raised his head, and an overhead light flashed in his glasses, making his eyes disappear. He too smiled, so I felt that it was all right.

They approached me, and I shook Mr. Chinh's hand first. "I am so happy you have come to visit us," I said.

I would have said more—I had a little speech in my head about my wife's love for him, and how she is so sorry she is not at the airport, and how much his great-grandchildren want to see him. But my wife's cousin cut in before I had a chance. "This is Mr. Khanh," he said to the old man. "The one I told you about who would meet you."

Mr. Chinh nodded and looked at me and repeated my name. He spoke no more, and I looked to the cousin, who said, "I'm Huong," and he bowed to me very formally.

"I remember you," I said, and I offered my hand. He took it readily, but I knew from his formality that there could be things I did not know about Mr. Chinh. It is the custom of Vietnamese, especially of the old school of manners, not to tell you things that are unpleasant to hear. The world need not be made worse than it is by embracing the difficult things. It is assumed that you wish to hear that all is well, and many people will tell you this no matter what the situation really is. Huong struck me as being of this tradition—as surely his father must, too, for this is how an otherwise practical people learns an attitude such as this.

But I am a blunt man. Business has made me that way, particularly business in America. So I said to Mr. Huong, "Is there something wrong with Mr. Chinh?"

He smiled at me as if I were a child asking about the thunder. "I came with our dear uncle to make sure he traveled safely. He is very old."

I suddenly felt a little uncomfortable talking about the man as if he wasn't there, so I looked at him. He was leaning contentedly on his cane, gazing around the circle of gates. I bent nearer to him and said, "Mr. Chinh, do you like the airport?"

He turned to me at once and said, "This is a fine airport. The best I 20 have seen."

The man's voice was strong, and this reassured me. I liked his appreciation of the airport, which I too admired, so I said to Mr. Huong, "Is he a little frail, physically?"

"Yes," said Mr. Huong, happy, I suppose, to have words put in his mouth sufficient to answer my blunt question. I did not like this cousin Huong.

But I was compelled to ask, "Will you be coming to Lake Charles to join us?"

"No. I must decline your gracious invitation. I return by a flight later this day."

I was blunt again. "You came all this way never to leave the airport? Just 25 to return at once?"

Mr. Huong shrugged. "It is my pleasure to make sure our beloved uncle arrives safely. My father said that if you should wish to discuss Uncle Chinh's permanent home after perhaps a week or so, he will await your call."

I didn't know the details of all that, except that I was prepared for my wife's sake and the sake of our country's family tradition to make him part of our household. So I just nodded and took Mr. Chinh by the arm and said a brief goodbye to Mr. Huong, and the old man and I started off for the baggage check.

Mr. Chinh was enchanted with the airport, gawking about as we moved, and his interest was so intense and his pleasure so evident from the little clucks and nods he made that I did not try to speak with him. Twice he asked me a question, once about where they would take the luggage, answered by our arrival at the carousel, which caused him to laugh loudly when the bell rang and the silver metal track began to run. Mr. Chinh stood at the opening, and he watched each bag emerging through the plastic flaps as closely as a customs inspector. The second question was if I had a car. And when I said yes, he seemed very pleased, lifting his cane before him and tapping it down hard. "Good," he said. "Don't tell me what kind. I will see for myself."

But in the parking garage, he was baffled. He circled the car and touched it gently with the rubber tip of his cane, touched it several places, on a taillight, a hubcap, the front bumper, the name on the grille. "I don't know this car," he said. "I don't know it at all."

"It's an Acura," I said.   30

He shook the name off as if a mosquito had just buzzed his ear. "I thought you would own a French car. A Citröen, I had predicted. A 15CV sedan."

"No, Mr. Chinh. It's an Acura. It's a very good car," and I stopped myself from telling him it was from Japan.

Mr. Chinh lifted his shoulders and let them drop heavily, like he was greatly disappointed and perhaps even a little scornful. I put his bags in the trunk and opened the door for him, and we made it out of the airport and back onto the two-lane highway before any more words were spoken. I was holding my eyes on the road, trying to think of small talk, something I'm not very good at, when Mr. Chinh finally said, "The inside is very nice."

I didn't understand. I glanced over to him, and he was running his hand along the dashboard, and I realized that he'd been thinking about the car all this time. "Good," I said. "I'm glad you like it."

"Not as nice as many others," he said. "But nice." 35

There's no car interior short of a Rolls that is nicer than my Acura, but I nodded at the old man, and I told myself that there was no need to debate with him or entertain him but just to be cordial to him. Let him carry the conversation, if he wished one. But the trip looked very long ahead of me. We hadn't even gotten out into the country of stump grinders and fruit stands. It was still franchised fast food and clusters of gas stations and minimalls and car dealerships. There were many miles to go.

Then up ahead I saw the work of a clever man, a car dealer who had dangled a big luxury car from the top of what looked like at least a seventy-foot crane. I said to Mr. Chinh, "There's something the Citröens don't do," and I motioned the man's attention to the car in the sky. He bent down and angled his head up to look, and his mouth gaped open. He said nothing but quickly shifted to the side window as we passed the car dealership, and then he turned around to watch out the back window until the car on the crane was out of sight.

I expected Mr. Chinh to remark on this. Perhaps a word on how no one would ever do such a thing to a French car. There would be no need. Something like that. But he said nothing, and after a time, I decided to appreciate the silence. I just concentrated on covering these miles before the old man would be reunited with the granddaughter he loved. I found that I myself was no longer comfortable with the old ways. Like the extended family. Like other things, too. The Vietnamese indirectness, for instance. The superstition. I was a good American now, and though I wished I could do more for this old man next to me, at least for my wife's sake, it was not an unpleasant thought that I had finally left Vietnam behind.

And I'd left behind more than the customs. I don't suppose that struck me as I was driving home from the airport. But it is clear to me now. I grew up, as did my wife, in Vung Tau. Both our families were pretty well off and we lived year-round in this seaside resort on the South China Sea. The French had called it Cap St. Jacques. The sand was white and the sea was the color of jade. But I say these things not from any vivid recollection, but from a thought in my head, as real only as lines from a travel brochure. I'd left behind me the city on the coast and the sea as well.

But you must understand that ultimately this doesn't have anything to 40 do with being a refugee in the United States. When I got to the two rivers again, Old and Lost, I could recognize the look of them, like a lake, but it was only my mind working.

Perhaps that is a bad example. What are those two rivers to me? I mention them now only to delay speaking of the rest of my ride with Mr.

Chinh. When we crossed the rivers, I suppose I was reminded of him some-how. Probably because of the earlier thoughts of the rivers as an omen. But now I tried once more to think of small talk. I saw a large curl of rubber on the shoulder of the road and then another a little later on, and I said to Mr. Chinh, "Those are retreads from trucks. In Vietnam some enterprising man would have already collected those to make some use of them. Here no one cares."

The old man did not speak, but after a few moments I sensed something beside me, and I glanced and found him staring at me. "Do we have far to go?" he asked.

"Perhaps an hour and a half," I said.

"May I roll down the window?"

"Of course," I said. I turned off the air conditioning, and as he made   45 faint grabbing motions at the door, I pressed the power button and lowered his window. Mr. Chinh turned his face to me with eyes slightly widened in what looked to me like alarm. "They're power windows," I said. "No handle."

His face did not change. I thought to explain further, but before I could, he turned to the window and leaned slightly forward so that the wind rushed into his face, and his hair — still more black than gray — rose and danced, and he was just a little bit scary to me for some reason. So I concentrated again on the road, and I was happy to let him stay silent, watching the Texas highway, and this was a terrible mistake.

If I'd forced him into conversation earlier, I would've had more time to prepare for our arrival in Lake Charles. Not that I could have done much, though. As it was, we were only fifteen minutes or so from home. We'd already crossed the Sabine River into Louisiana and I'd pointed it out to Mr. Chinh, the first words spoken in the car for an hour. Even that didn't start the conversation. Some time later the wandering of his own mind finally made him speak. He said, "The air feels good here. It's good when you can feel it on your face as you drive."

I naturally thought he was talking to me, but when I said, "Yes, that's right," he snapped his head around as if he'd forgotten that I was there.

What could I have said to such a reaction? I should have spoken of it to him right away. But I treated it as I would treat Mai waking from a dream and not knowing where she is. I said, "We're less than twenty miles from Lake Charles, Mr. Chinh."

He did not reply, but his face softened, as if he were awake now.   50

I said, "Mai can't wait to see you. And our children are very excited."

He did not acknowledge this, which I thought was rude for the grand-father who was becoming the elder of our household. Instead, he looked out the window again, and he said, "My favorite car of all was a Hotchkiss. I had a 1934 Hotchkiss. An AM80 tourer. It was a wonderful car. I would drive it from Saigon to Hanoi. A fine car. Just like the car that won the Monte Carlo rally in 1932. I drove many cars to Hanoi over the years. Citröen, Peugeot,

Ford, DeSoto, Simca. But the Hotchkiss was the best. I would drive to Hanoi at the end of the year and spend ten days and return. It was eighteen hundred kilometers. I drove it in two days. I'd drive in the day, and my driver would drive at night. At night it was very nice. We had the top down, and the moon was shining, and we drove along the beach. Then we'd stop and turn the lights on, and rabbits would come out, and we'd catch them. Very simple. I can see their eyes shining in the lights. Then we'd make a fire on the beach. The sparks would fly up, and we'd sit and eat and listen to the sea. It was very nice, driving. Very nice."

Mr. Chinh stopped speaking. He kept his face to the wind, and I was conscious of the hum of my Acura's engine, and I felt very strange. This man beside me was rushing along the South China Sea. Right now. He had felt something so strong that he could summon it up and place himself within it, and the moment would not fade, the eyes of the rabbits still shone, and the sparks still climbed into the sky, and he was a happy man.

Then we were passing the oil refineries west of the lake, and we rose on the I-10 bridge, and Lake Charles was before us, and I said to Mr. Chinh, "We are almost home now."

And the old man turned to me and said, "Where is it that we are going?" 55

"Where?"

"You're the friend of my nephew?"

"I'm the husband of Mai, your granddaughter," I said, and I tried to tell myself he was still caught on some beach on the way to Hanoi.

"Granddaughter?" he said.

"Mai. The daughter of your daughter Diem." I was trying to hold off the feeling in my chest that moved like the old man's hair was moving in the wind.

Mr. Chinh slowly cocked his head, and he narrowed his eyes, and he thought for a long moment and said, "Diem lost her husband in the sea."

"Yes," I said, and I drew a breath in relief.

But then the old man said, "She had no daughter."

"What do you mean? Of course she had a daughter."

"I think she was childless." 65

"She had a daughter and a son." I found that I was shouting. Perhaps I should have pulled off to the side of the road at that moment. I should have pulled off and tried to get through to Mr. Chinh. But it would have been futile, and then I would still have been forced to take him to my wife. I couldn't very well just walk him into the lake and drive away. As it was, I had five more minutes as I drove to our house, and I spent every second trying carefully to explain who Mai was. But Mr. Chinh could not remember. Worse than that. He was certain I was wrong.

I stopped at the final stop sign before our house, and I tried once more. "Mai is the daughter of Nho and Diem. Nho died in the sea, just as you said. Then you were like a father to Mai. . . . You carried her on your back."

"My daughter Diem had no children. She lived in Nha Trang."

"Not in Nha Trang. She never lived in Nha Trang."

Mr. Chinh shook his head no, refuting me with the gentleness of abso- 70
lute conviction. "She lived on the beach of Nha Trang, a very beautiful beach.
And she had no children. She was just a little girl herself. How could she have
children?"

I felt weak now. I could barely speak the words, but I said, "She had a
daughter. My wife. You love her."

The old man finally just turned his face away from me. He sat with his
head in the window as if he were patiently waiting for the wind to start up
again.

I felt very bad for my wife. But it wasn't that simple. I've become a
blunt man. Not like a Vietnamese at all. It's the way I do business. So I will
say this bluntly. I felt bad for Mai, but I was even more concerned for myself.
The old man frightened me. And it wasn't in the way you might think, with
my saying to myself, Oh that could be me over there sitting with my head
out the window and forgetting who my closest relatives are. It was different
from that, I knew.

I drove the last two blocks to our house on the corner. The long house
with the steep roof and the massively gnarled live oak in the front yard. My
family heard my car as I turned onto the side street and then into our driveway.
They came to the side door and poured out, and I got out of the car quickly,
intercepting the children. I told my oldest son to take the others into the house
and wait, to give their mother some time alone with her grandfather whom
she hadn't seen in so many years. I have good children, obedient children,
and they disappeared again even as I heard my wife opening the car door for
Mr. Chinh.

I turned and looked, and the old man was standing beside the car. My 75
wife embraced him, and his head was perched on her shoulder, and there was
nothing on his face at all, no feeling except perhaps the faintest wrinkling of
puzzlement. Perhaps I should have stayed at my wife's side as the old man
went on to explain to her that she didn't exist. But I could not. I wished to
walk briskly away, far from this house, far from the old man and his granddaughter. I wished to walk as fast as I could, to run. But at least I fought that
desire. I simply turned away and moved off, along the side of the house to the
front yard.

I stopped near the live oak and looked about, trying to see things. Trying
to see this tree, for instance. This tree as black as a charcoal cricket and with
great lower limbs, as massive themselves as the main trunks of most other
trees, shooting straight out and then sagging and rooting again in the ground.
A monstrous tree. I leaned against it, and as I looked away, the tree faded
within me. It was gone, and I envied the old man, I knew. I envied him driving
his Hotchkiss along the beach half a century ago. Envied him his sparks flying
into the air. But my very envy frightened me. Look at the man, I thought. He
remembered his car, but he can't remember his granddaughter.

And I demanded of myself: Could I? Even as I stood there? Could I
remember this woman whom I loved? I'd seen her just moments ago. I'd lived

with her for more than twenty years. And certainly if she was standing there beside me, if she spoke, she would have been intensely familiar. But separated from her, I could not picture her clearly. I could construct her face accurately in my mind. But the image did not burn there, did not rush upon me and fill me up with the feelings that I genuinely held for her. I could not put my face into the wind and see her eyes as clearly as Mr. Chinh saw the eyes of the rabbits in his headlights.

Not the eyes of my wife and not my country either. I'd lost a whole country, and I didn't give it a thought. Vung Tau was a beautiful city, and if I put my face into the wind I could see nothing of it clearly, not its shaded streets or its white sand beaches, not the South China Sea lying there beside it. I can speak these words, and perhaps you can see these things clearly because you are using your imagination. But I cannot imagine these things because I lived them, and to remember them with the vividness I know they should have is impossible. They are lost to me.

Until perhaps when I am as old as Mr. Chinh. Perhaps he, too, moved through his life as distracted as me. Perhaps only after he forgot his grand-daughter did he remember his Hotchkiss. And perhaps that was necessary. Perhaps he had to forget the one to remember the other. Not that I think he'd made that conscious choice. Something deep inside him was sorting out his life as it was about to end. And that is what frightens me the most. I am afraid that deep down I am built on a much smaller scale than the surface of my mind aspires to. When something finally comes back to me with real force, perhaps it will be a luxury car hanging on a crane or the freshly painted wall of a new dry cleaning store or the faint buzz of the alarm clock beside my bed. Deep down, secretly, I may be prepared to betray all that I think I love the most.

This is what brought me to the slump of grief against the live oak in my front yard. I leaned there, and the time passed, and then my wife crept up beside me. I turned to her, and she was crying quietly, her head bowed and her hand covering her eyes. 80

"I'm sorry," I said.

"I put him in the guest room," she said. "He thanked me as he would an innkeeper." She sobbed faintly, and I wanted to touch her, but my arm was very heavy, as if I was standing at the bottom of the sea. It rose only a few inches from my side. Then she said, "I thought he might remember after he slept."

I could neither reassure her with a lie nor make her face the truth. But I had to do something. I had thought too much about this already. A good businessman knows when to stop thinking and to act instead. I drew close to my wife, but only briefly did my arm rise and hold her. That was the same as all the other forgotten gestures of my life. Suddenly I surprised myself and my wife, too. I stepped in front of her and crouched down, and before either of us could think to feel foolish, I had taken Mai onto my back and straightened up, and I began to move about the yard, walking at first, down the long drooping lower branch of the oak tree and then faster along the sidewalk and then up the other side of the house, and I was going faster, and she only protested for a moment before she was laughing and holding on tighter, clinging with her legs about my waist and her arms around my neck, and I ran with her, ran as fast as I could so that she laughed harder, and I felt her clinging against me, pressing against me, and I felt her breath on the side of my face as warm and moist as a breeze off the South China Sea.

Suggestions for Writing and Discussion

1. Explain several ways that the title of this piece relates to this story. What connection do you think the author intended? Offer any support you can from the text as you answer this question.
2. In paragraph 2, Khanh details the types of small businesses on a stretch of his journey from Louisiana to Texas. From the details he provides, what inferences can you draw regarding this area and its residents?
3. Khanh begins this piece by telling the reader that he is a businessman, not a poet. Why do you think he begins this way? Do you think he is correct in his self-assessment? Explain.
4. Although both Mai and Khanh are from the same culture and have been in America the same length of time, compare the extent to which each has maintained or rejected her and his Vietnamese heritage.
5. From his first meeting with Mai's grandfather, Khanh informs us that he fears the old man. What is your reaction to the grandfather? Do you find him frightening? Sad? Strange? Or something else?

Suggestions for Extended Thinking and Research

1. The theme of crossing borders runs throughout this piece at various levels, both literal and symbolic. Identify several borders that are crossed and explain how they relate to what you see as the main theme of this story.
2. Interview several elderly people to discover what memories they value most in their lives. Consider talking with people in your community or perhaps visiting a local nursing home. Your greatest tasks will be to ask thoughtful, creative questions and, most of all, to listen carefully and sincerely to what the person you are interviewing is saying. After completing your interviews, write a paper describing what you have discovered.

DENISE LEVERTOV

What Were They Like?

> *Although she was born and brought up in Ilford, Essex, England, Denise Levertov emigrated to the United States in 1948 and has become known as an American writer. She has taught at several universities, including Tufts and Stanford, has served as poetry editor of the liberal journal* The Nation, *and was active in the protest movement against the Vietnam War during the 1960s and 1970s. This poem was written in 1964 and was first published in* Poems: 1960–1967.

Prereading/Journal-Writing Suggestion

What do you imagine your life would have been like if you had lived in Vietnam prior to 1960? How would you have spent your days? What would your family have been like? What do you imagine your country would have been like?

---

1) Did the people of Viet Nam
    use lanterns of stone?
2) Did they hold ceremonies
    to reverence the opening of buds?
3) Were they inclined to quiet laughter?   5
4) Did they use bone and ivory,
    jade and silver, for ornament?
5) Had they an epic poem?
6) Did they distinguish between speech and singing?

1) Sir, their light hearts turned to stone.   10
    It is not remembered whether in gardens
    stone lanterns illumined pleasant ways.
2) Perhaps they gathered once to delight in blossom,
    but after the children were killed
    there were no more buds.   15
3) Sir, laughter is bitter to the burned mouth.
4) A dream ago, perhaps. Ornament is for joy.
    All the bones were charred.
5) It is not remembered. Remember,
    most were peasants; their life   20
    was in rice and bamboo.
    When peaceful clouds were reflected in the paddies
    and the water buffalo stepped surely along terraces,
    maybe fathers told their sons old tales.

When bombs smashed those mirrors   25
there was time only to scream.
6) There is an echo yet
of their speech which was like a song.
It was reported their singing resembled
the flight of moths in moonlight.   30
Who can say? It is silent now.

Suggestions for Writing and Discussion

1. This poem divides into two sections: The first section raises questions and the second answers them. What type of person might be asking the questions in the first section? Why might this person be asking these questions in the first place? What do these questions imply about the speaker here?
2. In the second section, who might be answering the questions? What do the answers signify about this person?
3. Choose two images from this piece that you feel are most beautiful and two that are most painful. How might these contrasting images connect to the theme of the poem?
4. One speaker says, "It was reported their singing resembled/the flight of moths in moonlight." Ponder this metaphor and find all of the appropriate connections between singing and moths, between moths and the people of the poem.
5. Why do you think this poem contains only male images? The first speaker is a "Sir," and the responder says that "maybe fathers told their sons old tales." Why is there no mention of women anywhere?
6. In the final line, what does "It" refer to?

TOPICS FOR MAKING CONNECTIONS: CROSSING BORDERS

1. By referring to the pieces in this section on Vietnam and World War II, as well as tapping experiences from your own life, write an essay in which you adopt one of the following beliefs.
   A. Dwelling on the past can have a harmful effect on one's emotional and psychological growth.
   B. Those who forget the past can never learn from past experiences.
   C. Times change. The past has no bearing on who we are or where we're headed.
   D. Our thoughts and our lives are determined by those who came before us.
   E. The past is only one chapter in our history; the present is what really matters.
   F. Your own related thesis.

2. Write a dialogue in which you attempt to bridge the gap between any two authors or characters in this section. Here are some suggestions.
   Alice Bloom and the young blonde on the beach
   The Greek peasant woman and the young blonde
   Mustafa Nabil and the producer of *Hawaii Five-O*
   Paul Fussell and Michael Walzer

3. Choose any three pieces in this section and analyze what cultural values, in general, Americans are depicted as having.

4. Choose the one piece in this section that you enjoyed reading the most. Evaluate both the reading and your response as a reader in order to come to some conclusions about how writing can move readers in general as well as you, specifically.

5. Compare and contrast the opening strategies used by three of the essayists in this section. What conclusions can you draw about what a good introduction ought to do in order to be effective?

6. By referring to at least three pieces in this section, analyze the role that fear plays in shaping and directing our individual choices and beliefs.

7. By referring to at least three sources in this section, write an argument claiming that certain human characteristics cross all cultural boundaries.

8. "Am I my brother's keeper?" Assume and synthesize the roles of three characters or authors in this section as you attempt to answer this biblical question.

9. Besides firsthand experience, how else can we come to understand the world around us? Refer to several sources in this section as well as your own experience in order to answer this question.

10. Write an essay on how a particular movie or television show affected your view of a specific event in history: the Vietnam War, the bombing of Hiroshima, the Jewish holocaust, the assassination of President Kennedy.

11. From this section, nominate one person as your hero and explain why, from the list of candidates, you chose this person.

12. Inherent in the concept of democracy is the notion that America is owned and therefore guided by individuals. Write an essay in which you prove this to be either a true picture of America or an outrageous fallacy.

13. Write an essay, using the sources in this section, in which you argue for or against the proposition that the evils in America are mostly stereotypical masculine traits of aggression, greed, and power.

14. Refer to at least three pieces in this section as you write an essay in which you argue for your image of the "ideal American citizen."

15. Write an essay on one piece in this section that made you change your way of thinking, one that altered your previous assumptions on a topic. Analyze why this piece of writing had such an effect on you, and explain how you have changed as a result.

16. Interview someone you know who has been the victim of war — the drug war, the Vietnam War, World War II, the censorship war, and so on. Write an essay in which you attempt to draw some conclusions about the source of injustice and the power of the individual.

INDEX